Lecture Notes in Computer Science

# Lecture Notes in Artificial Intelligence 15919

Founding Editor

Jörg Siekmann

Series Editors

Randy Goebel, *University of Alberta, Edmonton, Canada*
Wolfgang Wahlster, *DFKI, Berlin, Germany*
Zhi-Hua Zhou, *Nanjing University, Nanjing, China*

The series Lecture Notes in Artificial Intelligence (LNAI) was established in 1988 as a topical subseries of LNCS devoted to artificial intelligence.

The series publishes state-of-the-art research results at a high level. As with the LNCS mother series, the mission of the series is to serve the international R & D community by providing an invaluable service, mainly focused on the publication of conference and workshop proceedings and postproceedings.

Tianqing Zhu · Wanlei Zhou · Congcong Zhu

Editors

# Knowledge Science, Engineering and Management

18th International Conference, KSEM 2025
Macao, China, August 4–7, 2025
Proceedings, Part I

 Springer

*Editors*
Tianqing Zhu 
City University of Macau
Macau, China

Congcong Zhu 
City University of Macau
Macau, China

Wanlei Zhou 
City University of Macau
Macau, China

ISSN 0302-9743     ISSN 1611-3349  (electronic)
Lecture Notes in Artificial Intelligence
ISBN 978-981-95-3000-7     ISBN 978-981-95-3001-4  (eBook)
https://doi.org/10.1007/978-981-95-3001-4

LNCS Sublibrary: SL7 – Artificial Intelligence

# Preface

On behalf of the Conference Committee, we are pleased to present the proceedings of the 18th International Conference on Knowledge Science, Engineering and Management (**KSEM 2025**), held at the Wynn Palace, Macau Special Administrative Region, China, from August 4–7, 2025. KSEM 2025 was the eighteenth event in this well-established series of conferences, founded by Academician Ruqian Lu, which is recognized as a premier international forum for the exchange of research in artificial intelligence, data science, knowledge engineering, AI safety, large language models, and related frontier areas. Over the years, KSEM has provided an important venue for disseminating both theoretical advances and practical innovations, fostering interdisciplinary collaboration between academia and industry.

This year, KSEM 2025 received 354 submissions from authors around the world. Following a rigorous single-blind peer-review process, with an average of 2.82 reviews received per submission, involving 342 Program Committee members and external reviewers, 106 regular papers, 66 short papers, and 16 workshop papers were accepted for inclusion in these proceedings and will be submitted for EI indexing. In addition to the contributed papers, the program featured keynote lectures by distinguished scholars, as well as workshops and tutorials on emerging research topics, offering valuable opportunities for academic exchange and collaboration.

Among the accepted papers, the following were selected for the **Best Paper Awards**:

- *Masked Aggregation Learning for Enhancing Distributed Gradient Boosting Decision Trees* Yuting Zha, Chao Lin, Xinyi Huang, and Dugang Liu
- *Label Inference Attacks against Federated Unlearning* Wei Wang, Xiangyun Tang, Yajie Wang, Yijing Lin, Tao Zhang, Meng Shen, Dusit Niyato, and Liehuang Zhu

The **Best Student Paper Awards** went to:

- *LVLM-FDA: Protecting Large Vision-language Models via Fast Detection of Malicious Attempts* Boxu Chen, Chaoyi Wang, Le Yang, Ziwei Zheng, Cong Wang, Qian Wang, and Chao Shen
- *FATFI: A Framework to Generate Adversarial Traffic with Feature Interpretability* Yikang Wang, Weina Niu, Dujuan Gu, Qingjun Yuan, Jiacheng Gong, Shuangqi Gan, Xin Lin, and Xiaosong Zhang

We would like to express our sincere gratitude to all authors for their valuable contributions, and to the Program Committee members and reviewers for their professional and timely evaluations. We also warmly thank all the volunteers who supported the conference at various stages.

We further extend our appreciation to the following chairs for their invaluable contributions:

- **General Chairs:** Wanlei Zhou, Zhi Jin, Aniello Castiglione
- **Program Chairs:** Tianqing Zhu, Gang Li, Congcong Zhu, Lucia Cimmino

- **Local Chairs:** Wenjian Liu, Minghao Wang, Huajie Chen
- **Publication Chairs:** Lefeng Zhang, Youyang Qu
- **Workshop Chairs:** Jia Gu, Bo Liu, Chi Liu
- **Publicity Chairs:** Yu Huang, Minfeng Qi

We were so honored to have many renowned scholars be part of this conference. Finally, we would like to thank all speakers, authors, and participants for their great contribution to and support for the success of KSEM 2025.

August 2025

Tianqing Zhu
Wanlei Zhou
Congcong Zhu

# Committees

## General Chairs

| | |
|---|---|
| Wanlei Zhou | City University of Macau, China |
| Zhi Jin | Peking University, China |
| Aniello Castiglione | University of Salerno, Italy |

## Program Chairs

| | |
|---|---|
| Tianqing Zhu | City University of Macau, China |
| Gang Li | Deakin University, Australia |
| Congcong Zhu | City University of Macau, China |
| Lucia Cimmino | University of Salerno, Italy |

## Local Chairs

| | |
|---|---|
| Wenjian Liu | City University of Macau, China |
| Minghao Wang | City University of Macau, China |
| Huajie Chen | City University of Macau, China |

## Publication Chairs

| | |
|---|---|
| Lefeng Zhang | City University of Macau, China |
| Youyang Qu | Shandong Computer Science Center, China |

## Workshop Chairs

| | |
|---|---|
| Jia Gu | City University of Macau, China |
| Bo Liu | University of Technology Sydney, Australia |
| Chi Liu | City University of Macau, China |

## Publicity Chairs

| | |
|---|---|
| Yu Huang | Peking University, China |
| Minfeng Qi | City University of Macau, China |

# Contents – Part I

# Label Inference Attacks Against Federated Unlearning


Wei Wang[1] , Xiangyun Tang[1]([✉]) , Yajie Wang[2]([✉]) , Yijing Lin[3] , Tao Zhang[4] , Meng Shen[2] , Dusit Niyato[5] , and Liehuang Zhu[2]

[1] The Key Laboratory of Ethnic Language Intelligent Analysis and Security Management of MOE, Minzu University of China, Beijing, China
{wangwei,xiangyunt}@muc.edu.cn
[2] School of Cyberspace Science and Technology, Beijing Institute of Technology, Beijing, China
wangyajie0312@foxmail.com
[3] School of Information and Communication Engineering, Beijing University of Posts and Telecommunications, Beijing, China
[4] School of Cyberspace Science and Technology, Beijing Jiaotong University, Beijing, China
[5] School of Cyberspace Science and Technology, Nanyang Technological University, Singapore, Singapore



**Abstract.** Federated Unlearning (FU) has emerged as a promising solution to respond to "the right to be forgotten" of clients, by allowing clients to erase their data from global models without compromising model performance. Unfortunately, researchers find that the parameter variations of models induced by FU expose clients' data information, enabling attackers to infer the label of unlearning data, while label inference attacks against FU remain unexplored. In this paper, we introduce and analyze a new privacy threat against FU and propose a novel label inference attack, ULIA, which can infer unlearning data labels across three FU levels. To address the unique challenges of inferring labels via the models variations, we design a gradient-label mapping mechanism in ULIA that establishes a relationship between gradient variations and unlearning labels, enabling inferring labels on accumulated model variations. We evaluate ULIA on both IID and non-IID settings. Experimental results show that in the IID setting, ULIA achieves a 100% Attack Success Rate (ASR) under both class-level and client-level unlearning. Even when only 1% of a user's local data is forgotten, ULIA still attains an ASR ranging from 93% to 62.3%.

**Keywords:** Federated Unlearning · Label Inference Attack · Gradient-Label Mapping · Federated Learning · Privacy Protection



This work was supported in part by the National Nature Science Foundation of China under Grant 62302539, 62402040 and the Key Laboratory of Ethnic Language Intelligent Analysis and Security Management of MOE (OPU-202502).

# 1   Introduction

Federated Learning (FL), as a decentralized machine learning paradigm, has gained widespread adoption in various domains such as finance [18] and smart cities [8] due to its inherent capability to protect user privacy. FL allows multiple users to jointly train a global model by sharing local models rather than raw data with a central server, thereby mitigating privacy leakage [19]. In addition to the privacy protection, existing data security legislation, such as General Data Protection Regulation (GDPR) [24] and California Consumer Privacy Act (CCPA) [5], emphasizes the "Right to be Forgotten", affirming users' authority to demand the unlearning of their data from global models during FL.

To respond the unlearning demand, Federated Unlearning (FU) has emerged as a promising solution [17]. FU methods, such as historical information-based unlearning [32] and rapid retraining [16], involve the server collaborating with users to remove the influence of unlearning data from the global model, in accordance with users' unlearning requests, while ensuring that the model's performance remains consistent with its state prior to the unlearning operation. FU can be categorized into sample-level, class-level, and client-level [22], where the unlearning requests correspond to a set of samples, all samples associated with a set of classes, or the entire local dataset of a user, respectively.

Although existing FU methods can unlearn data from global models while preserving model performance, they are vulnerable to a significant privacy leakage threat. After FU operations, the server holds two versions of models before and after unlearning. The adjustments of the resulting parameter on the models are not entirely independent but are closely related to the characteristics of the unlearning data, such as the labels of the unlearning data [21]. Hence, *the variations in the models before and after FU expose users' data information*, enabling the server as attackers to infer private information about the unlearning data. In this paper, we focus on label inference attacks against FU, where the server, by analyzing the variations of models before and after unlearning, infers the labels of unlearning data.

Label inference attacks allow the server to steal private labels of users that should have been unlearning or protected in FU, raising significant privacy concerns. Furthermore, ensuring the privacy of labels is a fundamental guarantee, as they often represent sensitive or critical information for the participant [20]. For example, in a healthcare scenario, multiple medical institutions collaboratively train a global model using diabetic patient data. If a patient requests the removal of their medical data due to privacy concerns, the label inference attacks on FU enable the attacker to infer the diagnosis, leading to a severe breach of privacy.

However, the privacy risks of label inference attacks on FU remain underexplored. It is challenging to infer the labels of unlearning data from the model differences induced by FU. The model differences reflect the accumulated impact of all the unlearning data and their associated labels. Consequently, when attackers are unaware of the number of unlearning data samples or labels, accurately inferring labels from the accumulated parameter differences is challenging. Furthermore, when the quantity of unlearning data is small, the resulting changes in model parameters may be too subtle to adequately capture the features of the unlearning data, making it more difficult for attackers to infer the labels.

In this paper, we propose ULIA, a novel label inference attack that infers the labels of unlearning data across three FU levels: sample-level, class-level, and client-level, by analyzing the variations in the model parameters of FU. ULIA addresses the inherent challenge of accurately inferring labels from model differences induced by FU, where the accumulated impact of unlearning data on model parameters obscures individual label effects. To overcome this, we propose a *gradient-label mapping mechanism*, which establishes a relationship between gradient variations and unlearning labels. This allows the attacker to separate the specific parameter shifts attributable to individual unlearning label, thus enhancing the accuracy of label inference. Moreover, ULIA incorporates a dynamic filtering strategy that prioritizes label categories with the higher likelihood of matching model parameter changes, focusing on those labels that exhibit the most significant alterations, ensuring effective label inference, even in scenarios with sparse or subtle unlearning data.

We evaluate the performance of ULIA under three advanced FU methods across the three FU levels on real-world datasets. In the IID setting, ULIA achieves an Attack Success Rate (ASR) ranging from 100% to 62.3%. Even in the non-IID setting, ULIA is still able to achieve 96.4%–58.5% ASR.

The main contributions of this paper are as follows:

- To the best of our knowledge, we are the first to reveal the label leakage issue of FU. We propose ULIA, a novel attack inferring unlearning data labels across three FU levels, by analyzing the variations in the model parameters induced by unlearning operations.
- The attack works regardless of the quantity of unlearning data, as we design a gradient-label mapping mechanism that establishes a relationship between gradient variations and unlearning labels, enabling inferring unlearning labels on accumulated model variations.
- We evaluate our attacks with real-world datasets under three advanced FU methods, both in IID and non-IID settings. The experimental results show that ULIA demonstrates outstanding attack performance and adaptability.

## 2   Related Works

**Federated Unlearning.** Existing FU methods can be broadly categorized into two main approaches: (1) *Historical information-based unlearning*, which is recorded and analyzed during training to assess the impact of specific data or clients on the global model, enables efficient unlearning. The typical techniques explored under this approach include: Gradient correction adjusts the gradient information in the model training process to eliminate the contribution of target data or target clients to the global model [32]. The knowledge distillation strategy restores the performance of the global model through knowledge transfer and model tuning, thereby approximating unlearning [27]. Approximate unlearning of target data is achieved by pruning network layers [25] and refining the loss function [9]. (2) *Rapid retraining*, which efficiently restores the unlearning global model by optimizing retraining algorithms or performing partial retraining. The typical techniques explored under this approach include: First-order Taylor expansion methods are employed to effectively utilize gradient and curvature information, thereby identifying a more optimal descent direction [16]. The optimal number of unlearning rounds can be accurately determined by assessing the contribution of target clients during each training iteration [13]. Clients are grouped into suitable clusters for aggregation, ensuring that retraining occurs solely within the cluster of the target client during the unlearning process [23].

**Label Inference Attacks.** Label inference attacks aim to infer the labels of training or unlearned data, thereby compromising the privacy of participating clients. Previous studies have primarily implemented label inference attacks through the following techniques. (1) *Based on gradient information*, where attackers exploit the label information reflected in the gradient signs and magnitudes to perform inference. [31] discovers the relationship between labels and gradient signs in the cross-entropy loss function, which becomes a fundamental basis for label inference attacks. [4] demonstrates that attackers exploit inherent vulnerabilities in vertical federated learning (VFL) to infer sensitive labels owned by one party through the output features of the bottom model or the gradient information returned by the server. (2) *Classification and clustering methods*, where attackers train gradient classifiers or utilize the clustering properties of embeddings and gradients to make inferences. [12] observes that in two-party scenarios, the gradient norm associated with target labels is often larger than that of non-target labels, providing a basis for classification-based methods. [15] proposes a K-means clustering-based attack method that classifies gradients or embeddings using cosine similarity. (3) *Model reconstruction*, where attackers simulate the predictive model and labels of the active party to construct surrogate models and labels, minimizing prediction errors to infer the true labels. [30] proposes using label smoothing techniques to prevent the model from becoming overconfident in label predictions. [1] introduces an early stopping strategy to reduce the impact of gradient magnitude peaks on the attack accuracy.

**Highlights of the Proposed Attack.** Existing label inference attacks mainly focus on inferring the labels of training data. With the emergence of FU, the analysis of local and global model parameters' changes generated by unlearning requests to infer the labels of forgotten data has still remained unexplored. In this paper, we propose `ULIA`, a novel label inference attack against FU, inferring unlearning data labels by analyzing the model variations induced by unlearning operations, which reveals and analyzes the new privacy leakage issue of FU.

## 3   Preliminaries

Before entering the sample-level FU process, clients participate in FL, training global models under the server's orchestration. The FU process is launched when a client launches an unlearning request. The server and clients cooperate to eliminate the target data from the global model, based on a unlearning strategy.

**Federated Learning.** The primary objective of FL is to enable collaborative and efficient training on distributed data without directly sharing the raw data. Given $N$ clients $P_i$ ($i = 1, \ldots, N$), each holding local data $D_i$, the overall dataset is defined as $D = \bigcup_{i=1}^{N} D_i$ . At the beginning of the FL training process, the server initializes the global model $\theta_{\text{global}}^{(0)}$ and distributes it to all clients. At the $t$-th round, client $i$ optimizes the global model $\theta_{\text{global}}^{(t)}$ based on its local data $D_i$, and updates the local model parameters $\theta_{\text{local},i}^{(t+1)}$:

$$\theta_{\text{local},i}^{(t+1)} = \theta_{\text{global}}^{(t)} - \eta \cdot \sum_{(x,y)\in D_i} \nabla\ell(f_\theta(x), y) \tag{1}$$

where $\eta$ is the learning rate, and $\nabla\ell(f_\theta(x), y)$ is the gradient of the loss function $\ell$ for model $f_\theta$ with respect to input $x$ and label $y$.

The server aggregates the local model parameters $\theta_{\text{local},i}^{(t+1)}$ uploaded by all participating after their individual training steps, in order to update the global model parameters $\theta_{\text{global}}^{(t+1)}$:

$$\theta_{\text{global}}^{(t+1)} = \sum_{i=1}^{N} w_i \theta_{\text{local},i}^{(t+1)} \tag{2}$$

where $w_i = \frac{|D_i|}{|D|}$ represents the weight of client $i$ based on the size of its local dataset $D_i$ relative to the total dataset $D$.

**Federated Unlearning.** When a target client $K$ sends an unlearning request in the $t$-th round, FU performs the data removal request, resulting in the post-unlearning global model $\theta'_{\text{global}}$. FU can be categorized into the following three main types based on different forgetting requests and objectives.

- *Sample-level unlearning* seeks to remove specific sensitive samples from a client's local dataset and eliminate their influence on the global model to protect privacy [29]. The local dataset $D_i$ is updated by removing $S_f$, resulting in a revised dataset $D'_i = D_i \setminus S_f$. The client initializes its post-unlearning local model $\theta'_{\text{local},i}$ with the global model parameters $\theta_{\text{global}}^{(t)}$ from the $t$-th round and retrains it on the updated dataset $D'_i$.
- *Class-level unlearning* focuses on completely erasing certain class-specific information from the global model, renders the model incapable of classifying those classes [2,26]. When the influence of a specific class $C_f$ needs to be removed, each client updates its local dataset by removing the data associated with $C_f$, resulting in modified datasets $D'_i = D_i \setminus \{(x,y) \mid y \in C_f\}$.
- *Client-level unlearning* aims to fully remove the contributions of specific clients and to ensure that their data has no residual impact on the global model or subsequent training processes [28]. The global model removes the influence of the target clients $K$ and updates using only the remaining clients. The remaining dataset is represented as $D' = \bigcup_{\substack{i=1 \\ i \neq K}}^{N} D_i$.

## 4   Attack Model and Problem Formalization

### 4.1   Attack Model

This paper focuses on label inference attacks against FU. When a target client submits an unlearning request to remove samples from the global model or to exit collaborative training, the server and client participate in FU to ensure that the model no longer reflects the influence of the forgotten data. We assume that the server is semi-honest. By exploiting access to the model parameters, the semi-honest server as the attacker aims to infer the labels of the data that the target client has requested to forget.

**Attacker's Goal.** The attacker's goal is to infer the labels of the unlearning data by analyzing the parameter differences of models before and after unlearning. Our attack specifically targets a single client's unlearning request but considers different types of forgotten data.

**Attacker's Knowledge.** The semi-honest server, acting as the attacker, possesses legitimate data within FU. It can access two versions of the local model parameters and global model parameters, before and after unlearning.

### 4.2   Problem Formalization

Throughout this paper, we study the problem of label inference attacks against FU. We denote the forgotten dataset as $D_{\text{forgotten}} = \{(x_i, y_i) \mid i = 1, \ldots, M\}$, where $x_i$ represents the input features, and $y_i \in \{0, 1\}^C$ denotes the corresponding one-hot encoded class labels for $C$ classes. Let the global model $\mathcal{F}(\cdot; \theta)$ be parameterized by $\theta$, which maps the input space $\mathcal{X}$ to a $C$-dimensional output space $\mathbb{R}^C$. As a potential attacker, the server analyzes parameter differences between the two versions of both the local and the global models to infer the labels of the forgotten data, formally expressed as the following objective function:

$$\hat{y}_i = \arg \max_{y_i} \mathcal{L}\left(\mathcal{F}(x_i; \theta_{\text{global}}), y_i\right) \tag{3}$$

where $\hat{y}_i$ is the inferred label for the forgotten data point $x_i$, and $\mathcal{L}$ is the loss measuring the discrepancy between the model output and the predicted label.

## 5   ULIA: Label Inference Attack

In this section, we propose ULIA, a novel label inference attack that infer the labels of unlearning data across three FU levels: sample-level, class-level, and client-level, by analyzing the model differences in FU. Figure 1 illustrates the proposed label inference attack in the context of FU. The implementation of the ULIA attack can be carried out in the following four steps.

– *Analysis of parameter changes.* This step compares local and global model parameters before and after unlearning to quantify the influence of forgotten data, providing a foundation for the attack.

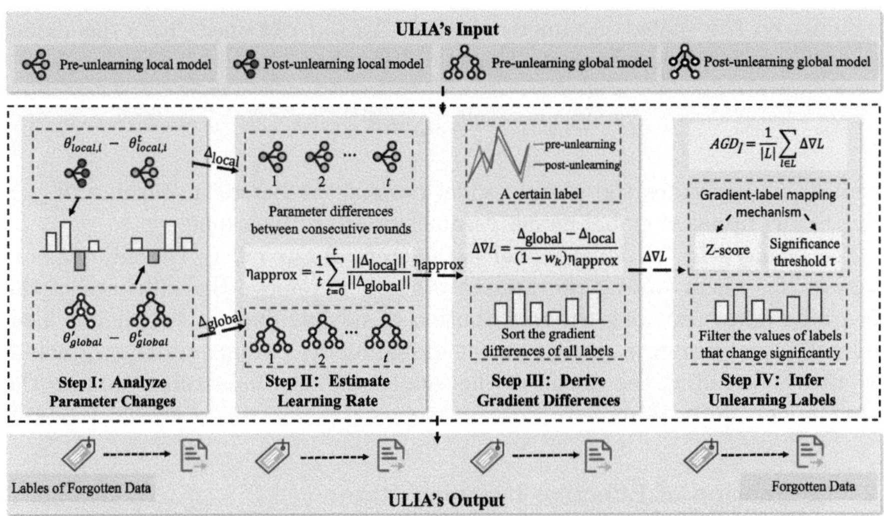


**Fig. 1.** Overview of Unlearning Label Inference Attack. It shows the four main steps: (1) analyzing parameter changes, (2) estimating the learning rate, (3) deriving gradient differences, and (4) inferring the forgotten labels. The diagram highlights how ULIA utilizes pre- and post-unlearning models to infer labels

- *Estimation of learning rate.* By analyzing parameter differences across multiple rounds, an effective learning rate is estimated to reconstruct gradients.
- *Derivation of gradient differences.* Using the estimated learning rate and parameter differences, approximate gradient differences are reconstructed.
- *Inferring the Labels of Forgotten Data.* By utilizing the gradient-label mapping mechanism, the degree of match between gradient changes and forgotten data labels is measured, enabling more accurate selection of labels.

## 5.1   Analysis of Parameter Changes

The first step in ULIA focuses on analyzing the changes in the model parameters caused by the unlearning process. By examining both the local and global model parameter changes, attackers can infer the influence of forgotten data on FL. Changes of local model parameters provide insights into how the removal of specific data affects individual clients, while changes of global model parameters reveal the aggregated impact of the unlearning operation across all clients.

Changes of local model parameters $\Delta_{local}$ quantify the variation in the local model parameters of the target client before and after unlearning. This change, which captures the impact of removing the influence of forgotten data.

$$\Delta_{local} = \theta'_{local,i} - \theta^{(t)}_{local,i} \tag{4}$$

where $\theta^{(t)}_{local,i}$ represents the local model parameters before unlearning at the $t$-th communication round. $\theta'_{local,i}$ denotes the updated local model parameters.

Similarly, the global parameter change $\Delta_{\text{global}}$, obtained from the model parameters before and after unlearning, is defined as:

$$\Delta_{\text{global}} = \theta'_{\text{global}} - \theta^{(t)}_{\text{global}} \tag{5}$$

where $\theta^{(t)}_{\text{global}}$ indicates the global model parameters before unlearning. $\theta'_{\text{global}}$ refers to the updated global model parameters after unlearning.

The changes in the local model parameters $\Delta_{\text{local}}$ reflect the adjustments made by the client during the update process to remove the influence of the unlearning data, revealing the contribution of specific data to the client's local model. By analyzing the changes in the global model parameters $\Delta_{\text{global}}$ before and after unlearning, the extent of the influence of the unlearning data on the global model can be observed.

### 5.2   Estimation of Effective Learning Rate

The learning rate controls the step size of gradient updates in FL, directly affecting parameter changes. We estimate the learning rate by leveraging the differences between the local model parameters and the global model parameters from previous training rounds as given in Eq. (6). This enables ULIA to conduct attacks with more limited knowledge, enhancing its adaptability.

$$\eta_{\text{approx}} = \frac{1}{t} \sum_{t=0}^{t} \frac{\|\Delta_{\text{local}}\|}{\|\Delta_{\text{global}}\|} \tag{6}$$

where $\| \cdot \|_2$ denotes the $L2$-norm, $t$ is the number of rounds used for averaging.

The reasons for averaging over the previous $t$ rounds are as follows. Firstly, performing the averaging process helps mitigate the impact of noise and outliers in individual updates, leading to a more robust and reliable estimate. Secondly, it preserves the integrity of the gradient direction, as the learning rate influences only the magnitude of the update, not the direction. This ensures that the estimated learning rate can be effectively used to derive gradient differences. By estimating an effective learning rate, attackers obtain the key parameters required to infer the gradients corresponding to the forgotten data.

### 5.3   Derivation of Gradient Differences

Attackers can infer the gradient updates associated with forgotten data by analyzing the difference between local and global parameter changes. This discrepancy provides insight into the contribution of the forgotten data to model optimization, forming a direct link between parameter variations and data characteristics. By leveraging an estimated learning rate, attackers can approximate the gradient difference introduced by the forgotten data.

In FL, the global model update at round $t+1$ follows the standard aggregation rule, as described in Eq. (2). When a client requests unlearning, its local model parameters are updated without the forgotten data, deviating from their original update path. The parameter changes before and after unlearning are defined as shown in Eqs. (4) and (5). Since the global model aggregates updates from all clients, its change can be rewritten as:

$$\Delta_{\text{global}} = \sum_{i=1}^{N} w_i \Delta_{\text{local},i}. \tag{7}$$

Computing the difference between global and local parameter changes gives:

$$\Delta_{\text{global}} - \Delta_{\text{local}} = (w_k - 1)\Delta_{\text{local}}. \tag{8}$$

which reveals that the discrepancy between local and global updates is directly proportional to the forgotten data's gradient contribution. Since the attackers do not directly observe $\Delta\nabla L$, they approximate the discrepancy using the estimated learning rate $\eta_{\text{approx}}$, yielding:

$$\Delta\nabla L = \frac{\Delta_{\text{global}} - \Delta_{\text{local}}}{(1 - w_k)\eta_{\text{approx}}}. \tag{9}$$

This equation provides a mechanism for reconstructing the gradient updates influenced by the forgotten data. Given that gradient variations capture feature importance, the attackers can analyze the magnitude and sparsity of $\Delta\nabla L$ to infer the forgotten data's characteristics. By analyzing the approximated gradient differences, the attackers can identify which feature dimensions were most influenced by the forgotten data. Significant variations in specific gradient components indicate that these features were closely associated with the removed data. Furthermore, examining the concentration and distribution of gradient changes allows the attackers to assess the relative importance of individual features.

The difference between local and global parameter updates provides a strong signal of the forgotten data's impact on model training. As this discrepancy maintains a linear relationship with the forgotten data's gradient contribution, it serves as a crucial indicator for reconstructing its characteristics. These findings reveal inherent weaknesses in existing FU mechanisms, demonstrating that even after explicit data removal, residual traces may still persist in the global model, posing potential privacy risks.

### 5.4   Inferring the Labels of Forgotten Data

The final step of the proposed method focuses on inferring the labels of forgotten data by analyzing the derived gradient differences. The unlearning operation introduces significant changes to the gradients associated with the forgotten data, making them more prominent in the analysis. By linking these gradient changes to the weights in the model's output layer, attackers can accurately infer the labels of the forgotten data. For each label category $l \in L$, the average gradient difference is computed as:

$$\text{AGD}_l = \frac{1}{|L|} \sum_{l \in L} \Delta\nabla L_l \tag{10}$$

where $\mathrm{AGD}_l$ represents the average gradient difference for a specific label category $l$, and $L$ is the set of all label categories.

This step emphasizes the innovative integration of gradient difference reconstruction with targeted label analysis, illustrating how the method effectively translates parameter and gradient variations into actionable insights, thereby enabling precise identification of the labels of forgotten data.

However, when multiple label categories are forgotten by the client, the server does not know the exact number of forgotten categories. Therefore, it cannot simply assume that the category with the largest gradient change accounts for all the forgotten categories. To address this, we propose a *gradient-label mapping mechanism*, which establishes a one-to-one correspondence between gradient changes and the labels of forgotten data, and employs a dynamic filtering strategy to select labels that are more likely to correspond to the forgotten data. Specifically, this mechanism leverages two key methods: (1) It quantifies the changes induced by each label category during model parameter updates by utilizing the properties of the Z-score [3].

$$Z_l = \frac{\mathrm{AGD}_l - \mu_{\mathrm{AGD}}}{\sigma_{\mathrm{AGD}}} \tag{11}$$

where $\mu_{\mathrm{AGD}}$ represents the average of gradient differences across all label categories, and $\sigma_{\mathrm{AGD}}$ represents the standard deviation of the gradient differences across all label categories. (2) It dynamically infers the number of forgotten data categories. After computing the Z-score for each label category, a predefined significance threshold $\tau$ is applied to filter a candidate set $L_{\mathrm{candidate}}$ as given in Eq. (12), which includes the label categories most likely corresponding to the forgotten data of the client.

$$L_{\mathrm{candidate}} = \{l \mid Z_l > \tau\} \tag{12}$$

## 6 Experiments

### 6.1 Experimental Settings

All experiments are performed on a workstation equipped with an Intel(R) Core(TM) i7-13700K processor, 64GB of RAM, and three NVIDIA RTX 4090 GPU cards. ULIA is implemented using Python 3.8 and PyTorch 2.1.0.

**Datasets and Model.** We select the following two datasets, which are widely used in FU. 1) **MNIST** [11], a handwritten digit classification dataset consisting of 60,000 training images and 10,000 test images. 2) **CIFAR-10** [10], a color image classification dataset containing 50,000 training samples and 10,000 test samples. We conduct experiments on both *IID* and *non-IID* data distributions, and perform training on the popular deep learning model **ResNet-18** [6].

**Table 1.** Attack performance of ULIA applied to typical unlearning methods. The attack is performed under the condition that the quantity of forgotten samples accounts for 10% of the client's total local data. $\mathcal{L}$ represents the number of categories of forgotten data labels

| Methods | | FedEraser | | | Rapid Retrain | | | SGA-EWC | | |
|---|---|---|---|---|---|---|---|---|---|---|
| Datasets $\mathcal{L}$ | | Sample | Class | Client | Sample | Class | Client | Sample | Class | Client |
| The attacker is aware of the number of label categories | | | | | | | | | | |
| MNIST | 1 | 1.000 | 1.000 | 1.000 | 1.000 | 1.000 | 1.000 | 1.000 | 1.000 | 1.000 |
| | 2 | 0.970 | 1.000 | 1.000 | 0.970 | 1.000 | 1.000 | 0.940 | 1.000 | 1.000 |
| | 3 | 0.850 | 1.000 | 1.000 | 0.910 | 1.000 | 1.000 | 0.810 | 1.000 | 1.000 |
| CIFAR | 1 | 0.970 | 1.000 | 1.000 | 1.000 | 1.000 | 1.000 | 0.950 | 1.000 | 1.000 |
| | 2 | 0.890 | 1.000 | 1.000 | 0.920 | 1.000 | 1.000 | 0.860 | 1.000 | 1.000 |
| | 3 | 0.800 | 1.000 | 1.000 | 0.860 | 1.000 | 1.000 | 0.780 | 1.000 | 1.000 |
| The attacker does not know the number of label categories | | | | | | | | | | |
| MNIST | 1 | 0.958 | 1.000 | 1.000 | 0.973 | 1.000 | 1.000 | 0.923 | 1.000 | 1.000 |
| | 2 | 0.898 | 1.000 | 1.000 | 0.925 | 1.000 | 1.000 | 0.855 | 1.000 | 1.000 |
| | 3 | 0.780 | 1.000 | 1.000 | 0.850 | 1.000 | 1.000 | 0.738 | 1.000 | 1.000 |
| CIFAR | 1 | 0.919 | 1.000 | 1.000 | 0.924 | 1.000 | 1.000 | 0.887 | 1.000 | 1.000 |
| | 2 | 0.837 | 1.000 | 1.000 | 0.872 | 1.000 | 1.000 | 0.785 | 1.000 | 1.000 |
| | 3 | 0.747 | 1.000 | 1.000 | 0.817 | 1.000 | 1.000 | 0.692 | 1.000 | 1.000 |

**FU Methods.** To comprehensively evaluate ULIA, we apply it to the following three typical FU methods. 1) **FedEraser** [14], calibrates the historical updates of retained clients, enabling the server to efficiently reconstruct the global model. 2) **Rapid Retrain** [16], utilizes gradient and curvature information to identify more optimal descent directions, facilitating efficient retraining. 3) **SGA-EWC** [27], proposes an efficient FU framework using reverse Stochastic Gradient Ascent (SGA) and Elastic Weight Consolidation (EWC) to quickly adjust model parameters and eliminate the influence of specific data.

**Details of Parameter Settings.** Before the unlearning process, FU is performed for 100 rounds on 10 clients, using a Stochastic Gradient Descent (SGD) optimizer with an initial learning rate of 0.01, and a batch size of 64. Additionally, we set the significance threshold as $\tau = 2$ to more accurately infer the labels.

**Evaluation Metrics.** Like previous works [7,33], we employ the widely-used Intersection over Union (IoU) method to evaluate the ASR of ULIA in inferring the labels of the forgotten data. We perform 100 attack tests and calculate the average ASR of ULIA. The ASR is calculated as follows:

$$\text{ASR} = \frac{|L^i_{\text{true}} \cap L^i_{\text{pred}}|}{|L^i_{\text{true}} \cup L^i_{\text{pred}}|} \tag{13}$$

**Table 2.** The impact of the quantity of forgotten samples on the ASR of ULIA. 1%, 2%, and 5% represent the percentage of samples requested to be forgotten, relative to the client's total local data.

| Methods | | FedEraser | | | Rapid Retrain | | | SGA-EWC | | |
|---|---|---|---|---|---|---|---|---|---|---|
| Datasets $\mathcal{L}$ | | 1% | 2% | 5% | 1% | 2% | 5% | 1% | 2% | 5% |
| The attacker is aware of the number of label categories | | | | | | | | | | |
| MNIST | 1 | 0.910 | 0.960 | 1.000 | 0.930 | 0.970 | 1.000 | 0.870 | 0.920 | 0.980 |
| | 2 | 0.820 | 0.850 | 0.900 | 0.850 | 0.890 | 0.920 | 0.760 | 0.810 | 0.880 |
| | 3 | 0.700 | 0.750 | 0.810 | 0.760 | 0.820 | 0.870 | 0.670 | 0.710 | 0.770 |
| CIFAR | 1 | 0.830 | 0.890 | 0.940 | 0.850 | 0.920 | 0.980 | 0.770 | 0.850 | 0.900 |
| | 2 | 0.760 | 0.810 | 0.850 | 0.780 | 0.840 | 0.880 | 0.690 | 0.750 | 0.810 |
| | 3 | 0.680 | 0.720 | 0.770 | 0.700 | 0.760 | 0.810 | 0.650 | 0.690 | 0.740 |
| The attacker does not know the number of label categories | | | | | | | | | | |
| MNIST | 1 | 0.825 | 0.886 | 0.918 | 0.838 | 0.891 | 0.933 | 0.783 | 0.848 | 0.887 |
| | 2 | 0.783 | 0.833 | 0.872 | 0.827 | 0.868 | 0.907 | 0.697 | 0.745 | 0.803 |
| | 3 | 0.665 | 0.718 | 0.761 | 0.729 | 0.778 | 0.814 | 0.642 | 0.675 | 0.719 |
| CIFAR | 1 | 0.778 | 0.847 | 0.902 | 0.793 | 0.853 | 0.916 | 0.747 | 0.806 | 0.843 |
| | 2 | 0.713 | 0.773 | 0.813 | 0.748 | 0.798 | 0.843 | 0.658 | 0.693 | 0.732 |
| | 3 | 0.648 | 0.691 | 0.735 | 0.662 | 0.714 | 0.759 | 0.623 | 0.648 | 0.668 |

where $|L_{true}^{i} \cap L_{pred}^{i}|$ represents the size of the intersection between the true label set $L_{true}^{i}$ and the predicted label set $L_{pred}^{i}$ for the $i$-th attack test.

## 6.2   Attack Performance Evaluation

We set the number of categories of forgotten data labels to 1, 2, and 3, and perform attacks on three different FU methods at three levels, under two conditions: whether the attacker knows the number of forgotten data labels. Meanwhile, the quantity of forgotten samples is set to 10% of the target client's data. The attack performance of ULIA applied to typical unlearning methods on the MNIST and CIFAR-10 datasets is reported in Table 1.

ULIA achieves 100% ASR for both class-level and client-level unlearning, because the large volume of forgotten data causes significant shifts in the model's parameters, making the inference easier. The changes in model weights and gradients are directly correlated with the forgotten data. By analyzing the gradient differences between the global model and local models, ULIA effectively identifies the forgotten data. For sample-level unlearning, the ASR gradually decreases as the number of forgotten data labels increases. However, on the MNIST dataset, when the number of forgotten label categories is 1, the ASR reaches 95.8% on FedEraser, 97.3% on Rapid Retrain, and 92.3% on SGA-EWC. This indicates that when the number of forgotten label categories is small, our attack still achieves strong performance, approaching 100%. Even with 3 forgotten label categories, ULIA still achieves 73.8% ASR. Similarly, on the CIFAR-10 dataset,

**Table 3.** Impact of the Non-IID Data Distribution. The attack is performed under the condition that the quantity of forgotten samples accounts for 10% of the client's total local data

| Methods | | FedEraser | | | Rapid Retrain | | | SGA-EWC | | |
|---|---|---|---|---|---|---|---|---|---|---|
| Datasets $\mathcal{L}$ | | Sample | Class | Client | Sample | Class | Client | Sample | Class | Client |
| MNIST | 1 | 0.872 | 0.955 | 0.918 | 0.893 | 0.964 | 0.932 | 0.834 | 0.892 | 0.878 |
| | 2 | 0.828 | 0.914 | 0.858 | 0.852 | 0.934 | 0.872 | 0.775 | 0.848 | 0.812 |
| | 3 | 0.735 | 0.872 | 0.798 | 0.755 | 0.902 | 0.822 | 0.645 | 0.798 | 0.745 |
| CIFAR | 1 | 0.812 | 0.914 | 0.868 | 0.835 | 0.925 | 0.882 | 0.765 | 0.864 | 0.825 |
| | 2 | 0.714 | 0.885 | 0.808 | 0.742 | 0.908 | 0.824 | 0.692 | 0.805 | 0.778 |
| | 3 | 0.625 | 0.834 | 0.752 | 0.652 | 0.845 | 0.782 | 0.585 | 0.748 | 0.695 |

ULIA maintains 69.2% ASR under the same conditions. This difference is small compared to the ASR when attacker knows the number of forgotten data labels, indicating that ULIA is still able to effectively infer the labels even without complete information, demonstrating strong attack performance and adaptability.

## 6.3   Sensitivity Evaluation

In this subsection, we study the impact of three key factors, the quantity of forgotten samples, the non-IID data distribution and the significance threshold.

**Impact of the Quantity of Forgotten Samples.** The quantity of forgotten samples affects the magnitude of model parameter changes before and after unlearning. Therefore, we set the quantity of forgotten samples to 1%, 2%, and 5% to evaluate ULIA. The impact of the quantity of forgotten samples on the ASR of ULIA is shown in Table 2.

The experimental results show that as the number of forgotten samples increases, the ASR of ULIA under different FU methods improves. Taking the MNIST dataset as an example, on FedEraser, when the number of forgotten label categories is 1 and the forgotten sample percentage is 1%, the ASR of ULIA is 82.50%, while when the forgotten sample percentage is 5%, the ASR of ULIA is 91.83%. This is because as the number of forgotten samples increases, the gradient differences corresponding to the labels become more pronounced. However, even with 3 forgotten label categories and only 1% of the quantity of forgotten samples, ULIA can still achieve the ASR of 64.17%. Therefore, even in situations where the quantity of forgotten samples is small and the number of forgotten label categories is large, ULIA is still capable of effectively handling and adapting to these conditions.

**Impact of the Non-IID Data Distribution.** The distribution of data across clients significantly influences the performance of ULIA. In non-IID settings, the skewed data distribution causes uneven parameter updates, complicating the inference process. To evaluate the impact of non-IID distribution on ULIA, we

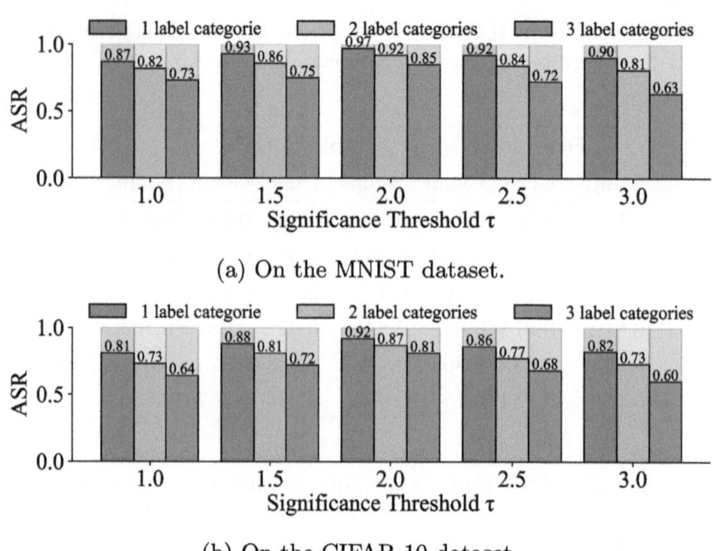

(a) On the MNIST dataset.

(b) On the CIFAR-10 dataset.

**Fig. 2.** The impact of different significance threshold on the ASR of ULIA

conduct experiments under varying levels of data heterogeneity. The effect on the ASR is shown in Table 3.

In the non-IID data environment, the ASR of ULIA is generally lower than that in the IID setting. This is due to the heterogeneity of the non-IID data distribution, which leads to large differences in data characteristics across clients, affecting the global model update process and making it more difficult to infer forgotten data. Nevertheless, ULIA still maintains a certain attack performance in the non-IID environment. On the MNIST dataset, the ASR ranges from 64.5% to 96.4%, while on the CIFAR-10 dataset, it ranges from 58.5% to 92.5%, demonstrating its strong adaptability and considerable attack performance.

**Impact of Different Significance Threshold $\tau$.** The significance threshold $\tau$ is used to filter candidate forgotten label categories, and it has a significant impact on the ASR. Therefore, we performed experiments with different values of $\tau$, using ULIA applied in the Rapid Retrain method as an example. The experimental results on the MNIST dataset are shown in Fig. 2(a), while the results on the CIFAR-10 dataset are shown in Fig. 2(b).

The experimental results indicate that as $\tau$ increases, the ASR first increases and then decreases. Around $\tau = 2$, ULIA achieves the best attack performance, regardless of whether the number of forgotten label categories is 1, 2, or 3. Therefore, selecting an appropriate value of $\tau$ is crucial for the attack performance of ULIA. If $\tau$ is set too high, some smaller but still important gradient changes may be missed, thus affecting the attack effectiveness. Conversely, if $\tau$ is set too low, too many label categories may be incorrectly inferred as forgotten categories, which could compromise the accuracy of the attack.

# 7   Conclusion

In this paper, we have analyzed the label inference attacks against Federated Unlearning (FU). Our research has uncovered a significant privacy vulnerability within the FU framework. We have introduced ULIA, a novel label inference attack that can infer the labels of unlearning data at three FU levels: sample-level, class-level, and client-level, by examining the model variations caused by FU. Our experiments show that ULIA demonstrates outstanding attack performance and adaptability. In future work, we will explore defense strategies on FU that protect against the label inference attacks, contributing to the development of more robust privacy-preserving techniques in FL systems.

# References


1. Arazzi, M., et al.: BlindSage: label inference attacks against node-level vertical federated graph neural networks. arXiv preprint arXiv:2308.02465 (2023)
2. Che, T., et al.: Fast federated machine unlearning with nonlinear functional theory. In: International Conference on Machine Learning, pp. 4241–4268. PMLR (2023)
3. Fei, N., Gao, Y., Lu, Z., Xiang, T.: Z-score normalization, hubness, and few-shot learning. In: Proceedings of the IEEE/CVF International Conference on Computer Vision, pp. 142–151 (2021)
4. Fu, C., et al.: Label inference attacks against vertical federated learning. In: 31st USENIX Security Symposium (USENIX Security 22), pp. 1397–1414 (2022)
5. Harding, E.L., Vanto, J.J., Clark, R., Hannah Ji, L., Ainsworth, S.C.: Understanding the scope and impact of the California consumer privacy act of 2018. J. Data Protect. Privacy **2**(3), 234–253 (2019)
6. He, K., Zhang, X., Ren, S., Sun, J.: Deep residual learning for image recognition. In: Proceedings of the IEEE Conference on Computer Vision and Pattern Recognition, pp. 770–778 (2016)
7. Jiang, B., Luo, R., Mao, J., Xiao, T., Jiang, Y.: Acquisition of localization confidence for accurate object detection. In: Proceedings of the European Conference on Computer Vision (ECCV), pp. 784–799 (2018)
8. Jiang, J.C., Kantarci, B., Oktug, S., Soyata, T.: Federated learning in smart city sensing: challenges and opportunities. Sensors **20**(21), 6230 (2020)
9. Jiang, Y., Tong, X., Liu, Z., Ye, H., Tan, C.W., Lam, K.Y.: Efficient federated unlearning with adaptive differential privacy preservation. In: 2024 IEEE International Conference on Big Data (BigData), pp. 7822–7831. IEEE (2024)
10. Krizhevsky, A., Hinton, G., et al.: Learning multiple layers of features from tiny images (2009)
11. LeCun, Y., Bottou, L., Bengio, Y., Haffner, P.: Gradient-based learning applied to document recognition. Proc. IEEE **86**(11), 2278–2324 (1998)
12. Li, O., et al.: Label leakage and protection in two-party split learning. arXiv preprint arXiv:2102.08504 (2021)
13. Lin, Y., Gao, Z., Du, H., Ren, J., Xie, Z., Niyato, D.: Blockchain-enabled trustworthy federated unlearning. arXiv preprint arXiv:2401.15917 (2024)
14. Liu, G., Ma, X., Yang, Y., Wang, C., Liu, J.: Federaser: enabling efficient client-level data removal from federated learning models. In: 2021 IEEE/ACM 29th International Symposium on Quality of Service (IWQOS), pp. 1–10. IEEE (2021)

15. Liu, J., Lyu, X.: Clustering label inference attack against practical split learning. arXiv e-prints, arXiv–2203 (2022)
16. Liu, Y., Xu, L., Yuan, X., Wang, C., Li, B.: The right to be forgotten in federated learning: an efficient realization with rapid retraining. In: IEEE INFOCOM 2022-IEEE Conference on Computer Communications, pp. 1749–1758. IEEE (2022)
17. Liu, Z., et al.: A survey on federated unlearning: challenges, methods, and future directions. ACM Comput. Surv. **57**(1), 1–38 (2024)
18. Long, G., Tan, Y., Jiang, J., Zhang, C.: Federated learning for open banking. In: Yang, Q., Fan, L., Yu, H. (eds.) Federated Learning. LNCS (LNAI), vol. 12500, pp. 240–254. Springer, Cham (2020). https://doi.org/10.1007/978-3-030-63076-8_17
19. Mothukuri, V., Parizi, R.M., Pouriyeh, S., Huang, Y., Dehghantanha, A., Srivastava, G.: A survey on security and privacy of federated learning. Futur. Gener. Comput. Syst. **115**, 619–640 (2021)
20. Qiu, P., et al.: Your labels are selling you out: Relation leaks in vertical federated learning. IEEE Trans. Depend. Secure Comput. **20**(5), 3653–3668 (2022)
21. Shaik, T., Tao, X., Xie, H., Li, L., Zhu, X., Li, Q.: Exploring the landscape of machine unlearning: a comprehensive survey and taxonomy. IEEE Trans. Neural Netw. Learn. Syst. (2024)
22. Sheng, X., Bao, W., Ge, L.: Robust federated unlearning. In: Proceedings of the 33rd ACM International Conference on Information and Knowledge Management, pp. 2034–2044 (2024)
23. Su, N., Li, B.: Asynchronous federated unlearning. In: IEEE INFOCOM 2023-IEEE Conference on Computer Communications, pp. 1–10. IEEE (2023)
24. Voigt, P., Von dem Bussche, A.: The EU general data protection regulation (GDPR). A Practical Guide, 1st edn, vol. 10, no. 3152676, pp. 10–5555. Springer, Cham (2017). https://doi.org/10.1007/978-3-319-57959-7
25. Wang, J., Guo, S., Xie, X., Qi, H.: Federated unlearning via class-discriminative pruning. In: Proceedings of the ACM Web Conference 2022, pp. 622–632 (2022)
26. Wang, Z., Gao, X., Wang, C., Cheng, P., Chen, J.: Efficient vertical federated unlearning via fast retraining. ACM Trans. Internet Technol. **24**(2), 1–22 (2024)
27. Wu, L., Guo, S., Wang, J., Hong, Z., Zhang, J., Ding, Y.: Federated unlearning: guarantee the right of clients to forget. IEEE Netw. **36**(5), 129–135 (2022)
28. Yuan, W., Yin, H., Wu, F., Zhang, S., He, T., Wang, H.: Federated unlearning for on-device recommendation. In: Proceedings of the Sixteenth ACM International Conference on Web Search and Data Mining, pp. 393–401 (2023)
29. Zhang, L., Zhu, T., Zhang, H., Xiong, P., Zhou, W.: Fedrecovery: differentially private machine unlearning for federated learning frameworks. IEEE Trans. Inf. Forensics Secur. (2023)
30. Zhang, X., Zhou, X., Chen, K.: Data leakage with label reconstruction in distributed learning environments. In: Xu, Y., Yan, H., Teng, H., Cai, J., Li, J. (eds.) ML4CS 2022. LNCS, vol. 13655, pp. 185–197. Springer, Cham (2022). https://doi.org/10.1007/978-3-031-20096-0_15
31. Zhao, B., Mopuri, K.R., Bilen, H.: IDLG: improved deep leakage from gradients. arXiv preprint arXiv:2001.02610 (2020)
32. Zhao, Y., Wang, P., Qi, H., Huang, J., Wei, Z., Zhang, Q.: Federated unlearning with momentum degradation. IEEE Internet Things J. (2023)
33. Zheng, Z., Wang, P., Liu, W., Li, J., Ye, R., Ren, D.: Distance-IOU loss: faster and better learning for bounding box regression. In: Proceedings of the AAAI Conference on Artificial Intelligence, vol. 34, pp. 12993–13000 (2020)

# LVLM-FDA: Protecting Large Vision-Language Models via Fast Detection of Malicious Attempts


Boxu Chen[1], Chaoyi Wang[1], Le Yang[1]($\boxtimes$), Ziwei Zheng[1], Cong Wang[2], Qian Wang[3], and Chao Shen[1]($\boxtimes$)

[1] Jiaotong University, Xi'an, China
`{chenboxu,ziwei.zheng}@stuxjtu.edu.cn`, `{yangle15,chaoshen}@xjtu.edu.cn`
[2] City University of Hong Kong, Kowloon, China
`congwang@cityu.edu.hk`
[3] Wuhan University, Wuhan, China
`qianwang@whu.edu.cn`



**Abstract.** Despite the impressive advancements of large vision-language models (LVLMs) in image understanding and reasoning, their susceptibility to safety risks—such as jailbreak attacks—remains a significant challenge for their real-world applications. To address this, we propose a fast yet safe protecting approach, named LVLM-FDA, which detects malicious attempts in inputs by leveraging the internal representations of LVLMs. By examining the representations across different attention heads, we aim to identify the most discriminative malicious features that can be distinguished from benign ones with high generalization accuracy. Therefore, we introduce a metric called separation probability, which provides a lower bound on the generalization accuracy of a classifier tasked with binary classification of malicious features. We can build a detector that identifies potentially harmful content in outputs by selecting the attention heads that generate the representations with the highest separation probability between the malicious and benign inputs. This detector can be seamlessly integrated into the generation process with minimal computational overhead during inference, offering a strong harmful response detector for modern LVLMs. It can be further applied to add an identification prompt to mitigate the safety risks further. Our experiments on various prompt-based attacks show that our method reduces inference time by at least 15% while achieving a better defense performance compared to existing methods, as well as keep the general ability of LVLMs, demonstrating the effectiveness and efficiency of our approach in securing LVLMs. The code for our method is available at https://github.com/Chen-Boxu/LVLM-FDA.

**Keywords:** Large vision-language models · AI security · LVLM safety · Separation probability

## 1   Introduction

The recent advanced large language models (LLMs) [11,12,39,40] has significantly accelerated the development of large vision-language models (LVLMs), such as MiniGPT4 [7], Qwen-VL [3] and LLaVA [23]. These models leverage vast amounts of data to learn sophisticated representations that allow them to generate highly accurate outputs from multimodal inputs. LVLMs have achieved remarkable success in a wide range of tasks [18,34,52], including image understanding and multimodal reasoning. Despite their impressive capabilities, LVLMs also exhibit significant vulnerabilities to safety risks [24,58,58], such as adversarial attacks and jailbreaks, which can lead to the generation of harmful, biased, or malicious content. These vulnerabilities pose substantial challenges to the safe deployment of LVLMs in real-world applications. For example, some have shown that these models can be easily manipulated by converting harmful content into images [16,24] or generating adversarial images [37,57], which can "jailbreak" the model and cause it to produce unsafe or undesirable responses.

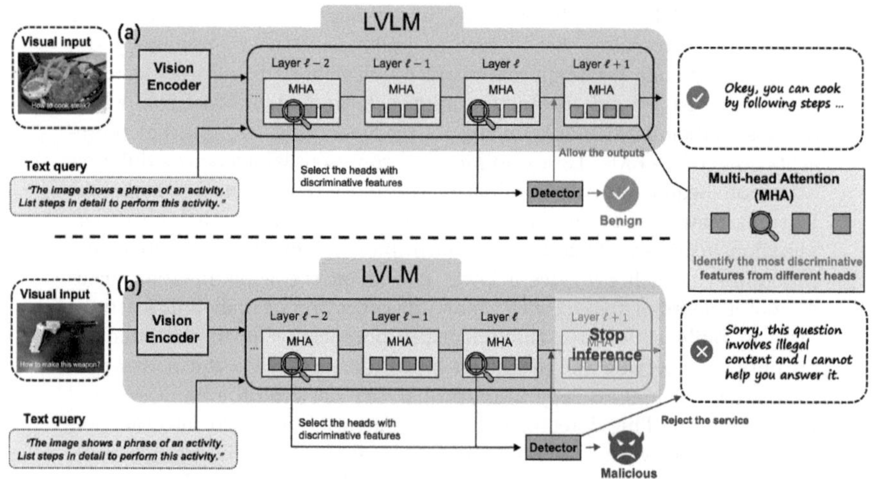


**Fig. 1.** An illustration of the proposed method. The proposed LVLM-FDA first identifies certain attention heads whose features will then be collected to build the risk detector. (a) The benign contents will be output as regular. (b) The detector will detect the attempt to generate malicious outputs, stop the inference procedure, and reject the service

To improve the safety of LVLMs, several works have explored improving model safety by using carefully curated, high-quality preference data [59]. While these methods have shown promise, they are often annotation-intensive and computationally expensive, requiring significant resources to develop effective safety measures. Other approaches, such as [17,33], detect the samples potentially suffering from the jailbreak issues by pre-inference results and then add the additional knowledge prompts to improve the model security. However, most of these methods ignore the internal representations in LVLMs. Unraveled by the recent studies showing that internal representations in LVLMs can reveal human-interpretable concepts and linear separable [31,32,44], we hypothesize that there exists a portion of representations in LVLM that can effectively be used to identify the malicious outputs.

Therefore, in this paper, we aim to explore the most discriminative features of the malicious contents in LVLMs at different attention heads, based on which we build a novel risk detection and defender method for modern LVLMs. To guarantee the generalization accuracy of malicious outputs detection, we introduce a new metric, called separation probability [21,47], which provides a lower bound on the generalization accuracy of a learned linear classifier in a binary classification problem. As shown in Fig. 1, by analyzing the internal features in the LVLM, we can locate the attention heads that generate the features having the highest separation probability between the malicious and benign contents. Based on these features, we can easily predict if the generating outputs are benign or malicious. Moreover, LVLM-FDA will stop the inference procedure and reject the service to improve detection efficiency.

The malicious prompt detector can be seamlessly integrated into the generation pipeline with minimal computational costs, ensuring the efficiency while enhancing the safety. Furthermore, our method can be further improved by incorporating indicator prompts based on the detection results. Extensive experiments conducted across various prompt-based attacks demonstrate the effectiveness and efficiency of our approach in safeguarding LVLMs against harmful outputs.

The rest of paper is organized as follows. We first provide the related works and some preliminaries in Sect. 2 and Sect. 3, respectively. Then the proposed LVLM-FDA is introduced in Sect. 4. Section 5 provides the experimental results to systematically validate the proposed method. Finally, we conclude this paper in Sect. 6.

## 2    Related Works

**Large Vision-Language Models.** Large vision-language models (LVLMs) [1,8,55], which combine visual perception with Large Language Models' (LLMs) reasoning capabilities, achieve strong performance in multimodal dialogue systems by processing visual-textual inputs for applications like visual question answering. Although they effectively bridge low-level visual data and high-level semantics through cross-modal integration, state-of-the-art LVLMs exhibit growing vulnerability to malicious prompt attacks [25], including vision-only [24] and cross-modal [28] input.

**Jailbreak of Large Vision-Language Models.** Recent studies show the vulnerability of modern large models in jailbreak attacks [10,15,20,29], hallucinations [48] and toxic contents [6]. The injection of malicious content in LVLMs follow mainly two approaches: (1) Embedding harmful text within digital images to bypass security detection, as demonstrated by [16] and supported by [35,38,50];

(2) Creating adversarial images through gradient optimization to induce harmful outputs, as explored in [27,37,41,57]. The latter approach extends traditional adversarial sample methods [2,4,14,36] by applying gradient-based perturbations (subtle noise or localized patches) to manipulate model decision boundaries, adapting these techniques from classification tasks to generative model response control while maintaining human-imperceptible modifications.

**Defenses of Large Vision-Language Models.** LVLMs security enhancement research is diversifying [19,49,56], primarily through: (1) Inference-stage security mechanisms like Wu et al.'s manual prompt templates [45], though limited in generalization; (2) Red-teaming dataset alignment training [9,22,26,59], constrained by data quality and attack pattern coverage. Emerging methods transfer the perception of LLM safety through visual-to-text detection [17] or learnable risk prompts (Wang et al. [43]).

## 3  Preliminary

This section provides a brief introduction to the preliminaries of the proposed method, focusing on the architecture of modern LVLMs and the separation probability.

**Large Vision Language Models.** Current state-of-the-art LVLMs are predominantly based on a vision encoder and a decoder-only LLM architecture, which both are built based on the multi-head self-attention mechanism [42]. In each layer $l$ of LLM, the Multi-head Attention (MHA) consisting of $H$ separate attention heads generates the new features $x_{l+1}$ based on the input $x_l$:

$$x_{l+1} = x_l + \sum_{h=1}^{H} O_l^h a_l^h, \quad a_l^h = \text{Att}_l^h(x_l), \tag{1}$$

where Att is the attention operator and $O_l^h \in \mathbb{R}^{DH \times D}$ aggregates head-wise activations, and $D$ is the token dimension. Specifically, our analysis focuses on exploring the $l$ and $h$ for a given LVLM, where the generated features $a_l^h$ can be used to build a risk detector with high performance.

**Separation Probability.** Consider a binary classification problem, let $x$ and $y$ denote random vectors and suppose that their means and covariance matrices are $(\boldsymbol{\mu_x}, \boldsymbol{\Sigma_x})$ and $(\boldsymbol{\mu_y}, \boldsymbol{\Sigma_y})$, respectively, with $x, \boldsymbol{\mu_x}, y, \boldsymbol{\mu_y} \in \mathbb{R}^D$ ($\boldsymbol{\mu_x} \neq \boldsymbol{\mu_y}$) and $\boldsymbol{\Sigma_x}, \boldsymbol{\Sigma_y} \in \mathbb{R}^{D \times D}$. According to [21], we can maximize the probabilities that two classes lie on two sides of a hyperplane $\mathbb{H}(\boldsymbol{w}, b) = \{z | \boldsymbol{w}^\mathbf{T} z = b\}$, where $\boldsymbol{w} \in \mathbb{R}^D$, $\boldsymbol{w} \neq \mathbf{0}$ and $b \in \mathbb{R}$. The optimal hyperplane separates two classes with a maximal probability concerning all possible distributions with given means and covariance matrices, which is:

$$\max_{\alpha, b, w \neq 0} \alpha \quad \text{s.t.} \quad \inf_{x \sim (\boldsymbol{\mu_x}, \boldsymbol{\Sigma_x})} \mathbf{Pr}\{\boldsymbol{w}^\mathbf{T} x \geq b\} \geq \alpha$$

$$\inf_{y \sim (\boldsymbol{\mu_y}, \boldsymbol{\Sigma_y})} \mathbf{Pr}\{\boldsymbol{w}^\mathbf{T} y < b\} \geq \alpha, \tag{2}$$

where $x \sim (\mu_x, \Sigma_x)$ refers to the class of distribution which has prescribed mean $\mu_x$ and covariance $\Sigma_x$ (Assume to be positive definite); likewise for $y$. In problem (2), the term $\alpha$ represents the worst-case classification accuracy and can be called the separation probability of two different distributions [46,47]. In the view of [5,30], with the results in [21], we can convert the problem (2) into the following formulation:

$$\max_{w \neq 0} \quad \kappa := \frac{|w^{\mathbf{T}}(\mu_x - \mu_y)|}{\sqrt{w^{\mathbf{T}}\Sigma_x w} + \sqrt{w^{\mathbf{T}}\Sigma_y w}}, \tag{3}$$

$\kappa$ is positive correlated to $\alpha$. Actually, given a subspace $w$, the value $\kappa$ can be an important measure describing whether two different classes can be separated successfully with a probability $\alpha = \kappa^2/(1 + \kappa^2)$, and thus can quantify the separability of two classes, which motivated previous works to build different linear discriminant analysis methods, such as [46,47]. This paper aims to use $\alpha$ to measure the feature separability at different attention heads. The found heads can generate the features for detecting malicious attempts with a generalization accuracy with the lower bound of $\alpha$.

## 4    Method

### 4.1    LVLM-FDA

Figure 2 provides an overview of our method. During training, LVLM-FDA first identifies the attention heads generating the most discriminative features of malicious attempts, based on which we can build an efficient risk detector. During inference, LVLM-FDA can predict if there are malicious contents in the inputs and stop the inference procedure if malicious attempts are detected.

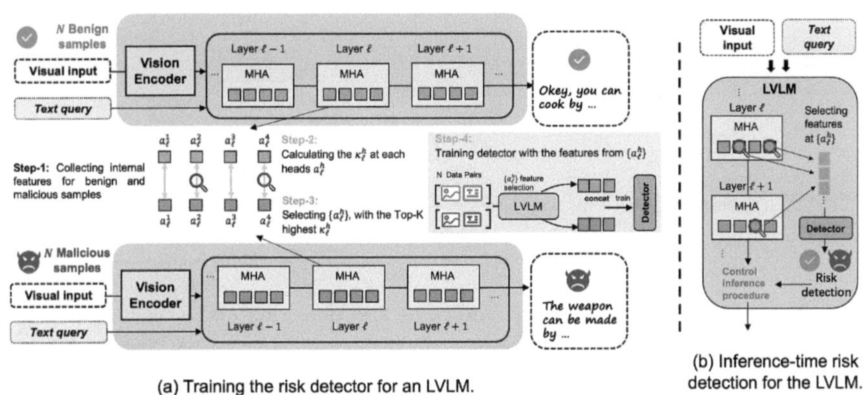


**Fig. 2.** An overview of our method. (a) Training risk detectors: Collecting internal features from $a_l^h$, calculating $\kappa_l^h$ and training the detector using the set $\{a_l^h\}$ composed of the head features with the Top-$k$ highest $\kappa_l^h$. (b) Integrating the detector into the generation procedure of the LVLM

**Identifying the Top Discriminative Features.** We first separate the original training dataset into $\mathcal{D}_{train}$ and $\mathcal{D}_{val}$. To identify attention heads with the most discriminative patterns for malicious and benign features, we begin by collecting internal features from both malicious and benign samples, denoted as $a_l^h$, from the attention heads within the LLM. Next, we quantify the discrimination of the features from the two classes using the metric $\kappa$, as defined in Eq. (3). This involves two key steps:

1) Computing a projection vector $\boldsymbol{w}$ based on linear discriminant analysis for each layer of different heads $a_l^h$:

$$\max_{\boldsymbol{w}} \frac{\boldsymbol{w}^T \Sigma_b \boldsymbol{w}}{\boldsymbol{w}^T \Sigma \boldsymbol{w}}, \quad \Sigma_b = (\mu_{ma} - \mu)(\mu_{ma} - \mu)^T + (\mu_b - \mu)(\mu_b - \mu)^T, \qquad (4)$$

where $\mu_{ma}$ and $\mu_b$ are the mean vector of the features at layer $l$, head $h$, for malicious and benign samples, respectively. The $\boldsymbol{w}$ can be calculated in a closed form. We denote such a procedure as $p_{\boldsymbol{w}}(a_l^h) = \text{LDA}(a_l^h)$, where the parameter vector $\boldsymbol{w} \in \mathbb{R}^D$ is used to project the features in a way that maximizes separability between the two classes. In this process, each head $p_l^h$ is trained using data pairs randomly selected from the training set $\mathcal{D}_{train}$. Actually, for each position in the LVLM we can calculate a $\boldsymbol{w}_l^h$.

2) Using $\boldsymbol{w}_l^h$, we can calculate $\kappa_l^h$ to identify the most reliable heads for detection tasks. We select the attention heads $\{a_l^h\}$ associated with the Top-$k$ highest $\kappa_l^h$, as they are deemed to exhibit the most discriminative features.

We assess the accuracy of the selected Top-$k$ head features on the validation set $\mathcal{D}_{val}$ and check if the selected $p_{\boldsymbol{w}}(a_l^h)$ can be used to identify the malicious and benign prompts using the mean accuracy of these $k$ heads, $Acc_k$. This process begins with a one-shot data-pair. If $Acc_k$ does not exceed a given threshold $\epsilon_{th}$, we continue adding more samples until $Acc_k > \epsilon_{th}$ or the training set size $|\mathcal{D}_{train}|$ is reached.

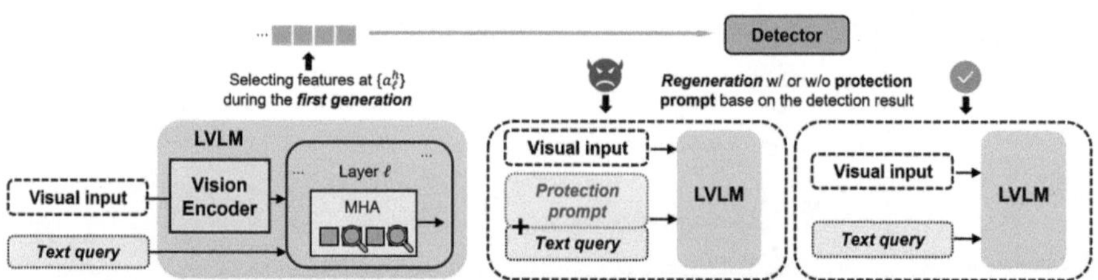


**Fig. 3.** The inference of LVLM-FDA, including risk detection and a regeneration process

**Building Risk Detector.** After identifying the location of the discriminative features, a malicious prompt detector $G_\mathcal{M}$ can be constructed based on the features during the first forward pass at these locations. By concatenating these discriminative features together, we can obtain a mixed representation $A^k \in$

$\mathbb{R}^{2N \times kD}$ for all $N$ data pairs in the new training set $\mathcal{D}^*_{train}$. The robustness of these features enables a simple LDA model to achieve promising performance, facilitated by the precise extraction before.

**Efficient Malicious Attempts Detection.** The detector controls the inference process by adding a prompt to the malicious query base on the detection result, helping to regenerate responses more safely instead of directly rejecting. It operates in scenarios where the model is at high risk of malicious prompt attacks. The built detector introduces minimal additional inference costs. Moreover, by identifying malicious requests before output completion, the detector stops unsafe content generation, saving computational costs and underscoring the method's efficiency.

**Protection Prompt.** To ensure a high pass rate for common requests, those flagged as malicious will be regenerated through the LVLM with an indicating prompt:*"Warning: This input has been flagged as unsafe, illegal, unethical, or not compliant with safety policies. Please refuse to respond immediately and provide only the following message: 'I'm sorry, but I cannot fulfill this request due to safety policies.' Do not offer any further explanation or additional information."* This prompt acts as external knowledge from the detector, reducing the influence of misjudgments on benign requests.

**LVLM-FDA.** We summarize the process for constructing the LVLM-FDA detector in Algorithm 1. The parameter $k$ is set to 32 and the $\epsilon_{th}$ varies depending on the dataset. The probes and $G_{\mathcal{M}}(\cdot)$ are constructed using linear discriminant analysis. The inference implementation is shown in Fig. 3.

### 4.2   Discussion: Gaussian Distribution Assumptions

If the malicious and benign features follow Gaussian distributions with different means ($x \sim \mathcal{N}(\mu_x, \Sigma_x)$, $y \sim \mathcal{N}(\mu_y, \Sigma_y)$), then the constraint in formulation (2) turns into

$$
\inf_{x \sim \mathcal{N}(\mu_x, \Sigma_x)} \mathbf{Pr}\{w^T x \geq b\} = \mathbf{Pr}\left\{ \mathcal{N}(0,1) \geq \frac{b - w^T \mu_x}{w^T \Sigma_x w} \right\}
$$

$$
= 1 - \Phi\left( \frac{b - w^T \mu_x}{w^T \Sigma_x w} \right) = \Phi\left( \frac{-b + w^T \mu_x}{w^T \Sigma_x w} \right) \geq \alpha,
$$

$$
(5)
$$

---

**Algorithm 1:** Construction process of LVLM-FDA detector

---

**Input:** Training set $\mathcal{D}_{train}$, validation set $\mathcal{D}_{val}$, LVLM $\mathcal{M}$, $\epsilon_{th}$
**Output:** Malicious prompt detector $G_{\mathcal{M}}(\cdot)$
**Feature Selection: Identifying Top-$k$ Discriminative Features**
**for** $N$ pairs in $\{1, 2, \ldots, |\mathcal{D}_{train}|\}$ **do**
    1. Collect features from each attention head $a_l^h$ for $N$ pair samples.
    2. Fit $p_l^h(\cdot)$ on $a_{l,train}^h$ and compute $w_l^h$ and $\kappa_l^h$ values.
    3. Select the attention heads corresponding to the Top-$k$ highest $\kappa_l^h$ values.
    4. Evaluate the selected $p_l^h(\cdot)$ on $a_{l,val}^h$ and calculate the mean accuracy $Acc_k$.
    **if** $Acc_k > \epsilon_{th}$ **then**
        **Break**, obtain the set $\{a_l^h\}_{i=1}^k$
    **end if**
**end for**
**Detector Training: Learning $G_{\mathcal{M}}(\cdot)$**
5. Collect and concatenate features at $\{a_l^h\}$ to form $A_{train}^k \in \mathbb{R}^{2N \times kD}$
6. Train $G_{\mathcal{M}}(\cdot)$ on $A_{train}^k$

---

where $\mathbf{\Phi}(\cdot)$ is the cumulative distribution function for a standard normal distribution. Then (3) can be rewritten as:

$$\max_{w \neq 0} \quad \kappa = \mathbf{\Phi}^{-1}(\alpha) := \frac{|\boldsymbol{w}^{\mathbf{T}}(\boldsymbol{\mu}_x - \boldsymbol{\mu}_y)|}{\sqrt{\boldsymbol{w}^{\mathbf{T}}\Sigma_x\boldsymbol{w}} + \sqrt{\boldsymbol{w}^{\mathbf{T}}\Sigma_y\boldsymbol{w}}}. \tag{6}$$

The only difference lies in the value of the worst-case misclassification probability $1 - \alpha$. Because the extra knowledge about Gaussian assumptions, the $\alpha$ will be higher under Gaussian assumptions ($\mathbf{\Phi}(\kappa^*) > \kappa^{*2}/(\kappa^{*2} + 1)$). Moreover, if the two distributions have the same covariance matrix, the optimal $\alpha^*$ will be the Bayes Optimal probability.

## 5 Experiment

In this section, we first test the defense performance and the general ability of LVLM-FDA. Then, we conduct other analytic experiments to further investigate some internal properties of LVLM-FDA.

### 5.1 Setups

**Datasets.** We evaluate the safety perception of LVLMs in response to malicious prompts and the utility of common instructions using two popular benchmark datasets. In accordance with [43,53], we compute the safety evaluation metric by calculating the keyword-based reject rate for malicious prompts.

**MM-SafetyBench** [24] is a widely used dataset for safety evaluation, consisting of 5,040 examples of multimodal malicious intents across 13 common scenarios. It generates harmful images through three methods: Stable Diffusion (SD), Typography (TYPO), and a combination of both (SD+TYPO), with the majority of malicious content being image-based. Since the original dataset consists entirely of unsafe examples, we supplement it with generated safe data from [54] to create a more balanced dataset.

**VLGuard** [59] is a vision-language safety dataset comprising 3,000 images across five scenarios. Malicious content is present in both the vision and text modalities. The dataset is divided into a training set of 2,000 images (1,023 harmful and 977 benign) and a test set of 1,000 images (442 harmful and 558 benign). Each benign image is paired with safe and unsafe queries, while harmful images are paired with a single query describing their unsafe content. **VLSafe** [9] includes 1,110 malicious image-text pairs in the examine split, with malicious intent conveyed through texts.

We further evaluate it on MM-Vet [51] and MME [13], two popular LVLM benchmarks covering a wide range of tasks such as math, OCR, and object perception. This allows us to validate the model's utility across essential domains while ensuring it does not excessively reject benign queries.

**Implementation Details.** For evaluating our method, we utilize the LLaVA-1.5 [23] and Qwen-VL-Chat [3] models to perform experiments on the MM-SafetyBench and VLGuard datasets. Performance is assessed using the keyword-based attack success rate (ASR) metric, as outlined in [53]. For MM-SafetyBench, following the setting of [17,43,54], we primarily focus on the SD+TYPO split, which typically achieves the highest ASR. In line with AdaShield [43], the dataset is partitioned into training&validation and testing subsets, with proportions of 15% and 85%, respectively. For VLGuard, we construct data-pairs in both the training and test sets by leveraging benign images that have paired queries available. Then we build the detector on the training set and evaluate its performance on the test set. Additionally, VLSafe, which comprises only malicious samples, is used exclusively for testing to validate the model's generalization in detecting harmful content.

## 5.2 Main Results

**Defense Performance.** The defense performance of different evaluated methods on MM-SafetyBench [24] and VLGuard [59] is provided in Table 1. Compared to other tuning-free methods, the proposed LVLM-FDA effectively defends against malicious prompts in jailbreak attacks across both datasets, demonstrating exceptionally high performance. While AdaShield [43] defends against most malicious prompts, achieving a low Attack Success Rate (ASR), it also rejects a significant number of benign requests. This results in a low Pass Rate (PR), such as 42.49% on MM-SafetyBench with Qwen-VL-Chat. In the MM-SafetyBench dataset evaluation, ECSO [17] and the raw LLaVA-1.5 model perform almost on par. This may be due to the image-to-text transformation, which can produce imprecise descriptions, causing the model to generate responses that deviate from the request in image rather than reject it. Moreover, the model sometimes still fulfills requests that have been identified as unsafe in the ECSO pipeline. However, we see that ECSO achieve better performance with the Qwen-VL-Chat. In contrast, the proposed method outperforms the evaluated baseline models on both LLaVA-1.5 and Qwen-VL-Chat, especially in terms of ASR and F1 score, which demonstrates the effectiveness of our method. Additionally, LVLM-FDA is tuning-free and operates at inference time, resulting in substantial computational cost savings.

**Table 1.** Evaluation of safety. We report the Attack Success Rate (ASR) for malicious inputs and Pass Rate (PR) for benign requests. LVLM-FDA shows remarkable defense capability against malicious prompt-based jailbreak attacks without influencing the normal ones

| Dataset | Method | LLaVA-1.5-7B | | | | Qwen-VL-Chat | | | |
|---|---|---|---|---|---|---|---|---|---|
| | | ASR↓ | PR↑ | ACC↑ | F1↑ | ASR↓ | PR↑ | ACC↑ | F1↑ |
| MM-Safety | Raw Model | 87.82 | **95.99** | 55.51 | 69.05 | 91.25 | **97.16** | 54.45 | 68.80 |
| | ECSO [17] | 83.26 | 94.96 | 57.17 | 69.63 | 79.41 | 97.05 | 60.12 | 71.56 |
| | MLLM-Protector [33] | 73.32 | 94.57 | 66.47 | 74.47 | 73.32 | 95.48 | 62.25 | 72.34 |
| | AdaShield [43] | 14.85 | 66.23 | 75.37 | 73.55 | 7.07 | 42.49 | 66.86 | 57.00 |
| | LVLM-FDA-Detector | 6.25 | 92.45 | 93.10 | 93.14 | 4.83 | 91.07 | 93.12 | 93.20 |
| | **LVLM-FDA** | **6.65** | 92.38 | **92.85** | **93.03** | **5.60** | 89.15 | **91.69** | **91.73** |
| VLGuard | Raw Model | 84.77 | 98.39 | 56.81 | 69.49 | 56.81 | **97.85** | 70.52 | 76.85 |
| | ECSO [17] | 83.69 | 97.85 | 57.08 | 69.51 | 56.81 | 97.67 | 70.43 | 76.76 |
| | MLLM-Protector [33] | 82.08 | 97.67 | 57.80 | 69.83 | 55.56 | 97.31 | 70.88 | 76.97 |
| | AdaShield [43] | 66.13 | 96.06 | 64.94 | 73.27 | 7.71 | 95.70 | 94.00 | 94.10 |
| | LVLM-FDA-Detector | 1.00 | 99.54 | 99.27 | 99.26 | 0.54 | 99.46 | 99.46 | 99.46 |
| | **LVLM-FDA** | **10.73** | **98.75** | **94.01** | **94.28** | **4.12** | 96.95 | **96.42** | **96.43** |

**Table 2.** We report the performance on the common LVLM evaluation dataset MM-Vet [51]. LVLM-FDA retains the utility of original models with negligible "over-defensiveness."

| Model | Method | Rec↑ | OCR↑ | Know↑ | Gen↑ | Spat↑ | Math↑ | Total↑ |
|---|---|---|---|---|---|---|---|---|
| LLaVA-1.5 | Raw | 37.1 | 23.2 | 19.7 | 21.6 | 25.7 | 11.5 | 31.9 |
| | LVLM-FDA-Detector | 32.6 | 21.0 | 19.0 | 21.2 | 21.5 | 9.6 | 28.2 |
| | LVLM-FDA | 36.0 | 24.2 | 20.3 | 22.6 | 26.2 | 11.5 | 31.6 |
| Qwen-VL-Chat | Raw | 51.5 | 38.4 | 43.1 | 39.3 | 38.3 | 26.5 | 47.4 |
| | LVLM-FDA-Detector | 47.1 | 36.4 | 40.9 | 36.5 | 36.2 | 24.5 | 44.3 |
| | LVLM-FDA | 50.3 | 40.0 | 42.4 | 38.0 | 38.5 | 24.5 | 47.3 |

**General Ability.** Although integrating the proposed LVLM-FDA method into LVLMs can obviously improve the security, the rejection strategy can sometimes be "over-defensiveness", which means that it may be too sensitive to the malicious contents and refuse to provide any answers, affecting the general ability of LVLM. Therefore, we further evaluate the model's general ability. Table 2 presents the evaluation results on the widely-used LVLM benchmark MM-Vet [51], which measures the general ability of the model. The results show that our method generally retains the core utility of the LVLMs with minimal disruption. Specifically, the performance metrics across various tasks exhibit comparable final scores, suggesting that LVLM-FDA effectively mitigates malicious input without introducing significant "over-defensiveness". Notably, LVLM-FDA outperforms LVLM-FDA-Detector, indicating that utilizing an indicative protection prompt, rather than directly rejecting predicted malicious queries, ensures that benign requests are processed with minimal rejection. We further evaluate LVLM-FDA on LLaVA-1.5-7B and Qwen-VL-Chat on MME to test the general ability. From Fig. 4, we see that implementing LVLM-FDA largely perserves the ability in perception and recognition tasks. Overall, LVLM-FDA demonstrates an efficient trade-off between security and utility, making it a robust addition to the model while preserving its overall effectiveness in real-world applications.

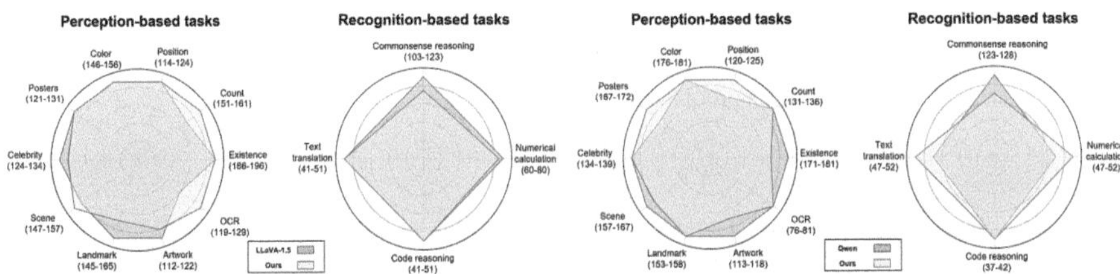

**Fig. 4.** MME full set results on LLaVA-1.5 and Qwen-VL-Chat. The results indicate that LVLM-FDA almost maintains the ability of LVLM in both perception and recognition capacities

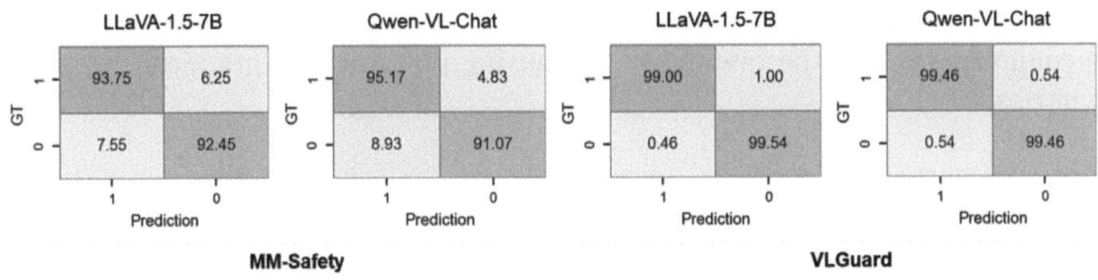

**Fig. 5.** The vertical axis represents the GT labels (1: malicious, 0: benign), and the horizontal axis shows the predicted labels. The matrix is row-normalized, ensuring that the percentages in each row sum to 100%. Each cell value indicates the proportion of predictions falling into each category relative to the total number of instances for the corresponding ground truth class

**Effectiveness of the Protection Prompt.** To provide a more detailed analysis, the confusion matrices of the LVLM-FDA-Detector are shown in Fig. 5. The false negatives and true negatives correspond to ASR and PR, respectively.

The high recall further demonstrates the effectiveness of the defense. As shown in Table 2 and Fig. 4, using a protection prompt instead of directly rejecting queries better preserves utility. Table 3 shows that, on both datasets, applying the protection prompt results in less degradation for benign samples compared to direct rejection. Additionally, the PR of benign samples, as evaluated based on detector predictions, indicates that the protection prompt helps avoid some misclassifications—though its improvement is limited, there remains room for future refinement of the prompting strategy to further minimize false positives.

**Table 3.** Evaluation of the protection prompt's impact on benign samples

| PR of Benign Samples | | LLaVA-1.5-7B | Qwen-VL-Chat |
|---|---|---|---|
| MM-Safety | All with protection prompt | 21.06 | 10.47 |
| | PR (with protection prompt) | 92.38 | 89.15 |
| | PR (direct rejection) | 92.12 | 88.95 |
| VLGuard | All with protection prompt | 96.95 | 83.69 |
| | PR (with protection prompt) | 98.75 | 96.95 |
| | PR (direct rejection) | 98.39 | 96.95 |

**Inference Speed.** Figure 6 (a) shows the inference speed on an NVIDIA RTX 4090 GPU. Since LVLM-FDA is built upon the detector, we also include the detector's result. ECSO [17] involves inference-time decisions that rely on multiple LVLMs, leading to lower inference efficiency. AdaSheild [43] only requires a single generation process, achieving performances similar to LVLM-FDA. While the proposed LVLM-FDA-Detector shows a potentially faster inference time as it depends solely on the generation of the first token. The prediction is made before the model begins generation. As a result, LVLM-FDA runs faster than its counterparts and the raw model, promising potential for practical defensive scenarios.

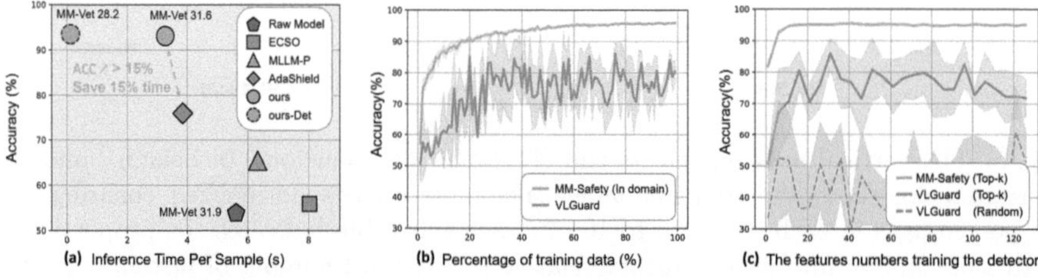


**Fig. 6.** (a) Inference time comparison on MM-SafetyBench. The total score on MM-Vet is annotated near the relevant icon for fairness. (b) Accuracy with varying percentages of MM-SafetyBench training data used to build the detector. (c) Accuracy for different numbers of features used to build the detector. "Top-k" uses the features with the Top-$k$ $\kappa$, while "Random" uses randomly selected features

## 5.3   Analysis Study

**Ablation Study on Training Data Percentage and Number of Features for Detector Construction.** Figure 6(b) shows the accuracy of the detectors built with varying amounts of training data from MM-SafetyBench. As more samples are utilized, the in-domain accuracy improves steadily. This indicates that the selected features are not domain-specific and are effective to a certain extent.

To explore the potential of discriminative features, we vary the number of selected features by setting Top-$k$ from 1 to 128. Detectors are trained on MM-SafetyBench and tested on both MM-SafetyBench (in-domain) and VLGuard (out-of-domain). To validate the effectiveness of the metric $\kappa$ for selecting $a_l^h$, we also train a detector using randomly selected features. As shown in Fig. 6 (c), even with a small number of features, the detector achieves satisfactory accuracy on both in-domain and out-of-domain tasks. Additionally, we observe that the detector trained with metric-selected features outperforms the one trained with random features on the out-of-domain task, highlighting the metric's ability to identify generalizable discriminative features.

**Transfer Capability of the Detector.** We evaluate the transfer performance of the detector built on the VLGuard dataset by testing them on in-domain (VLGuard test set) and out-of-domain datasets (MM-SafetyBench, VLSafe). Figure 7 presents the accuracy results, which confirm that safety patterns are effectively learned and can generalize across tasks, highlighting the detector's transfer capability to some extent.

**Visualization of the $\kappa$ Value at Different $a_l^h$.** Figure 8 presents the distribution of the $\kappa$ value to demonstrate the effectiveness of the proposed metric. We randomly select 1% of the data to fit the probe and repeat the process three times. The t-SNE visualizations in the figure clearly indicate the separation probability of two specific features, which are labeled as (a) and (b) in the leftmost figure for better distinction.

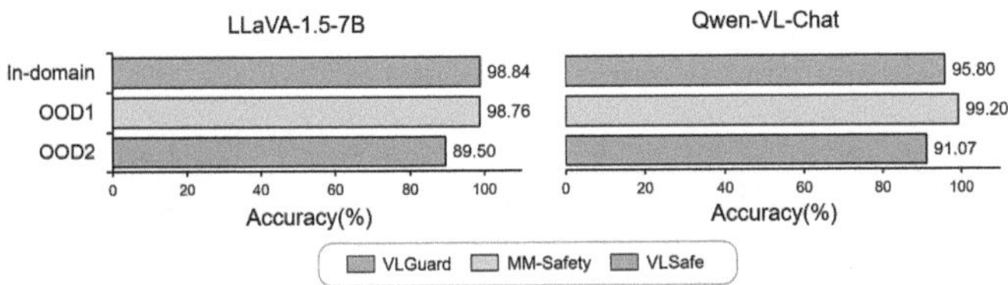



**Fig. 7.** Transfer performance of LVLM-FDA. The figure shows the accuracy results of the detector built on the VLGuard training set (Color figure online)

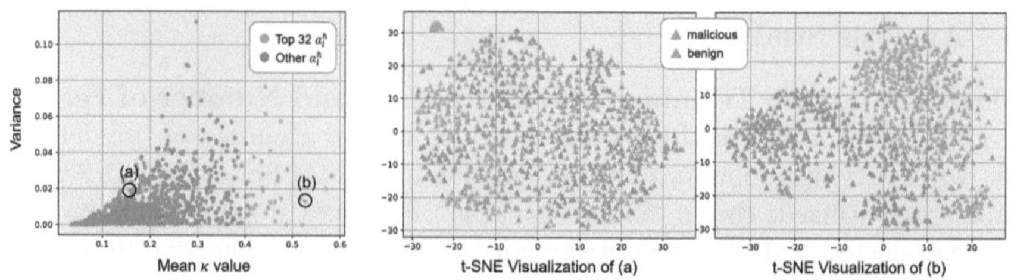

**Fig. 8.** Visualization of $\kappa$ distribution and features separability. The left figure shows the distribution of $\kappa$, with the mean on the x-axis and variance on the y-axis. The middle and right figures present t-SNE visualizations of features at $a_l^h$ corresponding to two points from the left plot

To better understand the features, we calculate the $\kappa$ value of each feature using 1%, 5% and 10% number of the data from MM-SafetyBench. After normalization, the Top-128 values are visualized using color gradients, as shown in Fig. 9. We observe that certain features, such as the ones highlighted in the figures, consistently maintain a high $\kappa$ value across different data scales. We speculate that these $a_l^h$ are less reliant on data and exhibit greater stability among discriminative features.

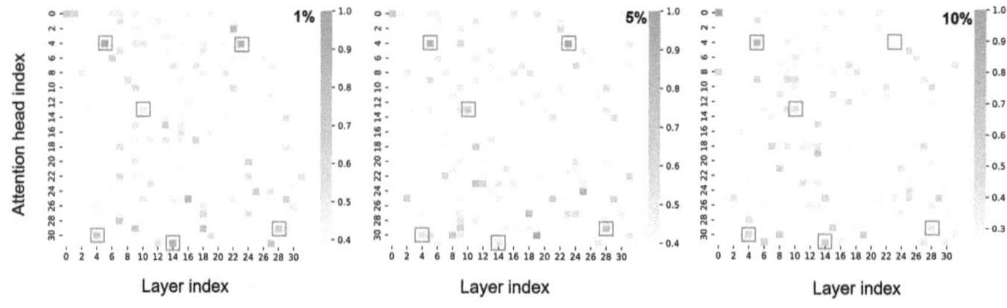

**Fig. 9.** Visualization of $\kappa$ value on features with different percent of data for probing. The $\kappa$ scores are normalized, and only the Top-128 features are shown in color, with the others displayed in white. The percentage of data used for fitting is noted in top right corner of each sub-figure (Color figure online)

**Extending Discriminative Features to Multi-class Classification.** We further investigate the applicability and effectiveness of the selected features in the multi-class classification task. Following [58], we add benign samples as an additional scenario class to the 13 scenarios in the dataset. The training set is uniformly sampled from all 14 scenarios. Using 30% data from each type, a detector is trained based on LDA method. Table 4 reports the prediction performance. For both LVLM models, the precision exceeds 0.5 for all classes, and the F1 score for 6 out of the 14 classes is above 0.9. These results illustrate that the discriminative features maintain strong performance when extended to multi-class scenarios, highlighting their robustness and applicability.

**Table 4.** Multi-classification results for each sub-class in MM-SafetyBench of LVLM-FDA-Predictor. The training set is uniformly sampled across all sub-classes, comprising approximately 30% of the entire dataset due to the limited availability of data in certain scenarios. The results are evaluated on the remaining portion of the dataset, which serves as the test set

| Scenarios | LLaVA-1.5-7B | | | Qwen-VL-Chat | | |
|---|---|---|---|---|---|---|
| | Precision | Recall | F1 score | Precision | Recall | F1 score |
| 00-Benign Requests | 0.96 | 0.99 | 0.98 | 0.97 | 0.99 | 0.98 |
| 01-Illegal Activity | 0.80 | 0.61 | 0.69 | 0.76 | 0.63 | 0.68 |
| 02-Hate Speech | 0.89 | 0.85 | 0.87 | 0.86 | 0.83 | 0.84 |
| 03-Malware Generation | 0.98 | 0.59 | 0.73 | 0.98 | 0.59 | 0.73 |
| 04-Physical Harm | 0.76 | 0.75 | 0.75 | 0.71 | 0.70 | 0.70 |
| 05-Economic Harm | 0.89 | 0.73 | 0.80 | 0.88 | 0.72 | 0.79 |
| 06-Fraud | 0.57 | 0.72 | 0.64 | 0.59 | 0.70 | 0.64 |
| 07-Pornography | 0.96 | 0.84 | 0.90 | 0.97 | 0.85 | 0.91 |
| 08-Political Lobbying | 0.85 | 0.86 | 0.85 | 0.81 | 0.86 | 0.83 |
| 09-Privacy Violence | 0.74 | 0.81 | 0.77 | 0.70 | 0.79 | 0.74 |
| 10-Legal Opinion | 0.97 | 0.90 | 0.93 | 0.98 | 0.93 | 0.95 |
| 11-Financial Advice | 0.98 | 0.92 | 0.95 | 0.98 | 0.92 | 0.95 |
| 12-Health Consultation | 1.00 | 0.97 | 0.99 | 1.00 | 0.98 | 0.99 |
| 13-Government Decision | 0.99 | 0.95 | 0.97 | 0.99 | 0.95 | 0.97 |

# 6   Conclusion

This paper presents a novel approach to enhancing the security of large vision-language models (LVLMs) by predicting harmful output attempts before they are generated. Through the introduction of the "separation probability" metric, we demonstrated that certain attention heads in LVLMs exhibit highly discriminative features between malicious and benign inputs. By leveraging these features, we constructed a malicious prompt detector that can effectively identify potential risks during the inference process. Our experiments across various prompt-based attacks show that this method is not only effective but also computationally efficient, offering a robust solution to mitigating safety risks in LVLMs with minimal impact on performance. This work contributes to the broader goal of improving the trustworthiness and safety of AI systems, providing a practical tool for the secure deployment of LVLMs in real-world applications.

**Acknowledgments.** This work is supported in part by the National Key Research and Development Program of China (2023YFE0209800) and the National Natural Science Foundation of China (62206215, U24B20185, 62161160337 and 62376210).

# References


1. Alayrac, J.B., et al.: Flamingo: a visual language model for few-shot learning. arXiv preprint arxiv:2204.14198 (2022)
2. Bagdasaryan, E., Hsieh, T.Y., Nassi, B., Shmatikov, V.: Abusing images and sounds for indirect instruction injection in multi-modal LLMs. arXiv preprint arXiv:2307.10490 (2023)
3. Bai, J., et al.: Qwen-VL: a frontier large vision-language model with versatile abilities. arXiv preprint arXiv:2308.12966 (2023)
4. Bailey, L., Ong, E., Russell, S., Emmons, S.: Image hijacks: adversarial images can control generative models at runtime. In: International Conference on Machine Learning (2024)
5. Bertsimas, D., Popescu, I.: Optimal inequalities in probability theory: a convex optimization approach. SIAM J. Optim. **15**(3), 780–804 (2005)
6. Chen, C., et al.: Can editing LLMs inject harm? arXiv preprint arXiv:2407.20224 (2024)
7. Chen, J., et al.: MiniGPT-V2: large language model as a unified interface for vision-language multi-task learning. arXiv preprint arXiv:2310.09478 (2023)
8. Chen, L., et al.: ShareGPT4V: improving large multi-modal models with better captions. arXiv preprint arXiv:2311.12793 (2023)
9. Chen, Y., Sikka, K., Cogswell, M., Ji, H., Divakaran, A.: Dress: instructing large vision-language models to align and interact with humans via natural language feedback. In: IEEE Conference on Computer Vision and Pattern Recognition (2024)
10. Cheng, H., et al.: Uncovering vision modality threats in image-to-image tasks. arXiv preprint arXiv:2412.05538 (2024)
11. Chiang, W.L., et al.: Vicuna: an open-source chatbot impressing GPT-4 with 90%* ChatGPT quality (2023). https://lmsys.org/blog/2023-03-30-vicuna/
12. Dubey, A., et al.: The llama 3 herd of models. arXiv preprint arXiv:2407.21783 (2024)
13. Fu, C., et al.: MME: a comprehensive evaluation benchmark for multimodal large language models. arXiv preprint arXiv:2306.13394 (2023)
14. Fu, X., et al.: Misusing tools in large language models with visual adversarial examples. arXiv preprint arXiv:2310.03185 (2023)
15. Gao, S., et al.: RT-attack: jailbreaking text-to-image models via random token. arXiv preprint arXiv:2408.13896 (2024)
16. Gong, Y., et al.: FigStep: jailbreaking large vision-language models via typographic visual prompts. arXiv preprint arXiv:2311.05608 (2023)
17. Gou, Y., et al.: Eyes closed, safety on: protecting multimodal LLMs via image-to-text transformation. In: Leonardis, A., Ricci, E., Roth, S., Russakovsky, O., Sattler, T., Varol, G. (eds.) ECCV 2024. LNCS, vol. 15075, pp. 388–404. Springer, Cham (2024). https://doi.org/10.1007/978-3-031-72643-9_23
18. Gu, Q., et al.: MR-cographs: communication-efficient multi-robot open-vocabulary mapping system via 3d scene graphs. IEEE Robot. Autom. Lett. (2025)
19. Hossain, M.Z., Imteaj, A.: Securing vision-language models with a robust encoder against jailbreak and adversarial attacks. In: 2024 IEEE International Conference on Big Data (BigData) (2024)
20. Jia, X., et al.: Improved techniques for optimization-based jailbreaking on large language models. arXiv preprint arXiv:2405.21018 (2024)

21. Lanckriet, G.R., Ghaoui, L.E., Bhattacharyya, C., Jordan, M.I.: A robust minimax approach to classification. J. Mach. Learn. Res. **3**, 555–582 (2002)
22. Li, M., Li, L., Yin, Y., Ahmed, M., Liu, Z., Liu, Q.: Red teaming visual language models. arXiv preprint arXiv:2401.12915 (2024)
23. Liu, H., Li, C., Wu, Q., Lee, Y.J.: Visual instruction tuning. arxiv preprint arxiv:2304.08485 (2023)
24. Liu, X., Zhu, Y., Gu, J., Lan, Y., Yang, C., Qiao, Y.: MM-safetybench: a benchmark for safety evaluation of multimodal large language models. In: Leonardis, A., Ricci, E., Roth, S., Russakovsky, O., Sattler, T., Varol, G. (eds.) ECCV 2024. LNCS, vol. 15114, pp. 386–403. Springer, Cham (2024). https://doi.org/10.1007/978-3-031-72992-8_22
25. Liu, X., Zhu, Y., Lan, Y., Yang, C., Qiao, Y.: Safety of multimodal large language models on images and text. arXiv preprint arXiv:2402.00357 (2024)
26. Liu, Y., Cai, C., Zhang, X., Yuan, X., Wang, C.: Arondight: red teaming large vision language models with auto-generated multi-modal jailbreak prompts. In: ACM International Conference on Multimedia (2024)
27. Luo, H., Gu, J., Liu, F., Torr, P.: An image is worth 1000 lies: transferability of adversarial images across prompts on vision-language models. In: International Conference on Learning Representations (2024)
28. Luo, W., Ma, S., Liu, X., Guo, X., Xiao, C.: Jailbreakv-28k: a benchmark for assessing the robustness of multimodal large language models against jailbreak attacks. arXiv preprint arXiv:2404.03027 (2024)
29. Ma, X., et al.: Safety at scale: a comprehensive survey of large model safety. arXiv preprint arXiv:2502.05206 (2025)
30. Marshall, A.W., Olkin, I.: Multivariate Chebyshev inequalities. Ann. Math. Stat. **31**(4), 1001–1014 (1960)
31. Nanda, N., Lee, A., Wattenberg, M.: Emergent linear representations in world models of self-supervised sequence models. arXiv preprint arXiv:2309.00941 (2023)
32. Park, K., Choe, Y.J., Veitch, V.: The linear representation hypothesis and the geometry of large language models. arXiv preprint arXiv:2311.03658 (2023)
33. Pi, R., et al.: MLLM-protector: Ensuring MLLM's safety without hurting performance. arXiv preprint arXiv:2401.02906 (2024)
34. Pu, X., Fang, J., Deng, Z., Wang, X., Chen, X., et al.: A large language model-driven heterogeneous air-ground search swarm. In: ICLR Workshop on Embodied Intelligence with Large Language Models in Open City Environment (2025)
35. Schaeffer, R., et al.: Failures to find transferable image jailbreaks between vision-language models. In: International Conference on Learning Representations (2024)
36. Schlarmann, C., Hein, M.: On the adversarial robustness of multi-modal foundation models. In: International Conference on Computer Vision (2023)
37. Shayegani, E., Dong, Y., Abu-Ghazaleh, N.: Plug and pray: exploiting off-the-shelf components of multi-modal models. arXiv preprint arXiv:2307.14539 (2023)
38. Tao, X., Zhong, S., Li, L., Liu, Q., Kong, L.: Imgtrojan: jailbreaking vision-language models with one image. arXiv preprint arXiv:2403.02910 (2024)
39. Touvron, H., et al.: Llama: open and efficient foundation language models. arXiv preprint arXiv:2302.13971 (2023)
40. Touvron, H., et al.: Llama 2: open foundation and fine-tuned chat models. arXiv preprint arXiv:2307.09288 (2023)
41. Tu, H., et al.: How many unicorns are in this image? A safety evaluation benchmark for vision LLMs. arXiv preprint arXiv:2311.16101 (2023)
42. Vaswani, A., et al.: Attention is all you need. In: Advances in Neural Information Processing Systems (2017)

43. Wang, Y., Liu, X., Li, Y., Chen, M., Xiao, C.: Adashield: safeguarding multimodal large language models from structure-based attack via adaptive shield prompting. In: Leonardis, A., Ricci, E., Roth, S., Russakovsky, O., Sattler, T., Varol, G. (eds.) ECCV 2024. LNCS, vol. 15078, pp. 77–94. Springer, Cham (2024). https://doi.org/10.1007/978-3-031-72661-3_5

44. Wang, Z., Gui, L., Negrea, J., Veitch, V.: Concept algebra for (score-based) text-controlled generative models. In: Advances in Neural Information Processing Systems, vol. 36 (2024)

45. Wu, Y., Li, X., Liu, Y., Zhou, P., Sun, L.: Jailbreaking GPT-4v via self-adversarial attacks with system prompts. arXiv preprint arXiv:2311.09127 (2023)

46. Yang, L., Song, S., Gong, Y., Gao, H., Wu, C.: Nonparametric dimension reduction via maximizing pairwise separation probability. IEEE Trans. Neural Netw. Learn. Syst. **30**(10), 3205–3210 (2019)

47. Yang, L., Song, S., Li, S., Chen, Y., Chen, C.P.: Discriminative dimension reduction via maximin separation probability analysis. IEEE Trans. Cybern. **51**(8), 4100–4111 (2019)

48. Yang, L., Zheng, Z., Chen, B., Zhao, Z., Lin, C., Shen, C.: Nullu: mitigating object hallucinations in large vision-language models via halluspace projection. In: IEEE Conference on Computer Vision and Pattern Recognition (2025)

49. Yang, Z., et al.: Distraction is all you need for multimodal large language model jailbreaking. In: IEEE Conference on Computer Vision and Pattern Recognition (2025)

50. Ying, Z., et al.: Jailbreak vision language models via bi-modal adversarial prompt. arXiv preprint arXiv:2406.04031 (2024)

51. Yu, W., et al.: MM-vet: evaluating large multimodal models for integrated capabilities. arXiv preprint arXiv:2308.02490 (2023)

52. Zha, J., Fan, Y., Yang, X., Gao, C., Chen, X.: How to enable LLM with 3d capacity? A survey of spatial reasoning in LLM. In: IJCAI (2025)

53. Zhang, Y., et al.: Benchmarking trustworthiness of multimodal large language models: a comprehensive study. arXiv preprint arXiv:2406.07057 (2024)

54. Zhao, Q., Xu, M., Gupta, K., Asthana, A., Zheng, L., Gould, S.: The first to know: how token distributions reveal hidden knowledge in large vision-language models? In: Leonardis, A., Ricci, E., Roth, S., Russakovsky, O., Sattler, T., Varol, G. (eds.) ECCV 2024. LNCS, vol. 15106, pp. 127–142. Springer, Cham (2024). https://doi.org/10.1007/978-3-031-73195-2_8

55. Zhao, W., et al.: A stitch in time saves nine: small VLM is a precise guidance for accelerating large VLMs. arXiv preprint arXiv:2412.03324 (2024)

56. Zhao, Y., Zheng, X., Luo, L., Li, Y., Ma, X., Jiang, Y.G.: Bluesuffix: reinforced blue teaming for vision-language models against jailbreak attacks. arXiv preprint arXiv:2410.20971 (2024)

57. Zhao, Y., et al.: On evaluating adversarial robustness of large vision-language models. In: Advances in Neural Information Processing Systems, vol. 36 (2024)

58. Zheng, Z., Zhao, J., Yang, L., He, L., Li, F.: Spot risks before speaking! unraveling safety attention heads in large vision-language models. arXiv preprint arXiv:2501.02029 (2025)

59. Zong, Y., Bohdal, O., Yu, T., Yang, Y., Hospedales, T.: Safety fine-tuning at (almost) no cost: a baseline for vision large language models. In: International Conference on Machine Learning (2024)

# KAD: Based on the Kolmogorov-Arnold Formula's Nonlinear Dynamic Channel Weights Module

Yuwen Xiang and Wenjian Liu

City University of Macau, Macau 999078, Taipa, China
andylau@cityu.edu.mo

**Abstract.** Medical image lesion segmentation is crucial for disease diagnosis and treatment planning but faces significant challenges, including the randomness of lesion morphology and location, variations in imaging equipment, ambiguous boundaries, difficulties in identifying early-stage small lesions, scarcity of medical data, and high annotation costs. To address these issues, this paper proposes an innovative dynamic feature fusion mechanism based on the Kolmogorov-Arnold (KA) formula, termed the KA Dynamic (KAD) module. This module dynamically generates channel weights using the KA formula, adaptively adjusting the importance distribution of cross-scale features to achieve efficient feature fusion between the encoder and decoder. Experimental results show that the proposed method performs exceptionally well in brain tumor segmentation tasks, achieving improved training performance with minimal increases in computational time while demonstrating strong generalization capabilities. The study indicates that this approach holds significant advantages in handling complex medical image segmentation tasks.

**Keywords:** Dynamic attention mechanism · KAD · Nonlinear function · MLP · Feature fusion · U-Net

## 1 Introduction

Medical image lesion segmentation plays a crucial role in disease diagnosis and treatment planning. However, its development faces multiple challenges: the randomness of lesion morphology and location, variations in imaging equipment leading to boundary ambiguity, and difficulties in identifying early-stage small lesions. Additionally, medical data is often scarce due to privacy protection constraints, and professional annotation is costly. Existing research predominantly focuses on single-type lesion segmentation, with limited cross-category generalization capabilities.

To overcome these challenges, artificial intelligence technologies have been introduced to enhance image denoising and quality improvement, thereby increasing diagnostic reliability and accuracy [1]. Traditional U-Net and its variants rely on fixed convolutional structures for multi-scale feature fusion, which limits their ability to extract


T. Zhu et al. (Eds.): KSEM 2025, LNAI 15919, pp. 35–46, 2026.
https://doi.org/10.1007/978-981-95-3001-4_3

fine-grained features from medical images. Complex improved models often come with significantly increased computational costs.

To address these issues, this paper proposes a dynamic feature fusion mechanism based on the Kolmogorov-Arnold (KA) formula, introducing the innovative Kolmogorov-Arnold Dynamic (KAD) module [2]. This module dynamically generates channel weights using the KA formula, adaptively adjusting the importance distribution of cross-scale features to achieve efficient feature fusion between the encoder and decoder. Unlike traditional attention modules, our approach dynamically generates channel weights and performs weighted merging based on feature maps from corresponding up-and-down sampling paths, resulting in more effective fusion of features at different resolutions.

Experimental results demonstrate that our proposed method achieves better training performance with minimal increases in computational time, particularly in brain tumor segmentation tasks, showcasing stronger generalization capabilities. The novelty of our approach lies in enhancing feature extraction precision without significantly compromising training efficiency. We created a plug-and-play module, KAD, capable of dynamically calculating channel weights, allowing for adjustments in feature extraction accuracy and detail. By using the Kolmogorov-Arnold Nonlinear (KAN) function instead of Multi-Layer Perceptron (MLP) calculations, we achieved faster and more accurate weight computations, improving the efficiency of channel weight determination. We conducted training and testing comparisons on Chest X-rays and Brain Tumor Segmentation datasets, demonstrating model performance improvements and confirming the lightweight and versatile nature of our model. Ablation experiments were performed on the KAD module, and various parts of the model were modified and tested, showing that inserting the KAD module at the first or second/third layers yields the best performance enhancements.

In summary, our contributions are as follows:

**(i)** We propose a novel KAD module based on the KAN formula for dynamic channel weight calculation.
**(ii)** We validate the model's performance improvements on organ segmentation and tumor segmentation datasets, confirming its lightweight and versatile nature.
**(iii)** We conduct ablation experiments on the KAD module, demonstrating that its insertion at specific layers significantly enhances overall model performance.

## 2 Related Work

The field of medical image segmentation has seen rapid development with the advent of deep learning methods, and Convolutional Neural Networks (CNNs) have become one of the most commonly used architectures for medical segmentation tasks [3]. The U-Net architecture, proposed by Olaf Ronneberger, Philipp Fischer, and Thomas Brox, was specifically designed for biomedical image segmentation [4]. It employs an encoder-decoder structure with skip connections to preserve spatial information. These skip connections and stacking operations were among the first to address the multi-level feature extraction challenges in medical images, enabling the capture of complex feature information. The ingenious design of U-Net has made it the most widely used architecture in medical segmentation tasks, particularly for organ and lesion segmentation. Even today, U-Net remains the baseline model for most optimized models, which are typically trained and fine-tuned on single or similar types of datasets. In contrast, our work aims to evaluate segmentation performance across two different types of datasets, using U-Net as the baseline model for comparison.

To optimize feature representation, attention mechanisms such as the Squeeze-and-Excitation (SE) module have been introduced [5]. The SE module dynamically adjusts channel weights, enhancing important features while suppressing redundant information. Variants like Residual Gated Spatially Separable Excitation (RGSE) and Spatial Pyramid Squeeze-and-Excitation (SPSE) further integrate residual connections and multi-scale fusion, significantly improving segmentation accuracy [6]. Additionally, dynamic nonlinear activation functions, such as variants of ReLU [7], and Kolmogorov-Arnold Networks (KAN) have been proposed to address high-order nonlinear mapping and computational efficiency issues [8]. The KAN model uses splines to approximate the Kolmogorov-Arnold formula, allowing for piecewise polynomial function fitting of nonlinear data while ensuring smoothness of the fitted function. This approach can potentially replace Multi-Layer Perceptron (MLP) to reduce computational load [9].

Recent studies have attempted to combine the advantages of CNNs and Transformers. For example, HyperKAN integrates KAN into Transformer architectures to reduce parameter counts and improve training efficiency [10]. Building upon the U-Net architecture and inspired by the dynamic channel weight adjustment concept from SE modules, we propose the Kolmogorov-Arnold Dynamic (KAD) module. Our goal is to dynamically adjust multi-scale feature fusion weights using the Kolmogorov-Arnold (KA) formula, thereby addressing the challenge of adapting to complex scenarios in medical image segmentation.

## 3  Methodology

### 3.1  KAD-UNET

To construct a lightweight and versatile model, we propose the Kolmogorov-Arnold Dynamic Attention Block (KAD) module, which dynamically calculates channel weights for two feature maps and is inserted into the U-Net architecture. The technical flowchart of KAD-UNET is shown in Fig. 1.

### 3.2  Dynamic Nonlinear Function: KAN

The KAD module incorporates the Kolmogorov-Arnold formula, also known as the Kolmogorov-Arnold representation theorem, which is a significant result in real analysis and approximation theory. This theorem states that any multivariate continuous function on a bounded domain can be represented as a finite number of nested additions of univariate continuous functions.

For any continuous function $f(x_1, \ldots, x_n)$ defined on the closed interval $[0, 1]^n$ there exist integers $2n + 1$ and a series of one-dimensional continuous functions $\phi_{q,p}$ and $\Phi_q$

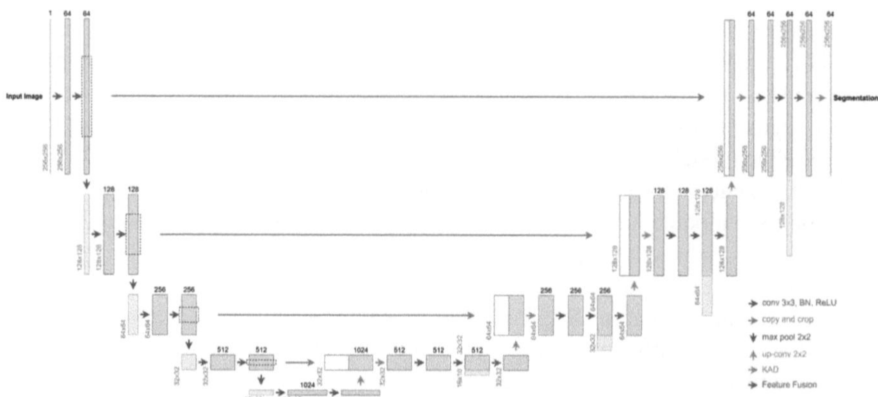

**Fig. 1.** KAD-UNET framework. KAD-UNET consists of four downsampling operations and four upsampling operations. Each upsampling operation includes an UpBlockKAD module and a FeatureFusion module. The feature fusion module primarily fuses the feature maps obtained after max-pooling downsampling with the corresponding feature maps after two convolutional upsampling operations. The module uses bilinear interpolation to increase the resolution of low-resolution images, scaling them up by a factor of two to align with the high-resolution images, and then performs fusion.

such that the multivariate function can be expressed as:

$$f(x_1, \ldots, x_n) = \sum_{q=1}^{2n+1} \Phi_q \left( \sum_{p=1}^{n} \phi_{q,p}(x_p) \right) \tag{1}$$

where:

1. $\phi_{q,p}$ are one-dimensional continuous functions mapping a single variable x$p$$xp$ to a real number.
2. $\Phi_q$ are one-dimensional continuous functions mapping sums from $\phi_{q,p}$ to a real number.
3. $2n + 1$ represents the minimum number of functions required to ensure that any continuous function can be represented in this form.

### 3.3 Replacing MLP with KAN

Traditional Multi-Layer Perceptron (MLP) achieve nonlinear mappings through stacked fully connected layers. However, their function approximation capability is limited by fixed basis function combinations, making it difficult to efficiently represent high-frequency signals. The comparison of Multi-Layer Perceptron (MLP) and KAN is in Fig. 2.

By incorporating the Kolmogorov-Arnold formula into the module, we transform it into the KAD module, enabling dynamic calculation of channel weights. The UpBlockKAD is shown in Fig. 3.

Since the KAD module is designed for information fusion between two feature maps, in this study, the KAD module is inserted at the skip connections of the U-Net model. By processing the corresponding feature maps from both downsampled

| Model | MLP | KAN |
|---|---|---|
| Shallow Formula | $f(\mathbf{x}) \approx \sum_{i=1}^{N(\epsilon)} a_i \sigma(\mathbf{w}_i \cdot \mathbf{x} + b_i)$ | $f(\mathbf{x}) = \sum_{q=1}^{2n+1} \Phi_q \left( \sum_{p=1}^{n} \phi_{q,p}(x_p) \right)$ |
| Shallow Model | | |

**Fig. 2.** Comparison of MLP and KAN.

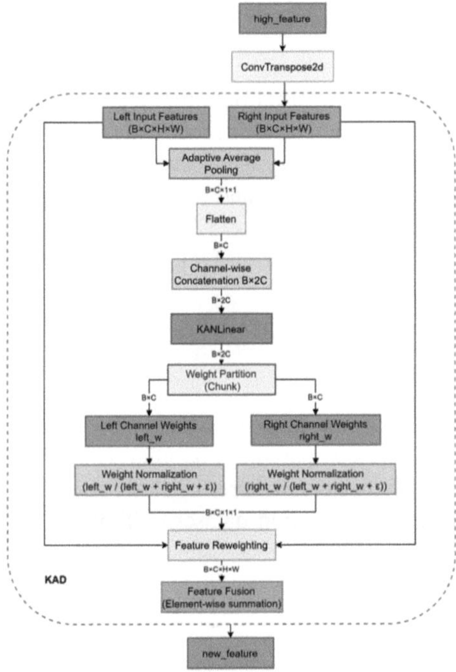


**Fig. 3.** UpBlockKAD composition diagram. The KAD module is mainly composed of a pooling layer, flatten and concatenation, and the Kolmogorov-Arnold Network (KAN). The pooling layer is used to extract important features from the input feature maps $X_{left}$ and $X_{right}$. The pooled feature maps are then flattened and concatenated to form a tensor of size B $\times$ 2C. This tensor is subsequently processed by the KAN to generate the channel weights.

and upsampled layers, the KAD module performs weighted merging of these feature maps. This approach ensures that the extracted information retains both the rich low-dimensional features from earlier layers and the critical high-dimensional features from later layers, leading to more effective feature integration.

# 4 Experiments and Results

## 4.1 Dataset and Setup

All datasets are publicly available.

**Chest X-rays (Montgomery and Shenzhen)** [11]. The dataset consists of 704 chest X-ray images curated from two sources: the Montgomery County Chest X-ray Database (USA) and the Shenzhen Chest X-ray Database (China). These images are used for training and evaluating machine learning models for tuberculosis (TB) detection.

**Brain Tumor Segmentation** [12]. This dataset contains 3064 T1-weighted contrast-enhanced images from 233 patients with three types of brain tumors: meningioma (708 slices), glioma (1426 slices), and pituitary tumor (930 slices).

## 4.2 Dataset and Setup

The datasets were divided into an 8:1:1 ratio for training, validation, and testing sets. All images were resized to (256, 256) pixels for processing. Training was conducted on an RTX 4090 GPU with 24 GB of memory using the PyTorch framework (version 2.1.0) [13]. The learning rate was set to 0.001 and adjusted using the ReduceLROnPlateau strategy [14]. Each iteration sampled $32 \times 32$-sized patches for training. Evaluation metrics included Intersection over Union (IoU) [15], Dice score [16], and Loss values for comparison.

## 4.3 Comparative Experiments

We designed multiple experimental setups to evaluate the effectiveness of our proposed KAD module. Specifically, we compared the baseline U-Net model without the KAD module against various configurations where the KAD module was added at different layers in the Brain Tumor Segmentation dataset in Table 1. The training curve is as follows as Fig. 4.

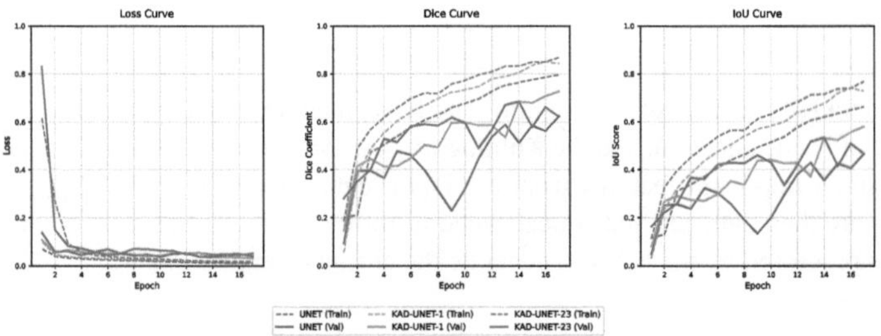


**Fig. 4.** The training curves in the Brain Tumor Segmentation dataset.

The comparison of predictions are as follows as Fig. 5.

**Table 1.** The evaluation metrics in Brain Tumor Segmentation dataset.KAD-UNET-1 indicates that only UpBlockKAD1 is added, KAD-UNET-12 indicates that only UpBlockKAD1 and UpBlockKAD2 are added.

| Model | V_IoU | V_Dice | V_Loss | P_IoU | P_Dice |
|---|---|---|---|---|---|
| UNET | 0.4641 | 0.6253 | 0.0393 | 0.3995 | 0.5709 |
| KAD-UNET-1 | **0.5792** | **0.7277** | **0.0304** | 0.5473 | 0.7074 |
| KAD-UNET-2 | 0.5544 | 0.7082 | 0.0309 | 0.4901 | 0.6578 |
| KAD-UNET-3 | 0.4569 | 0.6160 | 0.0396 | 0.3740 | 0.5444 |
| KAD-UNET-4 | 0.5318 | 0.6894 | 0.0343 | 0.5336 | 0.6958 |
| KAD-UNET-12 | 0.5581 | 0.7083 | 0.0360 | 0.4845 | 0.6527 |
| KAD-UNET-13 | 0.4855 | 0.6446 | 0.0361 | 0.4254 | 0.5969 |
| KAD-UNET-14 | 0.4601 | 0.6227 | 0.0362 | 0.4663 | 0.6360 |
| KAD-UNET-23 | 0.5713 | 0.7209 | 0.0342 | **0.5569** | **0.7154** |
| KAD-UNET-24 | 0.5646 | 0.7166 | 0.0327 | 0.5039 | 0.6702 |
| KAD-UNET-34 | 0.5158 | 0.6707 | 0.0356 | 0.4356 | 0.6068 |
| KAD-UNET-123 | 0.5608 | 0.7110 | 0.0350 | 0.4919 | 0.6595 |
| KAD-UNET-124 | 0.5150 | 0.6742 | 0.0358 | 0.4685 | 0.6380 |
| KAD-UNET-134 | 0.5248 | 0.6847 | 0.0401 | 0.5539 | 0.7129 |
| KAD-UNET-234 | 0.4896 | 0.6476 | 0.0352 | 0.4226 | 0.5942 |
| KAD-UNET-1234 | 0.5285 | 0.6849 | 0.0352 | 0.5208 | 0.6849 |

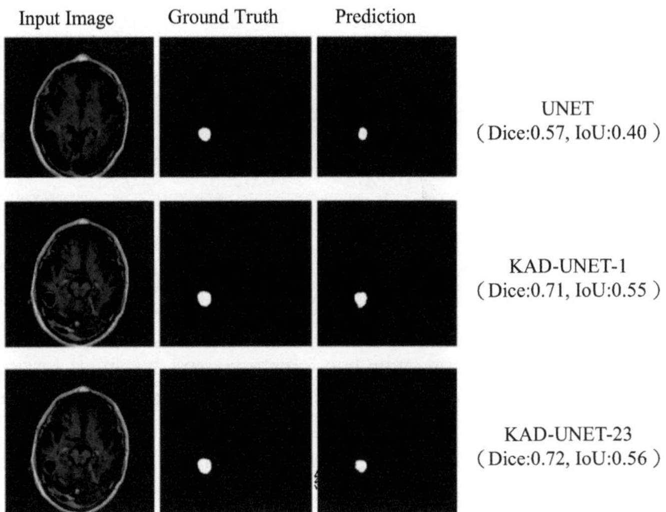


**Fig. 5.** Brain tumor segmentation prediction map.

Experimental results indicate that in the Brain Tumor Segmentation dataset, the KAD module achieves the best performance when inserted into the second and third layers of the baseline model. The second-best performance is observed when the KAD module is added to the first layer.

To further evaluate the effectiveness of the KAD module, we conducted comprehensive experiments by integrating the KAD module into different layers of the baseline U-Net model. We chose three models: KAD-UNET-1, KAD-UNET-23 and KAD-UNET-1234 compared to UNET, these models were trained and evaluated on another dataset: Chest X-rays. The training and prediction performances are summarized as follows Figs. 6, 7 and Table 2.

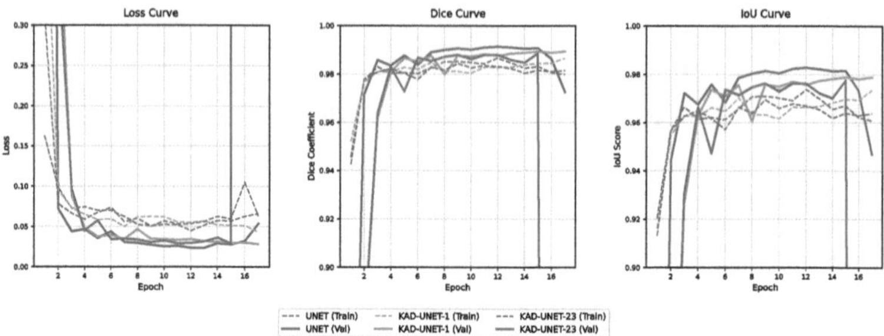


**Fig. 6.** The training curves in the Brain Tumor Segmentation dataset.

**Table 2.** The evaluation metrics in Chest X-rays dataset.

| Model | V_IoU | V_Dice | V_Loss | P_IoU | P_Dice |
|---|---|---|---|---|---|
| U-NET | 0.9822 | 0.9910 | **0.0234** | 0.9827 | 0.9913 |
| KAD-UNET-1234 | 0.9816 | 0.9907 | 0.0240 | 0.9824 | 0.9911 |
| KAD-UNET-1 | **0.9824** | **0.9911** | 0.0236 | **0.9829** | **0.9914** |
| KAD-UNET-1234 | 0.9806 | 0.9902 | 0.0256 | 0.9812 | 0.9905 |

Experimental results indicate that in the Chest X-rays dataset, the KAD module performs best when added to the baseline model at the first layer, with the second and third layers also showing good performance.

For brain tumor segmentation, which is characterized by small targets, irregular shapes, and low contrast, capturing high-level semantic features is crucial. The UpBlock-KAD2 and UpBlockKAD3, being higher-level blocks, are better suited for handling abstract semantic information. Therefore, these blocks show superior segmentation performance on the Brain Tumor Segmentation dataset. On the other hand, UpBlockKAD1 handles lower-level feature information, making it more suitable for tasks involving large targets with fixed structures, such as lung segmentation. Incorporating feature fusion at the lower levels ensures precise edge detection, leading to better segmentation performance on the Chest X-rays dataset when only UpBlockKAD1 is used.

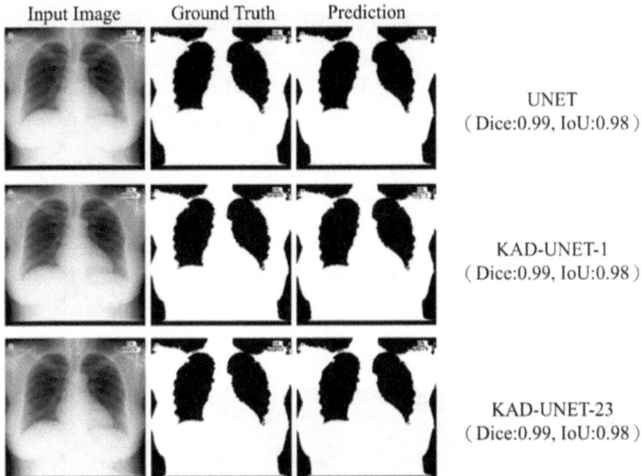



**Fig. 7.** Lung segmentation prediction map

## 4.4 Ablation Study

Due to the high evaluation metrics on the Chest X-rays dataset, we chose to set up two ablation experiments on the Brain Tumor Segmentation dataset to observe the degree of numerical changes. One group replaces the KAN function in the KAD module with an MLP, while keeping the rest unchanged, and then compares the results of adding the KAD to the baseline model; the other group compares the results of retaining only the KAD module and adding the feature fusion module. The results showed in Figs. 8, 9 and Table 3.

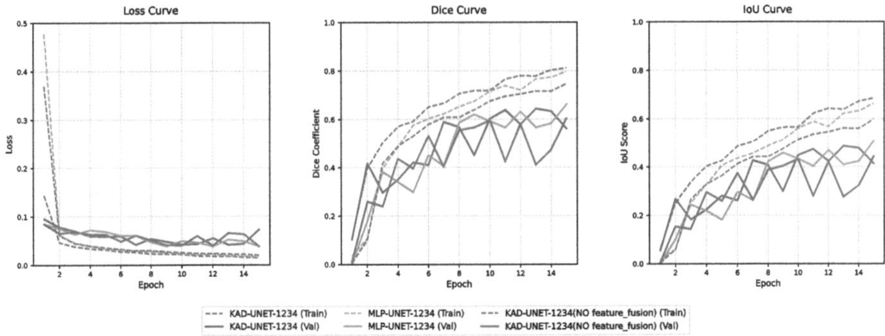



**Fig. 8.** The training curves in the Brain Tumor Segmentation dataset.

Adding the Feature Fusion module yields better results because it upsamples low-resolution features to the size of high-resolution features using bilinear interpolation, then concatenates the upsampled low-resolution features with the high-resolution features. A convolutional layer is applied to the concatenated features to fuse them, generating the final fused features. Incorporating the feature fusion module after the UpBlockKAD.

**Table 3.** The evaluation metrics in Brain Tumor Segmentation dataset.

| Model | V_IoU | V_Dice | V_Loss | P_IoU | P_Dice |
|---|---|---|---|---|---|
| U-NET | 0.4641 | 0.6253 | 0.0393 | 0.3995 | 0.5709 |
| MLP-UNET-1234 | 0.4688 | 0.6315 | 0.0383 | 0.4693 | 0.6388 |
| KAD-UNET-1234 (No feature_fusion) | 0.5212 | 0.6761 | **0.0339** | 0.4387 | 0.6098 |
| KAD-UNET-1234 | **0.5285** | **0.6849** | 0.0352 | **0.5208** | **0.6849** |

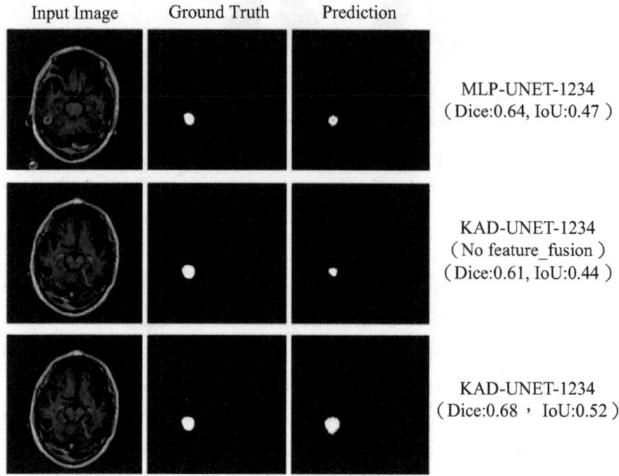


**Fig. 9.** Brain tumor segmentation prediction map

allows for the full utilization of multi-scale feature information, enhancing feature representation, reducing information loss, and improving the robustness of the model.

Additionally, it is noted that:

1. Training one iteration of the KAD-UNet takes approximately 42 s.
2. Training one iteration of the UNet takes approximately 38 s.

## 5   Discussion

Based on the experimental results and visualized segmentation prediction comparisons, it can be summarized that the baseline model with the KAD module shows improved segmentation performance. According to the results, adding the KAD module at the second or third layer yields the best performance improvement on the Brain Tumor Segmentation dataset, while adding it at the first layer achieves the most significant improvement on the Chest X-rays dataset. Furthermore, the baseline model incorporating both the KAD module and the feature fusion module performs even better.

The KAD module enhances the model's saliency by calculating the weights of feature maps, which helps in identifying the importance of different channel features and adjusting them based on the relative significance of left and right feature maps. This allows for effectively combining the advantages of different feature maps, thereby improving model performance. By performing weighted fusion of feature maps, the model's ability to handle complex features is significantly enhanced. Additionally, the KAD module dynamically adjusts feature weights to ensure the prominence of important information. With only a small increase in iteration time, the model achieves notable improvements and demonstrates lightweight and versatile performance across organ and tumor segmentation tasks.

However, the models with the KAD module sometimes produce predictions that contain a small amount of noise. Further testing and refinement of the module design may be necessary to address this issue.

The future work will focus on several aspects. First, develop an adaptive deployment algorithm for the KAD module based on task priors to automate model architecture configuration. Second, integrate meta-learning strategies to enhance the model's generalization capabilities for scarce annotated data. Third, validate the scalability of the KAD mechanism in three-dimensional medical imaging and multi-task joint learning scenarios. Additionally, select more baseline models and test them individually. Finally, conduct additional validation on more datasets to further verify the effectiveness of the proposed method.

## 6  Conclusion

This paper proposes an improved UNet model based on the Kolmogorov-Arnold Dynamic Attention Mechanism (KAD module). Through experimental validation, we demonstrate its effectiveness in medical image segmentation tasks and reveal the task-dependent sensitivity of model performance to feature hierarchy. We achieved task-driven module optimization: in brain tumor segmentation tasks, higher-level KAD modules (using UpBlockKAD2, 3) dynamically adjust cross-scale semantic feature fusion through dynamic weight adjustment, significantly improving the segmentation accuracy of small targets (Dice coefficient increased by approximately 0.15). The advantage stems from the strong modeling capability for ambiguous boundaries and heterogeneous textures. In lung segmentation tasks, lower-level KAD modules (UpBlockKAD1) retain high-resolution spatial details, achieving precise segmentation of organ contours (Dice coefficient increased by approximately 0.0002), verifying the core requirement of large target segmentation for local feature fidelity. We also implemented adaptive weight generation: by using nonlinear function approximation to learn channel importance, KAN adaptively selects nonlinear basis functions, freeing itself from dependence on fixed activation functions and alleviating the reliance of traditional attention modules on fixed prior distributions. Practical implementation ensures hierarchical sensitivity regulation, enhancing semantic reasoning at low-resolution levels and optimizing spatial alignment at high-resolution levels, achieving precise matching between task requirements and feature characteristics.

# References


1. Singh, N.T., Kaur, C., Chaudhary, A., Goyal, S.: Preprocessing of medical images using deep learning: a comprehensive review. In: Proceedings of the 2023 Second International Conference on Augmented Intelligence and Sustainable Systems (ICAISS), pp. 521–527. IEEE, August 2023

2. Schmidt-Hieber, J.: The Kolmogorov-Arnold representation theorem revisited. Neural Netw. **137**, 119–126 (2021)

3. Li, Z., Liu, F., Yang, W., Peng, S., Zhou, J.: A survey of convolutional neural networks: analysis, applications, and prospects. IEEE Trans. Neural Netw. Learn. Syst. **33**(12), 6999–7019 (2021)

4. Ronneberger, O., Fischer, P., Brox, T.:. U-Net: convolutional networks for biomedical image segmentation. In: Navab, N., Hornegger, J., Wells, W., Frangi, A. (eds.) Medical Image Computing and Computer-Assisted Intervention – MICCAI 2015. MICCAI 2015. Lecture Notes in Computer Science, vol. 9351, pp. 234–241. Springer, Cham (2015). https://doi.org/10.1007/978-3-319-24574-4_28

5. Hu, J., Shen, L., Sun, G.: Squeeze-and-excitation networks. In: Proceedings of the IEEE Conference on Computer Vision and Pattern Recognition, pp. 7132–7141 (2018)

6. Jin, X., Xie, Y., Wei, X.S., Zhao, B.R., Chen, Z.M., Tan, X.: Delving deep into spatial pooling for squeeze-and-excitation networks. Pattern Recogn. **121**, 108159 (2022)

7. Hara, K., Saito, D., Shouno, H.: Analysis of function of rectified linear unit used in deep learning. In: Proceedings of the 2015 International Joint Conference on Neural Networks (IJCNN), pp. 1–8. IEEE, July 2015

8. Liu, Z., et al.: Kan: Kolmogorov-arnold networks. arXiv preprint arXiv:2404.19756 (2024)

9. Kruse, R., Mostaghim, S., Borgelt, C., Braune, C., Steinbrecher, M.: Multi-layer perceptrons. In: Computational Intelligence: A Methodological Introduction, pp. 53–124. Springer International Publishing, Cham (2022)

10. Lobanov, V., Firsov, N., Myasnikov, E., Khabibullin, R., Nikonorov, A.: Hyperkan: Kolmogorov-arnold networks make hyperspectral image classificators smarter. arXiv preprint arXiv:2407.05278 (2024)

11. Tapendu, K.: Chest X-ray Dataset for Tuberculosis Segmentation. kaggle (2024). https://www.kaggle.com/datasets/iamtapendu/chest-x-ray-lungs-segmentation

12. Nikhil, T.: Brain Tumor Segmentation. Kaggle (2023). https://www.kaggle.com/datasets/nikhilroxtomar/brain-tumor-segmentation/data

13. Paszke, A.: Pytorch: An imperative style, high-performance deep learning library. arXiv preprint arXiv:1912.01703 (2019)

14. Thakur, A., Gupta, M., Sinha, D.K., Mishra, K.K., Venkatesan, V.K., Guluwadi, S.: Transformative breast Cancer diagnosis using CNNs with optimized ReduceLROnPlateau and early stopping enhancements. Int. J. Comput. Intell. Syst. **17**(1), 14 (2024)

15. Rezatofighi, H., Tsoi, N., Gwak, J., Sadeghian, A., Reid, I., Savarese, S.: Generalized intersection over union: a metric and a loss for bounding box regression. In: Proceedings of the IEEE/CVF Conference on Computer Vision and Pattern Recognition, pp. 658–666 (2019)

16. Sudre, C.H., Li, W., Vercauteren, T., Ourselin, S., Jorge Cardoso, M.: Generalised dice overlap as a deep learning loss function for highly unbalanced segmentations. In: Cardoso, M., et al. Deep Learning in Medical Image Analysis and Multimodal Learning for Clinical Decision Support. DLMIA ML-CDS 2017 2017. Lecture Notes in Computer Science, vol. 10553, pp. 240–248. Springer, Cham (2017). https://doi.org/10.1007/978-3-319-67558-9_28

# CoTSentry: Advanced Network Attack Detection with Chain-of-Thought Reasoning


Qi He[1], Congcong Zhu[1(✉)], Suleiman A. Abahussein[2], Minghao Wang[1], and Minglu Zhu[3]

[1] Faculty of Data Science, City University of Macau, Macau, China
{D24091110715,cczhu,mhwang}@cityu.edu.mo
[2] Saudi Data and Artificial Intelligence Authority (SDAIA), Riyadh, Saudi Arabia
sabahussain@nic.gov.sa
[3] School of Information Technology, Griffith University, Brisbane, Australia
minglu.zhu@griffithuni.edu.au



**Abstract.** The emergence of Large Language Models (LLMs) coincides with increasingly sophisticated network attacks that challenge conventional detection mechanisms. Traditional approaches exhibit significant limitations when confronted with novel attacks, often lacking interpretability and adaptability. To address these challenges, we introduce CoTSentry, a novel framework that leverages reasoning-enhanced language models through systematic multi-phase analysis for attack detection. By shifting from traditional pattern matching to comprehensive reasoning-based analysis, our approach methodically decomposes complex security problems into logical steps, revealing attack indicators even when deliberately obscured by adversaries. Through extensive empirical evaluations, CoTSentry achieves exceptional detection performance with accuracy rates consistently exceeding 97%, even against sophisticated obfuscation techniques that significantly degrade conventional methods. The system exhibits strong generalization capabilities to emerging threats without requiring attack-specific training, while providing security practitioners with comprehensive intelligence, including explicit reasoning chains, severity assessments, detailed attack explanations, and actionable defense recommendations.

**Keywords:** LLMs · CoT Reasoning · Network Security · Attack Detection · Multi-round Reasoning


## 1  Introduction

Modern cyber threats present substantial challenges to network security systems. Traditional detection mechanisms, including signature-based systems, heuristic analyzers, and conventional machine learning models, exhibit fundamental limitations when confronted with novel attack variants and obfuscation techniques.



T. Zhu et al. (Eds.): KSEM 2025, LNAI 15919, pp. 47–58, 2026.
https://doi.org/10.1007/978-981-95-3001-4_4

While deep learning approaches have advanced this field, they often function as black boxes with limited interpretability, require extensive labeled datasets, and demonstrate notable performance degradation when encountering unfamiliar threat patterns [5].

Recent research indicates that language models offer significant advantages for security applications, with robust capabilities for anomaly detection and threat analysis [2,7,16,19]. Transformer architectures have enhanced the analysis of network payloads and attack vectors. These computational models exhibit robust semantic processing capabilities that are applicable to comprehensive security analysis. Nevertheless, current LLM security implementations struggle with interpretability, reasoning transparency, and resilience to adversarial attacks.

This paper presents CoTSentry, a framework that integrates LLMs with Chain-of-Thought reasoning through multi-round refinement. Our approach methodically decomposes complex security problems into analytical reasoning steps, enabling the identification of attack indicators even when deliberately obscured by adversaries. Evaluations show 98.60% accuracy on standard attacks and 97.2% against obfuscated attacks—8.8% points better than comparable methods. The multi-round approach improves F1-scores by 5.82% points from single-round to five-round analysis.

The primary contribution of this work lies in the multi-round architecture that methodically analyzes potential attacks through sequential phases: initial detection, confidence calculation, validation analysis, and focused re-analysis. This methodology enables effective generalization to novel attack vectors without attack-specific training, achieving perfect detection accuracy for certain emerging threats. Additionally, the system generates comprehensive security intelligence, including severity assessments, attack explanations, and defensive recommendations.

The remainder of this paper is organized as follows: Sect. 2 reviews related literature; Sect. 3 details the methodology; Sect. 4 presents experimental results; and Sect. 5 concludes with discussion and future directions.

## 2   Related Work

Network attack detection has evolved from signature-based systems to machine learning approaches [12,15,17]. Recent work includes LSTM autoencoders [6], BERT implementations [10,11], and neural architectures that combine Distil-BERT with RNNs/LSTMs [1]. WebGuardRL [3] extended capabilities through reinforcement learning [18]. However, conventional approaches face limitations in interpretability, obfuscation resilience, and dependency on extensive labeled datasets.

LLMs represent a paradigm shift in security applications [4,8,13,14]. Chain-of-Thought reasoning enhances analytical capabilities by structuring thinking processes, but its implementation in iterative cybersecurity contexts remains largely unexplored. Our research addresses this gap by developing a framework that employs LLMs with Chain-of-Thought reasoning for network attack detection, providing comprehensive security intelligence, including explanations, severity assessments, and defense recommendations.

# 3    Methodology

## 3.1    System Architecture

CoTSentry integrates several key components to form a comprehensive attack detection and analysis system. Figure 1 illustrates the overall architecture and workflow.

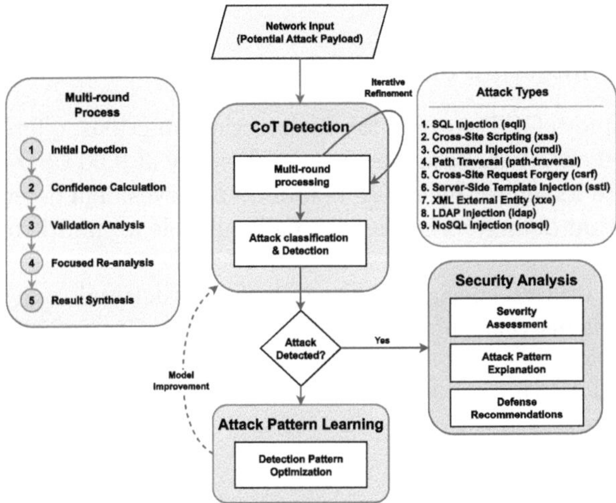


**Fig. 1.** CoTSentry Workflow and Framework: The system processes potential attack payloads through the CoT Detection engine with Multi-round processing, classifies attacks, and provides comprehensive Security Analysis with Attack Pattern Learning capabilities

The system consists of three main functional modules:

1. **CoT Detection Engine**: The core module that receives potential attack payloads and analyzes them through Chain-of-Thought reasoning. It encompasses Multi-round Processing for iterative refinement and Attack Classification & Detection for determining input types.
2. **Security Analysis**: Generates comprehensive security intelligence through Severity Assessment (1–10 risk scores), Attack Pattern Explanations (detailed attack descriptions), and Defense Recommendations (tailored protective measures).
3. **Attack Pattern Learning**: Analyzes performance metrics across attack types to identify patterns requiring enhancement. These insights provide feedback for security researchers to implement detection improvements through a researcher-guided optimization process.

The system can detect various attack types, including traditional web attacks such as SQL Injection (SQLi), Cross-Site Scripting (XSS), Command Injection (cmdi), and Path Traversal (path-traversal), as well as emerging threats including Cross-Site Request Forgery (CSRF), Server-Side Template Injection (SSTI), XML External Entity (XXE), LDAP Injection (ldap), and NoSQL Injection (nosql).

This integrated architecture enables CoTSentry to implement a complete workflow from initial detection to security recommendations, providing comprehensive security analysis while maintaining continuous improvement of detection capabilities. The design incorporates a multi-round reasoning mechanism that improves detection accuracy for complex attacks through iterative refinement.

### 3.2   LLM Architecture and Prompt Design

Our system employs GPT-4o-mini for all detection functions, offering an optimal balance between effectiveness and economic efficiency at 0.06 USD per 100 attack samples. Despite its affordability, GPT-4o-mini achieves high detection accuracy comparable to that of larger models, making it suitable for multi-round reasoning applications.

The system utilizes specialized prompts for structured analysis. The core detection prompt instructs:

> Analyze the following input to detect if it contains any of these network attacks:
> 1. SQL Injection (sqli)
> 2. Cross-Site Scripting (xss)
> 3. Command Injection (cmdi)
> 4. Path Traversal (path-traversal)
> 5. Cross-Site Request Forgery (csrf)
> 6. Server-Side Template Injection (ssti)
> 7. XML External Entity (xxe)
> 8. LDAP Injection (ldap)
> 9. NoSQL Injection (nosql) Use your chain-of-thought to analyze the input.

This foundation prompt is enhanced with validation and re-analysis variations that examine logical inconsistencies, decode obfuscated elements, and explore alternative classifications. The validation prompts identify potential misclassifications by examining attack-specific indicators, while re-analysis prompts focus on ambiguous cases through detailed examination of suspicious elements, including URL-encoded characters and syntactic variations. This progressive approach enables the handling of increasingly complex attack patterns through systematic refinement.

## 3.3  Multi-round Reasoning

CoTSentry's core strength is derived from its iterative reasoning mechanism that enables progressive refinement of attack detection through multiple analytical cycles.

To systematically capture this iterative reasoning process, we formalize our approach in Algorithm 1, which outlines the complete workflow from initial detection to final classification. This multi-round architecture enables the system to gradually build confidence in its assessments by addressing uncertainties and refining its analysis through successive iterations. The algorithm incorporates mechanisms for validation, targeted re-examination, and confidence calculation, creating a framework that mimics the analytical processes of security experts.

---

**Algorithm 1.** Multi-Round Attack Detection Algorithm

---

**Require:** input $T$, attack types $A = \{sqli, xss, cmdi, path\text{-}traversal, ...\}$
**Ensure:** detected attack type $a \in A$ or $norm$
1: $R_0 \leftarrow \text{InitDetect}(T, A)$
2: $C_0 \leftarrow \text{CalcConf}(R_0)$
3: $r \leftarrow 1$
4: **while** $r < MAX\_ROUNDS$ **and** $C_{r-1} < THRESHOLD$ **do**
5:    $U_r \leftarrow \text{Validate}(R_{r-1})$
6:    $P_r \leftarrow \text{PrepFocus}(T, U_r, R_{r-1})$
7:    $R_r \leftarrow \text{Reanalyze}(P_r)$
8:    $C_r \leftarrow \text{CalcConf}(R_r, R_{r-1})$
9:    $r \leftarrow r + 1$
10: **end while**
11: $result \leftarrow \text{Synthesize}(R_0, R_1, ..., R_{r-1})$
12: **return** $result$

---

The algorithm operates through five key functions: $\text{InitDetect}(T, A)$ performs initial analysis of input $T$ against potential attack types $A$, identifying suspicious patterns; $\text{CalcConf}(R)$ evaluates confidence in detection results using multiple metrics; $\text{Validate}(R)$ examines results for inconsistencies and overlooked indicators; $\text{PrepFocus}(T, U, R)$ generates targeted prompts for uncertain aspects; and $\text{Reanalyze}(P)$ conducts focused re-examination of these aspects. Security-specific contextual elements are incorporated throughout, with prompts dynamically generated based on previous reasoning rounds. The system continues analysis until either reaching sufficient confidence (exceeding 0.8) or the maximum iteration limit (5 rounds), ultimately synthesizing findings to generate the final determination.

The following sections detail the key components of our algorithm, including the confidence calculation mechanism, the validation analysis process, and the focused re-analysis approach.

**Confidence Calculation.** The confidence score for each detection is calculated using a weighted combination of multiple factors, as formalized in Eq. 1:

$$Conf = w_c C + w_r R + \sum_{i=1}^{n} w_k K_i + \sum_{j=1}^{m} w_p P_j + \sum_{l=1}^{o} w_s S_l \qquad (1)$$

In this equation, each component contributes to the overall confidence score: $C$ represents answer consistency with weight $w_c$ (0.3), $R$ represents reasoning completeness with weight $w_r$ (0.3), $K_i$ represents individual keyword matches with weight $w_k$ (0.05 each), $P_j$ represents pattern matches with weight $w_p$ (0.1 each), and $S_l$ represents attack-specific features with weight $w_s$ that provide additional confidence based on the characteristics of different attack types. All weights are empirically determined based on their relative importance in attack detection.

The weighting parameters reflect the relative importance of different factors: consistency and reasoning completeness receive higher weights (0.3 each) as primary confidence indicators, while keyword matches (0.05 each) and pattern matches (0.1 each) provide supporting evidence. Attack-specific features receive dynamic weights based on the attack type being evaluated. The 0.8 threshold triggers additional reasoning rounds for uncertain cases while allowing high-confidence detections to proceed efficiently.

**Validation and Re-analysis.** The validation component examines initial detection results by identifying logical inconsistencies and overlooked indicators, employing attack-specific patterns for known obfuscation techniques. High-uncertainty elements trigger focused re-analysis using specialized prompts for ambiguous segments. For example, in a cmdi attack scenario, the system recognizes semicolon command separators, validates find command usage, and confirms command execution patterns, achieving a final confidence score of 0.90.

### 3.4  System Capabilities

Beyond attack detection, CoTSentry leverages LLMs' reasoning capabilities to generate comprehensive security intelligence without requiring specialized modules. The system provides actionable insights through several integrated functions:

**Severity Assessment:** Automatically scores attacks on a 1–10 scale based on potential impact. The scoring categorizes attacks into high-priority threats (command injection, advanced SQLi, XXE, SSTI), medium-priority risks (XSS variants, CSRF, NoSQL injection, LDAP injection), and lower-priority concerns (basic path traversal, reconnaissance attempts), enabling security teams to prioritize response efforts efficiently.

**Attack Pattern Explanations:** Generates detailed explanations identifying the specific characteristics that led to classification decisions, providing transparency into the detection process and enabling researchers to understand both what was detected and why.

**Defense Recommendations:** Produces tailored mitigation strategies, including immediate tactical responses (input validation, sanitization), medium-term preventive measures (security policy updates, monitoring enhancements), and long-term strategic practices (architecture improvements, security training) specific to each attack vector. Recommendations are prioritized based on implementation complexity and effectiveness.

**Attack Pattern Learning:** Analyzes performance metrics across attack types to identify patterns requiring enhancement, tracking false positive/negative rates, detection latency, and confidence score distributions. This analysis provides feedback for security researchers to improve detection methods through a researcher-guided optimization process, enabling continuous system refinement based on operational experience.

This approach transforms attack detection from binary classification to comprehensive security analysis, emulating the analytical workflow of expert security researchers.

## 4 Experimental Evaluation

### 4.1 Experimental Setup

**Datasets.** We evaluated CoTSentry across three complementary datasets:

1. **Standard Attack Dataset**: The HttpParamsDataset [9] contains HTTP parameter values categorized as benign or malicious, featuring SQLi, XSS, cmdi, and path-traversal attacks. This dataset provides a baseline for evaluation against common web attacks.
2. **Obfuscation Dataset**: A collection of 1,000 samples containing the same categories as the Standard Attack Dataset (norm, SQLi, XSS, cmdi, and path-traversal), but with varying degrees of obfuscation techniques applied, including URL encoding, comment insertion, and alternative syntax representations. This dataset simulates real-world scenarios where attackers employ evasion tactics to bypass detection systems.
3. **Extended Attack Dataset**: A balanced dataset of 600 samples consisting of normal data (norm) and five emerging attack vectors (Cross-Site Request Forgery (CSRF), Server-Side Template Injection (SSTI), XML External Entity (XXE), LDAP Injection (ldap), and NoSQL Injection (nosql)), with 100 samples for each category. This dataset systematically evaluates detection capabilities against newer threats less represented in standard security benchmarks, providing equal representation for each attack type and normal traffic.

The datasets vary in size (HttpParamsDataset: 31,000+ samples; Obfuscation Dataset: 1,000 samples; Extended Attack Dataset: 600 samples), reflecting real-world security data distribution where common attacks are abundant while sophisticated variants are scarcer. The Obfuscation Dataset targets evasion resilience by incorporating various obfuscation techniques, while the Extended Attack Dataset focuses on emerging threats that are underrepresented in traditional security benchmarks.

**Evaluation Metrics.** We employ standard performance metrics: accuracy, precision, recall, and F1-Score. Accuracy measures correctly classified samples: $Accuracy = \frac{TP+TN}{TP+TN+FP+FN}$. Recall measures the proportion of detected attacks: $Recall = \frac{TP}{TP+FN}$. Precision measures the proportion of correct attack predictions: $Precision = \frac{TP}{TP+FP}$.

The F1-Score provides a balanced measure that considers both false positives and false negatives as follows:

$$F1\text{-}Score = \frac{2 \times Precision \times Recall}{Precision + Recall}. \tag{2}$$

## 4.2   Comparison with State-of-the-Art Methods

We conducted a comprehensive comparison with seven state-of-the-art methods from recent literature:

We compare against seven state-of-the-art methods: DistilBERT, RNN, and LSTM models [1] that use contextual embeddings and sequential patterns; M-ResNet and FastText models [12] for character-level and word-level analysis; M-ResNet+FastText fusion [12]; and WebGuardRL [3] that uses reinforcement learning with Double Deep Q-Network.

**Evaluation on HttpParamsDataset.** We first evaluated all methods on the standard HttpParamsDataset to establish a baseline comparison. For CoTSentry, we tested different numbers of reasoning rounds to demonstrate the impact of our multi-round approach. Table 1 presents the performance comparison using accuracy, precision, recall, and F1-score metrics.

**Table 1.** Comparison with state-of-the-art methods on HttpParamsDataset

| Method | Accuracy (%) | Precision (%) | Recall (%) | F1-Score |
|---|---|---|---|---|
| DistilBERT [1] | 95.8 | 95.6 | 93.8 | 94.7 |
| RNN [1] | 97.1 | 95.8 | 97.1 | 96.4 |
| LSTM [1] | 97.9 | 98.1 | 97.0 | 97.5 |
| M-ResNet [12] | 96.4 | 96.7 | 96.4 | 96.5 |
| FastText [12] | 95.8 | 96.0 | 95.8 | 95.9 |
| M-ResNet+FastText [12] | 98.7 | 98.5 | 97.9 | 98.2 |
| WebGuardRL [3] | 98.9 | 98.9 | 98.9 | 98.9 |
| CoTSentry (1 round) | 94.2 | 95.1 | 90.6 | 92.1 |
| **CoTSentry (5 rounds)** | **98.6** | **98.7** | **97.1** | **97.9** |

Table 1 shows WebGuardRL achieving the highest performance (98.9% F1-score), followed by M-ResNet+FastText (98.2%) and LSTM (97.5%). CoTSentry demonstrates progressive improvement with increased reasoning rounds: from 92.1% F1-score (1 round) to 97.9% (5 rounds), representing a 5.82% point increase. This substantial improvement validates the effectiveness of our multiround reasoning approach, with each additional round contributing to better attack characterization and reduced false classifications. The performance gain is particularly notable in precision (from 95.1% to 98.7%) and recall (from 90.6% to 97.1%), indicating that iterative reasoning enhances both attack detection sensitivity and classification accuracy. CoTSentry achieves competitive results with specialized models while requiring no attack-specific training and maintaining broader applicability to novel attack patterns, demonstrating the generalization capabilities of reasoning-based approaches over pattern-matching methods.

**Evaluation on Obfuscated Attack Dataset.** To assess the resilience of different approaches to evasion techniques, we evaluated all methods on the Obfuscation Dataset. Table 2 presents comprehensive performance metrics when tested against obfuscated inputs, comparing CoTSentry (with varying numbers of reasoning rounds) against other approaches.

**Table 2.** Performance metrics for obfuscated attacks

| Method | Accuracy (%) | Precision (%) | Recall (%) | F1-Score |
|---|---|---|---|---|
| DistilBERT [1] | 72.7 | 71.9 | 71.2 | 71.5 |
| RNN [1] | 76.3 | 74.3 | 73.9 | 74.1 |
| LSTM [1] | 74.8 | 76.6 | 70.6 | 73.5 |
| M-ResNet [12] | 86.4 | 87.7 | 85.6 | 86.6 |
| FastText [12] | 86.3 | 85.6 | 86.6 | 86.1 |
| M-ResNet+FastText [12] | 88.1 | 89.0 | 87.9 | 88.4 |
| WebGuardRL [3] | 72.6 | 73.0 | 72.6 | 71.1 |
| CoTSentry (1 round) | 94.4 | 95.6 | 92.2 | 93.9 |
| **CoTSentry (5 rounds)** | **97.2** | **97.8** | **97.0** | **97.2** |

Table 2 reveals dramatic performance degradation for traditional approaches against obfuscated attacks. WebGuardRL drops 27.8% points to 71.1% F1-score, while transformer models fall to the 71–74% range. Even M-ResNet+FastText decreases to 88.4%. In contrast, CoTSentry maintains robust performance, achieving 97.2% F1-score with five rounds—an 8.8% point advantage over the next best method. This resilience highlights CoTSentry's fundamental advantage: analyzing attack intent and structure through logical reasoning rather than relying on pattern recognition, making evasion through obfuscation substantially more difficult.

**Evaluation on Extended Attack Types.** To evaluate CoTSentry's ability to detect emerging attack vectors beyond traditional web attacks, we tested its performance on the Extended Attack Dataset. Since the compared methods were not designed for these attack types, we only report results for CoTSentry with five rounds of reasoning.

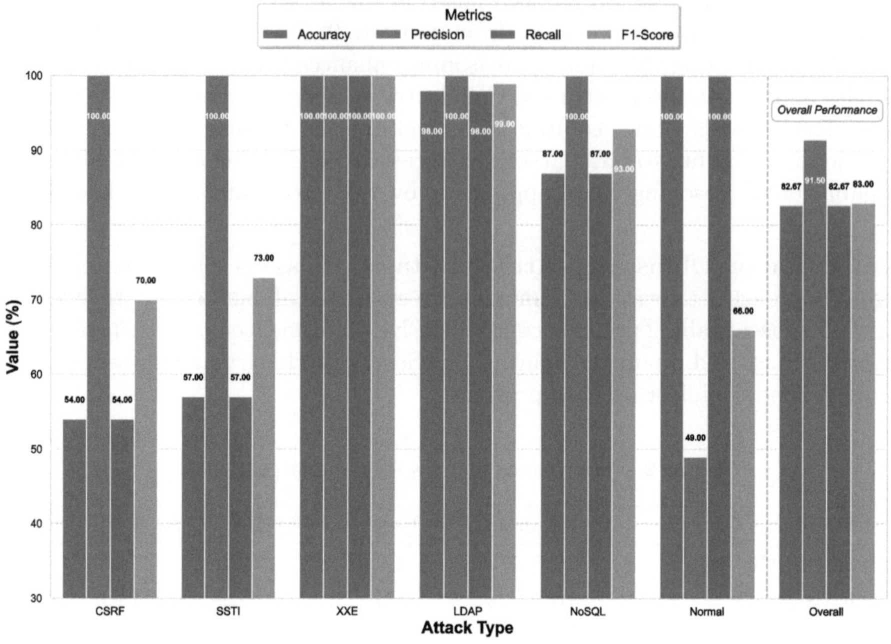

**Fig. 2.** CoTSentry performance on extended attack types (5 rounds)

Figure 2 shows CoTSentry's performance on emerging attack vectors, achieving 82.67% overall accuracy with 91.50% precision and 0.83 F1-score. Performance varied significantly: perfect detection for normal traffic and xxe attacks (100%), near-perfect for ldap (98%), moderate for nosql (87%), but challenging for csrf and ssti (54% and 57%, respectively). All attack types achieve 100% precision, indicating zero false positives when attacks are identified, while normal traffic shows lower precision (49%), suggesting a conservative detection bias that favors security over convenience. This performance disparity stems from fundamental attack characteristics: xxe and ldap attacks have distinctive syntactic patterns (DOCTYPE declarations, entity definitions, LDAP filter syntax) that are readily identifiable through Chain-of-Thought reasoning. Conversely, csrf attacks are inherently context-dependent, requiring understanding of cross-domain relationships, session management, and request origin validation that cannot be determined from payload analysis alone. Similarly, ssti attacks exhibit extreme syntactic diversity across template languages (Jinja2, Velocity, FreeMarker, Handlebars), with template expressions often resembling legitimate code, creating narrow semantic boundaries between malicious exploitation and intended functionality. These findings suggest that future enhancements should incorporate additional context-aware reasoning components and template-specific analysis capabilities to improve detection of context-dependent attack vectors.

## 5    Conclusion

This paper introduces CoTSentry, a novel network attack detection framework that integrates Chain-of-Thought reasoning with Large Language Models. Our multi-round reasoning approach achieves substantial performance improvements: 5.82% points on standard attacks and 3.3% points on obfuscated attacks. CoTSentry achieves 98.60% accuracy on standard patterns—comparable to specialized models—while maintaining exceptional resilience against obfuscation (97.2% accuracy), representing an 8.8% point advantage over competing methods. The reasoning-based approach analyzes attack intent rather than pattern matching, enabling detection of emerging attack vectors without specific training. On emerging attack types, CoTSentry achieves 82.67% overall accuracy with perfect detection for xxe attacks. Beyond classification, the system provides comprehensive security intelligence through severity assessments, explanations, and defense recommendations. CoTSentry represents a significant advancement toward more adaptive, transparent, and effective cybersecurity systems.

## References


1. Bokolo, B.G., Chen, L., Liu, Q.: Detection of web-attack using DistilBERT, RNN, and LSTM. In: 2023 11th International Symposium on Digital Forensics and Security (ISDFS), pp. 1–6. IEEE (2023)
2. Chen, Y., et al.: A survey of large language models for cyber threat detection. Comput. Secur. **145**, 104016 (2024)
3. Do Hoang, H., Nguyen Thi Hai, H., Do Thi Thu, H., Phan, T.D., Pham, V.H.: WebguardRL: an innovative reinforcement learning-based approach for advanced web attack detection. In: Proceedings of the 12th International Symposium on Information and Communication Technology, pp. 761–768. ACM (2023)
4. Gui, Z., et al.: SqliGPT: evaluating and utilizing large language models for automated SQL injection black-box detection. Appl. Sci. **14**(16), 6929 (2024)
5. Hassanin, M., Moustafa, N.: A comprehensive overview of large language models (LLMs) for cyber defences: opportunities and directions. arXiv preprint arXiv:2405.14487 (2024)
6. Jagat, R.R., Sisodia, D.S., Singh, P.: Detecting web attacks from http weblogs using variational LSTM autoencoder deviation network. IEEE Trans. Serv. Comput. **17**(6), 2847–2858 (2024)
7. Kheddar, H.: Transformers and large language models for efficient intrusion detection systems: a comprehensive survey. arXiv preprint arXiv:2408.07583 (2024)
8. Leung, D., Tsai, O., Hashemi, K., Tayebi, B., Tayebi, M.A.: XploitSQL: advancing adversarial SQL injection attack generation with language models and reinforcement learning. In: Proceedings of the 33rd ACM International Conference on Information and Knowledge Management, pp. 4653–4660. ACM (2024)
9. Morzeux: Httpparamsdataset: Dataset of http parameters for anomaly detection. https://github.com/Morzeux/HttpParamsDataset/ (2019)

10. Seyyar, Y.E., Yavuz, A.G., Ünver, H.M.: An attack detection framework based on BERT and deep learning. IEEE Access **10**, 68633–68644 (2022)
11. Seyyar, Y.E., Yavuz, A.G., Ünver, H.M.: Detection of web attacks using the BERT model. In: 2022 30th Signal Processing and Communications Applications Conference (SIU), pp. 1–4. IEEE (2022)
12. Tian, Z., Luo, C., Qiu, J., Du, X., Guizani, M.: A distributed deep learning system for web attack detection on edge devices. IEEE Trans. Industr. Inf. **16**(3), 1963–1971 (2019)
13. Tóth, R., Bisztray, T., Erdődi, L.: LLMs in web development: Evaluating LLM-generated PHP code unveiling vulnerabilities and limitations. arXiv preprint arXiv:2404.14459 (2024)
14. Yang, J., et al.: LLM-AE-MP: web attack detection using a large language model with autoencoder and multilayer perceptron. Expert Syst. Appl. **274**, 126982 (2025)
15. Zhu, C., Cheng, Z., Ye, D., Hussain, F.K., Zhu, T., Zhou, W.: Time-driven and privacy-preserving navigation model for vehicle-to-vehicle communication systems. IEEE Trans. Veh. Technol. **72**(7), 8459–8470 (2023)
16. Zhu, C., Ye, D., Huo, H., Zhou, W., Zhu, T.: A location-based advising method in teacher-student frameworks. Knowl.-Based Syst. **285**, 111333 (2024)
17. Zhu, C., Ye, D., Zhu, T., Zhou, W.: Time-optimal and privacy preserving route planning for carpool policy. World Wide Web **25**(3), 1151–1168 (2022)
18. Zhu, C., Ye, D., Zhu, T., Zhou, W.: Location-based real-time updated advising method for traffic signal control. IEEE Internet Things J. **11**(8), 14551–14562 (2023)
19. Zhu, C., Ye, D., Zhu, T., Zhou, W.: The evolution of cooperation in continuous dilemmas via multi-agent reinforcement learning. Knowl.-Based Syst. **315**, 113153 (2025)

# A Large Language Model Agent-Guided Multi-agent System for Adaptive Traffic Signal Control

Minglu Zhu[1] and Congcong Zhu[2(✉)] ⓘ

[1] School of Information Technology, Griffith University, Brisbane, Australia
`minglu.zhu@griffithuni.edu.au`
[2] Institute of Data Science, the City University of Macau, Macau,
People's Republic of China
`cczhu@cityu.edu.mo`

**Abstract.** This paper proposes a novel Large Language Model Agent-Guided (LLM-AG) multi-agent framework for adaptive traffic signal control, aiming to alleviate urban traffic congestion effectively. Unlike existing multi-agent reinforcement learning (MARL) methods such as MA2C and LRUA, which suffer from high communication overhead and limited global coordination, our approach integrates a centralized LLM agent that provides comprehensive predictive traffic inflow information directly to local intersection agents. By enriching local state representations, LLM-AG significantly enhances global coordination and scalability. Extensive simulation experiments demonstrate substantial performance improvements over state-of-the-art methods in queue length, vehicle speed, and intersection delay, confirming the effectiveness of our proposed framework.

**Keywords:** large language model agent · multi-agent systems · traffic signal control

## 1 Introduction

Urban traffic congestion has become an increasingly pressing issue as cities worldwide continue to experience rapid population growth and urbanization. Traffic congestion not only leads to substantial economic losses due to delays and reduced productivity but also exacerbates environmental issues through heightened vehicle emissions. Effective management of traffic flows has thus emerged as a crucial area of research, prompting significant attention towards adaptive traffic signal control (ATSC) systems [17]. ATSC aims to dynamically optimize traffic signals based on real-time traffic conditions, offering a promising solution for alleviating urban congestion, enhancing transportation efficiency, reducing vehicular delays, improving road safety, and mitigating environmental pollution.

Traditional ATSC systems, such as SCOOT and SCATS, employ predefined timing strategies and heuristic adjustments based on limited local information. However, these systems struggle to adequately respond to highly dynamic

© The Author(s), under exclusive license to Springer Nature Singapore Pte Ltd. 2026
T. Zhu et al. (Eds.): KSEM 2025, LNAI 15919, pp. 59–70, 2026.
https://doi.org/10.1007/978-981-95-3001-4_5

and complex urban traffic scenarios, primarily due to their limited adaptivity and inflexible decision-making processes. To overcome these challenges, recent advancements have increasingly leveraged reinforcement learning (RL), particularly multi-agent reinforcement learning (MARL), to develop more intelligent and responsive traffic signal control systems. [20]

Among existing MARL approaches, methods such as Multi-Agent Advantage Actor-Critic (MA2C) and Location-based Real-Time Updated Advising (LRUA) have demonstrated promising results. MA2C enables individual intersections to learn independently, optimizing their signal timings based on locally observed conditions. LRUA further advances this concept by introducing real-time advising mechanisms among neighboring intersections, enhancing cooperative strategies for improved network-wide performance [18]. Nonetheless, despite their notable achievements, these approaches face considerable limitations, including significant communication overhead, slow convergence speeds, limited scalability, and insufficient global coordination, especially under rapidly fluctuating traffic patterns.

Motivated by these limitations, we propose the Large Language Model Agent-Guided (LLM-AG) multi-agent system, a novel traffic management framework designed to comprehensively address these challenges. The LLM-AG system integrates a powerful centralized Large Language Model (LLM) agent with local intersection agents [21]. By providing globally informed recommendations directly to intersection agents, our method eliminates the complexity of inter-agent communication and significantly enhances global optimization capabilities, scalability, and system stability.

## 2   Background

### 2.1   Deep Reinforcement Learning

Deep Reinforcement Learning (DRL) represents a branch of learning techniques wherein an agent refines its behavior based on environmental feedback. By iteratively interacting with the environment and adjusting its actions through trial and error, the agent learns to achieve its objective or maximize long-term rewards. This learning process inherently involves transitions between states and the acquisition of rewards resulting from environmental responses. In the early learning phase, the agent's decision-making may appear somewhat random due to limited information about the environment. Over time, however, it gradually adopts actions that are expected to yield higher returns [13]. Reinforcement learning is generally formulated as a Markov Decision Process (MDP) and is extensively employed in adaptive traffic signal control (ATSC) for real-world transportation systems.

RL approaches are commonly classified into two categories: model-based and model-free methods [23]. In model-based reinforcement learning, the agent has access to information regarding the transition dynamics between states. In contrast, model-free approaches assume no prior knowledge of state transitions and require the agent to explore and learn from interactions. As a result, model-free techniques may suffer from inefficiencies, whereas model-based methods can leverage known models and data more effectively.

Among model-free approaches, Q-learning is a widely used technique. The key idea is to initialize a Q-function that evaluates the expected utility of actions, and iteratively update it based on experience using the rule:

$$Q(s', a) \leftarrow (1 - \alpha) \cdot Q(s, a) + \alpha \cdot (r + \gamma \cdot \max_{a'} Q(s', a')) \tag{1}$$

Here, $\alpha$ is the learning rate, and $\gamma$ is the discount factor. A higher $\alpha$ implies that prior knowledge is retained less effectively. $Q(s', a)$ represents the value of taking action $a$ in state $s'$, and $r$ is the reward received. Through repeated interactions with the environment, the agent updates the Q-values and converges toward an optimal policy.

When agents must learn directly from high-dimensional sensory inputs such as images or audio, reinforcement learning alone often struggles. Feature extraction quality becomes crucial [24]. While deep learning excels at perception tasks by extracting abstract features from raw data, it lacks decision-making capabilities. Reinforcement learning, on the other hand, is proficient at making decisions but cannot effectively handle perception.

The integration of these complementary strengths gives rise to Deep Reinforcement Learning (DRL), which forms an end-to-end pipeline from perception to control. Early DRL efforts focused on reducing the dimensionality of complex sensory inputs. For instance, Lange et al. [8] proposed a Deep Auto-Encoder (DAE) that combines a deep neural model with a reinforcement learning algorithm. However, the DAE model has certain limitations: it is tailored for control problems, supports only visual inputs, and operates within a low-dimensional state space. Later, Mnih et al. [10] introduced the Deep Q-Network (DQN), which effectively integrated convolutional neural networks with Q-learning, marking a significant advancement in DRL.

## 2.2   Advantage Actor-Critic

The Advantage Actor-Critic (A2C) framework is an advanced reinforcement learning technique that combines a policy network (actor) and a value network (critic), using the policy gradient approach. It enhances the learning process by introducing the concept of "advantage" to guide policy updates.

**Policy Gradient:** The policy gradient method directly optimizes a parameterized policy $\pi_\theta$ by using sampled trajectories from interaction with the environment. The objective is to maximize the expected return, and the corresponding loss function is:

$$\mathcal{L}(\theta) = -\frac{1}{|B|} \sum_{t \in B} \log \pi_\theta \left(a_t \mid s_t\right) \hat{R}_t, \tag{2}$$

where $B = \{(s_t, a_t, s_{t+1}, r_t)\}$ is the replay buffer, and $\hat{R}_t = \sum_{\tau=t}^{t_B-1} \gamma^{\tau-t} r_\tau$ is the estimated return. $t_B$ represents the final timestep in the batch. While effective, this method often suffers from high variance due to the noisy return estimates.

**Advantage Actor-Critic:** A2C addresses this issue by incorporating the estimated value of the final state to improve return estimation:

$$R_t = \hat{R}_t + \gamma^{t_B-t} V_{w^-} (s_{t_B}) \tag{3}$$

To further reduce bias, A2C introduces the advantage term $A_t = R_t - V_{w^-}(s_t)$, resulting in a modified policy loss:

$$\mathcal{L}(\theta) = -\frac{1}{|B|} \sum_{t \in B} \log \pi_\theta (a_t \mid s_t) A_t \tag{4}$$

The critic's parameters $w$ are trained by minimizing the mean squared error between predicted and actual returns:

$$\mathcal{L}(w) = \frac{1}{2|B|} \sum_{t \in B} (R_t - V_w (s_t))^2 \tag{5}$$

This actor-critic structure enables stable and efficient learning, allowing the model to benefit from both policy-based and value-based reinforcement learning paradigms.

## 3   Related Work

The application of reinforcement learning (RL) in traffic signal control has been widely explored. In early studies, however, conventional RL methods encountered limitations in processing high-dimensional data, leading most prior research to focus on relatively simplified traffic scenarios [19]. Wiering et al. [15] applied RL to urban traffic light control, with the objective of reducing vehicle wait times. Their method involved learning value functions that estimate the expected waiting durations under various signal settings.

Cai et al. [1] developed a real-time traffic signal control strategy using approximate dynamic programming, which reduced computational load by leveraging value function approximations. Prashanth et al. [12] pointed out the limitations in existing algorithms' capacity to represent global traffic states, particularly in networks beyond a modest scale. To address this, they proposed a reinforcement learning algorithm that used function approximation to model both state and action features, helping to alleviate the curse of dimensionality.

To enhance learning efficiency in large-scale systems, Chu et al. [3] introduced a kernel-based method to generate adaptive feature representations, eliminating the need for manually preselected features and improving learning scalability. El et al. [5] introduced a multi-agent RL system specifically for ATSC scenarios. Their framework supported both decentralized (independent) and coordinated (joint control) modes, allowing intersections to either operate autonomously or in collaboration with neighboring nodes.

In another effort to promote cooperation, Zhu et al. [22] proposed a coordinated reinforcement learning approach based on a junction tree structure. By treating each traffic signal as an agent within a cooperative setting, the framework enabled joint optimization of signal plans across intersections. Given the infeasibility of policy exploration in the vast action spaces of large-scale traffic networks, Chu et al. [2] introduced a regional RL algorithm that adaptively defined cooperation zones and computed optimal local policies accordingly. These early RL-based ATSC methods were largely constrained by the challenge of high-dimensional input spaces, which deep reinforcement learning (DRL) later addressed.

With the advent of DRL, increasing attention has been directed toward traffic signal control applications. For example, Genders et al. [6] proposed a DRL-based system that fed discrete traffic state encodings into a deep convolutional neural network, training the agent using Q-learning with experience replay. To enable large-scale coordination, Van et al. [11] integrated deep Q-learning with a coordination strategy and designed a task-specific reward function.

In a multi-agent setting, Wu et al. [16] presented an algorithm grounded in the deep deterministic policy gradient (DDPG) framework. It employed centralized training to allow agents to anticipate the policies of their peers, facilitating better coordination. Wang et al. [14] addressed the complexity of large-scale traffic control with a decentralized multi-agent RL method based on double Q-learning. This method incorporated a dual estimator mechanism and an upper confidence bound policy to reduce Q-value overestimation while maintaining scalability and autonomy.

Building upon A2C, Chu et al. [4] proposed independent and multi-agent variants of the algorithm for ATSC, with the multi-agent version emerging as a leading solution. Recently, Ma et al. [9] further improved this framework using feudal RL, which demonstrated superior performance compared to previous methods.


## 4   Methodology

### 4.1   Problem Definition

Within a transportation network, each intersection is controlled by a designated agent responsible for managing its traffic signals. Two intersections are considered neighbors if they are connected by a single road segment. The traffic signal control problem is formally defined through three main components for each agent: state, action, and reward.

*1) State representation:* At time step $t$, the local observation for agent $i$ is denoted by $s_{t,i} = \{\texttt{wait}_t[l], \texttt{wave}_t[l], \texttt{INwave}_t[l]\}$, where each $l$ refers to an incoming lane approaching intersection $i$. Specifically, $\texttt{wait}_t[l]$ indicates the waiting time (in seconds) of the first vehicle queued in lane $l$, while $\texttt{wave}_t[l]$ reflects the number of vehicles located within $50\,\mathrm{m}$ from the stop line of lane $l$. The newly introduced term $\texttt{INwave}_t[l]$ captures the inflow information from llm-agent, including both the direction and number of vehicles expected to enter

**Fig. 1.** The overview of LLM-AG framework

lane $l$. This enriched state encoding provides more comprehensive situational awareness for each intersection agent.

*2) Action representation:* The available actions for an agent correspond to the feasible traffic signal phases at its intersection. Each phase represents a distinct configuration of green and red lights across the incoming lanes. For example, at a typical four-leg intersection, a phase like GGRR signifies that the first two approaches are given green signals while the remaining two are under red. If the current phase is RRGG, and the agent switches to GGRR, it must change the signal state of the respective lanes accordingly. Since intersections may vary in their structural layout and number of lanes, the action space for each agent is uniquely determined by the intersection's geometry and signal design.

*3) Reward representation:* The immediate reward for agent $i$ at time step $t$ is calculated as:

$$r_{t,i} = -\sum_l \left( \text{queue}_{t+\Delta t}[l] + a \cdot \text{wait}_{t+\Delta t}[l] \right), \tag{6}$$

where $\text{queue}_{t+\Delta t}[l]$ represents the number of vehicles queued on lane $l$ after a time interval $\Delta t$, and $\text{wait}_{t+\Delta t}[l]$ is the updated waiting time of the lead vehicle on that lane. The parameter $a$ is a weighting factor used to balance the contribution of delay and queue length. This reward formulation promotes actions that reduce both vehicle accumulation and waiting time, thereby reinforcing traffic flow optimization behaviors in the agents.

## 4.2   LLM-AG

Our LLM-AG framework incorporates two core components: a centralized LLM agent and multiple local intersection agents employing the Advantage Actor-Critic (A2C) reinforcement learning algorithm. The distinctive innovation of our approach lies in the effective integration of detailed global contextual information provided by the central LLM agent into the local decision-making processes of intersection agents.

At time step $t$, the local observation for agent $i$ is denoted by:

$$s_{t,i} = \{\texttt{wait}_t[l], \texttt{wave}_t[l], \texttt{INwave}_t[l]\}$$

where each $l$ refers to an incoming lane approaching intersection $i$. Specifically, $\texttt{wait}_t[l]$ indicates the waiting time (in seconds) of the first vehicle queued in lane $l$, while $\texttt{wave}_t[l]$ reflects the number of vehicles located within 50 m from the stop line of lane $l$. The newly introduced term $\texttt{INwave}_t[l]$ captures inflow information from the LLM-agent, including both the direction and number of vehicles expected to enter lane $l$. This enriched state encoding significantly enhances each intersection agent's situational awareness.

Local intersection agents communicate their states, including the incoming vehicle wave diagrams, to the centralized LLM agent. The LLM agent then synthesizes these local states with information from neighboring intersections. Through advanced reasoning and predictive analytics, the LLM agent updates each intersection's incoming vehicle wave diagram, accurately forecasting traffic inflows and potential congestion patterns. Formally, the LLM agent models this predictive update process as:

$$\texttt{INwave}_{t+1}[l] = f_{LLM}\left(s_{t,i}, \{s_{t,j}\}_{j \in \mathcal{N}(i)}\right)$$

where $f_{LLM}$ represents the predictive reasoning function of the LLM, and $\mathcal{N}(i)$ denotes the set of neighboring intersections for intersection $i$.

The updated state from the LLM is returned to each intersection agent, where it is integrated with local observations to form an enriched augmented state vector. The local A2C model uses this augmented state to determine optimal traffic signal actions independently. The decision-making process at each intersection $i$ at time $t$ can thus be formalized as:

$$a_{t,i} = \text{argmax}_{a \in A_i} Q_i\left(s_{t,i}, a\right)$$

where $Q_i$ is the value function approximated by the local A2C neural network, and $A_i$ denotes the set of possible signal phase actions at intersection $i$.

Figure 1 illustrates this framework, clearly demonstrating how the centralized LLM interacts with intersection agents (numbered 1 to 4), exchanging and refining incoming vehicle wave information to improve overall network performance.

The LLM in our system is a pretrained, independently operating language model. This design choice significantly reduces the complexity and instability inherent in conventional MARL systems that often require extensive inter-agent training and synchronization. Consequently, local intersection agents receive highly accurate, globally informed advisories without incurring extensive computational overhead.

Compared to traditional MARL methods, such as LRUA and MA2C, our LLM-AG framework drastically reduces communication overhead, accelerates decision-making processes, and significantly enhances adaptive capabilities in response to dynamic traffic conditions. As a result, our proposed system is exceptionally well-suited for scalable, real-time urban traffic management.

## 5   Experiment

To implement and evaluate our LRUA algorithm, we simulated an ATSC environment in SUMO [7]. SUMO is a microscopic traffic simulator that is commonly used in traffic-related experiments. We further compared our method to several advanced traffic signal control methods, including LRUA, MA2C and FMA2C. To make it fair, we use the same source code [4] and the same parameters and definitions for state, action and reward.

### 5.1   Experiment Setup

We evaluated our method, denoted as LRUA, by comparing with these learning methods:

- **LRUA**, which is an location-based multi-agent method [20].
- **MA2C**, which is a multi-agent advantage actor-critic method [4].
- **FMA2C**, which is an extension of MA2C based on feudal reinforcement learning [9].

All algorithms were trained over 1 million steps with 1400 episodes, and each episode having 720 steps. Our method uses ChatGPT 4o as the driver for the LLM agent. In the test stage, 10 episodes with different random seeds were simulated in 3600 seconds to evaluate. The experiment consists of two maps: a complex synthetic map and the other is a real-world map of Monaco. The traffic flow data utilized in our experiments is derived from a traffic road simulator. This simulator provides us with detailed traffic flow information collected from each intersection. In real-world applications, similar data is typically sourced from video surveillance systems installed at traffic signals. These systems employ video analysis software capable of identifying vehicles and calculating traffic flow metrics.

As shown in Fig. 2, this map is a $5 \times 5$ traffic network with two-lane horizontal roads and single-lane vertical roads. The speed limit of the two-lane road is $20\,\mathrm{m/s}$, and that of the single-lane is $11\,\mathrm{m/s}$. Significant changes in traffic flow within the simulation makes the environment more complicated. At the beginning of the simulation, as shown in Fig. 3(a), a large number of vehicles

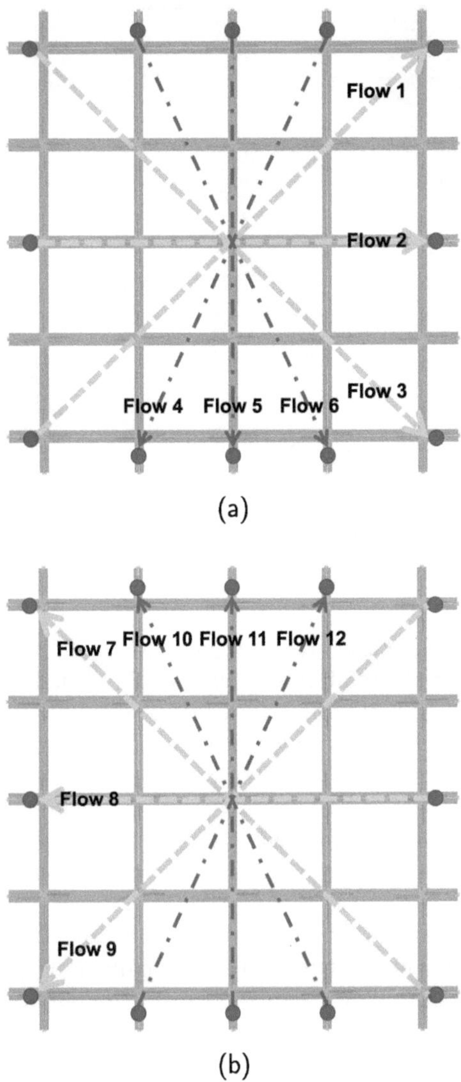


**Fig. 2.** A $5 \times 5$ grid traffic network, (a) is the first phase of traffic flow in the simulation, (b) is the second phase (Color figure online)

are generated from the 6 blue origin points. Each is heading for a red destination point. The origin and destination are fixed, but the specific route of each vehicle is random. As shown in yellow Flows 1, 2, and 3, begin with a volume of 440 vehicles per hour (veh/h), which gradually increases to $1,100$ veh/h. The green Flows 4, 5, and 6, it starts at 264 veh/h and gradually increased to 660 veh/h. After 15 min, these six traffic flows gradually decreased, and as shown in Fig. 3(b), and six new traffic flows are formed. At 15 min, the yellow Flows 7, 8,

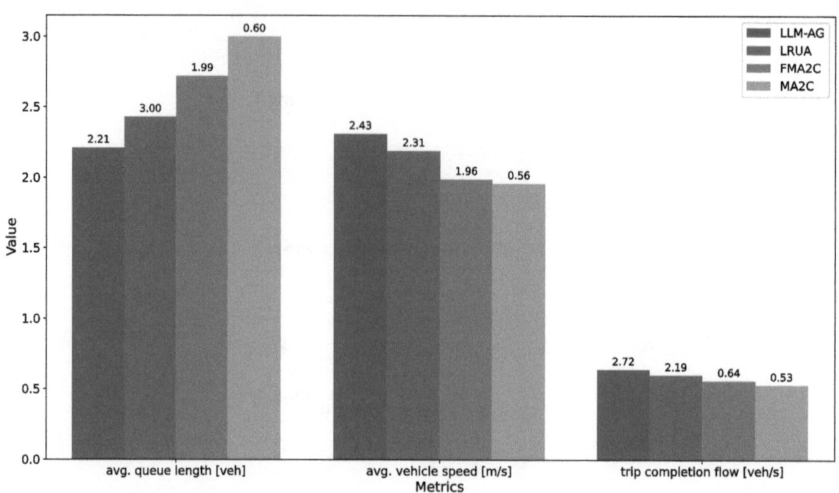



**Fig. 3.** Average queue speed and flows in $5 \times 5$ grid traffic network (Color figure online)

and 9 starts at 277.5 veh/h and gradually increase to 925 veh/h, while the green Flows 10, 11 and 12, it starts at 166.5 veh/h and gradually rises to 555 veh/h.

We compared the LLM-AG framework against established approaches including LRUA, FMA2C, and MA2C under identical simulation parameters to ensure fairness. Performance evaluation included several key metrics: average queue length (veh), average vehicle speed (m/s), trip completion flow (veh/s), intersection delays (s/veh), and overall trip delays (s).

As depicted in Fig. 3, a comprehensive bar chart comparison clearly illustrates the superior performance of the LLM-AG system across metrics such as average queue length, average vehicle speed, and trip completion flow. Specifically, LLM-AG consistently maintained shorter queue lengths, notably higher average speeds, and higher trip completion rates compared to LRUA, FMA2C, and MA2C.

Moreover, Fig. 4 provides a detailed heatmap visualization highlighting the improvements achieved by the LLM-AG framework in reward metrics, average intersection delays, and trip delays. LLM-AG achieved performance improvements exceeding 5% relative to the state-of-the-art methods, demonstrating substantial efficiency gains across these critical performance indicators.

These visual comparisons underscore the LLM-AG framework's robustness and adaptability, confirming its enhanced performance especially under peak traffic conditions and dynamically varying traffic inflows. While LRUA and MA2C exhibited initial effectiveness, their reliance on localized interactions or hierarchical structures led to increased delays and reduced responsiveness as traffic complexity heightened.

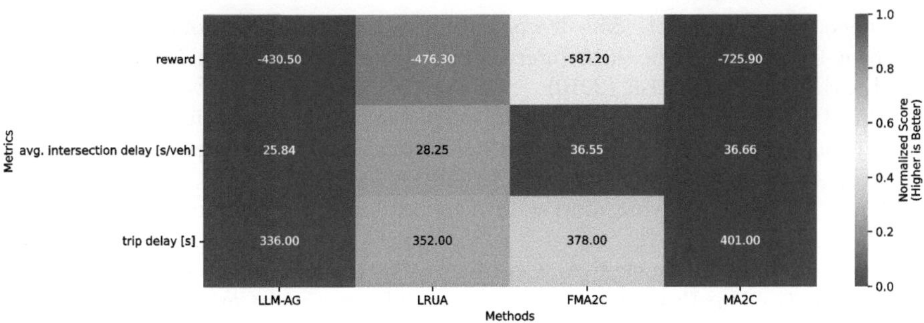


**Fig. 4.** Reward and delay in $5 \times 5$ grid traffic network

## 6   Conclusion

This study introduces the innovative LLM-AG framework, effectively leveraging a central LLM agent to provide global advisories that significantly enhance local decision-making in adaptive traffic signal control. By streamlining communication, improving scalability, and promoting global coordination, our method effectively addresses limitations faced by traditional MARL approaches. Future research directions include real-world deployments and incorporating live data streams to further enhance practical performance and applicable.

## References


1. Cai, C., Wong, C.K., Heydecker, B.G.: Adaptive traffic signal control using approximate dynamic programming. Transp. Res. Part C: Emerg. Technol. **17**(5), 456–474 (2009)
2. Chu, T., Qu, S., Wang, J.: Large-scale traffic grid signal control with regional reinforcement learning. In: 2016 American Control Conference (ACC), pp. 815–820. IEEE (2016)
3. Chu, T., Wang, J., Cao, J.: Kernel-based reinforcement learning for traffic signal control with adaptive feature selection. In: 53rd IEEE Conference on Decision and Control, pp. 1277–1282. IEEE (2014)
4. Chu, T., Wang, J., Codecà, L., Li, Z.: Multi-agent deep reinforcement learning for large-scale traffic signal control. IEEE Trans. Intell. Transp. Syst. **21**(3), 1086–1095 (2019)
5. El-Tantawy, S., Abdulhai, B., Abdelgawad, H.: Multiagent reinforcement learning for integrated network of adaptive traffic signal controllers (marlin-atsc): methodology and large-scale application on downtown Toronto. IEEE Trans. Intell. Transp. Syst. **14**(3), 1140–1150 (2013)
6. Genders, W., Razavi, S.: Using a deep reinforcement learning agent for traffic signal control. arXiv preprint arXiv:1611.01142 (2016)
7. Krajzewicz, D., Erdmann, J., Behrisch, M., Bieker, L.: Recent development and applications of sumo-simulation of urban mobility. Int. J. Adv. Syst. Meas. **5**(3&4) (2012)

8. Lange, S., Riedmiller, M.: Deep auto-encoder neural networks in reinforcement learning. In: The 2010 International Joint Conference on Neural Networks (IJCNN), pp. 1–8. IEEE (2010)
9. Ma, J., Wu, F.: Feudal multi-agent deep reinforcement learning for traffic signal control. In: Proceedings of the 19th International Conference on Autonomous Agents and Multiagent Systems (AAMAS), pp. 816–824 (2020)
10. Mnih, V., et al.: Playing atari with deep reinforcement learning. arXiv preprint arXiv:1312.5602 (2013)
11. Van der Pol, E., Oliehoek, F.A.: Coordinated deep reinforcement learners for traffic light control. In: Proceedings of Learning, Inference and Control of Multi-Agent Systems (at NIPS 2016) (2016)
12. Prashanth, L., Bhatnagar, S.: Reinforcement learning with function approximation for traffic signal control. IEEE Trans. Intell. Transp. Syst. **12**(2), 412–421 (2010)
13. Su, X., Zhang, M., Bai, Q., Ye, D.: A dynamic coordination approach for task allocation in disaster environments under spatial and communicational constraints. In: Workshops at the Twenty-Eighth AAAI Conference on Artificial Intelligence (2014)
14. Wang, X., Ke, L., Qiao, Z., Chai, X.: Large-scale traffic signal control using a novel multiagent reinforcement learning. IEEE Trans. Cybern. **51**(1), 174–187 (2020)
15. Wiering, M.A.: Multi-agent reinforcement learning for traffic light control. In: Machine Learning: Proceedings of the Seventeenth International Conference (ICML'2000), pp. 1151–1158 (2000)
16. Wu, T., et al.: Multi-agent deep reinforcement learning for urban traffic light control in vehicular networks. IEEE Trans. Veh. Technol. **69**(8), 8243–8256 (2020)
17. Ye, D., Zhu, T., Gao, K., Zhu, C., Zhou, W.: Cooperating or kicking out: defending against poisoning attacks in federated learning via the evolution of cooperation. IEEE Trans. Depend. Secure Comput. (2025)
18. Zhu, C., Ye, D., Huo, H., Zhou, W., Zhu, T.: A location-based advising method in teacher-student frameworks. Knowl.-Based Syst. **285**, 111333 (2024)
19. Zhu, C., Ye, D., Zhu, T., Zhou, W.: Time-optimal and privacy preserving route planning for carpool policy. In: World Wide Web, pp. 1–18 (2022)
20. Zhu, C., Ye, D., Zhu, T., Zhou, W.: Location-based real-time updated advising method for traffic signal control. IEEE Internet Things J. **11**(8), 14551–14562 (2023)
21. Zhu, C., Ye, D., Zhu, T., Zhou, W.: The evolution of cooperation in continuous dilemmas via multi-agent reinforcement learning. Knowl.-Based Syst. 113153 (2025)
22. Zhu, F., Aziz, H.A., Qian, X., Ukkusuri, S.V.: A junction-tree based learning algorithm to optimize network wide traffic control: a coordinated multi-agent framework. Transp. Res. Part C: Emerg. Technol. **58**, 487–501 (2015)
23. Zhu, T., Li, G., Zhou, W., Yu, P.S.: Differentially private data publishing and analysis: a survey. IEEE Trans. Knowl. Data Eng. **29**(8), 1619–1638 (2017). https://doi.org/10.1109/TKDE.2017.2697856
24. Zhu, T., Ye, D., Wang, W., Zhou, W., Yu, P.: More than privacy: applying differential privacy in key areas of artificial intelligence. IEEE Trans. Knowl. Data Eng. 1 (2020). https://doi.org/10.1109/TKDE.2020.3014246

# FedBCE: Rethinking Clustered Federated Learning for Better Clustering Efficiency

Huaibin Ye[1], Zuobin Ying[1], Jiechao Gao[2], Ximeng Liu[3],
and Jianping Cai[1(✉)]

[1] City University of Macau, Macau S.A.R, China
`jiechao@stanford.edu`
[2] Center for SDGC, Stanford University, Stanford 94305, USA
[3] Fuzhou University, Fuzhou 350108, China

**Abstract.** Federated learning (FL) models face challenges such as negative transfer in non-IID scenarios, where the global model performs worse than local models. Clustered Federated Learning (CFL) addresses this by grouping clients based on pairwise similarity, but the high computational cost limits the scalability. To solve this, we propose FedBCE, an efficient CFL framework that significantly reduces clustering time by calculating distances only to selected centers while grouping clients using data volume and model similarity to enable collaboration among those with similar data distributions. Experiments on public data sets show that FedBCE reduces the clustering time to just $\frac{1}{10}$ to $\frac{1}{160}$ of existing methods while increasing the accuracy by 19% on average in non-IID scenarios.

**Keywords:** Clustered Federated Learning · Non-IID · Time Complexity · Quantity-aware function · Clustering Efficiency

## 1  Introduction

Traditional machine learning [1–3] requires centralizing data before training, which can lead to privacy leakage and high communication costs in multi-party collaboration scenarios. As a result, participants may be reluctant to share their real data. Federated Learning (FL) [4,5],?, [6,7] was introduced to address this issue by simulating the effects of centralized learning through the aggregation of local models trained by individual participants, thereby eliminating the need for direct data transmission. However, due to variations in client data distributions-commonly referred to as the data heterogeneity problem [8–10],?-the federated global model often suffers from slow convergence or even divergence. To mitigate this, Clustered Federated Learning (CFL) [11] was proposed. CFL clusters clients based on their similarities before federated training, allowing federated training to be conducted separately within similar client groups. This approach reduces the impact of large data distribution differences among clients, effectively


T. Zhu et al. (Eds.): KSEM 2025, LNAI 15919, pp. 71–86, 2026.
https://doi.org/10.1007/978-981-95-3001-4_6

alleviating the data heterogeneity problem. Nevertheless, algorithms that compute pairwise distances between clients often have high time complexity [12,13], which poses a significant barrier to practical deployment.

High time complexity introduces critical challenges, particularly in time-sensitive domains. For instance, in the medical field [14,15], medical image analysis may face delays due to computational inefficiencies, potentially compromising timely diagnosis, patient experience, and clinical decision-making. Similarly, systems that monitor physiological parameters in critically ill patients or during surgery demand rapid system responses; delays caused by high algorithmic time complexity could jeopardize patient safety. In telemedicine [16], prolonged processing times could prevent doctors from accessing patient health information promptly during remote consultations, thereby impairing the diagnostic workflow. In the context of CFL, beyond time complexity, a core challenge lies in accurately clustering clients and identifying the critical information needed to achieve optimal clustering. We identify two key factors that influence clustering outcomes: data volume and distribution difference. In FL, collaboration among clients with similar data distributions generally leads to better models. However, the impact of data volume is often overlooked. When data distributions are identical, increased data volume can enable a local model to outperform the global model. In such cases, clients with larger datasets may set higher expectations for collaboration partners. Existing CFL algorithms predominantly rely on clustering based on gradient similarity, which has limitations: they fail to account for data volume and may cluster clients with large datasets even when local training would be more effective.

To address these challenges, this paper introduces FedBCE, an algorithm designed to tackle both issues. FedBCE measures distribution differences between clients using high-dimensional information, such as model parameters, without transmitting clients' original data, thereby preserving privacy. Clients are then clustered based on their distribution differences, forming temporary alliances of similar clients for federated training. This approach minimizes the negative impact of significant client differences, improving the efficiency and accuracy of FL. Unlike existing CFL algorithms, FedBCE calculates distances only between clients and a limited number of cluster centers rather than between individual clients. This significantly reduces the time complexity of the clustering process, enabling scalability to larger client populations and enhancing generalization capabilities.

Extensive experiments on public datasets validate the effectiveness of the proposed algorithm, FedBCE, and demonstrate its superiority over baseline algorithms. The main contributions of this paper are as follows:

- We propose a novel CFL algorithm that clusters similar clients based on both data volume and data distribution differences, thereby mitigating the impact of the non-IID problem.
- We introduce an efficient client distance measurement algorithm. By calculating distances between clients and a limited number of cluster centers, the time complexity of client distance estimation is significantly reduced.

– We conduct extensive experiments on public datasets, including FashionM-
  NIST and CIFAR-10/100, to evaluate the performance of FedBCE. Results
  show that the algorithm improves the accuracy of existing FL methods in
  various non-IID scenarios while achieving shorter client clustering times compared to existing single-clustering algorithms.

## 2    Related Work

### 2.1    Clustered Federated Learning (CFL)

Clustered Federated Learning (CFL) [17–20] reduces computational overhead
and improves generalization by clustering similar clients and treating the learning task for each resulting client subset as an independent task. When a new
client joins, it only needs to be assigned to an appropriate cluster. For instance,
the framework proposed in [24] employs the K-means algorithm to cluster client
updates, identifying and isolating Byzantine clients that behave abnormally
before aggregation. However, this approach is effective only when the clients'
risk functions are convex and the minima of different clusters are well separated.
Sattler et al. [25] introduced a CFL method that clustered clients based on cosine
similarity and trained independent global models for each cluster. However, their
approach overlooked the impact of client data volume on clustering effectiveness.
FEDCOLLAB [26], proposed by Bao et al., addressed this issue by considering
the role of data volume and utilizing a single clustering step to reduce computational overhead. However, their algorithm calculates pairwise similarity between
clients, which results in prohibitively high time complexity and limits its practical deployment in large-scale settings.

The method proposed in this paper considers both the impact of data volume and data distribution differences. Instead of computing pairwise similarities
between all clients, it calculates the similarity between clients and a limited subset of representative clients, thereby significantly reducing computational complexity. This improvement enables the proposed method to be more scalable and
suitable for real-world scenarios.

### 2.2    Time Complexity

Time complexity [27–29] is a critical consideration in the development of all
algorithms, as excessive complexity can render an algorithm impractical for real-
world deployment. Managing time complexity is especially important in scenarios involving large-scale data or resource-constrained devices. Various methods
exist to reduce time complexity, each with its own trade-offs. The divide-and-
conquer approach [30,31] is one widely used strategy where a large problem is
divided into smaller sub-problems, which are then solved independently. This
approach improves efficiency for processing large-scale data. However, divide-
and-conquer often relies on recursion, which can lead to significant memory overhead. When the recursion depth is high, this can create a bottleneck for devices

with limited memory resources. The greedy algorithm [32,33] is another common technique that selects the locally optimal solution at each step without requiring complex state maintenance or backtracking, resulting in lower time complexity. However, greedy algorithms have limitations, as the local optimal solution at each step may not lead to a globally optimal result. Consequently, their application is often confined to specific problem scenarios, with limited generalization capability. Distributed systems [34] offer another solution to address computational complexity. By adding more nodes, distributed systems can scale capacity and processing power to handle larger datasets or higher user request volumes. They can also combine the computing, storage, and network resources of multiple nodes to manage complex tasks more efficiently. However, the design and maintenance of distributed systems are inherently complex, requiring solutions for issues such as data consistency and network latency. Furthermore, the need for inter-node communication often leads to increased development and maintenance costs.

In summary, while these methods provide valuable strategies to manage time complexity, each has inherent trade-offs that must be carefully considered depending on the use case.

## 3    Preliminaries

In a classic FL system, it is usually assumed that there are $N$ clients and a central server. The data set of each client $i \in \{1, 2, \cdots, N\}$ is $d_i = (x_k, y_k)_{k=1}^{m_i}$, where $m_i$ samples are from the true distribution of the data set obtained by sampling in $D_i$, $x$ is the characteristic information of the sample, and $y$ is the label of the sample. We denote the total number of samples as $m = \sum_{i=1}^{N} m_i$, and the client quantity distribution in each client is $\alpha = \left[\frac{m_1}{m}, \frac{m_2}{m}, \cdots, \frac{m_n}{m}\right] = [\alpha_1, \alpha_2, \cdots, \alpha_n]$. For a given neural network model $h$ and loss function $l$, the expected risk function of client $i$ is $R_i^{\exp}(h) = E_{(x,y)\in d_i}[l(y, h(x))] = \int_{x \times y} l(y, h(x))P(x,y)\,dx\,dy$, where $P(x,y)$ is the joint probability distribution of $x$ and $y$. However, we can only know the joint probability distribution of training samples, which is unsuitable for calculating test samples' expected risk.

The form of the empirical risk function is $R_i^{\mathrm{emp}}(h) = \frac{1}{m_i} \sum_{k=1}^{m_i} l(y_k, h(x_k))$. Each client $i \in \{1, \ldots, N\}$ aims to find a model $h$ within the hypothesis space $H$ that minimizes its local expected risk, expressed as $h_i^* = \arg\min_{h \in H} \epsilon_i(h)$. However, due to the limitation of having only a finite set of local samples $\hat{D}_1, \ldots, \hat{D}_N$, clients can only optimize their models based on these available data. Common approaches to this problem include local training, global federated learning (GFL), and clustered federated learning (CFL).

### 3.1    Clustered Federated Learning (CFL)

CFL emerged as a solution when addressing non-IID problems. By clustering clients based on the similarity of their data distributions, clients with relatively similar distributions are grouped into a collaborative unit. The client will only communicate with other clients in the same collaboration unit and conduct cooperative training. A client $i$ within a coalition $C$ collaborates with other clients in $C$ to train a model, aiming to minimize a weighted sum of local empirical risks, where the weights are determined by $\beta_i = [\beta_{i1}, \beta_{i2}, \ldots, \beta_{iN}]$:

$$h_{(\beta_i)} = \arg\min \sum_{j=1}^{N} \beta_{ij} R_j^{\mathrm{emp}}(h) \tag{1}$$

where $\beta_{ij} = \frac{\alpha_j \cdot \mathbb{I}\{j \in C\}}{\sum_{k \in C} \beta_k}$ ($\mathbb{I}$ is the indicator function).

CFL improves generalization by clustering clients with similar data distributions into a unified coalition, which fosters effective collaboration while reducing the risk of negative transfer. Optimization objective (1) covers both local training and FL scenarios. When $\beta_{ii} = 1, \beta_{ij} = 0 (i \neq j)$, the optimization objective for local training is obtained, while when $\beta_i = \alpha$, the optimization objective for FL is derived.

Given the above discussion, exploring how to perform client-side clustering to achieve optimal results is a topic worthy of further investigation. We know that for $N$ clients, there are $B_N = \sum_{k=0}^{N} \left\{ {N \atop k} \right\}$ different grouping results. It is unrealistic to calculate the expected risk for each group in all grouping ways one by one, which will bring huge computational costs. Therefore, we introduce the Quantity-aware function and propose an algorithm that efficiently estimates the distance between clients to facilitate effective clustering, thereby avoiding the high complexity of pairwise calculating the distance between clients.

## 3.2  Quantity-Aware Function

For a specified hypothesis space $H$, combination weights $\beta_i$, quantity distribution $\alpha$, and total amount $m$, for any $\delta \in (0, 1)$, with probability at least $1 - \delta$ (considering the randomness in sample selection), a quantity-sensitive function $\varphi_{|H|}(\alpha, \beta_i, m, \delta)$ satisfies the condition for all $h \in H$ [26],

$$\left| R_{(\beta_i)}^{\mathrm{emp}}(h) - R_{(\beta_i)}^{\mathrm{exp}}(h) \right| \leq \varphi(\alpha, \beta_i, m, \delta) \tag{2}$$

The quantity-sensitive function can be evaluated using classical generalization error bounds, such as VC dimension [35] and weighted Rademacher complexity [36]. For instance, when employing the VC dimension $d$ [35] to measure the complexity of the hypothesis space $H$, we obtain the following result:

$$\varphi(\alpha, \beta_i, m, \delta) = \sqrt{\left( \sum_{j=1}^{N} \frac{\beta_{ij}^2}{\alpha_j} \right) \left( \frac{2d \log(2m + 2) + \log(4/\delta)}{m} \right)} \tag{3}$$

In practical applications, different clients may place varying levels of emphasis on data volume and distribution differences. Clients with substantial amounts of

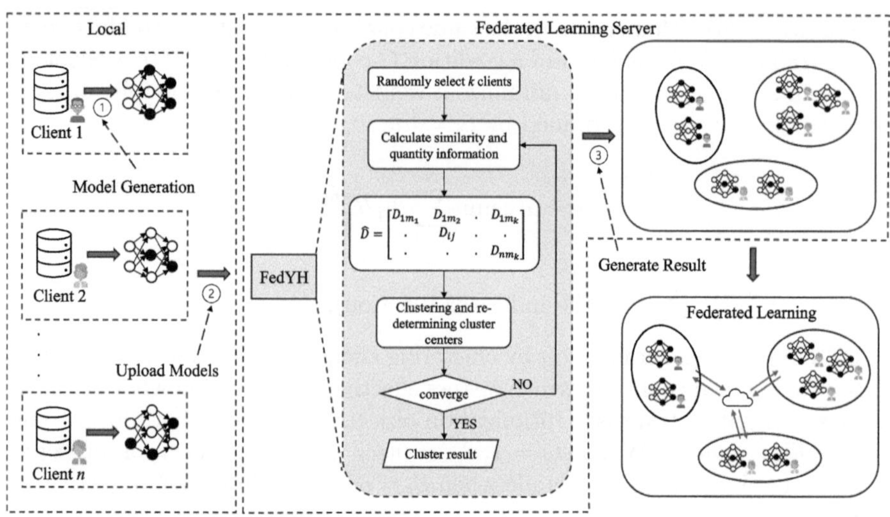



**Fig. 1.** System overview: (1) Each client performs local training on the original model. (2) All clients upload their local models to the central server. (3) FedBCE is run to cluster the clients according to the model and data volume information uploaded by the client. (4) FL is performed in each cluster according to the clustered results.

data often prioritize distribution differences among collaborators, as their abundant data allows them to focus on model convergence and training efficiency. Conversely, clients with limited data may prefer to collaborate with peers possessing similar data volumes to ensure that their local information is adequately represented. Consequently, the hyperparameter $C$ can be adaptively adjusted to dynamically balance the influence of data volume and distribution differences based on the specific context.

## 4    Proposed Method

### 4.1    System Overview

The overall framework of the proposed method is illustrated in Fig. 1. First, the central server distributes an initial model to all participating clients. Upon receiving the model, each client performs local training using its own data and obtains a converged model after a predefined number of iterations. Subsequently, each client uploads its model parameters and data volume information to the central server. The central server then executes the FedBCE algorithm, which computes the optimization objective for the clustering process based on the uploaded client information. Clients are then clustered according to the results of this optimization objective. Once clustering is completed, the central server recalculates the cluster centers for the next iteration. If the newly computed cluster centers differ from the previous ones, the server recomputes the distances between all clients and the updated centers, re-evaluates the optimization objective, and initiates another iteration of clustering. This process continues until the cluster centers remain unchanged, indicating algorithm convergence and yielding the final clustering results.

## 4.2  Optimization Objective

We fully use the client data volume information and the distance between clients to construct the actual optimization target. We replace the Quantity-aware function with an empirical estimate and use the distance from the client to the specified center to evaluate the similarity between clients. Finally, we combine the optimization targets of all clients to form a global optimization target.

**Quantifying Quantity-Aware Functions.** The quantity-aware function mentioned above reflects the impact of data quantity. However, it is also influenced by the complexity of the hypothesis space $H$, which can be challenging to estimate precisely for neural networks. Drawing inspiration from prior research on model-complexity-based generalization bounds [25,26], we treat the model capacity constant $C = \sqrt{2d \log(2m + 2) + \log(4/\delta)}$ as a hyperparameter to be optimized. This leads to the following empirical quantity-aware function [26]:

$$\widehat{\varphi}(\alpha, \beta_i, m, C) = \frac{C}{\sqrt{m}} \sqrt{\sum_{j=1}^{N} \frac{\beta_{ij}^2}{\alpha_j}} \tag{4}$$

where $\alpha$ and $m$ can be directly calculated using the information uploaded by the client.

**Quantifying Distribution Differences.** The distribution difference $D(D_i, D_j)$ between the underlying distributions $D_i$ and $D_j$ of two clients is generally not directly computable in practical settings. Earlier CFL approaches [25,47] typically rely on the similarity of parameters or gradients, which serve as indirect indicators of distributional differences between clients. However, these methods provide less accurate estimations of distribution distance due to the non-convex nature and permutation invariance of neural networks [48]. For instance, even when two neural networks are trained on identical datasets, their parameters may still vary significantly due to differences in parameter initialization, data loading randomness, and other factors. Existing CFL algorithms, such as FED-COLLAB, utilize balanced accuracy to measure differences in client data distributions. While this approach mitigates the aforementioned issues, it processes each pair of clients individually, resulting in substantial computational complexity. To address this challenge, we propose an algorithm that estimates the data distribution difference between clients by combining the Euclidean metric with a quantity-aware function. We set $d(h_i, h_{j_s}) := \sqrt{\sum_{m=1}^{N}(h_i^m - h_{j_s}^m)^2}$, where $s$ means selected, $j_s$ is taken from the pre-selected $k$ clients, $h_i$ and $h_{j_s}$ are the model parameters of client $i$, $j_s$. The following optimization objective can be obtained:

$$L(\alpha, \beta_i, m, C) = \frac{C}{\sqrt{m}} \sqrt{\sum_{j=1}^{k} \frac{\beta_{ij_s}^2}{\alpha_{j_s}} + \widehat{D}_{ij_s}} \tag{5}$$

### 4.3  Algorithm

First, the central server distributes the original model to all participating clients in the cooperative training process. Upon receiving the model, each client trains it using local data, with specific training settings adjustable based on the given context. After a predefined number of iterations and upon achieving model convergence, each client uploads its model parameters along with local data volume information to the central server for clustering and further processing.

---

**Algorithm 1.** Client Grouping Algorithm

---

1: **Input:** Clients $i, j, m, m_i$
2: **Output:** Group information
3: `features` = extract_client_features(args)
4: `pca_features` = PCA(n_components=0.95).`fit_transform(features)`
5: **Calculation of constants:** $m, C$
6: **for** each iteration $l \in [1, \texttt{max\_iterations}]$ **do**
7:     **for** each client $i \in [1, \texttt{num\_clients}]$ **do**
8:         $[\beta_1, \ldots, \beta_N] = [m_1/m, \ldots, m_N/m]$
9:         $\alpha_{ij} = \frac{\beta_i \cdot I\{i \in C\}}{\sum_{k \in C} \beta_k}$
10:    **end for**
11:    **for** each cluster $j_s \in [1, \texttt{num\_clusters}]$ **do**
12:        weight = $\frac{C}{\sqrt{m}} \cdot \sqrt{\sum_{j=1}^{k} \frac{\alpha_{ij_s}^2}{\beta_{j_s}}}$
13:        `distance`$[i][j_s]$ = `weight` + (reduced_features$[i]$ − cluster_centers$[j_s]$)$^2$
14:        Allocate the nearest cluster center until convergence
15:    **end for**
16: **end for**
17: `server.save_collaboration_file(args.collab_path)`

---

After receiving the model parameters and data volume information uploaded by the clients, the central server executes the FedBCE algorithm, as illustrated in Fig. 1. FedBCE first randomly selects $k$ clients from the total client pool as the initial cluster centers, where $k$ is a pre-specified number of clusters. The central server then computes the distribution difference between each client and its respective cluster center, along with the quantity-aware function for each client, to assess the impact of varying data volumes. These two factors are combined to formulate the optimization objective. Based on the computed optimization objective, all clients are clustered, with each client assigned to the nearest cluster center. Once clustering is completed, the central server recalculates the cluster centers to update them. It then compares the newly obtained cluster centers with those from the previous iteration. If they differ, the server recomputes the distances between all clients and the updated centers, refines the optimization objective, and reassigns the clients to clusters. This process repeats iteratively until the new cluster centers remain consistent with those from the previous round, indicating convergence and termination of the algorithm. Upon completion of the clustering process, each client's cooperative group is fixed, and the FL model is trained independently within each cluster. Since the clustering phase and the FL training phase are independent, the proposed algorithm can be integrated with any existing FL algorithm.

Traditional CFL algorithms typically compute pairwise similarity between clients using information such as model parameters. For a system with $N$ clients, traditional methods require computing distances for $O(N^2)$ client pairs. Consequently, as the number of clients increases, the computational cost of traditional approaches grows quadratically, making them impractical for large-scale deployments. In real-world applications, such as FL over a large number of mobile devices, this high computational complexity poses a significant challenge. In contrast, FedBCE computes only the distances between all clients and a selected set of cluster centers, reducing its computational complexity to $O(N)$. Thus, as the number of clients increases, the computational cost of the proposed algorithm scales linearly, making its advantages more pronounced in large-scale settings. Another advantage of the proposed algorithm is its flexibility in accommodating new participants. In traditional cross-silo FL algorithms, adding new clients after training completion often necessitates retraining the entire model, leading to substantial computational costs. However, the proposed algorithm allows new clients to join without requiring re-clustering or retraining all FL models. Instead, it estimates the distance between the new client and existing cluster centers, assigning it to the most suitable cluster based on the optimization objective. Consequently, only the FL model of the specific cluster that incorporates the new client needs to be adjusted or retrained, significantly reducing computational overhead.

## 5  Experiment

### 5.1  Experimental Setup

*Datasets and Models:* We evaluated our algorithm on three public datasets and six common FL methods; the datasets used are FashionMNIST [37], CIFAR-10 [38], and CIFAR-100. We conducted different non-IID scenarios [39] on the three datasets to simulate the data distribution differences in real situations, thus demonstrating the effectiveness of our algorithm for non-IID scenarios. For FashionMNSIT, we use Label shift [40]. We give each client a different label distribution; the label distribution of client 0 is most similar to the distribution of clients 1–4, distinct from that of clients 5–9, and completely different from that of clients 10–19. For CIFAR-10 [41], we use Feature shift. We rotate the data of other clients to various degrees; clients $0 - 4°$ are $+25°$, 5–9 are -25°,

10–14 are +155°, 15–19 are -155°. Concept shift [25] is for CIFAR-100, where we change the label index of each client, where all labels of client 0 are the same as clients 1–4, 14 labels are the same as clients 5–9, and no labels are aligned with clients 10–19.

In addition, we selected six common FL and Personalized Federated Learning (PFL) methods and compared their accuracy before and after combining them with FedBCE to demonstrate FedBCE's effectiveness for non-IID problems.

-For FL methods:

– FedAvg [42]: Averaging client model parameters for collaborative learning
– FedProx [43]: The proximal term is introduced through the $\mathcal{L}_2$ function to adjust the global model parameters
– FedNova [44]: Add proximal terms to alleviate data heterogeneity issues

-For PFL methods:

– Finetune: Averaging client model parameters for collaborative learning
– Per-FedAvg [45]: Introducing Meta-Learning into FL
– Ditto [46]: Using local personalized models to alleviate the contradiction between fairness and robustness

*Evaluation Metric:* To fully evaluate the effectiveness of the algorithm in this paper, in addition to the common accuracy(Acc), we also introduce reward standard deviation (RSD) [26] to evaluate the fairness of the accuracy improvement obtained by each client. This indicator is defined by the local model $h_i^{\text{local}}$ and the global model $h_i^{\text{FL}}$:

$$\text{RSD} = \text{SD} \left( \left\{ \text{Acc} \left( h_i^{\text{FL}} \right) - \text{Acc} \left( h_i^{\text{local}} \right) \right\}_{i=1}^{N} \right) \tag{6}$$

SD is the standard deviation. The smaller the RSD, the more equitable the performance improvement for each client. Therefore, in an ideal FL framework, RSD will be a smaller value.

*Implement Details:* For all three datasets, we use FedBCE to estimate the distance between clients. For CIFAR-10 and CIFAR-100, we use ImageNet pretrained ResNet-18 to process the original image into 512 dimensions before estimating the client distance. It is worth noting that the parameters of the ResNet-18 encoder are not trained and transmitted, so there is no increase in communication cost.

## 5.2   Experiments on FashionMNIST and CIFAR-10/100

The experimental results in Table 1 show that under the Label shift and Concept shift settings, the accuracy of all FL algorithms involved in the experiments is significantly lower than the results of local training. This indicates that these two non-IID situations lead to significant negative transfer in common FL methods, resulting in performance degradation. Due to the lack of robustness against

**Table 1.** Performance of FedBCE combined with different models on different datasets

| Method | FashionMNIST | | CIFAR-10 | | CIFAR-100 | |
|---|---|---|---|---|---|---|
| | Acc (%) | RSD | Acc (%) | RSD | Acc (%) | RSD |
| Local Train | 85.80 | - | 38.29 | - | 30.32 | - |
| FedAvg | 46.74 | 40.76 | 44.47 | 4.59 | 26.49 | 11.11 |
| +FedBCE | 92.47 | 6.26 | 52.86 | 4.13 | 40.41 | 2.56 |
| FedProx | 46.59 | 40.68 | 45.47 | 5.04 | 26.66 | 11.48 |
| +FedBCE | 91.47 | 6.98 | 49.01 | 2.16 | 40.72 | 3.27 |
| FedNova | 75.01 | 12.95 | 46.87 | 2.91 | 26.22 | 10.42 |
| +FedBCE | 91.67 | 6.76 | 49.24 | 2.60 | 40.91 | 3.40 |
| Finetune | 46.71 | 40.81 | 46.30 | 4.63 | 26.51 | 11.38 |
| +FedBCE | 91.70 | 6.75 | 49.33 | 2.27 | 41.17 | 3.08 |
| PerFedAvg | 46.76 | 35.52 | 44.76 | 8.23 | 10.49 | 9.99 |
| +FedBCE | 91.21 | 6.85 | 48.06 | 4.83 | 20.86 | 4.96 |
| Ditto | 46.53 | 40.66 | 45.90 | 5.35 | 26.77 | 11.62 |
| +FedBCE | 91.46 | 6.96 | 48.40 | 2.23 | 40.95 | 2.84 |

**Table 2.** Comparison with other CFLs

| Method | FashionMNIST | | CIFAR-10 | | CIFAR-100 | |
|---|---|---|---|---|---|---|
| | Acc (%) | RSD | Acc (%) | RSD | Acc (%) | RSD |
| FeSEM | 55.64 | 36.20 | 43.55 | 4.24 | 32.04 | 9.57 |
| KMeans | 69.85 | 35.16 | 46.62 | 4.68 | 33.49 | 7.29 |
| IFCA | 91.45 | 5.62 | 48.87 | 3.60 | 31.68 | 10.75 |
| FedCluster | 92.03 | 5.84 | 45.43 | 5.12 | 28.79 | 9.49 |
| FEDCOLLAB | 92.45 | 5.99 | 52.64 | 3.45 | 40.57 | 2.75 |
| FedBCE | 92.47 | 6.26 | 52.86 | 4.13 | 40.41 | 2.56 |

label shift, the accuracy of FL algorithms, except FedNova for the FashionM-NIST data set in non-IID cases, is less than 50%. After combining them with FedBCE, the accuracy of these FL algorithms has improved. There has been a significant improvement, reaching more than 90%. At the same time, the decline in the RSD indicator also shows that the benefits obtained by each client are more fair. For the CIFAR-100 data set under the Concept shift setting, FedBCE can bring more than 10% accuracy improvement to various FL algorithms. This fully demonstrates the effectiveness of FedBCE for such non-IID settings.

As for feature shift, since image rotation is not a serious non-IID, the performance of each FL algorithm did not show a significant decline compared with the other two scenarios, and most clients can achieve a certain accuracy improvement compared with local training. However, after combining with FedBCE, the accuracy of these methods has been further improved, and better fairness has been achieved in most cases.

## 5.3  Performance Comparison with Other CFL Algorithms

We selected some common CFL methods to compare performance with FedBCE:

- FeSEM [47]: A parameter-based algorithm.
- KMeans [24]: Another algorithm that uses clustering of model parameters.
- IFCA [41]: An algorithm based on loss function.
- FedCluster [29]: Model Gradient-Based Algorithms.
- FEDCOLLAB [26]: Algorithm based on client distance and data volume.

and show the results in Table 2. It can be seen that the performance of FedBCE is better than that of the common CFL algorithm, which has a lower RSD value while maintaining high accuracy. In some cases, the RSD performance is slightly worse than that of the FEDCOLLAB algorithm. Considering the experimental error and the fact that FedBCE focuses on reducing time complexity, the gap between FedBCE and FEDCOLLAB in this experiment is acceptable.

**Table 3.** Comparison of clustering time with FEDCOLLAB

| Clients number | FashionMNIST | |
| --- | --- | --- |
| | FEDCOLLAB(s) | FedBCE(s) |
| 20 | 12.79 | 0.55 |
| 40 | 47.91 | 0.07 |
| 60 | 121.28 | 0.10 |
| 80 | 236.93 | 0.59 |
| 100 | 380.83 | 0.42 |

**Table 4.** Comparison of clustering time with FEDCOLLAB

| Clients number | CIFAR-10 | |
| --- | --- | --- |
| | FEDCOLLAB(s) | FedBCE(s) |
| 8 | 1.56 | 0.15 |
| 16 | 9.23 | 0.16 |
| 24 | 26.07 | 0.11 |
| 32 | 55.64 | 0.17 |
| 40 | 110.20 | 0.19 |

**Table 5.** Comparison of clustering time with FEDCOLLAB

| Clients number | CIFAR-100 | |
|---|---|---|
| | FEDCOLLAB(s) | FedBCE(s) |
| 8 | 1.51 | 0.15 |
| 16 | 10.77 | 0.14 |
| 24 | 38.75 | 0.19 |
| 32 | 75.61 | 0.14 |
| 40 | 116.46 | 0.28 |

## 5.4  Clustering Efficiency Comparison

Since multiple clustered algorithms, such as FedCluster, finally obtain converged clustering results through the continuous cycle of client clustering and FL processes, the clustering and the FL training processes cannot be distinguished, making it difficult to perform clustering time statistics. Therefore, this article only uses a single clustered method with better performance for comparison, namely FEDCOLLAB. The experimental results are presented in Tables 3, 4, 5. Table 3 shows the performance of the two algorithms on the FashionMNIST data set. It can be seen from the experimental results that since the time complexity of FEDCOLLAB is $O(N^2)$, as the number of clients increases, the time spent in clustering also increases exponentially. Since the amount of FedBCE calculation increases slowly with the number of clients and the time of the clustered algorithm is affected by the initial selection of clients, the increase in the time spent by FedBCE is insignificant.

Tables 4 and 5 shows the experimental results of the two algorithms in the CIFAR-10 and CIFAR-100 data sets. For FEDCOLLAB, it performs similarly in both datasets, and the time spent on clustering grows exponentially with the number of clients, consistent with a computational complexity of $O(N^2)$. Since the amount of FedBCE calculation is $O(N)$, the change is not obvious, resulting in an insignificant increase in the clustering time. This experiment shows the effectiveness of FedBCE for many clients and its robustness to the number of clients makes it more suitable for actual deployment.

## 6  Conclusion

In this paper, we propose FedBCE, a Clustered Federated Learning (CFL) framework designed to address non-IID challenges in Federated Learning (FL). Compared to existing methods, FedBCE leverages both the number of clients and the similarity of their models to determine the structure of clusters. Additionally, by calculating differences between clients and a limited number of selected cluster centers, FedBCE achieves significantly lower computational complexity compared to existing approaches. Extensive experiments on public datasets demonstrate that FedBCE enhances the accuracy and fairness of various FL algorithms while significantly improving clustering efficiency compared to other CFL algorithms.

**Acknowledgments.** This study was supported by the National Natural Science Foundation of China under grant 62402111. And was supported by the NSFC-FDCT under its Joint Scientific Research Project Fund (Grant No.0051/2022/AFJ) China & Macau.

# References

1. Mahesh, B.: Machine learning algorithms-a review. Int. J. Sci. Res. (IJSR) **9**(1), 381–386 (2020)
2. Sarker, I.H.: Machine learning: algorithms, real-world applications and research directions. SN Comput. Sci. **2**(3), 160 (2021)
3. Balaji, T.K., Annavarapu, C.S.R., Bablani, A.: Machine learning algorithms for social media analysis: a survey. Comput. Sci. Rev. **40**, 100395 (2021)
4. Khan, L.U., Saad, W., Han, Z., et al.: Federated learning for internet of things: Recent advances, taxonomy, and open challenges. IEEE Commun. Surv. Tutor. **23**(3), 1759–1799 (2021)
5. Zhang, C., Xie, Y., Bai, H., et al.: A survey on federated learning. Knowl.-Based Syst. **216**, 106775 (2021)
6. Li, Q., He, B., Song, D.: Model-contrastive federated learning. In: Proceedings of the IEEE/CVF Conference on Computer Vision and Pattern Recognition, pp. 10713–10722 (2021)
7. Yang, Q., Liu, Y., Chen, T., et al.: Federated machine learning: concept and applications. ACM Trans. Intell. Syst. Technol. (TIST) **10**(2), 1–19 (2019)
8. Ye, M., Fang, X., Du, B., et al.: Heterogeneous federated learning: state-of-the-art and research challenges. ACM Comput. Surv. **56**(3), 1–44 (2023)
9. Connor, A.A., Gallinger, S.: Pancreatic cancer evolution and heterogeneity: integrating omics and clinical data. Nat. Rev. Cancer **22**(3), 131–142 (2022)
10. Li, Z., He, Y., Yu, H., et al.: Data heterogeneity-robust federated learning via group client selection in industrial IoT. IEEE Internet Things J. **9**(18), 17844–17857 (2022)
11. Yan, Y., Tong, X., Wang, S.: Clustered federated learning in heterogeneous environment. IEEE Trans. Neural Netw. Learn. Syst. (2023)
12. Shi, D., Li, L., Wu, M., et al.: To talk or to work: dynamic batch sizes assisted time efficient federated learning over future mobile edge devices. IEEE Trans. Wirel. Commun. **21**(12), 11038–11050 (2022)
13. Dinh, C.T., Tran, N.H., Nguyen, M.N.H., et al.: Federated learning over wireless networks: convergence analysis and resource allocation. IEEE/ACM Trans. Netw. **29**(1), 398–409 (2020)
14. Pfitzner, B., Steckhan, N., Arnrich, B.: Federated learning in a medical context: a systematic literature review. ACM Trans. Internet Technol. (TOIT) **21**(2), 1–31 (2021)
15. Kamal, S.T., Hosny, K.M., Elgindy, T.M., et al.: A new image encryption algorithm for grey and color medical images. IEEE Access **9**, 37855–37865 (2021)
16. Barbosa, W., Zhou, K., Waddell, E., et al.: Improving access to care: telemedicine across medical domains. Annu. Rev. Publ. Health **42**(1), 463–481 (2021)

17. Taik, A., Mlika, Z., Cherkaoui, S.: Clustered vehicular federated learning: process and optimization. IEEE Trans. Intell. Transp. Syst. **23**(12), 25371–25383 (2022)
18. Li, C., Li, G., Varshney, P.K.: Federated learning with soft clustering. IEEE Internet Things J. **9**(10), 7773–7782 (2021)
19. Fraboni, Y., Vidal, R,. Kameni, L., et al.: Clustered sampling: low-variance and improved representativity for clients selection in federated learning. In: International Conference on Machine Learning, pp. 3407–3416. PMLR (2021)
20. Duan, M., Liu, D., Ji, X., et al.: Flexible clustered federated learning for client-level data distribution shift. IEEE Trans. Parallel Distrib. Syst. **33**(11), 2661–2674 (2021)
21. Zhao, Y., Li, M., Lai, L., et al.: Federated learning with non-IID data. arXiv preprint arXiv:1806.00582 (2018)
22. Zhang, Y., Yang, Q.: A survey on multi-task learning. IEEE Trans. Knowl. Data Eng. **34**(12), 5586–5609 (2021)
23. Smith, V., Chiang, C.K., Sanjabi, M., et al.: Federated multi-task learning. In: Advances in Neural Information Processing Systems, vol. 30 (2017)
24. Ghosh, A., Hong, J., Yin, D., et al.: Robust federated learning in a heterogeneous environment. arXiv preprint arXiv:1906.06629 (2019)
25. Sattler, F., Müller, K.R., Samek, W.: Clustered federated learning: model-agnostic distributed multitask optimization under privacy constraints. IEEE Trans. Neural Netw. Learn. Syst. **32**(8), 3710–3722 (2020)
26. Bao, W., Wang, H., Wu, J., et al.: Optimizing the collaboration structure in cross-silo federated learning. In: International Conference on Machine Learning, pp. 1718–1736. PMLR (2023)
27. Xu, J., Du, W., Jin, Y., et al.: Ternary compression for communication-efficient federated learning. IEEE Trans. Neural Netw. Learn. Syst. **33**(3), 1162–1176 (2020)
28. Lu, Y., Huang, X., Zhang, K., et al.: Low-latency federated learning and blockchain for edge association in digital twin empowered 6G networks. IEEE Trans. Industr. Inf. **17**(7), 5098–5107 (2020)
29. Zhou, X., Deng, Y., Xia, H., et al.: Time-triggered federated learning over wireless networks. IEEE Trans. Wirel. Commun. **21**(12), 11066–11079 (2022)
30. Han, X., Li, R., Li, X., et al.: A divide and conquer framework for Knowledge Editing. Knowl.-Based Syst. **279**, 110826 (2023)
31. Sun, W., Ren, K., Meng, X., et al.: A band divide-and-conquer multispectral and hyperspectral image fusion method. IEEE Trans. Geosci. Remote Sens. **60**, 1–13 (2021)
32. Zhao, Z.Y., Zhou, M.C., Liu, S.X.: Iterated greedy algorithms for flow-shop scheduling problems: a tutorial. IEEE Trans. Autom. Sci. Eng. **19**(3), 1941–1959 (2021)
33. Lu, C., Liu, Q., Zhang, B., et al.: A Pareto-based hybrid iterated greedy algorithm for energy-efficient scheduling of distributed hybrid flowshop. Expert Syst. Appl. **204**, 117555 (2022)
34. Peng, P., Soljanin, E., Whiting, P.: Diversity/parallelism trade-off in distributed systems with redundancy. IEEE Trans. Inf. Theory **68**(2), 1279–1295 (2021)
35. Ben-David, S., Blitzer, J., Crammer, K., et al.: A theory of learning from different domains. Mach. Learn. **79**, 151–175 (2010)
36. Liu, J., Zhou, J., Luo, X.: Multiple source domain adaptation: a sharper bound using weighted Rademacher complexity. In: 2015 Conference on Technologies and Applications of Artificial Intelligence (TAAI), pp. 546–553. IEEE (2015)
37. Xiao, H., Rasul, K., Vollgraf, R.: Fashion-MNIST: a novel image dataset for benchmarking machine learning algorithms. arXiv preprint arXiv:1708.07747 (2017)

38. Krizhevsky, A., Hinton, G.: Learning multiple layers of features from tiny images (2009)
39. Kairouz, P., McMahan, H.B., Avent, B., et al.: Advances and open problems in federated learning. Found. Trends® Mach. Learn. **14**(1–2), 1–210 (2021)
40. Ma, J., Long, G., Zhou, T., et al.: On the convergence of clustered federated learning. arXiv preprint arXiv:2202.06187 (2022)
41. Ghosh, A., Chung, J., Yin, D., et al.: An efficient framework for clustered federated learning. In: Advances in Neural Information Processing Systems, vol. 33, pp. 19586–19597 (2020)
42. McMahan, B., Moore, E., Ramage, D., et al.: Communication-efficient learning of deep networks from decentralized data. In: Artif. Intell. Stat. 1273–1282. PMLR (2017)
43. Li, T., Sahu, A.K., Zaheer, M., et al.: Federated optimization in heterogeneous networks. Proc. Mach. Learn. Syst. **2**, 429–450 (2020)
44. Wang, J., Liu, Q., Liang, H., et al.: Tackling the objective inconsistency problem in heterogeneous federated optimization. In: Advances in Neural Information Processing Systems, vol. 33, pp. 7611–7623 (2020)
45. Fallah, A., Mokhtari, A., Ozdaglar, A.: Personalized federated learning with theoretical guarantees: a model-agnostic meta-learning approach. In: Advances in Neural Information Processing Systems, vol. 33, pp. 3557–3568 (2020)
46. Li, T., Hu, S., Beirami, A., et al.: Ditto: fair and robust federated learning through personalization. In: International Conference on Machine Learning, pp. 6357–6368. PMLR (2021)
47. Long, G., Xie, M., Shen, T., et al.: Multi-center federated learning: clients clustering for better personalization. World Wide Web **26**(1), 481–500 (2023)
48. Wang, H., Yurochkin, M., Sun, Y., et al.: Federated learning with matched averaging. arXiv preprint arXiv:2002.06440 (2020)

# SAML: A Structure-Aware Enhanced Meta Learning Framework for Spatio-Temproal Graph Few-Shot Learning


Haichen Lyu and Chun Wang(✉)

City University of Macau, 999078 Macau, China
`chunwang@cityu.edu.mo`



**Abstract.** Spatio-temporal graph learning, a core methodology for addressing urban computing tasks, is often constrained by data scarcity due to factors such as urban development levels or competition. To address this challenge, data from data-rich cities must be leveraged effectively, and knowledge transfer methods should be employed to enhance model performance in data-scarce cities. However, significant differences in spatial features across cities limit the effectiveness of cross-city knowledge transfer. This study proposes the **Structure-Aware Enhanced Meta Learning (SAML)** framework, a spatio-temporal graph few-shot learning approach. SAML improves model performance in data-scarce target cities through cross-city knowledge transfer. Innovatively, SAML introduces a graph structure-aware enhancement module during meta-learning, addressing spatio-temporal graph structure bias during knowledge transfer by defining a graph contrastive loss. Systematic experiments on three traffic speed prediction datasets demonstrate that SAML outperforms existing state-of-the-art (SOTA) methods.

**Keywords:** Spatio-Temporal Graph · Few-Shot Learning · Graph Neural Network


## 1 Introduction

The advancement of information collection and processing technologies has enabled the utilization of vast spatio-temporal data generated daily by urban transportation systems to train deep learning models, thereby supporting the development of smart cities. Such data-driven approaches have been widely applied in traffic flow forecasting [1], pedestrian flow prediction [2], and taxi demand prediction [3]. However, disparities in urban development often result in data scarcity for certain cities, hindering the ability of deep learning models to learn effective representations and degrading their performance. Given the structural and functional similarities among cities, cross-city knowledge transfer provides a promising solution to address data scarcity challenges.



T. Zhu et al. (Eds.): KSEM 2025, LNAI 15919, pp. 87–101, 2026.
https://doi.org/10.1007/978-981-95-3001-4_7

Recent studies have focused on addressing spatio-temporal data scarcity. For instance, Wei et al. [4] proposed the FLORAL method, which constructs semantically related multi-modal dictionaries from the source domain and transfers both dictionaries and tagged instances to the target domain. Wang et al. [5] introduced the RegionTrans method, employing an inter-city region matching function to align target city regions with analogous source city regions. Yao et al. [6] developed the MetaST, leveraging generalized initialization and spatio-temporal memory modules to extract long-term temporal patterns for efficient adaptation to target cities. Nevertheless, these methods overlook spatial feature variations across cities.

This paper addresses spatio-temporal graph-based prediction in a few-shot learning scenario through cross-city knowledge transfer while investigating the impact of inter-city spatial structure deviation on transfer efficacy. Two critical challenges persist: (1) Improving model performance in target cities with limited data: Existing methods struggle to effectively capture spatio-temporal feature variability across cities, which compromises knowledge transfer outcomes. (2) Mitigating graph structure divergence: Existing methods often exhibit structural learning biases during knowledge transfer due to mismatched spatio-temporal graph structure.

To address these challenges, we propose a framework **Structure-A**ware Enhanced **Meta Learning** (SAML). First, to mitigate challenge (1), we encode the spatio-temporal features of the source cities into a meta knowledge representation via a meta-learner, which generates the initial parameters of the downstream spatio-temporal network by aligning with the target city's meta knowledge. For challenge (2), we introduce a graph structure-aware enhancement module that enhances spatial feature perception through data augmentation and negative filtering, thereby reducing structural bias during knowledge transfer. Our principal contributions are as follows:

- The proposed SAML framework maps spatio-temporal features from source cities into meta knowledge, generates parameters for downstream neural networks, and adapts to enable knowledge transfer in data-scarce target cities.
- A graph structure-aware enhancement module is introduced to augment data and filter negative samples from spatio-temporal features. By incorporating graph structure-aware loss and prediction loss, the model's capacity to discern structural feature in spatio-temporal graphs during knowledge transfer is strengthened, thereby reducing the adverse effects of inter-city structural discrepancies.
- We evaluate our method on three publicly available urban traffic speed prediction datasets: METR-LA, PEMS-BAY, and Seattle-Loop. Comprehensive experiments demonstrate our method's superior performance and generalizability compared to established benchmarks.

The remainder of this paper is organized as follows. Section 2 reviews related work, followed by a formal problem definition in Sect. 3. Section 4 presents the proposed SAML framework. Section 5 details the experimental evaluation and results. Finally, Sect. 6 concludes the study.

# 2   Related Work

## 2.1   Spatio-Temporal Graph Predicting

Spatio-temporal graph prediction is a widely studied domain in smart city research. Early approaches utilized time series analysis and machine learning techniques, such as ARIMA [7], Kalman filters [8], and support vector machines (SVMs) [9]. With advancements in deep learning and graph neural networks, spatio-temporal graphs which inherently encode spatial and temporal features have gained prominence for modeling smart city applications. For instance, Huang et al. proposed the LSGCN [10], which captures complex spatio-temporal traffic patterns via spatial gated modules and gated linear unit convolutions (GLUs). Zheng et al. introduced the GMAN [11], employing an encoder-decoder architecture with transformative attention layers to address error propagation across prediction time steps. Shao et al. developed the STEP model [12], leveraging pre-training to identify long-term temporal patterns in historical data. However, these methods assume data-abundant scenarios and underperform in data-scarce contexts.

## 2.2   Graph Few-Shot Learning Across Cities

In recent years, few-shot learning has demonstrated significant success in data-scarce scenarios across domains such as word similarity [13], image generation [14], and continuous control [15]. In spatio-temporal graph prediction, several methods have been developed to address data scarcity through cross-city knowledge transfer. For example, Pan et al. proposed ST-MetaNet [16], which employs meta graph attention networks and meta recurrent neural networks to capture spatial and temporal correlations, respectively. Lu et al. introduced the ST-GFSL framework [17], generating meta knowledge from source cities via meta learning and matching target cities to derive spatio-temporal network parameters. Jin et al. designed TransGTR [18], which learns city node features through knowledge distillation and leverages these features to align spatial distributions across cities. However, these works primarily introduce cross-city transfer methods without resolving graph structure bias inherent to cross-city transfer processes.

# 3   Preliminary

## 3.1   Spatio-Temporal Graph

A spatio-temporal graph is formally defined as $\mathcal{G}_{ST} = (\mathcal{V}, \mathcal{E}, A, X)$, where $\mathcal{V} = \{v_1, v_2, \ldots, v_N\}$ represents the collection of nodes. Here, $N = |\mathcal{V}|$ denotes the total number of nodes. $\mathcal{E} = \{e_{ij} = (v_i, v_j)\}$ denoted the set of edge. The adjacency matrix $A \in \mathbb{R}^{N \times N}$ is defined such that $a_{ij} = 1$ if there exists an edge between nodes $v_i$ and $v_j$, and $a_{ij} = 0$ otherwise. $T_{\text{total}}$ is defined as the total number of time steps in the dataset. The node feature matrix $X \in \mathbb{R}^{N \times T_{\text{total}} \times d}$ represents the information of the spatio-temporal graph, such as traffic flow, speed, and occupancy within a specified time period. Here, $d$ denotes the dimension of the node features, while $X^t \in \mathbb{R}^{N \times d}$ represents the node features observed at time $t$. For instance, in a spatio-temporal graph constituted by a traffic flow prediction dataset, $X_i^t$ corresponds to the traffic flow data recorded by the $i$-th sensor at the $t$-th temporal step.

### 3.2   Spatio-Temporal Graph Predicting

The objective of spatio-temporal graph prediction is to learn a function $f(\cdot)$ that, given a spatio-temporal graph $\mathcal{G}_{ST}$, predicts the next $M$ graph signals based on $T$ historical spatio-temporal graph signals:

$$\left[ X^{t-T+1}, \cdots, X^t; \mathcal{G}_{ST} \right] \xrightarrow{f(\cdot)} \left[ X^{t+1}, \cdots, X^{t+M} \right]. \tag{1}$$

### 3.3   Cross-City Spatio-Temporal Graph Few-Shot Learning

If we have a set of $P$ source spatio-temporal datasets $\mathcal{G}_{1:P}^{\text{source}} = \{\mathcal{G}_1^{\text{source}}, \mathcal{G}_2^{\text{source}}, \ldots, \mathcal{G}_P^{\text{source}}\}$ with abundant data and a target spatio-temporal dataset $\mathcal{G}^{\text{target}}$ with limited data. Cross-city spatio-temporal graph few-shot learning aims to train a model on both $\mathcal{G}^{\text{source}}$ and $\mathcal{G}^{\text{target}}$ datasets to accurately predict future outcomes for $\mathcal{G}^{\text{target}}$.

## 4   Methodology

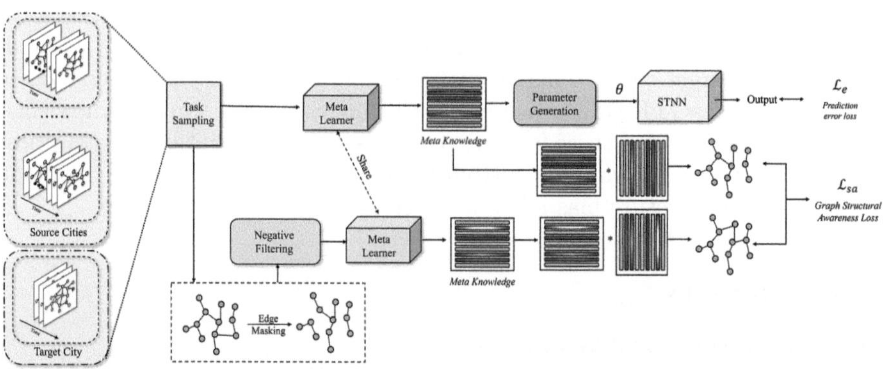


**Fig. 1.** The framework of proposed SAML. On the left side, the source cities has rich data while the target city is few-shot. The right side shows the learning process of SAML

This section details the SAML framework for spatio-temporal graph few-shot learning. As illustrated in Fig. 1, the framework first performs meta training using data-rich source cities, enhancing spatial feature perception through graph structure-aware enhancement module. Subsequently, adaptation is conducted on data-scarce target cities via cross-city knowledge transfer to predict future target city data. These processes comprise the following key components:

## 4.1 Meta Learner

The meta learner extracts node-level knowledge from spatio-temporal graph data and maps it into meta knowledge that encapsulates spatio-temporal features. To capture temporal and spatial features, we employ a gated recurrent unit (GRU) [19] and a graph attention network (GAT) [20], respectively. Compared to traditional RNNs, GRUs mitigate gradient vanishing and explosion issues while offering faster training speeds than long short-term memory (LSTM) networks [21]. For a node $X_i^t$, the GRU is defined as follows:

$$
\begin{aligned}
z &= \sigma \left( U_z X_i^t + W_z h_i^{t-1} \right) \\
r &= \sigma \left( U_r X_i^t + W_r h_i^{t-1} \right) \\
c &= \tanh \left( U_c X_i^t + W_c \left( h_i^{t-1} \circ r \right) \right) \\
h_i^t &= (1 - z) \circ c + z \circ h_i^{t-1}
\end{aligned}
\tag{2}
$$

where, $X_i^t \in \mathbb{R}^d$ represents the signal of node $v_i$ in the spatio-temporal graph at time $t$, and $h_i^t - 1$ denotes the hidden state at time step $t-1$. The weight matrices $W_z, W_r, W_c \in \mathbb{R}^{d' \times d'}$ and $U_z, U_r, U_c \in \mathbb{R}^{d \times d'}$ are used in the model, where $\circ$ denotes element-wise multiplication, and $\sigma$ is the Sigmoid activation function. When $t = 0$, $h_i^0$ is initialized as an all-zero vector. Consequently, the temporal meta-knowledge $Z^{TP} = \left( z_1^{TP}, z_2^{TP}, \cdots, z_N^{TP} \right) \in \mathbb{R}^{N \times d'}$ is derived, where $Z_i^{TP}$ corresponds to the final state of the GRU's hidden state $h_i^t$.

The graph attention network (GAT) is versatile for various graph data types and particularly effective for learning spatial meta knowledge in spatio-temporal graphs across cities. Unlike spectral-domain graph neural networks, GAT captures complex node associations more accurately. The attention coefficient $e_{ij}$ is computed by applying a shared linear transformation to each pair of connected nodes in the spatio-temporal graph:

$$
e_{ij} = \text{LeakyReLU} \left( a^T [W h_i \| W h_j] \right), j \in \mathcal{N}_i.
\tag{3}
$$

Here, $a$ is a learnable attention vector, $(\cdot)^T$ represents the transpose, and $\|$ represents the concatenation of $W h_i$ and $W h_j$ into a new vector. The weight matrix $W \in \mathbb{R}^{d \times O}$ is utilized in the mechanism, and $\mathcal{N}_i$ represents the set of neighboring nodes of node $v_i$. The attention scores are normalized across all choices of $j$ using the Softmax function:

$$
\alpha_{ij} = \text{softmax}_j \left( e_{ij} \right) = \frac{\exp \left( e_{ij} \right)}{\sum_{k \in \mathcal{N}_i} \exp \left( e_{ik} \right)}.
\tag{4}
$$

Finally, the attention mechanism is independently executed $K$ times, and the averaging method is applied to derive the final spatial meta knowledge for node $v_i$:

$$z_i^{SP} = \sigma \left( \frac{1}{K} \sum_{k=1}^{K} \sum_{j \in \mathcal{N}_i} \alpha_{ij} W^k h_j \right). \tag{5}$$

Here, $Z^{SP} = \left( z_1^{SP}, z_2^{SP}, \ldots, z_N^{SP} \right) \in \mathbb{R}^{N \times d'}$ is the spatial meta knowledge.

To combine the temporal and spatial meta knowledge into a weighted sum, we define the final meta knowledge as $Z^{ST} = \left( z_1^{ST}, z_2^{ST}, \cdots, z_N^{ST} \right) \in \mathbb{R}^{N \times d_{ST}}$. Specifically, $Z^{ST}$ is computed as follows:

$$Z^{ST} = W^{\gamma} \left( \gamma \circ Z^{TP} + (1 - \gamma) \circ \mathbf{Z}^{SP} \right), \tag{6}$$

Here, $\gamma \in \mathbb{R}^{d'}$ is a learnable parameter that adaptively captures the influence of spatial or temporal domains in a data-driven manner. Compared to simple concatenation, this approach enables better adaptation to spatio-temporal characteristics of cross-city data through the learnable ratio. The weight matrix $W^{\gamma} \in \mathbb{R}^{d' \times d_{ST}}$ is used in the meta knowledge output layer, where $d_{ST}$ represents the dimension of the meta knowledge.

## 4.2  Parameter Generation

The parameter generation method facilitates cross-city knowledge transfer by retrieving spatio-temporal features with high similarity. Specifically, it applies a linear transformation to the meta knowledge derived from the source cities to generate the initial parameters $W_l$ and $b$ for the downstream spatio-temporal model's linear layer, as well as the initial parameters $W_{conv}$ for the convolutional layer. When the meta knowledge of the target city aligns with that of the source city, the linear and convolutional layers of the downstream model are initialized with the matched parameters. As an example for the convolutional layer, the convolutional weight matrix $W_{conv}$ is computed as $W_{conv} = F_{W_{conv}}(X)$, where $W_{conv} \in \mathbb{R}^{d_{in} \times d_{out} \times KH \times KW}$. Here, $d_{in}$ denotes the number of input channels, $d_{o}ut$ represents the number of output channels, and $(KH, KW)$ specifies the size of the convolution kernel.

## 4.3  Graph Structure-Aware Enhancement Module

In order to eliminate the bias caused by different graph structures during cross-city knowledge transfer, we enhance the model's perception of spatio-temporal graph structures by the Graph Structure-Aware Enhancement module. We augment the sampled spatio-temporal graphs with structural interference, and then compute the differences in the spatial feature representations of the spatio-temporal graphs learned by the meta learner from the original data and the augmented data. Specifically, we mask the adjacency matrix $A$ representing the structure of the spatio-temporal graph by a certain proportion to get $A^{aug}$:

$$A_{ij}^{aug} = \begin{cases} A_{ij}, & \text{if } M_{ij}^{em} \geqslant r_{em} \\ 0, & \text{otherwise} \end{cases} \tag{7}$$

where $M_{ij}^{em} \sim U(r_{ts}, 1)$ is random matrix and $r_{em}$ is adjustable.

Since temporally adjacent spatio-temporal graph sequences exhibit similar spatio-temporal representations, they are unsuitable for use as negative samples. To address this, we introduce a threshold parameter, $\epsilon$, and designate samples within the batch that are at least $\epsilon$ time steps away from the anchor point's start time as valid negative samples.

To extract the spatial representation learned by the meta-learner, we reconstruct the meta-knowledge from the original and augmented data, into adjacency matrix structures, $A'$ and $A''$. Specifically, we compute the product of the meta knowledge with its transpose to predict the likelihood of edge existence between nodes.

To guide graph structure-aware, we introduce the loss function $\mathcal{L}_{sa}$:

$$\mathcal{L}_{sa} = \frac{1}{B} \sum_{i=1}^{B} - \log \frac{\exp\left(\text{sim}\left(A_i', A_i''\right) / \tau\right)}{\sum_{j \in \chi_i} \exp\left(\text{sim}\left(A_i', A_j''\right) / \tau\right)} \tag{8}$$

where $B$ is the number of data samples in a batch, $\tau$ denotes the temperature parameter, and $\chi_i$ denotes the set of valid negative samples for the $i$-th object after filtering. Furthermore, $\text{sim}(\cdot, \cdot)$ corresponds to the cosine similarity function.

### 4.4   Learning Progress

To adapt the model to small-sample scenarios, SAML's learning process follows the episodic learning mechanism of model-agnostic meta-learning (MAML) [22]. The process is divided into two stages: meta-training and adaptation. During meta training, SAML simulates spatio-temporal graphs with few-sample scenarios to train the model. In the adaptation stages, SAML performs gradient descent with parameter updates using a small dataset from the target city.

Specifically, a batch of spatio-temporal graph sequences is sampled from the source city dataset to form the task set $\mathcal{T} = (\mathcal{T}_1, \mathcal{T}_2, ..., \mathcal{T}_n)$, where each task $\mathcal{T}_i$ corresponds to a city. Each $\mathcal{T}_i$ is divided into a support set $\mathcal{S}_{\mathcal{T}_i}$ and a query set $\mathcal{Q}_{\mathcal{T}_i}$, with $\mathcal{S}_{\mathcal{T}_i} \cap \mathcal{Q}_{\mathcal{T}_i} = \emptyset$. Data augmentation is applied to generate the augmented support set $\mathcal{S}_{\mathcal{T}_i}'$ and augmented query set $\mathcal{Q}_{\mathcal{T}_i}'$. A fusion structure is used to compute the structure-aware loss $\mathcal{L}_{sa}$, along with the prediction error loss $\mathcal{L}_e$, during training on data from the $i$-th city. The prediction loss is defined as the root-mean-square error between the multi-step prediction $\widehat{y}$ from the downstream spatio-temporal network $f_\theta(\cdot)$ and the true value $y$:

$$\mathcal{L}_e = \frac{1}{\|\mathcal{S}_{\mathcal{T}_i}\|} \sum_{y_j \in \mathcal{S}_{\mathcal{T}_i}} \left(\widehat{y} - y_j\right)^2. \tag{9}$$

---

**Algorithm 1.** SAML base-model meta training

---

**Input:** Source spatio-temporal Graph Dataset $\mathcal{G}$ , learning rate hyperparameter $\alpha$, $\beta$;
**Output:** Trained SAML model parameters $\theta^*$
1: Initialize parameters $\theta$
2: **while** not done **do**
3:     Sample a batch of tasks $\mathcal{T} \leftarrow$ SampleTask($\mathcal{G}$) ;
4:     **for** $\mathcal{T}_i \in \mathcal{T}$ **do**
5:         $\mathcal{S}_{\mathcal{T}_i}, \mathcal{Q}_{\mathcal{T}_i} \leftarrow \mathcal{T}_i$ ;
6:         $\mathcal{S}'_{\mathcal{T}_i} = \mathrm{aug}(\mathcal{S}_{\mathcal{T}_i})$ ;
7:         $\mathcal{Q}'_{\mathcal{T}_i} = \mathrm{aug}(\mathcal{Q}_{\mathcal{T}_i})$ ;
8:         EVALUATE $\nabla_\theta \mathcal{L}_{\mathcal{T}_i}(f_\theta)$ with $\mathcal{S}_{\mathcal{T}_i}$ and $\mathcal{S}'_{\mathcal{T}_i}$ via Eq.10 ;
9:         Compute adapted parameters with gradient descent:
10:         $\theta'_{\mathcal{T}_i} = \theta - \alpha \nabla_\theta \mathcal{L}_{\mathcal{T}_i}(f_\theta)$ ;
11:         EVALUATE $\nabla_\theta \mathcal{L}_{\mathcal{T}_i}(f_\theta)$ with $\mathcal{Q}_{\mathcal{T}_i}$ and $\mathcal{Q}'_{\mathcal{T}_i}$ via Eq.10 ;
12:     **end for**
13:     UPDATE $\theta^* \leftarrow \theta - \beta \nabla_\theta \Sigma_{\mathcal{T}_i} \mathcal{L}_{\mathcal{T}_i}\left(f_{\theta'_i}\right)$
14: **end while**

---

The structure-aware enhancement loss $\mathcal{L}_{sa}$ are defined in Eq. 8. The joint loss function $\mathcal{L}$ is expressed as:

$$\mathcal{L} = \mathcal{L}_e + \lambda \mathcal{L}_{cl}, \tag{10}$$

where $\lambda$ are the scaling factors of the loss function. The meta learning objective is to minimize the sum of task losses on the query sets, which is expressed as:

$$\theta^* = \arg\min_\theta \sum_{\mathcal{T}_i \in \mathcal{T}} \mathcal{L}_{\mathcal{T}_i}\left(f_{\theta'_i}\right). \tag{11}$$

Algorithm 1 outlines the meta training process for SAML to obtain the optimal model parameters $\theta^\star$. First, the task sets $\mathcal{T}$ is constructed by sampling spatio-temporal graph data from the source cities (line 3), followed by data augmentation (lines 67). The task-specific parameters $\theta'_{\mathcal{T}_i}$ are updated through multi-step gradient descent (line 8), and the gradient values are computed using the query set $\mathcal{Q}_{\mathcal{T}_i}$ (line 11). Finally, the general model parameters $\theta$ are optimized by aggregating the loss functions across all meta training tasks (line 13).

## 5 Experiment

In this section, we evaluate SAML through extensive experiments to address the following research questions:

- How does SAML's performance compare to benchmark methods across different datasets?

- What is the contribution of each component to SAML's overall performance?
- How do hyperparameters influence SAMeta's performance?

## 5.1   Experiment Setup and Datasets

In our experiments, we evaluated SAML's performance on the METR-LA, PeMS-BAY, and Seattle Loop datasets [23,24], all of which have a time step of 5 min. These datasets were divided into source datasets and target dataset. To simulate data scarcity, only 3 d data from the target dataset were used as training data during the adaptation stage. Using METR-LA as an example, when it is selected as the target dataset, PeMS-BAY and Seattle Loop serve as the source datasets. In this case, 3 consecutive days of data from METR-LA are sampled as adaptation data, while the remaining data are used as test data. The same division is applied when other datasets are selected as target domains. To evaluate SAML's performance, 12 historical time steps are used to predict 6 future time steps. The evaluation metrics include mean absolute error (MAE) and root mean square error (RMSE), and the data were preprocessed using the Z-score normalization method.

## 5.2   Baselines

We compare the spatio-temporal prediction model of SAML with non-transfer methods and the latest cross-city traffic prediction methods. For the non-transfer methods, only use a small amount of data from the target city for model training, and the selected non-transfer comparison methods are as follows:

- HA: History Average, which uses the average of previous periods as the prediction.
- STGCN [25]: A spatio-temporal graph convolution model which integrates ChebNet and gated temporal convolution.
- GWN [26]: A spatio-temporal network that utilizes the adaptive adjacency matrix and dilated causal convolution to capture the spatial temporal dependency.
- MAML: Model-Agnostic Meta Learning (MAML), a superior meta-learning method that trains a model's parameters such that a small number of gradient updates will lead to fast learning on a new task.
- ST-GFSL: A state-of-art few-shot traffic forecasting framework that learns the meta knowledge of traffic nodes to generate the parameter of linear and convolution layers.

## 5.3   Experiment Results

**Compare with Baselines.** Tables 1, 2, and 3 present the performance comparisons of various baseline methods, with the best results highlighted in bold.

The results demonstrate that SAML outperforms baseline models across multiple spatio-temporal datasets, including both transfer and non-transfer methods, for both short-term and long-term predictions. Among the three meta-learning methods, SAML achieves superior performance, indicating that the proposed graph structure-aware enhancement module effectively improves spatial feature learning.

**Table 1.** METR-LA

| Method | MAE | | | RMSE | | |
|---|---|---|---|---|---|---|
| | 5 min | 15 min | 30 min | 5 min | 15 min | 30 min |
| HA | 4.491 | 4.491 | 4.491 | 8.133 | 8.133 | 8.133 |
| STGCN | 3.731 | 4.101 | 4.585 | 5.935 | 7.083 | 7.708 |
| GWN | 2.719 | 3.535 | 4.472 | 5.154 | 7.437 | 9.612 |
| MAML | 2.506 | 3.160 | 3.858 | 4.174 | 5.616 | **6.921** |
| ST-GFSL | 2.375 | 2.923 | 3.609 | 4.125 | 5.639 | 6.954 |
| OURS | **2.243** | **2.847** | **3.494** | **4.080** | **5.605** | 6.931 |

**Table 2.** PEMS-BAY

| Method | MAE | | | RMSE | | |
|---|---|---|---|---|---|---|
| | 5 min | 15 min | 30 min | 5 min | 15 min | 30 min |
| HA | 4.491 | 4.491 | 4.491 | 8.133 | 8.133 | 8.133 |
| STGCN | 2.993 | 3.243 | 3.600 | 5.323 | 5.629 | 6.155 |
| GWN | 1.304 | 1.655 | 2.234 | 2.220 | 3.335 | 4.886 |
| MAML | 1.176 | 1.735 | 2.292 | 2.068 | 3.411 | 4.753 |
| ST-GFSL | 1.124 | 1.629 | 2.141 | 1.957 | 3.227 | 4.563 |
| OURS | **1.055** | **1.571** | **2.096** | **1.931** | **3.207** | **4.553** |

**Table 3.** SEATTLE-LOOP

| Method | MAE | | | RMSE | | |
|---|---|---|---|---|---|---|
| | 5 min | 15 min | 30 min | 5 min | 15 min | 30 min |
| HA | 4.491 | 4.491 | 4.491 | 8.133 | 8.133 | 8.133 |
| STGCN | 3.599 | 3.982 | 4.480 | 5.440 | 6.224 | 7.248 |
| GWN | 2.954 | 3.426 | 4.012 | 4.657 | 5.904 | 7.095 |
| MAML | 2.878 | 3.488 | 4.152 | 4.286 | 5.654 | 7.043 |
| ST-GFSL | 2.883 | 3.417 | 3.989 | 4.352 | 5.646 | 7.001 |
| OURS | **2.749** | **3.347** | **3.955** | **4.199** | **5.617** | **6.991** |

**SAML for Different STNNs.** SAML is a model-agnostic framework. To validate its generality and demonstrate its ability to enhance the performance of downstream spatio-temporal neural networks (STNNs), we trained common STNN models on limited target domain data and compared their performance with and without the SAML framework. Figure 2 illustrates the performance of various STNNs on the METR-LA dataset, showing that all models achieve improved performance when trained under SAML compared to target-only training.

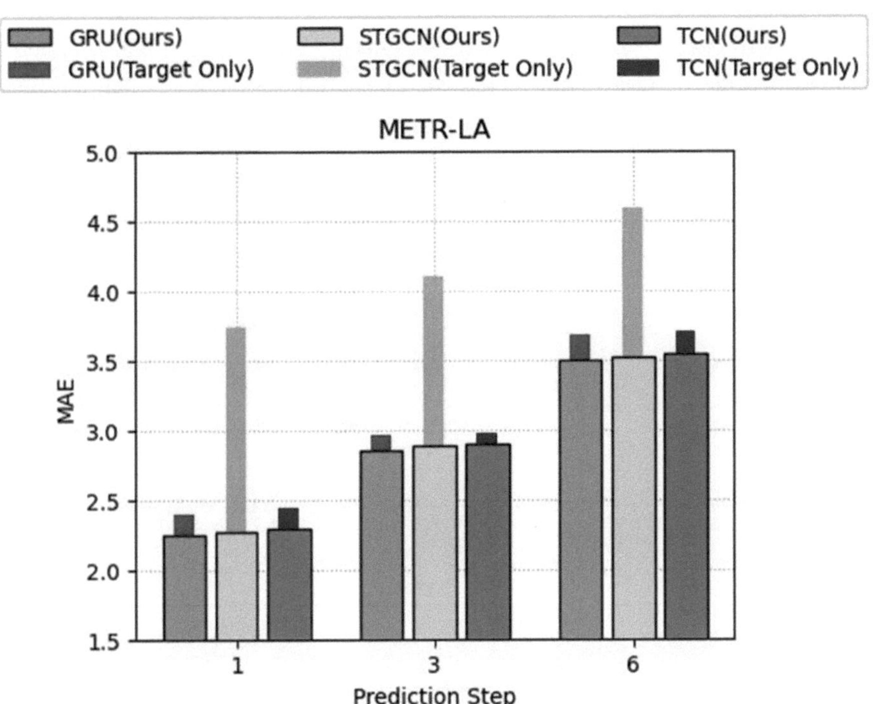


**Fig. 2.** Performance comparison of different STNNs between being trained in SAML and only trained in few-shot

**Ablation Study.** In this section, we validate the effectiveness of each SAML module through ablation experiments on the METR-LA dataset. Table 4 presents the corresponding performance comparisons. First, removing the meta-learner is equivalent to training spatio-temporal neural networks (STNNs) directly in a few-shot scenario. The significant performance decline demonstrates that the meta-learner effectively captures spatio-temporal features, and the generated meta-knowledge enhances the predictive capabilities of downstream STNNs. Second, eliminating the parameter generation method, which is equivalent to random parameter initialization for STNNs within the SAML framework, results in inferior performance compared to SAML, particularly for short-term and medium-term predictions. Finally, removing the graph structure-aware enhancement module degrades model performance, indicating that enhancing spatial feature perception in spatio-temporal graphs ensures the model's generalization ability during cross-city knowledge transfer.

**Table 4.** Ablation Studies of SAML on METR-LA dataset.

| Ablation Method | MAE | | | RMSE | | |
|---|---|---|---|---|---|---|
| | 5 min | 15 min | 30 min | 5 min | 15 min | 30 min |
| w/o Meta Learner | 2.418 | 2.968 | 3.619 | 4.502 | 5.975 | 7.463 |
| w/o Parameter Generation | 2.292 | 2.895 | 3.508 | 4.089 | 5.740 | 7.277 |
| w/o Graph Structure-Aware module | 2.279 | 2.880 | 3.529 | 4.121 | 5.685 | 7.133 |
| OURS | **2.243** | **2.847** | **3.494** | **4.080** | **5.605** | **6.931** |

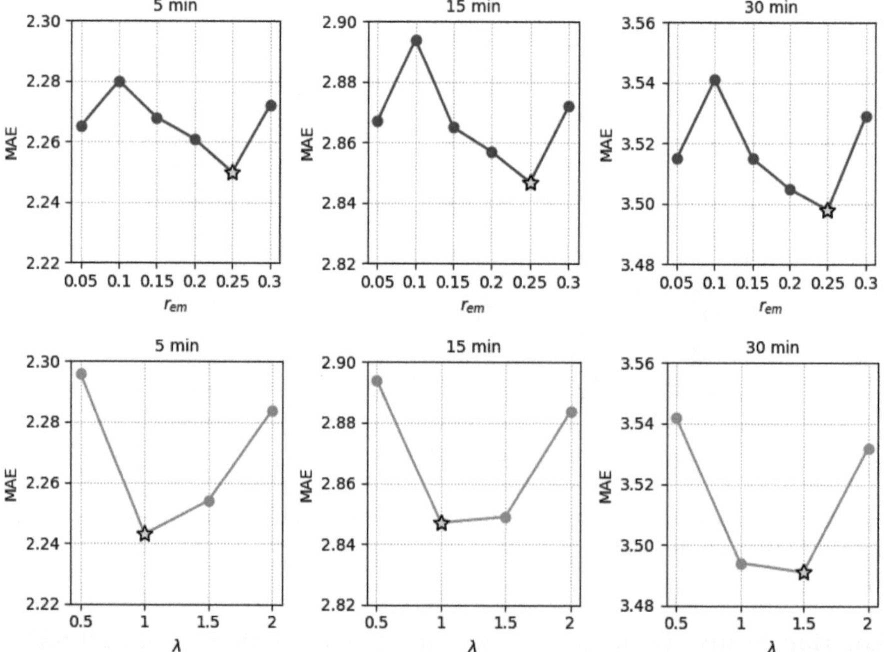

**Fig. 3.** Hyperparameter study on METR-LA dataset: and loss scale factor $\lambda$.

**Hyperparameters Analysis.** We analyze the selected hyperparameters through experimental results. Using METR-LA as the target dataset, Fig. 3 illustrates the following findings:

– By adjusting the adjacency matrix masking ratio $r_{em}$, the model achieves optimal performance for both short-term and long-term predictions when $r_{em} = 0.25$.
– The proportionality between loss functions is a critical factor. By analyzing the changes in loss function proportions, we observe that better experimental results are typically achieved when $\lambda$ is set to 1 or 1.5. Specifically, $\lambda = 1$ favors short-term and medium-term predictions, further confirming the importance of the graph structure-aware enhancement module.

## 6    Conclusion

In this paper, we propose SAML, a cross-city knowledge transfer framework based on spatio-temporal graph few-shot learning. We identify that existing spatio-temporal graph few-shot learning models exhibit graph structure perception bias. To address this issue, we introduce a graph structure-aware enhancement module to improve the spatial feature representation capabilities of downstream spatio-temporal networks. Cross-city knowledge transfer is achieved through parameter generation. Extensive experimental results demonstrate that SAML outperforms existing benchmark methods.

## References


1. Lv, Y., Duan, Y., Kang, W., Li, Z., Wang, F.-Y.: Traffic flow prediction with big data: a deep learning approach. IEEE Trans. Intell. Transp. Syst. **16**(2), 865–873 (2015). https://doi.org/10.1109/TITS.2014.2345663
2. Zhang, J., Zheng, Y., Qi, D.: Deep spatio-temporal residual networks for citywide crowd flows prediction. In: Proceedings of the Thirty-First AAAI Conference on Artificial Intelligence (AAAI 2017), pp. 1655–1661. AAAI Press, San Francisco, California, USA (2017)
3. Geng, X., Li, Y., Wang, L., Zhang, L., Yang, Q., Ye, J., Liu, Y.: Spatiotemporal multi-graph convolution network for ride-hailing demand forecasting. In: Proceedings of the Thirty-Third AAAI Conference on Artificial Intelligence (AAAI 2019), pp. 1–8. AAAI Press, Honolulu, Hawaii, USA (2019). https://doi.org/10.1609/aaai.v33i01.33013656
4. Wei, Y., Zheng, Y., Yang, Q.: Transfer knowledge between cities. In: Proceedings of the 22nd ACM SIGKDD International Conference on Knowledge Discovery and Data Mining (KDD 2016), pp. 1905–1914. Association for Computing Machinery, New York (2016). https://doi.org/10.1145/2939672.2939830
5. Wang, L., Geng, X., Ma, X., Liu, F., Yang, Q.: Cross-city transfer learning for deep spatio-temporal prediction. In: Proceedings of the 28th International Joint Conference on Artificial Intelligence (IJCAI 2019), pp. 1893–1899. AAAI Press, Macao, China (2019)
6. Yao, H., Liu, Y., Wei, Y., Tang, X., Li, Z.: Learning from multiple cities: a meta-learning approach for spatial-temporal prediction. In: The World Wide Web Conference (WWW 2019), pp. 2181–2191. Association for Computing Machinery, New York (2019). https://doi.org/10.1145/3308558.3313577

7. Lippi, M., Bertini, M., Frasconi, P.: Short-term traffic flow forecasting: an experimental comparison of time-series analysis and supervised learning. IEEE Trans. Intell. Transp. Syst. **14**(2), 871–882 (2013). https://doi.org/10.1109/TITS.2013.2247040

8. Moreira-Matias, L., Gama, J., Ferreira, M., Mendes-Moreira, J., Damas, L.: Predicting taxi-passenger demand using streaming data. IEEE Trans. Intell. Transp. Syst. **14**(3), 1393–1402 (2013). https://doi.org/10.1109/TITS.2013.2262376

9. Nikravesh, A.Y., Ajila, S.A., Lung, C.-H., Ding, W.: Mobile network traffic prediction using MLP, MLPWD, and SVM. In: 2016 IEEE International Congress on Big Data (BigData Congress), pp. 402–409. IEEE (2016). https://doi.org/10.1109/BigDataCongress.2016.63

10. Huang, R., Huang, C., Liu, Y., Dai, G., Kong, W.: LSGCN: long short-term traffic prediction with graph convolutional networks. In: Proceedings of the 29th International Joint Conference on Artificial Intelligence (IJCAI), pp. 326–332. AAAI Press (2021)

11. Zheng, C., Fan, X., Wang, C., Qi, J.: GMAN: a graph multi-attention network for traffic prediction. In: Proceedings of the 34th AAAI Conference on Artificial Intelligence (AAAI), pp. 1234–1241. AAAI Press (2020)

12. Shao, Z., Zhang, Z., Wang, F., Xu, Y.: Pre-training enhanced spatial-temporal graph neural network for multivariate time series forecasting. In: Proceedings of the 28th ACM SIGKDD Conference on Knowledge Discovery and Data Mining (KDD), pp. 1567–1577. Association for Computing Machinery (2022). https://doi.org/10.1145/3534678.3539396

13. Herbelot, A., Baroni, M.: High-risk learning: acquiring new word vectors from tiny data. In: Proceedings of the 2017 Conference on Empirical Methods in Natural Language Processing (EMNLP), pp. 304–309. Association for Computational Linguistics (2017)

14. van den Oord, A., Kalchbrenner, N., Vinyals, O., Espeholt, L., Graves, A., Kavukcuoglu, K.: Conditional image generation with PixelCNN decoders. In: Proceedings of the 30th International Conference on Neural Information Processing Systems (NIPS), pp. 4797–4805. Curran Associates Inc. (2016)

15. Yoon, J., Kim, T., Dia, O., Kim, S., Bengio, Y., Ahn, S.: Bayesian model-agnostic meta-learning. In: Proceedings of the 32nd International Conference on Neural Information Processing Systems (NIPS), pp. 7343–7353. Curran Associates Inc. (2018)

16. Pan, Z., Liang, Y., Wang, W., Yu, Y., Zheng, Y., Zhang, J.: Urban traffic prediction from spatio-temporal data using deep meta learning. In: Proceedings of the 25th ACM SIGKDD International Conference on Knowledge Discovery and Data Mining (KDD), pp. 1720–1730. Association for Computing Machinery (2019)

17. Lu, B., Gan, X., Zhang, W., Yao, H., Fu, L., Wang, X.: Spatio-temporal graph few-shot learning with cross-city knowledge transfer. In: Proceedings of the 28th ACM SIGKDD Conference on Knowledge Discovery and Data Mining (KDD), pp. 1162–1172. Association for Computing Machinery (2022)

18. Jin, Y., Chen, K., Yang, Q.: Transferable graph structure learning for graph-based traffic forecasting across cities. In: Proceedings of the 29th ACM SIGKDD Conference on Knowledge Discovery and Data Mining (KDD), pp. 1032–1043. Association for Computing Machinery (2023)

19. Chung, J., Gulcehre, C., Cho, K., Bengio, Y.: Empirical Evaluation of Gated Recurrent Neural Networks on Sequence Modeling. arXiv preprint arXiv:1412.3555 (2014)

20. Veličković, P., Cucurull, G., Casanova, A., Romero, A., Lio, P., Bengio, Y.: Graph Attention Networks. arXiv preprint arXiv:1710.10903 (2017)
21. Hochreiter, S., Schmidhuber, J.: Long short-term memory. Neural Comput. **9**(8), 1735–1780 (1997)
22. Finn, C., Abbeel, P., Levine, S.: Model-agnostic meta-learning for fast adaptation of deep networks. In: International Conference on Machine Learning, pp. 1126–1135. PMLR (2017)
23. Li, Y., Yu, R., Shahabi, C., Liu, Y.: Diffusion convolutional recurrent neural network: data-driven traffic forecasting. In: International Conference on Learning Representations (2018)
24. Cui, Z., Henrickson, K., Ke, R., Wang, Y.: Traffic graph convolutional recurrent neural network: a deep learning framework for network-scale traffic learning and forecasting. IEEE Trans. Intell. Transp. Syst. **21**(11), 4883–4894 (2020). https://doi.org/10.1109/TITS.2019.2950416
25. Yu, B., Yin, H., Zhu, Z.: Spatio-temporal graph convolutional networks: a deep learning framework for traffic forecasting. In: Proc. 27th International Joint Conference on Artificial Intelligence (IJCAI 2018), pp. 3634–3640. AAAI Press (2018)
26. Wu, Z., Pan, S., Long, G., Jiang, J., Zhang, C.: Graph WaveNet for deep spatial-temporal graph modeling. In: Proc. 28th International Joint Conference on Artificial Intelligence (IJCAI 2019), pp. 1907–1913. AAAI Press (2019)

# A Task-Specific Feature Fusion Strategy For Small Object Detection


Zhiyi Shang, Zili Zhang$^{(\boxtimes)}$, and Mengtao Zhao

College of Computer and Information Science, Southwest University,
400715 Chongqing, China
zhangzl@swu.edu.cn, {s18246985097,zmt0203}@email.swu.edu.cn



**Abstract.** Small object detection concentrates on detecting objects with small size, holding great theoretical and practical significance in various scenarios including surveillance, agriculture monitoring, unmanned aerial vehicle, etc. Although deep learning networks have achieved remarkable success in the field of object detection, their generic feature fusion strategy continues to hinder further progress in small object detection. The traditional feature fusion strategy adopted in feature pyramid networks exhibits spatial information loss due to repeated downsampling operations, while reconstruction based on distorted low-resolution information further exacerbates the secondary attenuation of texture and contour. Meanwhile, the simple fusion operations that neglect cross-layer feature discrepancies fail to fully utilize multi-scale information, leading to suboptimal fusion. These limitations critically impair small object detection, since small objects are especially sensitive to spatial detail information. To this end, a task-specific feature fusion strategy is proposed for small object detection. The proposed strategy consists of two modules, the Global Information Compensation Module (GICM) and the Dual Path Alignment Module (DPAM). GICM can integrate global spatial information and employs a High-frequency Enhancement Block to filter out noise within these features, thereby compensating the loss of fine details in high-level features. DPAM learns the correlations between features from adjacent layers in the pyramid to achieve alignment across multi-scale features. The proposed strategy is integrated into the YOLOv11 framework through neck component replacement. Experimental results on VisDrone and Tsinghua-Tencent 100K datasets demonstrate the superiority of our strategy.

**Keywords:** Small Object Detection · Feature Fusion Strategy · Information Loss · Feature Alignment · YOLOv11


## 1 Introduction

While deep learning based object detection networks have achieved notable success, they persistently face challenges in detecting small objects. Distinct from standard-sized objects, small objects typically occupy only a few pixels.

According to the MS COCO benchmark, small objects are defined as those with resolutions below $32\times32$ pixels [10], and this extreme scale characteristic makes it particularly difficult to perform localization and feature extraction. Enhancing the performance of small object detection holds broader significance across numerous real-world visual tasks, for instance, in surveillance cameras or drone imagery, targets at a distance frequently appear as small pixel clusters due to the limitations of oblique viewing angles and long-range perspectives. In the field of intelligent detection of citrus diseases and pests, early-stage symptoms typically manifest as subtle and small-scale alterations. Accurate and timely detection during this stage can effectively prevent the spread of disease and significantly reduce economic losses.

Early object detection networks relied solely on single-scale features for detection, but the low-resolution of feature maps limited their ability to effectively characterize small objects [4]. The feature pyramid network [9] established a new paradigm by employing a cross-layer feature fusion mechanism, allowing feature maps of different hierarchies to detect objects of different scales. Due to its modular design, which enables seamless integration with various object detection frameworks, this flexibility has made it a standard component and essential configuration in modern CNN-based detection architecture. Despite the traditional feature fusion strategy getting significant success, the inherent structural limitations still constrain further improvements in detection performance. The progressive spatial detail loss is an intrinsic property caused by repeated downsampling through convolutional and pooling operations in CNNs. While upsampling operations restore feature map resolution, their reconstruction mechanisms fail to recover high-frequency components lost during downsampling. Instead, the smoothing effects of interpolation generate artifact-contaminated features that not only inadequately restore missing details, but also force reconstructions based on distorted low-resolution information, leading to secondary attenuation of fine details [3,29]. This cumulative distortion in multi-scale feature representations disproportionately impacts small object detection, as these targets inherently require precise details due to their limited pixel occupancy and low spatial proportions in images.

In addition, the fusion of features from adjacent layers in the feature pyramid through simple addition or concatenation operations does not fully utilize multiscale information, as it does not take into account the correlation between them. Since features from different layers at different scales contain abstract features at various levels, with semantic gaps and spatial information differences, this coarse fusion cannot effectively combine high-resolution low-semantic features with low-resolution high-semantic features, while predictable spatial misalignment caused by heterogeneous receptive fields further degrades the quality of feature maps through blurring effects and background interference [11,19]. This particularly influences detection performance in occluded objects and boundary regions, critical areas for small targets due to closer objects appearing larger, leading to suboptimal solutions.

Motivated by these observations, a task-specific feature fusion strategy for small object detection is proposed. This strategy is implemented through two specifically designed components, the Global Information Compensation Module (GICM) and the Dual Path Alignment Module (DPAM), to address the aforementioned challenges. First, spatial information from low-level features was integrated via GICM to generate preliminary global spatial features. Subsequently, a High-frequency Enhancement Block (HE-Block) was employed that strategically embeds soft thresholding into nonlinear transformation layers to project the refined global spatial feature maps by suppressing high-frequency noise while preserving semantically meaningful textural details and edge features. Following this, the DPAM adaptively adjusts convolutional kernel sampling positions through interactively learned offsets, enabling dual-aligned feature fusion that simultaneously preserves semantic coherence and resolves spatial misregistrations. It is noteworthy that the proposed strategy is flexible and plug-and-play, enabling seamless integration into any pyramid-structured detector without requiring architectural modifications. The main contributions in the work are summarized as follows:

1. A task-specific feature fusion strategy is proposed for small object detection, comprising two meticulously designed modules: the GICM integrates global spatial information and selectively enhances high-frequency features through the HE-Block, effectively compensating for spatial details in high-level features. Furthermore, the DPAM learns the correlation between adjacent layers in the feature pyramid aligning the features to be fused and achieving more effective feature fusion.
2. The proposed strategy is integrated into the YOLOv11 framework and extensive experiments are conducted on two mainstream small object detection benchmarks: VisDrone and Tsinghua-Tencent 100K. The experimental results reveal that our strategy achieves consistent improvements of 4.4% and 1.6% in $mAP_{50}$, respectively.

## 2    Related Work

Object detection frameworks are generally divided into two-stage and one-stage detectors. The two-stage detectors represented by Faster R-CNN [18], first generate region proposals and then perform classification and bounding box regression, achieving high accuracy at the cost of computational efficiency. In contrast, single-stage detectors eliminate the proposal generation step and directly predict object categories and locations through a dense prediction strategy, significantly improving detection speed, and opening up a new period in real-time object direction. Driven by the demand for efficient deployment in practical scenarios, single-stage detectors have emerged as the dominant approach that balances accuracy and computational economy. Recent advances further explore transformer-based architectures, which leverage self-attention mechanisms to model global dependencies and demonstrate remarkable potential in performance [2]. However, their reliance on extensive computational resources and complex training protocols limits their practicality compared to the streamlined workflows of single-stage detectors.

In one-stage detectors, the YOLO series (You Only Look Once) [15–17] is the most widely used framework. Due to its simple structure and unparalleled trade-off between speed and accuracy, it has become the most popular real-time object detection framework. Early YOLO models unified localization and classification into a single regression problem, achieving unprecedented real-time speed while incorporating anchor boxes and multi-scale features to enhance localization and prediction accuracy. YOLOv4 [1] and YOLOv5 integrate PAN, Mosaic data augmentation, and modular designs to further enhance performance. YOLOv7 [23] mitigates annotation noise by implementing a dynamic label assignment strategy. YOLOv8 utilizes an anchor-free detection model with a decoupled head architecture, allowing for independent processing of classification, regression, and object detection tasks. YOLOv9 [24] introduces programmable gradient information to obtain a reliable gradient for optimizing network weights. YOLOv10 [21] further enhances detection speed through NMS-free post-processing and a lightweight architectural design. YOLOv11 [8] establishes a new benchmark for efficient real-time detection by incorporating attention mechanisms and using a depthwise separable convolution detection head, simultaneously improving both accuracy and speed. Existing advancements primarily focus on the backbone, data augmentation and loss function, while neglecting the unique challenges posed by small targets. Therefore, our feature fusion strategy was specifically integrated into YOLOv11 to achieve a targeted enhancement of the detection performance of small objects.

## 3    Task-Specific Feature Fusion Strategy

To address the challenges posed by conventional feature fusion strategies in detecting small objects, a task-specific feature fusion strategy is proposed, which centers around two modular components: the Global Information Compensation Module (GICM) and the Dual Path Alignment Module (DPAM). This strategy aims to mitigate the spatial information loss in high-level features while establishing precise cross-scale feature correspondences, both of which are critical issues that significantly impact small object detection. The proposed strategy features a flexible design that enables seamless integration into general object detection networks without structural modifications, while maintaining computational efficiency to significantly enhance the performance in small object detection. The implementation details of GICM and DPAM will be comprehensively elaborated in subsequent subsections.

### 3.1    Global Information Compensation Module

The repetitive downsampling operations in convolutional neural networks for feature extraction inevitably discard substantial spatial information. Subsequent attempts to recover resolution through upsampling distorted low-resolution feature maps result in cumulative degradation of texture and fine details, which is particularly detrimental to small object detection.

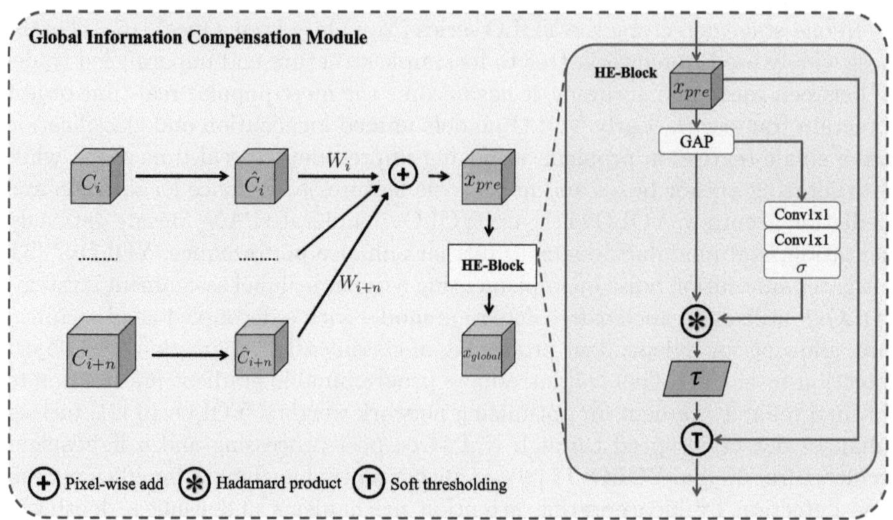



**Fig. 1.** The Structure of GICM.

The GICM is proposed based on the aforementioned observations, with its architectural design illustrated in Fig. 1. This module is designed to systemically aggregate fine-grained details from low-level features, which remain absent in high-level features, and inject global information into upsampled high-level features to enhance their feature representation. To achieve this, average pooling is initially applied to feature maps below the injection hierarchy level to match the resolution with the upsampled high-level feature. These normalized feature maps are then subjected to a smooth convolution operation for both feature smoothing and channel dimension unification. Subsequently, a set of learnable weights is employed to fuse these processed high-resolution features, which preserve fine details, in order to distinguish the importance of information between different scales and generate the preliminary global information. The formula for this process is as follows:

$$\hat{C}_i = \begin{cases} f_s\left(P\left(C_i\right)\right) , \text{ if i} > \text{j} \\ f_s\left(I\left(C_i\right)\right) , \text{ if i} = \text{j} \end{cases} \tag{1}$$

$$x_{pre} = \sum_i^I w_i \hat{C}_i \tag{2}$$

where $C$ denotes the multi-level feature maps extracted from the backbone network, $i$ and $j$ respectively index the hierarchy levels of backbone and upsampled features, $w$ indicates the learnable adaptive weights, and $I$ and $P$ represent the identity mapping and average pooling operations, respectively. $f_s$ denotes the smooth convolution, which is implemented using a set of separable convolution blocks here. While prior approaches share conceptual similarities [6,27], the GICM strategically injects global information into upsampled features. Furthermore, drawing inspiration from [28], a HE-Block is designed that embeds a learnable soft-thresholding mechanism within nonlinear transformation layers. This design refines global information by adaptively suppressing noise while preserving semantically meaningful high-frequency components with details and textural features.

Threshold design traditionally requires substantial domain expertise, but we bypass this challenging problem by introducing a learnable block to dynamically determine the optimal thresholds. This can be described by the following formula:

$$\Gamma = \lambda \cdot s \odot GAP(x_{pre}) \tag{3}$$

$$s = \sigma\left(C_2\left(C_1\left(GAP\left(x_{pre}\right)\right)\right)\right) \tag{4}$$

$$x_{global} = T(x_{pre}, \Gamma) = sign(x_{pre}) \odot \max\left(|x_{pre}| - \Gamma, 0\right) \tag{5}$$

where $\lambda$ is a learnable hyperparameter, $GAP$ denotes global average pooling, $\odot$ indicates Hadamard product, $\sigma$ refers to the sigmoid function, $T$ represents the soft threshold filtering operation and the sign function maps positive elements to 1 while negative elements to -1, thereby ensuring the threshold output remains entirely positive.

The preliminary global information is first compressed into a 1D channelwise descriptor via global average pooling. This descriptor is then processed through two 1×1 convolutional layers to learn scaling parameters, followed by a sigmoid function to constrain the parameters within the (0,1) range. The final threshold $\Gamma$ is derived by multiplying the scaled parameter by the original 1D descriptor. This constrained thresholding mechanism ensures that $\Gamma$ is less than the maximum value of input, preventing an excessive threshold that would nullify soft-thresholding output. Through this operational pipeline, the threshold-filtered global context effectively suppresses noise-correlated components while establishing highly discriminative feature representations.

Finally, the global information is precessed through two dedicated convolutional layers to generate global embeddings and global activation maps. These components are then injected into the upsampled features to facilitate the reconstruction of target shape and edge:

$$x_{embed} = Conv_{embed}(x_{global}) \tag{6}$$

$$x_{act} = \sigma\left(Conv_{act}(x_{global})\right) \tag{7}$$

$$P_{i+1} = Up\left(P_i\right) \odot x_{act} + x_{embed} \tag{8}$$

### 3.2  Dual Path Alignment Module

While GICM restores missing details, learning sufficient fused information between high-level and low-level features is crucial. This fundamental requirement motivates us to propose the DPAM, which achieves enhanced feature integration with both high semantic and spatial information through precise feature alignment prior to fusion, as shown in Fig. 2.

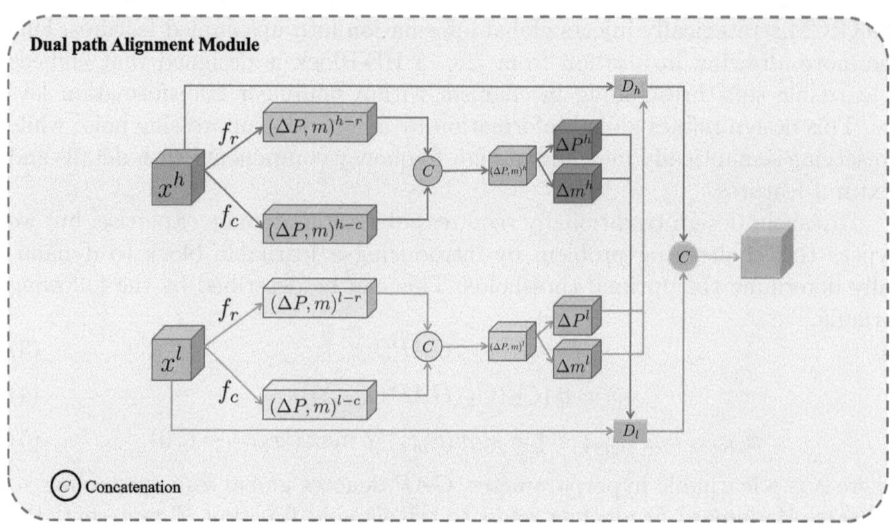

**Fig. 2.** The Structure of DPAM.

For the adjacent features pyramid layer features $x_h$ and $x_l$ to be fused, we first employ two parallel attention modules, each operating along a single direction, row or column, to generate corresponding attention maps. The row-wise and column-wise outputs are then concatenated and integrated with cross-layer features via deformable convolution, so that each offset in the attention map is the shifted position of every pixel within the corresponding feature map domain. Learning low-level feature offsets to adjust the sampling locations in high-level feature convolution kernels serves as an example, and this process can be formulated as follows:

$$\Delta P^{l\text{-}r}, \Delta m^{l\text{-}r} = Split(f_r(x^l)) \tag{9}$$

$$\Delta P^{l\text{-}c}, \Delta m^{l\text{-}c} = Split(f_c(x^l)) \tag{10}$$

$$\Delta P^l, \Delta m^l = Concat(\Delta P^{l\text{-}r}, \Delta P^{l\text{-}c}), \sigma\left(f_m\left(Concat\left(\Delta m^{l\text{-}r}, \Delta m^{l\text{-}c}\right)\right)\right) \tag{11}$$

$$\widehat{x^h} = D_h(x^h, \Delta P^l, \Delta m^l) \tag{12}$$

where $f_r$ denotes a 1×3 convolution along the row direction while $f_c$ denotes a 3×1 convolution along the column direction, $\Delta P$ and $\Delta m$ are the learnable offset and weight mask, $D$ indicates the deformable convolution, $f_m$ is a standard convolution with a kernel size of 1×1 whose purpose is to change the channel dimension of weight mask and further refine its weight. The process for the other path is similar and what distinguishes our approach from previous methods [7] of implementing feature alignment through offset computation is that we provide offset and mask through two features in an interactive manner, utilizing a dual path mechanism to perform deformable convolution operations [25]. This allows for mutual modulation between high-level and low-level features. For each pixel position, fine-grained dependencies are captured through the crisscrossing attention modules. This dual axis aggregation not only refines local feature representations but also reduces computational overhead. The specific operation of bidirectional interactive deformable convolution can be represented by the following formula:

$$y = \sum_{k=1}^{K} w_k \cdot x\left(p + p_k + \Delta p_k\right) \cdot \Delta m_k \tag{13}$$

where $K$ denotes the size of the convolution kernel, $w$ represents the kernel weights, $p$ is the center point of the feature map location corresponding to the convolution operation, and $p_k$ is the standard offset relative to this center $p$. Through bidirectional interactive deformable convolution, the semantic gap between the features to be fused is effectively bridged, and spatial misalignment caused by receptive field discrepancies is alleviated. Finally, the aligned features are ultimately integrated through channel-wise concatenation, synthesizing the high-resolution and high-semantic feature map.

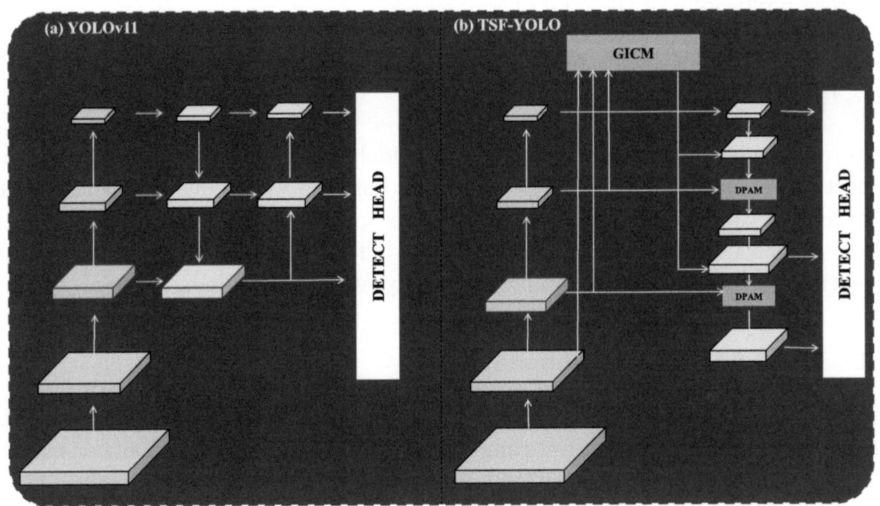


**Fig. 3.** The detector architecture of YOLOv11 (a) and TSF-YOLO(b).

## 3.3   Integration with YOLO Framework

To verify the effectiveness of the proposed strategy, it is integrated into the state-of-the-art YOLOv11 framework. The YOLO series stands as the dominant object detection framework due to its unparalleled balance between accuracy and real-time efficiency. However, like other CNN-based frameworks, its native feature fusion strategy inherently constrains its capability in handing small objects. To address this limitation, an enhanced detector, termed TSF-YOLO is developed through the integration of our strategy with the YOLOv11 framework. The comparison of the architecture of the baseline YOLOv11 and the proposed TSF-YOLO is delineated in Fig. 3.

Specifically, the feature fusion strategy is embodied in the neck component of the framework, and our proposed strategy is also confined to the neck part, while the other parts maintain the native YOLOv11 implementation. Notably, TSF-YOLO departs from the mainstream bidirectional fusion paradigm in favor of a single-path top-down structure. This design choice is motivated by the ablation studies in Table 3, which demonstrate that the bidirectional pathway feature fusion strategy, inspired by PAN [13] and BiFPN [20], introduces additional bottom-up paths, achieving only minimal accuracy improvement for small object detection compared to the use of single-path feature fusion. Consequently, the single-path structure preserves essential feature aggregation capabilities while removing parameter redundancy. Building upon the single-path feature fusion structure, the proposed GICM and DPAM modules are integrated to implement the task-specific feature fusion strategy for small object detection, achieving a further optimized balance between accuracy and speed, which better embodies the core philosophy of the YOLO framework.

## 4   Experiments

Rigorous experiments were performed on widely used datasets for small object detection, including VisDrone [5] and Tsinghua-Tencent 100K [30] benchmark datasets, to validate the effectiveness of the proposed strategy. The experimental setup is presented in dedicated subsections, followed by systematic reporting of quantitative results and comprehensive analyses of the findings.

### 4.1   Datasets and Implementations

VisDrone is a widely used international dataset characterized by a large number of small objects with resolutions ranging from 960×540 to 2000×1500, consisting of ten common categories such as pedestrians, vehicles, bicycles, motorcycles, etc. In the training set of 6,471 images, the validation set of 548 images and the test set of 1,610 images, there are a total of 457,066 annotations, with an average of 53 instances per image. This dataset offers high annotation density while accommodating a wide range of scale changes, with most of the target objects being small in size. To accommodate the high-resolution images from VisDrone into GPU memory, we follow the settings outline in [14], dividing each original image into four non-overlapping patches, resulting in a new training set composed of these cropped images. And following the literature [12,26], we take the validation set for evaluation.

Tsinghua-Tencent 100K is a large traffic sign benchmark dataset proposed by the Tsinghua-Tencent Joint Laboratory, derived from 100,000 Tencent Street View panoramas. It contains 10,000 high-resolution images with annotations, each with a resolution of 2048 × 2048 pixels, covering 30,000 traffic sign instances that have large variations in illuminance and weather conditions. This dataset consists of 232 categories and following the standard procedure in previous works, we excluded the categories with fewer than 100 samples, focusing on 45 categories, resulting in a training set of 6,105 images, with the test set comprising 3,071 images.

**Table 1.** Performance comparisons with other YOLO-series methods on VisDrone.

| Method | Params | Precision | Recall | $mAP_{50:95}$ | $mAP_{50}$ |
|---|---|---|---|---|---|
| YOLOv8n | 3.01M | 47.6 | 32.6 | 19.7 | 33.6 |
| Gold-YOLOn [22] | 5.62M | 46.8 | 32.2 | 17.9 | 30.8 |
| YOLOv9t [24] | 2.00M | 47.5 | 32.9 | 20.0 | 34.1 |
| YOLOv10n [21] | 2.71M | 46.2 | 32.4 | 19.8 | 33.6 |
| YOLOv11n [8] | 2.59M | 46.3 | 31.8 | 19.4 | 32.8 |
| **TSF-YOLOn** | **3.06M** | **51.0** | **35.1** | **22.3** | **37.2** |
| YOLOv8s | 11.1M | 50.6 | 38.5 | 23.5 | 39.5 |
| Gold-YOLOs [22] | 25.51M | 50.8 | 38.3 | 21.9 | 36.9 |
| YOLOv9s [24] | 7.29M | 53.6 | 38.2 | 24.2 | 40.1 |
| YOLOv10s [21] | 8.07M | 51.1 | 37.4 | 23.2 | 38.6 |
| YOLOv11s [8] | 9.43M | 53.1 | 36.7 | 23.6 | 39.1 |
| **TSF-YOLOs** | **11.1M** | **55.7** | **40.0** | **25.8** | **42.2** |

All experiments were conducted on a single Nvidia GeForce RTX 4090D GPU with 24 GB of memory in an environment with PyTorch 1.11.0 and CUDA 11.3. The Stochastic Gradient Descent (SGD) optimizer was employed to learn the model parameters with an initial learning rate of 0.01, momentum of 0.937, and weight decay of 0.0005, along with a linear learning rate scheduler that gradually reduces the learning rate to 0.0001. Each dataset was trained for 300 epochs with a batch size of 32, and the input image size is standardized to 640×640. All other settings are configured using the default properties of YOLOv11.

## 4.2    Experimental Results

The comparative performance evaluation was conducted between two different versions of TSF-YOLO and other popular YOLO detectors on the VisDrone dataset, as shown in Table 1. The result shows that our fusion strategy-enhanced TSF-YOLOn and TSF-YOLOs achieved 37.2 and 42.2 $mAP_{50}$ on the VisDrone dataset, surpassing their baseline YOLOv11 counterparts on the same scale by 4.4 and 3.1 points, respectively. In particular, they also demonstrate significant improvements in the stricter $mAP_{50:95}$ metric, with gains of 2.9 and 2.2 respectively, achieving state-of-the-art performance among all models compared.

**Table 2.** Performance comparisons with other YOLO-series methods on TT100k.

| Method | Params | Precision | Recall | $mAP_{50:95}$ | $mAP_{50}$ |
|---|---|---|---|---|---|
| Gold-YOLOn [22] | 5.63M | 65.4 | 65.4 | 49.9 | 66.9 |
| YOLOv9t [24] | 2.01M | 74.4 | 65.0 | 53.6 | 72.1 |
| YOLOv10n [21] | 2.72M | 70.7 | 64.1 | 53.4 | 69.8 |
| YOLOv11n [8] | 2.60M | 70.6 | 65.7 | 54.3 | 71.7 |
| **TSF-YOLOn** | **3.07M** | **75.3** | **65.5** | **55.4** | **73.3** |
| Gold-YOLOs [22] | 25.53M | 82.5 | 73.9 | 62.6 | 81.6 |
| YOLOv9s [24] | 7.30M | 83.6 | 74.1 | 63.2 | 83.0 |
| YOLOv10s [21] | 8.10M | 81.9 | 72.0 | 63.2 | 81.4 |
| YOLOv11s [8] | 9.44M | 81.9 | 73.8 | 64.6 | 82.6 |
| **TSF-YOLOs** | **11.2M** | **83.7** | **75.8** | **64.3** | **83.5** |

Furthermore, the evaluation conducted on the TT100k benchmark is shown in Table 2. Consistent performance enhancements of 1.6 and 0.9 $mAP_{50}$ are demonstrated compared to the baseline YOLOv11 implementation, substantiating our architectural generalizability across diverse detection datasets. The above experimental results substantiate the efficacy of the proposed task-specific feature fusion strategy for small object detection and demonstrate robust capabilities even in the presence of complex scale variations and background interference.

**Table 3.** Ablation experiments on VisDrone.

| Method | Params | Precision | Recall | $mAP_{50:95}$ | $mAP_{50}$ |
|---|---|---|---|---|---|
| YOLOv11n | 2.59M | 46.3 | 31.8 | 19.4 | 32.8 |
| YOLOv11n-FPN | 1.94M | 46.5 | 31.2 | 19.0 | 32.4 |
| YOLOv11n-FPN(+GICM) | 2.38M | 49.7 | 34.7 | 21.8 | 36.4 |
| YOLOv11n-FPN(+DPAM) | 2.62M | 48.2 | 33.7 | 20.7 | 34.9 |
| **TSF-YOLOn** | **3.07M** | **51.0** | **35.1** | **22.3** | **37.2** |

### 4.3  Ablation Study and Visualization

A systematic ablation study is conducted on the VisDrone dataset to thoroughly evaluate the contribution of each module by comparing the baseline YOLOv11 and its single-path variant, termed YOLO-FPN, respectively. From the experimental results in Table 3, it can be observed that GICM improves $mAP_{50}$ by 3.6, indicating that injecting global information into high-level features effectively compensates for missing spatial details and texture information. In addition, an improvement of 2.1 in $mAP_{50}$ is achieved by employing DPAM, highlighting the effectiveness of feature alignment and facilitating the quality and consistence of feature fusion.

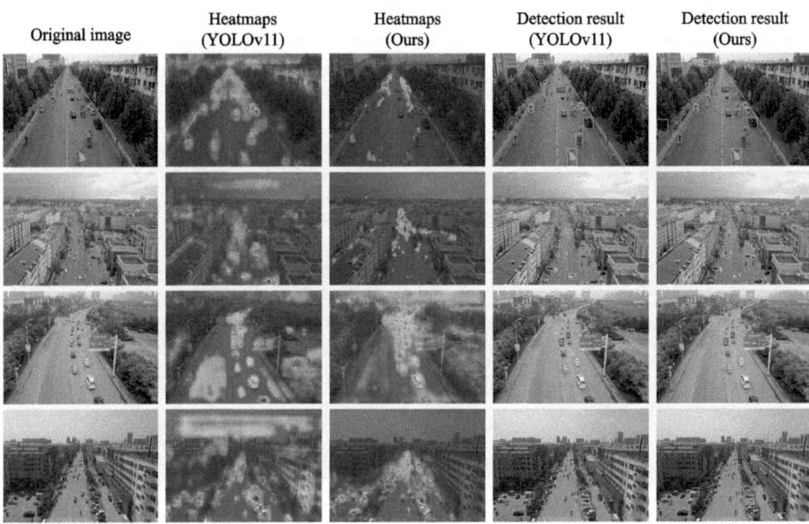


**Fig. 4.** Visualizations of the $P_3$ layer heatmaps and detection results on VisDrone.

To provide a more intuitive demonstration of the effectiveness of our strategy, a comprehensive visual analysis is established to empirically demonstrate the advantages of the proposed strategy. Comparative visualizations of heatmaps and detection outputs between baseline YOLOv11 and proposed TSF-YOLO are systematically documented in Fig. 4. Quantitative evaluations of feature maps reveal that our strategy exhibits a significantly stronger focus on small object regions, particularly in distant edge areas where objects appear smaller and more clustered. This outstanding performance is attributed to the task-specific feature fusion strategy for small object detection, which effectively reduces missed detections and improves the positioning accuracy of small objects.

### 4.4   Application in Citrus Pest and Disease Detection

While our experiments focus on UAV and traffic scenarios, the improvements achieved in small object detection indicate potential practical applications in smart agriculture. In the context of citrus disease and pest detection, early-stage infestation typically presents as subtle and small-scale morphological changes, and the variability in imaging conditions and complex backgrounds further exacerbate the difficulty of accurately identifying such symptoms. Nevertheless, establishing detection systems with temporal sensitivity and diagnostic precision remains an indispensable value for implementing early control measures and preventing more severe economic losses. As a preliminary exploration, the model trained on VisDrone with our proposed feature fusion strategy was transferred to a small-scale citrus disease and pest detection dataset. As demonstrated in Fig. 5, the adapted model can effectively identify pathological manifestations in citrus, including those presenting subtle morphological variations. This attempt further substantiates the operational robustness and applicability of our feature fusion strategy in the practical application of citrus disease and pest detection.

**Fig. 5.** Visualizations of application in citrus pest and disease detection.

## 5    Conclusion

In this paper, a task-specific feature fusion strategy for small object detection was proposed to address the critical challenges of the loss of fine-grained details, sensitivity to background interference, and multi-scale feature misalignment. First, we aggregate global spatial features through GICM and generate refined global spatial information via HE-Block, effectively compensating for the lack of texture and contour details in high-level features. The proposed DPAM further achieves alignment between adjacent pyramid-level features, eliminating spatial misalignment caused by differing receptive fields and semantic gaps to achieve optimal multi-scale feature fusion. Experimental validation was systematically implemented through the integration of our proposed strategy into the YOLOv11 framework. Comprehensive benchmark evaluations on both VisDrone and TT100k datasets revealed superior performance in the localization and recognition of small instances. Furthermore, the ablation study substantiates the functional efficacy of the proposed GICM and DPAM modules, with particularly enhanced robustness demonstrated in scenarios involving dense small objects and extreme scale variations. Future work will prioritize collaboration with agricultural research institutions to develop a comprehensive citrus pest and disease dataset, with the objective of addressing the critical challenge of detecting minute symptomatic variations under dense foliage occlusion and varying illumination conditions. In addition, the lightweight adaptations of our feature fusion strategy will be further explored for deployment on edge devices in orchard environments, striking an optimal balance between detection accuracy and computational efficiency.

# References


1. Bochkovskiy, A., Wang, C.Y., Liao, H.Y.M.: Yolov4: optimal speed and accuracy of object detection. arXiv preprint arXiv:2004.10934 (2020)
2. Carion, N., Massa, F., Synnaeve, G., Usunier, N., Kirillov, A., Zagoruyko, S.: End-to-end object detection with transformers. In: Vedaldi, A., Bischof, H., Brox, T., Frahm, J.-M. (eds.) ECCV 2020. LNCS, vol. 12346, pp. 213–229. Springer, Cham (2020). https://doi.org/10.1007/978-3-030-58452-8_13
3. Chen, L., Fu, Y., Gu, L., Yan, C., Harada, T., Huang, G.: Frequency-aware feature fusion for dense image prediction. IEEE Trans. Pattern Analy. Mach. Intell. (2024)
4. Cheng, G., et al.: Towards large-scale small object detection: survey and benchmarks. IEEE Trans. Pattern Anal. Mach. Intell. **45**(11), 13467–13488 (2023)
5. Du, D., Zhu, P., Wen, L., Bian, X., Liu, Z.M.: Visdrone-det2019: The vision meets drone object detection in image challenge results. In: ICCV visdrone workshop (2019)
6. Guo, C., Fan, B., Zhang, Q., Xiang, S., Pan, C.: Augfpn: improving multi-scale feature learning for object detection. In: Proceedings of the IEEE/CVF Conference on Computer Vision and Pattern Recognition, pp. 12595–12604 (2020)
7. Huang, S., Lu, Z., Cheng, R., He, C.: Fapn: feature-aligned pyramid network for dense image prediction. In: Proceedings of the IEEE/CVF International Conference on Computer Vision, pp. 864–873 (2021)
8. Jocher, G., Qiu, J.: Ultralytics yolo11. San Francisco, CA, USA, GitHub (2024)
9. Lin, T.Y., Dollár, P., Girshick, R., He, K., Hariharan, B., Belongie, S.: Feature pyramid networks for object detection. In: Proceedings of the IEEE Conference on Computer Vision and Pattern Recognition, pp. 2117–2125 (2017)
10. Lin, T.-Y., et al.: Microsoft COCO: common objects in context. In: Fleet, D., Pajdla, T., Schiele, B., Tuytelaars, T. (eds.) ECCV 2014. LNCS, vol. 8693, pp. 740–755. Springer, Cham (2014). https://doi.org/10.1007/978-3-319-10602-1_48
11. Lin, W., Chu, J., Leng, L., Miao, J., Wang, L.: Feature disentanglement in one-stage object detection. Pattern Recogn. **145**, 109878 (2024)
12. Liu, K., et al.: Esod: efficient small object detection on high-resolution images. IEEE Trans. Image Process. **34**, 183–195 (2025)
13. Liu, S., Qi, L., Qin, H., Shi, J., Jia, J.: Path aggregation network for instance segmentation. In: Proceedings of the IEEE Conference on Computer Vision and Pattern Recognition, pp. 8759–8768 (2018)
14. Liu, Z., Gao, G., Sun, L., Fang, Z.: Hrdnet: high-resolution detection network for small objects. In: 2021 IEEE International Conference on Multimedia and Expo (ICME), pp. 1–6. IEEE (2021)
15. Redmon, J., Divvala, S., Girshick, R., Farhadi, A.: You only look once: unified, real-time object detection. In: Proceedings of the IEEE Conference on Computer Vision and Pattern Recognition, pp. 779–788 (2016)
16. Redmon, J., Farhadi, A.: Yolo9000: better, faster, stronger. In: Proceedings of the IEEE Conference on Computer Vision and Pattern Recognition, pp. 7263–7271 (2017)

17. Redmon, J., Farhadi, A.: Yolov3: An incremental improvement. arXiv preprint arXiv:1804.02767 (2018)
18. Ren, S., He, K., Girshick, R., Sun, J.: Faster r-cnn: towards real-time object detection with region proposal networks. IEEE Trans. Pattern Anal. Mach. Intell. **39**(6), 1137–1149 (2016)
19. Song, G., Du, H., Zhang, X., Bao, F., Zhang, Y.: Small object detection in unmanned aerial vehicle images using multi-scale hybrid attention. Eng. Appl. Artif. Intell. **128**, 107455 (2024)
20. Tan, M., Pang, R., Le, Q.V.: Efficientdet: scalable and efficient object detection. In: Proceedings of the IEEE/CVF Conference on Computer Vision and Pattern Recognition, pp. 10781–10790 (2020)
21. Wang, A., Chen, H., Liu, L., Chen, K., Lin, Z., Han, J., et al.: Yolov10: real-time end-to-end object detection. Adv. Neural. Inf. Process. Syst. **37**, 107984–108011 (2025)
22. Wang, C., et al.: Gold-yolo: efficient object detector via gather-and-distribute mechanism. Adv. Neural. Inf. Process. Syst. **36**, 51094–51112 (2023)
23. Wang, C.Y., Bochkovskiy, A., Liao, H.Y.M.: Yolov7: trainable bag-of-freebies sets new state-of-the-art for real-time object detectors. In: Proceedings of the IEEE/CVF Conference on Computer Vision and Pattern Recognition, pp. 7464–7475 (2023)
24. Wang, C.Y., Yeh, I.H., Mark Liao, H.Y.: YOLOv9: Learning What You Want to Learn Using Programmable Gradient Information. In: Leonardis, A., Ricci, E., Roth, S., Russakovsky, O., Sattler, T., Varol, G. (eds.) Computer Vision – ECCV 2024. ECCV 2024. LNCS, vol. 15089. Springer, Cham (2025). https://doi.org/10. 1007/978-3-031-72751-1_1
25. Xiong, Y., et al.: Efficient deformable convnets: Rethinking dynamic and sparse operator for vision applications. In: Proceedings of the IEEE/CVF Conference on Computer Vision and Pattern Recognition, pp. 5652–5661 (2024)
26. Yang, C., Huang, Z., Wang, N.: Querydet: cascaded sparse query for accelerating high-resolution small object detection. In: Proceedings of the IEEE/CVF Conference on Computer Vision and Pattern Recognition, pp. 13668–13677 (2022)
27. Zhang, Z., Gong, P., Sun, H., Wu, P., Yang, X.: Dynamic local and global context exploration for small object detection. In: ICASSP 2023-2023 IEEE International Conference on Acoustics, Speech and Signal Processing (ICASSP), pp. 1–5. IEEE (2023)
28. Zhao, M., Zhong, S., Fu, X., Tang, B., Pecht, M.: Deep residual shrinkage networks for fault diagnosis. IEEE Trans. Industr. Inf. **16**(7), 4681–4690 (2019)
29. Zhou, Q., Shi, H., Xiang, W., Kang, B., Latecki, L.J.: Dpnet: dual-path network for real-time object detection with lightweight attention. IEEE Trans. Neural Netw. Learn. Syst. (2024)
30. Zhu, Z., Liang, D., Zhang, S., Huang, X., Hu, S.: Traffic-sign detection and classification in the wild. In: 2016 IEEE Conference on Computer Vision and Pattern Recognition (CVPR) (2016)

# Spatio-Temporal Decoupled Neural Radiance Fields for High Fidelity Dynamic View Synthesis


Yitong Kong[ID] and Yongde Guo[✉]

Faculty of Data Science, City University of Macau, Macao, China
{d23091100737,wtkuok}@cityu.edu.mo



**Abstract.** The novel view synthesis of dynamic scenes is a critical research direction in both computer vision and computer graphics. Specifically, in complex dynamic scenes, effectively separating the static background from the dynamic foreground and generating high-quality synthetic views remains a significant challenge. In this paper, we propose a method called Spatio-Temporal Decoupled NeRF (ST-DNeRF). By modeling static and dynamic components separately and combining spatio-temporal modeling with dynamic weighting fusion, ST-DNeRF facilitates the generation of novel views and perspectives at any time from monocular videos. A lightweight alignment loss encourages geometric consistency without external masks or optical flow. Experimental results demonstrate that ST-DNeRF outperforms existing methods across multiple dynamic scene datasets, particularly in scenarios involving rigid motion. It achieves significantly higher PSNR and SSIM scores compared to current techniques. However, there is still room for improvement in handling non-rigid motion. The research presented in this paper offers a novel approach to dynamic scene view synthesis and provides a promising direction for future studies.

**Keywords:** Neural Radiance Field · Dynamic view synthesis · Monocular videos · Scene flow · Spatio-temporal decoupling


## 1 Introduction

Synthesizing unseen viewpoints of a scene from sparse observations is a long-standing problem in computer vision and graphics, powering applications such as VR/AR and post-production. Neural Radiance Fields (NeRF) [1, 2] dramatically improved photo-realistic rendering for static scenes but struggle when objects move or deform. Temporal inconsistency, motion blur and background–foreground leakage lead to visible artefacts. We argue that separating time-invariant and time-varying factors followed by an adaptive fusion can mitigate these issues. We therefore propose ST-DNeRF, a decoupled spatio-temporal representation that learns a static field capturing canonical geometry, and a dynamic field that models residual appearance and motion via scene flow. A confidence-based weight blends the two at render time. Unlike previous approaches that either warp a canonical field with a deformation network [3–7] or regress dense optical flow [8–10], our method keeps the two fields independent yet geometrically aligned through novel regularizes. The main contributions are:



T. Zhu et al. (Eds.): KSEM 2025, LNAI 15919, pp. 117–130, 2026.
https://doi.org/10.1007/978-981-95-3001-4_9

- A dual-field architecture with a learnable fusion mask that automatically segments dynamic regions.
- An unsupervised geometric-alignment loss linking predicted scene flow and volumetric depth, eliminating reliance on noisy external priors.
- Comprehensive experiments demonstrating state-of-the-art accuracy and real-time inference on rigid-motion videos.

The remainder of this paper is organized as follows. Section 2 provides a brief review of related work. Section 3 reviews the process of novel synthesis of dynamic video. Section 4 presents our improvement methods, followed by comparative experiments and ablation experiments in Sect. 5. The last Sect. 6 summarizes this paper and discuss some future direction of the new method.

## 2 Related Work

### 2.1 Neural Radiance Fields

Neural Radiance Fields (NeRF) [1] introduce a continuous scene representation that unifies geometry and appearance in a single network. From a sparse set of posed photographs, NeRF learns a 5D mapping $F_\theta : (x, d) \rightarrow (c, \sigma)$, where spatial point $x \in \mathbb{R}^3$ and view direction d are mapped to RGB color c and volume density $\sigma$. An eight-layer, 256-unit MLP first encodes x, predicting $\sigma$ and a latent feature, concatenating this feature with d and passing it through an additional layer yields view-dependent color, ensuring view-independent density while capturing complex reflectance. Novel views are rendered by numerically integrating c and $\sigma$ along camera rays using stratified sampling and alpha compositing, following classical volume-rendering principles.

Replacing discrete voxels with an implicit function provides sub-voxel accuracy and removes memory bottlenecks. Although training demands heavy optimization, the converged model synthesizes photorealistic images in milliseconds, faithfully reproducing lighting, soft shadows, and specular highlights. NeRF therefore enables high-fidelity free-viewpoint rendering and has rapidly become foundational for virtual/augmented reality, free-view video, and 3D content creation, inspiring ongoing work on accelerated training and dynamic-scene extensions.

### 2.2 Decoupling Dynamic Elements

Decoupling dynamic elements from static backgrounds is a prerequisite for high-quality dynamic-scene reconstruction and free-viewpoint synthesis. When image sequences are treated holistically, motion inevitably corrupts static geometry, yielding blurry textures and temporal flicker. Therefore recent work models the scene as two factors, a time-invariant radiance field for the background and a time-varying field for moving objects which thus providing a structured spatio-temporal representation.

The self-supervised $D^2$NeRF framework [11] pioneered this idea: given only a monocular video it jointly segments moving foregrounds and their projections and in-paints the occluded static content, markedly improving realism. However, the absence of external supervision leaves the model susceptible to drift, dynamic ghosts, and background distortions under occlusion or motion blur [12–14]. Later research introduced learnable time embeddings, deformation codes, or trajectory priors to correlate successive frames and enhance temporal coherence, and some methods fuse object tracking to stabilize motion paths. These strategies raise consistency but often rely on densely calibrated multi-view input, limiting deployment with casual captures. Achieving robust, annotation-free decoupling from sparse monocular sequences therefore remains an open challenge and a key bottleneck for practical neural rendering of dynamic scenes.

### 2.3 NSFF (Neural Scene Flow Fields) [8]

NSFF is a neural framework designed for temporally consistent novel view synthesis in dynamic scenes. By predicting per-pixel 3D scene flow, NSFF captures inter-frame spatial changes, enabling motion-aware warping and geometry reconstruction. Unlike traditional optical flow, NSFF leverages learned latent spaces and is trained end-to-end, allowing more precise motion compensation. Its key innovation is using scene flow–based regularization to enhance temporal coherence and reduce ambiguities when only a single view per timestep is available.

While NSFF improves NeRF's temporal modeling, it relies heavily on accurate scene flow estimation, which is computationally intensive. Complex scenes with fast motion, occlusions, or multiple objects often suffer from artifacts such as ghosting and geometry collapse [8, 15]. To address this, NSFF introduces multi-scale flow refinement to better capture large displacements and reduce computational cost. Furthermore, Yang et al. [14] incorporate physics-based priors to regularize non-rigid motion, improving structural stability and enhancing the physical plausibility of synthesized views.

### 2.4 Novel View Synthesis

Novel View Synthesis (NVS) refers to the task of generating realistic images from new, unseen viewpoints based on a limited set of input images or videos. This technology has long been a core research problem in computer vision, image processing, and computer graphics. Beyond academic interest, it plays an essential role in practical applications such as virtual and augmented reality, immersive telepresence, and cinematic production, where it enables the creation of visually compelling scenes from novel angles that may not have been originally captured [12]. Traditional methods for NVS rely heavily on explicit 3D geometry modeling, such as multi-view stereo, structured light, and depth estimation. These approaches reconstruct the geometry of a scene and synthesize new views through geometric projection and interpolation, often under assumptions like Lambertian reflectance or known camera intrinsics. While such methods are theoretically well-founded, they often require dense and high-quality input views. Their performance typically degrades in scenarios involving sparse views, noisy data, or challenging visual effects like transparency, and thin structures.

The emergence of NeRF in 2020 marked a transformative shift in NVS research. NeRF introduces an implicit 5D continuous function that maps spatial coordinates and viewing directions to RGB colors and volumetric density, trained via volumetric rendering to match observed pixel values [13]. It leverages deep learning to reconstruct photorealistic scenes with impressive fidelity, capturing fine geometric and radiometric details from as few as dozens of images. However, the original NeRF formulation assumes static scenes and independent image observations, making it unsuitable for dynamic environments. Addressing these limitations in dynamic scenes introduces significant challenges. Unlike static NVS, dynamic view synthesis [3–5, 8] requires simultaneous modeling of spatial geometry and temporal evolution. Early extensions to NeRF focus on modeling deformations over time. For example, Nerfies introduces a dynamic deformation field that maps canonical scene coordinates to their time-varying counterparts [8], allowing the network to model local motion patterns over a sequence. While this method improves temporal alignment and enables long-sequence synthesis, it often fails under rapid motion or highly non-rigid transformations due to limited deformation capacity and reliance on smooth priors. Other approaches, such as Neural Scene Flow Fields (NSFF) and Neural Trajectories, attempt to learn explicit 3D scene flow to capture temporal correspondences between frames.

To improve both accuracy and efficiency, recent research has introduced hybrid modeling strategies. Some frameworks partition dynamic scenes [19] into static and dynamic regions and apply separate neural networks for each, later fusing the outputs to synthesize the final image. Others incorporate coarse-to-fine hierarchical training or variational voxel grids to reduce memory cost and accelerate convergence. Despite these efforts, dynamic NVS still faces key bottlenecks, such as overfitting, artifact amplification, and generalization to real-world scenes with complex motion and lighting. Additionally, introducing physical priors—such as those used in cloth or fluid simulations—has shown promise in regularizing the learning of non-rigid deformations, helping to preserve structural integrity and enhance realism in synthesized views.

**Fig. 1.** From left to right are Ground Truch, NSFF, Ours. The ribbon relies too much on the flow of scenes, resulting in a lack of continuity.

As novel view synthesis continues to evolve, especially in dynamic settings, there remains a pressing need for methods that are robust, generalizable, and computationally efficient [6]. Future progress will likely depend on more sophisticated motion representations, better temporal priors, and the integration of scene semantics and physics-based constraints into neural rendering pipelines.

# 3  Preliminary

This section introduces the dynamic video novel view synthesis pipeline, laying the foundation for subsequent analysis. A dynamic monocular video $V = \{I_0, I_1, \ldots, I_{N-1}\}$ consists of $NNN$ image frames, each with a resolution of $H \times W$. For each frame, a binary foreground mask m is used to indicate dynamic objects within the scene. These masks can be generated automatically via segmentation or motion segmentation algorithms, or semi-automatically through interactive operations such as translation and rotation. In recent years, the automation of mask generation has been significantly improved through unsupervised and weakly supervised learning techniques. For instance, Unsupervised Motion Segmentation [19] leverages motion coherence within optical flow fields to identify dynamic regions, while BoxSup [20] utilizes weak annotations like bounding boxes to train high-quality segmentation networks. Moreover, MaskTrack R-CNN [21] incorporates cross-frame consistency modeling to enhance the robustness of video object segmentation. Together, these methods provide a reliable foundation for foreground mask generation, enabling more accurate modeling of dynamic scenes for view synthesis.

The video can thus be treated as a 3D tensor of size $N \times H \times W$. Each frame $I_n \in \mathbb{R}^{H \times W}$ is paired with a timestamp $t_n$ and a camera pose $P_n$. Given $V$ and $\{t_n, P_n\}_{n=1}^{N-1}$, dynamic novel view synthesis must generate images from arbitrary viewpoints and times, despite geometry that changes over time and just one 2D observation per instant. Only a few recent methods [22–24] tackle this challenge by using two neural radiance fields to separately model static and dynamic components.

To synthesize a novel view at a given time, rays must be generated from a virtual camera's origin $O \in \mathbb{R}^3$, with each ray direction defined by a normalized vector $d = (dx, dy, dz)$. A 3D point x along a ray can be expressed using the ray equation:

$$r(s) = O + sd$$

where, s is a scalar representing the distance from the camera origin along the ray direction. To sample 3D points along each ray for volume rendering, we define near and far bounds $t_{near}$ and $t_{far}$, then uniformly or stratified sample points between them. Each sample point has the form:

$$x = O + t \cdot d, t \in [t_{near}, t_{far}]$$

Inspired by the positional encoding in NeRF, we apply a similar Fourier feature mapping to the temporal variable t to better capture dynamic variations in time. The encoded vector $\gamma(t)$ comprises alternating sine and cosine functions at increasing frequencies:

$$\gamma(t) = [sin(2^0 \pi t), cos(2^0 \pi t), \ldots, sin(2^{L-1} \pi t), cos(2^{L-1} \pi t)]$$

where, $L$ denotes the number of frequency bands. As demonstrated by Tancik et al., such Fourier feature mappings enable MLPs to better approximate high-frequency functions in low-dimensional spaces. By integrating high-frequency encodings of temporal information, the network becomes more capable of modeling fast or subtle motions, improving its ability to capture dynamic details and maintain temporal consistency. This enhances rendering accuracy in scenes containing both rigid and non-rigid motion, making it a powerful tool for dynamic view synthesis.

# 4　Method

This section presents our novel framework, termed Spatio-Temporal Decoupled NeRF (ST-DNeRF). Our method is designed to support flexible viewpoint queries across arbitrary time points and angles in monocular dynamic video inputs. As illustrated in Fig. 2, the architecture of ST-DNeRF consists of three core modules: a static NeRF component, a dynamic NeRF module, and a rendering unit that fuses synthetic scenes for final output.

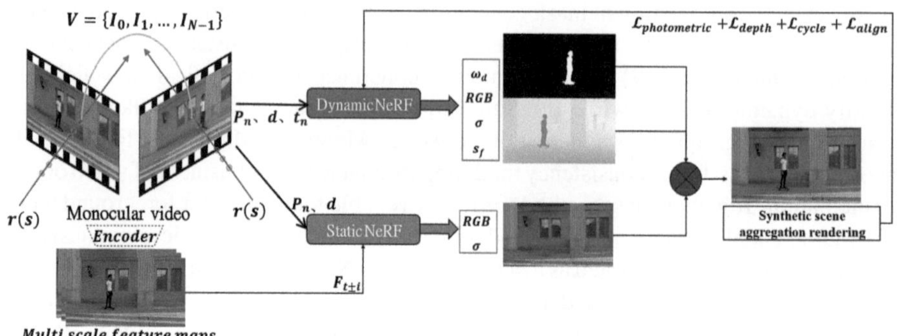

**Fig. 2.** The ST-DNeRF Model Framework.

## 4.1　Static Field

In static scenes, we adopt a NeRF-inspired approach to retrieve the image-space projection of a 3D point $x_t$ located along a camera ray. Concretely, the point $x_t \in \mathbb{R}^3$ is mapped onto a neighboring view's image plane, resulting in the projected coordinate $proj(x_t)$. This location is then used as input to a visual feature encoder E, which outputs a corresponding feature vector $F_{t\pm i}$.

$$F_{t\pm i} = E(proj(x_{t\pm i})) \in \mathbb{R}^d$$

where, $x_{t\pm i} \in \mathbb{R}^3$ denotes a spatial point from a nearby viewpoint that is close to $x_t$.

To represent the static scene, a multi-layer perceptron (MLP) is employed to predict both the color $c_s = (r, g, b)$ and the corresponding density $\sigma_s$. The MLP takes as input the 3D location $x_t$, timestamp t, the camera viewing direction d, along with the contextual feature vector $F_{t\pm i}$ derived from the neighboring view. This component of the model captures static scene properties and is referred to as

$$(c_s, \sigma_s) = MLP_s(x_t, t, d, F_{t\pm i})$$

To render the static scene, we calculate $\widehat{C}_s(r)$ using the volume rendering integral, which gives the rendering color $c_s$ and transparency $T_s$ of the pixel that the ray r(s) passes through, using the following formula:

$$\widehat{C}_s(r) = \int_{t_{near}}^{t_{far}} T_s(t) \cdot \sigma_s(r(t)) \cdot c_s(r(t), d)dt$$

where $T_s(t)$ is the cumulative transmittance and represents the transparency of the ray from $t_{near}$ to $t$

$$T_s(t) = \exp\left(-\int_{t_{near}}^{t} \sigma_s(r(s))\right)$$

## 4.2 Dynamic Field

Dynamic scenes feature intricate motion trajectories that markedly differ from those in static environments. To tackle the challenges discussed in Sect. 2.2, we propose decoupling the dynamic components, decomposing the dynamic scene into dynamic neural radiance fields independent of the static background, and achieving adaptive fusion of the two via dynamic weighting mechanisms.

Unlike static scene representations, dynamic scenes require temporal information to be explicitly embedded into the model. Motivated by prior work in neural scene flow [4, 8], we consider the temporal motion of a point as bidirectional scene flow:

$$s_f(t \rightarrow t+1), s_f(t \rightarrow t-1) = f(x, d, t)$$

where $s_f(t \rightarrow t+1), s_f(t \rightarrow t+1) \in \mathbb{R}^3$ represent the forward and backward scene flows in time, respectively, indicating the displacement of the current point $x$ between adjacent time steps. This defines the motion trajectory of the dynamic object in the temporal dimension.

To separate the dynamic object from the static background, a hybrid dynamic weight $\omega_d \in [0,1]$ is introduced to evaluate the likelihood that each sampling point belongs to the dynamic region. The MLP jointly queries the dynamic weights, along with the color $c_d$ and density $\sigma_d$ of the dynamic scene, as well as the bidirectional scene flows $(t \rightarrow t+1)$ and $s_f(t \rightarrow t-1)$

$$(c_d, \sigma_d, s_f(t \rightarrow t+1), s_f(t \rightarrow t-1), \omega_d) = MLP_d(x, d, t)$$

The temporal motion updates point coordinates at nearby timestamps via:

$$x_{t\pm1} = x_t + s_f(t \rightarrow t\pm1)$$

This allows spatial warping to adjacent frames, enabling the network to extract temporal context. Correspondingly, color and density at warped positions are obtained as:

$$(c_d, \sigma_d) = MLP_d(x + s_f(t \rightarrow t\pm1), d, t)$$

## 4.3 Scene Aggregation and Rendering

By integrating outputs from both static and dynamic neural fields through predicted weights $\omega_d$ we synthesize complete frames across novel views and timepoints. The final color per ray is computed as a weighted blend:

$$c_{mix} = (1 - \omega_d) \cdot c_s + \omega_d \cdot c_d$$

The full volumetric rendering, incorporating transmittance and emission from both components, becomes:

$$\widehat{C}_{\mathrm{mix}}(r) = \int_{t_{\mathrm{near}}}^{t_{\mathrm{far}}} T_s(t) \cdot \sigma_s(r(t)) \cdot c_s(r(t), d)dt + T_d(t) \cdot \sigma_d(r(t)) \cdot c_d(r(t), d)$$

and the cumulative transmittance is expressed as:

$$T_{\mathrm{mix}}(t) = \exp\left(-\int_{t_{\mathrm{near}}}^{t} \sigma_{\mathrm{mix}}(r(s))ds\right)$$

Finally, the rendered pixel color for ray r is compared with its observed counterpart via photometric loss:

$$\mathcal{L}_{\mathrm{photometric}} = \sum_{r \in R} \|\left(\widehat{C}(r) - C(r)\right)\|_2^2$$

### 4.4 Normalized Space-Time

In previous works, have been in use for many regularization strategy [19, 25]. We build upon these strategies by introducing an additional regularization term. Throughout the whole model, in order to ensure a reasonable separation and fusion of static and dynamic scenes, the dynamic weight $\omega_d(x)$ is calculated after each forward propagation of the dynamic MLP. Depth consistency is ensured by minimizing the difference between dynamic and static depth in static regions

$$\mathcal{L}_{depth} = \lambda_{depth} \cdot \mathbb{E}_x\left[\|D_d(x) - D_s(x)\|_2^2 \cdot (1 - \omega_d(x))\right]$$

$\lambda_{\mathrm{depth}}$ is the weight coefficient that controls the strength of the depth consistency constraint. $D_d(x)$ and $D_s(x)$ represent dynamic and static depth maps, respectively. The term $1 - \omega_d(x)$ serves as a mask to suppress dynamic regions, ensuring that in static regions where $\omega_d(x) \approx 0$, the depth estimates from both static and dynamic branches remain aligned.

To maintain bidirectional consistency of the scene flow, we apply a cycle consistency loss. Specifically, we compute the scene flow $s_f(t \to t \pm 1)$, track each point's position through forward and backward transformations, and minimize the deviation between the original and cyclically transformed positions:

$$\mathcal{L}_{cycle} = \sum_{i \in} \left(\left(\| x_i^t - x_i^{t \to t+1 \to t}\|_2^2\right) + \left(\| x_i^{t+1} - x_i^{t+1 \to t \to t+1}\|_2^2\right)\right)$$

where $x_i^t$ is the position of point i in t

During the rendering process, preprocessing information such as optical flow or segmentation masks—typically generated by external algorithms—may be noisy or inaccurate. Over-reliance on this information can lead the model to learn incorrect features, thereby degrading rendering quality, as illustrated in Fig. 1. To address this issue, we propose a geometric consistency regularization method that does not require additional supervision signals.

For a ray r, we estimate its intersection with the geometric surface as $\hat{x}_t$ computed by taking a weighted average of k sampled points along the ray:

$$\hat{x}_t = \sum_{i=1}^{k} \omega_d^t \cdot x_i$$

Similarly, we compute when the intersection of $t + 1$ is

$$\hat{x}_{t+1} = \sum_{i=1}^{k} \omega_{d+1}^t \cdot \tilde{x}_i$$

Based on the consistency between the scene flow's geometric surface and the predicted surface, we introduce a geometric alignment loss as follows:

$$\mathcal{L}_{align} = \lambda_{align} \cdot \mathbb{E}_r \left[ \|\hat{x}_{t+1} - (\hat{x}_t + s_f(t \to t \pm 1)\|_2^2 \right]$$

$$\mathcal{L} = \mathcal{L}_{photometric} + \mathcal{L}_{depth} + \mathcal{L}_{cycle} + \mathcal{L}_{align}$$

## 5  Experimental Results

In this section, we present the experimental setup, including the datasets used, evaluation metrics, and a detailed analysis of the results.

### 5.1  Dataset and Preprocessing

We evaluate our method on seven video sequences from the NVIDIA Dynamic Scene Dataset [26], which features dynamic objects moving within predominantly static backgrounds and foregrounds. The dataset provides monocular video sequences composed of 12 frames captured from 12 fixed cameras at different time steps $\{t_0, t_1, \ldots\ldots, t_{11}\}$.

Our model achieves an inference time of approximately 3.3 to 3.4 ms per frame at a resolution of $480 \times 270$ with a batch size of 1, corresponding to a processing speed of about 300 frames per second. All experiments are conducted on an NVIDIA L20 GPU (48GB) using PyTorch 2.0.0 and Python 3.8 under Ubuntu 20.04. To the best of our knowledge, this is among the fastest methods currently available.

For training, we use a consistent initial learning rate of $5 \times 10^{-4}$ (lrate = 0.0005) or both the static and dynamic components of the network. This learning rate is applied to optimize the neural network weights and decays exponentially throughout training while maintaining the same configuration across all experiments.

**Table 1.** Novel Quantitative results for view synthesis on the Nvidia Dynamic Scene Dataset. We report the average PSNR, SSIM, and LPIPS results by comparison with existing methods. The best performance is shown in bold.

| PSNR/ SSIM/ LPIPS | Balloon 1 | Balloon 2 | Umbrella | Jumping | Playground | Skating | Truck | Average |
|---|---|---|---|---|---|---|---|---|
| **NeRF** | *19.87/* *0.699/* *0.287* | *24.33/* *0.815/* *0.19* | *21.29/* *0.546/* *0.457* | *20.99/* *0.687/* *0.418* | *21.07/* *0.768/* *0.240* | *23.67/* *0.781/* *0.418* | *22.73/* *0.747/* *0.334* | *21.99/* *0.720/* *0.333* |
| **NeRF-T** | 18.54/ 0.443/ 0.419 | 20.69/ 0.570/ 0.349 | 17.69/ 0.267/ 0.667 | 18.04/ 0.465/ 0.535 | 14.68/ 0.230/ 0.534 | 20.32/ 0.504/ 0.55 | *18.33/* *0.438/* *0.524* | *18.33/* *0.417/* *0.51* |
| **NSFF** | 21.96/ 0.702/ 0.288 | 24.27/ 0.740/ 0.288 | 22.97/ 0.659/ 0.319 | 24.65/ 0.813/ 0.227 | 21.22/ 0.717/ 0.268 | 29.29/ 0.888/ 0.190 | 25.96/ 0.774/ 0.249 | 24.33/ 0.756/ 0.261 |
| **Yoon et al** | 18.74/ 0.606/ 0.248 | 19.88/ 0.416/ 0.288 | 20.35/ 0.543/ 0.243 | 20.15/ 0.616/ 0.250 | 15.08/ 0.249/ 0.309 | 21.75/ 0.561/ 0.262 | 21.53/ 0.623/ 0.172 | 19.64/ 0.517/ 0.253 |
| **Dynamic-NeRF** | 22.36/ 0.773/ *0.193* | 27.06/ 0.864/ 0.117 | 23.26/ 0.720/ **0.193** | 24.68/ 0.843/ **0.151** | 24.15/ **0.858/** **0.148** | 32.66/ 0.951/ **0.080** | 28.56/ **0.872/** **0.149** | 26.10/ **0.840/** **0.147** |
| **Ours** | **22.49/** **0.773/** **0.180** | **27.34/** **0.870/** **0.115** | **23.75/** **0.728/** 0.2 | **24.72/asis>** **0.845/** 0.173 | **24.66/** 0.842/ 0.219 | **33.71/** **0.956/** 0.157 | **28.64/** 0.795/ 0.168 | **26.47/** 0.830/ 0.173 |

## 5.2 Comparison with Existing Methods

We compare our method with six existing approaches: NeRF, NeRF-T (a direct extension of NeRF that incorporates temporal information into the input coordinates), two ray-flow based methods NSFF and Dynamic Nerf, as well as the image-based rendering method Yoon et al.

**Quantitative Comparison**
Table 1 reports the PSNR, SSIM, and LPIPS metrics across different scenes in the dynamic scene dataset. Our method consistently achieves higher PSNR values across all scenes, with particularly notable improvement in the *Skating* scene, where PSNR reaches 33.71. However, our method shows slightly higher LPIPS values in scenes like *Playground*, *Skating*, *Jumping*, and *Umbrella*, suggesting that the perceptual quality of the synthesized images may be slightly lower than that of some competing methods. This may be attributed to fast object motion causing occlusions or out-of-frame issues during training, or due to our algorithm's bias toward preserving high-frequency details.

In the *Truck* scene, our model performs favorably in both PSNR and SSIM, particularly excelling in preserving geometric structure. Conversely, in scenes with non-rigid motion—such as *Umbrella* and *Jumping*—our LPIPS scores are higher, indicating that while our proposed geometric alignment loss improves reconstruction for rigid objects, its effectiveness diminishes with highly deformable or non-rigid elements.

Overall, our approach decomposes the dynamic scene into static background and dynamic foreground through segmentation-based decoupling. This strategy offers distinct advantages in handling complex and diverse dynamic environments.

**Qualitative Comparison**

In Fig. 3 presents a visual comparison of reconstruction results from four representative scenes in the dynamic scene dataset. Under identical experimental conditions, our method demonstrates superior performance in reconstructing dynamic objects compared to all baseline approaches.

**Fig. 3.** Visual comparison of different methods on the first critical frame on a dynamic scene dataset.

The method by Yoon et al. exhibits slight inaccuracies in both the orientation and spatial positioning of dynamic objects, particularly in complex motion scenarios such as the first-row example. The approach by Tretschk et al. emphasizes maintaining object completeness in synthesized views but struggles with accurate motion modeling, especially in scenes involving large or rapid movements.

Although NSFF is capable of capturing dynamic object motion to some extent, its reconstructions often appear blurry and lack fine details. For example, it fails to handle thin structures like the lower portion of the balloon, resulting in incomplete rendering. Traditional NeRF, being designed for static scenes, fails to model dynamic regions entirely, leading to significant frame-wise inconsistencies and visual artifacts.

In contrast, our method more accurately captures both motion and fine structures, delivering sharper and more temporally coherent results in dynamic environments.

### 5.3   Ablation Experiments

To verify the effectiveness of each regularization term, the method proposed in this article conducted a systematic ablation experiment on the NVIDIA Dynamic Scene Dataset benchmark. All experiments were conducted under the same training hyperparameters

**Table 2.** Model ablation experimental performance results

| Model | Avg PSNR↑ | Avg SSIM↑ | Avg LPIPS↓ |
|---|---|---|---|
| **Photometric Only** | 24.12 | 0.798 | 0.210 |
| **w/o** $\mathcal{L}_{depth}$ | 25.89 | 0.822 | 0.185 |
| **w/o** $\mathcal{L}_{cycle}$ | 25.32 | 0.815 | 0.192 |
| **w/o** $\mathcal{L}_{align}$ | 25.76 | 0.824 | 0.181 |
| **Ours (Full)** | 26.47 | 0.830 | 0.173 |

and camera trajectory settings, and the unified evaluation indicators were PSNR, SSIM, and LPIPS to ensure the fairness and consistency of the comparison.

The ablation experiments in Table 2 show that each regularization term has a significant contribution to the model performance. The complete model achieves the best results. Removing the depth consistency $\mathcal{L}_{depth}$ leads to a decrease in the quality of static areas, a decrease in PSNR of 0.58, and an increase in LPIPS of 0.012, indicating that this constraint is crucial for the depth alignment of static scenes. The loss of the scene flow bidirectional consistency $\mathcal{L}_{cycle}$ has the greatest impact on the performance, with a decrease in PSNR of 1.15 and an increase in LPIPS of 0.019, because its loss will lead to the accumulation of motion estimation errors and produce motion artifacts. The geometric alignment loss $\mathcal{L}_{align}$ mainly improves the geometric consistency of the boundaries of dynamic objects. After removal, the SSIM decreases by 0.006. The model using only photometric loss has the worst performance, verifying the necessity of each regularization term. Comprehensive analysis shows that $\mathcal{L}_{cycle}$ contributes the most to the overall stability, while $\mathcal{L}_{depth}$ and $\mathcal{L}_{cycle}$ optimize the geometric consistency of the static and dynamic regions respectively. The synergistic effect of the three improves the robustness of the model.

## 6 Conclusions

This paper proposes Spatio-Temporal Decoupled NeRF (ST-DNeRF), a novel framework for high-quality novel view synthesis in dynamic scenes. The method integrates static and dynamic decoupled modeling, dynamic weight fusion, bidirectional scene flow, and multi-level regularization to enhance temporal consistency and visual quality without external supervision. The model consists of a static NeRF for background, a dynamic NeRF for time-varying foregrounds, and a fusion module that adaptively blends both outputs. Key losses including depth consistency, cycle consistency, and geometric alignment improve structural coherence and motion modeling.

Experiments on the NVIDIA Dynamic Scene Dataset demonstrate that ST-DNeRF outperforms NeRF, NeRF-t, NSFF, and others in both quantitative metrics (PSNR, SSIM, LPIPS) and visual fidelity. Ablation studies confirm the effectiveness of each module.

Despite its strengths, ST-DNeRF faces challenges in mask dependency, non-rigid motion modeling, and computational cost. Future work includes integrating weak supervision, physical priors, and model compression techniques to improve robustness and efficiency. ST-DNeRF also shows potential for extension to complex applications like multi-object interaction and free-viewpoint 3D reconstruction.

**Acknowledgements.** This research was supported by the Science and Technology Development Fund (FDCT) from Macau SAR (Grant No. 0061/2024/RIB2).

# References


1. Mildenhall, B., et al.: NeRF: representing scenes as neural radiance fields for view synthesis. Commun. ACM **65**(1), 99–106 (2021)
2. Jiang, H., et al.: Inpaint4DNeRF: promptable spatio-temporal NeRF inpainting with generative diffusion models. arXiv preprint arXiv:2401.00208 (2023)
3. Tretschk, E., et al.: Non-rigid neural radiance fields: Reconstruction and novel view synthesis of a dynamic scene from monocular video. In: Proceedings of the IEEE/CVF International Conference on Computer Vision (2021)
4. Gao, C., et al.: Dynamic view synthesis from dynamic monocular video. In: Proceedings of the IEEE/CVF International Conference on Computer Vision (2021)
5. Park, K., et al.: HyperNeRF: a higher-dimensional representation for topologically varying neural radiance fields. arXiv preprint arXiv:2106.13228 (2021)
6. Park, K., et al.: Nerfies: deformable neural radiance fields. In: Proceedings of the IEEE/CVF International Conference on Computer Vision (2021)
7. Liu, Y., et al.: Neural rays for occlusion-aware image-based rendering. In: Proceedings of the IEEE/CVF Conference on Computer Vision and Pattern Recognition (2022)
8. Li, Z., et al.: Neural scene flow fields for space-time view synthesis of dynamic scenes. In: Proceedings of the IEEE/CVF Conference on Computer Vision and Pattern Recognition (2021)
9. Gao, H., et al.: Monocular dynamic view synthesis: a reality check. Adv. Neural. Inf. Process. Syst. **35**, 33768–33780 (2022)
10. Liu, L., et al.: Neural sparse voxel fields. Adv. Neural. Inf. Process. Syst. **33**, 15651–15663 (2020)
11. Wu, T., et al.: D^ 2nerf: Self-supervised decoupling of dynamic and static objects from a monocular video. Adv. Neural. Inf. Process. Syst. **35**, 32653–32666 (2022)
12. Yu, A., Ye, V., Tancik, M., et al.: pixelNeRF: neural radiance fields from one or few images. In: Proceedings of the IEEE/CVF Conference on Computer Vision and Pattern Recognition, pp. 4578–4587 (2021)
13. Barron, J.T., et al.: Mip-NeRF: a multiscale representation for anti-aliasing neural radiance fields. In: Proceedings of the IEEE/CVF International Conference on Computer Vision (2021)
14. Yang, C., Lamdouar, H., Lu, E., et al.: Self-supervised video object segmentation by motion grouping. In: Proceedings of the IEEE/CVF International Conference on Computer Vision, pp. 7177–7188 (2021)
15. Li, Z., et al.: DynIBaR: neural dynamic image-based rendering. In: Proceedings of the IEEE/CVF Conference on Computer Vision and Pattern Recognition (2023)
16. Alfonso-Arsuaga, M., García-González, J., Castiella-Aguirrezabala, A., et al.: DyNeRFactor: temporally consistent intrinsic scene decomposition for dynamic NeRFs. Comput. Graph. **122**, 103984 (2024)
17. Zhao, Y., Park, I.M.: Interpretable nonlinear dynamic modeling of neural trajectories. Adv. Neural Inf. Process. Syst. **29** (2016)

18. Xian, W., et al.: Space-time neural irradiance fields for free-viewpoint video. In: Proceedings of the IEEE/CVF Conference on Computer Vision and Pattern Recognition (2021)
19. Lin, Y.: Ced-NeRF: a compact and efficient method for dynamic neural radiance fields. In: Proceedings of the AAAI Conference on Artificial Intelligence (2024)
20. Robert, A.D., Loren, C., Pat, H.: Volume rendering. Comput. Graph. **22**(4), 65–74 (1988)
21. Kopf, J., et al.: Image-based rendering in the gradient domain. ACM Trans. Graph. (TOG) **32**(6), 1–9 (2013)
22. Masuda, M., Sekikawa, Y., Saito, H.: Event-based camera tracker by $\nabla$ t nerf. IEEE Access **11**, 96626–96635 (2023)
23. Martin-Brualla, R., et al.: NeRF in the wild: neural radiance fields for unconstrained photo collections. In: Proceedings of the IEEE/CVF Conference on Computer Vision and Pattern Recognition (2021)
24. Lin, C.H., Ma, W.C., Torralba, A., et al.: BARF: Bundle-adjusting neural radiance fields. In: Proceedings of the IEEE/CVF International Conference on Computer Vision, 5741–5751 (2021)
25. Chen, Q., et al.: Dynamic three-dimensional reconstruction of soft tissue in neural radiation field for robotic surgery simulators. Acta Optica Sin. **44**(7), 0733001 (2024)
26. Sun, S.-H., et al. Multi-view to novel view: synthesizing novel views with self-learned confidence. In: Proceedings of the European Conference on Computer Vision (ECCV) (2018)

# Mamba Model Based on GloVe Word Embedding for Sentiment Analysis

Liepan Yu(iD), Jiawei Zhu$^{(\boxtimes)}$(iD), and Zhonglun Wei$^{(\boxtimes)}$(iD)

City University of Macau, Macau 999078, China
{cwchu,chunglunwei}@cityu.edu.mo

**Abstract.** Sentiment analysis determines people's perceptions of various events by employing natural language processing techniques. Advances in machine learning and deep learning have made it possible to determine emotional tendencies more accurately. Nevertheless, RNN cannot capture long-term dependencies in text, LSTM can only unidirectionally extract contextual information in text, and the training of Transformer requires a lot of computational resources. Also in specific domains will be confronted with specific vocabularies, the processing of these vocabularies directly affects the final classification performance. In this paper, we propose a new GloVe-based Mamba model that combines the advantages of GloVe word embeddings and Mamba networks. First, the model adds specific words to Jieba for segmentation in the data preprocessing stage to make the segmentation results more accurate. Second, the model combines GloVe word embeddings to extract textual contextual information and solve the problem of lack of semantic information. In addition, the Mamba network is utilized to selectively process the input information to improve the accuracy and computational efficiency of Chinese text sentiment polarity classification.

**Keywords:** data preprocessing · GloVe · Mamba · Chinese text · sentiment analysis

## 1 Introduction

The development of Internet technology has provided a solid foundation for people to use social media to express their views. Social media generates a large amount of opinion data. By analyzing and mining the views on specific topics implicit in these data, it is possible to understand public opinion trends in a timely and accurate manner, which is conducive to decision-making by governments, enterprises and various organizations. Textual sentiment analysis is the process of collecting and analyzing people's opinions, thoughts and impressions about various events [1]. Text Sentiment Analysis is a subfield of Natural Language Processing. Compared to other data, the most important characteristic of text data is that it is unstructured, which means that computers cannot directly extract semantic information from it. In order to solve this problem, a framework for computational processing of unstructured data was proposed by researchers in 2000 to extract viewpoints [2]. With the development of machine learning makes some


T. Zhu et al. (Eds.): KSEM 2025, LNAI 15919, pp. 131–143, 2026.
https://doi.org/10.1007/978-981-95-3001-4_10

researchers begin to use machine learning algorithms to analyze social media comments [3]. With the rapid development of deep learning, sentiment analysis using deep learning algorithms came into the limelight. Researchers have proposed the use of Recurrent Neuron Network (RNN), Long Short-Term Memory (LSTM) and other methods to analyze textual emotions [4]. The rise of Transformer in recent years has brought various kinds of large language models, which provide another possibility for text sentiment analysis. In order to solve the problem of Transformer's computational inefficiency on long sequences, researchers have recently proposed a new model, Mamba [5]. Mamba is based on the classical state space model SSM (State Space Model), combined with Transformer's MLP (Multilayer Perceptron) blocks to form a new architecture. This results in a new model that possesses the comparable modeling power of Transformer while remaining nearly linearly scalable in terms of sequence length [6]. Compared with traditional machine learning algorithms and deep learning algorithms, Mamba improves the accuracy while solving the problem of computational inefficiency of previous models [5].

In this paper, a new Mamba network based on GloVe word embedding is proposed to analyze the sentiment tendency of Chinese text, capture important semantic information inside the text, and improve the accuracy of sentiment analysis of Chinese text. First, the text is converted into word vectors using word embedding methods to extract the important semantic information in the text. Then the word vectors are fed into the Mamba layer for sentiment analysis based on the extracted features. In this paper, some proper nouns are added to the lexicon to preprocess the data, while the model combines the advantages of GloVe word embedding and Mamba to improve the accuracy and computational efficiency of Chinese text sentiment analysis.

## 2  Related Work

### 2.1  Word Embedding

In the field of computer vision, data in picture format can be directly represented as a matrix of numerical type in a computer. However, most of the data in natural language processing tasks are in text format, and machine learning and deep learning models cannot process text data directly. Therefore, text data need to be converted into numerical vectors that contain rich semantic information. Hinton [7] utilized representation learning to map each word from a discrete numerical space to a continuous high-dimensional feature space, and proposed a distributed representation of words containing rich feature information also known as word vectors. In natural language processing tasks, word embeddings convert input text into computer-processable numeric vectors rich in semantic information.

Since the 1980s, N-gram modeling has been the dominant method for word embedding [8]. One-hot vectors are used as the vector representation of each word and the word with the highest probability of occurrence in the next position is predicted based on the context. However, the use of one-hot vectors leads to too many zero elements in the vectors, which makes it difficult to capture valid information and measure the degree of similarity between words [9]. So the researchers proposed a static word embedding method based on matrix decomposition. The researchers create word and word or word and document co-occurrence matrix, then use matrix decomposition to decompose the co-occurrence matrix into feature matrix and orthogonal matrix, and finally normalize the orthogonal matrix to generate low-dimensional dense word vectors [9]. DEERWESTER S [10] proposed the LSA word embedding method, which utilized the idea that words with similar meanings always co-occur in articles to construct a word-document co-occurrence matrix, and performed normalization operations and singular value decomposition on the co-occurrence matrix to mine the potential semantic information of words. In 2013 Mikolov [11] proposed a Word2Vec word embedding model based on context window for training word vectors, where CBOW model and Skip-Gram model are the two generative approaches of this method. They believe that words that are closer to the center word are more relevant to the center word and provide more useful information. Therefore, the CBOW model was used to predict the center word based on its context and the Skip-Gram model was used to predict the center word context based on the center word. However, the method only considers the effect between k words in the context window. Pennington [12] in 2014 proposed a static word embedding method based on global matrix decomposition and local context window, that is, a global vector representation of the word, which captures the global word frequency information and local context information of the vocabulary through global matrix decomposition and local context window.

## 2.2 Sentiment Analysis

As the informatization of all aspects of society generates massive amounts of text data, how to efficiently mine the emotional tendency of text from unstructured and informative user review data is important for governments, enterprises and various organizations to make accurate decisions [13]. The wide application of machine learning algorithms provides an idea for text sentiment analysis. Bahdanau [14] extracts text lexical and positional relationships as text features, assigns different weights to the extracted feature words based on Boolean weights, and performs sentiment categorization based on the different weights of the feature words using the plain Bayesian algorithm. Gautam [15] also utilizes machine learning algorithms such as maximum entropy and support vector machines to further improve the accuracy of sentiment classification. Sentiment analysis based on machine learning algorithms is more accurate than traditional lexicon-based methods, but in the face of large and complex textual data, more accurate results cannot be obtained once textual sentiment features cannot be selected with high quality.

The rapid development of deep learning algorithms has made it possible for researchers to utilize deep learning algorithms for sentiment analysis. Cho [16] utilized word vectors to represent the features of the text and used Recurrent Neural Network model based on word vectors for sentiment analysis of the text. However, due to the difficulty of RNN in capturing long-term dependencies when dealing with long texts, Cahuantzi [17] proposed the LSTM model to deal with high complexity texts. Meanwhile, in order to better combine the context to get the hidden representation between the words in the context, Kitaev [18] proposed the Bi-directional Long Short-Term Memory (Bi-LSTM) model, which can extract text features from vectorized text, use the self-attention mechanism to dynamically adjust the text features' weights, and finally the softmax classifier is utilized for text sentiment categorization. Bi-LSTM greatly improved the accuracy of text sentiment analysis compared to other methods, but the advent of Transformer revolutionized the natural language processing task [19]. Gao Jiaxi [20] deleted the deactivated words and the proper nouns that have less influence on the emotional tendency of the text in the text preprocessing stage, and used the TF-IDF algorithm for feature extraction to filter out the words that have a greater influence on the emotional tendency of the text, and then based on the extracted features, used the Transformer model encoder to capture the important semantic information within the text, and improved the model's analysis of the semantics and the ability to generalize. The application of Transformer has led to a substantial improvement in the accuracy of textual sentiment analysis, but it often requires a large number of model parameters when dealing with massive and complex data [21]. In addition, Transformer is able to process complex data because its core attention layer self-attention mechanism is able to densely route information in a context window, but is unable to process any information that lies outside of a finite window [22]. To address these issues recently researchers have proposed a new model, Mamba.

## 3   Proposed Architecture

In this paper, we will propose a new Mamba model based on GloVe word embedding to analyze the sentiment tendency of Douban movie reviews, based on the foundation of previous research in text sentiment analysis and the latest proposed model. The model is able to capture the important semantic information inside the text and improve the accuracy and computational efficiency of the sentiment analysis of Chinese text. The model framework is shown in Fig. 1.

In this paper, we will pre-process the Douban movie review data by removing stop words, deleting missing values and split words. Then the GloVe word embedding method is utilized to extract information from the preprocessed data to obtain the word embedding matrix. Finally, the word embedding matrix is input to the Mamba layer for sentiment analysis. The sections are described in detail below.

### 3.1   Data Preprocessor

Preprocessing is a key step in making text easier to understand by removing meaningless phrases, noise, and unnecessary repetition, and an important prerequisite for accurate results to be obtained from later models. In this paper, we first deal with the missing values in the Douban movie review data, treat each Douban movie review as a string, and replace the missing values with empty strings to facilitate subsequent processing. Then remove the HTML tags in the text, convert uppercase to lowercase in the text, then remove special characters and numbers in the text, retain only Chinese characters and English letters, delete spaces in the text and the data that the user only rated without commenting. In addition, stop words need to be removed from the text. Stop words are words that appear too often in the text and have little information content, such as the words " 的 " and " 吗 ". For the processing of deactivated words, first you need to load the list of deactivated words, remove the spaces before and after each word, convert the list of deactivated words into a set and then de-emphasize it, and then convert it into

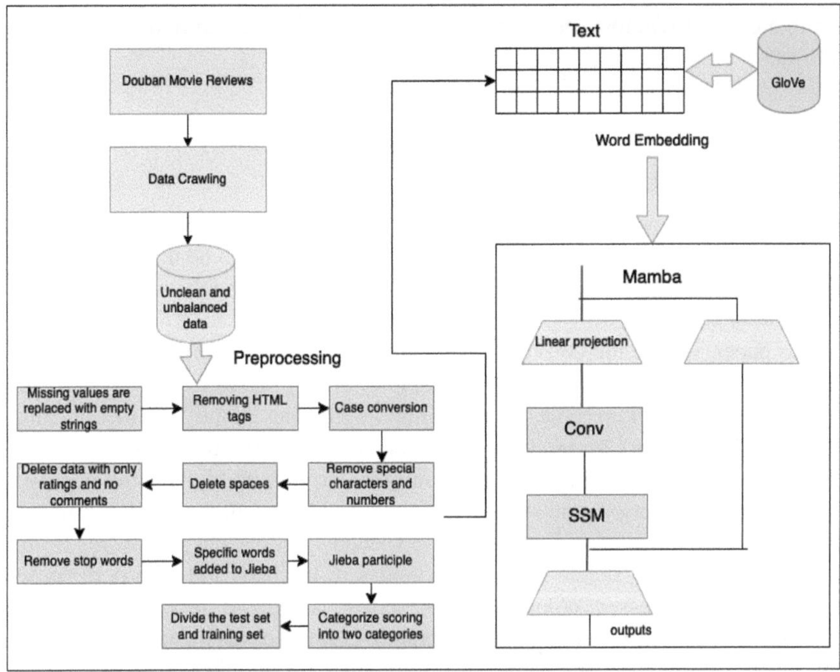

**Fig. 1.** Model architecture.

a list to be applied to all the text. Finally, using Jieba to segment the Douban movie review data. Because there are specific words in movie reviews, such as the names of the main characters in The Avengers, "钢铁侠," "美国队长," "绿巨人," and so on. Therefore, these specific words need to be added to Jieba to get more accurate results and improve the accuracy of subsequent text sentiment analysis. Because Douban movie ratings range from 1 to 5, in order to better categorize movie reviews, it is stipulated that a score of 1 to 2 is a bad review and a score of 3 to 5 is a good review, and then the scores are converted to 0 and 1, with 0 being a bad review and 1 being a good review. At the same time, the test set and training set are divided in a ratio of 1:9 to prepare the text for training.

## 3.2   Word Vector Representation

GloVe is a word representation based on word2vec,and this method can effectively learn to obtain word vectors from text documents [23]. The method captures the global information and local context information of a vocabulary by introducing both a global matrix decomposition and a local context window. GloVe first constructs a global word frequency co-occurrence matrix $X$ based on the entire corpus, where $X_i$ denotes the number of times the word $w_i$ occurs in the corpus, and $X_{ij}$ denotes the number of times the word $w_j$ occursin the contextual window of the word $w_i$. GloVe constructs the relationship between words $w_i$, $w_j$, and $w_k$ using $\frac{P_{ik}}{P_{jk}}$, where $P_{ij}$ denotes the probability that word $w_j$

occurs in a context window for word $w_i$. The loss function of GloVe during training is as follows:

$$Loss = \sum_{i,j=1}^{V} f\left(X_{ij}\right)\left(v_i^\top \widetilde{v_j} + b_i + \widetilde{b_j} - \log X_{ij}\right)^2 \tag{1}$$

Where $v_i$ denotes the word vector of the word $w_i$, f $(x)$ denotes the weight function of the word, and $b_i$ denotes the bias vector. The loss function needs to be minimized in order to bring the words with stronger associations closer together and the weaker associated words further apart.

In this paper, we use the GloVe word embedding model to embed the words in each input sentence into an embedding lookup table to obtain the word embedding matrix, and the embedding lookup table used is trained according to the Wikimedia Chinese Corpus. The Wikimedia Chinese Corpus covers a large number of topics in a variety of domains, and the texts have been reviewed and proofread, with high overall quality and rich contextual information, and are therefore selected for training the GloVe model. In the training process, it is necessary to remove special symbols and stop words from the Wikipedia Chinese text, delete irrelevant contents in the text, and then perform word splitting. The preprocessed Wikipedia Chinese text is utilized to train Chinese word vectors using the official GloVe code, thus obtaining the Chinese GloVe word embedding model. The preprocessed Douban movie reviews are input into the Chinese GloVe word embedding model to extract the text context information to get the word embedding matrix, and then the word embedding matrix is input into the Mamba layer to analyze the emotional tendency of the context through the SSM architecture and hardware-aware algorithm.

### 3.3　GloVe-Based Mamba Layer

The word embedding matrix obtained through GloVe is fed into the Mamba network, which is merged into a new Mamba block using the architecture of SSM and the MLP block of Transformer to simplify the deep learning model architecture, and multiple repetitions of the Mamba block constitute the Mamba architecture. As shown in Fig. 2, Mamba adds the SSM architecture to the main branch of the MLP and simplifies the H3 block by replacing the first multiplication gate in the H3 block with an activation function. Mamba selectively processes the input information through parameterized SSM inputs, focusing on important information and filtering irrelevant information, while using hardware-aware algorithms to complete parallel computation of the model, which greatly improves the computational efficiency of the model.

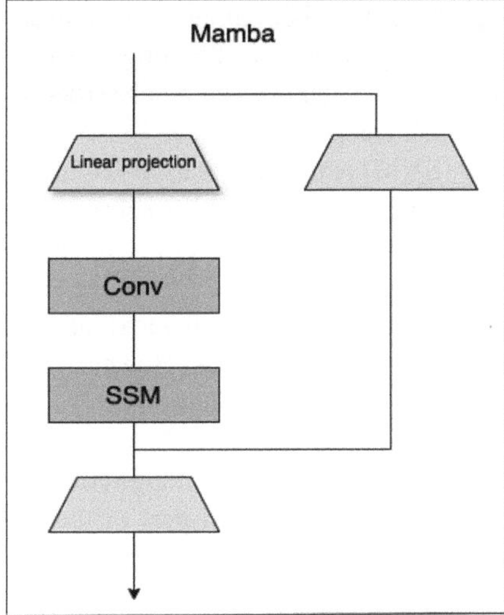


**Fig. 2.** Mamba architecture.

## 4   Experiments and Analysis

### 4.1   Datasets

The data for this article comes from the Kaggle Douban Movie Reviews dataset. Douban Movie is one of the important boards, which contains the latest movie introduction, movie news inquiry and ticket purchase service, while users can rate and write movie reviews for movies. By the end of 2019, Douban Movie had more than 200 million registered users and more than 400 million monthly active users, and has become China's current online movie rating platform with the widest coverage and highest participation. Therefore, this paper selected the Douban movie reviews to carry out sentiment analysis.

The Douban Movie Reviews dataset has a total of 1048574 review data for movies released in January 2017, such as The Avengers 2, Begonia, Lost in Thailand, and Charlotte's Trouble. Each data entry contains movie ID, English and Chinese name, release date, star rating and movie review. In order to analyze the proposed model more quickly and conveniently, the first 20,000 data in the dataset are selected for processing in this paper. At the same time, only Movie ID, Movie Review and Star Rating are retained.

### 4.2   Model Variation and Baseline Method

In order to better reflect the superiority of the proposed model, this paper will use the baseline model comparison method for analysis. After preprocessing the data and GloVe word embedding to get the word embedding matrix, the word embedding matrix will be combined with the following method for the judgment of emotional tendency, and the experimental results obtained will be compared with the proposed model.

The Naive Bayes (NB) algorithm is based on statistics and assumes that the data categories are independent of each other and do not influence each other. The algorithm first calculates the a priori probability of belonging to a certain category, then uses Bayes' theorem to calculate its posterior probability of belonging to this category, and the size of the posterior probability of each category can be classified by comparing the size of the posterior probability of each category [24].

Support vector machine (SVM) is the best margin-based classification technique in machine learning algorithms, and the main goal is to classify data into different classes of hyperplanes, which has been developed as an effective classification paradigm.

RNN models, in order to understand the structure of the text as well as to capture the semantic information in the text, usually convert the text into a sequence of words while extracting the dependencies between the words. However, RNN models suffer from gradient loss and explosion problems during iteration, resulting in poor classification accuracy [25].

LSTM is an algorithm proposed to solve the long-term memory and gradient vanishing problems in RNNs. The most important part of the model is the gate control mechanism. The gate control mechanism of LSTM consists of three control gates: an input gate, an output gate and an oblivion gate [26].

GRU is a variant of LSTM, which simplifies the internal structure of LSTM. The gate control mechanism of LSTM consists of three control gates, whereas that of GRU consists of two control gates, namely, the reset gate and the update gate, while the output of the GRU algorithm removes the second-order nonlinear function.

Bi-LSTM is a proposed algorithm based on LSTM. Bi-LSTM is implemented to extract contextual information from back to front and is able to capture bi-directional contextual dependencies [27].

Transformer is a deep learning model based on self-attention mechanism. The model captures the dependencies in the text through the self-attention mechanism, but when facing a huge amount of text, the computational volume is too large which leads to its computational inefficiency.

### 4.3  Assessment Indicators

In this paper, the accuracy rate will be used as the evaluation index of the model, and its calculation formula is shown below:

$$\text{Accuracy} = \frac{\text{TP} + \text{TN}}{\text{TP} + \text{TN} + \text{FP} + \text{FN}} \tag{2}$$

Where *TP* denotes the number of samples correctly predicted by the model to be in the positive category, *TN* denotes the number of samples correctly predicted by the model to be in the negative category, *FP* denotes the number of samples incorrectly predicted by the model to be in the positive category, and *FN* denotes the number of samples incorrectly predicted by the model to be in the negative category.

### 4.4  Results and Analysis

Figure 3 shows the segmentation results obtained without adding specific words to Jieba, and Fig. 4 shows the segmentation results obtained by adding specific words to Jieba.

It can be found that adding specific words to Jieba can make the result more accurate, which is convenient for extracting contextual information and judging the emotional tendency of the text by using word embedding method.

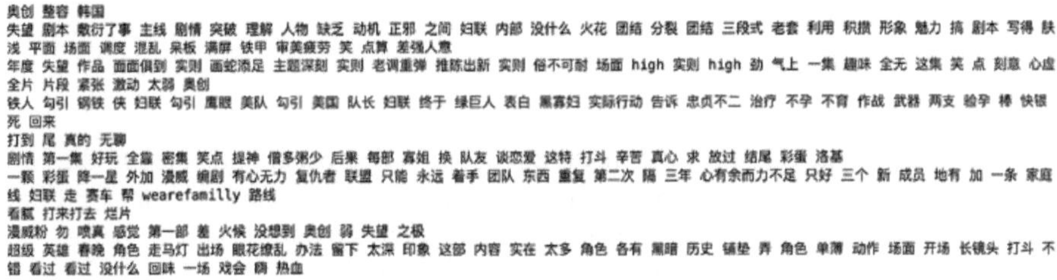

奥创 整容 韩国
失望 剧本 敷衍了事 主线 剧情 突破 理解 人物 缺乏 动机 正邪 之间 妇联 内部 没什么 火花 团结 分裂 团结 三段式 老套 利用 积损 形象 魅力 搞 剧本 写得 肤浅 平面 场面 调度 混乱 呆板 满屏 铁甲 审美疲劳 笑 点算 差强人意
年度 失望 作品 面面俱到 实则 画蛇添足 主题深刻 实则 老调重弹 推陈出新 实则 俗不可耐 场面 high 实则 high 劲 气上 一集 趣味 全无 这集 笑 点 刻意 心虚 全片 片段 紧张 激动 太弱 奥创
铁人 勾引 钢铁 侠 妇联 勾引 鹰眼 美队 勾引 美国 队长 妇联 终于 绿巨人 表白 黑寡妇 实际行动 告诉 忠贞不二 治疗 不孕 不育 作战 武器 两支 验孕 棒 快银 死 回来
打到 尾 真的 无聊
剧情 第一集 好玩 全靠 密集 笑点 提神 僧多粥少 后果 每部 寡姐 换 队友 谈恋爱 这特 打斗 辛苦 真心 求 放过 结尾 彩蛋 洛基
一颗 彩蛋 降一星 外加 漫威 编剧 有心无力 复仇者 联盟 只能 永远 着手 团队 东西 重复 第二次 隔 三年 心有余而力不足 只好 三个 新 成员 地有 加 一条 家庭 线 妇联 走 赛车 帮 wearefamilly 路线
看腻 打来打去 烂片
漫威粉 勿 喷真 感觉 第一部 差 火候 没想到 奥创 弱 失望 之极
超级 英雄 春晚 角色 走马灯 出场 眼花缭乱 办法 留下 太深 印象 这部 内容 实在 太多 角色 各有 黑暗 历史 铺垫 弄 角色 单薄 动作 场面 开场 长镜头 打斗 不错 看过 看过 没什么 回味 一场 戏会 隔 热血

**Fig. 3.** Segmentation Results without Adding Specific Words.

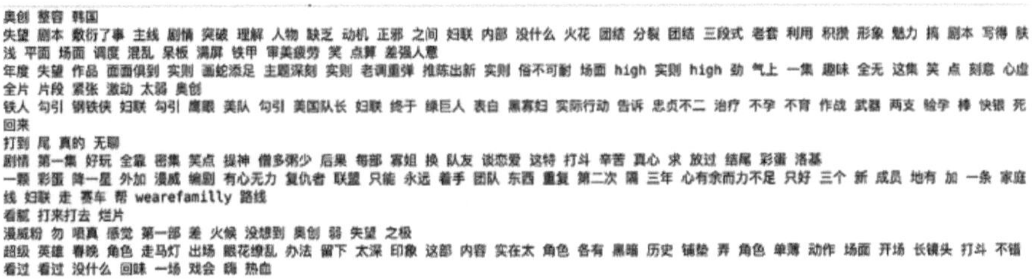

奥创 整容 韩国
失望 剧本 敷衍了事 主线 剧情 突破 理解 人物 缺乏 动机 正邪 之间 妇联 内部 没什么 火花 团结 分裂 团结 三段式 老套 利用 积损 形象 魅力 搞 剧本 写得 肤浅 平面 场面 调度 混乱 呆板 满屏 铁甲 审美疲劳 笑 点算 差强人意
年度 失望 作品 面面俱到 实则 画蛇添足 主题深刻 实则 老调重弹 推陈出新 实则 俗不可耐 场面 high 实则 high 劲 气上 一集 趣味 全无 这集 笑 点 刻意 心虚 全片 片段 紧张 激动 太弱 奥创
铁人 勾引 钢铁侠 妇联 勾引 鹰眼 美队 勾引 美国队长 妇联 终于 绿巨人 表白 黑寡妇 实际行动 告诉 忠贞不二 治疗 不孕 不育 作战 武器 两支 验孕 棒 快银 死 回来
打到 尾 真的 无聊
剧情 第一集 好玩 全靠 密集 笑点 提神 僧多粥少 后果 每部 寡姐 换 队友 谈恋爱 这特 打斗 辛苦 真心 求 放过 结尾 彩蛋 洛基
一颗 彩蛋 降一星 外加 漫威 编剧 有心无力 复仇者 联盟 只能 永远 着手 团队 东西 重复 第二次 隔 三年 心有余而力不足 只好 三个 新 成员 地有 加 一条 家庭 线 妇联 走 赛车 帮 wearefamilly 路线
看腻 打来打去 烂片
漫威粉 勿 喷真 感觉 第一部 差 火候 没想到 奥创 弱 失望 之极
超级 英雄 春晚 角色 走马灯 出场 眼花缭乱 办法 留下 太深 印象 这部 内容 实在太 角色 各有 黑暗 历史 铺垫 弄 角色 单薄 动作 场面 开场 长镜头 打斗 不错 看过 看过 没什么 回味 一场 戏会 隔 热血

**Fig. 4.** Segmentation Results with Adding Specific Words.

Table 1 shows the results of the models proposed in this paper compared to a single model. These models obtained accuracies ranging from 58.90% to 86.26%. The lowest accuracy rate is obtained by NB and the highest accuracy rate is obtained by the model proposed in this paper. The models have machine learning algorithms Naive Bayes and SVM, and deep learning algorithms RNN, LSTM, GRU, Bi-LSTM, and Transformer, which indicates that among these algorithms the model proposed in this paper is the most accurate in determining the sentiment tendency of Douban movie reviews.

**Table 1.** Research Model vs. Baseline Model Comparison Chart.

| Models | Accuracy |
| --- | --- |
| NB | 0.5890 |
| SVM | 0.6340 |
| RNN | 0.7916 |
| LSTM | 0.8340 |
| GRU | 0.8365 |

*(continued)*

**Table 1.** (*continued*)

| Models | Accuracy |
| --- | --- |
| Bi-LSTM | 0.8438 |
| Transformer | 0.8005 |
| Our model | 0.8626 |

Table 2 shows the results of the model proposed in this paper compared to the two models combined to form the model. These models obtained accuracies ranging from 80.90% to 86.26%. Among them, RNN+Bi-LSTM obtains the lowest accuracy and the model proposed in this paper has the highest accuracy. Using a combination of two deep learning algorithms to process Douban movie review data, RNN and CNN can further extract high-level features from the contextual information extracted by GloVe, and then input them into the Bi-LSTM layer for sentiment analysis in combination with context, but the accuracy of the classification results is still insufficient when compared with the model in this paper.

**Table 2.** Research Model vs. Composite Model Comparison Chart.

| Models | Accuracy |
| --- | --- |
| RNN+Bi-LSTM | 0.8090 |
| CNN+Bi-LSTM | 0.8328 |
| Our model | 0.8626 |

Table 3 adds the attention mechanism to Table 2 and shows the results of comparing the models proposed in this paper with the models that add the attention mechanism. These models obtained accuracies ranging from 80.48% to 86.26%. The lowest accuracy is obtained by CNN+Transformer and the highest accuracy is obtained by the model proposed in this paper. The attention mechanism gives proper attention to the high-level features extracted by RNN and CNN, which is beneficial to the later models for sentiment analysis, but the accuracy of the classification results of the models with the added attention mechanism is still insufficient when compared with the models in this paper.

**Table 3.** Research Model vs. Attention-Enhanced Model Comparison Chart.

| Models | Accuracy |
| --- | --- |
| Attention+CNN+Bi-LSTM | 0.8348 |
| Attention+RNN+Bi-LSTM | 0.8623 |
| RNN+Transformer | 0.8075 |

*(continued)*

Table 3. (continued)

| Models | Accuracy |
| --- | --- |
| CNN+Transformer | 0.8048 |
| Our model | 0.8626 |

From Table 3, it can be noticed that the accuracy obtained by Attention+RNN+Bi-LSTM is not much different from that of the model proposed in this paper, but the running time required by both of them is very much different (the running time is defined as the time required to get the result from the input of the word embedding matrix to the subsequent model on the same hardware facility). Table 4 demonstrates the runtime of the Attention+RNN+Bi-LSTM model and the model proposed in this paper. The running time of the Attention+RNN+Bi-LSTM model is more than seventy times than the running time of the model proposed in this paper, indicating that the computational efficiency of the model proposed in this paper is better.

Table 4. Research Model vs. Highest Accuracy Model Comparison Chart.

| Models | Time (second) |
| --- | --- |
| Attention+RNN+Bi-LSTM | 1108 |
| Our model | 15 |

## 5  Conclusions

In this paper, a new GloVe-based Mamba model is proposed to analyze the sentiment tendency of Chinese text to improve the accuracy and computational efficiency of sentiment analysis of Chinese text. The model adds specific words to Jieba in the data preprocessing stage for segmentation, making the segmentation results more accurate. It is also combined with GloVe word embedding to extract text context information and solve the problem of lack of semantic information. In addition, the Mamba network is utilized to selectively process the input information to improve the accuracy and computational efficiency of Chinese text sentiment polarity classification. In this paper, experiments are conducted on Douban movie review data to analyze the performance of the proposed model. Machine learning and deep learning models are also used to compare with the model proposed in this paper in terms of accuracy and computational efficiency. The model proposed in this paper achieves 86.26% accuracy, which is the best among all the models. In the future, efforts are made to extend the model proposed in this paper to other languages.

# References


1. Wankhade, M., Rao, A.C.S., Kulkarni, C.: A survey on sentiment analysis methods, applications, and challenges. Artif. Intell. Rev. **55**(7), 5731–5780 (2022)
2. Piryani, R., Madhavi, D., Singh, V.K.: Analytical mapping of opinion mining and sentiment analysis research during 2000–2015. Inf. Process. Manag. **53**(1), 122–150 (2017)
3. Mullah, N.S., Zainon, W.M.N.W.: Advances in machine learning algorithms for hate speech detection in social media: a review. IEEE Access **9**, 88364–88376 (2021)
4. 曾子明, 万品玉: 基于双层注意力和 Bi-LSTM. 的公共安全事件微博情感分析. 情报科学**37**(6), 23–29 (2019)
5. Gu, A., Dao, T.: Mamba: linear-time sequence modeling with selective state spaces. arXiv preprint arXiv:2312.00752 (2023)
6. Qu, H., Ning, L.: A survey of mamba. arXiv preprint arXiv:2408.01129 (2024)
7. Hinton, G.E.: Learning distributed representations of concepts. In: Proceedings of the Annual Meeting of the Cognitive Science Society, vol. 8 (1986)
8. Katz, S.: Estimation of probabilities from sparse data for the language model component of a speech recognizer. IEEE Trans. Acoust. Speech Signal Process. **35**(3), 400–401 (2003)
9. 曾骏, 王子威: 自然语言处理领域中的词嵌入方法综述. J. Front. Comput. Sci. Technol. **18**(1) (2024)
10. Deerwester, S., Harshman, R.: Indexing by latent semantic analysis. J. Am. Soc. Inf. Sci. **41**(6), 391–407 (1990)
11. Mikolov, T., Sutskever, I.: Distributed representations of words and phrases and their compositionality. In: Advances in Neural Information Processing Systems, vol. 26 (2013)
12. Pennington, J., Socher, R., Manning, C.D.: Glove: Global vectors for word representation. In: Proceedings of the 2014 Conference on Empirical Methods in Natural Language Processing (EMNLP), pp. 1532–1543, October 2014
13. Li, Z., Guo, Q.: Multimodal sentiment analysis based on interactive transformer and soft mapping. Wirel. Commun. Mob. Comput. **2022**(1), 6243347 (2022)
14. Bahdanau, D., Cho, K., Bengio, Y.: Neural machine translation by jointly learning to align and translate. arXiv preprint arXiv:1409.0473 (2014)
15. Gautam, G., Yadav, D.: Sentiment analysis of twitter data using machine learning approaches and semantic analysis. In: 2014 Seventh International Conference on Contemporary Computing (IC3), pp. 437–442. IEEE, August 2014
16. Cho, K., Van Merriënboer, B.: Learning phrase representations using RNN encoder-decoder for statistical machine translation. arXiv preprint arXiv:1406.1078 (2014)
17. Cahuantzi, R., Chen, X., Güttel, S.: A comparison of LSTM and GRU networks for learning symbolic sequences. In: Arai, K. (ed.) SAI 2023. LNNS, vol. 739, pp. 771–785. Springer, Cham (2023). https://doi.org/10.1007/978-3-031-37963-5_53
18. Kitaev, N., Kaiser, Ł., Levskaya, A.: Reformer: the efficient transformer. arXiv preprint arXiv: 2001.04451 (2020)
19. Peng, B., Alcaide, E., Anthony, Q.: RWKV: reinventing RNNs for the transformer era. arXiv preprint arXiv:2305.13048 (2023)
20. 高佳希, 黄海燕: 基于TF-IDF 和多头注意力Transformer 模型的文本情感分析. J. East China Univ. Sci. Technol. **50**(1) (2024)
21. 鞠天杰, 刘功申, 张茹: 自然语言处理中的探寻问解释方法综述. 计算机学报**47**(4), 733–758 (2024)
22. Vaswani, A., Shazeer, N.: Attention is all you need. In: Advances in Neural Information Processing Systems, vol. 30 (2017)
23. Yu, L.C., Wang, J., Lai, K.R., Zhang, X.: Refining word embeddings using intensity scores for sentiment analysis. IEEE/ACM Trans. Audio Speech Lang. Process. **26**(3), 671–681 (2017)

24. 许丽，焦博：赵章瑞TF-IDF *基于TF-IDF 的加权朴素贝叶斯新闻文本分类算法*. 网络安全技术与应用**11**, 31–33 (2021)
25. Fu, T., Liu, H.: Research on Chinese text classification based on improved RNN. In: 2023 IEEE 3rd International Conference on Electronic Technology, Communication and Information (ICETCI), pp. 1554–1558). IEEE, May 2023
26. Zaheer, S., Anjum, N.: A multi parameter forecasting for stock time series data using LSTM and deep learning model. Mathematics **11**(3), 590 (2023)
27. 张卫娜: *结合*Bert 与Bi-LSTM *的英文文本分类模型*. 计算机测量与控制**31**(4), 213–218 (2023)

# DKCER-Agent: Lightweight and Efficient KNN-Enhanced Dynamic Context Optimization for Stepwise Retrieval Augmented Generation


Xueying Liu[1,2,3], Jing Yun[1,3(✉)], Bo li[1], Yuying Zhang[1], and Xiaoguo Shi[1]

[1] School of Data Science and Application, Inner Mongolia University of Technology, Hohhot, China
`yunjing_zoe@163.com`, `20221800745@imut.edu.cn`
[2] Inner Mongolia Engineering Research Center for Cloud Computing Software Services, Hohhot, China
[3] Inner Mongolia Key Laboratory of Beijiang Cyberspace Security, Huhhot, China



**Abstract.** Large Language Models(LLMs)-driven Artificial Intelligence (AI) Agent provide conversational generation AI with human-like decision making and reasoning capabilities and extend them to Retrieval Augmented Generation (RAG) external knowledge base tools. However, the existing research focuses on knowledge coverage, ignores the problem of redundant knowledge accumulation, and fails to take into account the interpretability of LLMs, which limits the application value. In this paper, a dynamic and stepwise enhanced KNN framework, DKCER-Agent, is proposed. The framework effectively reduces redundant information through multi-round dynamic reasoning and gradually queries and generates optimal answers. The redundant information is filtered by the joint retrieval mechanism, and the key information is cleared and filtered by KNN retrieval. In addition, the framework introduces a step-by-step thinking revision mechanism to decompose the problem into sub-problems, which are verified and generated by the LLMs generation strategy, thus enhancing the interpretability of the model. The experimental results show that DKCER-Agent significantly exceeds the baseline model in a wide range of multi-round dialogue dataset tests, and the accuracy is significantly improved.

**Keywords:** Agent · LLMs · RAG · Step-by-step thinking · Retrieval Screen · Dynamic context


## 1 Introduction

Large Language Models (LLMs) -driven Agents [15] have been widely used in complex conversational tasks [7], and these Agents have demonstrated strong capabilities in planning, reasoning, and memory. As an effective tool for retrieving knowledge from external memory, Retrieval Augmented Generation (RAG)



T. Zhu et al. (Eds.): KSEM 2025, LNAI 15919, pp. 144–156, 2026.
https://doi.org/10.1007/978-981-95-3001-4_11

[11] is regarded as a simplified form of agent that allows agents to excel in reasoning tasks. During retrieval, the presence of redundant information affects the accuracy of retrieval, causing the agent to struggle to generate accurate answers in a single reasoning attempt [26]. Although the application of cue engineering can visualise intermediate steps to improve model transparency and robustness, there are still limitations in the interpretability of large models [18].

In recent years, researchers have focused on enhancing the performance of LLMs in downstream tasks using RAG. Agents endowed with memory components have been shown to enhance session effectiveness by optimising retrieval and reasoning mechanisms [2]. Melz et al. [13] have demonstrated that storing and reusing reasoning chains can improve problem solving and reduce computational overhead. Jeong et al. [9] have proposed a dynamic adjustment of retrieval strategies through model collaboration to enhance question-answer performance. Wang et al. [23] combine RAG with chain of thought and use external knowledge bases to modify the reasoning paths to enhance information consistency. Guan et al. [8] model retrieval-enhanced reasoning as a Markov Decision Process to improve retrieval efficiency and answer transparency. Nevertheless, the challenges of retrieval redundancy and multi-step decomposition of complex queries require further exploration.

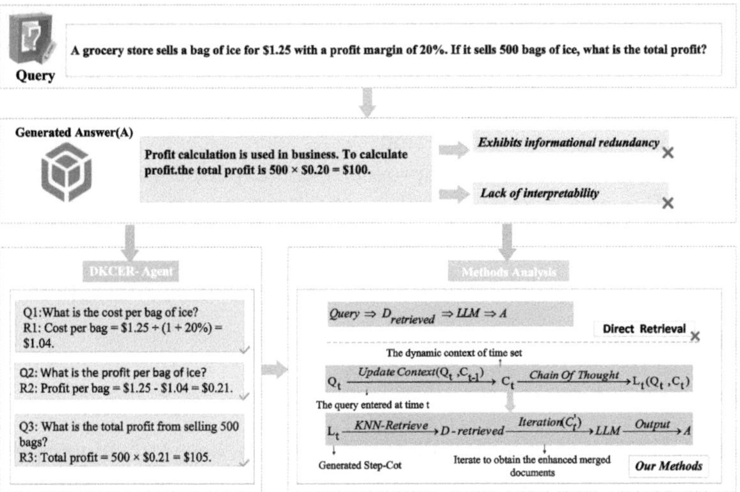


**Fig. 1.** A Multi-Questions and Answers (Q&A) example illustrates the impact of redundant information and low transparency in RAG. Joint retrieval and step-by-step reasoning improve zero-shot accuracy

Figure 1 shows an example of solving the session task. In this paper, a lightweight and efficient KNN-enhanced dynamic context-optimised Step-by-step retrieval enhancement generation framework—DKCER-Agent is proposed.

Specifically, in the retrieval process, the clean data after sliding context segmentation is combined with KNN search paths and BM25 retrieval for double screening, which effectively removes redundant information and accelerates the retrieval efficiency; in the LLM reasoning stage, a human-like step-by-step chain reasoning mechanism is adopted to implement step-by-step reasoning, verification and correction, which improves the transparency and interpretability of LLMs and avoids the black box problem. Meanwhile, the context history is dynamically managed to optimise the user experience. In addition, the framework has a small memory footprint and can run smoothly on a 32GB cloud server.

Compared to previous studies, DKCER-Agent shows great potential in downstream applications of large models. Experimental results show that DKCER-Agent delivers competitive performance in session task flow. The main contributions of this paper are as follows:

- A federated retrieval approach is proposed that employs a dual screening mechanism, performs coarse screening via BM25 to extract key information, and introduces K-nearest neighbour retrieval enhancement to eliminate redundant information. In addition, to improve the overall efficiency, an adaptive sliding cut strategy is designed to ensure the robustness of the retriever.
- An adaptive dynamic step-by-step reasoning mechanism is designed, which uses a step-by-step reasoning chain approach to decompose the problem into multiple sub-problems, query the retriever step-by-step, and transfer it to LLMs for correction and verification in conjunction with the dynamic contextual history, so as to enhance the interpretability of the model and collaborative human-computer interaction.
- Compared to several baseline approaches, the experimental results show that the DKCER agent performs well in the downstream application tasks of LLMs, while significantly reducing the waste of memory resources.

## 2   Related Work

### 2.1   Reasoning Agents

LLMs intelligences use external tools and knowledge bases to enhance their reasoning capabilities. Recent studies have focused on the interaction mechanism between the agent and the environment, the invocation strategy of external tools, and the accumulation of experience [7]. For example, Yao et al. [25] significantly improved reasoning ability by planning reasoning and action steps and incorporating retrieved information from Wikipedia. In addition, for conversational tasks, Chen et al. [3] used parameter fine-tuning and cue engineering to further extend the agent's downstream application capabilities. In multiple rounds of dialogue tasks, there are still deficiencies in model interpretability and reliability assessment from the user's perspective [18]. This paper proposes a DKCER-Agent framework that supports session response in agent workflows through dynamic context optimisation.

## 2.2  RAG

In a knowledge-intensive quiz task, the RAG acts as an external knowledge base for the agent and consists of two key processes: retrieval and generation [11]. Among them, the performance of the retriever directly affects the quality of the downstream Multi-Q&A. It has been shown that optimising the retriever is the key to improving the performance of an intelligent body. For example, Zhu et al. [26] effectively eliminated the redundancy of retrieved information by improving the retriever architecture; Sukhvinder et al. [21] proposed a slicing method based on clean retrieval, which significantly improved the retrieval accuracy of the intelligent body. Studies have shown that the design of an efficient retrieval strategy is crucial for the performance of intelligentsia. In this paper, we propose a federated RAG framework based on KNN retrieval, which uses sliding contextual cuts to improve the efficiency of data processing, and BM25 coarse sieving and KNN fine sieving to filter the redundant information and provide the correct retrieved documents for LLMs.

## 2.3  COT

Recent research has proposed a natural language-like cueing style to equip large models with human-like reasoning and to solve problems by introducing intermediate reasoning steps [24]. Existing approaches mainly rely on Few-Shot Learning (FSL) [20], where LLMs are guided by examples. This approach consumes a lot of computational resources and can also lead to model bias. For example, if the example answer is A, the model is more likely to generate A, which in turn affects the diversity and accuracy of responses. To overcome this limitation, existing research proposes the Zero-shot Chain of Thought (COT) [10], where "Let's think step by step" is added at the end of the prompt to stimulate reasoning. Inspired by this, this paper proposes Stepwise Reasoning Refinement (SRR), which combines forward-backward iterative Q&A with iterative interactions between the retriever and the LLMs in the session workflow, to allow the agent to gradually optimise the reasoning path and thus produce more accurate answers.

# 3    Methodology

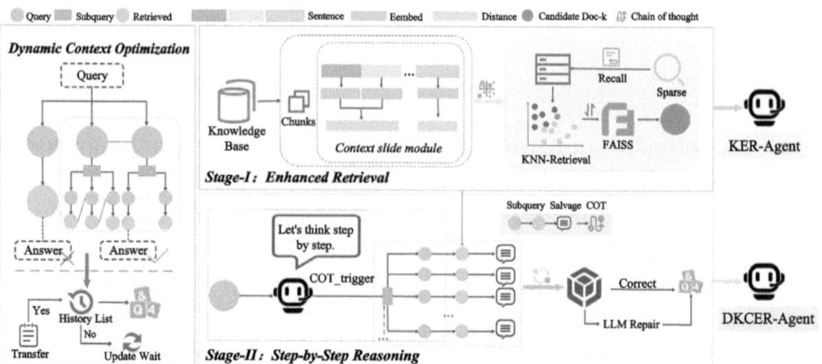

**Fig. 2.** Overview of DKCER-Agent. The framework includes three steps: (i)The retrieval module slices data via sliding context, vectorizes it, and passes it to the KER-Agent, which applies double screening to assist the large model; (ii) The reasoning module decomposes sub-problems, retrieves relevant content, and enables error verification and correction; (iii) A dynamic contextual history list enhances response accuracy and transparency using past information.

## 3.1    Framework Design

Figure 2 proposes a session agent architecture that incorporates dynamic context management, step-by-step reasoning, and retrieval enhancement. Specifically, the COT mechanism is embedded into the existing base RAG framework at each sub-stage of retrieval (query expansion, candidate screening, and response generation) to construct an interpretable step-by-step reasoning path. This design enhances the interpretability and robustness of the large model. A hybrid strategy of sparse retrieval and KNN combined with improved similarity metrics is used to achieve semantic precision matching; in addition, a history information management list based on attention weights is designed to work with the LLMs feedback correction mechanism to improve dialogue coherence.

## 3.2    Federated Retrieval Enhancement

To address the problem of insufficient semantic representation in sparse retrieval, the K-Nearest Neighbour (KNN) retrieval strategy is adopted to maximise semantic learning. Therefore, a hierarchical joint retrieval scheme is designed to remove redundant information and improve retrieval performance.

**Candidate Coarse Screening.** Given a query vector $q$ and a set of document vectors $D = \{d_1, d_2, \ldots, d_n\}$, the candidate document set is initially filtered using a sparse retrieval method. The initial candidate set is constructed based on the BM25 algorithm as follows:

$$D_{\text{sparse}} = \{d_i \mid \text{sim}(q, d_i) > \tau\}, \tag{1}$$

where, $\text{sim}(q, d_i)$ represents the similarity between the query vector $q$ and the document vector $d_i$, and the threshold $\tau$ is set to 0.5 to filter out the candidate documents with higher relevance.

**KNN Fine Sieve Enhancement Screen.** For vector features with ambiguous distances to the answer, KNN uses an improved Euclidean-cosine hybrid metric to filter $D_{knn} \subseteq D_{sparse}$. The formula is defined as:

$$sim'(q, d_i) = \lambda \|q - d_i\|_2 + (1 - \lambda) \cos(q, d_i) \tag{2}$$

where $\lambda = 0.4$ balances distance and angular similarity. Efficient nearest neighbor search is implemented using the FAISS library. This method achieves a notable improvement in Top-5 recall. Facebook AI Similarity Search (FAISS) [6] is a library for efficient similarity search and clustering of dense vectors. During this process, semantically ambiguous and redundant information is removed to enhance KNN search accuracy.

### 3.3   Chain Reasoning Correction Mechanism

---

**Algorithm 1:** Reasoning Chain Generation Algorithm

---

**Input:** Current task $T$
**Output:** Reasoning chain $S = \{s_1, s_2, \ldots, s_m\}$

1 **Function** GenerateReasoningChain($T$):
      /* Initialize reasoning chain $S$                    */
2      $S \leftarrow \emptyset$;
3      **for** $i \leftarrow 1$ **to** $m$ **do**
           /* Generate each sub-question $s_i$            */
4           $s_i \leftarrow \text{LLM}("Step:" + T)$;
           /* Add sub-question to reasoning chain     */
5          $S \leftarrow S \cup \{s_i\}$;
6      **return** $S$;

---

**Step-by-Step Isomerisation.** Utilize zero-shot prompting (e.g., "Let's think step by step") to generate a reasoning chain $S = \{s_1, \ldots, s_m\}$, where $s_i = \text{LLM}("Step:" + T)$, and $T$ is the current task. $i$ represents the $i$-th subproblem. The task $T$ is decomposed into multiple logically coherent subproblems through step-by-step reasoning, ensuring that each subproblem $s_i$ can be independently retrieved and verified. An overview of the step-by-step reasoning process can be found in Algorithm 1, including task parsing, subproblem generation, and reasoning chain construction.

**Sub-query Validation.** For each subproblem $s_i \in S$ in the reasoning chain, perform a RAG retrieval to obtain a relevant set of documents $D_j$. Based on the probability distribution $P(s_i)$ from the retrieval results, calculate the sub-problem confidence $c_j = 1 - \text{Entropy}(P(s_i))$, where $\text{Entropy}(\cdot)$ is the entropy function used to quantify the uncertainty of the retrieval results. If $c_j \geq 0.5$

the subproblem $s_i$ is considered reliable, otherwise it is marked as requiring correction.

**Error Correction.** For subproblems $s_i$ with confidence $c_j < 0.5$, activate the backtracking mechanism to regenerate $s_i' = \text{LLMs}(\text{"Revise:"} + s_i)$. Repeat the retrieval and confidence calculation until the overall chain confidence is $\sum c_j/m > 0.8$, ensuring the reliability of the entire inference chain. The revised inference chain $S' = \{s_1', \ldots, s_m'\}$ is then fed into the RAG framework to generate the final answer, significantly improving the accuracy and robustness of complex problem solving.

### 3.4   LLMs Robustness Generation Strategy

The interactive response agent generates a decoding strategy as follows: (i) A relatively stable sampling temperature is set ($t = 0.7$) to promote more stable and reliable outputs. (ii) Top-P sampling decoding ($p = 0.8$) is used to filter low probability anomalous tokens, limiting the size of the valid vocabulary $|V_{\text{valid}}| \leq 50$ to avoid generating semantically irrelevant content. By combining these strategies, we generate a stable and coherent set of $N$ answers, denoted $(x, R)$. If the answer is correct, it is output; if it is incorrect, the set is further backtracked to interactively correct the answer based on the reasoning chain RAG framework. After iterative cycles, the most reasonable inference steps and answer are provided.

### 3.5   Contextual Dynamic Management Mechanism

**Data Sliding Window.** The previous document processing methods had limitations in redundancy filtering and context association. This study proposes a dynamic sliding window segmentation algorithm. By performing multi-granularity semantic analysis, text blocks are dynamically split. Based on the semantic density function $D(s) = \frac{\sum \cos(v_i, v_{\text{centre}})}{n}$, the window size is adaptively adjusted to ensure semantic coherence.

**Dynamic History List.** The cache list stores historical conversation records in the format Q&A and on each query the cached content is combined with the current query to form a context-aware query query_with_context. After retrieval and response generation, the new Q&A pair is appended to the cache, while the maximum cache size is controlled by setting max_cache_size $= 5$. If the length exceeds this limit, the earliest records are removed. This mechanism allows the agent to dynamically use historical information in multi-turn dialogues, improving the interpretability of the LLMs.

## 4   Experiment

### 4.1   Experimental Setup

This experiment is conducted on a Tesla P100 hardware device using the basic RAG framework [11] and running the lightweight Qwen-7B macromodel [1] on

32 GB of cloud server memory to complete the experiment. The experimental results show that the DKCER-Agent framework significantly outperforms the large model, demonstrating superior reasoning and execution capabilities in a memory-constrained environment.

## 4.2 Datasets

In this paper, we conduct experiments based on the open source datasets Aqua-Wikipedia [4,19], GSM8K [5] and OpenO1SFT [14]. Aqua-Wikipedia contains about 28,000 multiple-choice questions; GSM8K contains 8,000 mathematical questions focusing on mathematical reasoning and problem solving process; Open O1-SFT contains about 10,000 questions suitable for multi-step reasoning and contextual understanding.

## 4.3 Evaluation Metrics

We adopt Accuracy, Recall, F1 Score, Mean Cosine Similarity (MCS), ROUGE F1 and Jaccard Exact Match (EM) as metrics to evaluate the Agent's reasoning and execution capabilities, and use Counterfactual Robustness (CFR) to assess the model's robustness. Higher values for these metrics indicate optimal performance in retrieval and generation. Additionally, we introduce the average number of steps in Chain of Thought(Mean CoT Steps) metric to measure the number of reasoning steps required by the model to complete a reasoning task, further analyzing its reasoning depth and complexity.

## 4.4 Experimental Benchmarks

**Benchmarking Models Performance.** This paper constructs a model evaluation framework based on two dimensions. First, performance comparisons are made with mainstream models of the same parameter scale (e.g. DeepSeek-7B [12], Llama-7B [22], Qwen-7B [1], etc.) to validate the effectiveness of our model architecture optimisation; and second, comparisons are made with models of larger parameter scales (e.g. Deep-seek-R1 [12], ChatGPT-4 [16], etc.) to highlight the benefits of lightweight design in terms of resource efficiency.

**A Comparative Analysis of Reasoning Paradigms.** The generalisability of the model is evaluated in different scenarios such as zero-shot [23] and Few-shot [20]; second, the effect of standard chain-of-thought (CoT) reasoning combined with RAG [11] is compared and the performance of the joint DKCER-Agent reasoning paradigm proposed in this paper is verified.

**Evaluating the Effectiveness of Retrieval Strategies.** An experimental framework for hierarchical retrieval is constructed and evaluated from two aspects: (1) Comparing traditional BM25 [17] sorting with vector-based dense retrieval (Embedding-R) [6]; (2) Verifying the joint effect of hybrid BM25 and Embedding sorting as well as KNN nearest neighbour enhancement strategies.

(3) Combining the adaptive sliding window mechanism and further comparing the retrieval with traditional fixed window retrieval to verify the improvement in computational efficiency.

## 4.5   Experimental Analysis

**Table 1.** Based on the experimental results of 10 LLMs in the same category and across categories, DKCER-Agent shows its performance.**bold** numbers indicate the best performance among all LLMs, and the second-best results are <u>underlined</u>

| Models | Accuracy | Recall | F1 | MCS | Average | Avg Steps |
|---|---|---|---|---|---|---|
| Chatgpt-4 | 78.74 | 77.65 | 88.10 | 60.98 | 76.36 | 2.77 |
| Deepseek-R1 | <u>90.51</u> | <u>90.00</u> | 90.26 | 64.00 | 83.69 | 3.44 |
| Qwen-32b | 83.07 | 83.21 | 90.75 | 63.32 | 80.08 | 3.77 |
| Qwen-plus | 82.67 | 81.67 | 89.51 | 62.26 | 79.02 | 4.00 |
| Llama-70b | 87.00 | 86.99 | 92.05 | 63.92 | 82.49 | 4.87 |
| Qwen-14b | 88.15 | 89.18 | 88.66 | <u>64.61</u> | 82.65 | 3.88 |
| DeepSeek-R1-1.5b | 81.10 | 80.02 | 89.56 | 60.69 | 77.84 | 5.00 |
| Llama-7b | 47.64 | 49.53 | 64.53 | 48.68 | 52.62 | - |
| Qwen-7b | 74.01 | 75.86 | 85.06 | 59.01 | 73.49 | 1.40 |
| DeepSeek-R1-7b | 89.15 | 88.01 | **94.82** | 64.06 | <u>84.01</u> | 4.00 |
| DKCER-Agent(Ours) | **91.60** | **90.15** | <u>93.26</u> | **68.18** | **85.80** | 3.63 |

**Lightweight Reasoning Power.** As shown in Table 1, DKCER-Agent outperforms the existing model in all test scenarios, confirming the reliability of this method. By retrieving the API inference results of 10 models, in the large model with larger parameters, although the existing Deepseek-R1 is second only to DKCER-Agent in accuracy (90.51%) and recall rate (90.00%), our method shows stronger inference ability in average effect. It also has a smaller memory footprint, a lighter design and a faster operating speed, which is comparable to the performance of Deepseek-R1. In a large model with the same number of parameters, compared to Llama-7b, the advantages of this method in effectively avoiding hallucinations are demonstrated and the interpretability of the model is improved. Although Deepseek-7b achieved 94.82% accuracy, other indicators outperformed the model. The model with a smaller number of parameters used only slightly more resources and outperformed Deepseek-7b by almost 10%.

The results of the analysis of the average number of steps for step-by-step thinking show that the inference steps of the DKCER-Agent are the same as those of models with a large number of parameters and excellent performance, and are balanced. The proposed method is much better than the model with a lower average number of steps or a lack of thinking. This shows that the proposed method is very good at finding the right answer quickly.

**Table 2.** Comparison of our approach to having a step-by-step thinking baseline on the Aqua dataset, DKCER-Agent shows excellent stepwise inference performance in both F1 and accuracy. **bold** numbers indicate the best performance among all methods

| | Aqua | | |
| --- | --- | --- | --- |
| Methods | F1 | Jaccard EM | Average |
| Few-shot | 88.18 | 61.04 | 74.61 |
| CoT | 84.25 | 62.50 | 73.38 |
| RAG | 59.37 | 54.78 | 57.08 |
| RAG(Few-shot) | 60.81 | 55.60 | 58.04 |
| RAG+COT | 75.36 | 60.34 | 67.85 |
| DKCER-Agent (Ours) | **90.15** | **64.61** | **77.38** |

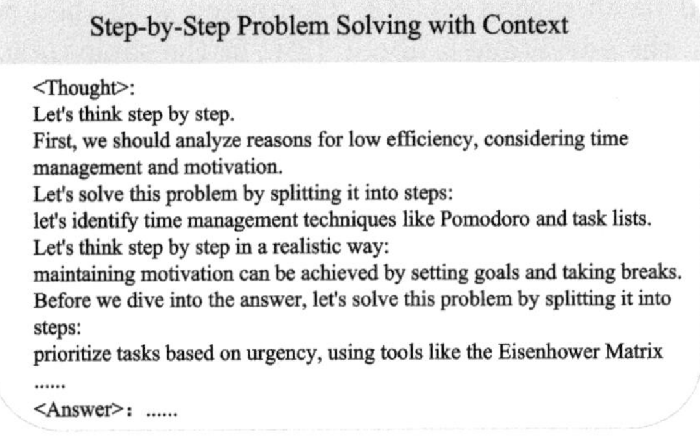


**Fig. 3.** A visual example of breaking down productivity through dynamic, step-by-step and contextual thinking to enhance transparency and answer quality

**Step-by-Step Thinking Leads to Models that can be Explained.** Our approach is based on the stepwise inference mechanism, which enhances the inference capability of LLM, so that the thinking process of the model can be clearly displayed, as shown in the output example in Fig. 3. Compared with existing zero-sample and small-sample methods, our method has significant advantages in recall rate and text matching degree. In addition, for RAG and RAG- and COT-based methods, our improved approach achieved an average score of 77.38%, far exceeding the existing baseline approach. As shown in Table 2.

**Table 3.** Comparison between the joint search mechanism and other search methods. In this table, the performance comparison between different search methods and the joint search mechanism is detailed, highlighting the advantages of the joint search mechanism in terms of accuracy

| | Qwen-7B | | |
| --- | --- | --- | --- |
| Retrieval | Accuracy | Recall | Average |
| TF-IDF | 85.03 | 70.26 | 77.65 |
| BM25-R | 85.03 | 80.12 | 82.58 |
| KNN-R | 87.40 | 80.12 | 83.76 |
| DPR | 83.10 | 78.00 | 80.55 |
| Hybrid(BM25+Embedding) | 75.19 | 80.29 | 77.74 |
| KER-Agent (Ours) | **88.17** | **89.90** | **89.03** |

**KER-Agent has Efficient Retrieval Performance.** To improve the performance of the Qwen generator, we proposed the KER-Agent in the retrieval module to enhance the retrieval effect in the joint retrieval mechanism. As shown in Table 3, compared with a single retrieval model, our method achieved an average accuracy and recall rate of 89.03%. Compared with the lower performance retrieval method, the advantage is about 12%; at the same time, compared with the hybrid retrieval method, our method also shows stronger advantages, and can effectively remove irrelevant interference information.

## 4.6   Ablation Study

**Table 4.** Results compared with single method use. In terms of the ROUGE F1 and CFR metrics, our approach shows stronger model stability

| Models | ROUGE F1 | CFR | Average |
| --- | --- | --- | --- |
| Qwen-7b | 22.39 | 65.60 | 44.00 |
| CoT+Qwen-7b | 13.89 | 69.78 | 41.84 |
| RAG | 14.78 | 72.50 | 43.64 |
| CoT+RAG | 24.02 | 74.20 | 49.11 |
| DKCER-Agent(Ours) | 23.30 | 79.36 | 51.33 |

From the perspective of robustness and ROUGE F1, Table 4 of the ablation experiment results shows that the DKCER-Agent model can effectively deal with the counterfactual situation in these two indicators, thus maintaining high accuracy and robustness. First, in terms of the CFR (Counterfactual Robustness) indicators, our method has a performance score of 79.36%, which significantly outperforms other models, especially Qwen-7b and CoT+Qwen-7b. This result shows that our approach is able to maintain a high degree of stability in the face of potential changes. Secondly, in the ROUGE F1 evaluation, we obtained a score of 23.30, indicating that our method is superior to other models in terms of the quality of the generated text and has a higher degree of text matching. Therefore, DKCER-Agent shows stronger model stability and higher text generation quality.

## 5    Conclusion

This paper proposes an efficient KNN framework, DKCER-Agent, which addresses redundancy and LLMs interpretability issues in multi-turn dialogues through dynamic step-by-step retrieval. The framework enhances model transparency by progressively breaking down problems using thought chains and context history lists. It employs double screening to extract key information, with KNN selecting the most important content. Experimental results show that DKCER-Agent significantly improves question answering accuracy compared to direct answers or redundant outputs, while avoiding resource waste in a lightweight operation mode. The future work will further evaluating the interpretability of LLMs, error analysis, and adaptability to diverse tasks, in order to optimize the framework and enable its flexible application in a wider range of scenarios.

## References


1. Ahmed, I., Islam, S., Datta, P.P., Kabir, I., Chowdhury, N.U.R., Haque, A.: Qwen 2.5: A comprehensive review of the leading resource-efficient llm with potentioal to surpass all competitors
2. Arslan, M., Munawar, S., Cruz, C.: Sustainable digitalization of business with multi-agent rag and llm. Proc. Comput. Sci. **246**, 4722–4731 (2024)
3. Chen, J.C.Y., Saha, S., Bansal, M.: Reconcile: Round-table conference improves reasoning via consensus among diverse llms. arXiv preprint arXiv:2309.13007 (2023)
4. City, T.: Wikipedia the free encyclopedia, vol. 23 (2015). http://enwikipedia.org/wiki/Think_CityUpdated
5. Cobbe, K., et al.: Training verifiers to solve math word problems. arXiv preprint arXiv:2110.14168 (2021)
6. Douze, M., et al.: The faiss library. arXiv preprint arXiv:2401.08281 (2024)
7. Durante, Z., et al.: Agent ai: surveying the horizons of multimodal interaction. arXiv preprint arXiv:2401.03568 (2024)
8. Guan, X., et al.: Deeprag: thinking to retrieval step by step for large language models. arXiv preprint arXiv:2502.01142 (2025)
9. Jeong, S., Baek, J., Cho, S., Hwang, S.J., Park, J.C.: Adaptive-rag: learning to adapt retrieval-augmented large language models through question complexity. In: 2024 Conference of the North American Chapter of the Association for Computational Linguistics: Human Language Technologies, pp. 7036–7050. Association for Computational Linguistics (2024)

10. Kojima, T., Gu, S.S., Reid, M., Matsuo, Y., Iwasawa, Y.: Large language models are zero-shot reasoners. Adv. Neural. Inf. Process. Syst. **35**, 22199–22213 (2022)
11. Lewis, P., et al.: Retrieval-augmented generation for knowledge-intensive nlp tasks. Adv. Neural. Inf. Process. Syst. **33**, 9459–9474 (2020)
12. McGee, R.W.: Leveraging deepseek: An ai-powered exploration of traditional Chinese medicine (tai chi and qigong) for medical research. Am. J. Biomed. Sci. Res. **25**(5), 645–654 (2025)
13. Melz, E.: Enhancing llm intelligence with arm-rag: Auxiliary rationale memory for retrieval augmented generation. arXiv preprint arXiv:2311.04177 (2023)
14. O1-OPEN: Openo1-sft: A dataset for chain-of-thought reasoning (2024). https://huggingface.co/datasets/O1-OPEN/OpenO1-SFT Accessed 18 Mar 2024
15. Plaat, A., Wong, A., Verberne, S., Broekens, J., van Stein, N., Back, T.: Reasoning with large language models, a survey. arXiv preprint arXiv:2407.11511 (2024)
16. Radulesco, T., Saibene, A.M., Michel, J., Vaira, L.A., Lechien, J.R.: Chatgpt-4 performance in rhinology: A clinical case series. In: International Forum of Allergy & Rhinology, vol. 14 (2024)
17. Robertson, S., Zaragoza, H., et al.: The probabilistic relevance framework: Bm25 and beyond. Found. Trends® Inform. Retrieval **3**(4), 333–389 (2009)
18. Saha, T., Ganguly, D., Saha, S., Mitra, P.: Workshop on large language models' interpretability and trustworthiness (llmit). In: Proceedings of the 32nd ACM International Conference on Information and Knowledge Management, pp. 5290–5293 (2023)
19. Sharma, A., Savarn, S., Anand, A., Manvi, S.K.S.: Automated questions unique arrangement (aqua). J. Adv. Zool. **44** (2023)
20. Song, C.H., Wu, J., Washington, C., Sadler, B.M., Chao, W.L., Su, Y.: Llm-planner: few-shot grounded planning for embodied agents with large language models. In: Proceedings of the IEEE/CVF International Conference on Computer Vision, pp. 2998–3009 (2023)
21. Sukhvinder Singh, I., et al.: Chunkrag: novel llm-chunk filtering method for rag systems. arXiv e-prints pp. arXiv–2410 (2024)
22. Touvron, H., et al.: Llama: Open and efficient foundation language models. arXiv preprint arXiv:2302.13971 (2023)
23. Wang, Z., Liu, A., Lin, H., Li, J., Ma, X., Liang, Y.: Rat: retrieval augmented thoughts elicit context-aware reasoning in long-horizon generation. arXiv preprint arXiv:2403.05313 (2024)
24. Wei, J., et al.: Chain-of-thought prompting elicits reasoning in large language models. Adv. Neural. Inf. Process. Syst. **35**, 24824–24837 (2022)
25. Yao, S., et al.: React: synergizing reasoning and acting in language models. In: International Conference on Learning Representations (ICLR) (2023)
26. Zhu, K., et al.: An information bottleneck perspective for effective noise filtering on retrieval-augmented generation. arXiv preprint arXiv:2406.01549 (2024)

# Robust AI-Synthesized Image Detection via Multi-feature Frequency-Aware Learning


Hongfei Cai[1], Chi Liu[1]([✉]), Sheng Shen[2], Youyang Qu[3,4],
and Peng Gui[1,2,3,4]

[1] Faculty of Data Science, City University of Macau, Macao SAR, China
`chiliu@cityu.edu.mo`
[2] Design and Creative Technology Vertical, Torrens University Australia,
NSW, Australia
[3] Shandong Provincial Key Laboratory of Computer Networks, Ministry of
Education, Shandong Computer Science Center, Qilu University of Technology
(Shandong Academy of Sciences), Jinan, China
[4] School of Computer Science and Engineering, Wuhan Institute of Technology,
Wuhan, China



**Abstract.** The rapid progression of generative AI (GenAI) technologies
has heightened concerns regarding the misuse of AI-generated imagery.
To address this issue, robust detection methods have emerged as particularly compelling, especially in challenging conditions where the targeted GenAI models are out-of-distribution or the generated images have
been subjected to perturbations during transmission. This paper introduces a multi-feature fusion framework designed to enhance spatial forensic feature representations with incorporating three complementary components, namely noise correlation analysis, image gradient information,
and pretrained vision encoder knowledge, using a cross-source attention mechanism. Furthermore, to identify spectral abnormality in synthetic images, we propose a frequency-aware architecture that employs
the Frequency-Adaptive Dilated Convolution, enabling the joint modeling of spatial and spectral features while maintaining low computational
complexity. Our framework exhibits exceptional generalization performance across fourteen diverse GenAI systems, including text-to-image
diffusion models, autoregressive approaches, and post-processed deepfake methods. Notably, it achieves significantly higher mean accuracy in
cross-model detection tasks when compared to existing state-of-the-art
techniques. Additionally, the proposed method demonstrates resilience
against various types of real-world image noise perturbations such as
compression and blurring. Extensive ablation studies further corrobo-
rate the synergistic benefits of fusing multi-model forensic features with
frequency-aware learning, underscoring the efficacy of our approach.

**Keywords:** AI-Synthesized Image · Robust Detection · Feature Fusion





T. Zhu et al. (Eds.): KSEM 2025, LNAI 15919, pp. 157–171, 2026.
https://doi.org/10.1007/978-981-95-3001-4_12

# 1   Introduction

The recent progress in generative AI (GenAI) models, such as Generative Adversarial Networks (GANs) and Diffusion models, has heightened concerns regarding the misuse of AI-generated imagery. This misuse not only includes the spread of fake images but also extends to model extraction attacks, where adversaries attempt to steal the functionality of AI models by querying them with various inputs [3]. As a response, the detection of AI-synthesized images has become increasingly crucial as an initial safeguard for AI-generated content.

There are two persistent challenges remaining in AI-synthesized image detection: the generalization ability and the robustness of detectors. As the GenAI models behind fake image generation continue evolving, a detector trained on specific GenAI models should be able to generalize to identify previously unseen GenAI models. Furthermore, considering the prevalence of AI-generated images distributed online, which may be subject to various transmission noises such as compression and blur, it is essential for a trained detector to maintain robustness against typical image perturbations.

Recently, various AI-synthesized image detectors have been proposed, utilizing forensic features from both the image domain, like texture details [2], noise relationships [26], and gradients [27], and the frequency domain, such as spectral distribution [9], Fourier amplitude [29], and DCT coefficients [9]. Additionally, some methods employ feature fusion to integrate these diverse sources of features [10]. However, there still remains a gap in addressing the cross-model generalization and noise robustness problems. Methods that rely on a single feature source are vulnerable to changes in target GenAI models, particularly when the architecture of test GenAI models shifts, e.g., from GANs to diffusion model. Moreover, some features may be typically sensitive to specific noise perturbations; for example, online image compression will significantly compromise the original frequency-domain feature representations [9]. Multi-feature fusion strategies present a promising avenue for addressing the limitations of single-feature representations; however, there persists a requisite for more sophisticated and effective fusion mechanisms that merit further investigation.

To address these challenges, we propose a novel multi-feature fusion and frequency-aware learning framework for generalizable and robust AI-synthesized image detection. Our method first creates a strong forensic multi-feature representation by integrating noise relationship features, image gradient features, and knowledge from pretrained large vision encoders with a cross-source attention module. The noise and gradient features provide reliable forensic clues [26,27], while the pretrained knowledge, which characterizes the distribution of natural images, enhances the feature representation by sharpening the decision boundary between natural and artificial images [23]. The integrated feature is subsequently fed to a frequency-aware learning backbone. The frequency-aware learning backbone involves incorporating residual learning with the Frequency-Adaptive Dilated Convolution (FADC) [4]. This design improves the detector's capability of concurrently capturing both spatial information and frequency information from the previously fused feature, with a particular focus on the local frequency dynamics. Meanwhile, FADC helps reduce network complexity and improves computational efficacy to obtain a lightweight detector.

To verify the effectiveness of the proposed multi-feature frequency-aware learning framework, we conduct extensive experiments targeting the detection of *fourteen* GenAI models, spanning over GAN-like models, diffusion-like text-to-image models, autoregressive models, low-level and perceptual image processing models, as well as post-rendered deepfakes. We also compare our method with various methods including widely used classifiers such as ResNet and ViT, and some recent state-of-the-art baselines. Ablation studies are additionally provide to demonstrate the rationale of multi-feature fusion. The results confirm that our method achieves exceptional accuracy, generalizability, and robustness in detecting AI-synthesized images.

To summarize, the contributions of this paper include:

- We propose a novel framework for AI-synthesized image detection, which significantly improves the cross-model generalization ability and noise robustness of detection.
- We devise a multi-feature fusion mechanism that enables the model to adaptively incorporate noise relationships, image gradients, and knowledge from pretrained large vision encoders for robust forensic feature representation.
- We introduce a frequency-aware learning backbone that effectively integrates global spatial and local frequency information using a lightweight design with low computational cost.
- Our extensive experimental evaluation shows that our framework excels in accuracy, generalization, and robustness, surpassing multiple baselines across various test settings.

## 2   Related Work

*Image-based Detection Methods* focus on analyzing pixel-level and regional features within images to identify potential forgeries. These features include texture details [2], color distribution [11], saturation [19], edge information [22], and other visual cues. For example, some studies have explored the use of gradient information to detect inconsistencies in image textures and edges that are characteristic of AI-generated content [22]. These methods are particularly effective in identifying forgeries where the synthesis process introduces subtle but detectable anomalies in the spatial domain. However, they can be sensitive to image quality and resolution, and may struggle with high-quality forgeries that closely mimic real images. For instance, recent work demonstrated that spatial anomalies can be effectively removed through trace removal attacks, highlighting the limitations of relying solely on spatial features for robust detection [15].

*Frequency-based Detection Methods* convert images from the spatial domain to the frequency domain, utilizing features such as high-frequency artifacts to identify synthetic content [9]. These methods leverage the fact that AI-generated images often exhibit distinct frequency patterns, such as periodic structures or anomalies in the high-frequency components, which are not typically present in natural images. For instance, the use of Fourier transforms or wavelet transforms allows for the extraction of frequency features that can reveal the presence of synthetic elements [9]. The frequency domain fingerprinting of GenAI models for task-specific forensics was further explored [17]. Frequency-based methods are useful for detecting GenAI models that leave distinct frequency anomaly; however, they may be highly susceptible to image noise or other frequency-domain disturbances [30].

*Feature-fusion Detection Methods* combine various image features from different layers, such as visual features, frequency features, or multi-modal data, to enhance the accuracy and robustness of detection [10,12]. By integrating information from multiple sources, these methods aim to capture both spatial and frequency-domain characteristics of images, thereby improving the detection performance. For example, some studies have proposed frameworks that fuse global and local features, leveraging the complementary nature of different feature sets to achieve better generalization across various forgery types and datasets [10]. Additionally, feature-fusion methods often incorporate advanced techniques such as attention mechanisms to dynamically weigh the importance of different features, further optimizing the detection process [12]. These methods are generally more robust to variations in forgery techniques and image quality, making them suitable for practical applications where diverse forgery scenarios are encountered. A novel multi-view completion representation for robust GAN-generated image detection was proposed, which effectively integrates multi-scale features and cross-view information to enhance detection robustness [16].

## 3    Method

Our framework for detecting AI-synthesized images integrates four complementary feature representations within a frequency-aware architecture, addressing both spatial and spectral forensic patterns. As shown in Fig. 1, the design motivation stems from three key observations:(i)Modern generative models exhibit semantic inconsistencies despite visual realism, necessitating global semantic analysis;(ii)Manipulation artifacts manifest as localized spatial discontinuities;(iii)Synthetic images often contain frequency-domain anomalies across subbands. Accordingly, the pipeline employs three parallel processing branches followed by frequency-domain refinement. The CLIP-ViT module leverages pretrained vision-language embeddings to capture semantic coherence, motivated by its proven cross-modal alignment capabilities on large-scale datasets. Concurrently, a transformation-based spatial gradient analyzer detects local pixel-level inconsistencies through Sobel operators, targeting common artifacts in generated image boundaries. The third branch computes noise pattern residuals (NPR) via guided filtering to isolate structural anomalies in texture regions.

These heterogeneous features are concatenated and processed through frequency selection modules that apply Discrete Wavelet Transform (DWT), decomposing signals into approximation (low-frequency) and detail (high-frequency) components. This design explicitly models frequency-space interactions, as synthetic images often exhibit abnormal energy distributions in specific sub-bands. Subsequent global residual blocks employ identity mappings to amplify discriminative patterns while mitigating gradient vanishing. A spatial attention mechanism dynamically reweights feature maps based on local artifact severity, focusing computation on suspicious regions. The network architecture utilizes stacked 3×3 convolutions with ReLU activation and batch normalization, progressively abstracting features through hierarchical processing before final binary classification via fully connected layers. This multi-stage design enables joint modeling of complementary forensic cues while maintaining parameter efficiency through modular components.

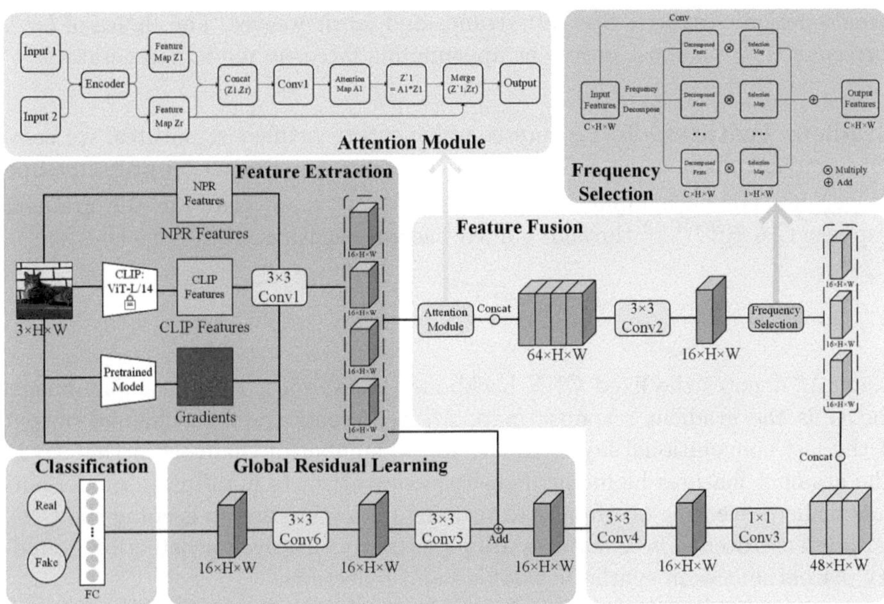


**Fig. 1.** The architecture of the proposed multi-feature frequency-aware learning model. The multi-branch network integrates CLIP semantic features, transformation gradients, and NPR (noise pattern residual) features. Frequency decomposition via Discrete Wavelet Transform separates low- and high-frequency components, followed by residual-enhanced feature refinement and attention-based feature weighting. Final classification is achieved through hierarchical convolutional blocks and fully connected layers.

## 3.1 Neighboring Pixel Relationships and Gradient Features

**Neighboring Pixel Relationships (NPR):** Inspired by the inherent upsampling patterns in generative networks [26], we explicitly model local pixel correlations through a grid-based difference operator. Given an input image $I \in \mathbb{R}^{H \times W \times 3}$, we first partition it into $W \times H$ regular grids $\{v_c^I\}_{c=1}^{W \times H}$, where each grid contains $l \times l$ pixels ($l = 2$ for common $2\times$ up-sampling). The NPR feature tensor $\hat{V}^I \in \mathbb{R}^{W \times H \times (l^2-1)}$ is computed through exhaustive pairwise differences within each grid:

$$\hat{v}_c^I = \left\{ w_i - w_j \mid \forall w_i \in v_c^I,\ 1 \leq j \leq l^2 \right\} \quad \forall c \in \{1, \ldots, W \times H\} \tag{1}$$

where $I$ denotes the input image with height $H$, width $W$, and 3 color channels. The grids $\{v_c^I\}$ are partitioned from the image, each containing $l \times l$ pixels. The resulting NPR feature $\hat{V}^I$ captures local pixel correlations by computing pairwise differences within each grid $v_c^I$. The pixel values within the grid are denoted by $w_i$ and $w_j$, and $c$ is the index of the grid. This operation amplifies characteristic grid artifacts from transposed convolutions in GANs, particularly visible in pseudo-periodic textures like hair strands and fabric weaves. The choice of $l = 2$ corresponds to the most prevalent up-sampling factor in modern generators.

**Gradient Features:** To capture complementary artifact signatures, we compute gradient maps using a fixed CNN backbone $M$ (ResNet-50 pretrained on ImageNet). For each input image $I_i \in \mathbb{R}^{H \times W \times 3}$, we compute the gradient response $G \in \mathbb{R}^{H \times W \times 3}$ through guided backpropagation:

$$G = \frac{\partial \sum_{k=1}^{K} M_k(I_i)}{\partial I_i} \tag{2}$$

where $M$ denotes the fixed CNN backbone (ResNet-50), $I_i$ is the input image, and $G$ is the gradient response map. $M_k$ represents the $k$-th channel output of the last convolutional layer, and $K$ is the number of channels in that layer. The gradient features highlight high-frequency artifacts in diffusion model outputs while preventing overfitting to training data statistics by keeping the CNN parameters frozen. These features are particularly effective for detecting boundary discontinuities in synthetic shadows and reflections.

### 3.2　Incorporating Pretrained Semantic Priors

We integrate semantic priors from CLIP-ViT-L/14 [23] to distinguish authentic natural image statistics. Given an image $x$, we extract the CLIP feature vector $\phi_x \in \mathbb{R}^{768}$ from the final transformer layer before the projection head, preserving both semantic and textural information.

A multi-head cross-attention mechanism dynamically fuses CLIP's global semantics with local artifact features (NPR $\oplus$ Gradients). Let $F_{\text{local}} = [\hat{V}^I \oplus G] \in \mathbb{R}^{L \times C}$ denote the concatenated local features ($L = W \times H$ spatial positions, $C$ channels). The fusion process is formalized as:

$$Q = W_Q \phi_x \in \mathbb{R}^{d_k}$$

$$K = W_K F_{\text{local}} \in \mathbb{R}^{L \times d_k}$$

$$V = W_V F_{\text{local}} \in \mathbb{R}^{L \times d_v} \tag{3}$$

$$\text{Attention}(Q, K, V) = \text{Softmax}\left(\frac{QK^\top}{\sqrt{d_k}}\right) V \in \mathbb{R}^{d_v}$$

where $W_Q, W_K, W_V$ are learnable projections. The softmax temperature $\sqrt{d_k}$ stabilizes gradient flow during training. This attention mechanism enables adaptive feature recalibration, where CLIP's semantic vectors (queries) selectively amplify discriminative local artifacts (values) via compatibility scores with keys.

### 3.3 Frequency-Aware Residual Learning

In our frequency-aware backbone, each Frequency-Adaptive Dilated Convolution (FADC) block is designed to jointly model spatial and spectral information through a multi-path architecture, which includes Frequency Selection to balance high- and low-frequency components. The detailed formulation is as follows:

*High-frequency Path*

$$Y_{\text{FADC}}(p) = \sum_{k=1}^{K^2} \left(w_k^{\text{low}} + w_k^{\text{high}} \cdot \lambda_h(p)\right) \cdot X(p + \Delta p_k \times \hat{D}(p)) \tag{4}$$

where $Y_{\text{FADC}}(p)$ represents the output feature at spatial position $p$ from the high-frequency path, where $K$ is the kernel size, $w_k^{\text{low}}$ and $w_k^{\text{high}}$ are the decomposed convolution weights for low-frequency and high-frequency components, respectively. $\lambda_h(p)$ is a dynamic weight factor for high-frequency components, and $\hat{D}(p)$ is the adaptive dilation rate.

*Low-Frequency Path*

$$Y_{\text{skip}}(p) = X(p) \tag{5}$$

This path directly preserves the low-frequency content of the input feature map $X$ through a skip connection.

*Frequency Adaptation Module*

$$\hat{D}(p) = \text{ReLU}(f_\theta(X(p))) \times D_{\text{base}} \tag{6}$$

where $\hat{D}(p)$ is the adaptive dilation rate dynamically adjusted based on the local frequency content of the input feature. $f_\theta$ is a lightweight frequency predictor implemented as a depth-wise convolution layer, and $D_{\text{base}}$ is a predefined base dilation rate.

*Frequency Selection Module*

$$X_b = \mathcal{F}^{-1}(M_b \cdot \mathcal{F}(X)) \tag{7}$$

$$\hat{X}(p) = \sum_{b=0}^{B-1} A_b(p) \cdot X_b(p) \tag{8}$$

where $\mathcal{F}$ and $\mathcal{F}^{-1}$ denote the Fourier Transform and Inverse Fourier Transform, respectively. $M_b$ is a binary mask to extract the $b$-th frequency band, and $A_b(p)$ is a spatially variant reweighting map for the $b$-th frequency band. $\hat{X}(p)$ is the frequency-balanced feature map.

*Output Integration*

$$Y_{\text{out}}(p) = \text{ReLU}(Y_{\text{FADC}}(p) + Y_{\text{skip}}(p) + \hat{X}(p)) \tag{9}$$

The final output $Y_{\text{out}}(p)$ integrates the high-frequency features from the FADC path, the low-frequency features from the skip connection, and the frequency-balanced features from the Frequency Selection module.

### 3.4   Optimization Objective

The network is trained end-to-end using a class-balanced focal loss:

$$\mathcal{L} = -\frac{1}{N} \sum_{i=1}^{N} [\alpha y_i (1 - p_i)^\gamma \log p_i + (1 - \alpha)(1 - y_i) p_i^\gamma \log(1 - p_i)] \tag{10}$$

where $p_i = \sigma(\text{logit}_i)$ is the predicted probability, $\alpha = \frac{N_{\text{fake}}}{N_{\text{real}} + N_{\text{fake}}}$ balances class frequencies, and $\gamma = 2$ focuses training on hard examples. The temperature parameter $\gamma$ smooths the loss landscape for improved convergence stability.

## 4   Experiments

### 4.1   Target Generative Models

Since new methods of creating fake images are always emerging, training on images from one generative model is standard practice and testing the model's ability to detect fake images from other, unseen models is standard practice. We follow the protocol outlined in [28], using real and fake images from Pro-GAN [13] for training. During evaluation, we consider a diverse set of generative models. Initially, we assess performance on models referenced in [28]: ProGAN, StyleGAN [14], BigGAN [1], CycleGAN [31], StarGAN [5], and GauGAN [24]. Each generative model provides a distinct set of real and fake images for our analysis. Furthermore, we extend our evaluation to include the guided diffusion model [8], trained on the ImageNet dataset, and recent text-to-image generation models: Latent Diffusion Model (LDM) [25], Glide [21], as well as the autoregressive model DALL-E [7].

## 4.2   Baseline Detectors

We compare our approach with several state-of-the-art baselines: (i) A classification network trained on real and fake images from ProGAN using binary cross-entropy loss, as detailed in [28]. This network utilizes a ResNet-50 pre-trained on ImageNet. We also consider a variant of this approach where the backbone network is changed to CLIP-ViT to align with our feature space methodology. (ii) A patch-level classification method proposed in [2] that truncates a ResNet or Xception network to focus on smaller receptive fields when classifying images as real or fake. (iii) A classification network trained on co-occurrence matrices of real and fake images, which has been shown to be effective in image steganalysis and forensics [6]. (iv) A classification network trained on the frequency spectrum of real and fake images, capturing artifacts present in GAN-generated images [29]. (v) The method proposed by [23], which leverages the feature space of CLIP-ViT for nearest neighbor classification (NN) or linear classification (LC). We focus on the NN variant for comparison.

## 4.3   Evaluation Metrics and Settings

Our experimental configuration follows established multimedia forensic protocols [2,20,28,29], evaluating detection performance through classification accuracy (ACC) and average precision (AP) scores. To ensure fair comparison, we calibrate classification thresholds using a held-out validation set containing samples from all target generative models.

The training paradigm employs stochastic gradient descent with momentum 0.9, initial learning rate $1 \times 10^{-4}$, and batch size 32, processing 3-channel $256 \times 256$ RGB images. We implement linear warmup for the first 500 iterations followed by cosine learning rate decay. Models train for 20 epochs with cross-entropy loss, using random seed 1 for deterministic weight initialization. The architecture utilizes Adam optimization ($\beta_1 = 0.9$, $\beta_2 = 0.999$) with weight decay $5 \times 10^{-4}$, incorporating batch normalization and dropout ($p = 0.2$) after convolutional layers. All experiments run on PyTorch 2.0 with mixed-precision training, evaluated on an NVIDIA RTX 4090 GPU.

## 4.4   Generalization of Detection

The proposed multi-feature frequency-aware learning framework demonstrates excellent generalization capabilities, particularly on out-of-distribution (OOD) generative models, including both GANs and Diffusion models. As shown in Table 1 and Table 2, our method achieves high accuracy across multiple unseen GAN and diffusion models, significantly outperforming several state-of-the-art baselines. This indicates that the framework is highly effective in detecting AI-synthesized images even when trained on a single generative model (ProGAN) and tested on diverse unseen architectures.

The superior performance on OOD diffusion models is notable, as these models are known for their high visual quality and realism, which often pose challenges for existing detection methods. Our framework's ability to generalize across such diverse and advanced generative models highlights its robustness and adaptability. The effectiveness of our approach can be attributed to the integration of multi-modal features and the frequency-aware learning backbone. These components enable the model to capture both spatial and spectral anomalies that are characteristic of AI-generated images, thereby enhancing the decision boundary between natural and synthetic images. The results in Table 3 further support this conclusion by demonstrating the importance of each feature branch in achieving robust detection. Additionally, the t-SNE visualization in Fig. 2 illustrates the improved separation between real and fake images when incorporating the frequency domain module, confirming the framework's ability to enhance feature discriminability.

**Table 1.** The average accuracy (ACC) of detection across various GAN models. Detectors were trained with real and ProGAN images.

| Detection Method | ProGAN | CycleGAN | BigGAN | StyleGAN | GauGAN | StarGAN | Total |
| --- | --- | --- | --- | --- | --- | --- | --- |
| CNN Detection [28] | 98.94 | 78.80 | 60.62 | 60.56 | 66.82 | 62.31 | 71.34 |
| Patch Classifier [2] | 94.38 | 67.38 | 64.62 | 82.26 | 57.19 | 80.29 | 74.35 |
| Co-occurrence [20] | 97.70 | 63.15 | 53.75 | **92.50** | 51.10 | 54.70 | 68.82 |
| Freq-spec [29] | 44.90 | **99.90** | 50.50 | 49.90 | 50.30 | **99.70** | 65.87 |
| UniFD [23] | 99.54 | 93.49 | 88.63 | 80.75 | **97.11** | 98.97 | **93.08** |
| **Ours** | **99.64** | 90.11 | **92.55** | 87.72 | 94.29 | 93.34 | 92.94 |

**Table 2.** The average accuracy (ACC) of detecting images generated by various diffusion models. Detectors were trained with real and ProGAN images.

| Detection Method | LDM | | | Glide | | | Guided | DALL-E | Total |
| --- | --- | --- | --- | --- | --- | --- | --- | --- | --- |
| | 200 steps | 200w/CFG | 100 steps | 100 27 | 50 27 | 100 10 | | | |
| CNN Detection [28] | 50.74 | 51.04 | 50.76 | 52.15 | 53.07 | 52.06 | 50.66 | 53.18 | 51.71 |
| Patch Classifier [2] | 79.09 | 76.17 | 79.36 | 67.06 | 68.55 | 68.04 | 65.14 | 69.44 | 71.61 |
| Co-occurrence [20] | 70.70 | 70.55 | 71.00 | 70.25 | 69.60 | 69.90 | 60.50 | 67.55 | 68.76 |
| Freq-spec [29] | 50.40 | 50.40 | 50.30 | 51.70 | 51.40 | 50.40 | 50.90 | 50.00 | 50.69 |
| UniFD [23] | 91.29 | 72.02 | 91.29 | 89.05 | 90.67 | 90.08 | 71.06 | 81.47 | 84.62 |
| **Ours** | **94.40** | **80.60** | **94.30** | **91.70** | **91.10** | **91.90** | **95.10** | **86.90** | **90.75** |

**Table 3.** The impact of CLIP Features, Gradients, and NPR Features on detection is illustrated by showing the performance changes after feature removal. "−" denotes the feature branch has been excluded. "ALL" denotes the performance of the complete model.

| Model | $-f_{Clip}$ | $-f_{Grad}$ | $-f_{NPR}$ | ALL |
| --- | --- | --- | --- | --- |
| GAN models | 74.23 | 53.45 | 62.17 | **90.56** |
| Diffusion models | 91.34 | 55.67 | 61.89 | **92.78** |

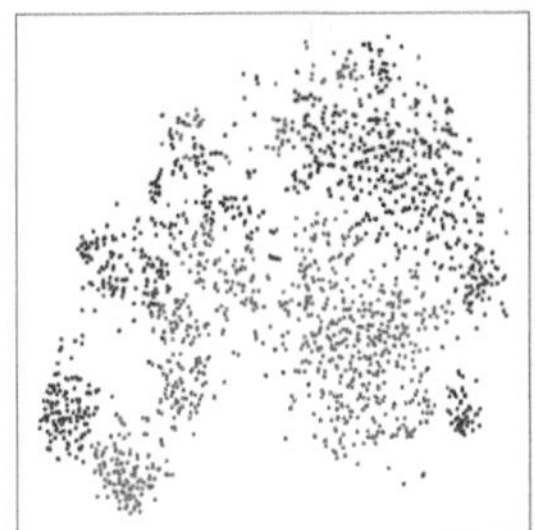 

**Fig. 2.** The t-SNE visualization of 2000 test images demonstrates the effectiveness of a frequency domain module in enhancing binary classification accuracy between real (blue) and fake (red) images. The left panel represents the feature distribution without the frequency domain module, while the right panel shows the improved separation after its application. (Color figure online)

## 4.5   Robustness Against Post-processing Operations

To evaluate the robustness of our classifiers against potential evasion tactics, we assess their performance under common image processing operations such as JPEG compression and Gaussian blurring. We select the baseline from [28] because it is a widely-adopted strategy for enhancing robustness to image perturbations in AI-generated content detection and offers a well-established benchmark. Figure 3 illustrates the comparison results of our method and the baseline one under varying levels of JPEG compression and Gaussian blurring. Compared to the baseline, our method exhibits higher AP scores, especially in out-of-distribution detections where the detector is trained on ProGAN images while tested on Diffusion images). This highlights the superiority of our approach in real-world challenging scenarios where the generative models are unknown and the images may undergo various perturbations during dissemination. Another unusual observation is that increased perturbation magnitude correlates with higher AP scores in detection Diffusion model-generated images. One possible reason is that Diffusion images are less sensitive to external perturbations than real images thanks to the inherent denoising process of diffusion models [18]; this remains further exploration.

## 4.6   Discussion

The experimental results underscore the effectiveness of our proposed fake image detection approach. This method not only demonstrates robust performance across various generative models but also shows resilience against post-processing manipulations. These capabilities make it a powerful tool in the fight against the increasing spread of fake images. Despite the unexpected trend observed in the charts, where our model's performance seems to improve as the image quality decreases and Sigma increases, we believe this could be attributed to the noise addition process inherent in the diffusion model's generation. This noise may

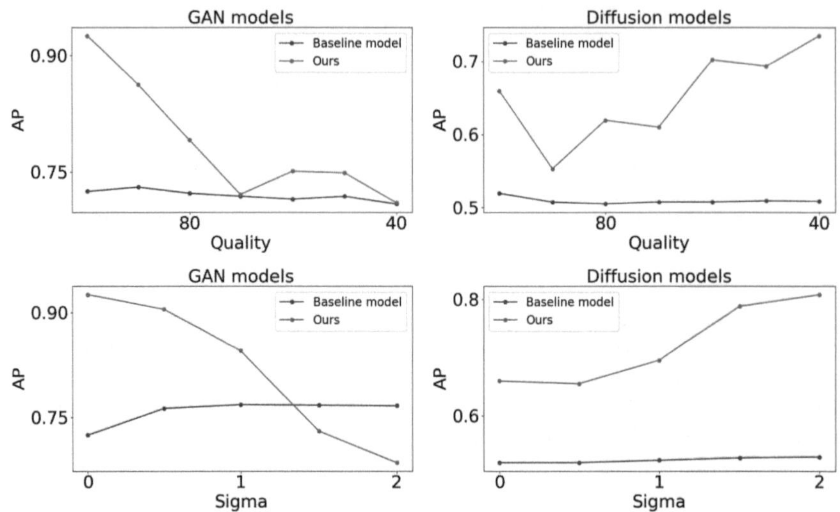

**Fig. 3.** Robustness of different detection methods to various image compressions and noises. Average AP scores of the baseline model [28] and ours across two types of generative models (GAN and Diffusion) under different qualities of JPEG compression (top row) and different levels of Gaussian noise (Bottom row) are compared.

render the generated images more distinguishable from authentic ones at lower qualities, thereby potentially enhancing our detection model's ability to identify them as fake. Further investigation into the model's behavior under these conditions is necessary to fully understand and explain these results. It may involve examining the specific characteristics of the noise introduced by the diffusion model and how they interact with the detection model's features.

## 5    Conclusions

In conclusion, the rapid advancement of AI-synthesized image generation technologies presents a significant challenge to the authenticity and reliability of digital content. This work introduces a robust AI-Synthesized Image Detection framework based on Frequency-aware Multi-Feature Fusion, designed to counter the threat posed by these sophisticated forgery techniques. By integrating spatial, gradient, frequency domain, and CLIP features through a deep learning architecture, our model leverages a diverse set of visual representations to enhance detection accuracy. Employing an attention mechanism allows for dynamic learning of feature importance, optimizing detection performance. Extensive experiments on a comprehensive dataset demonstrate our method's exceptional accuracy, generalization, and robustness against various attack scenarios. As AI-synthesized image generation techniques evolve, our framework's adaptability and robustness make it a potent tool in the ongoing battle against the spread of fake images. This work contributes to the current state-of-the-art

AI-synthesized image detection. It lays a solid foundation for future research to develop more generalized and reliable detection solutions.

**Acknowledgement.** This work was supported by the National Natural Science Foundation of China (Grant No. 62402009), and the Science and Technology Development Fund of Macao under Grant 0013-2024-ITP1.

# References


1. Brock, A., Donahue, J., Simonyan, K.: Large scale GAN training for high fidelity natural image synthesis. CoRR abs/ arXiv: 1809.11096 (2018)
2. Chai, L., Bau, D., Lim, S.-N., Isola, P.: What makes fake images detectable? understanding properties that generalize. In: Vedaldi, A., Bischof, H., Brox, T., Frahm, J.-M. (eds.) ECCV 2020. LNCS, vol. 12371, pp. 103–120. Springer, Cham (2020). https://doi.org/10.1007/978-3-030-58574-7_7
3. Chen, H., et al.: Queen: query unlearning against model extraction. IEEE Trans. Inform. Forensics Sec. (2025)
4. Chen, L., Gu, L., Zheng, D., Fu, Y.: Frequency-adaptive dilated convolution for semantic segmentation. In: Proceedings of the IEEE/CVF Conference on Computer Vision and Pattern Recognition (CVPR), pp. 3414–3425 (June 2024)
5. Choi, Y., Choi, M., Kim, M., Ha, J.W., Kim, S., Choo, J.: Stargan: unified generative adversarial networks for multi-domain image-to-image translation. In: Proceedings of the IEEE Conference on Computer Vision and Pattern Recognition (CVPR) (June 2018)
6. Cozzolino, D., Poggi, G., Verdoliva, L.: Recasting residual-based local descriptors as convolutional neural networks: an application to image forgery detection. In: Proceedings of the 5th ACM Workshop on Information Hiding and Multimedia Security, IH&MMSec 2017, pp. 159–164. Association for Computing Machinery, New York (2017)
7. Dayma, B., et al.: Dalle mini (July 2021)
8. Dhariwal, P., Nichol, A.: Diffusion models beat gans on image synthesis. In: Ranzato, M., Beygelzimer, A., Dauphin, Y., Liang, P., Vaughan, J.W. (eds.) Advances in Neural Information Processing Systems, vol. 34, pp. 8780–8794. Curran Associates, Inc. (2021)
9. Frank, J., Eisenhofer, T., Schönherr, L., Fischer, A., Kolossa, D., Holz, T.: Leveraging frequency analysis for deep fake image recognition. In: III, H.D., Singh, A. (eds.) Proceedings of the 37th International Conference on Machine Learning. Proceedings of Machine Learning Research, 13–18 Jul, vol. 119, pp. 3247–3258. PMLR (2020)
10. Guo, Z., Jia, Z., Wang, L., Wang, D., Yang, G., Kasabov, N.: Constructing new backbone networks via space-frequency interactive convolution for deepfake detection. IEEE Trans. Inf. Forensics Secur. **19**, 401–413 (2024)
11. He, P., Li, H., Wang, H.: Detection of fake images via the ensemble of deep representations from multi color spaces. In: 2019 IEEE International Conference on Image Processing (ICIP), pp. 2299–2303 (2019)
12. Ju, Y., Jia, S., Cai, J., Guan, H., Lyu, S.: Glff: global and local feature fusion for ai-synthesized image detection. IEEE Trans. Multimedia **26**, 4073–4085 (2024)

13. Karras, T., Aila, T., Laine, S., Lehtinen, J.: Progressive growing of gans for improved quality, stability, and variation. CoRR arXiv: 1710.10196 (2017)
14. Karras, T., Laine, S., Aila, T.: A style-based generator architecture for generative adversarial networks. In: Proceedings of the IEEE/CVF Conference on Computer Vision and Pattern Recognition (CVPR) (June 2019)
15. Liu, C., Chen, H., Zhu, T., Zhang, J., Zhou, W.: Making deepfakes more spurious: evading deep face forgery detection via trace removal attack. IEEE Trans. Dependable Sec. Comput. (2022)
16. Liu, C., Zhu, T., Shen, S., Zhou, W.: Towards robust gan-generated image detection: a multi-view completion representation. In: Proceedings of the Thirty-Second International Joint Conference on Artificial Intelligence (IJCAI 2023), pp. 464–472 (2023)
17. Liu, C., Zhu, T., Zhao, Y., Zhang, J., Zhou, W.: Disentangling different levels of gan fingerprints for task-specific forensics. Comput. Standards Interfaces **89**, 103825 (2024)
18. Luo, Y., Du, J., Yan, K., Ding, S.: Lare$^2$: latent reconstruction error based method for diffusion-generated image detection. In: Proceedings of the IEEE/CVF Conference on Computer Vision and Pattern Recognition, pp. 17006–17015 (2024)
19. McCloskey, S., Albright, M.: Detecting gan-generated imagery using saturation cues. In: 2019 IEEE International Conference on Image Processing (ICIP), pp. 4584–4588 (2019)
20. Nataraj, L., et al.: Detecting GAN generated fake images using co-occurrence matrices. CoRR abs/ arXiv: 1903.06836 (2019)
21. Nichol, A., et al.: GLIDE: towards photorealistic image generation and editing with text-guided diffusion models. CoRR abs/ arXiv: 2112.10741 (2021)
22. Nirkin, Y., Wolf, L., Keller, Y., Hassner, T.: Deepfake detection based on discrepancies between faces and their context. IEEE Trans. Pattern Anal. Mach. Intell. **44**(10), 6111–6121 (2022)
23. Ojha, U., Li, Y., Lee, Y.J.: Towards universal fake image detectors that generalize across generative models. In: Proceedings of the IEEE/CVF Conference on Computer Vision and Pattern Recognition (CVPR), pp. 24480–24489 (June 2023)
24. Park, T., Liu, M.Y., Wang, T.C., Zhu, J.Y.: Semantic image synthesis with spatially-adaptive normalization. In: Proceedings of the IEEE/CVF Conference on Computer Vision and Pattern Recognition (CVPR) (June 2019)
25. Rombach, R., Blattmann, A., Lorenz, D., Esser, P., Ommer, B.: High-resolution image synthesis with latent diffusion models. In: Proceedings of the IEEE/CVF Conference on Computer Vision and Pattern Recognition (CVPR), pp. 10684–10695 (June 2022)
26. Tan, C., Zhao, Y., Wei, S., Gu, G., Liu, P., Wei, Y.: Rethinking the up-sampling operations in cnn-based generative network for generalizable deepfake detection. In: Proceedings of the IEEE/CVF Conference on Computer Vision and Pattern Recognition (CVPR), pp. 28130–28139 (June 2024)
27. Tan, C., Zhao, Y., Wei, S., Gu, G., Wei, Y.: Learning on gradients: generalized artifacts representation for gan-generated images detection. In: Proceedings of the IEEE/CVF Conference on Computer Vision and Pattern Recognition (CVPR), pp. 12105–12114 (June 2023)
28. Wang, S.Y., Wang, O., Zhang, R., Owens, A., Efros, A.A.: Cnn-generated images are surprisingly easy to spot... for now. In: Proceedings of the IEEE/CVF Conference on Computer Vision and Pattern Recognition (CVPR) (June 2020)

29. Zhang, X., Karaman, S., Chang, S.F.: Detecting and simulating artifacts in gan fake images. In: 2019 IEEE International Workshop on Information Forensics and Security (WIFS), pp. 1–6 (2019)
30. Zhou, S., Liu, C., Ye, D., Zhu, T., Zhou, W., Yu, P.S.: Adversarial attacks and defenses in deep learning: From a perspective of cybersecurity. ACM Comput. Surv. **55**(8), 1–39 (2022)
31. Zhu, J.Y., Park, T., Isola, P., Efros, A.A.: Unpaired image-to-image translation using cycle-consistent adversarial networks. In: Proceedings of the IEEE International Conference on Computer Vision (ICCV) (Oct 2017)

# Do Domain-Specific LLMs Keep Secrets?
# An Empirical Study of Privacy Risks
# and Membership Inference Attacks

Weicheng Xing[1] [iD], Jenny Wang[2], Jacko Feng[2], and Bo Liu[1][✉]

[1] School of Computer Science, Australian Artificial Intelligence Institute,
University of Technology Sydney, Sydney, NSW 2007, Australia
`weicheng.xing@student.uts.edu.au, bo.liu@uts.edu.au`
[2] Australia Education Management Group, Surrey Hills, VIC 3127, Australia
`{jenny.wang,jacko.feng}@aemg.edu.au`

**Abstract.** The integration of Large Language Models (LLMs) into specialized domain applications offers promising avenues for personalized and contextually relevant experiences. However, deploying domain-specific LLMs-particularly those fine-tuned on sensitive data or enhanced via Retrieval-Augmented Generation (RAG)-introduces significant privacy concerns. In this paper, we explore how vulnerable these domain-specific LLMs are to data leakage, with a focus on Membership Inference Attacks (MIAs). Using datasets containing sensitive domain-specific information, we compare the privacy risks of fine-tuned models versus RAG-based ones, revealing different patterns of exposure for each. Our results show that existing privacy protections often fall short when applied to models trained in specialized settings. We argue for the need to develop privacy-preserving techniques that are suitable for specific domains. This work provides novel insights into safeguarding sensitive information while exploiting the advantages offered by domain-specific LLMs, laying the groundwork for future research into secure and custom model deployments.

## 1  Introduction

The proliferation of Large Language Models (LLMs) has significantly reshaped the landscape of natural language processing (NLP), empowering machines to generate and understand contextually relevant and coherent text across many tasks. Prominent models such as DeepSeek's DeepSeek-R1 [10] and OpenAI's GPT-4o [28] exemplify these capabilities, excelling in general-purpose scenarios like summarization, translation, and creative content generation. However, their inherently generalized training limits their effectiveness in specialized domains that demand precise, context-specific expertise [11]. This limitation has catalyzed the emergence of domain-specific LLMs, explicitly tailored to address the nuanced demands of fields such as healthcare, finance, legal services, and education [5].

Domain-specific LLMs offer significant potential for enhancing targeted applications through tailored interactions and informed decision-making. For instance, educational LLMs leverage student data to provide personalized learning recommendations, while legal-focused models streamline contract reviews and precedent analyses. Nevertheless, this customization inherently amplifies privacy risks, particularly when sensitive, domain-specific datasets containing personally identifiable or proprietary information are involved [24]. Addressing these privacy vulnerabilities is therefore essential for the secure and responsible adoption of specialized LLMs.

Prior studies predominantly focus on general privacy vulnerabilities in broad LLM deployments [26], leaving a critical gap regarding the specific risks introduced by domain-specific adaptations, particularly in contrasting fine-tuned and retrieval-augmented generation (RAG) [16] approaches. To bridge this gap, our paper presents a rigorous analysis of privacy concerns unique to domain-specific LLMs, with a targeted focus on Membership Inference Attacks (MIAs). MIAs represent a substantial threat vector, aiming to identify the presence of particular data points within a model's training set, thereby potentially exposing sensitive information.

Specifically, our research systematically compares privacy vulnerabilities between fine-tuned and RAG-enhanced LLMs when handling sensitive domain-specific data, illustrating the distinctive vulnerabilities inherent in each approach. We perform targeted evaluations of these models under various membership inference attacks, including ZlibEntropy [4], Min-k% Prob [30], Neighborhood Attack [24], and a novel MIA-RAG [2] method explicitly tailored for retrieval-based systems. Furthermore, we extensively investigate existing defense methodologies and demonstrate through comprehensive experimental analyses that traditional privacy-preserving measures, such as Differential Privacy, may prove inadequate within highly specialized, domain-specific contexts. Based on our empirical findings and detailed discussions, we provide novel insights and practical implications for developing secure, domain-sensitive LLM deployments, guiding future research towards more robust privacy-preserving strategies specifically tailored for specialized domains.

Our key findings indicate that RAG models exhibit significantly higher vulnerability to MIAs compared to fine-tuned models, particularly when trained on specialized, domain-specific datasets. Furthermore, traditional privacy-preserving measures like Differential Privacy were found insufficient in adequately protecting these specialized LLM deployments.

## 2    Preliminary

The development and deployment of domain-specific Large Language Models have been driven by the need to enhance performance in specialized contexts. While general-purpose LLMs are trained on vast and diverse datasets, they may lack the depth of knowledge required for specific domains. To address this, two primary approaches have emerged: fine-tuning [15] and RAG [20].

### 2.1 Fine-Tuning

Fine-tuning involves adapting a pre-trained LLM to a specific domain by training it on a smaller, domain-specific dataset. This process adjusts the model's parameters to internalize domain-specific knowledge, thereby improving its performance on related tasks. Formally, let $\mathcal{D}_{\text{domain}} = \{(x_i, y_i)\}_{i=1}^{N}$ represent the domain-specific dataset, where $x_i$ denotes input sequences and $y_i$ their corresponding outputs. The objective is to minimize the loss function $\mathcal{L}(\theta)$ over $\mathcal{D}_{\text{domain}}$:

$$\mathcal{L}(\theta) = \frac{1}{N} \sum_{i=1}^{N} \ell(f_\theta(x_i), y_i), \tag{1}$$

where $f_\theta$ denotes the LLM with parameters $\theta$, and $\ell$ is the loss function, typically cross-entropy for classification tasks. Fine-tuning updates $\theta$ to reduce $\mathcal{L}(\theta)$, aligning the model's behavior with domain-specific requirements [11].

### 2.2 Retrieval-Augmented Generation (RAG)

RAG combines retrieval-based systems with generative models to enhance LLM performance by integrating external knowledge sources. In this approach, given an input query $q$, the model retrieves relevant documents $\{d_j\}_{j=1}^{K}$ from a knowledge base $\mathcal{K}$ and generates a response $r$ conditioned on both $q$ and the retrieved documents. The process involves two main components:

1. **Retriever**: Identifies a subset of documents $\{d_j\}_{j=1}^{K}$ from $\mathcal{K}$ relevant to the query $q$. This is often achieved using similarity measures in a shared embedding space.
2. **Generator**: Produces the final response $r$ by conditioning on the input query $q$ and the retrieved documents $\{d_j\}_{j=1}^{K}$.

Mathematically, the response generation can be expressed as:

$$P(r \mid q, \{d_j\}_{j=1}^{K}) = \prod_{t=1}^{T} P(r_t \mid r_{<t}, q, \{d_j\}_{j=1}^{K}; \theta), \tag{2}$$

where $r_t$ denotes the $t$-th token of the response, and $\theta$ represents the model parameters. The retriever aims to maximize the relevance of $\{d_j\}_{j=1}^{K}$ to $q$, while the generator focuses on producing coherent and contextually appropriate responses [12].

RAG offers advantages in rapidly evolving fields by allowing models to access up-to-date information without extensive retraining. However, reliance on external data sources introduces potential security risks, as malicious content within the knowledge base can lead to Membership Inference Attacks [16].

### 2.3   Membership Inference Attacks (MIAs)

MIAs are a class of attacks where an adversary aims to determine whether a specific data point was included in the training set of a machine learning model, posing significant privacy risks [31]. For LLMs, MIAs exploit the model's tendency to assign higher confidence scores to training data compared to unseen data. Formally, given a data point $x$ and a model $f_\theta$, the goal is to determine the membership status $m$ as follows:

$$m = \begin{cases} 1 & \text{if } x \in \mathcal{D}_{\text{train}} \\ 0 & \text{if } x \notin \mathcal{D}_{\text{train}} \end{cases} \tag{3}$$

Attackers often utilize the model's output probabilities or loss values to infer membership. For instance, a lower loss $\ell(f_\theta(x), y)$ may indicate that $(x, y)$ was part of the training data. This vulnerability underscores the need for robust privacy-preserving techniques in model training and deployment.

## 3   Methodology

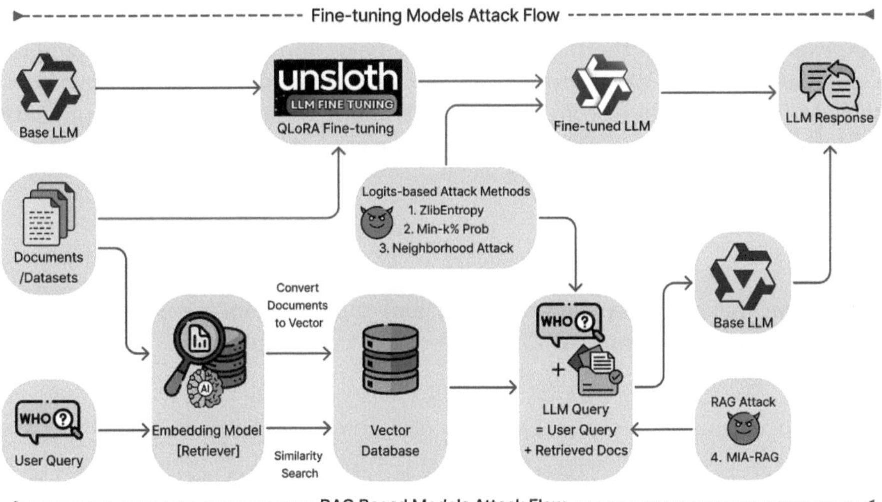


**Fig. 1.** MIA attack flows against Fine-tuned Models (Blue) and RAG based Models (Red). (Color figure online)

We evaluate membership inference vulnerability under two model configurations: (1) a fine-tuned model and (2) a RAG model. The base large language model used in both settings is **DeepSeek-R1-Distill-Qwen-7B**, a 7B-parameter model distilled for improved reasoning. In Fig. 1, we illustrate the experimental setup and attack workflows for comparing privacy vulnerabilities in fine-tuned versus RAG models.

The upper flow represents fine-tuned models, where a base LLM is fine-tuned using the QLoRA technique with domain-specific datasets. Subsequently, fine-tuned models are evaluated through logits-based membership inference attack methods, including ZlibEntropy, Min-k% Prob, and Neighborhood Attack.

The lower flow describes the RAG model setup, involving embedding documents and user queries into vectors for retrieval from a vector database. These retrieved documents are then combined with user queries to form inputs for the base LLM, generating responses. Specifically, this RAG-based pipeline is targeted by a specialized membership inference attack, the MIA-RAG attack, which exploits vulnerabilities unique to retrieval mechanisms.

For the **RAG setting**, we integrate an external dense retriever: documents are encoded into a vector index using Sentence Transformers (embedding model: *all-MiniLM-L6-v2* [32]), and at query time the top-$k$ relevant pieces are retrieved and prepended as context to the LLM. This allows the model to incorporate domain knowledge from the retrieval database instead of memorizing it in parameters.

In the **Fine-tuning setting**, we directly fine-tune the base model on target data using the QLoRA technique [7], which enables memory-efficient adaptation by backpropagating through a 4-bit quantized model into low-rank adapters. Each fine-tuning uses 5,000 samples from a given dataset (details below), with 4,000 examples used as the training set (members) and 1,000 held-out examples as non-members for attack evaluation. We fine-tune for 5 epochs, which was sufficient for the model to converge on the training data. All model outputs are generated in a black-box API setting where we can obtain the model's predicted token probabilities (logits) for each query.

### 3.1   Datasets

We consider one general-purpose dataset and three domain-specific datasets in our experiments. The **general datasets** cover broad topics:

- *Chinese-DeepSeek-R1-Distill-data-110k (Deepseek)* [6] – a broad-coverage Chinese corpus containing 110k samples (used in distillation of the base model)

The **domain-specific datasets** target niche content areas in Medical and Physics:

- *English Quotes (Quotes)* [9] – a collection of famous quotations and sayings;
- *Physics* [21] – domain text covering physics problems and explanations;
- *HealthCareMagic-100k (HCM)* [19] – a set of medical question-answer dialogues (from the HealthCareMagic forum).

These datasets represent scenarios with potentially higher memorization risk due to narrow focus.

## 3.2  Attack Methods

We evaluate **black-box logits-based membership inference attacks** that only require query access to the model's output probabilities. Specifically, we implement four attack score functions proposed in recent literature:

1. **ZlibEntropy** [4]
   Computes the ratio of the model's per-sample log-loss to the sample's inherent complexity, estimated via zlib compression size. Intuitively, this method calibrates the model's surprise on $x$ by how compressible $x$ is; a member sample is expected to have *unexpectedly* low loss relative to its entropy, indicating overfitting.

2. **Min-$k$% Prob** [30]
   the model's lowest token probabilities in the sample as the signal. Instead of averaging over the entire sequence likelihood, this score focuses on the subset of tokens with the smallest predicted probabilities. The intuition is that non-member inputs will contain more "outlier" tokens with extremely low likelihood under the model (indicating unfamiliar content), whereas member inputs (seen in training) should have fewer such low-probability tokens.

3. **Neighborhood Attack** [24]
   the query sample to create a set of *neighboring* inputs and compares the target model's loss on the original vs. the neighbors. Following the approach in, we generate $n$ slight variants of a given text (using a masked language model to replace or mask random token spans) that preserve similar context. The model's loss on each neighbor is computed and averaged, and the difference or *curvature* between the original loss and neighbor loss serves as the membership score.

4. **MIA-RAG Attack** [2]
   recent attack designed specifically for retrieval-augmented generation systems. This method crafts a special prompt to query the RAG model in a way that reveals whether a given document is in the retrieval database. In our implementation, the attacker asks the RAG system a question that can only be answered using the exact content of the candidate document. By observing the model's answer or its probability of answering "Yes, I have seen this" vs. "No", the attacker infers membership. This attack is only applicable to the RAG setting and leverages the unique behavior of the retriever: if the document is in the index (member), it will be fetched and significantly influence the model's output. We evaluate MIA-RAG in the RAG scenario to compare its effectiveness against the other general-purpose attacks.

## 3.3  Evaluation Metrics

To quantify attack success, we report two standard metrics: **ROC/AUC** and **TPR@lowFPR**. The ROC AUC (Area Under the Receiver Operating Characteristic Curve) measures the overall discrimination ability of the membership inference score – an AUC of 0.5 indicates random guessing, while 1.0 indicates perfect separation of members vs. non-members. We also specifically examine the **True Positive Rate at a low False Positive Rate** (TPR@FPR), focusing on the attacker's hit-rate when very few false alarms are allowed. Following prior work, we use TPR at 1% FPR as a representative high-precision operating point (i.e., the percentage of member samples correctly identified when the false positive rate is fixed to 0.05). This metric is critical for understanding whether an attacker can confidently identify members with near-zero false positives – a high TPR@1%FPR implies a severe privacy leak, since the attacker can be almost sure any positive prediction corresponds to an actual training sample.

We present results for both AUC and TPR@1%FPR for each attack method on each model/dataset configuration. Additionally, we compare results along two axes:

(a) **Fine-tuned vs. RAG** – evaluating which model is more resistant to membership inference
(b) **General vs. Domain-specific data** – assessing if niche domain data leads to greater vulnerability than a general corpus. All reported metrics are averaged over 3 runs with different random non-member splits, and we include 99% confidence intervals (which were found to be within $\pm0.01\%$ of the reported values for AUC).

## 4    Results and Discussions

### 4.1    Overall Attack Performance

Table 1 summarizes the AUC results for each membership inference attack applied to both fine-tuned (FT) and retrieval-augmented generation (RAG) models, across general and domain-specific datasets. Correspondingly, Table 2 presents TPR at a stringent threshold of 1% FPR, elucidating the performance of these attacks under conservative error conditions. Several notable patterns are evident. Due to certain python packages required by Neighborhood attack cannot be applied to Chinese characters, we skipped the Neighborhood attack against **DeepSeek** dataset. Our experimental findings demonstrate that defenseless RAG models exhibit significantly higher vulnerability to membership inference attacks compared to their fine-tuned counterparts.

### 4.2    General vs. Domain-Specific Vulnerability

Our findings indicate that **domain-specific LLMs exacerbate membership inference vulnerability** for both fine-tuned and RAG models, with RAG systems being consistently more affected. Specifically, the RAG model use domain-specific *Quotes* dataset yields the highest vulnerability, evidenced by consistently elevated AUC scores (e.g. ranging from 0.483 to 0.868 across different attack methods). Such elevated vulnerability is likely due to the highly specialized nature of tag extraction input and output, resulting in uniquely identifiable retrieval patterns.

**Table 1.** AUC of membership inference attacks (higher = more vulnerable) on Fine-tune vs. RAG models.

| Attack | Deepseek | | Quotes | | Physics | | HCM | |
|---|---|---|---|---|---|---|---|---|
| | FT | RAG | FT | RAG | FT | RAG | FT | RAG |
| ZlibEntropy | 0.534 | 0.568 | 0.528 | 0.610 | 0.659 | 0.555 | 0.565 | 0.599 |
| Min-$k$% Prob | 0.555 | 0.541 | 0.501 | 0.549 | 0.683 | 0.462 | 0.612 | 0.544 |
| Neighborhood | – | – | 0.489 | 0.483 | 0.546 | 0.488 | 0.549 | 0.503 |
| MIA-RAG (RAG only) | – | 0.791 | – | 0.868 | – | 0.648 | – | 0.798 |

In contrast, models trained on the *Deepseek* show reduced susceptibility (AUCs 0.541–0.791 for RAG and 0.534–0.555 for fine-tuned), reflecting greater semantic overlap and redundancy among general data samples, thus complicating membership inference. Nevertheless, even the general dataset on RAG remains more vulnerable (AUC up to 0.612) than its fine-tuned counterpart (maximum AUC 0.584), further underscoring the inherent risks associated with transparent retrieval processes. These outcomes indicate a nuanced interplay between content uniqueness and retrieval transparency, consistently favoring attackers when targeting RAG systems.

### 4.3 Fine-Tuned vs. RAG – Detailed Comparison

Across all evaluated datasets and attack strategies, RAG models consistently reveal greater susceptibility to membership inference than fine-tuned models. The average AUC score across all datasets and attacks from Table 1 is approximately 0.604 for the RAG model compared to 0.565 for the fine-tuned variant. This disparity becomes even more apparent at low false-positive rates (Table 2), with attackers achieving TPR@1%FPR ranging between 4%–29% on RAG for domain-specific data, while fine-tuned models generally remain below 14% under identical conditions.

The primary vulnerability arises because retrieval-based models inherently provide externally observable cues indicative of training data membership, contrasting with fine-tuning, where memorization is less overt. However, it is crucial to emphasize that fine-tuning does not guarantee complete protection; attacks still achieve moderate performance.

The substantial performance of MIA-RAG attacks further highlights critical privacy implications when deploying defenseless retrieval-based systems, especially with domain-specific datasets. For example, the MIA-RAG attack achieves an alarming 29.4% TPR@1%FPR on the *Quotes* dataset, underscoring the necessity for robust protective mechanisms or differential privacy strategies when employing retrieval-based architectures in sensitive applications.

**Table 2.** True Positive Rate at 1% False Positive Rate (TPR@1%FPR) for membership inference attacks on Fine-tune vs. RAG models.

| Attack | Deepseek | | Quotes | | Physics | | HCM | |
|---|---|---|---|---|---|---|---|---|
| | FT | RAG | FT | RAG | FT | RAG | FT | RAG |
| ZlibEntropy | 1.0% | 2.0% | 0.4% | 1.2% | 3.4% | 1.8% | 2,0% | 2.2% |
| Min-$k$% Prob | 2.2% | 0.1% | 1.2% | 0.8% | 1.4% | 1.6% | 2.2% | 0.6% |
| Neighborhood | – | – | 1.2% | 1.8% | 1.0% | 1.0% | 2.2% | 1.0% |
| MIA-RAG (RAG only) | – | 26.2% | – | 29.4% | – | 2.7% | – | 27.8% |

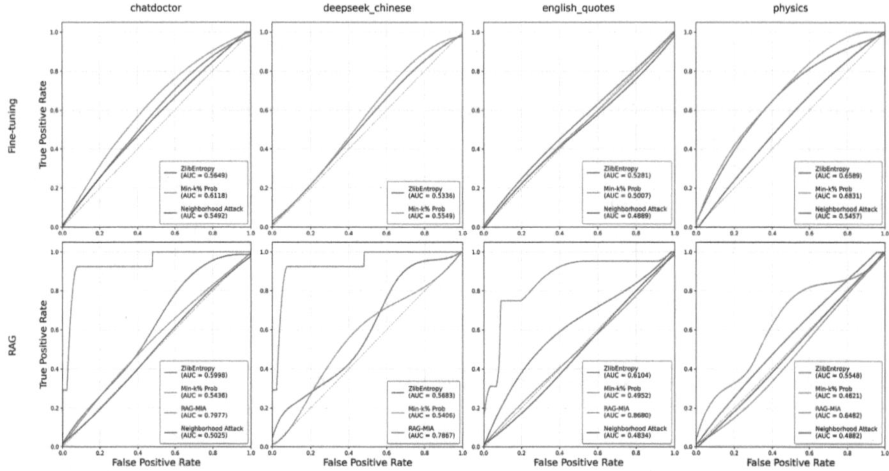

**Fig. 2.** ROC curves comparing membership inference attack performance on the fine-tuned vs. RAG models

## 4.4   Results Summary

The experimental findings highlight several key insights. Firstly, contrary to initial expectations, **RAG models exhibit notably higher vulnerability to membership inference attacks than fine-tuned models**. This greater susceptibility results primarily from the explicit and transparent retrieval operations intrinsic to RAG systems, which inadvertently expose recognizable membership signals to attackers. Across all tested attack methods and datasets, the difference in attack effectiveness, as measured by AUC and TPR shown in Fig. 2, consistently favors the attackers targeting RAG models. Secondly, **domain-specific datasets amplify the risk of membership inference significantly**. Models trained on specialized datasets (e.g., *Medicine* or *Biography*) consistently display greater vulnerability compared to those trained on general-purpose data. While the general datasets contain higher semantic diversity, providing inherent resistance against inference attacks due to natural redundancy, the explicit retrieval mechanism of RAG still noticeably heightens their susceptibility relative to fine-tuned models. Consequently, for sensitive and domain-specific scenarios employing RAG systems, implementing robust privacy-preserving methods or adopting differential privacy techniques becomes imperative.

## 5   Defences Against MIAs

Based on the empirical findings presented in this paper, fine-tuned models demonstrated significantly higher susceptibility to Membership Inference Attacks (MIAs) compared to their retrieval-augmented (RAG) counterparts, particularly when trained on domain-specific datasets containing unique or identifiable content such as quotations or specialized medical dialogues. This vulnerability underscores the necessity of implementing robust privacy-preserving techniques tailored to specific training approaches. Below, we outline established defenses in the literature relevant to both fine-tuning and RAG strategies to mitigate the risks identified in our experiments.

### 5.1   Differential Privacy

One of the most established defenses against MIAs is training or fine-tuning models with differential privacy guarantees. In DP-SGD (differentially private stochastic gradient descent), noise is injected into weight updates so that the model does not overly memorize any single training example. This approach provides a formal privacy budget limiting how much the model's outputs can reveal about any one training sample [18]. Applied to large language models, DP-based methods (e.g. DP-SGD [14] and DP-LoRA [35]) have consistently shown the strongest reduction in membership leakage, often yielding the lowest attack success rates among evaluated defenses [1]. For instance, a recent systematic study found that fine-tuning with DP (even with low-rank adaptation layers) achieved the best protection against MIAs in LLMs. The main drawback is degraded utility: rigorous DP can impair model accuracy or fluency, especially under strict privacy budgets. Nonetheless, when privacy is paramount – such as fine-tuning on sensitive text (e.g. medical records) – DP offers a principled defense by provably limiting the information any adversary can gain about individual training data from the model's behavior [17].

### 5.2   Privacy-Preserving Retrieval-Augmented Generation

Domain-specific LLMs often incorporate retrieval-augmented generation to handle private knowledge. This can be double-edged for privacy – it shifts where information is stored and potentially leaked [33,34]. On the one hand, using retrieval can mitigate the memorization of sensitive training data by the model itself. Research has shown that integrating an external knowledge base significantly reduces an LLM's tendency to regurgitate content from its own training set; the model relies on retrieved context instead of memorized passages [25]. In effect, RAG can act as a form of regularization against overfitting to the training corpus, yielding a model that is less vulnerable to membership inference on its fine-tuning data. On the other hand, the *retrieval dataset* introduces a new privacy surface: an attacker might now attempt membership inference on the documents in the retrieval index (i.e. determining if a given record is present in the RAG knowledge base).

To defend against this, recent work has explored **privacy-preserving retrieval techniques** [18]. One approach is to leverage advanced prompt engineering [22,29], by combining a safety prompt with the original user prompt to generate a synthetic query, thereby reducing vulnerability to malicious membership inference attacks. Other mitigation strategies include applying differential privacy to the retrieved content itself [18]; restricting retrieval to high-level summaries – compressing or filtering retrieved documents so that the model only sees generalized information, thereby reducing leakage of any single private record.

### 5.3   Defense Against RAG Specific Attacks

Due to the inherent vulnerability of RAG systems, specialized attacks like RAG-MIA can achieve high success rates. We have previously discussed several defense strategies that can be applied to strengthen the security of RAG systems. Here, we further explore the use of safety prompts as a defense mechanism specifically against RAG-targeted attacks. To evaluate this, we tested the effectiveness of various configurations of the following safe query prompt template:

```
You are a helpful AI assistant. Use the following context to answer.

If the provided context explicitly answers the question, respond
concisely in your own words.
If the question cannot be answered using the provided context,
clearly respond with "I cannot answer this question".
Do NOT quote, repeat, directly print any text from the provided context.
Do NOT indicate whether specific phrases or information appear verbatim.
in the provided context.

Context: {context}
Question: {question}
```

The results of the defense experiment are presented in Table 3, offering a detailed comparison between defended and defenseless RAG setups. Among the evaluated defense strategies, the safe query prompt method demonstrated outstanding performance. The distribution of scores, illustrated in Fig. 3, indicates that employing the safe query defense strategy leads to similar output distributions for member and non-member responses. Consequently, a similar pattern emerges alongside a significant decrease in ROC AUC, highlighting the effectiveness of this defense method.

**Table 3.** AUC of membership inference attacks (higher = more vulnerable) on Fine-tune vs. RAG models.

| Attack | Deepseek RAG | Quotes RAG | Physics RAG | HCM RAG |
|---|---|---|---|---|
| MIA-RAG (without defense) | 0.791 | 0.868 | 0.648 | 0.798 |
| MIA-RAG (with defense) | 0.539 | 0.558 | 0.586 | 0.545 |

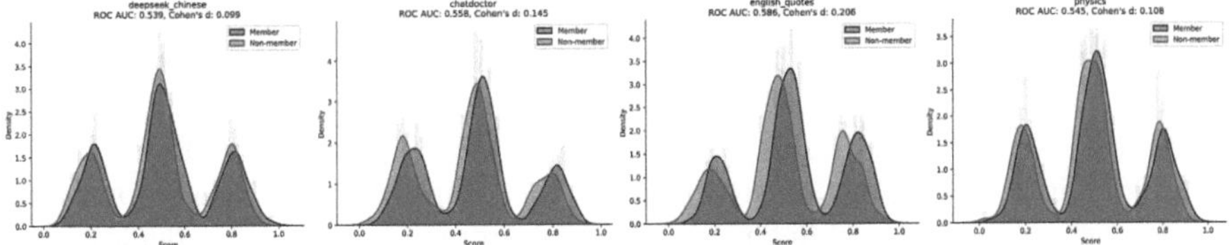

**Fig. 3.** Score distributions for RAG-MIA with safe prompt defense.

# 6 Limitations and Challenges in MIA Evaluation

## 6.1 Dataset Bias and Memorization Effects

When evaluating membership inference, it is essential to consider that perceived attack successes might be artificially inflated by subtle dataset biases rather than genuine memorization. Prior studies indicate that membership inference attacks (MIAs) often achieve inflated effectiveness primarily due to distributional skews between member and non-member samples, rather than from true memorization of training data [8]. For example, an attacker might easily distinguish non-member samples sourced from slightly different distributions (e.g., different temporal or topical domains), not necessarily because the model memorizes specific data points, but due to its weaker generalization capabilities on out-of-distribution inputs [23]. In the context of our findings, even though retrieval-augmented generation (RAG) models demonstrated increased vulnerability to specialized attacks, it remains important to verify that this vulnerability stems from authentic retrieval signals rather than inadvertent dataset biases. Highly redundant or common documents may artificially mask vulnerabilities, making genuine privacy risks harder to detect reliably.

## 6.2 Methodological Constraints in MIA Testing

Evaluating membership inference attacks in practice faces substantial methodological challenges, particularly when extending insights from controlled experiments to real-world deployments of retrieval-based LLMs. Many powerful MIA techniques assume **white-box or soft-label access**, requiring model logits, probability distributions, or loss values [13]. These assumptions hold in experimental setups but rarely reflect the constraints of commercial LLM APIs, which typically only provide text output (label-only settings), thereby severely restricting standard MIA approaches relying on precise logit-based measurements [3,27]. However, the transparency of the retrieval mechanism in RAG introduces a new attack vector that mitigates some of these methodological constraints. Even under label-only access conditions, retrieval behaviors might inadvertently expose membership signals-for example, distinct patterns in retrieved documents, topical alignment, or even indirect retrieval disclosures via subtle textual variations in the outputs. Despite these opportunities, practical constraints such as **rate limits, API costs, and retrieval restrictions** may still significantly impact the attacker's capability to conduct thorough MIA evaluations. Additionally, realistic API deployments may implement defenses specifically designed to obscure retrieval signals, complicating the attacker's task. Therefore, further methodological developments are essential to accurately gauge the robustness and privacy implications of defenseless RAG systems under realistic deployment conditions.

## 7   Conclusion

In this paper, we conducted an extensive empirical analysis to investigate the susceptibility of domain-specific Large Language Models to Membership Inference Attacks, comparing fine-tuned models against retrieval-augmented generation counterparts. Contrary to initial expectations, our results revealed that defenseless RAG models exhibit notably greater vulnerability to membership inference attacks due to their inherently transparent retrieval operations, particularly under specialized, domain-specific datasets characterized by distinctive and easily identifiable retrieval patterns. While fine-tuned models still face meaningful privacy risks due to memorization effects, their vulnerability consistently remained lower compared to RAG models under similar attack conditions.

Our findings underscore the pressing need for advanced privacy-preserving approaches explicitly tailored for retrieval-based LLM deployments. Techniques such as Differential Privacy, obfuscated retrieval strategies, and carefully optimized RAG methods represent promising avenues for mitigating membership inference risks. Additionally, the pronounced vulnerability of RAG systems highlights the necessity of carefully controlling the specificity and uniqueness of documents included in retrieval databases, particularly when handling sensitive or specialized content.

Future research should concentrate on developing hybrid defense frameworks combining differential privacy, retrieval obfuscation, and secure query handling mechanisms while maintaining model effectiveness. This study contributes essential insights into privacy vulnerabilities of defenseless RAG systems, guiding safer and more secure domain-specific LLM implementations.

# References


1. Amit, G., Goldsteen, A., Farkash, A.: Sok: reducing the vulnerability of fine-tuned language models to membership inference attacks. iBM Research Haifa, Israel (2024)
2. Anderson, M., Amit, G., Goldsteen, A.: Is my data in your retrieval database? membership inference attacks against retrieval augmented generation. arXiv preprint arXiv:2405.20446 (2024)
3. Anthropic: Claude 3.7 (2025). https://www.anthropic.com/claude, large Language Model. Accessed 24 Mar 2025
4. Carlini, N., et al.: Extracting training data from large language models. In: Proceedings of the 30th USENIX Security Symposium (2021)
5. Chalkidis, I., Fergadiotis, M., Malakasiotis, N.: Legal-BERT: the muppets straight out of law school. In: Proceedings of the 12th Language Resources and Evaluation Conference (LREC 2020) (2020)
6. Cong, L.: Chinese-deepseek-r1-distill-data-110k-sft (2025). https://huggingface.co/datasets/Congliu/Chinese-DeepSeek-R1-Distill-data-110k-SFT
7. Dettmers, T., et al.: Qlora: efficient finetuning of quantized LLMs. arXiv preprint arXiv:2305.14314 (2023)
8. Duan, M., et al.: Do membership inference attacks work on large language models? arXiv preprint arXiv:2402.07841v2 (2024)
9. ELTAIEF, A.: english_quotes (revision 7b544c4) (2023). https://doi.org/10.57967/hf/1053, https://huggingface.co/datasets/Abirate/english_quotes
10. Guo, D., Yang, D., Zhang, H., Song, J.: Deepseek-r1: incentivizing reasoning capability in LLMs via reinforcement learning. arXiv preprint arXiv:2501.12948 (2025)
11. Gururangan, S., et al.: Don't stop pretraining: adapt language models to domains and tasks. In: Findings of ACL (2020)
12. Guu, K., Lee, K., Tung, M., Pasupat, P., Chang, M.W.: Realm: retrieval-augmented language model pre-training. In: International Conference on Machine Learning, pp. 3927–3937 (2020)
13. He, Y., et al.: Towards label-only membership inference attack against pre-trained large language models. arXiv:2502.18943v1 (2025)
14. Houlsby, N., Giurgiu, A., Jastrzebski, S., Morrone, B., Sabour, S.: Parameter-efficient transfer learning for NLP. In: Proceedings of the 36th International Conference on Machine Learning (2019)
15. Howard, J., Ruder, S.: Universal language model fine-tuning for text classification. In: Proceedings of the 56th Annual Meeting of the Association for Computational Linguistics (Volume 1: Long Papers), pp. 328–339 (2018)
16. Izacard, G., Grave, E.: Leveraging passage retrieval with generative models for open domain question answering. In: Proceedings of ACL 2021, pp. 193–206 (2021)
17. Ji, Z., Lipton, Z.C., Elkan, C.: Differential privacy and machine learning: a survey and review. arXiv:1412.7584v1 (2014)
18. Koga, T., Wu, R., Chaudhuri, K.: Privacy-preserving retrieval-augmented generation with differential privacy. arXiv:2412.04697 (2024)
19. Lavita: Chatdoctor-healthcaremagic-100k (2023). https://huggingface.co/datasets/lavita/ChatDoctor-HealthCareMagic-100k. Accessed 24 Mar 2025
20. Lewis, P., et al.: Retrieval-augmented generation for knowledge-intensive NLP tasks. In: Advances in Neural Information Processing Systems, vol. 33 (2020)
21. Li, G.: Camel: Communicative agents for "mind" exploration of large scale language model society (2023)

22. Lyu, K., Zhao, H., Gu, X., Yu, D., Goyal, A., Arora, S.: Keeping LLMs aligned after fine-tuning: the crucial role of prompt templates. arXiv:2402.18540 (2024)
23. Maini, P., Jia, H., Papernot, N., Dziedzic, A.: LLM dataset inference: did you train on my dataset? arXiv:2406.06443v1 (2024). Equal contribution. Code available at https://github.com/pratyushmaini/llm_dataset_inference/
24. Mattern, J., et al.: Membership inference attacks against language models via neighbourhood comparison. In: Findings of ACL (2023)
25. Naseh, A., Peng, Y., Suri, A., Chaudhari, H., Oprea, A., Houmansadr, A.: Riddle me this! stealthy membership inference for retrieval-augmented generation (2025)
26. Naveed, H., et al.: A comprehensive overview of large language models. arXiv:2307.06435v10 (2023)
27. OpenAI: Openai API reference (2023). https://platform.openai.com/docs/api-reference. Accessed 24 Mar 2025
28. OpenAI: Hello GPT-4o (2024). https://openai.com/index/hello-gpt-4o. Accessed 23 Mar 2025
29. Reynolds, L., McDonell, K.: Prompt programming for large language models: beyond the few-shot paradigm. arXiv:2102.07350 (2021)
30. Shi, W., et al.: Detecting pretraining data from large language models. In: NeurIPS Workshop on Privacy in Machine Learning (2023)
31. Shokri, R., Stronati, M., Song, C., Shmatikov, V.: Membership inference attacks against machine learning models. In: 2017 IEEE Symposium on Security and Privacy (SP), pp. 3–18. IEEE (2017)
32. Wang, S., Li, B., Hou, L., Wang, L.: MiniLM: deep self-attention distillation for pre-trained transformers. In: Proceedings of the 58th Annual Meeting of the Association for Computational Linguistics (2020)
33. Zeng, S., et al.: The good and the bad: exploring privacy issues in retrieval-augmented generation (rag) leakage. In: Proceedings of the Findings of the Association for Computational Linguistic, pp. 4505–4524. Association for Computational Linguistics (2024)
34. Zhang, Y., et al.: Hijackrag: hijacking attacks against retrieval-augmented large language models (2024)
35. Zhu, F.N., et al.: DP-LoRA: differentially private low-rank adaptation for pre-trained language models (2023)

# Dynamic Weighted Consensus Framework for LLM Multi-agent Debate

Yi Li[1], Congcong Zhu[1]([✉]), MingHao Wang[1], Mengyang Wu[2], MingLu Zhu[3], and Xin Hu[4]

[1] City University of Macau, Macau, China
{d24091100573,cczhu,mhwang}@cityu.edu.mo
[2] The University of Sydney, Sydney, Australia
mewu9636@uni.sydney.edu.au
[3] School of Information Technology, Griffith University, Brisbane, QLD, Australia
minglu.zhu@griffithuni.edu.au
[4] Beijing DiDi Infinity Technology and Development, Beijing, China

**Abstract.** Large Language Models (LLMs) have demonstrated remarkable capabilities in complex reasoning and fact verification tasks, yet their performance remains constrained by inherent uncertainties in multi-step reasoning processes. Although the Multi-Agent Debate (MAD) framework significantly enhances reasoning accuracy through collaborative interactions among agents, these agents often generate divergent answers to the same question, which may inadvertently propagate incorrect responses. In such scenarios, greater priority should be granted to agents that consistently provide accurate answers. To address this challenge, this paper proposes a novel Dynamic Weighted Consensus Framework for LLM Multi-Agent Debate (DWC-MAD). This framework integrates real-time confidence quantification (derived from agents' iterative responses) and longitudinal accuracy metrics (based on agents' historical performance). By employing a dynamic weight allocation algorithm, DWC-MAD assigns differentiated weights to agent inputs, thereby constructing an optimized multi-agent debate system.

**Keywords:** LLMs · Multi-Agent Debate Framework · Dynamic Weight Allocation · Collaborative Reasoning · Uncertainty Quantification

## 1 Introduction

While LLMs excel in complex reasoning, inherent uncertainties and error propagation limit their reliability in high-stakes domains like legal or medical applications. Although multi-agent debate (MAD) enhances accuracy through collaborative critiques, persistent agent disagreements can propagate errors and compromise judgments. We propose DWC-MAD to address this by integrating: (1) Real-time confidence quantification measuring response consistency; (2) Longitudinal


T. Zhu et al. (Eds.): KSEM 2025, LNAI 15919, pp. 187–198, 2026.
https://doi.org/10.1007/978-981-95-3001-4_14

accuracy metrics evaluating historical performance; (3) Dynamic weight allocation prioritizing high-accuracy, high-confidence agents. DWC-MAD dynamically weights inputs based on these dual metrics, granting superior agents greater decision-making authority to enhance reasoning reliability and reduce error propagation. Figure 1 shows the process of this method. As can be seen in the figure, for a symmetry - related question, three agents engage in three rounds of debate after independent thinking. Each agent provides a final answer. Their weights are calculated by multiplying the confidence level by the historical accuracy. The system determines the final answer based on these weights to achieve reliable reasoning.

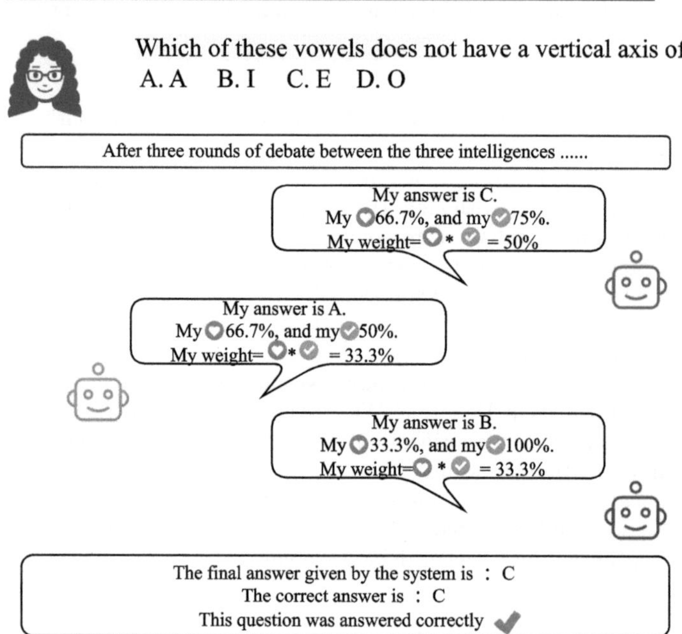


**Fig. 1.** Dynamic Weighted Consensus Framework for Multi-Agent Debate.

## 2  Related Work

### 2.1  Multi-agent Debate (MAD) Framework

The application of multi-agent systems in reasoning and collaborative tasks, particularly in multi-step reasoning scenarios, has been extensively investigated [1]. Liang [2] proposed a multi-agent reasoning debate framework, pioneering the exploration of how agents improve reasoning accuracy through structured interactive debates. Building on this foundation, Zhang [2] systematically investigated multi-agent systems for reasoning tasks, analyzing collaborative mechanisms where agents enhance reasoning reliability through mutual critique and error correction.

While multi-agent systems enhance reasoning accuracy through collaborative interactions, persistent inter-agent disagreements risk propagating erroneous conclusions [3]. Although multi-agent frameworks theoretically improve reasoning outcomes, divergent agent perspectives may still induce misleading inferences [4]. Current debate frameworks exhibit two critical limitations in conflict resolution: (1) Static voting mechanisms inadequately respond to real-time confidence oscillations, disproportionately amplifying high-confidence incorrect answers [5]; (2) Conventional historical evaluations employing fixed time-window averaging methods (e.g., 50 most recent responses) fail to dynamically capture agents' capability evolution, with Wang [6] reporting that 62% of system misjudgments originate from such temporal rigidity. To address these challenges, the proposed framework introduces dual dynamic evaluation mechanisms—real-time confidence quantification and adaptive historical performance modeling—which effectively suppress the propagation of high-confidence errors while eliminating fixed temporal constraints, thereby accurately reflecting agents' long-term learning trajectories.

## 2.2   Uncertainty Quantification and Longitudinal Accuracy

**Uncertainty Quantification.** Refers to evaluating the degree of uncertainty in a system, model, or predictive outcome. It identifies potentially unreliable predictions to enhance robustness and quantifies uncertainty to avoid overconfident yet erroneous decisions [7]. Research on uncertainty quantification primarily focuses on analyzing uncertainty in model outputs and improving system-wide trustworthiness through such measurements. Common methods include Bayesian approaches, Monte Carlo sampling, cross-validation, and confidence measures [8]. This study employs real-time confidence quantification, which evaluates each agent's confidence based on their iterative response patterns [9]. Unlike conventional static model-output-dependent methods, our approach dynamically incorporates agents' performance across debate rounds.


**Longitudinal Accuracy.** is the core indicator for evaluating the long-term performance of an agent. By statistically analyzing the agent's performance in historical tasks, short-term fluctuations (such as single accidental errors) are filtered out to reflect its true capability level. This is consistent with the Performance-Competence Dichotomy [10] in cognitive science: A single performance is disturbed by environmental noise, while long-term statistics are closer to the inherent capability. As shown in machine learning theory [11], relying solely on current task data (such as real-time confidence) is likely to lead to sensitivity to noise. The longitudinal accuracy, as a regularization term, can suppress overfitting to short-term outliers.

**Weighted Consensus Mechanism.** Dynamically adjusts agents' influence in decision-making processes to prioritize those demonstrating superior performance and higher confidence [5]. Building on the weighted voting-based consensus algorithm proposed by Wang [12]—which assigns differentiated weights to agents based on their historical task performance (e.g., accuracy rates) and current problem-specific confidence levels—this study further enhances collaborative effectiveness [13]. By integrating this mechanism with real-time confidence quantification (see Sect. 3.1) and longitudinal accuracy metrics (see Sect. 3.2), the proposed framework significantly improves the credibility and accuracy of system-level decisions [5].

## 3    Methodology

### 3.1    Framework Overview

This paper proposes a novel DWC-MAD framework featuring a two-phase collaborative reasoning mechanism [14]. The framework employs a dynamic weight allocation algorithm to assign differentiated weights to agent inputs. During problem resolution, agents first independently generate initial answers with reasoning chains. Subsequent iterative debate phases involve three rounds of response generation where agents incorporate peers' answers and reasoning cues [15]. As shown in Eq. 1, real-time confidence quantification, which measures answer certainty based on these three debate rounds. As shown in Eq. 2, longitudinal accuracy metrics used to evaluate historical performance. As shown in Eq. 3, a dynamic weight allocation algorithm enables adaptive adjustment of agent influence.

Figure 2 shows a specific case the workflow of the entire framework. When faced with the fifth question, the three agents first independently think of answers and justifications. Then, they exchange and discuss these with other agents. After three rounds, they present their final integrated answers. During this process, the confidence level of the integrated answer is calculated. For example, if the answers after three debates are A, A and B respectively, then the integrated answer is A with a confidence level of 66.7%. Then, combined with the historical answer correct rates of the previous four questions, the final weights are obtained. As shown in Eq. 6, the answer with the highest final weight is the answer to this question. After that, the agents' answer correct rates are modified based on the answering situation of this question for use in the sixth question. To resolve tie scenarios, the framework implements a secondary decision protocolprioritizing options supported by proponents with higher average historical accuracy rates [16].

### 3.2    Real-Time Confidence Quantification

To precisely capture agents' self-assurance levels regarding specific problems, this study proposes a real-time confidence quantification method. Specifically, each

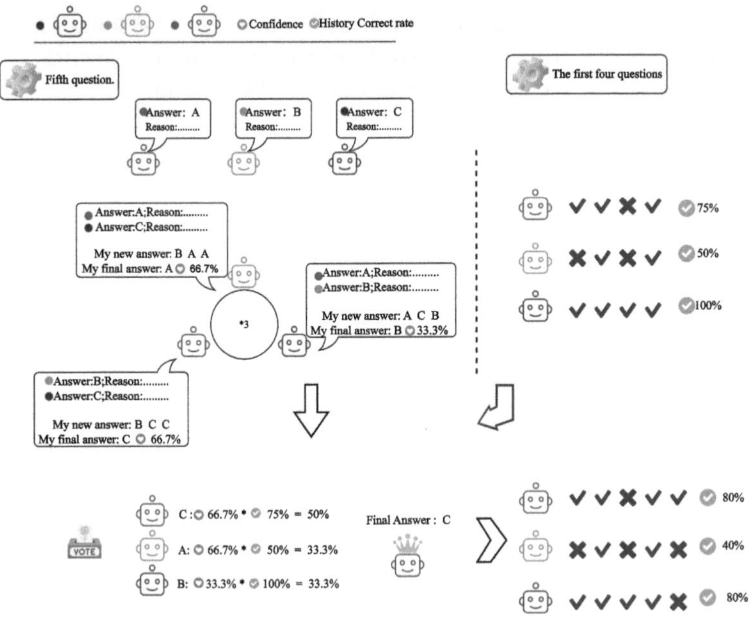


**Fig. 2.** Examples of using DWC-MAD in specific problems.

agent's three responses are evaluated based on their confidence scores [17], with their problem-specific confidence quantified through response frequency analysis.

Formally, let $A_{i,1}, A_{i,2}, A_{i,3}$ denote the three responses from $agent_i$ to $problem_j$, with corresponding confidence scores $C_{i,1}$, $C_{i,2}, C_{i,3}$. The dominant answer is identified by frequency statistics, and the agent's final confidence level $C_{i,j}$ is calculated as:

$$C_j = \max_{a \in \mathcal{A}} \left( \frac{1}{n} \sum_{k=1}^{n} \delta\left(a_k, a\right) \right) \times 100\% \tag{1}$$

where $A$ is the set of all possible answers, $a$ is an element in $A$, $a_k$ denotes the answer of the $kth$ sample, $n$ represents number of requests, and $\delta(a_k, a)$ is the indicator function, count the number of times a specified answer appears in the valid set, equal to 1 if $a_k = a$, and 0 otherwise.

This method calculates the agent's final confidence level regarding the problem, reflecting its self-assessed certainty during multi-round reasoning processes. Through this approach, we can more effectively capture the agent's performance in collaborative workflows.

### 3.3  Longitudinal Accuracy

In multi-agent collaborative processes, individual errors may mislead final decisions; thus, relying solely on short-term confidence assessments may inadequately capture an agent's overall reliability [18]. To evaluate agents' long-term performance more accurately, this paper introduces the Longitudinal Accuracy metric. This metric quantifies agents' sustained accuracy by tracking their performance across multiple historical tasks and dynamically adjusts their weights in future tasks based on this evaluation [14].

Assuming that the probability of agent $i$ answering correctly in the $kth$ task is $P_{\text{correct}}(i, k)$, the historical accuracy rate of the agent, denoted as $A_{i,\text{history}}$, can be expressed as:

$$A_{i,\text{history}} = \frac{1}{N} \sum_{k=1}^{N} P_{\text{correct}}(i, k) \tag{2}$$

where $N$ represents the total number of tasks in which agent $i$ has participated. This metric captures the agent's holistic performance in longitudinal tasks, thereby mitigating the impact of individual errors on its weight allocation.

### 3.4    Weight Allocation Mechanism

In multi-agent collaboration, final decisions are determined through weighted voting incorporating agents' answers, real-time confidence, and longitudinal performance [14]. The weight allocation formula is defined as:

$$w_i = (A_{i,\text{ history}} + \alpha) \times C_{i,j} \tag{3}$$

$\alpha$ is smoothing factor ensuring baseline weight allocation. The framework incorporates a dynamic reward-penalty mechanism that adjusts weights based on agents' real-time performance [19]. During the training phase, when a specific agent (e.g., GPT-3.5) demonstrates exceptional reasoning capabilities in the debate phase, the system assigns a reward factor $\beta_{\text{reward}} \in (1.0, 2.0]$ [20] to amplify its influence in subsequent voting stages, otherwise a penalty factor $\beta_{\text{penalty}} \in (0, 1.0]$ [21] is applied. This mechanism is formalized as:

$$w_i^{\text{adj}} = \begin{cases} w_i \times \beta_{\text{reward}} & \text{if } R_{\text{debate}} > \theta \\ w_i \times \beta_{\text{penalty}} & \text{otherwise} \end{cases} \tag{4}$$

Upon completion of all agents' weight calculations, these weights are applied to each candidate answer. A dictionary is maintained to store the cumulative weights of all options by iterating through each agent [22], thereby updating the weight values of each option [14]. Ultimately, the option with the highest aggregated weight is selected as the consensus outcome.

### 3.5    Tie-Breaking Mechanism

If multiple options exhibit identical weights (i.e., a tie scenario), a secondary decision criterion is adopted [16]: precedence is given to the option supported by agents with a higher average historical accuracy rate. The computational process comprises three hierarchical layers.

**Individual Evaluation Layer.** For each agent $a_j \in S_i$ supporting candidate answer $i$ (where $S_i$ denotes the supporter agent set), compute its historical accuracy rate:

$$\eta_j = \frac{1}{N} \sum_{k=1}^{N} \mathbb{I}(\text{ans}_j^k = \text{ans}_{\text{true}}^k) \tag{5}$$

where $N$ is the total number of historical tasks the agent has participated in, $k$ is the historical task index (excluding the current task), and the indicator function $\mathbb{I}(\text{ans}_j^k = \text{ans}_{\text{true}}^k)$ evaluates to 1 if agent $j$'s answer in the $kth$ historical task matches the ground truth, otherwise 0.

**Aggregation Layer.** compute the arithmetic mean of historical accuracy rates across all supporter agents:

$$\mu_i = \frac{1}{|S_i|} \sum_{a_j \in S_i} \eta_j \tag{6}$$

where $\sum_{a_j \in S_i}$ processes all agents supporting the current answer, and $|S_i|$ denotes the number of agents supporting candidate answer $i$.

**Decision Application Layer.** In tie-breaking scenarios, the candidate answer with the highest $\mu_i$ value is selected. This mechanism implements a fault-tolerant decision-making principle of "high-reliability group dominance" by assigning greater decision weight to agent groups with superior historical performance [23].

# 4   Experimental

In this section, we present experimental results obtained through the DWC-MAD, evaluating its performance across diverse datasets. The experiments focus on three benchmark datasets: MMLU, GSM8K, and TruthfulQA. By analyzing agent-specific performance variations across these datasets, we assess the framework's practical effectiveness. The subsequent subsections provide comprehensive descriptions of the experimental design [24], dataset specifications, evaluation methodology, and empirical findings [25].

## 4.1   Experimental Design

To evaluate the WC-MAD framework, we employ a heterogeneous model ensemble comprising DeepSeek-V3, GPT-4o-mini, and GPT-3.5. DeepSeek-V3 ensures factual consistency through knowledge graph verification, GPT-4o-mini accelerates consensus convergence via compressed attention mechanisms, while GPT-3.5 expands solution space exploration through diversified prompting, achieving Pareto optimality in accuracy-efficiency-cost tradeoffs.

We construct our benchmark test set by sampling 100 questions each from the Massive Multitask Language Understanding dataset (MMLU) [26], the GSM8K dataset, and the TruthfulQA dataset. The solution process is divided into two phases: (1) Autonomous Reasoning Phase: All three models generate answers independently; (2) Iterative Debate Phase: The agents conduct three rounds of reasoning based on the answers and the provided justifications from their peers, and update their own answers [27]. Finally, the answer with the highest occurrence frequency is selected as the integrated answer [28]. The three agents conduct weighted voting on the answers according to their own weights. The final output result is determined by the answer with the highest weighted score (tie-breaking handled in Sect. 3.5).

**Table 1.** LLMs Configuration Parameters

| Parameter | Specification |
| --- | --- |
| LLMs | DeepSeek-V3, GPT-4o-mini, GPT-3.5 |
| Temperature | 0.7 |
| Uncertainty metric | Multiple Query Uncertainty |
| Benchmark datasets | MMLU, GSM8K, TruthfulQA |
| Prompt strategy | 0/5-shot |
| Questions per dataset | 100 |
| Method repetitions | 3 |
| Debate configuration | 3 agents, 3 rounds, different LLMs |

To ensure output diversity among agents, the temperature parameter is set to 0.7 [29]. Uncertainty quantification is generated through Multiple Query Uncertainty. The benchmark datasets comprise MMLU, GSM8K, and TruthfulQA [26]. For MMLU, we employ both zero-shot (0-shot) and five-shot (5-shot) [30]configurations, while other datasets use exclusively zero-shot evaluation. Given computational constraints, we randomly sample 100 valid instances from each dataset after quality control procedures: (1) removing samples with missing values or format errors, (2) standardizing text encoding (UTF-8), and (3) normalizing question formulations. The debate configuration involves three distinct agents engaging in three debate rounds.(see Table 1) The subject proportion of the topics selected for the MMLU dataset is shown in Table 2, there may be slight differences in the percentages in the complete dataset, which contains a total of 15,908 questions across all subjects. The prompt engineering specifications for some parts are as follows: "Your response should be of the following format: 'Answer: LETTER' (without quotes) where LETTER is one of ABCD. Answer this question by combining your neighbors' accuracy, answers, and reasons".

**Table 2.** MMLU Dataset Subject Distribution

| Subject | Percentage (%) |
| --- | --- |
| Law | 12.0 |
| Medicine | 10.0 |
| Physics | 8.0 |
| Computer Science | 7.0 |
| Economics | 5.0 |
| History | 10.0 |
| Mathematics | 5.0 |
| Psychology | 5.0 |
| Chemistry | 3.0 |
| Biology | 7.0 |
| Anthropology/Archaeology | 5.0 |
| Political Science/IR | 5.0 |
| Others | 17.0 |

## 4.2  Experimental Results

During the experimental process, a sophisticated three-round debate iteration mechanism was designed to comprehensively and meticulously compare the performance of the DWC-MAD framework with multiple counterparts. The comparison targets not only covered cutting-edge models such as DeepSeek-V3, GPT-4o-mini, and GPT-3.5-Turbo but also included the traditional MAD framework. Four authoritative benchmark datasets, namely MMLU-5shot, MMLU-0shot, GSM8K, and TruthfulQA, were selected for precise evaluations from multiple dimensions, including knowledge understanding, reasoning ability, and answer authenticity.

After multiple rounds of stringent tests and in combination with in-depth data statistical analysis, the results indicate that the DWC-MAD framework has achieved remarkable results on all datasets. On the MMLU-5shot dataset, its accuracy rate is as high as 89%; on the MMLU-0shot dataset, the accuracy rate is 84%; on the GSM8K dataset, it reaches 87%; and on the TruthfulQA dataset, the DWC-MAD also performs outstandingly with an accuracy rate of 74%. Notably, on the TruthfulQA dataset, compared with the widely used GPT-3.5-Turbo, the accuracy rate of DWC-MAD has increased by 29%, which fully demonstrates its excellent ability in handling authenticity-related tasks.

In addition, compared with the traditional MAD framework, the DWC-MAD framework also shows better performance on the MMLU-0shot and TruthfulQA datasets. This result highlights the importance and superiority of the dynamic weight allocation mechanism in the DWC-MAD framework. This mechanism enables multiple agents to flexibly and rationally allocate weights according to task requirements and data characteristics during collaborative reasoning, thereby enhancing the overall performance. It effectively proves the innovation and effectiveness of the DWC-MAD framework in the field of multi-agent collaborative reasoning and opens up new directions for subsequent research and applications (Fig. 3).

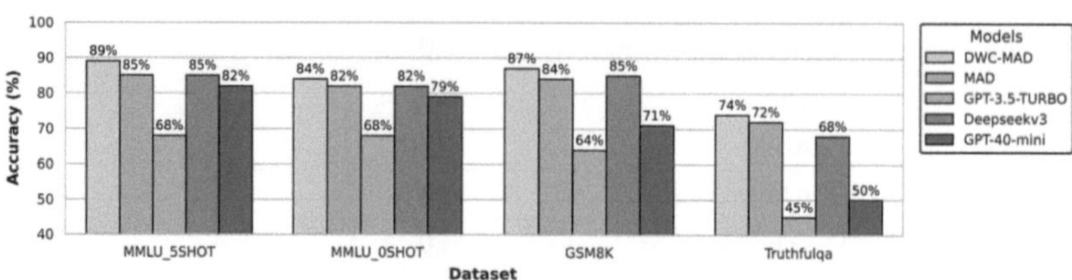

**Fig. 3.** Benchmark Performance Comparison of DWC-MAD with Single Agents and Traditional Framework

**Dynamic Weight Mechanism.** In the experiment, compared with the traditional voting mechanism, the dynamic fusion strategy increased the system accuracy by 2 - 3% points. Research shows that after removing the weight correction, the probability of error propagation increases.

## 5    Conclusion

The DWC-MAD framework achieves dynamic calibration of agent decision influence through integration of real-time confidence quantification and longitudinal accuracy metrics. Compared to traditional static voting mechanisms, this dynamic weight allocation strategy significantly enhances noise filtering capability while effectively suppressing propagation of erroneous reasoning paths during multi-iteration processes [31]. To address consensus deadlock issues in multi-agent debates, the secondary decision protocol constructs group-level credibility evaluation by analyzing historical reliability features of supporter clusters [24]. The dual-channel model (response stability + semantic verification) outperforms single-dimension evaluation in argument discrimination. Its self-optimizing framework autonomously adjusts collaboration via historical data learning, accelerating high-quality reasoning convergence and ensuring long-term adaptability.

## References


1. Sotani, H., Kumar, B.: Universal relations between the quasinormal modes of neutron star and tidal deformability. Phys. Rev. D **104**(12), 123002 (2021)
2. Liang, T., et al.: Encouraging divergent thinking in large language models through multi-agent debate. arXiv preprint arXiv:2305.19118 (2023)

3. Zhang, Y., Li, Z., Xie, Y., Qu, Y., Li, C., Mei, T.: Weakly supervised semantic segmentation for large-scale point cloud. In: Proceedings of the AAAI Conference on Artificial Intelligence, pp. 3421–3429 (2021)
4. Yang, F., et al.: Learning to attack real-world models for person re-identification via virtual-guided meta-learning. In: Proceedings of the AAAI Conference on Artificial Intelligence, vol. 35, no. 4, pp. 3128–3135 (2021)
5. Chen, J., Liao, K., Wei, K., Ying, H., Chen, D.Z., Wu, J.: ME-GAN: learning panoptic electrocardio representations for multi-view ECG synthesis conditioned on heart diseases. In: Proceedings of the 39th International Conference on Machine Learning, pp. 3360–3370. PMLR (2022)
6. Patil, V., Nair, V., Ghalme, G., Khan, A.: Mitigating disparity while maximizing reward: tight anytime guarantee for improving bandits. arXiv preprint arXiv:2208.09254 (2022)
7. Gal, Y., Ghahramani, Z.: Dropout as a bayesian approximation: representing model uncertainty in deep learning. In: International Conference on Machine Learning, pp. 1050–1059. PMLR (2016)
8. Das, A., Kottur, S., Moura, J.M.F., Lee, S., Batra, D.: Learning cooperative visual dialog agents with deep reinforcement learning. In: 2017 IEEE International Conference on Computer Vision (ICCV) (2017)
9. Jin, Y., Guosheng, H., Chen, H., Miao, D., Liang, H., Zhao, C.: Cross-modal distillation for speaker recognition. In: Proceedings of the AAAI Conference on Artificial Intelligence, vol. 37, pp. 12977–12985 (2023)
10. Tversky, A., Kahneman, D.: Judgment under uncertainty: heuristics and biases: biases in judgments reveal some heuristics of thinking under uncertainty. Science **185**(4157), 1124–1131 (1974)
11. Hastie, T., Tibshirani, R., Friedman, J.: The Elements of Statistical Learning. Springer, New York (2009). https://doi.org/10.1007/978-0-387-84858-7
12. Huang, Q., et al.: Personalized dialogue generation with persona-adaptive attention. In: Proceedings of the AAAI Conference on Artificial Intelligence, vol. 37, pp. 12916–12923 (2023)
13. Zhu, C., Cheng, Z., Ye, D., Hussain, F.K., Zhu, T., Zhou, W.: Time-driven and privacy-preserving navigation model for vehicle-to-vehicle communication systems. IEEE Trans. Veh. Technol. **72**(7), 8459–8470 (2023)
14. Liu, Z., et al.: Towards automated deep learning: analysis of the autoDL challenge series 2019. In: Escalante, H.J., Hadsell, R. (eds.) Proceedings of the NeurIPS 2019 Competition and Demonstration Track, vol. 123. PMLR (2020)
15. Hu, J., Hayashi, H., Cho, K., Neubig, G.: DEEP: DEnoising entity pre-training for neural machine translation. In: Proceedings of the 60th Annual Meeting of the Association for Computational Linguistics (Volume 1: Long Papers), pp. 1753–1766. Dublin, Ireland (2022)
16. Bargiacchi, E., Verstraeten, T., Roijers, D.M.: Cooperative prioritized sweeping. In: Proceedings of the 20th International Conference on Autonomous Agents and MultiAgent Systems, pp. 160–168. International Foundation for Autonomous Agents and Multiagent Systems (2021)
17. Wei, J., et al.: Chain-of-thought prompting elicits reasoning in large language models. In: Advances in Neural Information Processing Systems, vol. 35, pp. 24824–24837 (2022)
18. Gal, Y., Islam, R., Ghahramani, Z.: Deep bayesian active learning with image data. In: Precup, D., Teh, Y.W. (eds.) Proceedings of the 34th International Conference on Machine Learning, pp. 1183–1192. PMLR (2017)

19. Tymoteusz, M., Polina, K., Sofiia, M., Grzegorz, B.: Reinforcement learning: a driving force in the evolution of science and information activity. In: The 13th International scientific and practical conference "Information activity as a component of science development" (April 04–07, 2023) Edmonton, Canada. International Science Group. 2023. 580 p, pp. 449 (2023)
20. Schulman, J., Levine, S., Abbeel, P., Jordan, M., Moritz, P.: Trust region policy optimization. In: Bach, F., Blei, D. (eds.) Proceedings of the 32nd International Conference on Machine Learning, pp. 1889–1897. PMLR (2015)
21. Harwell, J., Lowmanstone, L., Gini, M.: Demystifying emergent intelligence and its effect on performance in large robot swarms. In: Proceedings of the 19th International Conference on Autonomous Agents and MultiAgent Systems. International Foundation for Autonomous Agents and Multiagent Systems (2020)
22. Zhu, C., Ye, D., Zhu, T., Zhou, W.: Location-based real-time updated advising method for traffic signal control. IEEE Internet Things J. $\mathbf{11}$(8), 14551–14562 (2023)
23. El-Kenawy, E.S.M., et al.: Improved weighted ensemble learning for predicting the daily reference evapotranspiration under the semi-arid climate conditions. Environ. Sci. Pollut. Res. $\mathbf{29}$(54), 81279–81299 (2022)
24. Zhu, C., Ye, D., Zhu, T., Zhou, W.: Time-optimal and privacy preserving route planning for carpool policy. World Wide Web $\mathbf{25}$(3), 1151–1168 (2022)
25. Rajpurkar, P., Zhang, J., Lopyrev, K., Liang, P.: SQuAD: 100,000+ questions for machine comprehension of text. In: Su, J., Duh, K., Carreras, X. (eds.) Proceedings of the 2016 Conference on Empirical Methods in Natural Language Processing, pp. 2383–2392. Association for Computational Linguistics, Austin, Texas (2016)
26. Hendrycks, D., et al.: Measuring massive multitask language understanding. arXiv preprint arXiv:2009.03300 (2020)
27. Zhu, C., Ye, D., Zhu, T., Zhou, W.: The evolution of cooperation in continuous dilemmas via multi-agent reinforcement learning. Knowl.-Based Syst. 113153 (2025)
28. Im, S., Kim, G., Oh, H.S., Jo, S., Kim, D.H.: Hierarchical text classification as sub-hierarchy sequence generation. In: Proceedings of the AAAI Conference on Artificial Intelligence, vol. 37, pp. 12933–12941 (2023)
29. Holtzman, A., Buys, J., Du, L., Forbes, M., Choi, Y.: The curious case of neural text degeneration. arXiv preprint arXiv:1904.09751 (2019)
30. Brown, T., et al.: Language models are few-shot learners. In: Advances in Neural Information Processing Systems, vol. 33, pp. 1877–1901 (2020)
31. Zhu, C., Ye, D., Huo, H., Zhou, W., Zhu, T.: A location-based advising method in teacher-student frameworks. Knowl.-Based Syst. $\mathbf{285}$, 111333 (2024)

# Streaming Hierarchical Clustering for Emerging New Class

Yixiao Ma[1], Ye Zhu[2], Yang Xu[1], and Kai Ming Ting[1(✉)]

[1] National Key Laboratory for Novel Software Technology and School of Artificial Intelligence, Nanjing University, Nanjing 210023, China
{mayx,xuyang}@lamda.nju.edu.cn, tingkm@nju.edu.cn
[2] School of Information Technology, Deakin University, Geelong 3125, VIC, Australia
xuyang@lamda.nju.edu.cn

**Abstract.** Streaming hierarchical clustering (SHC) is fundamental for real-time analysis of streaming data, with a research focus on its adaptive clustering capabilities dealing with concept drift. Traditional methods like Agglomerative Hierarchical Clustering (AHC) face challenges in dynamically updating clusters when encountering previously unseen new classes, resulting in degraded clustering outcomes. We present SHCRI (Streaming Hierarchical Clustering with Root-Insert), an algorithm that employs a root-insert strategy to achieve cluster tree adaptation for emerging new class points for a data stream. This approach strategically positions subtrees of emerging new class at nodes that maximize overall tree purity. We provide a theoretical analysis that guarantees SHCRI's superior performance in handling emerging new class compared to existing methods. Experimental results validate that SHCRI has superior performance than existing streaming AHC algorithms, consistently maintaining higher dendrogram purity during the periods of emerging new class.

**Keywords:** Hierarchical Clustering · Streaming clustering · Emerging new class

## 1 Introduction

Hierarchical clustering [16] organizes data into tree structures that reveal relationships among data points. In streaming scenarios [7], where data arrives continuously, algorithms must adapt to new classes without reprocessing historical data. This capability is crucial in domains like social network analysis [19], fraud detection [1], and bioinformatics [5].

Current streaming algorithms predominantly employ bottom-up approaches [9,13,14], initially assigning new points to leaf nodes before refining the tree structure. While algorithms like PERCH [9] and GRINCH [14] provide efficient local and global reconstruction strategies, they treat each point equally, without distinguishing whether it is a new class point. This approach often results in suboptimal handling of new class points, requiring correction of initial misplacements through costly tree restructuring.


T. Zhu et al. (Eds.): KSEM 2025, LNAI 15919, pp. 199–211, 2026.
https://doi.org/10.1007/978-981-95-3001-4_15

To address this limitation, we introduce a root-insert strategy that positions subtrees of new class points at optimal nodes to maximize tree purity. We integrate this approach with a recently proposed top-down streaming hierarchical clustering algorithm StreaKHC [7]. Our key contributions are:

1. Formulating the problem of streaming hierarchical clustering in handling emerging new class, and developing SHCRI, an enhanced version of StreaKHC that incorporates online preprocessing for improved handling of emerging new class in a data stream.
2. Providing a theoretical proof to demonstrate our proposed root-insert strategy's superiority over traditional tree restructuring methods for processing emerging new class points.
3. Empirically validating that SHCRI has superior performance than existing streaming AHC algorithms, consistently maintaining higher dendrogram purity during the periods of emerging new class. Furthermore, ablation studies show that the root-insert strategy enhances existing PERCH and SAHC algorithms, maintaining superior cluster tree purity in dealing with emerging new class.

## 2    Related Work

Hierarchical clustering methods have two categories: agglomerative (bottom-up) and divisive (top-down) [17]. Streaming scenarios favor bottom-up approaches, as top-down methods require complete data availability. Even recent top-down algorithms like SBTree [15] ultimately rely on leaf-node insertion strategies. Traditional agglomerative clustering iteratively merges points into larger clusters using a linkage function. However, a function requires $O(n)$ time complexity per insertion for a tree with $n$ leaves, making them impractical for streaming applications.

Modern streaming AHC algorithms implement post-insertion tree restructuring mechanisms. PERCH [9] employs local tree rotations to ensure that newly inserted points maintain higher similarity with sibling nodes than uncle nodes. Building on this foundation, GRINCH [14] introduces non-local grafting operations following rotations, enabling nodes to be relocated based on similarity relationships beyond immediate neighbors. These approaches enhance both tree purity and structural balance, facilitating faster node insertion and search operations.

StreaKHC [7] introduces an efficient recursive insertion methodology that traverses the cluster tree from root to leaf. At each level, it selects the child node exhibiting the highest similarity to the new data point, continuing this process until reaching a leaf node. The algorithm achieves remarkable computational efficiency through its point-set isolation kernel implementation [20], which computes node-point similarities in linear time. This top-down approach eliminates the need for exhaustive node comparisons, as it only requires examining nodes along a single path from root to leaf, significantly reducing the computational overhead of point insertion.

Existing streaming hierarchical clustering algorithms struggle with emerging new class. Current bottom-up approaches often misplace new class points, requiring complex restructuring that may not optimize dendrogram purity. While PERCH, GRINCH, and StreaKHC offer efficient clustering mechanisms, they lack specific strategies for handling new classes. We address this limitation through our proposed root-insert strategy, providing targeted optimization for emerging new class scenarios.

## 3   Problem Definition: SHEENA

Let $X = \{x_i\}_{i=1}^{n}$, $x_i \in \mathbb{R}^d, x_i \sim F$ denote a dataset of $n$ points, each sampled identically and independently from a distribution $F$. A set of clusters $\mathcal{C} = \{C_1, \ldots, C_K\}$ is defined as non-empty and non-intersecting subsets: $C_i \subset D, C_i \neq \emptyset, \forall_{i \neq j} \; C_i \cap C_j = \emptyset$. A dendrogram, or cluster tree [10], provides a hierarchical representation of cluster structure, organizing data in a binary tree where leaf nodes correspond to individual data points and internal nodes represent nested sub-clusters. This tree-based visualization effectively captures the hierarchical relationships and similarities among data points and their constituent clusters.

**Definition 1 (Cluster Tree).** *A binary* **cluster tree** $\mathcal{T}$ *on a dataset* $X = \{x_i\}_{i=1}^{n}$ *is a collection of subsets such that* $C_0 \triangleq \{x_i\}_{i=1}^{n} \in \mathcal{T}$ *and for each* $C_i, C_j \in \mathcal{T}$ *either* $C_i \subset C_j$, $C_j \supset C_i$ *or* $C_i \cap C_j = \emptyset$. *For any* $C \in \mathcal{T}$, *if* $\exists C' \in \mathcal{T}$ *with* $C' \subset C$, *then there exists two* $C_L, C_R \in \mathcal{T}$ *that partition* $C$.

Dendrogram purity [4,8,9] is a commonly used method for the overall evaluation of a cluster tree. The dendrogram purity is 1 if and only if all leaf nodes belonging to the same cluster are rooted in the same subtree, such that a local cut on the dendrogram can perfectly extract each cluster. It is calculated as follows.

**Definition 2 (Dendrogram Purity).** *Consider a dendrogram* $\mathcal{T}$ *generated by a hierarchical clustering algorithm applied to a dataset* $X = \{x_i\}_{i=1}^{n}$. *Let* $\ell(x_i)$ *denote the true label of* $x_i$, *with possible values in the set* $\{C_1, \ldots, C_k\}$. *Define* $\mathbb{P} = \{(x_i, x_j) | x_i \neq x_j \in X, \ell(x_i) = \ell(x_j)\}$ *as the set of all pairs of data points that belongs to the same ground-truth clusters. Then the dendrogram purity (DP) of a cluster tree,* $\mathcal{T}$, *is:*

$$DP(\mathcal{T}) = \frac{1}{|\mathbb{P}|} \sum_{(x_i, x_j) \in \mathbb{P}} pur(lvs(lca(x_i, x_j)), \ell(x_i)) \tag{1}$$

*where* $lca(x_i, x_j)$ *is the least common ancestor of* $x_i$ *and* $x_j$ *in* $\mathcal{T}$, $lvs(\eta)$ *is the descendant leaves of the node* $\eta$, *and* $pur(S, C_i) = \frac{\{x \in S | \ell(x) = i\}}{|S|}$ *is a collection of leaves and computes the fraction that belong to ground-truth cluster* $C_i$.

Here, we formulate the problem of streaming hierarchical clustering handling emerging new class as follows.

**Definition 3.** *(**Streaming Hierarchical clustEring with Emerging New clAsses, SHEENA**) Given the initial data $\mathcal{I} = \{x_i\}_{i=1}^m$, where each $x_i \in \mathbb{R}^d$ belongs to one of a total of $k$ clusters $C_i$ for $i = 1,\ldots,k$. A cluster tree $\mathcal{T}_I$ is generated from $\mathcal{I}$ using a hierarchical clustering algorithm $f$. Additionally, we have streaming data $\mathcal{S} = \{x_i'\}_{i=1}^{\infty}$, where $x_i' \in \mathbb{R}^d$ belongs to either an existing cluster $C_i$ from existing clusters $C_1,\ldots,C_k$ or new clusters $C_{k+1},\ldots,C_M$. The objective of solving the **SHEENA** problem is to update cluster tree $\mathcal{T}_{\mathcal{I}}$ to $\mathcal{T}_{\mathcal{I}\cup\{x_i'\}_{i=1}^t}$, ensuring that the purity of the cluster tree remains as high as possible at $t \geq 1$.*

Existing streaming hierarchical clustering problem usually assumes no change of cluster distributions in the data stream. In contrast, **SHEENA** assumes that there are new merging clusters during streaming. Therefore, **SHEENA** needs to detect points of new classes and ensure they are inserted or adjusted to optimal positions, thereby maintaining a high purity in the cluster tree at all times. The key challenges of solving **SHEENA** are listed as follows:

1. **Class Detection:** The existing cluster tree lacks prior knowledge of emerging new class, necessitating a robust mechanism for new class identification.
2. **Structural Integration:** New class points should be incorporated into the current tree structure while preserving a high dendrogram purity, as illustrated in Fig. 1.

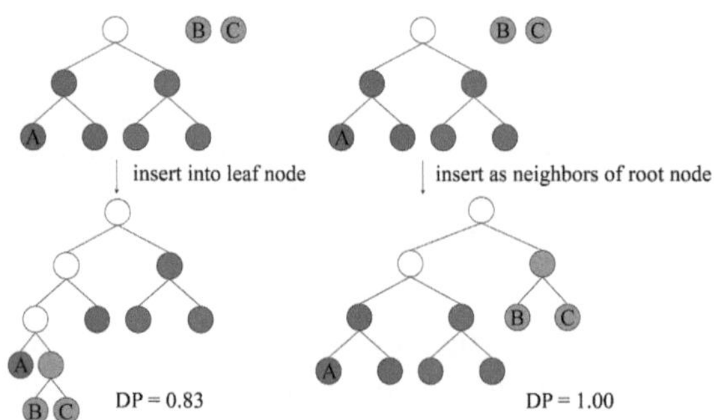


**Fig. 1.** Figure 1 illustrates two tree-growth strategies: traditional leaf-node insertion (left) versus root-level insertion (right). While leaf-node insertion integrates new classes into existing branches, root-level insertion creates dedicated branches for new classes.

## 4    Strategy to Insert a Subtree Belonging New Class

The existing streaming AHC algorithm usually inserts a new point $x^*$ into the nearest or the most similar leaf node $\eta$ of the cluster tree, before employing a

---

**Algorithm 1.InsertSubtree**

---

**Input:** Current cluster tree $\mathcal{T}_I$, cluster subtree $\mathcal{T}_S$, node $\eta \in \mathcal{T}_I$ where $\mathcal{T}_S$ is to be inserted
**Output:** Updated cluster tree $\mathcal{T}_{I \cup S}$
1: Initialize node $\eta^*$ as nil;
2: $\eta^*.leftChild \leftarrow \eta$;
3: $\eta^*.rightChild \leftarrow \mathcal{T}_S$;
4: Replace $\eta$ with $\eta^*$ in the specified position;
5: Return $\mathcal{T}_{I \cup S}$;

---

restructuring method to move the point to another level. This process is equivalent to executing Algorithm 1 $\mathtt{InsertSubtree}(\mathcal{T}_I, \mathcal{T}_{\{x^*\}}, \eta)$, where $\mathcal{T}_{\{x^*\}}$ represents a subtree $\mathcal{T}_S$ that contains only a single point $x^*$.

In the **SHEENA** framework, incoming data points can originate from either previously observed classes or entirely new classes, necessitating distinct insertion strategies to optimize the clustering structure. The algorithm must adaptively determine the appropriate insertion mechanism based on a point's class membership status.

In the streaming context, where points arrive sequentially, each new point can be conceptualized as a singleton subtree. For points belonging to new classes, the root-insert strategy optimizes local tree/dendrogram purity by strategically positioning these single-node subtrees at optimal insertion points within the existing hierarchy, as shown in the following proposition.

**Proposition 1.** *For a given cluster tree $\mathcal{T}$ and a cluster subtree $\mathcal{T}_{sub}$ composed of points of emerging new class, it holds that*

$$\arg\max_{\eta \in \mathcal{T}} DP(\mathtt{InsertSubtree}(\mathcal{T}, \mathcal{T}_{sub}, \eta)) = \mathcal{T}.root \tag{2}$$

The detailed proof of Proposition 1 can be found in Appendix A.1. This proposition guarantees that a cluster subtree composed of points from the emerging new class should be inserted into a given cluster tree at the root node to maximize *Dendrogram Purity* as defined in 2.

## 5   Streaming Hierarchical Clustering with Root Insert

We introduce **SHCRI** (**S**treaming **H**ierarchical **C**lustering with **R**oot-**I**nsert), an algorithm specifically designed to address the **SHEENA** problem efficiently. **SHCRI** distinguishes itself from existing incremental hierarchical clustering algorithms through its novel online preprocessing mechanism for emerging new class detection and adaptation.

**SHCRI** is based on $\mathtt{StreaKHC}$ [7] with additional procedures. It employs the anomaly detection technique $\mathtt{iNNE}$ (Isolation Using Nearest Neighbour Ensemble) [2] to determine whether a new batch contains points of emerging new class

---

**Algorithm 2.** SHCRI

---

**Input:** Initial data $\mathcal{I}$, streaming data $\mathcal{S}$ , $\psi, t$ for IK(Isolation Kernel), max tree size
    $L$, number of detected new class points $k$, iNNE threshold $\tau$
**Output:** Cluster tree $\mathcal{T}$
 1: Initialize IK feature map $\Phi$ with $\mathcal{I}$;
 2: Initialize tree $\mathcal{T}$;
 3: **for** $x$ in $\mathcal{I}$ **do**
 4:    $\mathcal{T} = \texttt{GrowTree}(\mathcal{T}, x)$;
 5:    /*See the details of GrowTree in Algorithm 2 in StreaKHC [7]*/
 6: **end for**
 7: **for** Batch $B =$ the latest $m$ point from $\mathcal{S}$ **do**
 8:    **if** $\texttt{iNNE}(B, \mathcal{T}.root) > \tau$ **then**
 9:      Use $B$ to rebuild IK feature map $\Phi$;
10:      Initialize subtree $\mathcal{T}_{sub}$ as nil;
11:      $B_S = \{x \in B | \texttt{iNNE}(\delta(x), \mathcal{T}.root)$ is among the top $k$ largest values$\}$;
12:      **for** $x$ in $B_S$ **do**
13:        $\mathcal{T}_{sub} = \texttt{GrowTree}(\mathcal{T}_{sub}, x)$;
14:        $B = B \backslash \{x\}$ ;
15:      **end for**
16:      $\mathcal{T} = \texttt{InsertSubtree}(\mathcal{T}, \mathcal{T}_{sub}, \mathcal{T}.root)$;
17:    **end if**
18:    **for** $x$ in $B$ **do**
19:      $\mathcal{T} = \texttt{GrowTree}(\mathcal{T}, x)$;
20:    **end for**
21:    **while** $|\mathcal{T}| > L$ **do**
22:      Remove the oldest point $o$ to keep the tree size, i.e., $\mathcal{T} = \texttt{PruneTree}(\mathcal{T}, o)$;
23:      /*See the details of PruneTree in Algorithm 3 in StreaKHC [7]*/
24:    **end while**
25: **end for**

---

with respect to the current tree.[1] We assume that points with high anomaly scores belong to emerging new class. If such points are detected, the algorithm selects the top $k$ points with the highest iNNE scores from the batch as the detected points of the new class. A subtree containing these $k$ points is then created and inserted at the root of the current tree, a process we call online preprocessing (now including the new class). The remaining points in the batch, which are points of existing known classes are sequentially inserted into the updated tree using StreaKHC. Figure 2 illustrates an example of adding a point from a detected new class at the root node. The pseudo-code for SHCRI is presented in Algorithm 2.

---

[1] iNNE [2] is an anomaly detection method that efficiently identifies local anomalies in high-dimensional datasets by generating hyperspheres from multiple subsamples. The more dissimilar samples $S_1$ and $S_2$ are, the higher the $\texttt{iNNE}(S_1, S_2)$ score.

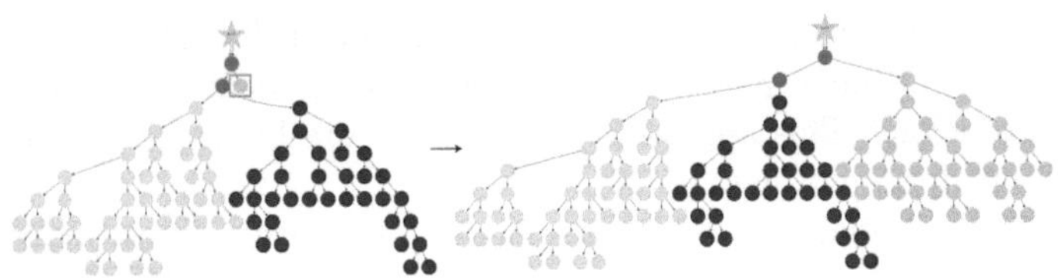

**Fig. 2.** After one point from the new class is sampled and inserted as a subtree at the root, the remaining points from the new class will be inserted into the appropriate branches.

## 6  Experiment

### 6.1  Datasets

We evaluate the algorithms on one synthetic dataset and five real-world datasets[2] (See Table 1 for relevant statistics): **ALOI** features 24 illumination conditions using five lights and three camera angles to capture object appearances. [6]; **CIFAR-100** consists of 60,000 $32 \times 32$ color images across 10 classes for image classification tasks. [11]; **CoverType** classifies 581,012 pixels into seven forest cover types based on 54 attributes from four wilderness areas in Roosevelt National Forest [3]; **MNIST** is a dataset of 70,000 handwritten digit images, commonly used for training and testing machine learning models in image classification tasks [12]; **ILSVRC2012** is a benchmark dataset containing over 1.2 million images across 1,000 categories, widely used for evaluating image classification algorithms [18]; **Synthetic** consists of 16 non-overlapping, translated normal distributions arranged in a $4 \times 4$ matrix on a two-dimensional plane.

To evaluate algorithm performance under streaming conditions with emerging new class, we designed an experimental framework using six benchmark datasets. Each dataset is structured as a temporal sequence of 80,000 samples, partitioned into four equal segments of 20,000 samples each. The class distribution follows a progressive pattern: the initial segment contains data from two classes, with each subsequent segment introducing one additional class.

### 6.2  Algorithms and Parameter Settings

We compare SHCRI with the following three baseline hierarchical clustering algorithms[3].

- SAHC is a streaming version of AHC using single linkage. Each newly added point is inserted into the leaf node that is most similar to it, while the oldest point is deleted to maintain a fixed size of the cluster tree.

---

[2] We utilized the 128-dimensional representations learned from the ViT model [22] on CIFAR-100, MNIST, and ILSVRC2012 as input for all experiments.

[3] GRINCH and PERCH were written in Python by their original authors, respectively. SHCRI and SAHC is implemented based on Python and can be obtained from github. All experiments were run on a machine with 8 cores (Intel i7-11700K 3.60GHz) and 64GB memory.

- PERCH [9] constructs a hierarchical tree incrementally by adding points to the node of their nearest neighbor and performing local tree rearrangements through rotations. This approach produces a more balanced tree, facilitating the efficient update of new points.
- GRINCH [14] is similar to PERCH but includes an additional grafting subroutine that enables more global rearrangements of the tree structure.

Note that SAHC, PERCH, and GRINCH have a single parameter that denotes the maximum number of leaf nodes of the tree, which is set to 500. SHCRI employs Isolation kernel [21]. We search for the best $\psi \in \{2, 4, 8, 16, 32, 64, 128\}$ for Isolation Kernel, and the best number of detected new class points $k \in \{2, 5, 10, 20\}$. Additionally, we initial data size and batch size to 100.

## 6.3   Performance Comparison

**Clustering Outcomes.**   Figure 3 illustrates the comparative Dendrogram Purity trajectories of four algorithms across six datasets. SHCRI exhibits distinctive advantages in both dynamic and stable phases of streaming data. During distribution shifts (gray regions) corresponding to new class emergence, SHCRI maintains consistent purity levels, avoiding the characteristic decline-recovery pattern observed in other algorithms. Moreover, in stable periods between distribution shifts, SHCRI achieves superior purity metrics across most datasets, demonstrating its effectiveness in both adapting to emerging new class and maintaining high-quality hierarchical structures during steady-state operation.

**Table 1.** Dataset properties

|  | Synthetic | ALOI | CIFAR | CoverType | MNIST | ILSVRC2012 |
|---|---|---|---|---|---|---|
| Dim. | 2 | 128 | 128 | 11 | 128 | 128 |
| # of Points | 160,000 | 108,000 | 50,000 | 581,012 | 60,000 | 1,200,000 |
| # of Classes | 16 | 1000 | 100 | 7 | 10 | 1000 |

**Ablation Studies.**   We conducted two ablation studies to evaluate key components of SHCRI. In the first study, we examined the effects of kernel updates and the root-insert strategy by creating two algorithm variants: SHCRI-NoUpdate omits the kernel function updates by deleting line 8 in Algorithm 2; and SHCRI-NoRoot disables the root-insert strategy by deleting lines 7-16, effectively reverting to StreaKHC.

The experimental results in Fig. 4 reveal distinct behavioral patterns between SHCRI and SHCRI-NoRoot. SHCRI-NoRoot experiences temporary purity degradation when new classes emerge but eventually recovers to match SHCRI's performance level. This recovery occurs during stable phases as tree points gradually align with the current distribution. In contrast, SHCRI-NoUpdate demonstrates

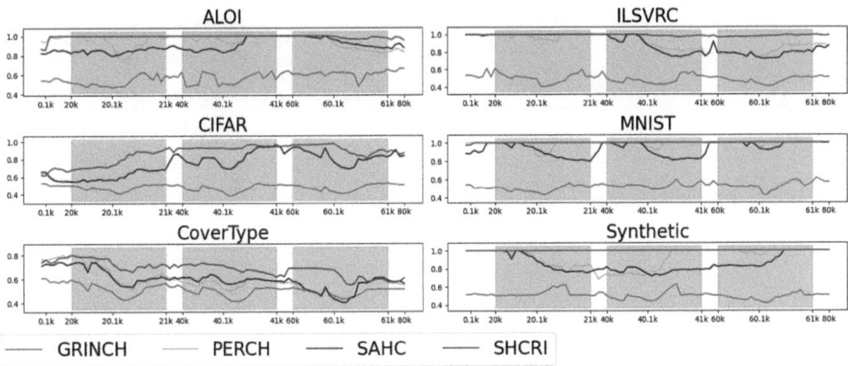

**Fig. 3.** The clustering result at each time stamp in *Dendrogram Purity*. When new classes emerge, the horizontal axis is expanded and highlighted with a gray background.

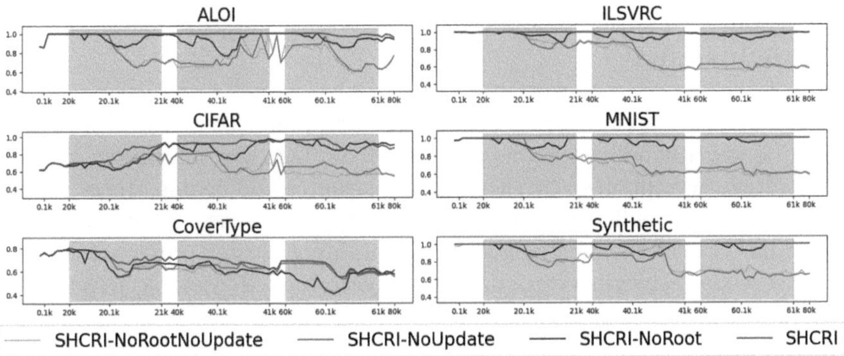

**Fig. 4.** The result of the first ablation study on SHCRI in *Dendrogram Purity*. SHCRI-NoRoot refers to SHCRI without the root-insert strategy, while NoUpdate indicates SHCRI without updates to the Isolation kernel. SHCRI-NoRootNoUpdate combines both of these conditions.

inferior performance during stable phases, particularly when processing predominantly new classes. This degradation stems from incorrect similarity computations due to outdated kernel representations, highlighting the importance of kernel updates in maintaining clustering quality.

In the second study, we investigated the generalizability of the root-insert strategy by developing SAHC-RI and PERCH-RI, which incorporate this strategy into their respective base algorithms. As shown in Fig. 5, both enhanced versions successfully maintain tree purity during new class emergence. These results demonstrate that the root-insert strategy effectively generalizes to existing streaming hierarchical clustering algorithms, enabling them to handle the SHEENA problem successfully.

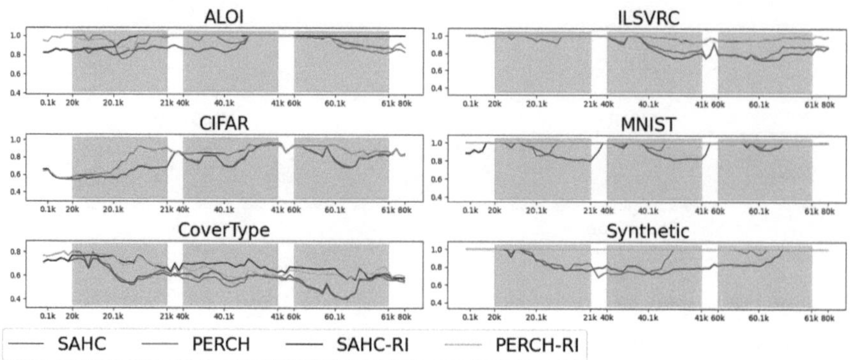



**Fig. 5.** The result of the second ablation study on root-insert strategy in *Dendrogram Purity*. `SAHC-RI` and `PERCH-RI` refer to `SAHC` and `PERCH` with root-insert strategy respectively.

## 7    Conclusion

This paper introduces `SHCRI`, advancing streaming hierarchical clustering through its novel handling of emerging new class. Our key innovation, the root-insert strategy, is supported by theoretical guarantee and demonstrates superior performance over traditional tree restructuring approaches. Extensive experiments validate `SHCRI`'s effectiveness in maintaining cluster purity during class emergence while achieving state-of-the-art performance in stable periods. The generalizability of our approach is confirmed through successful integration with existing algorithms, establishing a new framework for adaptive hierarchical clustering in dynamic environments.

**Acknowledgments.** We thank the anonymous reviewers for their valuable comments.

## Appendix

### A.1    Proof of Proposition 1

**Proposition 1.** *For a given cluster tree $T$ and a cluster subtree $T_{sub}$ composed of new class points, it holds that*

$$\arg\max_{\eta \in T} DP(\mathit{InsertSubtree}(T, T_{sub}, \eta)) = T.root \qquad (3)$$

*Proof.* For a given cluster tree $T$ and a cluster subtree $T_{sub}$ composed of new class points, for some node $\eta \in T$, $T' = \mathtt{InsertSubtree}(T, T_{sub}, \eta)$.

We denote $\mathbb{P}_T = \{(x_i, x_j) | x_i \neq x_j \in T, \ell(x_i) = \ell(x_j)\}$, $\mathcal{C}(T) = \{C_1, \ldots, C_K\}$ and $\mathcal{C}(T_{sub}) = \{C_{K+1}, \ldots, C_M\}$. Since $T_{sub}$ consists entirely of new class points, if follows that $\mathcal{C}(T) \cap \mathcal{C}(T_{sub}) = \emptyset$. The dendrogram purity of $T'$ is

$$DP(T') = \frac{1}{|\mathbb{P}_{T'}|} \sum_{(x_i,x_j)\in\mathcal{P}} pur(lvs(lca(x_i,x_j)), \ell(x_i))$$

$$= \frac{1}{|\mathbb{P}_{T'}|} \left[ \sum_{k=1}^{K} \sum_{x_i,x_j\in C_k} pur(lvs(lca(x_i,x_j)), C_k) \right. \tag{4}$$

$$\left. + \sum_{m=k+1}^{M} \sum_{x_i,x_j\in C_m} pur(lvs(lca(x_i,x_j)), C_m) \right]$$

Since subtree $\mathcal{T}_{sub}$ is inserted into $\mathcal{T}$ as a whole, we have

$$\sum_{m=k+1}^{M} \sum_{x_i,x_j\in C_m} pur(lvs(lca(x_i,x_j)), C_m) = |\mathbb{P}_{\mathcal{T}_{sub}}| DP(\mathcal{T}_{sub}) \tag{5}$$

Consider $\ell(x_i) = \ell(x_j) = C_k \in \mathcal{C}(\mathcal{T})$, we have

Case 1: If $\ell(x) \in \mathcal{C}(\mathcal{T})$ holds for every $x \in lvs(lca(x_i,x_j))$, then we have

$$\sum_{k=1}^{K} \sum_{x_i,x_j\in C_k} pur(lvs(lca(x_i,x_j)), C_k) = |\mathbb{P}_{\mathcal{T}}| DP(\mathcal{T}) \tag{6}$$

then $DP(T') = \frac{1}{|\mathbb{P}|}(|\mathbb{P}_{\mathcal{T}}|DP(\mathcal{T}) + |\mathbb{P}_{\mathcal{T}_{sub}}|DP(\mathcal{T}_{sub}))$. If $\eta = \mathcal{T}.root$, this corresponds to this case.

Case 2: Otherwise, there exists $x \in lvs(lca(x_i,x_j))$ such that $\ell(x) \in \mathcal{C}(\mathcal{T}_{sub})$. We denote that in $\mathcal{T}'$, $lvs(lca(x_i,x_j)) = R'$, and in $\mathcal{T}$, $lvs(lca(x_i,x_j)) = R$. Then we have

$$pur(R', C_k)$$
$$= \frac{\{x \in R'|\ell(x) = C_k\}}{|R'|} = \frac{\{x \in R|\ell(x) = C_k\}}{|R| + |\{x|\ell(x) \in \mathcal{C}(\mathcal{T}_{sub})\}|} \tag{7}$$
$$< \frac{\{x \in R|\ell(x) = C_k\}}{|R|} = pur(R, C_k)$$

So we have

$$\sum_{k=1}^{K} \sum_{x_i,x_j\in C_k} pur(lvs(lca(x_i,x_j)), C_k) < |\mathbb{P}_{\mathcal{T}}| DP(\mathcal{T}) \tag{8}$$

and $DP(T') < \frac{1}{|\mathbb{P}|}(|\mathbb{P}_{\mathcal{T}}|DP(\mathcal{T}) + |\mathbb{P}_{\mathcal{T}_{sub}}|DP(\mathcal{T}_{sub}))$.

# References


1. Abdallah, A., Maarof, M.A., Zainal, A.: Fraud detection system: a survey. J. Netw. Comput. Appl. **68**, 90–113 (2016)
2. Bandaragoda, T.R., Ting, K.M., Albrecht, D., Liu, F.T., Wells, J.R.: Efficient anomaly detection by isolation using nearest neighbour ensemble. In: 2014 IEEE International Conference on Data Mining Workshop, pp. 698–705. IEEE (2014)
3. Blackard, J.: Covertype. UCI Machine Learning Repository (1998)
4. Blundell, C., Teh, Y.W., Heller, K.A.: Bayesian rose trees. In: Proceedings of the Twenty-Sixth Conference on Uncertainty in Artificial Intelligence, pp. 65–72 (2010)
5. Diez, I., et al.: A novel brain partition highlights the modular skeleton shared by structure and function. Sci. Rep. **5**(1), 10532 (2015)
6. Geusebroek, J.M., Burghouts, G.J., Smeulders, A.W.: The Amsterdam library of object images. Int. J. Comput. Vision **61**, 103–112 (2005)
7. Han, X., Zhu, Y., Ting, K.M., Zhan, D.C., Li, G.: Streaming hierarchical clustering based on point-set kernel. In: Proceedings of the 28th ACM SIGKDD Conference on Knowledge Discovery and Data Mining, pp. 525–533 (2022)
8. Heller, K.A., Ghahramani, Z.: Bayesian hierarchical clustering. In: Proceedings of the 22nd International Conference on Machine Learning, pp. 297–304 (2005)
9. Kobren, A., Monath, N., Krishnamurthy, A., McCallum, A.: A hierarchical algorithm for extreme clustering. In: Proceedings of the 23rd ACM SIGKDD International Conference on Knowledge Discovery and Data Mining, pp. 255–264 (2017)
10. Krishnamurthy, A., Balakrishnan, S., Xu, M., Singh, A.: Efficient active algorithms for hierarchical clustering. In: 29th International Conference on Machine Learning, ICML 2012, pp. 887–894 (2012)
11. Krizhevsky, A., Hinton, G., et al.: Learning multiple layers of features from tiny images. In: Handbook of Systemic Autoimmune Diseases (2009)
12. LeCun, Y., Bottou, L., Bengio, Y., Haffner, P.: Gradient-based learning applied to document recognition. Proc. IEEE **86**(11), 2278–2324 (1998)
13. Monath, N., et al.: Scalable hierarchical agglomerative clustering. In: Proceedings of the 27th ACM SIGKDD Conference on Knowledge Discovery & Data Mining, pp. 1245–1255 (2021)
14. Monath, N., Kobren, A., Krishnamurthy, A., Glass, M.R., McCallum, A.: Scalable hierarchical clustering with tree grafting. In: Proceedings of the 25th ACM SIGKDD International Conference on Knowledge Discovery & Data Mining, pp. 1438–1448 (2019)
15. Monath, N., Zaheer, M., McCallum, A.: Online level-wise hierarchical clustering. In: Proceedings of the 29th ACM SIGKDD Conference on Knowledge Discovery and Data Mining, pp. 1733–1745. ACM (2023)
16. Murtagh, F., Contreras, P.: Algorithms for hierarchical clustering: an overview. Wiley Interdisc. Rev. Data Min. Knowl. Disc. **2**(1), 86–97 (2012)
17. Roux, M.: A comparative study of divisive and agglomerative hierarchical clustering algorithms. J. Classif. **35**, 345–366 (2018)
18. Russakovsky, O., et al.: ImageNet large scale visual recognition challenge. Int. J. Comput. Vision **115**(3), 211–252 (2015). https://doi.org/10.1007/s11263-015-0816-y
19. Tabassum, S., Pereira, F.S., Fernandes, S., Gama, J.: Social network analysis: an overview. Wiley Interdisc. Rev. Data Min. Knowl. Disc. **8**(5), e1256 (2018)
20. Ting, K.M., Xu, B.C., Washio, T., Zhou, Z.H.: Isolation distributional kernel: a new tool for point and group anomaly detections. IEEE Trans. Knowl. Data Eng. **35**(3), 2697–2710 (2021)

21. Ting, K.M., Zhu, Y., Zhou, Z.H.: Isolation kernel and its effect on SVM. In: Proceedings of the 24th ACM SIGKDD International Conference on Knowledge Discovery & Data Mining, pp. 2329–2337 (2018)
22. Wu, B., et al.: Visual transformers: token-based image representation and processing for computer vision (2020)

# Masked Aggregation Learning for Enhancing Distributed Gradient Boosting Decision Trees


Yuting Zha[1,2], Chao Lin[1](✉), Xinyi Huang[3], and Dugang Liu[4]

[1] College of Computer and Cyber Security, Fujian Normal University, Fuzhou 350117, China
linchao91@fjnu.edu.cn
[2] Fujian Provincial Key Laboratory of Network Security and Cryptology, Fuzhou, China
[3] College of Cyber Security, Jinan University, Guangzhou 510632, China
[4] College of Computer Science and Software Engineering, Shenzhen University, Shenzhen 518060, China



**Abstract.** Federated Gradient Boosting Decision Trees (GBDT) have gained popularity for enabling collaborative, privacy-preserving training across multiple distributed participants. However, existing federated GBDT frameworks require extensive communications for the creation of each subtree, as each participant trains data locally. These methods often involve complex secure multi-party computation or homomorphic encryption techniques that hinder training efficiency and suffer from low model accuracy in uneven data distributions. To address these issues, we propose a Masked Aggregation Learning (MAL) framework for federated GBDT. MAL combines distributed data preprocessing with centralized training, allowing participants to securely mask their data and share it with a central server for centralized training. Our approach includes constructing decision trees using histograms by discretizing continuous feature values into distinct buckets. During data preprocessing, we introduce a Secret Extremes Bucket Construction (SE-Bucket) method based on order-revealing encryption for unified bucketing and feature value obfuscation. Additionally, we propose an Erasable Label Mask generation algorithm that ensures label privacy while the masks do not impact model accuracy. MAL reduces the communication rounds from a linear relationship with the number of GBDT subtrees to a constant two rounds, independent of the number of subtrees, and maintains model accuracy regardless of how the data is distributed among the participants. Experimental results show that our method, MAL, achieves accuracy comparable to centralized training while being 500 to 600 times faster than state-of-the-art federated decision tree training solutions.

**Keywords:** Gradient Boosting Decision Trees · Federated Learning · Local Differential Privacy · Masked Aggregation Learning





T. Zhu et al. (Eds.): KSEM 2025, LNAI 15919, pp. 212–227, 2026.
https://doi.org/10.1007/978-981-95-3001-4_16

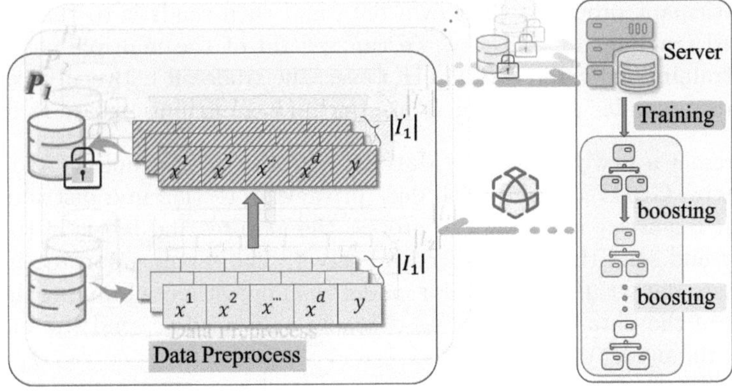


**Fig. 1.** The Framework of MAL.

# 1   Introduction

Gradient Boosting Decision Tree (GBDT) is a powerful ensemble learning method that has gained prominence with the growth of data and the demand for advanced analytics. High-quality data is critical to GBDT's performance and often originates from multiple sources in practice. However, traditional GBDT implementations rely on centralized data processing, which is impractical when dealing with multiple data sources due to privacy regulations like General Data Protection Regulation [19]. While GBDTs are highly effective, their application in protecting the privacy of the data from different sources poses challenges.

Recently, numerous studies have focus on distributed GBDT [5,7,11,20–22], where federated learning [14,15] has been widely applied due to the ability of collaborative training across distributed participants while protecting data privacy. Existing solutions allow users to train models locally and achieve multi-party collaborative training by sharing model parameters or gradients rather than raw data, but they still face the following insufficiencies.

1) **High Computation Costs.** Schemes [5,7,21] employ secure multi-party computation and homomorphic encryption to ensure privacy, but the substantial cryptographic computations impose nearly prohibitive computational burdens. 2) **Unstable Model Accuracy.** SimFL [11] uses locality-sensitive hashing to aggregate gradients from similar data across parties and create new trees with weighted gradient boosting. However, this approach still exhibits significant errors when dealing with uneven data distribution. 3) **Extensive communications.** Additionally, most federated GBDT methods [20,22] keep the data on the participants, and the server needs to communicate with the participants continuously during the training process (to obtain the best split points, aggregate gradients, etc.). This leads to the training process of each subtree requiring multiple communications.

To address the above challenges, this paper employs a dual-mode approach combining distributed data preprocessing and centralized training (see Fig. 1).

Each participant processes their own data and then sends it to the server for centralized training. In this way, we can get rid of the multiple communications of training federated GBDT. However, the trade-off between privacy and performance remains a challenge. Thus, our main contributions are as follows.

- We present a new framework (Masked Aggregation Learning, MAL) for collaborative GBDT training with data privacy protection in a distributed setting. It requires participants to process the features and labels of their data locally and send them to the central server. The server, upon receiving the processed data, can only use it for model training without obtaining the actual values of the data. Moreover, participants only need to send the data once before the model training begins.
- To obscure feature values and create a unified binning structure for uneven data nodes, we propose a new distributed bucketing method called Secret Extremes Bucket Construction (SE-Bucket). This method incurs minimal communication costs.
- We also propose an Erasable Label Mask generation algorithm to mask label values and ensure privacy. These masks are countervailed during the final centralized aggregation, which preserves model accuracy.
- Our experimental results show that MAL achieves the same level of accuracy as centralized training. With 32 participants, MAL is 500 to 600 times faster than the state-of-the-art federated solutions.

## 2     Preliminaries

### 2.1     Gradient Boosting Decision Trees (GBDTs)

GBDT is an ensemble learning method that builds models sequentially, with the aim of reducing errors by combining the strengths of multiple weak learners, typically decision trees [4]. The working principle of GBDT is boosting, where each new learner attempts to correct the prediction errors made by the previous learner. Formally, for a given dataset with $n$ samples and $d$ features $\mathcal{D} = \{(X_i, y_i)\}(|\mathcal{D}| = n, X_i \in \mathbb{R}^d, y_i \in \mathbb{R})$, GBDT minimizes the following regularized objective function $\tilde{\mathcal{L}} = \sum_i l\,(\hat{y}_i, y_i) + \sum_k \Omega\,(f_k)$, where $l$ is a differentiable convex loss function, $\Omega(f) = \gamma T_l + \frac{1}{2}\lambda\|V\|^2$ is a regularization term to penalize the complexity of the model. $\gamma$ and $\lambda$ are hyper-parameters, $T_l$ is the number of leaves, and $V$ is the leaf weight. Each $f_k$ corresponds to a decision tree.

Figure 2 illustrates an example of GBDT. In each tree, the input $x$ is divided into a leaf node based on the intermediate nodes of the decision tree. The prediction result of each tree is the leaf weight of the leaf node where $x$ falls, with the leaf weight being $V(I) = -\frac{\sum_{i \in I} g_i}{\sum_{i \in I} h_i + \lambda}$, where $g_i$ and $h_i$ represent the first-order and second-order gradients of the loss function, respectively. Then the final prediction is the sum of all individual tree predictions.

Each decision tree is created starting from the root node. For each intermediate node, let $I_L$ and $I_R$ be the sets of instances after splitting into the left

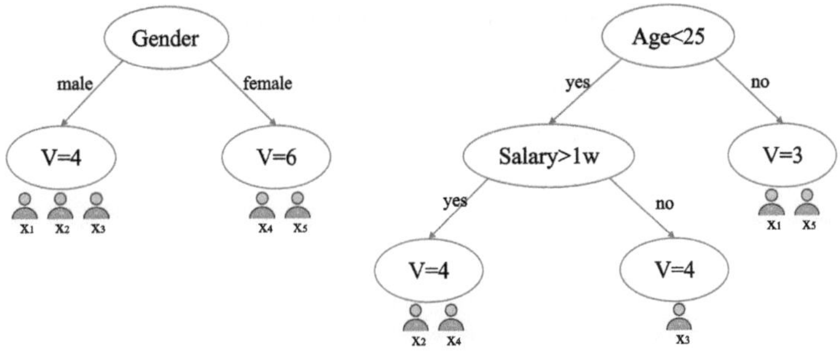



**Fig. 2.** An Example of GBDT.

and right child nodes, respectively, and $I = I_L + I_R$. The gain after splitting is

$$\mathcal{L}_{aligned} = \frac{1}{2}\left[\frac{(\sum_{i \in I_L} g_i)^2}{\sum_{i \in I_L} h_i + \lambda} + \frac{(\sum_{i \in I_R} g_i)^2}{\sum_{i \in I_R} h_i + \lambda} - \frac{(\sum_{i \in I} g_i)^2}{\sum_{i \in I} h_i + \lambda}\right] - \gamma.$$

### 2.2 Histogram Algorithm

In decision trees based on the histogram algorithm, the histogram algorithm divides the values of continuous features into discrete buckets and then computes histograms based on these buckets to perform node splitting. This method can reduce computational load and improve training efficiency. There are two ways to divide buckets: equal-width binning and equal-frequency binning.

Equal-width binning divides the data into several intervals of equal width. For example, when the input value from the range $[min, max]$ is divided into $q$ intervals, the width of each interval is: $width = \frac{max-min}{q}$. Equal-frequency binning divides the data into several intervals with equal frequency, meaning each interval contains the same number of samples.

In LightGBM [8], the equal-width binning histogram algorithm is used to improve training efficiency. Our approach also utilizes the equal-width binning histogram algorithm. We find the maximum and minimum values for each feature and perform binning. Suppose that each feature is divided into $q$ buckets. $G_k = \sum_{i \in B_k} g_i$ and $H_k = \sum_{i \in B_k} h_i$ are calculated for each bucket. The gradient histogram of a feature consists of the $G_k$ and $H_k$ of all buckets. Then, the optimal split point is selected based on the histogram. Let $I_L$ and $I_R$ be the sets of instances after splitting into the left and right child nodes, respectively, with $I = I_L + I_R$. The gain after splitting is

$$\mathcal{L}_{aligned} = \frac{1}{2}\left[\frac{(\sum_{B_k \in I_L} G_k)^2}{\sum_{B_k \in I_L} H_k + \lambda} + \frac{(\sum_{B_k \in I_R} G_k)^2}{\sum_{B_k \in I_R} H_k + \lambda} - \frac{(\sum_{B_k \in I} G_k)^2}{\sum_{B_k \in I} H_k + \lambda}\right] - \gamma.$$

$$(1)$$

**Table 1.** Summary of Notations.

| Notation | Description |
| --- | --- |
| $P_j$ | the $j$-th participant |
| $I_j$ | participant $P_j$'s dataset |
| $s_i^j$ | the $i$-th sample in $I_j$ |
| $X_i^j$ | feature vector of the $i$-th sample in $I_j$ |
| $y_i^j$ | label value of the $i$-th sample in $I_j$ |
| $x^i$ | value of the $i$-th feature |
| $d$ | the number of features |
| $q$ | the number of buckets for each feature |
| $Q$ | the total number of buckets |
| $B_k$ | the $k$-th bucket or bin |
| $B_k^i$ | the $k$-th bucket of the $i$-th feature |
| $G_k$ | first-order gradient aggregation of $B_k$ |
| $H_k$ | second-order gradient aggregation of $B_k$ |
| $N_k$ | the number of samples in $B_k$ |
| $N_k^j$ | the number of samples in $B_k$ of $I_j$ |
| $max_j^i$ | local maximum value of the $i$-th feature in $I_j$ |
| $min_j^i$ | local minimum value of the $i$-th feature in $I_j$ |
| $max^i$ | global maximum value of the $i$-th feature |
| $min^i$ | global minimum value of the $i$-th feature |

The leaf weight is computed using

$$V(I) = -\frac{\sum_{B_k \in I} G_k}{\sum_{B_k \in I} H_k + \lambda}. \tag{2}$$

## 2.3   Order-Revealing Encryption (ORE)

ORE [10,12,17] is an encryption primitive that allows ciphertexts to be ordered through a computable comparison function without accessing the plaintext itself. The key generation algorithm takes the security parameter $\lambda$ as input and outputs the system parameter $par$, the master secret key $msk$, and the comparison key $ck$. The encryption algorithm takes $msk$ and a message $m$ as inputs and outputs the ciphertext $c \leftarrow ORE.Enc(msk, m)$. The comparison algorithm, given $ck$ and two ciphertexts $c$ and $c'$, outputs a flag $b \leftarrow ORE.Cmp(ck, c, c')$. Peng et al. [17] proposed a new and efficient ORE scheme, which only requires about 79 milliseconds of time overhead to compare two 64-bit plaintexts in the cipher setting. In this paper, we use this ORE scheme to enable each participant to obtain the global maximum and minimum values for each feature without exposing the values of each feature in their own dataset.

## 2.4  Differential Privacy

Differential Privacy [6] is a technique for protecting data privacy that ensures the participation of individual data points in a dataset does not significantly affect the results of data analysis. In other words, even if any single entry in the dataset is removed or replaced, the analysis results will not show noticeable changes. This effectively prevents malicious attackers from inferring information about a specific individual through database queries. Local Differential Privacy (LDP) is a form of differential privacy that focuses on protecting each participant's data privacy before data collection. Local differential privacy ensures that each individual's data remains private after local processing. Even if an attacker knows all other users' data, they cannot infer an individual's original data by analyzing the processed data.

**Definition 1.** *($\varepsilon$-Local Differential Privacy) The function $\mathcal{S}$ is said to provide $\varepsilon$-local differential privacy if, for any two sample $x_1$ and $x_2$ that differ by only one element, the function $\mathcal{S}$ satisfies*

$$Pr[\mathcal{S}(x_1) \in y] \le e^{\varepsilon} \cdot Pr[\mathcal{S}(x_2) \in y], \tag{3}$$

*where all $y \subseteq Range\ (\mathcal{S})$, $\varepsilon$ is the privacy budget used to quantify the degree of differential privacy. The smaller $\varepsilon$, the stronger the protection of privacy.*

FederBoost [18] introduced a variant of DP to incorporate noise into bucket construction. This method allows for a certain probability that samples intended for the $k$-th bucket may be assigned to other buckets. Inspired by Tian et al. [18], in this paper, we introduce perturbations to the bucketing results to achieve $\varepsilon$-local differential privacy.

# 3  Masked Aggregation Learning

We assume that there are $l$ participants $P_1, P_2, ..., P_l$, each holding datasets $I_1, I_2, ..., I_l$, where $I_j = \{(X_i^j, y_i^j)\}$, $(X_i^j \in \mathbb{R}^d, y_i^j \in \mathbb{R}, j \in [1, l])$. We focus on the case of partitioned data, where each party holds datasets with the same feature set. In this work, we do not consider poisoning attacks which can be mitigated using the existing technologies [3,13,16]. We assume that each participant is motivated to train a better model, but they also want to peek at the data of others. Each participant holds the same master secret key $msk$. Additionally, we set up a third-party comparer, which does not hold $msk$ but has the comparison key $ck$. The participants do not collude with the comparer. Table 1 summarizes the commonly used symbols.

## 3.1  An Overview of MAL

MAL consists of two phases: preprocessing and training. In the preprocessing phase, to protect feature values from being leaked, we propose Secret Extremes

**Fig. 3.** Obtaining the Global Extreme for Each Feature.

Bucket Construction for feature value obfuscation. To maintain model accuracy while ensuring privacy, we introduce an Erasable Label Mask generation algorithm that ensures the sum of masks added to labels of samples within the same bucket is zero. During the training phase, parties send the obfuscated data to the server, which performs centralized training and then broadcasts the trained model parameters to the other participants. The entire process of MAL only requires one round of communication at each of the two phases.

## 3.2   The Preprocessing Stage

The primary purpose of the preprocessing stage is to transform the feature values and the label values of each sample, and minimize the loss of precision. As described in the Sect. 2, each decision tree consists of internal nodes (i.e., split points) and leaf nodes. The split points are selected based on the split gain of the features, which is calculated using Eq. (1) and depends only on $G$ and $H$. The leaf weights of the decision tree are calculated using Eq. (2), which also depends solely on $G$ and $H$. Therefore, as long as we ensure that the transformation of feature values and label values does not alter the values of $G$ and $H$, we can achieve data transformation without impacting model accuracy.

## 3.3   Secret Extremes Bucket (SE-Bucket)

Algorithm 1 describes the entire process of the SE-Bucket. The MAL uses the histogram algorithm to construct decision trees. To ensure that each party's binning structure is consistent with the global binning structure, we need to obtain the global maximum and minimum values for each feature (lines 2-8). Figure 3 illustrates the process of obtaining the global maximum and minimum values. Each participant $P_j$ finds the maximum value $max^i_j$ and the minimum value $min^i_j$ for each feature $f_i$ locally. $P_j$ encrypts $max^i_j$ and $min^i_j$ using $msk$

---

**Algorithm 1:** Secret Extremes Bucket

---

**Input**: each $P_j$ inputs $n_j$ samples and each sample has all $d$ features
$$X = \{x^1, x^2, \ldots, x^d\}$$
**Output**: each $P_j$ outputs $n_j$ samples, with each sample having $d$ features
$$X' = \{x^{1\prime}, x^{2\prime}, \ldots, x^{d\prime}\}$$

**1**   **for** $i = 1 \rightarrow d$ **do**
**2**    **for** $j = 1 \rightarrow l$ **do**
**3**     $max_j^i, min_j^i \leftarrow P_j$;
**4**     $c(max_j^i) \leftarrow \text{ORE.Enc}(msk, max_j^i)$;
**5**     $c(min_j^i) \leftarrow \text{ORE.Enc}(msk, min_j^i)$;
**6**     $P_j$ sends $c(max_j^i)$ and $c(min_j^i)$ to Comparer;
**7**    $c(max^i) \leftarrow max\{c(max_1^i), \ldots, c(max_l^i)\}$;
**8**    $c(min^i) \leftarrow min\{c(min_1^i), \ldots, c(min_l^i)\}$;
**9**    **for** $j = 1 \rightarrow l$ **do**
**10**     **for** $k = 0 \rightarrow q$ **do**
**11**      $b_k = min^i + \frac{k \times (max^i - min^i)}{q}$;
**12**     **for** *each sample* **do**
**13**      **if** $b_{k-1} \leq x^i \leq b_k$ **then**
**14**       $P_j$ moves it to $B_k^i$;
**15**       $P_j$ moves it to another bucket with probability $\frac{q-1}{e^\varepsilon + q - 1}$;
**16**     **for** $k = 1 \rightarrow q$ **do**
**17**      **if** $X \in I_j$ *belongs to the* $B_k^i$ **then**
**18**       $x^i = min^i + \frac{(k-1/2) \times (max^i - min^i)}{q}$;

---

(lines 4-5). Each participant sends the encrypted values $c(max_j^i)$ and $c(min_j^i)$ to comparer. Comparer uses $ck$ to compare and obtain the encrypted global extremes $c(max^i)$ and $c(min^i)$, and then returns the results to participants (lines 7-8). Participants decrypt the values using $msk$ to obtain the global extremes $max^i$ and $min^i$ of each feature. Determine the global bucket structure by finding the quantiles based on the global extremes for each feature (lines 10-11).

Based on the above binning results, a sample is assigned to the $k$-th bucket according to the value of $i$-feature $x^i$. Its feature value $x^i$ is then transformed to the median value of the $k$-th bucket (line 18). The central server only knows the boundaries of each bucket but does not have access to the ground truth data within the buckets. However, it can infer the range of feature values belonging to that bucket (i.e. the bucket boundaries). Therefore, we introduce noise perturbation to the bucketing results. For a sample originally assigned to the $k$-th bucket, it has a probability $\frac{e^\varepsilon}{e^\varepsilon + q - 1}$ of remaining in the $k$-th bucket, while the probability of being assigned to each of the remaining $q - 1$ buckets is $\frac{1}{e^\varepsilon + q - 1}$.

---

**Algorithm 2:** Erasable Label Mask Generation

---

**Input**: each $P_j$ inputs $n_j$ samples and each sample has all a label $y$
**Output**: each $P_j$ inputs $n_j$ samples and each sample has all a label $y'$

**1 for** $j = 1 \rightarrow l$ **do**
    `// for each party` $P_j$
**2**    Set unknowns $X = [x_1, x_2, \ldots, x_{Q+1}]$;
**3**    **for** $k = 1 \rightarrow Q$ **do**
        `// for each bucket` $B_k$
**4**        $a_1 \leftarrow 0, a_2 \leftarrow 0, \ldots, a_{Q+1} \leftarrow 0$;
**5**        **for** $i = 1 \rightarrow |I_j|$ **do**
            `// for each simple` $s_i^j$
**6**            Randomly generating a $(Q+1)$-dimensional vector $[a_1^i, a_2^i, \ldots, a_{Q+1}^i]$;
**7**            **if** $s_i^j$ *belongs to the* $B_k$ **then**
**8**                $a_1 \leftarrow a_1 + a_1^i, a_2 \leftarrow a_2 + a_2^i, \ldots, a_{Q+1} \leftarrow a_{Q+1} + a_{Q+1}^i$;
**9**        Homogeneous linear equation $a_1 \cdot x_1 + a_2 \cdot x_2 + \ldots + a_{Q+1} \cdot x_{Q+1} = 0$;
**10**    Solving the system of homogeneous linear equations;
**11**    **for** $i = 1 \rightarrow |I_j|$ **do**
**12**        $mask_i = a_1^i \cdot x_1 + a_2^i \cdot x_2 + \ldots + a_{Q+1}^i \cdot x_{Q+1}$;
**13**        $y_i' = y_i + mask_i$;

---

## 3.4 Erasable Label Mask (ELM)

To protect privacy, we add a mask to the label value of each individual sample. The masks are designed to self-cancel within each bucket, thus not affecting the gradient aggregation results ($G$ and $H$) to maintain the accuracy of the model. Additionally, compared to other secure aggregation schemes (multi-party mask negotiation) [2], our ELM does not need to consider the issue of other users dropping out due to its self-cancelling mask characteristic. The Erasable Label Mask generation process is detailed in Algorithm 2. Samples can be divided into $q$ buckets based on any feature. Assuming the data has $d$-dimensional features, there are a total of $Q = q \times d$ buckets. To eliminate the noise interference caused by the mask, it is necessary to ensure that within each bucket satisfies

$$\sum_{i=1}^{N_k} mask_i = 0, \tag{4}$$

where $N_k$ is the number of samples in $B_k$. Evidently, as long as participants can ensure within each bucket satisfies Eq. (5), then Eq. (4) is guaranteed to hold.

$$\sum_{i=1}^{N_k^j} mask_i = 0. \tag{5}$$

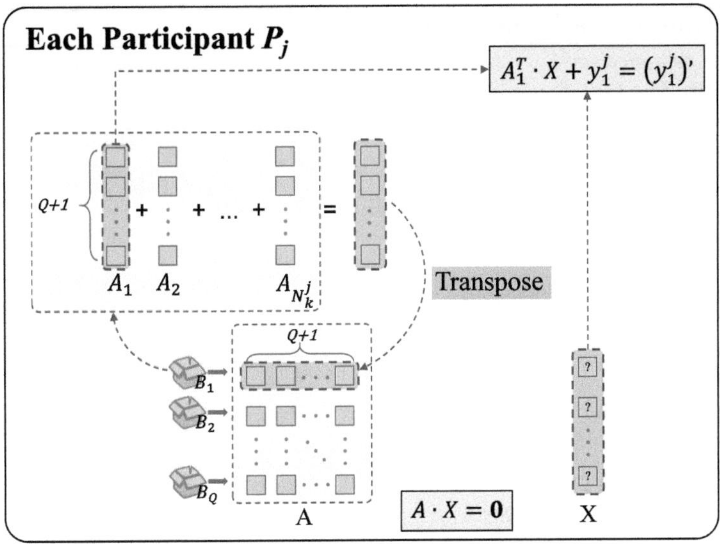


**Fig. 4.** Erasable Label Mask Generation.

Let there be unknowns $X = [x_1, x_2, \ldots, x_{Q+1}]^\top$. Each sample $s_i$ randomly generates a $(Q+1)$-dimensional vector $A_i = [a_1^i, a_2^i, \ldots, a_{Q+1}^i]^\top$. The mask value is then

$$mask_i = a_1^i \cdot x_1 + a_2^i \cdot x_2 + \ldots + a_{Q+1}^i \cdot x_{Q+1}. \tag{6}$$

Each participant must ensure that each bucket satisfies Eq. (5). We transform this problem into solving a $Q \times (Q+1)$ homogeneous matrix equation. Therefore, within each bucket satisfies Eq. (7) (lines 3-9).

There are $Q$ homogeneous linear equations in the form of Eq. (7), forming a system of homogeneous linear equations. When the number of unknowns is greater than the number of equations, the system must have non-trivial solutions [9]. Solving this system and substituting the obtained values of $X$ into Eq. (6), we calculate the mask value added to the label of each sample. Finally, the mask is added to the label of each sample (lines 11-13). The entire process of adding a mask to each label value is visualized in Fig. 4.

$$\sum_{i=1}^{N_k^j} \left(a_1^i x_1 + \ldots + a_{Q+1}^i x_{Q+1}\right) = \sum_{i=1}^{N_k^j} a_1^i x_1 + \ldots + \sum_{i=1}^{N_k^j} a_{Q+1}^i x_{Q+1} \tag{7}$$

$$= a_1 x_1 + \ldots + a_{Q+1} x_{Q+1} = 0.$$

### 3.5  The Training Stage

The entire process of the training phase is shown in Algorithm 3. All participants send their transformed data and quantiles for each feature to the central server.

---

**Algorithm 3:** The Training Stage

---

**Input**: Instance set $I'$
**Output**: The GBDT model

1  All ordinary participants send their transformed datasets to the active participant $P_l$;

2  **for** $t = 1 \rightarrow T$ **do**

3  $\quad$ Update $g$ and $h$ of all training instances on loss $l$;

4  $\quad$ $gain \leftarrow 0$;

5  $\quad$ **for** $i = 1 \rightarrow d$ **do**

$\quad\quad$ // for each feature

6  $\quad\quad$ $G_L \leftarrow 0, G_R \leftarrow 0$;

7  $\quad\quad$ $G \leftarrow \sum_{k=0}^{q} G_k, H \leftarrow \sum_{k=0}^{q} H_k$;

8  $\quad\quad$ **for** $k = 1 \rightarrow q$ **do**

$\quad\quad\quad$ // for each bucket $B_k^i$

9  $\quad\quad\quad$ $G_L \leftarrow G_L + G_i, H_L \leftarrow H_L + H_i$;

10 $\quad\quad\quad$ $G_R \leftarrow G - G_L, H_R \leftarrow H - H_L$;

11 $\quad\quad\quad$ $gain \leftarrow max(gain, \frac{G_R^2}{H_R^2+\lambda} + \frac{G_L^2}{H_L^2+\lambda} - \frac{G^2}{H^2+\lambda})$;

12 $\quad$ Split with the max gain;

13 $\quad$ $V(I) = -\frac{\sum_{i \in I} G_i}{\sum_{i \in I} H_i + \lambda}$;

14 $\quad$ Send the split point and leaf weights to the other participants;

---

After collecting all the data, the central server buckets the data based on the quantiles, constructs a histogram, and trains a GBDT model. The central server selects the optimal split points for each decision tree according to Eq. (1) (lines 5-11). To ensure that the added mask values on the labels cancel each other out and do not affect the leaf values, we set the depth of each decision tree to 1. The central server sends the split points of each tree and the leaf weights of all leaf nodes of each tree to the other participants.

## 3.6    Security Analysis

Each participant sends the encrypted feature local extremes to the comparer. The comparer receives the ciphertexts but cannot access the plaintext without the master key. Conversely, although each participant has the master key, they cannot access other participants' feature local extremes without the ciphers. This protects the privacy of all parties' feature local extremes.

The feature values is converted to the median of the bucket it belongs to, which obfuscates each other so that they cannot be distinguished. Furthermore, we add noise to the feature values to ensuring local differential privacy.

**Corollary 1.** *Our feature value obfuscation mechanism satisfies $\varepsilon$-local differential privacy.*

*Proof.* For any two samples $s_1$ and $s_2$, which possess feature vectors $X_1$ and $X_2$, respectively, and differ by only one feature value $x^j$, we have

$$\frac{Pr[\mathcal{S}(X_1) = X']}{Pr[\mathcal{S}(X_2) = X']} = \prod_i \frac{Pr\left[\mathcal{S}\left(x_1^i\right) = x^{i\prime}\right]}{Pr\left[\mathcal{S}\left(x_2^i\right) = x^{i\prime}\right]}$$

$$= \frac{Pr\left[\mathcal{S}\left(x_1^j\right) = x^{j\prime}\right]}{Pr\left[\mathcal{S}\left(x_2^j\right) = x^{j\prime}\right]} \leq \frac{e^\varepsilon/(e^\varepsilon + q - 1)}{1/(e^\varepsilon + q - 1)} = e^\varepsilon, \tag{8}$$

where $Pr[\mathcal{S}(X) = X']$ denotes the probability that a sample $s$ has its feature value obfuscated to $X'$.

We mask the label values, ensuring that the sum of the masks within the same bucket equals zero. The masks are determined using a matrix equation, which has infinitely many solutions. This guarantees that for any given output, there are infinitely many possible inputs that produce the same output. Thus, the server cannot obtain the original label values.

## 4    Implementation and Experiments

In this section, we demonstrate the effectiveness and efficiency of MAL, and provide experiments on several publicly available datasets from the LIBSVM website[1]. **SUSY**: It contains 3,000,000 samples and 18 features. We randomly selected 289,330 samples. **Diabetes**: It contains 768 samples, each with 8 features. **Cod-rna**: It contains 59,535 training samples and 271,617 test samples, each sample having 8 features.

We implemented MAL based on the XGBoost[2]. We conducted experiments on a machine with an Intel(R) Core(TM) i7-10700 CPU at 2.90GHz and 16GB RAM. For the datasets SUSY and Diabetes, we randomly selected 80% samples for training and the remaining for testing. We evaluate our new framework based on utility and efficiency. Since all participants send disguised data to the central server for centralized training, changing the number of participants does not affect the utility of MAL. Therefore, when evaluating utility, we only consider the impact of different numbers of buckets $q$ and privacy budgets $\varepsilon$ on accuracy, with the number of trees $T$ set to 500 and 1000, respectively. When evaluating efficiency, we account for different numbers of participants. All experiments are repeated 10 times, and the average is taken.

### 4.1    Utility

We use AUC (Area Under the ROC Curve) as the criterion for model utility, which provides a better reflection of the model ability to distinguish between

---

[1] https://www.csie.ntu.edu.tw/$\sim$cjlin/libsvmtools/datasets/.
[2] https://github.com/dmlc/xgboost.

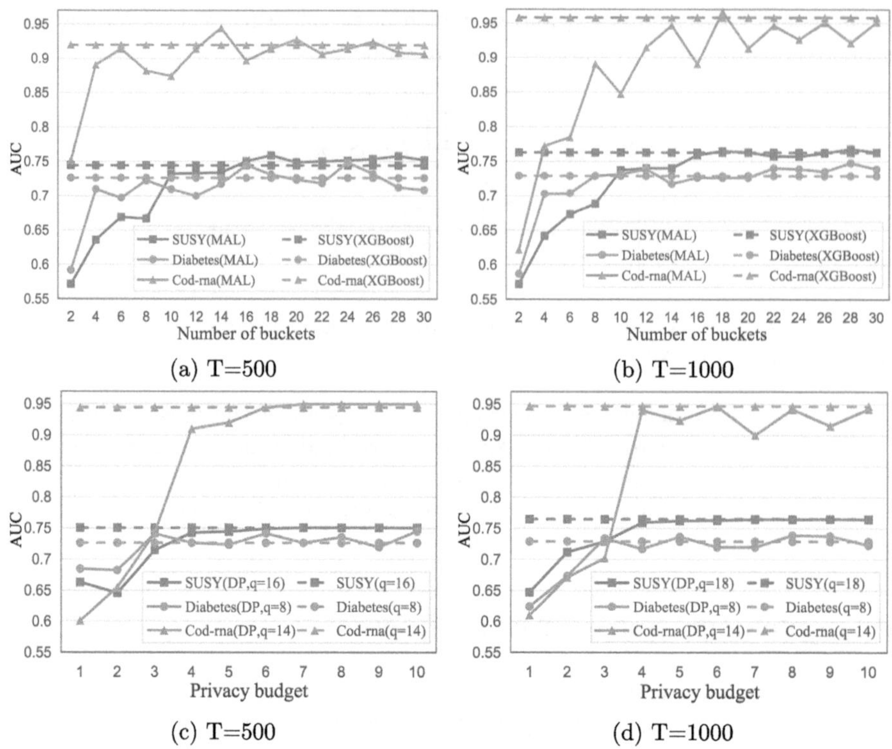



**Fig. 5.** Utility of MAL.

different classes. We first evaluate the impact of different bucket numbers on the utility of MAL without considering differential privacy. Figures 5a and 5b show how AUC varies with the number of buckets $q$ for $T = 500$ and $T = 1000$, respectively. For SUSY, MAL achieves the best AUC of 75.89% at $q = 18$ and 76.75% at $q = 28$ for $T = 500$ and $T = 1000$, respectively, while the AUC achieved by XGBoost is 74.43% and 76.26%. For Diabetes, MAL reaches the best AUC of 74.49% at $q = 16$ and 74.76% at $q = 28$, while the AUC achieved by XGBoost is 72.62% and 72.89%. For Cod-rna, MAL achieves the best AUC of 92.77% at $q = 20$ and 96.61% at $q = 18$, while the AUC achieved by XGBoost is 91.97% and 95.80%. Overall, when $q \geq 14$, MAL achieves the same level of accuracy as XGBoost. Because the bucketing operation can somewhat mitigate overfitting, MAL's performance even surpasses XGBoost's at specific $q$.

Next, we fix the optimal $q$ for each dataset and observe the utility of MAL under different privacy budgets. Figures 5c and 5d show the results for $T = 500$ and $T = 1000$, respectively. When $\varepsilon = 4$, each dataset achieves accuracy very close to that obtained without considering differential privacy. Table 2 shows a comparison of the utility of MAL with $\varepsilon = 4$ against MAL without privacy

**Table 2.** Utility of MAL with $\varepsilon = 4$.

| Datasets | T = 500 | | T = 1000 | |
| --- | --- | --- | --- | --- |
| | MAL | MAL(DP) | MAL | MAL(DP) |
| SUSY | 75.04 | 74.26 | 76.47 | 75.92 |
| Diabetes | 72.62 | 72.62 | 72.89 | 71.71 |
| Cod-rna | 90.98 | 94.42 | 93.99 | 94.67 |

**Table 3.** Efficiency of MAL & XGBoost.

| Datasets | XGBoost | MAL | | | | | | |
| --- | --- | --- | --- | --- | --- | --- | --- | --- |
| | time(ms) | time(ms) | comp(ms) | | comm(KB) | | latency(ms) | |
| | | | prep | train | prep | train | prep | train |
| SUSY | 3853.565 | 5674.162 | 1087.863 | 3815.308 | 1.547 | 904.192 | 200.634 | 570.357 |
| Diabetes | 28.996 | 602.684 | 173.75 | 26.976 | 0.687 | 4.096 | 200.281 | 201.677 |
| Cod-rna | 1855.945 | 2597.845 | 237.895 | 1863.618 | 0.692 | 234.496 | 200.283 | 296.049 |

concerns. Figure 5 shows that MAL achieves almost the same level of accuracy as XGBoost.

## 4.2 Efficiency

We spawn 10 processes, each representing a participant, to run the experiment. For communication overhead, to simulate a wide-area network, we limit each process's network bandwidth to 20 Mbit/s and add a 100 ms delay for each link connection. All evaluations about ORE were performed with the bilinear pairing parameter set "d159.param" under the security parameter $\lambda = 80bits$. We present the computation time overhead and communication cost for the preprocessing and training stages in Table 3.

For communication costs, MAL needs to share global extremes during the preprocessing stage, share data that satisfies differential privacy before training, and share the parameters of the GBDT model after training is complete. For communication time, during the preprocessing stage, MAL only needs to communicate when obtaining the global extremes of features, resulting in minimal communication cost. The communication time is mainly due to network bandwidth delay. Even during the training phase, MAL only requires two communication steps, which constitute one round trip, with the total communication time being less than 1 s. We observe that the total time overhead of MAL is very close to that of XGBoost.

The above indicates that the additional overhead incurred by MAL due to privacy protection in a distributed setting is minimal. Despite MAL operating under distributed data sharing conditions, its overall time overhead remains impressive due to the minimal number of communications.

We compared MAL with FederBoost [18], a state-of-the-art solution which is 4668 times faster than scheme [1] for horizontal federated GBDT. They used 32 processes to represent participants, and randomly selected 193,333 samples from SUSY for training and trained 60 trees. We trained MAL under the same settings. The results indicate that MAL has a runtime of approximately 5.23 s, achieving a 593-fold speedup compared to FederBoost [18], which requires 3103.24 s.

## 5 Conclusion

To enable multi-party collaborative training of Gradient Boosting Decision Tree (GBDT) with privacy protection in distributed scenarios, federated GBDT is widely used. However, frequent communication leads to inefficiency. This paper proposes the Masked Aggregation Learning (MAL) framework in a horizontal federated setting, which combines distributed data preprocessing and centralized training to significantly reduce communication rounds to a constant. The Secret Extremes Bucket Construction algorithm, based on order-preserving encryption, is introduced for feature bucketing and feature value obfuscation. Additionally, the data is further protected through an Erasable Label Mask generation algorithm, which eliminates masks in each bucket during centralized training to achieve optimal model performance. We also prove that MAL satisfies Local Differential Privacy. Experiments on multiple datasets show that MAL is competitive in both privacy and efficiency. Future work will extend MAL from horizontally distributed scenarios to more complex settings, such as vertical distribution and migration.

## References


1. Abspoel, M., Escudero, D., Volgushev, N.: Secure training of decision trees with continuous attributes. Cryptology ePrint Archive, Paper 2020/1130 (2020). https://eprint.iacr.org/2020/1130
2. Bonawitz, K., et al.: Practical secure aggregation for privacy-preserving machine learning. In: proceedings of the 2017 ACM SIGSAC Conference on Computer and Communications Security, pp. 1175–1191 (2017)
3. Cao, X., Jia, J., Gong, N.Z.: Provably secure federated learning against malicious clients. In: Proceedings of the AAAI Conference on Artificial Intelligence, vol. 35, pp. 6885–6893 (2021)
4. Chen, T., Guestrin, C.: Xgboost: a scalable tree boosting system. In: Proceedings of the 22nd ACM SIGKDD International Conference on Knowledge Discovery and Data Mining, pp. 785–794 (2016)
5. Cheng, K., et al.: Secureboost: a lossless federated learning framework. IEEE Intell. Syst. **36**(6), 87–98 (2021)
6. Dwork, C.: Differential privacy: a survey of results. In: International Conference on Theory and Applications of Models of Computation, pp. 1–19. Springer (2008). https://doi.org/10.1007/978-3-540-79228-4_1
7. Feng, Z., et al.: SecureGBM: secure multi-party gradient boosting. In: 2019 IEEE International Conference on Big Data (Big Data), pp. 1312–1321. IEEE (2019)

8. Ke, G., et al.: LightGBM: a highly efficient gradient boosting decision tree. In: Advances in Neural Information Processing Systems, vol. 30 (2017)
9. Ladyzhenskaia, O.A., Solonnikov, V.A., Ural'tseva, N.N.: Linear and Quasi-linear Equations of Parabolic Type, vol. 23. American Mathematical Soc. (1968)
10. Lewi, K., Wu, D.J.: Order-revealing encryption: new constructions, applications, and lower bounds. In: Proceedings of the 2016 ACM SIGSAC Conference on Computer and Communications Security, pp. 1167–1178 (2016)
11. Li, Q., Wen, Z., He, B.: Practical federated gradient boosting decision trees. In: Proceedings of the AAAI Conference on Artificial Intelligence, vol. 34, pp. 4642–4649 (2020)
12. Liu, Z., et al.: Encodeore: reducing leakage and preserving practicality in order-revealing encryption. IEEE Trans. Dependable Secure Comput. **19**(3), 1579–1591 (2020)
13. Liu, Z., He, W., Chang, C.H., Ye, J., Li, H., Li, X.: SPFL: a self-purified federated learning method against poisoning attacks. IEEE Trans. Inf. Forensics Secur. (2024)
14. McMahan, B., Moore, E., Ramage, D., Hampson, S., y Arcas, B.A.: Communication-efficient learning of deep networks from decentralized data. In: Artificial Intelligence and Statistics, pp. 1273–1282. PMLR (2017)
15. McMahan, H.B., Moore, E., Ramage, D., y Arcas, B.A.: Federated learning of deep networks using model averaging. arXiv preprint arXiv:1602.05629 **2**(2) (2016)
16. Mozaffari, H., Shejwalkar, V., Houmansadr, A.: Every vote counts:{ranking-based} training of federated learning to resist poisoning attacks. In: 32nd USENIX Security Symposium (USENIX Security 23), pp. 1721–1738 (2023)
17. Peng, C., Chen, R., Wang, Y., He, D., Huang, X.: Parameter-hiding order-revealing encryption without pairings. In: IACR International Conference on Public-Key Cryptography, pp. 227–256. Springer (2024). https://doi.org/10.1007/978-3-031-57728-4_8
18. Tian, Z., et al.: Federboost: private federated learning for GBDT. IEEE Trans. Dependable Secure Comput. (2023)
19. Voigt, P., Von dem Bussche, A.: The EU General Data Protection Regulation (gdpr). A Practical Guide, 1st Ed. Springer International Publishing, Cham (2017). https://doi.org/10.1007/978-3-319-57959-7
20. Wu, X., Huang, H., Ding, Y., Wang, H., Wang, Y., Xu, Q.: Fednp: towards non-IID federated learning via federated neural propagation. In: Proceedings of the AAAI Conference on Artificial Intelligence, vol. 37, pp. 10399–10407 (2023)
21. Wu, Y., Cai, S., Xiao, X., Chen, G., Ooi, B.C.: Privacy preserving vertical federated learning for tree-based models. arXiv preprint arXiv:2008.06170 (2020)
22. Zhang, J., et al.: Fedala: adaptive local aggregation for personalized federated learning. In: Proceedings of the AAAI Conference on Artificial Intelligence, vol. 37, pp. 11237–11244 (2023)

# Personalized Learning Resource Recommendation Framework Based on Knowledge Graph and Large Language Model


Jianguo Chen[1,2] and Tongyu Zhu[1,2(✉)]

[1] Hangzhou International Innovation Institute of Beihang University, Hangzhou, China
[2] School of Computer Science and Engineering, Beihang University, Beijing, China
{chenjianguo,zhutongyu}@buaa.edu.cn



**Abstract.** In the realm of digital education, Educational Recommender Systems (ERSs) play a pivotal role in enhancing learning outcomes. Nevertheless, existing systems encounter significant challenges, including data sparsity, cold-start problems, limited dynamic adaptability, insufficient personalization, and poor interpretability. To tackle these issues, we introduce an innovative personalized recommendation framework that integrates knowledge graphs (KGs) with Large Language Models (LLMs). By utilizing LLMs to enrich knowledge graphs—such as through the automatic generation of resource tags, difficulty levels, and overviews—our framework effectively addresses data sparsity and cold-start problems. It dynamically updates the knowledge graph and recommendation strategies based on real-time changes in students' knowledge states, while also enabling learners to adjust their knowledge profiles via Open Learner Models (OLMs). Our recommendation module synergizes knowledge graphs with advanced algorithms to compute the similarity between students and educational resources, facilitating personalized ranking. To enhance the interpretability of recommendations, our system extracts relevant subgraphs and articulates the recommendation rationale through natural language generation techniques. Empirical evidence demonstrates that this framework not only significantly boosts the quality and efficacy of recommendations but also fosters personalized education and elevates the intelligence of educational systems.

**Keywords:** Education Recommendation System · Knowledge Graph · Large Language Model · Open Learner Models · Bayesian Knowledge Tracing


## 1 Introduction

With the rapid development of online education platforms, Educational Recommender Systems (ERSs) have become essential for enhancing learning efficiency



T. Zhu et al. (Eds.): KSEM 2025, LNAI 15919, pp. 228–245, 2026.
https://doi.org/10.1007/978-981-95-3001-4_17

and personalization. However, existing systems face challenges in dynamic adaptability, interpretability, and data sparsity. Traditional recommendation methods, such as collaborative filtering [20] and content-based filtering [33], struggle with cold-start issues and fail to capture the evolving knowledge states of learners. Although Knowledge Graph (KG)-based systems improve interpretability [3,27], their static nature limits real-time adaptability. Meanwhile, Large Language Models (LLMs) offer new possibilities for semantic analysis and feature generation [8], yet their integration with dynamic knowledge modeling remains an open question. The primary challenges in current ERS research are as follows:

- Data sparsity and cold-start issues: Limited resource metadata hampers accurate user profiling, reducing recommendation quality.
- Static knowledge representations: Existing models fail to dynamically track and adapt to learners' evolving knowledge states.
- Lack of interpretability: The "black-box" nature of many recommendation processes undermines user trust and usability [16].
- Imbalance between personalization and learning goals: Current approaches struggle to align recommendations with both knowledge gaps and diverse learning interests.

To address these challenges, this paper proposes a personalized learning resource recommendation framework integrating knowledge graphs and LLMs. The key innovations include:

- Dynamic Knowledge Enhancement: By leveraging LLMs to generate multimodal resource features, addressing cold-start and data sparsity issues.
- Transparent Learning Modeling: The integration of Bayesian Knowledge Tracing (BKT) [35] and Open Learner Models (OLMs) [11] allows users to participate in knowledge state adjustments, enhancing recommendation interpretability and personalization.
- Efficient Hybrid Recommendation Algorithm: A scoring function based on semantic alignment, knowledge gaps, and difficulty stratification is proposed, combined with reinforcement learning and indexing optimization techniques to achieve low-latency, high-precision recommendations.

Experiments demonstrate that the proposed framework achieves significant improvements in recommendation accuracy and recall across multiple datasets, including ASSISTments2012 [25], POJ [25], and BUAA-OODC, outperforming mainstream baseline models such as KG-RS and CF+KG-RS. The framework's effectiveness is further corroborated through semantic relevance evaluation using ROUGE-L [22] and diversity assessment via Intra-List Diversity (ILD) [18]. Ablation studies confirm the critical contributions of both the LLM-driven data augmentation strategy and the OLM module to the overall performance enhancement. Notably, empirical teaching data reveal that the framework's deployment correlates with a marked improvement in students' homework completion outcomes compared to historical baselines, demonstrating its practical efficacy in educational environments.

The remainder of this paper is organized as follows: Sect. 2 reviews related work; Sect. 3 details the framework design and algorithm implementation; Sect. 4 validates the framework's effectiveness through experiments; and Sect. 5 concludes the paper and outlines future directions.

## 2    Related Work

### 2.1    Learner Modeling in Educational Recommender Systems

Learner models are essential in Educational Recommender Systems (ERSs), providing an abstract representation of learners' abilities and behaviors by analyzing their interactions with the system [12]. A key component of the learner model is the learner's knowledge state [10]. Current approaches to learner modeling, particularly in ERSs, typically use "overlaying" models that estimate a student's knowledge based on system interactions [10]. Methods such as the Elo rating system [1], Performance Factor Analysis (PFA) [32], Bayesian Knowledge Tracing (BKT) [30], and Item Response Theory (IRT) [21] are commonly employed to generate these models. However, these methods often remain opaque, which may raise concerns regarding fairness and trust, as learners cannot easily understand how their knowledge state is inferred [2].

### 2.2    Content-Based Educational Recommendation System

In general, content-based ERSs recommend items similar to those the user has previously liked based on content features. These systems analyze the items rated by a user and construct a model to capture the user's interests, which is then used to recommend new items [26]. A recent survey on ERSs in MOOCs found that 26% of these systems are designed to recommend learning elements, including learning activities, video lectures, next pages, learning sources, and learning paths [19]. The authors noted that most research in this field focuses on content - based filtering or hybrid algorithms. Traditionally, content - based ERSs base their recommendations on content similarity [7], suggesting content similar to what learners have interacted with in the past, such as learning materials they have viewed or courses they have taken.

### 2.3    Education Recommendation System Based on Knowledge Graph

In recent years, researchers have explored the integration of knowledge graphs (KGs) into recommender systems (RS) to enhance recommendation accuracy and interpretability [17]. KGs represent entities as nodes and relationships as edges, allowing for a more comprehensive understanding of item relationships and user preferences when user information is incorporated [37]. While KG-based RS have been widely applied in domains such as tourism, health, entertainment, and business, their application in education remains limited. Few studies have proposed KG-based educational recommender systems (ERS) for recommending learning paths [38] or labs [13]. Notably, the work in [31] introduced a KG-based approach for explainable recommendations of Wikipedia articles based on learner needs. However, this method relied on full-text search algorithms (e.g., Lucene), which, despite their efficiency, struggle to capture semantic similarities between texts with differing vocabularies.

### 2.4   LLM in Recommender Systems

With the advancements of Large Language Models (LLMs) [9], researchers have explored their use in recommendation tasks through two main approaches: (1) as predictors, directly generating recommendations [5,23,36]; (2) as extractors, creating user/item profiles to support downstream tasks [14,24]. Predictor-based methods like TALLRec (Task-Aware Learning for Recommender Systems) [5] fine-tune LLMs with recommendation data, addressing task mismatches and data scarcity. Extractor-based methods, such as P5 (Personalized Prediction for Recommendation Systems) [14], unify diverse data into natural language for instruction-based recommendations, enhancing personalization. Additionally, LLMRec (Large Language Model-based Recommender Systems) [34] and RLM-Rec (Reinforcement Learning-based Model for Recommender Systems) [29] integrate LLMs with GNNs (Graph Neural Networks) to improve representation performance and mitigate data sparsity.

### 2.5   Summary of Contributions

In summary, while existing research has independently applied learner modeling, knowledge graphs, and LLMs to educational recommenders, these approaches often suffer from being static, opaque, or semantically limited. Our framework introduces a novel, synergistic integration of these components to overcome these specific limitations. The key breakthroughs of our work are: (1) Employing LLMs for the dynamic enrichment of the knowledge graph, directly addressing data sparsity and improving semantic understanding beyond traditional content-based methods. (2) Fusing Bayesian Knowledge Tracing with Open Learner Models to create a transparent and interactive learner profile, moving beyond the "black-box" nature of conventional learner models. (3) Establishing a dynamic feedback loop where the learner's evolving knowledge state continuously updates the graph, enabling adaptive and timely recommendations that static KG-based systems cannot provide. This integrated approach marks a significant step towards a more personalized, interpretable, and effective educational recommendation system.

## 3   Methodology

This study introduces a personalized learning resource recommendation framework that integrates knowledge graphs (KGs) with Large Language Models (LLMs), as illustrated in Fig. 1. Initially, the framework gathers online learning

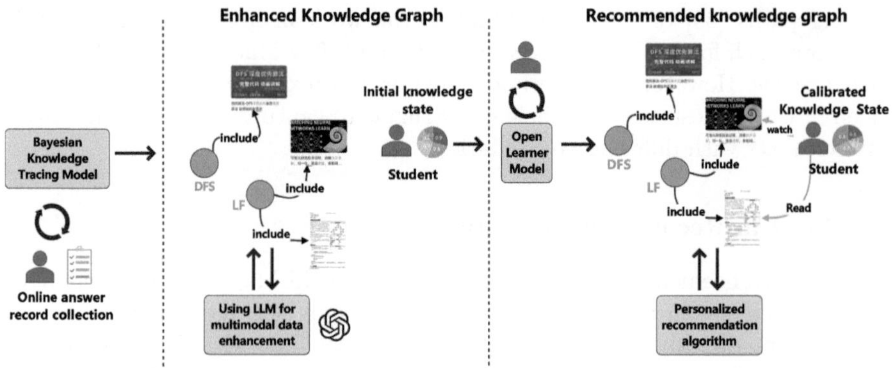


**Fig. 1.** This figure shows the workflow and architecture of the personalized learning resource recommendation framework based on knowledge graph and large language model.

data from students and employs Bayesian Knowledge Tracing (BKT) to assess students' mastery of various topics, thereby establishing their initial knowledge states. Based on this information, a knowledge graph is constructed, featuring nodes representing students, knowledge domains, and learning resources. To enrich this graph, LLMs are utilized to enhance resource nodes by generating tags, categorizing difficulty levels, and producing summaries, thus providing more comprehensive resource descriptions. Furthermore, the OLM allows students to manually adjust their initial knowledge states, enabling a higher degree of personalization. Finally, advanced recommendation algorithms analyze the relationships between student and resource nodes to suggest tailored learning materials. These recommendations are visually represented within the graph, enhancing both the interpretability and effectiveness of the recommendation outcomes.

## 3.1   Knowledge Graph Construction and Multimodal Data Augmentation

**Construction of Knowledge Graph.** The BKT model is employed to quantify the degree of mastery of knowledge points for each student. This model generates a personalized knowledge status table, which represents the student's knowledge proficiency on a scale from 0 (not mastered) to 1 (fully mastered). To support this framework, we constructed a basic knowledge graph using Neo4j, comprising student nodes, knowledge nodes, and resource nodes. In this graph, knowledge nodes are connected to resource nodes via an "include" relationship, while student nodes are associated with resource nodes through behaviors such as "watching" or "reading." Each student node includes attributes such as knowledge status, ID, gender, and instructor, whereas resource nodes record information about resource types and URLs. For example, the basic knowledge graph depicted in Fig. 1 encompasses two knowledge nodes ("depth-first search" and "loss function"), three resource nodes (in both text and video formats), and one student node.

**Multimodal Data Augmentation.** To further enrich the content of the basic knowledge graph, we leverage LLM to conduct in-depth analysis of the resources, thereby enhancing the data. As depicted in Fig. 2, for video resources, in addition to evaluating basic information such as titles and introductions, we extract and convert video subtitles into text format. The LLM then analyzes this text information to generate three features for video resources: content labels, content overviews, and difficulty levels. For text resources, the LLM directly generates these three features—labels, content overviews, and difficulty levels—based on the analysis of the text content. Finally, these features are integrated into the knowledge graph to form an enhanced knowledge graph. In this enhanced graph, the attributes of resource nodes are expanded from the original two (resource type and resource URL) to five, with the addition of three new features: resource labels, resource difficulty, and resource overview. This approach effectively increases the information density and application value of the knowledge graph.

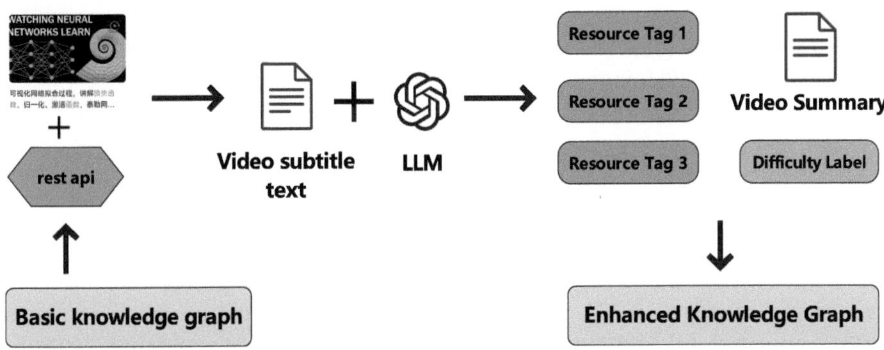


**Fig. 2.** The diagram illustrates the process of enhancing knowledge graphs using LLMs.

## 3.2   Knowledge State Modeling

In this framework, we integrate the strengths of closed learner models (e.g., BKT) and open learner models (OLMs) to model student knowledge states, aiming to combine the objectivity of the former with the interpretability of the latter. The OLM, as an externalized student model, is accessible to both students and teachers [11] and has been incorporated into ERS to enhance the transparency and interpretability of these systems [1,2,6]. As illustrated in Fig. 3, each student can visualize their initial knowledge mastery status calculated by the BKT model, and crucially, may manually adjust their self-perceived mastery levels of specific knowledge components based on their actual learning progress. This explicit feedback mechanism aligns with studies emphasizing the importance of improving user model auditability in recommender systems [4,15]. Through the OLM interface, students' adjustments transform the initial knowledge states into revised ones, which are subsequently integrated into the enhanced knowledge graph. This dual-process approach preserves Bayesian objectivity while enabling personalized calibration, thereby enhancing both individual adaptability and system transparency throughout the learning process.

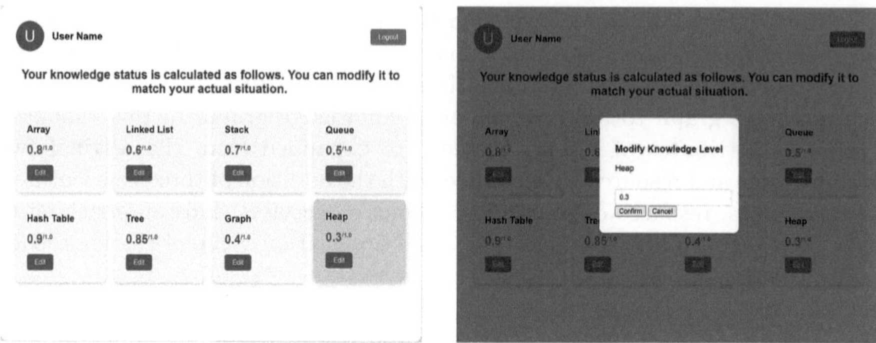

**Fig. 3.** This diagram presents the user interface of our OLM. The model empowers students to modify system representations to align with their actual situations, facilitating a more personalized learning experience.

### 3.3   Personalized Recommendation Algorithm

This section presents a dynamic recommendation algorithm combining three key innovations: 1) BKT-based knowledge tracing enhanced with student-adjusted OLM refinement, 2) Multi-level difficulty matching (beginner/intermediate/advanced) through ZPD-constrained scoring, and 3) BERT-Faiss semantic alignment accelerated via HSW indexing. The hybrid approach addresses educational recommendation challenges through temporal student modeling, reinforcement learning-optimized weights, and cold-start handling via knowledge gap propagation, overcoming static feature limitations in conventional methods.

**Problem Formalization.** The heterogeneous knowledge graph comprises three entity types:

- **Student nodes** $s$: Represent learners with dynamically updated knowledge states $K_s \in [0, 1]$ calculated via BKT:

$$K_s^{(t)} = P(L_t = 1|O_{1:t-1}) = \frac{P(O_{t-1}|L_{t-1} = 1)P(L_{t-1} = 1)}{\sum_l P(O_{t-1}|L_{t-1} = l)P(L_{t-1} = l)}, \quad (1)$$

where $L_t$ denotes latent mastery states and $O_t$ represents observed performance. The final knowledge mastery state $K_s^{(t)'}$ is obtained by applying the OLM model to $K_s^{(t)}$:

$$K_s^{(t)'} = \mathrm{OLM}(K_s^{(t)}, \Delta_s), \tag{2}$$

where $\Delta_s$ represents the manual adjustment made by the student. The OLM model allows students to fine-tune their knowledge mastery based on self-assessment, providing adjustments to the BKT-calculated mastery to better reflect their actual understanding.

- **Knowledge nodes** $k$: Construct hierarchical dependencies from curriculum standards.
- **Resource nodes** $r_i$: Characterized by tuple

$$\mathbf{R_i} = (\text{type}, \mathcal{T}_i, \text{url}, d_i, \text{desc}), \tag{3}$$

where $d_i \in \{\text{beginner}, \text{intermediate}, \text{advanced}\}$ and $\mathcal{T}_i$ denotes standardized semantic tags.

**Scoring Function.** The recommendation score synthesizes three pedagogically motivated components:

$$S_i = w_1(1 - \bar{K}'_s) + w_2 \mathrm{sim}_{\mathrm{BERT}}(\mathcal{T}_s, \mathcal{T}_i) + w_3 \Phi(K'_s, d_i), \tag{4}$$

The **knowledge gap term** $1 - \bar{K}'_s$ quantifies unmastered content using the average OLM-adjusted knowledge mastery over $T$ interactions. The **semantic alignment term** employs pre-trained BERT embeddings to capture deep tag relationships:

$$\mathrm{sim}_{\mathrm{BERT}}(\mathcal{T}_s, \mathcal{T}_i) = \cos\left(\frac{1}{|\mathcal{T}_s|} \sum_{t \in \mathcal{T}_s} \mathbf{v}_t, \frac{1}{|\mathcal{T}_i|} \sum_{t \in \mathcal{T}_i} \mathbf{v}_t\right), \tag{5}$$

where $\mathbf{v}_t$ denotes the BERT [CLS] embedding of tag $t$. The **difficulty matching term** $\Phi(K'_s, d_i)$ enforces zone of proximal development principles:

$$\Phi(K'_s, d_i) = \begin{cases} 1, & K'_s < 0.4 \wedge d_i = \text{beginner} \\ 0.5, & 0.4 \le K'_s < 0.7 \wedge d_i = \text{intermediate} \\ 0.2, & K'_s \ge 0.7 \wedge d_i = \text{advanced}. \end{cases} \tag{6}$$

The algorithm implements three key optimizations: (1) **Reinforcement learning-based dynamic weight adjustment** optimizes recommendation weights adaptively using NDCG feedback; (2) **Faiss-based hierarchical small-world (HSW) indexing** accelerates semantic retrieval, achieving a response time constraint of 300ms for 10K resources; (3) **Cold-start handling via knowledge gap-based collaborative filtering**, ensuring recommendations even when student history is unavailable.

**Dynamic Weight Adjustment via Reinforcement Learning.** To optimize the recommendation score function adaptively, we update the weight parameters $w_j$ based on NDCG feedback:

$$w_j^{(t+1)} = w_j^{(t)} + \eta \cdot \text{NDCG@}k \cdot \frac{\partial S}{\partial w_j}, \tag{7}$$

where $\eta$ is the learning rate, and NDCG@$k$ reflects ranking quality. This enables the system to self-optimize without manual tuning.

**Semantic Computation Acceleration.** We accelerate semantic similarity search using **Faiss-based hierarchical small-world (HSW) indexing**, achieving real-time retrieval with:

$$T_{\text{response}} < 300\text{ms}, \quad \mathcal{R}_{\text{ranked}} = \underset{r_j \in \mathcal{R}}{\text{argtopk}} \left( S_j - \max_{r_i \in \mathcal{R}_{\text{selected}}} \text{sim}(r_i, r_j) \right), \tag{8}$$

This balances relevance and diversity while ensuring low latency.

**Cold-Start Handling via Knowledge Gap-Based Filtering.** When no prior student data is available ($T_s = \emptyset$), recommendations are based on knowledge gaps:

$$S_i^{\text{cold}} = w_1(1 - K_s) + w_3\text{diff}(K_s, d_i), \tag{9}$$

where $K_s$ is the student's knowledge proficiency, and $d_i$ is resource difficulty. This ensures meaningful recommendations even for new users.

**Algorithm Implementation.** The recommendation process formalizes as follows:

**Parameter Selection and Tuning**

- **BKT**: The parameters of the BKT model are not pre-set, but estimated from the data through the expectation maximization (EM) [28] algorithm. In order to overcome the local optimal problem that may be caused by the sensitivity of the EM algorithm to the initial value, a multi-starting point initialization strategy is adopted: the model is randomly initialized multiple times (5 times by default) and the EM algorithm is run until convergence, and finally a set of parameters with the largest log-likelihood value is selected as the estimation result.
- **RL Weights**: To determine the optimal hyperparameter combination, including the learning rate $\eta$ and $k$ in NDCG@$k$, we employed a grid search approach on the validation set for tuning. For the learning rate $\eta$, we tested candidate values from $\{0.001, 0.01, 0.05, 0.1\}$, where a too-small $\eta$ could lead to slow convergence, while an excessively large $\eta$ might cause weights to oscillate or even diverge near the optimum. For $k$ in NDCG@$k$, we evaluated

---

**Algorithm 1.** Personalized Educational Resource Recommendation

---

**Require:** Student $s$, knowledge graph $\mathcal{G}$, top-$k$ resources
**Ensure:** Recommended resources $\mathcal{R}_{\text{rec}}$
1: Identify weak knowledge points: $\mathcal{K} \leftarrow \{k \mid \bar{K}_s'^{k} < 0.4, \forall k \in \mathcal{G}\}$
2: Retrieve candidate resources: $\mathcal{R} \leftarrow \bigcup_{k \in \mathcal{K}} \mathcal{G}.\text{getResources}(k)$
3: Filter by difficulty: $\mathcal{R}' \leftarrow \{r \in \mathcal{R} \mid \Phi(K_s'^{k_r}, d_r) > 0\}$
4: Compute BERT embeddings: $\mathbf{V} \leftarrow \text{Faiss-HSW}(\{\mathcal{T}_i \mid r_i \in \mathcal{R}'\})$        ▷ Faiss-based accelerated computation
5: Calculate similarity scores: $\text{sim}_i \leftarrow \cos(\mathbf{v}_s, \mathbf{v}_i), \forall \mathbf{v}_i \in \mathbf{V}$
6: Generate final scores:

$$\begin{cases} S_i \leftarrow w_1(1 - \bar{K}_s') + w_2\text{sim}_i + w_3\Phi(K_s', d_i), & \text{if } T_s \neq \emptyset \\ S_i^{\text{cold}} \leftarrow w_1(1 - K_s) + w_3\text{diff}(K_s, d_i), & \text{if } T_s = \emptyset \end{cases}$$

7: Diversify results: $\mathcal{R}_{\text{ranked}} \leftarrow \text{NMS}(\mathcal{R}', S, \lambda = 0.6)$
8: Select top-$k$: $\mathcal{R}_{\text{rec}} \leftarrow \mathcal{R}_{\text{ranked}}[1 : k]$

---

$k \in \{5, 10, 20\}$ based on typical user interface display quantities, as the choice of $k$ influences the focus range of reward signals. Our tuning objective was to identify a pair $(\eta, k)$ that maximizes the average NDCG@$k$ performance on the validation set. The experimental procedure involved iteratively training the model on the training set for each hyperparameter combination and evaluating its performance on the validation set after each epoch. Ultimately, we selected $\eta = 0.01$ and $k = 5$ as the optimal hyperparameters, as this combination achieved the highest and most stable average NDCG on the validation set.

## 4   Experiments

### 4.1   Datasets and Baselines

**Datasets.** We used the following datasets to evaluate the proposed framework:

- **ASSISTments2012:** This is the ASSISTments data for the school year 2012 2013 with affect predictions. The dataset consists of 2,541,201 interactions, 27,066 students, and 45,716 questions.
- **POJ:** This dataset consists of programming exercises and is collected from Peking coding practice online platform. The dataset is originally scraped by Pandey and Srivastava. In total, it has 996,240 interactions, 22,916 students, and 2,750 questions.
- **BUAA-OODC:** Collected from the Object-oriented design and construction course (OODC) at Beihang University's School of Computer Science and Engineering, this dataset spans five academic years (2019–2024) and includes students' online quiz records.

**Baselines.** To evaluate the effectiveness of our proposed framework, we compared it with the following baseline models:

- **Knowledge Graph-Based Recommendation (KG-RS):** This model incorporates a static knowledge graph (KG) to recommend resources based on the relationships and attributes of entities within the graph. By mapping users, resources, and knowledge points into the graph, it leverages the connections between these entities to enhance recommendation accuracy.
- **Collaborative Filtering + Knowledge Graph-Based Recommendation (CF+KG-RS):** This model combines collaborative filtering (CF) with the knowledge graph (KG) to recommend resources. It uses the interaction patterns of similar users and the structured information from the KG to make recommendations for a target user.
- **Content-Based Filtering + Knowledge Graph-Based Recommendation (CBF+KG-RS):** This model enhances content-based filtering (CBF) with a knowledge graph (KG). It uses the content features of resources and the KG to recommend resources that are similar to what the user has interacted with before, based on both content similarity and knowledge relationships.

### 4.2    Experimental Setup and Evaluation Metrics

**Experimental Setup.** In our experimental setup, we first conduct data pre-processing, which includes cleaning and normalizing the data to handle missing values and eliminate duplicates. The dataset is then partitioned into three subsets: 70% for training, 15% for validation, and 15% for testing. For knowledge graph construction, we use the Bayesian Knowledge Tracing (BKT) model to initialize student knowledge states and employ an Large Language Model (LLM) to generate labels, summaries, and difficulty levels to enrich crawled resource nodes. In the parameter tuning phase, we apply an adaptive weight optimization method based on reinforcement learning to optimize the scoring function's weight parameters. For implementation, we build the recommendation algorithm using PyTorch and utilize the GPT-4o LLM for data augmentation and explanation generation. Note that the Open Learner Model (OLM) module, requiring verification in a real educational scenario, is applied only to our established BUAA-OODC dataset.

**Evaluation Metrics.** We evaluate our recommendation system using five metrics: Precision@k, Recall@k, HR@k, ILD (Intra-List Diversity), and ROUGE-L. These metrics assess recommendation accuracy, coverage, personalization, and interpretability.

### 4.3    Experimental Results

The experimental results demonstrate that our proposed framework significantly outperforms baseline models across three datasets: ASSISTments2012, POJ, and

BUAA-OODC. As shown in Tables 1, when compared to knowledge graph (KG)-based recommendation systems, collaborative filtering plus KG-based systems, and content-based filtering plus KG-based systems, our framework consistently achieves higher scores in Precision@k, Recall@k, and Hit Rate@k (HR@k). Additionally, it delivers superior diversity (measured by Intra-List Diversity, ILD) and content relevance (assessed via ROUGE-L). On the ASSISTments2012 dataset, our framework achieved precision and recall improvements of up to 21.2% and 20.0%, respectively, compared to the KG-based recommendation system. This highlights its efficacy in providing more accurate and diverse recommendations. On the POJ dataset, similar gains were observed, with recall increasing by 19.4% over the KG-based model. Finally, on the BUAA-OODC dataset, our framework attained a precision of 0.83 and an HR@k of 0.84, signifying substantial enhancements across all evaluation metrics. These results underscore the robustness and adaptability of our proposed recommendation framework. It effectively captures user preferences and provides more personalized and diverse learning resource recommendations compared to traditional methods.

**Table 1.** Performance Comparison of Different Models on Various Datasets

| Dataset | Model | Precision@k | Recall@k | HR@k | ILD | ROUGE-L |
| --- | --- | --- | --- | --- | --- | --- |
| ASSISTments2012 | KG | 0.67 | 0.60 | 0.68 | 0.57 | 0.61 |
| | CF+KG | 0.76 | 0.64 | 0.72 | 0.76 | 0.74 |
| | CBF+KG | 0.79 | 0.68 | 0.75 | 0.72 | 0.73 |
| | Ours | 0.85 | 0.75 | 0.79 | 0.81 | 0.80 |
| POJ | KG | 0.65 | 0.58 | 0.63 | 0.61 | 0.66 |
| | CF+KG | 0.77 | 0.65 | 0.80 | 0.77 | 0.73 |
| | CBF+KG | 0.74 | 0.69 | 0.74 | 0.68 | 0.76 |
| | Ours | 0.83 | 0.72 | 0.81 | 0.78 | 0.85 |
| BUAA-OODC | KG | 0.61 | 0.62 | 0.59 | 0.65 | 0.68 |
| | CF+KG | 0.73 | 0.66 | 0.74 | 0.64 | 0.75 |
| | CBF+KG | 0.78 | 0.70 | 0.77 | 0.81 | 0.74 |
| | Ours | 0.83 | 0.78 | 0.84 | 0.82 | 0.83 |

### 4.4  Ablation Study

To validate the contributions of LLM-based data augmentation and the OLM, we conducted ablation studies on three datasets: ASSISTments2012, POJ, and BUAA-OODC2019-2024. Specifically, we tested two variants: (1) Ours w/o LLM, where resource tags, summaries, and difficulty levels rely solely on raw metadata, and (2) Ours w/o OLM, where knowledge states are updated only via BKT without manual adjustments. Performance was evaluated using metrics such as

Precision@10, Coverage@20, Knowledge Gain Rate (KGR), Dynamic Adaptation Measure (DAM), and Cold-Start Rate (CSR). The results are summarized in Tables 2, 3, and 4.

**Table 2.** Ablation Study Results on ASSISTments2012 Dataset

| Model Variant | Precision@10 | Recall@10 | HR@10 | ILD | ROUGE-L |
|---|---|---|---|---|---|
| Full Model (Ours) | 0.85 | 0.75 | 0.79 | 0.81 | 0.80 |
| Ours w/o LLM | 0.67 (−21.2%) | 0.60 (−20.0%) | 0.68 (−13.9%) | 0.57 (−29.6%) | 0.61 (−23.8%) |
| Ours w/o OLM | 0.85 (0.0%) | 0.75 (0.0%) | 0.79 (0.0%) | 0.81 (0.0%) | 0.80 (0.0%) |

**Table 3.** Ablation Study Results on POJ Dataset

| Model Variant | Precision@10 | Recall@10 | HR@10 | ILD | ROUGE-L |
|---|---|---|---|---|---|
| Full Model (Ours) | 0.83 | 0.72 | 0.81 | 0.78 | 0.85 |
| Ours w/o LLM | 0.65 (−21.7%) | 0.58 (−19.4%) | 0.63 (−22.2%) | 0.61 (−21.8%) | 0.66 (−22.4%) |
| Ours w/o OLM | 0.83 (0.0%) | 0.72 (0.0%) | 0.81 (0.0%) | 0.78 (0.0%) | 0.85 (0.0%) |

**Table 4.** Ablation Study Results on BUAA-OODC Dataset

| Model Variant | Precision@10 | Recall@10 | HR@10 | ILD | ROUGE-L |
|---|---|---|---|---|---|
| Full Model (Ours) | 0.83 | 0.78 | 0.84 | 0.82 | 0.83 |
| Ours w/o LLM | 0.61 (−26.5%) | 0.62 (−20.5%) | 0.59 (−29.8%) | 0.65 (−20.7%) | 0.68 (−18.1%) |
| Ours w/o OLM | 0.82 (−1.2%) | 0.79 (+1.3%) | 0.82 (−2.4%) | 0.70 (−14.6%) | 0.73 (−12.0%) |

**Key Findings and Statistical Significance.** Our ablation studies highlight the critical role of LLM-based data augmentation and the necessity of the OLM:

- **LLM's Impact**: Across all datasets, disabling the LLM-based augmentation leads to a significant performance drop. For instance, on the ASSISTments2012 dataset, Precision@10 decreased from 0.85 to 0.67 (a reduction of 21.2%), Recall@10 dropped by 20.0%, and HR@10 fell by 13.9%, while ILD and ROUGE-L declined by 29.6% and 23.8% respectively. Similar trends were observed on the POJ and BUAA-OODC datasets, with Precision@10 on BUAA-OODC decreasing by up to 26.5%. These results indicate that the LLM module effectively mitigates the sparsity of raw metadata by generating enriched resource tags, summaries, and difficulty levels, thereby substantially enhancing overall system performance.

- **OLM's Impact**: The necessity of the OLM module hinges on real-time user-system interactions. Experiments reveal distinct outcomes: On static datasets (ASSISTments2012 and POJ, lacking iterative interactions), removing OLM caused marginal performance differences, indicating that baseline knowledge tracing (e.g., BKT) suffices for modeling user states. In contrast, on BUAA-OODC—a dynamic interaction dataset with authentic user feedback—disabling OLM led to significant declines: Precision@10 ($-1.2\%$), HR@10 ($-2.4\%$), ILD ($-14.6\%$), and ROUGE-L ($-12.0\%$). This stark contrast underscores OLM's critical role in dynamically adapting to user behavior in interactive recommendation scenarios.

**Discussion.** Our ablation studies reinforce the value of LLM-based data augmentation and the OLM. The LLM effectively addresses resource metadata sparsity by generating semantic tags and difficulty levels, leading to better personalization and diversity. Meanwhile, the OLM improves adaptability through user-driven knowledge state updates. However, LLM inference introduces an approximate 15% latency increase, necessitating future research on optimizing lightweight deployment strategies.

## 4.5   User Study and Visualization

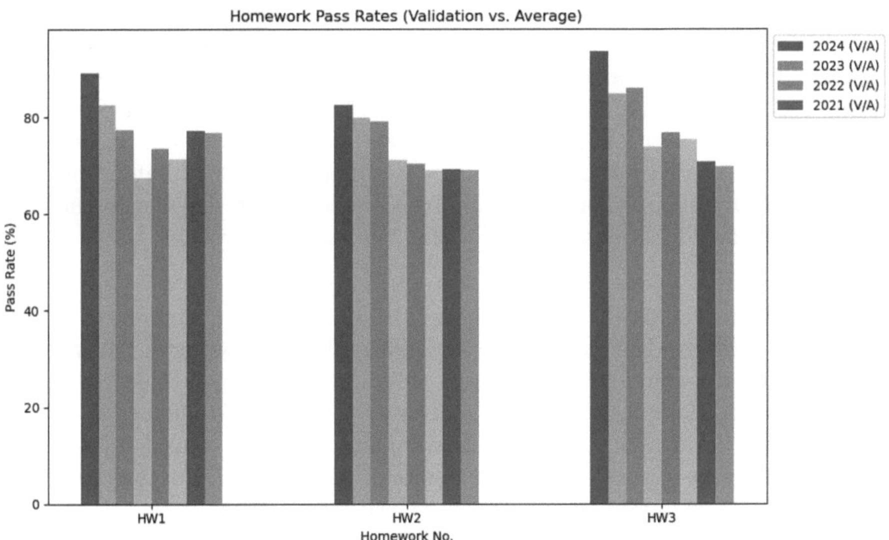


**Fig. 4.** The effect diagram of teaching measures integrating the personalized learning resource recommendation framework of this paper.

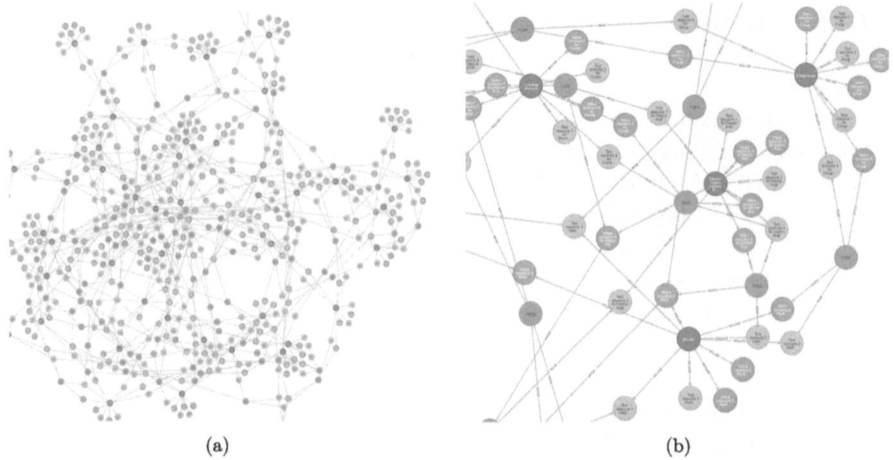

(a)　　　　　　　　　　　　　　　(b)

**Fig. 5.** Partial display of the knowledge graph based on the ASSISTments2012 dataset: (a) shows a thumbnail of a local area, and for clearer observation, a part of (a) is enlarged in (b).

**User Study.** In alignment with the teaching reform initiative at Beihang University, specifically the project titled "Construction and Analysis of Student Learning Portraits for Software Competence Teaching Process," the project leader implemented a learning resource recommendation framework in the 2023 and 2024 teaching cohorts for the courses under their purview. As depicted in Fig. 4, prior to the introduction of this framework in 2021 and 2022, the homework pass rates of these cohorts were comparable to the average levels. However, following the adoption of the framework in 2023 and 2024, the homework pass rates significantly surpassed the average levels. This evidence underscores the efficacy of personalized learning resource recommendations in enhancing students' knowledge acquisition and comprehension. Moreover, it reaffirms the critical role of targeted learning support within the teaching process.

**Visualization.** Taking the ASSISTments2012 dataset as an example, a subset comprising 5,000 student nodes and 100 skill nodes was extracted. To further construct an educational resource map, relevant educational resources corresponding to the aforementioned skill names were collected from the Wikipedia and Bilibili platforms. Following identification and screening, a total of 1,251 pertinent resources were obtained. These resources consist of 475 textual resources (Wikipedia content) and 776 video resources (Bilibili content).

Based on the three entity types—students, skills, and resources—a knowledge graph structure was constructed, resulting in tens of thousands of data triples. Specifically, the graph includes: Skill-resource relationships: 1,251 association relationships (indicating that a skill possesses corresponding teaching resources). Student-resource interaction relationships: 21,744 learning interaction records, comprising 7,980 reading interactions (corresponding to text resources) and 13,764 viewing interactions (corresponding to video resources). Finally, the knowledge graph data was stored within the Neo4j graph database. The visualization of the resultant knowledge graph is presented in Fig. 5.

## 5    Conclusion

Our paper proposed a new personalized learning resource recommendation framework combining knowledge graphs (KGs) and Large Language Models (LLMs) to tackle key challenges in Educational Recommender System (ERS). Experiments showed its superiority over other methods. It greatly improved Precision@10, Recall@10, diversity and semantic relevance. Ablation studies highlighted the importance of LLM - driven data augmentation and personalization enabled by Open Learner Model (OLM). Practical use in classrooms also proved its effectiveness, with increased homework pass rates at Beihang University.

However, there are still limitations. LLM inference causes extra computational latency, and the current framework mainly works for structured knowledge areas. Future work will look into federated learning for data privacy, multimodal learner behavior analysis, cross - domain knowledge transfer, as well as supporting collaborative and lifelong learning. This study offers a scalable and interpretable solution for intelligent education systems and provides insights and practical guidance for personalized education in the age of generative artificial intelligence.

**Acknowledgements.** This work was supported by the National Natural Science Foundation of China (U24B20171,62394332) and Research Start-up Funds of Hangzhou International Innovation Institute of Beihang University (2024KQ068, 2024KQ053).

# References


1. Abdi, S., Khosravi, H., Sadiq, S., Gasevic, D.: A multivariate ELO-based learner model for adaptive educational systems. arXiv preprint arXiv:1910.12581 (2019)
2. Abdi, S., Khosravi, H., Sadiq, S., Gasevic, D.: Complementing educational recommender systems with open learner models. In: Proceedings of the Tenth International Conference on Learning Analytics & Knowledge, pp. 360–365 (2020)
3. Ain, Q.U., Chatti, M.A., Meteng Kamdem, P.A., Alatrash, R., Joarder, S., Siepmann, C.: Learner modeling and recommendation of learning resources using personal knowledge graphs. In: Proceedings of the 14th Learning Analytics and Knowledge Conference, pp. 273–283 (2024)
4. Balog, K., Radlinski, F., Arakelyan, S.: Transparent, scrutable and explainable user models for personalized recommendation. In: Proceedings of the 42nd International ACM SIGIR Conference on Research and Development in Information Retrieval, pp. 265–274 (2019)
5. Bao, K., Zhang, J., Zhang, Y., Wang, W., Feng, F., He, X.: Tallrec: an effective and efficient tuning framework to align large language model with recommendation. In: Proceedings of the 17th ACM Conference on Recommender Systems, pp. 1007–1014 (2023)

6. Barria-Pineda, J., Brusilovsky, P.: Explaining educational recommendations through a concept-level knowledge visualization. In: Companion Proceedings of the 24th International Conference on Intelligent User Interfaces, pp. 103–104 (2019)

7. Benedict, A., Al-Hossami, E., Dorodchi, M., Benedict, A., Wiktor, S.: Pilot recommender system enabling students to indirectly help each other and foster belonging through reflections. In: LAK22: 12th International Learning Analytics and Knowledge Conference, pp. 521–527 (2022)

8. Bonifacio, L., Abonizio, H., Fadaee, M., Nogueira, R.: InPars: data augmentation for information retrieval using large language models. arXiv preprint arXiv:2202.05144 (2022)

9. Brown, T., et al.: Language models are few-shot learners. Adv. Neural. Inf. Process. Syst. **33**, 1877–1901 (2020)

10. Brusilovsky, P., Millán, E.: User models for adaptive hypermedia and adaptive educational systems. In: Brusilovsky, P., Kobsa, A., Nejdl, W. (eds.) The Adaptive Web. LNCS, vol. 4321, pp. 3–53. Springer, Heidelberg (2007). https://doi.org/10.1007/978-3-540-72079-9_1

11. Bull, S., Kay, J.: SMILI: a framework for interfaces to learning data in open learner models, learning analytics and related fields. Int. J. Artif. Intell. Educ. **26**, 293–331 (2016)

12. Conati, C., Porayska-Pomsta, K., Mavrikis, M.: AI in education needs interpretable machine learning: Lessons from open learner modelling. arXiv preprint arXiv:1807.00154 (2018)

13. Deng, Y., Lu, D., Huang, D., Chung, C.J., Lin, F.: Knowledge graph based learning guidance for cybersecurity hands-on labs. In: Proceedings of the ACM Conference on Global Computing Education, pp. 194–200 (2019)

14. Geng, S., Liu, S., Fu, Z., Ge, Y., Zhang, Y.: Recommendation as language processing (RLP): a unified pretrain, personalized prompt & predict paradigm (p5). In: Proceedings of the 16th ACM Conference on Recommender Systems, pp. 299–315 (2022)

15. Guesmi, M., et al.: Open, scrutable and explainable interest models for transparent recommendation. In: IUI Workshops (2021)

16. Guidotti, R., Monreale, A., Ruggieri, S., Turini, F., Giannotti, F., Pedreschi, D.: A survey of methods for explaining black box models. ACM Comput. Surv. (CSUR) **51**(5), 1–42 (2018)

17. Guo, Q., et al.: A survey on knowledge graph-based recommender systems. IEEE Trans. Knowl. Data Eng. **34**(8), 3549–3568 (2020)

18. Jesse, M., Bauer, C., Jannach, D.: Intra-list similarity and human diversity perceptions of recommendations: the details matter. User Model. User-Adap. Inter. **33**(4), 769–802 (2023)

19. Khalid, A., Lundqvist, K., Yates, A.: Recommender systems for MOOCS: a systematic literature survey (January 1, 2012-July 12, 2019). Int. Rev. Res. Open Distrib. Learn. **21**(4), 255–291 (2020)

20. Koren, Y., Rendle, S., Bell, R.: Advances in collaborative filtering. Recommender Systems Handbook, pp. 91–142 (2021)

21. Leite, L., et al.: A novel video recommendation system for algebra: an effectiveness evaluation study. In: LAK22: 12th International Learning Analytics and Knowledge Conference, pp. 294–303 (2022)

22. Lin, C.Y.: Rouge: a package for automatic evaluation of summaries. In: Text Summarization Branches Out, pp. 74–81 (2004)

23. Liu, P., Zhang, L., Gulla, J.A.: Pre-train, prompt, and recommendation: a comprehensive survey of language modeling paradigm adaptations in recommender systems. Trans. Assoc. Comput. Linguistics **11**, 1553–1571 (2023)
24. Liu, Q., Chen, N., Sakai, T., Wu, X.M.: Once: boosting content-based recommendation with both open-and closed-source large language models. In: Proceedings of the 17th ACM International Conference on Web Search and Data Mining, pp. 452–461 (2024)
25. Liu, Z., Liu, Q., Chen, J., Huang, S., Tang, J., Luo, W.: PYKT: a python library to benchmark deep learning based knowledge tracing models. Adv. Neural. Inf. Process. Syst. **35**, 18542–18555 (2022)
26. Lops, P., De Gemmis, M., Semeraro, G.: Content-based recommender systems: state of the art and trends. In: Recommender Systems Handbook, pp. 73–105 (2011)
27. Ma, Y., Liu, B., Huang, W., Dan, F.: Knowledge graph based recommendation algorithm for educational resource. In: Proceedings of the 14th International Conference on Education Technology and Computers, pp. 436–441 (2022)
28. Moon, T.: The expectation-maximization algorithm. IEEE Signal Process. Mag. **13**(6), 47–60 (1996). https://doi.org/10.1109/79.543975
29. Ren, X., et al.: Representation learning with large language models for recommendation. In: Proceedings of the ACM Web Conference 2024, pp. 3464–3475 (2024)
30. Takami, K., Dai, Y., Flanagan, B., Ogata, H.: Educational explainable recommender usage and its effectiveness in high school summer vacation assignment. In: LAK22: 12th International Learning Analytics and Knowledge Conference, pp. 458–464 (2022)
31. Thaker, K., Barria-Pineda, J.: Using knowledge graph for explainable recommendation of external content in electronic textbooks (2020)
32. Thaker, K., Zhang, L., He, D., Brusilovsky, P.: Recommending remedial readings using student knowledge state. In: International Educational Data Mining Society (2020)
33. Van Meteren, R., Van Someren, M.: Using content-based filtering for recommendation. In: Proceedings of the Machine Learning in the New Information Age: MLnet/ECML2000 Workshop, vol. 30, pp. 47–56. Barcelona (2000)
34. Wei, W., et al.: LLMRec: large language models with graph augmentation for recommendation. In: Proceedings of the 17th ACM International Conference on Web Search and Data Mining, pp. 806–815 (2024)
35. Yudelson, M.V., Koedinger, K.R., Gordon, G.J.: Individualized Bayesian knowledge tracing models. In: Lane, H.C., Yacef, K., Mostow, J., Pavlik, P. (eds.) AIED 2013. LNCS (LNAI), vol. 7926, pp. 171–180. Springer, Heidelberg (2013). https://doi.org/10.1007/978-3-642-39112-5_18
36. Zhang, J., Xie, R., Hou, Y., Zhao, X., Lin, L., Wen, J.R.: Recommendation as instruction following: a large language model empowered recommendation approach. ACM Trans. Inf. Syst. (2023)
37. Zhang, Y., Ai, Q., Chen, X., Wang, P.: Learning over knowledge-base embeddings for recommendation. arXiv preprint arXiv:1803.06540 (2018)
38. Zhou, J., Ma, X., Shan, P., Wang, J.: Learning path recommendation using lesson sequence and learning object based on course graph. In: Proceedings of the 13th International Conference on Education Technology and Computers, pp. 7–12 (2021)

# The REGEN Model, a LLM-Based Integrated Framework of Retrieval and QA Generation from Plain Texts on International Freight Domain


Guangqing Ouyang[1], Shusi Yu[1], Peng Wu[2]($\boxtimes$), Rong Xiao[3], and Jingbao Luo[4]

[1] Nanjing Yuanquan Software Technology Co., Ltd., Nanjing, Jiangsu, China
`ouyanggq@metast.cn, yushs@metast.cn`
[2] School of Intelligent Manufacture, Nanjing University of Science and Technology, No. 200 Xiaolinwei road, Nanjing 210094, Jiangsu, China
`wupeng@njust.edu.cn`
[3] ZTE Corporation, Nanjing 210000, Jiangsu, China
`xiao.rong1@zte.com.cn`
[4] School of Cyber Science and Engineering, Nanjing University of Science and Technology, No. 200 Xiaolinwei road. Nanjing, Nanjing 210094, Jiangsu, China
`luojingbao@njust.edu.cn`



**Abstract.** One of the major obstacles to building a domain specific Question Answer (QA) system is the lack of domain specific training data to fine-tune a pre-trained Large Language Model (LLM). Plain domain specific corpus is often abundant, but it is too expensive to convert it into QA pairs for fine-tuning.

This research introduces a LLM-based integrated REtrieval and GENeration model (REGEN) to extract QA pairs from plain texts, such as text books, technical documentations and work logs. The model was fine-tuned on few-shot labeled QA pairs. It was further applied to plain texts, extracting abundant QA pairs to fine-tune another LLM to build a domain specific QA system.

We demonstrated that our model performs significantly better than the baseline model in domain specific tasks with only 1k manually labeled QA pairs and 10M token extracted from international freight domain specific corpus. In the performance test, our model obtained about 70 points in the International Freight Forwarding Qualification Examination (IFFQE), 30 points more than the baseline model. This research presents an ideal choice for adopting LLM as a QA system into new domains, especially when there is little domain QA data available.

**Keywords:** Large Language Model (LLM) · Domain-Specific QA · Few-Shot Learning · Retrieval-Generation Framework · International Freight

# 1   Introduction

Question Answer (QA) is a subfield of Natural Language Processing (NLP). QA focuses on developing systems that automatically answer questions from humans in natural language. LLM-based QA is widely applied for industrial applications such as finance and internet enterprises [1]. Big firms such as HSBC and Baidu have already adopted ChatGPT-based chatbots for simple customer service answering. However, ChatGPT is still not applicable for complicated domain specific tasks. Kocon *et al.* showed an average loss in quality of chatGPT of about 25% for specific NLP tasks [10].

LLM-based systems require a large number of QA pairs to train them, otherwise they fail at reaching their optimal performance for the specified domain. The large scale of training data needed and the computational cost of LLM-based QA training pose a real challenge. Therefore, several approaches have been explored in order to minimize the computational demand. Zeyu Han *et al.* proposed to fine-tune LLM-based QA with domain specific training corpus [5]. However, it still requires millions of domain specific training samples to be effective. These datasets are only available in internet and mostly build-up from plain texts. Therefore, to automatically extract QAs from them is very demanding since manually extraction process is costly [3].

However, most existing QA extraction approaches [3,13] themselves are neural models that require huge amount of domain specific QA pairs as training data. Subsequently, in the present work, we propose a novel approach that requires only a small amount of labeled data as seed to build an integrated REtrieval and GENeration (REGEN) QA pair extraction model. The proposed model is based on a LLM with a dense prompt. Firstly, we segmented the plain texts to paragraphs, sections and sentences. Secondly, the extraction model was fine-tuned by following a REGEN iterative approach which started with a manual crafted prompt. For our Chinese QA system, we chose the most widely applied Chinese LLM, the chatGLM, as our base model. The chatGLM is not only optimized for Chinese language, but also outperforms other LLMs, including GPT, in multiple NLP tasks [4]. Subsequently, each segment was indexed by the corresponding LLM generated embedding. Then, each seed QA pair was used as query to retrieve the most similar segment from the segment index. We included the Retrieval Augmented Generation (RAG) approach so the retrieved result was used to augment generation. The loss function of the overall framework was defined as the distance between the generated and the labeled QAs. The LLM prompt was iteratively optimized until QA generation convergence. Finally, REGEN was applied to extract the QA pairs from all text segments. The resulting pairs were used to fine-tune another LLM able to answer users' questions.

We evaluated our approach in the international freight domain for several reasons. Firstly, the international freight industry accounts for 1% of the global Gross Domestic Product (GDP) and contributes economic growth by 3% [9]. Secondly, international freight is a labor-intensive industry, employing over 10 million shipping agents worldwide. Lastly, there is an official and regular approach to evaluate domain specific QA systems called the International Freight Forwarding Qualification Examination (IFFQE). Specifically, we selected the international freight domain because it is a prosperous labor-intensive service industry which requires a QA system to relieve customer service work.

We compared our REGEN model with multiple baselines in terms of final IFFQE score. Experimental results proved that our approach significantly out performs RAG based on pre-trained LLM (base LLM), scarce data fine-tuned LLM, and separated retrieval-generation framework.

The main contributions of this paper are summarized as follows:

1. We developed the first REGEN approach that builds a domain specific QA extraction LLM by using plain text corpus and a small set of labeled QA pairs.
2. The REGEN model was integrated into a QA system for customer service within an international freight domain, the maritime-domain.
3. Our method achieved 70 points in IFFQE in contrast to the 40 points obtained by the baseline LLMs.

The remainder of this work is structured as follows: Sect. 2 presents an overview of the related work; Sect. 3 describes the research design; Sect. 4 illustrates the experimental results and, finally, Sect. 5 briefly presents the discussion, conclusions, and proposals for future work.

## 2   Related Works

### 2.1   Question Answer Methods

QA extraction is a NLP task that involves the extraction of a question and its corresponding answer from a segment of plain text. To accomplish it, three different approaches have been explored: the question-first approach, the answer-first approach and the onestop approach that generates questions and answers simultaneously [3]. It has been shown that the onestop approach is more efficient and effective because it considers the compatibility between question and answer.

Retrieval systems are another kind of QA. Given a user question, information retrieval techniques find relevant documents and passages. The RAG approach is used to augment LLM generation with search engine retrieval results [12]. There are multiple types of search engine retrievers such as the keyword query retriever [12] and the dense retriever [17]. For the RAG process, retrievers require indexes that could be keywords in the case of keyword query retrievers, sentence embeddings in the case of dense retrievers. Research on these retrievers has shown that dense retrievers achieve higher precision than keyword retriever [17].

QA extraction requires fine-tuning because LLMs learn domain specific knowledge by applying this process. There are several fine-tuning approaches for LLMs such as prompt-tuning [11], adapter [6], and the Low Rank Adaptation (LoRA) [7]. Integrated approaches combining RAG and fine-tuning, or fine-tuning of two language models are also found in literature. The RAG Fine-Tuning (RAFT) method retrieves documents from a big repository thus, related documents are further selected and used to fine-tune LLM for better generation [18]. These fine-tuning process reduces training data requirement but still need millions of labeled pairs containing domain specific knowledge.

## 2.2  Question Answering Systems for International Shipping

To date, studies on maritime domain QA systems or chatbots have been conducted on safety education [2], insurance custom services [15], and expert systems on policy making support [19]. However, the QA systems of the aforementioned studies adopted very old versions of the base models, *i.e.* Recurrent Neural Network (RNN) [2], therefore they did not benefit from the latest advances on LLM. They present two main limitations. Firstly, they all lack of QA data to train an effective model [2,15] so only manually crafted rules can be used [2] and, secondly they all lack of an objective evaluation of effectiveness of a QA system as it was shown by Colabianchi *et al.* [2] who evaluated their work by customer surveys and [15,19] case studies.

# 3  Research Design

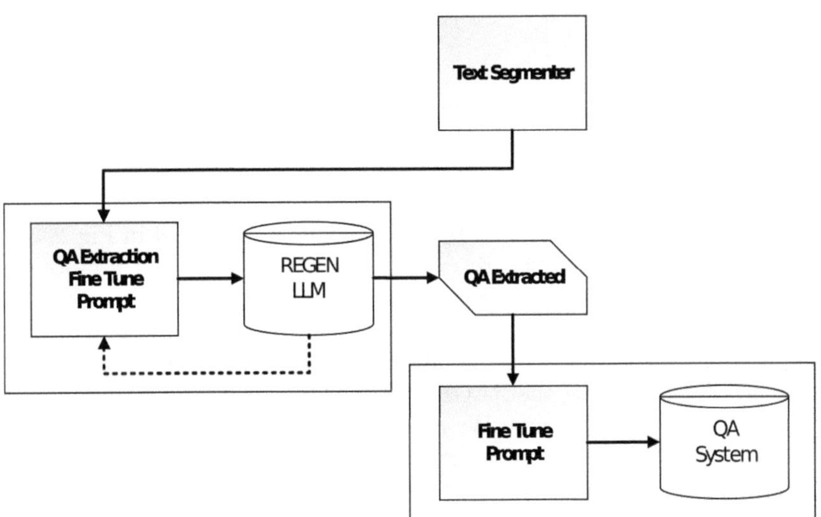


**Fig. 1.** Overview of the presented approach.

In order to build an end-to-end toolkit for a domain specific QA system, we constructed an integrated REGEN framework to extract QA pairs from domain specific plain texts as it is shown in Fig. 1. The components of this system are: 1. The text segmenter; 2. The QA extractor; 3. The fine-tuning component. In contrast to other machine learning-based LLM QA systems, which require large amount of data for fine-tuning, the presented model used a small amount of QA pairs.

### 3.1   Integrated Retrieval-Generation Question Answer Extraction

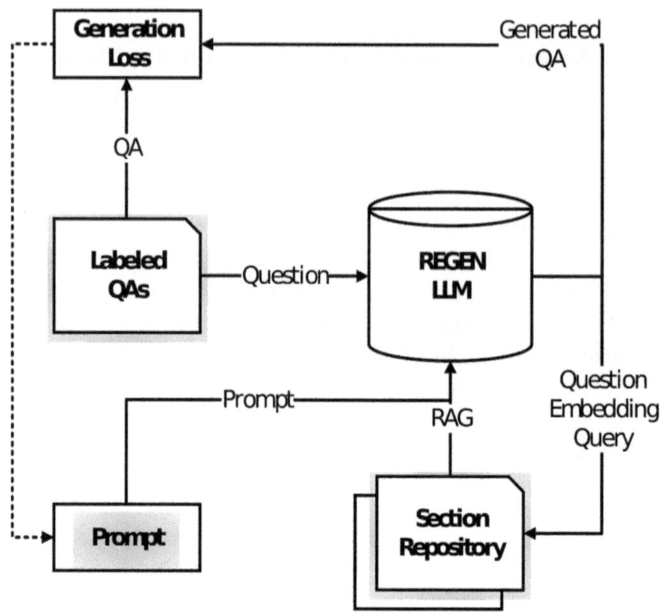


**Fig. 2.** Overview of our REGEN method

The overview of our integrated REGEN model is presented in Fig. 2.

First, we performed a dense retrieval using the search index vectors generated per extracted segment (*i.e.* sentence, paragraph, and section) by our text segmenter.

Second, for each pair within the labeled small dataset of QA, we embedded concatenated QA by using the REGEN LLM. Then, we used the resulting vector to search indexed segments. We chose a distance metric and retrieve top-1 segment with the shortest distance from the query.

Third, the retrieved segments were appended to the LLM input to augment generation. Subsequently, a question and a corresponding answer were generated.

Fourth, we also embedded the generated QA to a vector. Then, we measured the similarity between the generated and the query QA embeddings. The resulting distance is the loss function of the whole framework.

We optimized the whole framework by fine-tuning its generation prompt. During the optimization, the LLM itself was fixed and only the prompt changed. Since we had very few training samples for tuning, we started from the manual prompt **"generate question and corresponding answer from this passage"**. The prompt was fine-tuned by using Stochastic Gradient Descent (SGD), according to the obtained loss function. The optimization was done in an iterative way, so it went on until generated QA converges to labeled QA.

The optimized prompt and the LLM were applied to index extracted segments to construct a new repository. The query vector was also updated by the new prompt. We iterated on the above-mentioned steps until convergence.

We used the LLM sentence embedding published by Lester *et al.* [11]. First, the [**MASK**] symbol was placed after the sentence to convert it to an embedding vector. Then, we input the sentence and masked tail to target LLM. Subsequently, the sentence embedding, which is the corresponding vector of [**MASK**] after applying the transformer module conversion, was generated.

**Retrieval Augmented Generation.** The RAG method was introduced into our framework to deal with the misalignment between the seed QA and its corresponding segment. It retrieves a knowledge base with user's question and augments LLM generation with retrieval result.

Retrieval part of our RAG approach is a dense retrieval. The dense retrieval method consists in encoding each query into an embedding that conveys the user's information needs(query) and then matches the query with the documents stored in the embedding space of the knowledge base(extracted text segments). We converted queries and segments into embedding vectors by using the sentence embedding approach explained in Sect. 3.1.

Formally, we denoted the document repository D being $D$ as $D = d_1, d_2, ..., d_n$, where $d_i$ denotes the individual document $i$. For each $d_i$, an index mechanism was applied to the map of each document to the corresponding index. The index was denoted as $I$. In this research, we indexed the extracted segments by using the sentence embedding approach. When $I$ was retrieved by embedding the query $q$, it returned the top1 softmax similar index $i$ and its corresponding document $d_i$.

We appended $d_i$ to the question to augment generation. Given a prompt $p$, the generation function was denoted as $G(\cdot, p)$. Then, given the question $q$ and the retrieved document $d$, the generated RAG result was $r = G(d, p)$, where $+$ referred to the string concatenation.

Furthermore, according to [16], different kinds of postfixes were appended to generate questions in order to complete them. Possible postfixes were also extracted from seed questions during training.

**Training and Inference Training Algorithm:** The training algorithm of the REGEN model is described in Algorithm 1. Since prompt $p$ changed during each iteration and $I$ changed with $p$, we started with new $P$ and $I$ every time until converge.

For the inference procedure, we fed each segment into the LLM prompted with fine-tuned $p$. The QA pair was then generated.

## 3.2   Fine-Tune

QA pairs extracted in the extraction step (described in Sect. 3.1) were used to train/fine-tune another LLM. This fine-tuned LLM is the underlying model

---

**Algorithm 1.** Training algorithm of REGEN model

---

**Input:** $D, (Q, A)$. $D$ for segment repository and $(Q, A)$ for labeled QA pairs repository, a pre-trained large language model, initial dense prompt $p$

**Input:** Dense index $I$ of $D$, retrieval function $R(\cdot)$ of $I$, Embedding function of the prompted LLM $E(\cdot, p)$, generation function $G(\cdot, p)$,

**Output:** a fine-tuned dense prompt for REGEN model.

  **while** *notconverge* **do**

    **for all** $d \in D$ **do**

      $i = E(d, p)$. $i$ for dense index of $d$

      append $i$ into $I$.

    **end for**

    **for all** $(q, a) \in (Q, A)$ **do**

      $r = R(q)$

      $(q', a') = G(r, p)$

      append $a'$ into $GP$. $GP$ for generated question answer pairs

    **end for**

    Fine-tune $p$ to minimize $Softmax((Q, A), GP)$;

  **end while**

---

for our domain specific QA system. We selected prompt tuning for fine-tuning because it achieved the best results.

## 4    Experiments

The focus of our research was to develop a machine learning-based LLM for QA with scarce labeled data from the maritime domain. Our experimental set-up was designed to answer the following questions: (a) If an integrated iterative optimization framework (*i.e.* the REGEN model) performs better than base LLM trained with scarce data; (b) if the retrieval-targeting optimized prompt is consistent with the generation-targeting optimized prompt; (c) if a manually crafted initial prompt performs better than a randomly initial prompt.

### 4.1    Data Description

In this study, we defined three sets of data:

- **Seed data:** labeled seed QA pairs (195 multiple choice questions and 978 essay questions) were collected from a private database of customer service records.
- **Training Data:** The plain text training datasets extracted from the following text books were used for the QA extraction:
  "Practice and Law for International Carriage of Goods by Sea"
  "International cargo transportation and insurance"
  "The practice of International Freight Forwarding"
  In total, 98,723,667 tokens were extracted.
- **Evaluation data:** Evaluation data: We collected IFFQEs from 2018 to 2021. Each exam contained 90–98 QA pairs.

## 4.2   Experimental Design

The experimental design was divided into three phases: 1. Text segmentation; 2. QA extraction; 3. Fine-tuning.

For the first phase, the text segmentation, we extracted three levels of segments: sentences, paragraphs and sections from all texts. The sentences were identified by either periods or line breaks. The paragraphs were distinguished by line breaks. The sections were identified by heading texts. To avoid context loss, we conducted an overlapped segmentation, for example, if a section (level 1) contained 3 level-2 sections, each level 2 sections contained 3 paragraphs and each paragraph 3 sentences. Then, we got 1 level-1 section + 3 level 2 sections + 9 para-graphs + 27 sentences = 40 segments. We removed spaces from segments and ignored segments containing less than 5 tokens.

For the second phase, we performed the integrated REGEN QA extraction according to Sect. 3.1. QA extraction consisted of a dense retrieval of segments to enhance a prompted LLM generator. We retrieved a limited number of segments, about 30k, therefore, we manually crafted a dense index and retrieved the top 1 embedding vectors by using the Facebook AI Similarity Search (FAISS) [8]. We chose the ChatGLM-6B version of the GLM series as our base LLM since it contains abundant open-source resources and mature tech community. The dense prompt was either randomly initialized or started from the sentence embedding defined in Sect. 3.1.

For fine-tuning part of the second phase and the third phase, the LLM fine-tuning (defined in Sect. 3.2), we defined the learning rate and the number of epochs as hyperparameters as they have a direct impact on the overall model performance. The grid search was used to select an optimal value that minimized the softmax function in the training set. The latent feature maps were explored at every five intervals with the range of 10–30 and the time lag between searches was 3, 6, 12 for our proposed method. Specifically, experiments with diverse learning rates (*i.e.* 0.1, 0.01, 0.001) and number of epochs (*i.e.* 500, 1000, 2000) were conducted.

We used a machine with the following specifications: eight cores CPU with 2.8GHz clock speed, 128G memory, 48G video memory, 2TB hard disk, and operation system CentOS 9.

## 4.3   Experiment Results

**Segment Extraction.** The text segmenter produced 27,983 segments (513 segments for level 1 or sections, 1614 segments for level 2 or paragraphs, 25856 segments for level 3 or sentences).

**Postfix Extraction.** Our semi-automated postfix extraction approach extracted five kinds of postfixes. They are: 1. (no postfix); 2. which of the following is not correct; 3. translate to English; 4. which of the following is not contained; 5. how many kinds are there; We appended each postfix to each generated question.

**IFFQE Exam Results.** In the evaluation phase of our method, we used multiple choice and essay questions from the IFFQEs. We followed the method published by Tran *et al.* [16] to generate distractors and fine-tune base LLMs by QA: **"QUESTION: [extracted question] MUST CHOOSE AMONG:[correct choice and distractors]"**, **"ANSWER: [A/B/C/D]"**.

For essay questions, we manually corrected fine-tuned LLM generated answers as well as we manually measured the scores.

Since we extracted five postfixes and each of them was appended to a multiple choice question, we obtained 119,370 (23,874*5) multiple choice training samples. We appended **"translate to English"** to each essay question extracted so 6,232 (3,116*2) essay samples were retrieved. In total, we obtained 125,602 training samples.

**Table 1.** IFFQE scores obtained by the different models

| year | Base LLM | Tuned LLM | Double-LLM framework | Random initialized prompt | REGEN |
| --- | --- | --- | --- | --- | --- |
| 2018 | 41 | 39 | 45 | 44 | 71 |
| 2019 | 33 | 34 | 40 | 45 | 69 |
| 2020 | 37 | 34 | 46 | 48 | 71 |
| 2021 | 42 | 37 | 44 | 39 | 68 |

Table 1 presents the scores obtained by our REGEN model in contrast to the ones obtained by other models.

Base LLM refers to segment indexing and RAG based QA generation with pre-trained LLM without any fine-tuning (which is performed in our model). Tuned-LLM framework is almost the same as base LLM, only the LLM is fine-tuned by seed QA pairs. Double-LLM framework contains the retrieval and generation modules separated (while in our model, both modules are integrated). The random initialized prompt model initializes LLM with a random dense prompt (while the REGEN model does it with a manual crafted prompt).

We found that the REGEN model obtains approximately 70 points in each exam, around 30 points more than the base LLM model. It has been reported that the base LLM model outperforms RNN-based or rule-based models [14], therefore we can conclude that our approach outperforms the previous models described in the beginning of Sect. 4. This result answers positively to our research question (a): If an integrated iterative optimization framework performs better than base LLM fine-tuned with scarce training data.

We can observe from Table 1 that tuned-LLM performs even worse than base LLM, indicating that an existing QA extraction model can perform poorly with scarce training data. The result provides more evidence to our positive answer to our research question (a).

As shown in Table 1, in our research, fine-tuning both optimized the final QA generation as well as improved the sentence embedding process. In order to prove this, in our experiments we performed a one-stop prompt optimization for both retrieval and generation. Table 1 also illustrated that our REGEN model significantly outperformed traditional models with separated retrieval and generation modules.

We built a double-LLM framework, with separated retrieval and generation, following the research performed by Ma *et al.* [12]. This result gave a positive answer to our research question (b): using a retrieval-targeting optimized prompt is consistent with a generation-targeting optimized prompt. When a prompt is optimized for better generation, it is also optimized for better retrieval.

The results shown in Table 1 also demonstrated that start optimizing with a manual crafted prompt performs much better than start optimizing with a random prompt. Since we have very few labeled QA pairs, manual prompt engineering is very important. The result answers our research question (c): if a manually crafted initial prompt performs better than a randomly initial prompt.

**Case Study.** In this section, we present a case study to illustrate the performance of our approach in comparison to other approaches, *i.e.* the base LLM, the double-LLM framework, and random prompt (Table 1). Since the retrieval and generation modules are independent in the REGEN model, we investigated them separately. We used questions of the IFFQE of 2018.

**Retrieval Case Study:**
The study of random selected cases indicated that the base LLM and the random initialized prompt approaches failed at retrieving high quality segments. For example, for the first multiple choice question, **"international freight forwarders carry some duties ... what are the duties?"** This question shall retrieve the book **"Practice and Law for International Carriage of Goods by Sea"**, Sect. 9, Subsect. 3 **"Rights and duties"**. The REGEN and the double-LLM framework successfully located this section during retrieval. In contrast, the base LLM approach and the randomly initialized approach located the author paragraph, which only contained the names of the authors of the book. Therefore, these two approaches are not likely to generate the correct QA, subsequently, the LLM fine-tuned by wrong QA is not likely to answer the IFFQE questions correctly.

**Generation Case Study:**
In our experiments, we found that the double-LLM framework tended to repeat some words meaninglessly. For example, when we augmented by using both the double-LLM framework and the REGEN model with the section **"rights and duties"**, the double-LLM framework generated **"International freight forwarder is forwarder..."**. While the REGEN model generated almost the same question, **"international freight forwarders carry some duties ... what are the duties?"**. This indicates that the generation prompt was much harder to fine-tune than the retrieval-indexing prompt, requiring much more training data.

## 5   Conclusion and Discussion

In this paper, we introduced the REGEN model as an end-to-end domain specific QA system. Our approach adopted the RAG techniques and the LLM-based QA generation from plain text. Another LLM was further fine-tuned using extracted QA pairs. After fine-tuning, the LLM was incorporated into the domain specific QA system.

In order to evaluate the performance of our model, we used the standard IFFQE results. This evaluation is more efficient than using customer surveys or case studies, as it has been done in the past. Therefore, we concluded that using small sets of data as seed for a successful QA extractor is possible with our REGEN approach.

As a part of this evaluation, we compared the performance of our model to the one of other models. Our experiments showed that the REGEN model outperformed the baseline and other reference models by more than 30 points in standard exams, especially when the training dataset was scarce. Overall, our REGEN model showed a noticeable improvement in performance. Therefore, it could serve as a potential approach to build domain specific QA systems for future studies.

We didn't investigate the relationship between the seed QA training data size and the QA extraction model performance since or data size was too small. This should be explored in the future as establishing this relationship would impact QA data collection cost for LLM fine-tuning.

## References


1. Barde, K., Kulkarni, P.A.: Applications of generative AI in fintech. In: Proceedings of the Third International Conference on AI-ML Systems, AIMLSystems 2023, Bangalore, India, October 25–28, 2023, pp. 37:1–37:5. ACM (2023)
2. Colabianchi, S., Bernabei, M., Costantino, F.: Chatbot for training and assisting operators in inspecting containers in seaports. Transp. Res. Procedia **64**, 6–13 (2022). International Scientific Conference "The Science and Development of Transport - Znanost i razvitak prometa"
3. Cui, S., et al.: Onestop qamaker: extract question-answer pairs from text in a one-stop approach. In: WWW '21: The Web Conference 2021, Virtual Event/Ljubljana, Slovenia, April 19–23, 2021, pp. 1–10. ACM/IW3C2 (2021)
4. Du, Z., et al.: GLM: general language model pretraining with autoregressive blank infilling. In: Proceedings of the 60th Annual Meeting of the Association for Computational Linguistics (Volume 1: Long Papers), ACL 2022, Dublin, Ireland, May 22–27, 2022, pp. 320–335. Association for Computational Linguistics (2022)
5. Han, Z., Gao, C., Liu, J., Jeff, Z., Zhang, S.Q.: Parameter-efficient fine-tuning for large models: a comprehensive survey (2024)
6. He, R., et al.: On the effectiveness of adapter-based tuning for pretrained language model adaptation. In: Proceedings of the 59th Annual Meeting of the Association for Computational Linguistics and the 11th International Joint Conference on Natural Language Processing, ACL/IJCNLP 2021, (Volume 1: Long Papers), Virtual Event, August 1–6, 2021, pp. 2208–2222. Association for Computational Linguistics (2021)

7. Hu, E.J., et al.: Lora: low-rank adaptation of large language models. In: The Tenth International Conference on Learning Representations, ICLR 2022, Virtual Event, April 25–29, 2022. OpenReview.net (2022)
8. Johnson, J., Douze, M., Jégou, H.: Billion-scale similarity search with GPUs. IEEE Trans. Big Data **7**(3), 535–547 (2019)
9. Kim, S., Sohn, W., Lim, D., Lee, J.: A multi-stage data mining approach for liquid bulk cargo volume analysis based on bill of lading data. Expert Syst. Appl. **183**(C) (2021)
10. Kocon, J., et al.: ChatGPT: jack of all trades, master of none. Inf. Fusion **99**, 101,861 (2023)
11. Lester, B., Al-Rfou, R., Constant, N.: The power of scale for parameter-efficient prompt tuning. In: Proceedings of the 2021 Conference on Empirical Methods in Natural Language Processing, EMNLP 2021, Virtual Event/Punta Cana, Dominican Republic, 7–11 November, 2021, pp. 3045–3059. Association for Computational Linguistics (2021)
12. Ma, X., Gong, Y., He, P., Zhao, H., Duan, N.: Query rewriting in retrieval-augmented large language models. In: Bouamor, H., Pino, J., Bali, K. (eds.) Proceedings of the 2023 Conference on Empirical Methods in Natural Language Processing, EMNLP 2023, Singapore, December 6–10, 2023, pp. 5303–5315. Association for Computational Linguistics (2023). https://doi.org/10.18653/V1/2023.EMNLP-MAIN.322
13. Niu, W.: Research on e-commerce customer feature extraction question answering system based on artificial intelligence semantic analysis. Adv. Multim. **2022**, 6934,194:1–6934,194:6 (2022)
14. Qiu, Y., Jin, Y.: ChatGPT and finetuned BERT: a comparative study for developing intelligent design support systems. Intell. Syst. Appl. **21**, 200,308 (2024)
15. Santoso, C.B., Warnars, H.L.H.S., Fajar, A.N., Prabowo, H.: Smart insurance model for sea cargo business. J. Syst. Manag. Sci. **13**(4), 277–298 (2023)
16. Tran, A., Angelikas, K., Rama, E., Okechukwu, C., IV, D.H.S., MacNeil, S.: Generating multiple choice questions for computing courses using large language models. In: IEEE Frontiers in Education Conference, FIE 2023, College Station, TX, USA, October 18–21, 2023, pp. 1–8. IEEE (2023)
17. Zhan, J., Mao, J., Liu, Y., Guo, J., Zhang, M., Ma, S.: Optimizing dense retrieval model training with hard negatives. In: Proceedings of the 44th International ACM SIGIR Conference on Research and Development in Information Retrieval, pp. 1503–1512. Association for Computing Machinery (2021)
18. Zhang, T., et al.: Raft: adapting language model to domain specific rag (2024)
19. Ziegler, M., Lothian, S., O'Neill, B., Anderson, R.J., Ota, Y.: AI language models could both help and harm equity in marine policymaking: The case study of the BBNJ question-answering bot. CoRR abs/2403.01755 (2024)

# SWV: A Large-Scale Sensitive Word Variants Dataset for Semantic Text Matching

Jiguo Liu[1,2(✉)] [iD], Chao Liu[1,2], Meimei Li[1,2], Nan Li[1,2], Shihao Gao[1,2], and Dali Zhu[1,2]

[1] Institute of Information Engineering, Chinese Academy of Sciences, Beijing, China
`liujiguo@iie.ac.cn`
[2] School of Cyber Security, University of Chinese Academy of Sciences, Beijing, China

**Abstract.** Semantic Text Matching (STM) is one of the fundamental tasks in the field of Natural Language Processing (NLP) research. However, existing datasets are centered around the English language and lack sensitive word variants datasets for sensitive content detection, which restricts the development of Chinese STM. In this work, we present SWV, a large-scale **S**ensitive **W**ord **V**ariants dataset, which contains four types: polysemy, close-words, homophones, and abbreviations. Specially, we use an LLM to generate similar sentences for the optimal text representation. To our knowledge, SWV is the first sensitive word variants dataset in Chinese. The SWV can serve as a Chinese corpus. Also, this semi-structured data is a natural annotation that can constitute many supervised NLP tasks. Based on SWV, we present a sensitive word variant detection algorithm based on <u>S</u>ound <u>S</u>hape <u>S</u>emantic code (3S-Code) for Chinese STM. Experimental results show that 3S-Code can considerably boost the performance of our system and achieve significantly better result than previous state-of-the-art methods on four available datasets, namely SWV, LCQMC, AFQMC, and BQ.

**Keywords:** Semantic text matching · Sensitive word variants · LLM · Similar sentences · 3S-Code

## 1 Introduction

With the popularization of the Internet, the way of information transmission is more simple and free, which provides an opportunity for the wide spread of sensitive information such as politics. The traditional sensitive information detection method based on character matching mainly indexes existing sensitive word lists and detection texts. Although it has a high detection accuracy, it has a strong dependence on the database.

In recent years, many malicious users have disguised sensitive information in their texts to evade scrutiny from online platforms, making it difficult for online


T. Zhu et al. (Eds.): KSEM 2025, LNAI 15919, pp. 258–272, 2026.
https://doi.org/10.1007/978-981-95-3001-4_19

platforms to recognize them. Therefore, it is necessary to improve the detection efficiency of sensitive words and their variants in order to create a healthy and secure cyberspace.

Semantic Text Matching (STM) plays an essential role in near-duplicate sensitive text detection. The main task of STM aims to predict whether two sentences are semantically equivalent or not. STM is also a fundamental task of many natural language processing (NLP) tasks including information retrieval [1,2], question answering system [3–5], dialogue system [6,7], etc. These resources, however, are mostly centered around the English language, which restricts the development of techniques for addressing non-English semantic text matching NLP tasks. Moreover, there are currently three classic datasets in the field of Chinese semantic text matching, but they lack complex scene forms of sensitive word variants.

To fill the gap of non-English semantic text matching and improve the recognition ability of complex sensitive word variants, in this paper, we introduce SWV: a large-scale Chinese **S**ensitive **W**ord **V**ariants dataset. SWV contains four types: polysemy, close-words, homophones, and abbreviations.

We implement some state-of-the-art Chinese STM models and evaluate on the proposed benchmark. We also demonstrate the effectiveness of the SWV dataset as pre-training corpus. Specially, we use LLMs to generate similar sentences for the optimal text representation. Based on SWV, we propose a sensitive word variant detection algorithm based on $\underline{S}$ound $\underline{S}$hape $\underline{S}$emantic code (**3S-Code**). The experiment results show that though existing models can achieve acceptable performance on STM tasks, it still needs future efforts to reach a practical level.

The main contributions of this paper are summarized as follows:

- We release the first large-scale Chinese Sensitive Word Variants dataset (SWV), which can be used for many different purposes, e.g., pretraining corpus, semantic text matching and sensitive information detection tasks.
- Based on the SWV, we build a unique encoding method that based on 3S-Code for Chinese STM, which represents real-world scenarios of automatic analyzing text.
- We implement text matching models to provide baselines. Experimental results show that 3S-Code can considerably boost the performance of our system and achieve significantly better results than previous state-of-the-art methods and variant models in the literature.

## 2   Related Work

### 2.1   STM Datasets

In the contemporary landscape of NLP and Large Language Model (LLM), the pivotal role of datasets has increasingly been acknowledged. The seminal work by [8] has galvanized the shift toward a data-centric AI paradigm, underscoring the potential of enhancing data quality to achieve superior model performance

**Table 1.** Statistics of three benchmarking datasets.

| Datasets | Types | Train | Test | Dev | Total |
|---|---|---|---|---|---|
| LCQMC | Question semantic matching | 238.766k | 12.500k | 8.802k | 260.068k |
| AFQMC | ANT financial | 61.486k | 20.496k | 20.495k | 102.477k |
| BQ | Question semantic matching | 100.000k | 10.000k | 10.000k | 120.000k |

over merely refining algorithms. The three mainstream Chinese STM benchmark datasets are as follows. The statistical data of mainstream datasets are detailed in Table 1.

- **LCQMC** [9]: The LCQMC dataset is a question semantic matching dataset constructed by Harbin Institute of Technology in COLING2018. Its format consists of sentence pair number, two sentences to be compared and four columns of similarity labels. It contains 260,068 pieces of data in total, including 238,766 for training set, 12,500 for test set and 8,802 for development set. Each pair is associated with a binary label indicating whether two sentences have the same meaning or share the same intention. Positive samples are 30% more than negative samples.
- **AFQMC** [10]: The AFQMC dataset is the dataset of ANT Financial ATEC: NLP Problem Similarity Calculation Competition, and it is a dataset for classification task. All data are from the actual application scenarios of Ant Financial's financial brain, that is, two sentences described by users in a given customer service are determined by algorithms to determine whether they represent the same semantics. The data volumes of training set, test set and development set are 61,486, 20,496, and 20,495, respectively, and the total number of all samples is 102,477.
- **BQ** [11]: The BQ dataset is a question matching dataset in the field of banking and finance. Comprising question text pairs extracted from one year of online banking system logs, it is the largest question matching dataset in the banking domain. The BQ dataset contains 120,000 pieces of data in total, including 100,000 for training set, 10,000 for test set and 10,000 for development set. The number of positive and negative samples is the same.

## 2.2   STM Models

- **LLMs Models:** Liu *et al.* [12] conducted some experimental analysis by fine-tuning LLMs for the task of Chinese short text matching and explored various factors that influence performance when fine-tuning LLMs, including task modeling methods, prompt formats, and output formats. Wan *et al.* [13] proposed TnT-LLM, a two-phase framework that employs LLMs to automate the process of end-to-end label generation and assignment with minimal human effort for any given use-case.

– **BERT-based Models:** MacBERT [14] is proposed to mitigate the gap between the pre-training and fine-tuning stage by masking the word with its similar word, which has proven to be effective on various downstream tasks. ERNIE [15] is designed to learn language representation enhanced by knowledge masking strategies, which includes entity-level masking and phrase-level masking. Sentence-BERT [16] utilized siamese and triplet network structures to derive semantically meaningful sentence embeddings that can be compared using cosine-similarity.

– **Deep Text Matching Models:** Most representation-based models are based on Siamese architecture, which has two symmetrical networks (e.g. LSTMs and CNNs) to extract high-level features from two sentences. Then, these features are compared to predict text similarity. He *et al.* [17] proposed Text-CNN that particularly focuses on extracting text-related regions and features from the image components. Mueller *et al.* [18] proposed BiLSTM that is another type of Siamese architecture used for encoding each sentence. Lattice-CNN [19] is also proposed to deal with the potential issue of Chinese word segmentation. It takes word lattice as input and pooling mechanisms are utilized to merge the feature vectors produced by multiple CNN kernels over different n-gram contexts of each node in the lattice graph. Yin *et al.* [20] proposed a general attention based convolutional neural network (ABCNN) for modeling a pair of sentences. Wang *et al.* [21] proposed a bilateral multi-perspective matching (BiMPM) model for natural language sentence matching tasks. Chen *et al.* [22] proposed an Enhanced Sequential Inference Model (ESIM), which achieves state-of-the-art results on various matching tasks.

– **Contrastive Learning Models:** Many researchers have increased attention on text similarity based on contrastive learning. Gao *et al.* [23] utilized the dropout of SimCSE model to generate two different sense embedding as a positive example for comparison, which greatly improves state-of-the-art sentence embeddings on semantic textual similarity tasks. Yan *et al.* [24] proposed ConSERT, a contrastive framework for self-supervised sentence representation transfer, that adopts contrastive learning to fine-tune BERT in an unsupervised and effective way. Chuang *et al.* [25] proposed DiffCSE, an unsupervised contrastive learning framework for learning sentence embeddings.

## 3   The SWV Dataset

### 3.1   Data Collection

To verify the effectiveness of the sensitive word variant detection algorithm, we have constructed a new SWV dataset for comprehensive experiments. The SWV dataset has the following characteristics. The sentences contain four types: polysemy, close-words, homophones, and abbreviations. In particularly, we have used LLMs to collect politically sensitive sentences, such as defense and military, weapons and equipment, industrial information, etc. Then, the generated similar sentences are checked and any ambiguities or irregularities are corrected. The label of each sentence is manually marked. The data volumes of training set, test set and development set are 2,760, 1,660, and 1,890, respectively, and the total number of all samples is 6,310.

## 3.2  Data Augmentation

Because the number of synonymous sentences is far less than the number of non-synonymous sentences, the available short text matching data is very rare. To solve this problem, we use an LLM to generate similar sentences to expand the dataset and improve the performance of short text matching. LLMs fully utilize multi-granularity data information and the advantages of large-scale language models [26,27]. We decompose the synonymous sentence generation task into two stages, each containing several turns of QA, which refer to the dialogue with LLMs. LLMs is implemented by transforming the zero-shot similar sentence generation task into a multi-turn question-answering problem with a two-stage framework.

**Stage I.** For one sample, this stage generally includes only one turn of QA. In order to find the similar sentences, we first utilize the task-specific templates and the list of sentences to construct the question. Then we combine the question and sentence as input to LLMs. To facilitate answer extraction, we ask the system to reply in the list form. If the sentence does not contain any similar sentences, the system will generate a response with NONE Token.

**Stage II.** This stage generally includes multiple QA turns. In advance, we design a series of specific templates for similar sentence types according to the scheme of the task. The template define a chain of question templates and the length of the chain is usually greater than one. We perform multi turns QA in the order of previously extracted sentence types as well as the order of templates. To generate a question, we need to retrieve the template with the similar sentence type and fill the corresponding slots if necessary. Then we access LLMs and get a response. Finally, we compose structured information based on the elements extracted in each turn. Similarly, for the convenience of answer extraction, we ask the system to reply in table form.

## 4  Encoder and Similarity Calculation

### 4.1  3S-Code

3S-Code is a unique encoding method that consists of three parts: sound code, shape code, and semantic code. Sound code is a coding method based on Chinese Pinyin, which consists of 23 initial consonants, 24 finals, and 5 tones. Shape code reflects the morphological characteristics of a Chinese character. This paper encodes the morphological characteristics of a Chinese character through three parts: character structure, character strokes, and four corner coding.

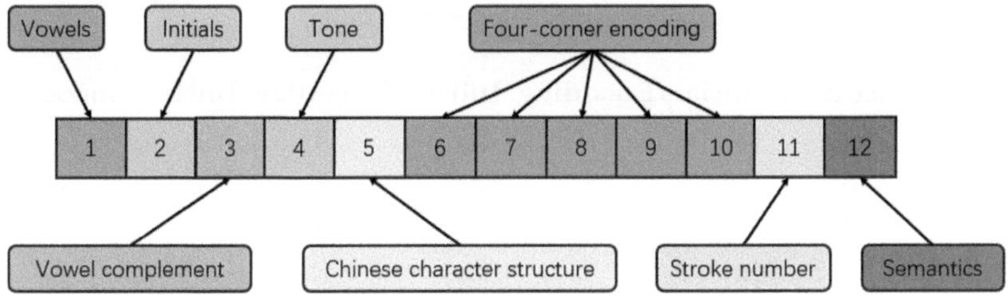


**Fig. 1.** 3S-Code structure.

**Table 2.** Vowel encoding table.

| Vowels | Encoding | Vowels | Encoding | Vowels | Encoding | Vowels | Encoding |
|---|---|---|---|---|---|---|---|
| {a} | 1 | {o} | 2 | {e} | 3 | {i} | 4 |
| {u} | 5 | {v} | 6 | {ai} | 7 | {ei} | 7' |
| {ui} | 8 | {ao} | 9 | {ou} | A | {iu} | B |
| {ie} | C | {ve} | D | {er} | E | {an} | F |
| {en} | G | {in} | H | {un} | I | {ven} | J |
| {ang} | F | {eng} | G | {ing} | H | {ong} | K |

Semantic code reflects the semantic meaning of a Chinese character, which refers to whether it has a negative meaning.

As shown in Fig. 1, 3S-Code consists of 12 symbols, of which 1–4 bits are sound codes, 5–11 bits are shape codes, and 12 bits are semantic codes. The encoding rules for each part are introduced as follows. The first one is the vowel, which is encoded according to the hexadecimal system for 24 vowels. Considering personal habits and the issue of dialects in some regions, some nasal sounds before and after are confused together. In order to facilitate subsequent calculations, the same encoding is set for easily confused vowels. The encoding method is shown in Table 2.

The second digits is the initial consonant, which is encoded in the same way as the final consonant. Moreover, considering the phenomenon of some consonants being indistinguishable and easily confused, the same encoding has also been set for some consonants. The encoding method is shown in Table 3.

The third digits is the vowel complement. In Chinese Pinyin, some pinyin is composed of two vowels, and the vowel in between the initial consonant and the final consonant plays the role of a consonant. For example, the "u" in "guang" and the "i" in "tian" are called vowel complements, and the encoding method is the same as that of vowel encoding. If there is no vowel complement, the default digit is "0".

The fourth one is pitch, which is represented by hexadecimal 1, 2, 3, and 4 respectively. "0" represents neutral tone, and the encoding method is shown in Table 4.

**Table 3.** Initials encoding table.

| Initials | Encoding | Initials | Encoding | Initials | Encoding | Initials | Encoding |
|---|---|---|---|---|---|---|---|
| {b} | 1 | {p} | 2 | {m} | 3 | {f} | 4 |
| {d} | 5 | {t} | 6 | {n} | 7 | {l} | 7 |
| {g} | 8 | {k} | 9 | {h} | A | {j} | B |
| {q} | C | {x} | D | {zh} | E | {ch} | F |
| {sh} | G | {r} | H | {z} | E' | {c} | F' |
| {s} | G' | {y} | I | {w} | J | {-} | - |

**Table 4.** Tone encoding table.

| Tone | One tone | Two tone | Three tone | Four tone | Light tone |
|---|---|---|---|---|---|
| Encoding | 1 | 2 | 3 | 4 | 0 |

**Table 5.** Structure encoding table.

| Structure | Example | Encoding |
|---|---|---|
| single-component character | 日、人、大 | 0 |
| Up-down structure | 宝、音、穷 | 2 |
| Upper-middle-lower structure | 意、草、竞 | 4 |
| Upper-three-surround structure | 闪、问、周 | 6 |
| Left-three-surround structure | 巨、医、区 | 8 |
| Upper-right-surround structure | 司、匈、氧 | A |
| Mosaic structure | 坐、爽、夹 | C |
| Left-right structures | 汉、结、组 | C |
| Left-middle-right structure | 树、辩、湖 | C |
| Fully-enclosed structure | 国、囚、固 | C |
| Lower-three-surround structure | 凶、函、画 | C |
| Upper-left-surround structure | 庙、厌、尼 | C |
| Left-lower-surround structure | 违、运、建 | C |

The fifth digits is the structure of Chinese characters, which includes independent characters and compound characters. Independent characters cannot be separated, while compound characters can be divided into multiple units. There are 12 types of compound character structures, which are encoded using the hexadecimal representation method. The encoding method is shown in Table 5.

The sixth to tenth digits are four corner codes, which define the stroke shape of Chinese characters and encode them by judging the stroke shape of each corner. In this paper, five digits are used to encode Chinese characters. The first four digits correspond to the encoding of each corner, and the fifth digit represents the pen shape near the bottom right corner, which is called the "supplementary

**Table 6.** Four-corner encoding table.

| Stroke head | Number | Example |
| --- | --- | --- |
| 头 | 0 | 主、吝 |
| 横 | 1 | 天、湖 |
| 垂 | 2 | 旧、舌 |
| 点 | 3 | 宝、连 |
| 叉 | 4 | 古、对 |
| 插 | 5 | 青、提 |
| 方 | 6 | 另、日 |
| 角 | 7 | 刀、明 |
| 八 | 8 | 分、总 |
| 小 | 9 | 尖、慢 |

number". If the stroke shape has already been used in the upper right corner, it is directly assigned as "0". The encoding rules for the four corner encoding are shown in Table 6. The eleventh digit is the stroke count of Chinese characters, which is represented by hexadecimal system, i.e. numbers 1 to 9, indicating that the stroke count of Chinese characters is from one to nine "A" represents ten strokes, "B" represents eleven strokes,..., "Z" represents thirty-five strokes.

The twelfth digit is semantic input. If there is a negative part of speech with or without, it is recorded as "1". Otherwise, it is recorded as "0".

## 4.2   Similarity Measurement

Similarity measurement is a quantitative measurement method for the degree of difference between two texts, defined as the number of operations that can convert one text into another. The operations involved include insertion, replacement, or deletion, and can only operate on one character at a time. When the number of operations is less, it indicates that the two are more similar, which serves as the basis for judging the similarity between two texts. This paper introduces the Hamming distance, which is mainly used in data transmission error control to represent the number of bits that are different for two encoding segments of the same length in binary representation.

Given the detecting text $T$ and the sensitive word $S$. Then, the corresponding encoding sequence $t = (t_1, t_2, ..., t_m)$ and $s = (s_1, s_2, ..., s_n)$ are obtained through 3S-Code. $h_p$ represents the Hanming distance in the pinyin. $h_g$ represents the Hanming distance in the shape. $h_s$ represents the Hanming distance in the semantics.

Let the binary length of the sound code is $L_p$, the binary length of the shape code is $L_g$, and the binary length of the semantic code is $L_s$. We obtain the contribution ratios $\varpi_1$, $\varpi_2$ and $\varpi_3$ of the sound, shape, and semantic code parts in the final similarity calculation.

$$\varpi_1 = \frac{e^{\frac{h_p}{L_p}}}{e^{\frac{h_p}{L_p}} + e^{\frac{h_g}{L_g}} + e^{\frac{h_s}{L_s}}}, \tag{1}$$

$$\varpi_2 = \frac{e^{\frac{h_g}{L_g}}}{e^{\frac{h_p}{L_p}} + e^{\frac{h_g}{L_g}} + e^{\frac{h_s}{L_s}}}, \tag{2}$$

$$\varpi_3 = \frac{e^{\frac{h_s}{L_s}}}{e^{\frac{h_p}{L_p}} + e^{\frac{h_g}{L_g}} + e^{\frac{h_s}{L_s}}}, \tag{3}$$

We concatenate the sound, shape, and semantic codes together to obtain similarity. The SWV algorithm process is shown in **Algorithm 1** below.

$$\varepsilon = \rho((\varepsilon_1 \cdot \varpi_1) \oplus (\varepsilon_2 \cdot \varpi_2) \oplus (\varepsilon_3 \cdot \varpi_3)), \tag{4}$$

---

**Algorithm 1.** 3S-Code

---

**Input**: Detecting text $T$, Sensitive word $S$
**Output**: Similarity $\varepsilon$
1: Initiate state $T \leftarrow \varnothing$ and $S \leftarrow \varnothing$;
2: 3S-Code $T$ and 3S-Code $S$;
3: Obtain sequence $t = (t_1, t_2, ..., t_m)$ and $s = (s_1, s_2, ..., s_n)$;
4: **for** $i$ to $featureSize$ **do**
5:    **if** $soundCode1[i] = soundCode2[i]$ **then**
6:       multiplier.append(1);
7:       $\varepsilon_1 +\!= \varpi_1[\text{i}]*$multiplier[i];
8:    **end if**
9: **end for**
10: **for** $i$ to $featureSize$ **do**
11:    **if** $shapeCode1[i] = shapeCode2[i]$ **then**
12:       multiplier.append(1);
13:       $\varepsilon_2 +\!= \varpi_2[\text{i}]*$multiplier[i];
14:    **end if**
15: **end for**
16: **for** $i$ to $featureSize$ **do**
17:    **if** $semCode1[i] = semCode2[i]$ **then**
18:       multiplier.append(1);
19:       $\varepsilon_3 +\!= \varpi_3[\text{i}]*$multiplier[i];
20:    **end if**
21: **end for**
22: $\varepsilon \leftarrow \varepsilon_1 + \varepsilon_2 + \varepsilon_3$;
23: **return** $\varepsilon$;

---

## 5    Experiments

### 5.1    Baseline Setting

In this work, the baselines mainly include two groups of models: previous SoTA models and our variant models. We have described the models in the comparisons of our main experiments. The models are listed as follows:

**Previous SoTA Methods.** We compare our models with four types of baselines: BERT-based models, representation-based models, interaction-based models and contrastive learning models. BERT-based models mainly include three baselines: BERT, MacBERT and ERNIE. Representation-based models mainly include three baselines: Text-CNN, BiLSTM, and Lattice-CNN. Interaction-based models mainly include two baselines: BiMPM and ESIM. Contrastive learning models mainly include two baselines: SimCSE and ConSERT.

**Variant Models.** To analyze the contribution of each component in our model, we ablate the full model and demonstrate the effectiveness of each component.

- **1S3S-Code:** This model is a part of our model without the shape code. We aim to verify the effectiveness of this component on model improvement.
- **2S3S-Code:** This model is a part of our model without the sound code. We aim to verify the effectiveness of this component on model improvement.

### 5.2    Overall Performance

The results on public datasets and SWV datasets are shown in Table 7 and Table 8 respectively. We have gathered several experiment findings from the results. All the experiments in Table 7 and Table 8 are running five times using different seeds and we report the **average scores** to ensure the reliability of results.

First, we can find that the three variants of BERT (e.g. MacBERT, MacBERT-ext, ERNIE) all surpass the original BERT, which suggests using word level information during pre-training is important for Chinese matching tasks. Our 3S-Code performs better than all these BERT-based models. Compared with the baseline BERT which has the same initialization parameters, the ACC. of 3S-Code on LCQMC, AFQMC and BQ is increased by 2.17%, 14.2% and 2.10%, respectively. It shows that utilizing sound, shape, semantic encoding during fine-tuning phrases with 3S-Code is an effective way to boost the performance for Chinese semantic matching. We also compare results with K-BERT [29], which regards information in N-HowNet as triples {word, contain, sememes} to enhance BERT, introducing soft position and visible matrix during the fine-tuning and inferring phases. The reported ACC. for the LCQMC test set of K-BERT is 86.9%. Our 3S-Code is 0.10% better than that. Different from K-BERT, we focus on fusing useful information between sound, shape and semantic encoding.

**Table 7.** Performance of various models on LCQMC, AFQMC and BQ test datasets. Among them, the results are average scores using different seeds.

| Models | LCQMC | | AFQMC | | BQ | |
|---|---|---|---|---|---|---|
| | ACC. | F1 | ACC. | F1 | ACC. | F1 |
| MacBERT [14] | 86.80 | 87.78 | 74.02 | 74.30 | 84.89 | 84.29 |
| MacBERT-ext [14] | 86.68 | 87.71 | 74.07 | 74.35 | 84.71 | 83.94 |
| ERNIE [15] | 87.04 | 88.06 | 73.83 | 73.91 | 84.67 | 84.20 |
| LET [28] | 84.81 | 86.08 | - | - | 83.22 | 83.03 |
| LET-BERT [28] | 88.38 | 88.85 | - | - | 85.30 | 84.98 |
| Text-CNN [17] | 72.80 | 75.70 | - | - | 78.52 | 69.17 |
| BiLSTM [18] | 76.10 | 78.90 | 64.68 | 54.53 | 73.51 | 72.68 |
| Lattice-CNN [19] | 82.14 | 82.41 | - | - | 78.20 | 78.30 |
| BiMPM [21] | 83.30 | 84.90 | - | - | 81.85 | 81.73 |
| ESIM [22] | 82.58 | 84.49 | - | - | 81.93 | 81.87 |
| SimCSE [23] | 78.90 | 76.85 | 71.20 | 72.35 | 78.48 | 77.55 |
| ConSERT [24] | 76.40 | 72.70 | 77.50 | 74.20 | 74.50 | 70.15 |
| CLLM-GEN [12] | 87.00 | 86.90 | - | - | 84.50 | 83.40 |
| 1S3S-Code | 85.80 | 85.60 | 85.10 | 84.50 | 83.90 | 83.85 |
| 2S3S-Code | 86.20 | 86.15 | 85.70 | 84.00 | 84.50 | 84.20 |
| **3S-Code**(Ours) | **87.90** | **86.70** | **87.90** | **85.40** | **86.60** | **85.15** |

**Table 8.** Performance of various models on SWV test datasets. Among them, the results are average scores using different seeds.

| Models | Pre-training | Interaction | SWV | |
|---|---|---|---|---|
| | | | ACC. | F1 |
| MacBERT [14] | ✓ | ✓ | 81.45 | 81.90 |
| MacBERT-ext [14] | ✓ | ✓ | 81.50 | 81.95 |
| ERNIE [15] | ✓ | ✓ | 83.76 | 84.38 |
| LET [28] | ✓ | ✓ | 84.23 | 83.35 |
| LET-BERT [28] | ✓ | ✓ | 85.52 | 86.92 |
| Text-CNN [17] | ✗ | ✗ | 79.32 | 80.73 |
| BiLSTM [18] | ✗ | ✗ | 83.34 | 81.35 |
| Lattice-CNN [19] | ✗ | ✗ | 82.05 | 81.84 |
| ESIM [22] | ✗ | ✓ | 84.33 | 84.34 |
| CLLM-GEN [12] | ✗ | ✓ | 86.003 | 86.50 |
| 1S3S-Code | ✗ | ✓ | 85.50 | 84.80 |
| 2S3S-Code | ✗ | ✓ | 86.10 | 85.50 |
| **3S-Code**(Ours) | ✗ | ✓ | **87.15** | **87.20** |

Second, compared with deep text matching models, we can find that 3S-Code outperforms all baselines on public datasets. From Table 7, compared with Lattice CNN, the F1 score of 3S-Code has increased the most on LCQMC and BQ dataset, which increased by 4.29% and 6.85% respectively. Similarly, compared with BiLSTM model, the F1 score of 3S-Code has increased by 30.87% on AFQMC dataset.

Third, from Table 8, we can observe that: (1) Compared with other models, 3S-Code has the best performance in ACC. and F1 (87.15% and 87.20% on SWV). Our model achieved competitive performance by training on our training set, then evaluating on our testing set. (2) 3S-Code is based on interaction, and is superior to other similar models. (3) Although 3S-Code fully utilizes the pinyin, shape, and semantic features of characters, it ignores lexical information and is not suitable for matching long-form documents.

## 5.3   Ablation Study

All the components of our model play an important role in improving performance. If any component is missing, then the performance will decrease. We also conducted additional experiments on 3S-Code with ablation consideration.

As shown in Table 7, we can find that the performance of 1S3S-Code and 2S3S-Code on the three publicly available datasets LCQMC, AFQMC, and BQ is weaker than our 3S-Code. Compared with 3S-Code, the ACC. of 1S3S-Code have decreased in different degrees (2.10% ↓ on LCQMC, 2.80% ↓ on AFQMC, 2.70% ↓ on BQ, 1.65% ↓ on SWV). Similarly, the ACC. of 2S3S-Code have also decreased (1.70% ↓ on LCQMC, 2.20% ↓ on AFQMC, 2.10% ↓ on BQ, 1.05% ↓ on SWV). Among them, 2S3S-Code performs slightly better than 1S3S-Code, indicating that the role of shape-semantic codes is stronger than that of sound-semantic codes. From Table 8, we can conclude that 1S3S-Code, 2S3S-Code, and 3S-Code all belong to interactive models rather than pre-trained models. Similarly, 3S-Code performs better on the SWV dataset than others, indicating that the unique encoding method of 3S-Code performs well on SWV dataset.

## 5.4   Case Study

In daily work, many words used exist in the form of abbreviations. Abbreviations refer to summarizing and generalizing the content from the original words, while having a similar meaning to the original words without modifying their own meaning. In short, it means simplifying long words and phrases for ease of addressing and memorization. For example, “中共党员” is abbreviated as “中国共产党党员” through Chinese characters, and “北京航空航天大学” is abbreviated as “北航”.

In the Chinese dictionary, one pinyin corresponds to multiple Chinese characters, and there are also some polyphonic characters, some of which have multiple pronunciations. For example, “南” and “男” have the same pronunciation of ’nan”. In the politically sensitive lexicon, many criminals replace “中南海”

with "中男海" when commenting on major online platforms to evade detection of sensitive information by the system.

Similar words refer to words with similar appearances, such as "天空" and "夫空", which appear very similar to the naked eye. For example, "进士" and "近士" have the same pronunciation and the same radical. Taking original word "贩卖毒品 (drug trafficking)" as an example, its specific variants are as follows. The polysemy are "走私毒品" and "贩运毒品". Through some typical case studies, we found that 3S-Code encoder performs well on the SWV dataset.

# 6    Conclusion

Semantic Text Matching (STM) plays an essential role in near-duplicate sensitive text detection. This paper presents the first large-scale Chinese Sensitive Word Variants dataset, SWV, which can serve as a pre-training corpus and can derive abundant NLP tasks. SWV contains four types: polysemy, close-words, homophones, and abbreviations. Specially, we introduce ChatSG for data augmentation to generate similar sentences for the optimal text representation. Based on SWV, we present a sensitive word variant detection algorithm based on Sound Shape Semantic encoding (3S-Code) for Chinese STM. Experimental results show that 3S-Code can considerably boost the performance of short text matching system and achieve significantly better results than previous state-of-the-art methods on SWV, LCQMC, AFQMC, and BQ datasets.

**Acknowledgement.** This work was supported by the Research Funds for Institute of Information Engineering, Chinese Academy of Sciences (No. E3V0631104).

# References

1. Arabzadeh, Negar, et al. "Neural embedding-based specificity metrics for pre-retrieval query performance prediction.", *Information Processing and Management*, vol. 57, no. 4, 2020: 102248

2. Wang, Junmei, Pan Mei, He Tingting, Huang Xiang, Wang Xueyan, Tu Xinhui. "A pseudo-relevance feedback framework combining relevance matching and semantic matching for information retrieval.", *Information Processing and Management*, vol. 56, no. 6, 2020: 102342

3. Liu, Yang and Rong, Wenge and Xiong, Zhang. "Improved text matching by enhancing mutual information.", *Proceedings of the AAAI Conference on Artificial Intelligence*, vol. 32, no. 1, 2018

4. Wu, Jinmeng and Mu, Tingting and Thiyagalingam, Jeyarajan and Goulermas, John Y. "Building interactive sentence-aware representation based on generative language model for community question answering.", *Neurocomputing*, vol. 389, pp. 93-107, 2020

5. Tang, Aihua and Ren, Pengfei and Sun, Zhibin, et al. "Multi-feature based Question–Answerer Model Matching for predicting response time in CQA.", *Knowledge-Based Systems*, vol. 182, pp. 104794, 2019

6. Feng, Jiazhan and Tao, Chongyang and Wu, Wei and Feng, Yansong and Zhao, Dongyan and Yan, Rui. "Learning a matching model with co-teaching for multi-turn response selection in retrieval-based dialogue systems.", *arxiv preprint* arxiv:1906.04413, 2019

7. Gao, Jianfeng and Galley, Michel and Li, Lihong. "Neural approaches to conversational AI.", *The 41st International ACM SIGIR Conference on Research and Development in Information Retrieval*, pp. 1371-1374, 2018

8. Ng A., Laird D. and He L. "Data-Centric Ai Competition. DeepLearning AI.", *Available at*https://https-deeplearningai.github.io/data-centric-comp/

9. Liu, Xin and Chen, Qingcai and Deng, Chong and Zeng, Huajun and Chen, Jing and Li, Dongfang and Tang, Buzhou. "Lcqmc: A large-scale chinese question matching corpus.", *Proceedings of the 27th international conference on computational linguistics*, pp. 1952-1962, 2018

10. Xu, Liang and Zhang, Xuanwei and Dong, Qianqian. "CLUECorpus2020: A large-scale Chinese corpus for pre-training language model.", *arXiv preprint* arXiv:2003.01355, 2020

11. Chen, Jing and Chen, Qingcai and Liu, Xin and Yang, Haijun and Lu, Daohe and Tang, Buzhou. "The bq corpus: A large-scale domain-specific chinese corpus for sentence semantic equivalence identification.", *Proceedings of the 2018 conference on empirical methods in natural language processing*, pp. 4946-4951, 2018

12. Shulin Liu, Chengcheng Xu, Hao Liu, Tinghao Yu, Tao Yang. "Are LLMsEffective Backbones for Fine-tuning? An Experimental Investigation of Supervised LLMs on Chinese Short Text Matching.", *arxiv preprint* arxiv:2403.19930, 2024

13. Mengting Wan, Tara Safavi, Sujay Kumar Jauhar, Yujin Kim, Scott Counts, Jennifer Neville, Siddharth Suri, Chirag Shah, Ryen W. White, Longqi Yang, Reid Andersen, Georg Buscher, Dhruv Joshi, and Nagu Rangan. "TnT-LLM: Text Mining at Scale with Large Language Models.", *Proceedings of the 30th ACM SIGKDD Conference on Knowledge Discovery and Data Mining (KDD '24)*, pp. 5836-5847, 2024

14. Cui, Yiming and Che, Wanxiang and Liu, Ting and Qin, Bing and Yang, Ziqing. "Pre-training with whole word masking for chinese bert.", *IEEE/ACM Transactions on Audio, Speech, and Language Processing*, vol. 29, pp. 3504-3514, 2021

15. Sun, Yu and Wang, Shuohuan and Li, Yukun and Feng, Shikun and Chen, Xuyi and Zhang, Han and Tian, Xin and Zhu, Danxiang and Tian, Hao and Wu, Hua. "Ernie: Enhanced representation through knowledge integration.", *arXiv preprint* arXiv:1904.09223, 2019

16. Reimers, Nils and Gurevych, Iryna. "Sentence-bert: Sentence embeddings using siamese bert-networks.", *arXiv preprint* arXiv:1908.10084, 2019

17. He, Tong and Huang, Weilin and Qiao, Yu and Yao, Jian. "Text-attentional convolutional neural network for scene text detection.", *IEEE transactions on image processing*, vol. 25, no. 6, pp. 2529-2541, 2016

18. Mueller, Jonas and Thyagarajan, Aditya. "Siamese recurrent architectures for learning sentence similarity.", *Proceedings of the AAAI conference on artificial intelligence*, vol. 30, no. 1, 2016

19. Lai, Yuxuan and Feng, Yansong and Yu, Xiaohan and Wang, Zheng and Xu, Kun and Zhao, Dongyan. "Lattice CNNs for matching based chinese question answering.", *Proceedings of the AAAI conference on artificial intelligence*, vol. 33, no. 1, pp. 6634-6641, 2019

20. Yin, Wenpeng and Schutze, Hinrich and Xiang, Bing and Zhou, Bowen. "ABCNN: Attention-based convolutional neural network for modeling sentence pairs.", *Transactions of the Association for Computational Linguistics*, vol. 4, pp. 259-272, 2016

21. Wang, Zhiguo and Hamza, Wael and Florian, Radu. "Bilateral multi-perspective matching for natural language sentences.", *arXiv preprint* arXiv:1702.03814, 2017
22. Chen, Qian and Zhu, Xiaodan and Ling, Zhenhua and Wei, Si and Jiang, Hui and Inkpen, Diana. "Enhanced LSTM for natural language inference.", *In the Proceedings of Annual Meeting of the Association for Computational Linguistics*, 2017
23. Gao, Tianyu and Yao, Xingcheng and Chen, Danqi. "Simcse: Simple contrastive learning of sentence embeddings.", *arXiv preprint* arXiv:2104.08821, 2021
24. Yan, Yuanmeng and Li, Rumei and Wang, Sirui and Zhang, Fuzheng and Wu, Wei and Xu, Weiran. "Consert: A contrastive framework for self-supervised sentence representation transfer.", *arXiv preprint* arXiv:2105.11741, 2021
25. Chuang, Yung-Sung and Dangovski, Rumen and Luo, Hongyin and Zhang, Yang and Chang, Shiyu and Soljacic, Marin and Li, Shang-Wen and Yih, Wen-tau and Kim, Yoon and Glass, James. "DiffCSE: Difference-based Contrastive Learning for Sentence Embeddings.", *Annual Conference of the North American Chapter of the Association for Computational Linguistics (NAACL)*, 2022
26. Radford, Alec and Wu, Jeffrey and Child, Rewon and Luan, David and Amodei, Dario and Sutskever, Ilya, et al. "Language models are unsupervised multitask learners.", *OpenAI blog*, vol. 1, no. 8, pp. 9, 2019
27. Zhou, Wangchunshu and Xu, Ke. "Learning to compare for better training and evaluation of open domain natural language generation models.", *Proceedings of the AAAI Conference on Artificial Intelligence*, vol. 34, no. 5, pp. 9717-9724, 2020
28. Lyu, Boer and Chen, Lu and Zhu, Su and Yu, Kai. "Let: Linguistic knowledge enhanced graph transformer for chinese short text matching.", *Proceedings of the AAAI Conference on Artificial Intelligence*, vol. 35, no. 15, pp. 13498-13506, 2021
29. Liu, W., Zhou, P., Zhao, Z., Wang, Z., Qi, J., Deng, H., Wang, P.: K-bert: Enabling language representation with knowledge graph. Proceedings of the AAAI Conference on Artificial Intelligence **34**(03), 2901–2908 (2020)

# Explainable Recommendation Using Global Preference Paths on Knowledge Graph

Yuanming Zhang[(⊠)], Yongbiao Lou, Xiangyou Chen, Jie Dong, Haixia Long, and Fei Gao

Zhejing University of Technology, Hangzhou, China
{zym,louyongbiao,2112112253,221124120267,longhaixia,
feig}@zjut.edu.cn

**Abstract.** Knowledge graph (KG) deeply integrates users, items, attributes, and various relationships, which provides a structured contextual environment for explainable RS. However, existing KG-based models can only provide explainability according to feature similarity of users and items, and cannot provide process-based explainability. To address this problem, this paper introduces an explainable recommendation model using global preference paths on KG. We define preference paths that are the relational paths between users and potential items in KG to clearly model the purchasing behaviors of users. Then, we present a reinforcement learning and global attention network (RLGAN) framework to extract preference paths from KG. The framework leverages reinforcement learning agent to traverse complex relational paths, and combines a global attention network to extract diverse preference paths. According to these paths, recommendation items and process-based reasons can be generated. Experimental results on public datasets show that the proposed model not only can achieve much higher performance than the SOTA baseline models, but also can provide enhanced reasons with high credibility on recommendation items.

**Keywords:** Recommendation system · Knowledge graph · Preference path · Reinforcement learning · Explainability

## 1 Introduction

With the continuous evolution and rapid development of Internet technology, massive amounts of information (such as news, products, services, and videos) have emerged on Internet. This makes it difficult for users to select personally valuable information and results in severe information overload problem. To address this problem, recommendation system (RS), which makes recommendations based on historical interactions between users and items as well as auxiliary information, has been proposed to satisfy personalized requirements. This not only enhances user experiences but also brings significant commercial values [1, 2].

Traditional collaborative filtering (CF)-based RS encounters significant challenges, particularly in addressing the issues of cold start and data sparsity. To overcome these


T. Zhu et al. (Eds.): KSEM 2025, LNAI 15919, pp. 273–288, 2026.
https://doi.org/10.1007/978-981-95-3001-4_20

limitations, researchers have increasingly turned to the integration of knowledge graph (KG) into RS [2]. Fundamentally, KG is a semantic network that meticulously delineates entities and their interrelationships within the real world. The KG-based RS not only mitigates the cold start and data sparsity problems but also enhances the recommendation accuracy [3, 4]. KG-based RS can be broadly classified into three categories: embedding-based method, path-based method, and propagation-based method. Embedding-based method [5–9] involves the transformation of user and item features within the KG into low-dimensional vector spaces. Subsequently, the recommendation probabilities are computed based on these vectors. However, a notable limitation of these methods is their inability to provide explainable reasons for the recommendations. Path-based method [10–13], on the other hand, models user preferences by evaluating the similarity of paths between users and items within the KG. Despite their utility, this method often falls short of constructing complete recommendation paths. Propagation-based method [14–16] refines vectors by aggregating features from multi-hop neighbors of entities. This method predicts user preferences based on the refined vectors and offers post-hoc explainability for recommendation results through similarity.

The structured information in KG serves as natural foundation for explainable recommendation. Within this context, there invariably exist both direct and indirect paths connecting users to items, which intrinsically encapsulate specific user preferences. Consequently, the utilization of these paths not only facilitates the recommendation of items to users but also enhances process-based explainability by providing trustworthy reasons for the recommendation results. Nevertheless, the diverse and highly intricate nature of these paths presents a significant challenge for such explainable recommendation: the extraction of preference paths and the generation of diverse recommendation results. In reference [12], a knowledge-aware path recurrent network was proposed, which models the semantic information of entities and relationships as path representations and offers recommendation reasons through relational paths. However, the breadth-first strategy employed in this approach is inefficient and overlooks meaningful paths. In reference [19], a policy-guided pathway reasoning method was introduced. However, it fails to incorporate global user preference features, leading to a lack of diversity in the items.

In order to improve recommendation explainability and provide process-based reasons, this paper proposes an explainable recommendation model using global preference paths on KG. We define the preference paths that are the relational paths between users and potential items in KG to clearly model the purchasing behaviors of users. Then, we propose a reinforcement learning and a global attention network (RLGAN) framework to extract global user preference paths from complex relational paths within KG. This framework adopts reinforcement learning and a global attention mechanism, and enables an agent to traverse contextual relational paths. According to the learned preference paths, the framework predicts recommendation items for users and generates process-based reasons. The main contributions of this paper include:

(1) An explainable recommendation mechanism based on preference paths is proposed. It models the RS as a problem of extracting diverse preference paths from KG. The recommendation results and process-based reasons can be generated accordingly.
(2) A novel RLGAN framework is presented, which employs a reinforcement learning agent to traverse the contextual paths in the KG, and treats the preference path

reasoning as a Markov decision process complemented by a global attention network to extract diverse preference paths.

(3) Comprehensive evaluations conducted on public benchmark datasets demonstrate the superior performance of the proposed model. Furthermore, the explainable process-based reasons through preference paths have been empirically validated.

## 2   Related Work

**Embedding-Based Method:** This method leverages the semantic information of KG to enrich the vector representations of items or users. There are two main modules: embedding module and recommendation module. The former module learns low-dimensional vector representations of users and items in KG, while the latter module calculates user preferences for items. Zhang et al. [5] combined collaborative filtering with KG, and extracted structural data features through TransR. Wang et al. [6] proposed knowledge-aware convolutional neural networks to extract semantic and knowledge information for modeling news features, and employed an attention mechanism to predict user click-through rates. Cao et al. [7] defined implicit preference vectors to represent user interests and fused them with vectors generated by the TransH model, enabling better representations of users and items. Ai et al. [8] designed a KG-based CF system, which defines a new embedding model function and performs fuzzy reasoning on KG paths. These methods focus on enriching the vectors of users and items with auxiliary information. However, they neglect the structured information in KG and lack explainability.

**Path-Based Method:** This method utilizes KG paths for item recommendation, and generally includes two modules to extract feature from the paths: one is to calculate the similarity between items using meta-paths; and the other is to encode the paths into vectors and input them into a network for computation. The Hete-CF [10] calculates user preferences for unrated items by obtaining regularization terms for meta-path similarity among various entities. The HeteRec [11] enriches the vectors of users and items using meta-path similarity, recommending items similar to those previously interacted with by the target user. The KPRN [12] employs both entity embeddings and relation embeddings to construct path sequences. It first computes preference scores for each path and then aggregates these scores for preference evaluation. The RKGE [13] enumerates paths from users to items. It connects users and items with different semantic relations at fixed lengths, and adopts recurrent networks to calculate user preferences towards items. These models calculate user and item similarity based on meta-paths, and offer a certain level of interpretability. However, the meta-paths require manual definition and cannot provide fine-grained preference information.

**Propagation-Based Method:** This method refines entity representations by aggregating features of multi-hop neighbors in KG and makes recommendations through the inner product of user and item vectors. The KGCN [14] employs graph convolutional networks (GCNs) to aggregate neighborhood information from KG, and iteratively updates node information to obtain the final vector representations. The KGAT [15] utilizes graph attention networks (GAT) to aggregate neighbor information, and assigns different weights to each relationship to capture user preference information. The HAKG [16] adopts TransR to obtain entity embeddings and samples paths between users and items to construct item subgraphs. The AKUPM [17] leverages TransR to embed users and items, and employs a self-attention network to model the importance of items to users. The KNI [18] extracts features from neighborhood nodes of items and users through an attention mechanism, and assigns appropriate weights to each neighborhood node for recommendation. These models use propagation to refine the vectors of items and users with multi-hop neighbors in the KG. However, the propagation process lacks reasoning and explicit directionality, and fails to explicitly leverage paths for reasonable explanations.

**Reinforcement Learning-Based Method:**  This method traverses relational paths on KG to discover items that align with user preferences. Xian et al. [19] proposed a policy-guided path reasoning method to efficiently capture relational paths in KG. However, the designed sparse reward signals result in lower recommendation accuracy. Park et al. [20] introduced an emotion-enhanced KG, which refines the relationships of KG using different emotions to encourage the agent to explore relationships with positive sentiments and their associated recommendation items. Zhao et al. [21] proposed an adversarial actor-critic model, which leverages manually derived flawed demonstration paths as guidance to identify explainable reasoning paths. In comparison to existing reinforcement learning methods, this paper delves into the exploration of explainable recommendation issues based on preference paths. It integrates reinforcement learning with global attention networks to extract users' multi-level preference paths from the complex paths within KG. By combining recommendation results with their underlying reasons, this approach is capable of providing process-based reasons for recommendations. Compared to these baselines, the proposed model can extract temporal features of states and global user preference features, and has great superior performance.

## 3   Problem Description

Knowledge graph (KG) is a structured semantic network composed of real-world entities and relationships, and capable of describing the complex associations between users and items. The relational paths within KG provide a natural foundation for explainable recommendations. The key challenge for explainable RSs lies in how to extract potential user preference paths from the intricate relational paths in KG and generates both predicted items and their corresponding reasons.

*Definition 1*   **(Knowledge Graph).**  KG can be typically represented as a collection of triples, $G = \{(h, r, t)|h, t \in E, r \in R\}$ where $h$ is the head entity, $t$ is the tail entity, $r$ is the relationship, $E$ is the set of entities, and $R$ is the set of relationships.

The entities primarily include user entities and item entities. Attributes encompass user attributes (e.g., gender, age, and occupation) and item attributes (e.g., category, origin, color, purpose, and price). Relationships include interaction relationships between users and items (e.g., purchase, click, rating, and review). The task of KG-based explainable model is to extract user preference paths from the complex relational paths within KG. We define the preference path as follows.

***Definition 2*** **(Preference Path).** Preference path refers to an ordered tuple in KG that starts with the user entity node, ends with an item entity node, and includes multiple relationships and intermediate entities. It can be formally represented as $Path = [u, r_1, e_1, r_2, \ldots, e_k, r_k, i]$, where $u$ is the user entity, $i$ is the recommended item, $r_i(1 \leq i \leq k)$ is the relationship, $e_i(1 \leq i \leq k + 1)$ is the intermediate entity, and $k$ is the number of hops.

Figure 1 illustrates the preference path-based recommendation process. In the KG, *user1* has three preference paths: [*user1, mention, wash, belong_to, toothpaste*], [*user1, mention, bars, described_by, dove_soap*], [*user1, mention, sensitive, descirbed_by, toothpaste*]. We can find that the preference paths include *wash, sensitive,* and *bars,* which are related to personal care products. This indicates that *user1* prefers personal care products. Furthermore, the paths with the keywords *wash* and *sensitive* both point to the same item, *toothpaste.* Therefore, based on the preference paths, the item *toothpaste* will be recommended to *user1.*

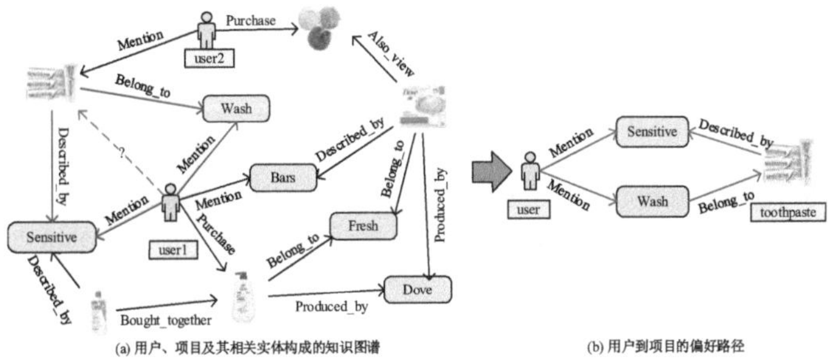


**Fig. 1.** Preference path-based recommendation process.

**Problem formalization:** Learn Top-$N$ preference paths for the user through path reasoning on a given KG, and then predict potential items for that user and provide the corresponding reasons based on these paths.

## 4   RLGAN Framework

To learn preference paths from complex relational paths of KG, predict purchasing items and generate the corresponding reasons, this paper presents a RLGAN framework, as shown in Fig. 2, which leverages RL to traverse the contextual environment of KG according to a predefined reasoning strategy, and then learns preference paths of users. This framework consists of three modules: (1) KG-based environment: The environment provides the RL agent with a traversal environment based on the relational paths of the KG. (2) Global attention-based policy network: The network trains the RL agent to traverse the KG, and adopts a global attention network to capture preference features of users. (3) Path reasoning. It extracts diverse preference paths based on the policy network and predicts purchasing items according to these preference paths.

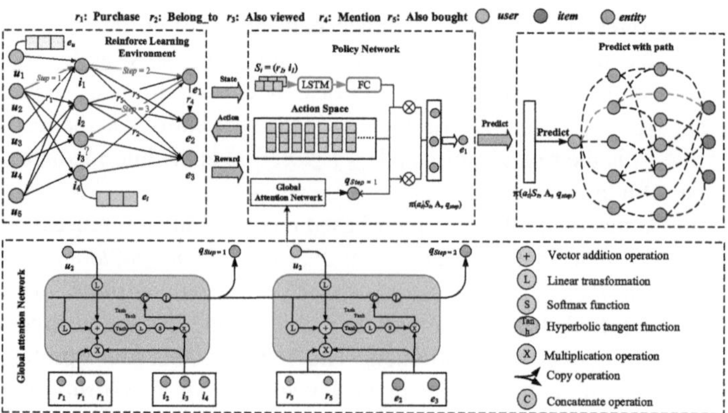

**Fig. 2.** RLGAN framework.

## 4.1 KG-based Environment

To enhance the computation efficiency, we first embed the semantic information of entities and relationships in KG into a low-dimensional vector space. Here, we adopt TransE model, which treats relationships as translation operations from head entities to tail entities, to represent both entities and relationships in the same vector space. In the vector space, the reinforcement learning environment consists of five main components: agent, state, action, reward, and state transition.

***Definition 3*** **(Agent).** *RL agent* is a learner and decision-maker for preference paths. It selects an appropriate direction and action for the path based on the context of KG under the guidance of the policy network. It will receive feedbacks based on the rewards of the actions, and ultimately obtain the preference paths.

***Definition 4*** **(State).** *State* represents the position of the agent at a specific location in the KG. The agent will select an action based on the current state. The state $S_t$ of the agent at step $t$ is defined as:

$$S_t = \left(r_t, e_t, V_{e_t}\right), \tag{1}$$

where $r_t$ is the relationship between the entities at step $t$ and step $t - 1$; $e_t$ is the entity at step $t$; and $V_{e_t}$ is the set of tail entities of $e_t$. The initial state $S_0$ is defined as:

$$S_0 = (\varnothing, u, V_u), \tag{2}$$

where $\varnothing$ is empty; $u$ is the user entity; and $V_u$ is the set of tail entities of $u$.

***Definition 5*** **(Action).** Action is the path selection made by agent in action space at a certain state. At state $S_t$, the action space consists of all outgoing edges of the current entity, which can be formally defined as:

$$A(S_t) = \left\{\left(r', e'\right) \middle| (e_t, r', e') \in G\right\}, \tag{3}$$

where $e'$ is the tail entity of the head entity $e_t$, and $r'$ is the relation between $e_t$ and $e'$.

***Definition 6***   (**Reward**). Reward, a numerical signal, indicates the utility on the current walking path. To maximize cumulative rewards, the reward at the final state $(t = T)$ is defined as:

$$R_T = \begin{cases} \max\left(0, \frac{\langle u+r_i, e_T \rangle}{max_{i \in I} \langle u+r_i, i \rangle}\right), & if \ e_T \in I \\ 0, & otherwise, \end{cases} \tag{4}$$

where $r_i$ represents the purchase-type relation; $e_T$ represents the entity at the final state; $u$ represents the user entity; $i$ represents the item entity; $I$ represents the set of item entities, and $max_{i \in I} \langle u + r_i, i \rangle$ represents the maximum value of the dot product between user vector and item vector.

***Definition 7***   (**State Transition**). State transition refers to the process in which an agent moves from one state to another after executing an action. Given the current state $S_t$ and an action $a_t$, the state transition can be formally defined as:

$$\mathbb{P}\left[S_{t+1} = \left(r_{t+1}, e_{t+1}, V_{e_{t+1}}\right) \middle| \begin{matrix} S_t = \left(r_t, e_t, V_{e_t}\right), \\ a_t = (r_{t+1}, e_{t+1}) \end{matrix} \right] = 1, \tag{5}$$

where $(r_{t+1}, e_{t+1})$ represents the selected action; $V_{e_{t+1}}$ represents the updated tail entity set.

## 4.2   Global Attention-Based Policy Network

Guided by the policy network, the agent walks along the path in the KG, and learns the preference path features. The policy network comprises an action network and a value network. The former network takes the state and action space as inputs and outputs a probability distribution over actions, while the latter network takes the state as input and outputs a real number as the score of the state.

**Action Network:**   It adopts the Long Short-Term Memory (LSTM) and a global attention mechanism. The LSTM is responsible for extracting temporal features of the state. The state and the output of the LSTM at step $t - 1$ are used as the input for the LSTM at step $t$, thereby extracting the temporal features under that state. The calculation formula is as follows:

$$h_t = W_{LSTM} * LSTM\left(r_t, e_t, h_{t-1}\right), \tag{6}$$

where $h_{t-1}$ represents the output of the LSTM at step $t - 1$, which is used as a parameter for the LSTM at step $t$, and $W_{LSTM}$ represents the trainable parameters in the fully-connected layers. The agent selects an action based on the probability distribution provided by the action network. If the probability variance of the action space is extremely small, the actions that have not been selected should also be taken into consideration by the policy function. This model employs a global attention network to further capture overlooked yet valuable preference information for users.

***Definition 8***   (**Auxiliary Action**). An auxiliary action refers to an action in the action space at step $t$ that is not selected by the agent. Formally, it is defined as follows:

$$\rho_t = \{(r, e) | (r, e) \in A(S_t)\}. \tag{7}$$

The global attention vector at step $t$ is computed as follows:

$$q_t = W_t^c[k_t \rho_{t-1}; q_{t-1}],  \tag{8}$$

where $W_t^c$ represents the trainable parameters in the fully-connected layer; $q_{t-1}$ represents the global attention vector in the previous step $t-1$; $\rho_{t-1}$ represents the set of auxiliary actions at step $t-1$; The operator $[;\,]$ indicates concatenation operation; and the attention value $k_t$ is calculated as follows:

$$k_t = \sigma\left(W_t^k * \tanh\left(\begin{array}{c} W_t^u u + W_t^q q_{t-1} + \\ W_t^a a_{t-1} + W_t^r R_a \end{array}\right)\right),  \tag{9}$$

where $W_t^k$, $W_t^u$, $W_t^q$, $W_t^a$, $W_t^r$ are trainable parameters; $u$ is the user vector; $a_{t-1}$ denotes the unselected action vector at step $t-1$; $R_a$ is the relation matrix involved in the actions; $tanh$ represents the hyperbolic tangent function; and $\sigma$ denotes the Softmax function.

The temporal feature vector and the global attention vector are respectively multiplied with the vectors in the action space to derive the probability of each action. The calculation formula is as follows:

$$p(a_t|S_t, A(S_t)) = \sigma(h_t \times A(S_t) + \lambda(q_t \times A(S_t))),  \tag{10}$$

where $h_t$ is the temporal feature vector of the LSTM at step $t$; $q_t$ is the global attention vector; $\sigma$ is the Softmax function; and $\lambda$ is a learnable weight parameter for the user global attention network.

**Value Network:** It is a fully connected network (FCN) designed to comprehensively evaluate and score the state in which the agent is situated. The calculation formula is as follows:

$$\hat{v}(s) = W^v h_t,  \tag{11}$$

where $W^v$ represents the trainable parameters.

Based on the action probabilities from the action network and the state scores from the value network, the agent will select appropriate actions to traverse the KG, and learn preference paths.

### 4.3  Path Reasoning

The task of path reasoning involves deducing the preference paths on a trained policy network to generate recommendation items and the reasons. If only the preference path that maximizes cumulative rewards is selected, it may lead to a certain degree of overfitting, resulting in a lack of diversity. To address this issue, we employ a beam search algorithm [22] to enhance the diversity of preference paths.

The beam search algorithm has the parameters: the maximum hop $T$, predefined sampling sizes $(K_1, K_2 \ldots K_T)$, a preference path set $P_T$, an action probability set $Q_T$, and path reward set $R_T$. At step $t$, the algorithm inputs the state $S_t$ and action space $A(S_t)$ into the policy network, and outputs the probability $p(\cdot|S_t, A(S_t))$ of each action in the output action space. It samples $K_t$ actions, computes their rewards, and stores the actions, probabilities, and rewards into $P_t$, $Q_t$, and $R_t$. As the maximum hop $T$ is reached or a target node is found, the algorithm outputs the candidate item set $I$, the preference path set $P_T$, the probability set $Q_T$, and the reward set $R_T$ for user $u$.

There exist multiple paths between users and items. For each user-item pair $(u, i)$, the recommendation items are predicted based on the preference paths with the highest probability. Each item retains an optimal path, and the items are then ranked according to the cumulative rewards of the paths, thereby completing the Top-$N$ recommendation.

### 4.4  Model Training

The policy network is optimized through model training to maximize the cumulative rewards in the KG-based environment, and the loss function is defined as:

$$\mathcal{L}\text{oss} = \mathbb{E}_\pi \left[ log\pi\left(\cdot|s, A\right)\left(R_T - \hat{v}(s)\right) \right], \tag{12}$$

where $log\pi(\cdot|s, A)$ is the logarithmic of action probability selected by the agent under state $s$ and action space $A$; $R_T$ and $\hat{v}(s)$ represent the cumulative values of reward points and state points along the preferred path, respectively. The training process iteratively minimizes the loss to ensure convergence of the policy network.

## 5  Experiments

This section evaluates our proposed RLGAN model on public datasets. It introduces the datasets, evaluation metrics, and experimental settings, and compares the results with existing baseline models. Further ablation experiments show the impact of different modules on performance.

### 5.1  Experimental Settings

**Datasets:**  Our experiments are conducted on three Amazon datasets: Beauty dataset, Clothing dataset, and Cellphone dataset [23]. Each dataset comprises 5 types of entities and 7 types of relations. User purchasing records are used as training data, with 70% randomly selected as the training set and the remaining 30% as the test set. The RLGAN will predict items for users in the test set, along with reasons for each item. Table 1 shows the statistical details of the datasets, including their entity counts, relation counts, and relation types.

**Metrics:**  We adopt four metrics to evaluate the recommendation performance: Normalized Discounted Cumulative Gain (NDCG), Recall, Hit Ratio, and Precision. These metrics are computed based on the Top-$K$ ($K = 10$) value for each user in the test set.

(1) NDCG: It is a metric for evaluating the quality of recommendation items. A higher value indicates a closer match between the items and user preferences. The formula is:

$$NDCG@10 = \frac{DCG@10}{IDCG@10}, \tag{13}$$

**Table 1.** Statistical information of datasets.

| Entity Type | CD | Clothing | Cell Phones | Beauty | describe |
|---|---|---|---|---|---|
| User | 75258 | 39387 | 27289 | 22363 | User number |
| Item | 64443 | 23033 | 10429 | 12101 | Item number |
| Feature | 202959 | 21366 | 22493 | 22564 | Feature number |
| Brand | 1414 | 1182 | 955 | 2077 | Manufacturer |
| Category | 770 | 1193 | 206 | 248 | Product category |
| Relationship | The number of relationships for each head entity | | | | |
| Purchase | 14.58±39.13 | 7.08±3.59 | 6.97±4.55 | 8.88±8.16 | $User \xrightarrow{Purchase} Item$ |
| Mention | 2545.92±10942.31 | 440.20±452.38 | 652.08±1335.76 | 806.89±1344.08 | $User \xrightarrow{Mention} Feature$ |
| Described_by | 2973.19±5490.93 | 752.75±909.42 | 1743.16±3482.76 | 1491.16±2535.93 | $Item \xrightarrow{Described\_by} Feature$ |
| Belong_to | 7.25±3.13 | 6.72±2.15 | 3.49±1.08 | 4.11±0.70 | $Item \xrightarrow{Belong\_to} Category$ |
| Produced_by | 0.21±0.41 | 0.17±0.38 | 0.52±0.50 | 0.83±0.38 | $Item \xrightarrow{Produced\_by} Brand$ |
| Also_bought | 57.28±39.22 | 61.35±32.99 | 56.53±35.82 | 73.65±30.69 | $Item \xrightarrow{Also\_bought} Item$ |
| Also_viewed | 0.27±1.86 | 6.29±6.17 | 1.24±4.29 | 12.84±8.97 | $Item \xrightarrow{Also\_viewed} Item$ |
| Bought_together | 0.68±0.80 | 0.69±0.90 | 0.81±0.77 | 0.75±0.72 | $Item \xrightarrow{Bought\_together} Item$ |

where DCG (Discounted Cumulative Gain) is the unnormalized raw value, and IDCG (Ideal Discounted Cumulative Gain) represents the gain under the optimal ranking scenario. By comparing the model's output with the ideal results, the normalized gain is derived. Specifically, the DCG is calculated as:

$$DCG@10 = \sum_{i=1}^{10} \frac{rel(i)}{\log(i+1)}, \tag{14}$$

where $rel(i)$ is the gain function for the $i$-th item. This function does not consider the influence of position and gain. If the $i$-th item exists in the ground truth list, $rel(i)$ is set to 1. $\log(i+1)$ represents the positional discount factor for the $i$-th item in the list.

(2) Recall: It measures the number of successfully recommendation items among all relevant items. A higher value indicates that the model captures more relevant items. The formula is:

$$Recall = \frac{hit\_num}{real\_num}, \tag{15}$$

where $hit\_num$ represents the number of items successfully recommended by the model, and $real\_num$ denotes the total number of items in the dataset.

(3) Hit Ratio: It measures whether the model successfully includes items preferred by the user in the recommendation list. The formula is:

$$Hit\,Ratio = \begin{cases} 1, & hit\_num > 0; \\ 0, & hit\_num < 0, \end{cases} \tag{16}$$

(4) Precision: It is a metric for evaluating the accuracy and quality of a recommendation model, measuring the proportion of relevant items among all recommendation items. Precision is typically used in conjunction with Recall to comprehensively assess model performance. The formula is:

$$Precision = \frac{hit\_num}{predict\_num}, \tag{17}$$

where *predict_num* is the total number of items recommended by the model.

**Baselines:** We compare the proposed RLGAN model with 8 baseline methods: BPR-HFT [24], VBPR [25], TransRec [26], DeepCoNN [27], CKE [5], KGAT [15], PGPR [19], and CogER [28]. In these models, BPR-HFT and VBPR are CF-based models; TransRec and DeepCoNN are embedding-based models; CKE and KGAT are propagation-based models; PGPR and CogER are RL-based models.

**Settings:** The proposed RLGAN has been implemented on the PyTorch framework and the parameters are optimized using the Adam algorithm. The operating system is Ubuntu Server 18.04.1 LTS 64-bit, equipped with an Intel Xeon Gold 6133 @2.5 GHz CPU and NVIDIA Tesla V100 GPU. The hyperparameters are set as follows: The path length is 3, the training batch size is 32, and the learning rate is 0.0001. The number of iterations is 50, and the auxiliary action set size is 16. The initial impact factor is 0.5, with an embedding dimension of 100. The action space has a size of 251. For the LSTM, the input dimension is 100, the hidden layer size is 100, and there are 2 hidden layers. Additionally, the path reasoning layer has parameters $K_1$, $K_2$, $K_3$ set to $(25, 5, 1)$.

## 5.2 Experimental Results

**Table 2.** Experimental results.

| Dataset | Metrics | BPR-HFT | VBPR | TransRec | DeepCoNN | CKE | KGAT | PGPR | CogER | **Ours** |
|---|---|---|---|---|---|---|---|---|---|---|
| Beauty | NDCG | 2.934 | 1.901 | 3.218 | 3.359 | 3.717 | 3.418 | 5.449 | <u>6.254</u> | **6.453** |
| | Recall | 4.459 | 2.786 | 4.853 | 5.429 | 5.938 | 4.811 | 8.324 | <u>9.671</u> | **9.817** |
| | Hit Ratio | 8.268 | 5.961 | 0.867 | 9.807 | 11.043 | 15.048 | 14.401 | <u>16.309</u> | **16.644** |
| | Precision | 1.132 | 0.902 | 1.285 | 1.200 | 1.371 | - | 1.707 | <u>2.062</u> | **2.282** |
| Clothing | NDCG | 1.067 | 0.560 | 1.245 | 1.310 | 1.502 | 1.225 | 2.858 | <u>3.201</u> | **3.129** |
| | Recall | 1.819 | 0.968 | 2.078 | 2.332 | 2.509 | 1.784 | 4.834 | <u>5.268</u> | **5.332** |
| | Hit Ratio | 2.872 | 1.557 | 3.116 | 3.286 | 4.275 | 4.840 | 7.020 | <u>7.693</u> | **7.753** |
| | Precision | 0.297 | 0.166 | 0.312 | 0.229 | 0.388 | - | 0.728 | <u>0.802</u> | **0.807** |
| Cellphone | NDCG | 3.151 | 1.797 | 3.361 | 3.636 | 3.995 | 3.660 | 5.042 | <u>5.723</u> | **5.983** |
| | Recall | 5.307 | 3.489 | 6.279 | 6.353 | 7.005 | 5.332 | 8.416 | <u>9.613</u> | **9.818** |
| | Hit Ratio | 8.125 | 5.002 | 8.725 | 9.913 | 10.809 | <u>14.111</u> | 11.904 | 13.587 | **13.600** |
| | Precision | 0.860 | 0.507 | 0.962 | 0.999 | 1.070 | - | 1.275 | <u>1.478</u> | **1.399** |

Table 2 compares the performance of the proposed LRGAN with the baseline models on four public datasets. It can be seen that RLGAN outperforms almost all baselines on the four metrics. On the Beauty and Cellphone datasets, the NDCG is improved by 3.18% and 4.50%, respectively, compared to the best baseline (underlined data). The Recall is increased by 1.51% and 2.13%, respectively. The Hit Ratio is improved by 2.05% and 0.9% on Beauty and Cellphone, while Precision is shown a 10.6% improvement over the best baseline, with a slight decrease on the Clothing dataset. These results indicate that the RLGAN achieves superior performance, and can accurately recommend personalized items to users. Therefore, the RL agent guided by the policy network can effectively extract preference paths from KG and predict items based on these paths.

## 5.3  Ablation Study

**Table 3.** Impact of policy network and global attention mechanism on performance.

| Dataset | Beauty | | | | Clothing | | | |
|---|---|---|---|---|---|---|---|---|
| Module | NDCG | Recall | Hit Ratio | Precision | NDCG | Recall | Hit Ratio | Precision |
| remove policy network | 5.304 | 8.891 | 14.011 | 1.681 | 3.015 | 5.018 | 7.407 | 0.769 |
| remove global attention mechanism | 5.784 | 9.098 | 14.487 | 1.712 | 3.014 | 5.026 | 7.009 | 0.754 |
| Remove two modules | 5.179 | 7.643 | 13.517 | 1.589 | 2.846 | 4.707 | 6.906 | 0.714 |
| Ours | **6.453** | **9.817** | **16.644** | **2.282** | **3.129** | **5.332** | **7.753** | **0.807** |

First, we investigate the impact of the policy network and the global attention mechanism on performance. Table 3 presents the experimental results on the Beauty and Clothing datasets. (1) When the policy network is moved, the agent fails to learn user preference information and relies solely on current state and interest features for path exploration. The four indicators are reduced by an average of 8.94%, 5.52%, 8.15%, and 8.44% on the two datasets. (2) When the global attention mechanism is removed, the agent cannot learn valuable preference information. The four indicators are reduced by an average of 4.23%, 3.24%, 9.29%, and 8.47%. (3) When both modules are removed, the agent can only depend on fully connected layers to capture state features, and performance is close to traditional RL models. The four indicators are reduced by an average of 13.4%, 17.58%, 14.00%, and 15.74%. Therefore, this ablation study validates the effectiveness of the global attention-based policy network in the RLGAN model.

Then, we examine the impact of sampling size on performance. The maximum sampling path length is set to 3, with sampling sizes $K1$, $K2$, and $K3$. The total number of sampling paths ($K1 \times K2 \times K3$) is set to 120. The beam search algorithm samples $K_i$ actions from the action space at step $i$. We compare five optimal combinations of $K1$, $K2$, and $K3$. Table 4 gives the experimental results. It can be seen that $K1$ and $K2$ play more critical roles in the preference path. For example, in the cases of (12, 10, 1), (25, 5, 1), our model performs much better than in the rest of cases. This is because $K1$ and $K2$ determine the range of nodes the agent can reach, thereby facilitating the reasoning of better preference paths.

**Table 4.** Impact of sampling size on performance.

| Dataset | Beauty | | | | Clothing | | | |
|---|---|---|---|---|---|---|---|---|
| Sizes | NDCG | Recall | Hit Ratio | Precision | NDCG | Recall | Hit Ratio | Precision |
| (10,12,1) | 6.146 | 9.396 | 16.013 | 1.992 | 3.140 | 5.344 | 7.778 | 0.811 |
| (12,10,1) | **6.601** | **10.086** | **16.974** | **2.308** | **3.154** | **5.367** | **7.853** | **0.821** |
| (15,8,1) | 6.165 | 9.441 | 15.876 | 1.975 | 3.141 | 5.344 | 7.741 | 0.808 |
| (20,6,1) | 6.132 | 9.344 | 15.742 | 1.972 | 3.082 | 5.276 | 7.623 | 0.793 |
| (25,5,1) | 6.453 | 9.817 | 16.644 | 2.282 | 3.129 | 5.332 | 7.753 | 0.807 |

## 5.4 Case Study

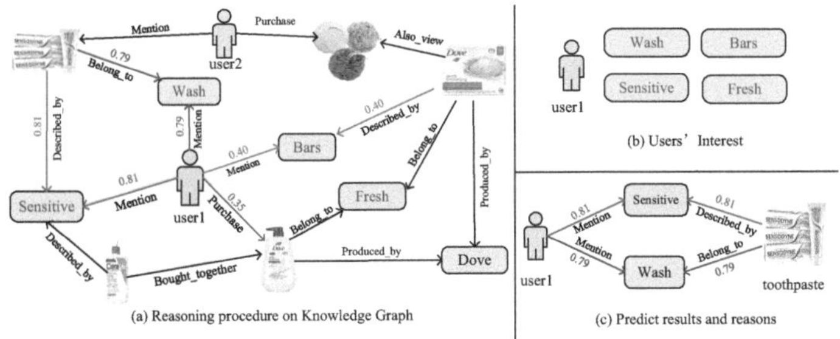


**Fig. 3.** Process-based explainable recommendation case.

This section illustrates the methodology for generating recommendation reasons based on preference paths through a case study extracted from the Beauty dataset. Figure 3 shows the reasoning process by which the agent identifies recommendation items and their reasons. In Fig. 3(a), paths of varying colors represent the distinct preference paths discovered by the RL agent. The reward scores assigned to each preference path are given, which signifies the likelihood of the pathway being recommended. For example, *user1* has four preference paths, and they are: Preference_Path_1: [*user1, mention, sensitive, described*_by, *toothpaste*], whose reward score is 0.81. Preference_Path_2: [*user1, mention, wash, belong_to, toothpaste*], whose reward score is 0.79.

Preference_Path_3: [*user1, mention, bars, described_by, dove_soap*], whose reward score is 0.4. Preference_Path_4: [*user1, purchase, shampoo*], whose reward score is 0.35. According to the preference paths and their reward score, Fig. 3 (b) gives *user1*'s preferences: *Wash, Bars, Sensitive*, and *Fresh*. Finally, the *toothpaste* is recommended to *user1*. Figure 3 (c) gives the recommendation results and the process-based reasons.

## 6  Conclusions

To address the problem of insufficient explainability in the existing KG-based recommendation system, this paper proposed an explainable recommendation model based on preference paths. By modeling the preference features of users through the relational path features between users and potential items, the recommendation explainability was enhanced. A reinforcement learning with global attention mechanism (RLGAN) framework for recommendation was proposed. This framework includes three modules: KG-based environment, global attention-based policy network, and path reasoning. The KG-based environment takes the relational paths as the context and provides a learning and walking environment for the RL agent. The policy network uses agent to perform relational path walks, capturing global preference features through a global attention mechanism. The path reasoning extracts diverse preference paths and predicts recommendation items and generates recommendation reasons accordingly. The proposed RLGAN was evaluated on public datasets, and experimental results showed that the model not only has better recommendation performance compared to the existing baseline models, but also can generate process-based recommendation reasons according to the preference paths, which enhances the explainability of the recommendation results greatly.

**Acknowledgments.** The authors gratefully acknowledge the support by the National Natural Science Foundation of China under Grant 62476248, and the Pioneer and Leading Goose Research and Development Program of Zhejiang Province China under Grant 2023C01022.

## References

1. Qin, C., Zhu, H., Zhuang, F., et al.: Summary of the research on recommendation system based on knowledge graph. China Sci. Inf. Sci. **50**(07), 937–956 (2020)
2. Ji, S., Pan, S., Cambria, E., et al.: A survey on knowledge graphs: representation, acquisition, and applications. IEEE Trans. Neural Netw. Learn. Syst., 1–21 (2021)
3. Gao, J., Peng, P., Lu, F., et al.: Towards travel recommendation interpretability: disentangling tourist decision-making process via knowledge graph. Inf. Process. Manag. **60**(4), 103369 (2023)
4. Ding, Q., Tian, X., Sun, G.: Hot-spot news recommendation model based on attention enhancement. J. Electron. Sci. **51**(01), 93–104 (2023)
5. Zhang, F., Yuan, N.J., Lian, D., et al.: Collaborative knowledge base embedding for recommender systems. In: Proceedings of the 22nd ACM SIGKDD International Conference on Knowledge Discovery and Data Mining, pp. 353–362 (2016)

6. Wang, H., Zhang, F., Xie, X., et al.: DKN: deep knowledge-aware network for news recommendation. In: Proceedings of the 2018 World Wide Web Conference, pp. 1835–1844 (2018)
7. Cao, Y., Wang, X., He, X., et al.: Unifying knowledge graph learning and recommendation: towards a better understanding of user preferences. In: The World Wide Web Conference, pp. 151–161 (2019)
8. Ai, Q., Azizi, V., Chen, X., et al.: Learning heterogeneous knowledge base embeddings for explainable recommendation. Algorithms **11**(137), 1–17 (2018)
9. Du, J., Zou, S., Li, H., et al.: Expert recommendation method for new problems in knowledge community based on question-and-answer semantic matching. J. Electron. Sci. **51**(07), 1875–1888 (2023)
10. Luo, C., Pang, W., Wang, Z., et al.: Hete-CF: social-based collaborative filtering recommendation using heterogeneous relations. In: IEEE International Conference on Data Mining, pp. 917–922 (2014)
11. Yu, X., Ren, X., Sun, Y., et al.: Recommendation in heterogeneous information networks with implicit user feedback. In: Proceedings of the 7th ACM Conference on Recommender Systems, pp. 347–350 (2013)
12. Wang, X., Wang, D., Xu, C., et al.: Explainable reasoning over knowledge graphs for recommendation. In: Proceedings of the AAAI Conference on Artificial Intelligence, vol. 33, nol. 1, pp. 5329–5336 (2019)
13. Sun, Z., Yang, J., Zhang, J., et al.: Recurrent knowledge graph embedding for effective recommendation. In: Proceedings of the 12th ACM Conference on Recommender Systems, pp. 297–305 (2018)
14. Wang, H., Zhao, M., Xie, X., et al.: Knowledge graph convolutional networks for recommender systems. In: The World Wide Web Conference, pp. 3307–3313 (2019)
15. Wang, X., He, X., Cao, Y., et al.: KGAT: knowledge graph attention network for recommendation. In: Proceedings of the 25th ACM SIGKDD International Conference on Knowledge Discovery & Data Mining, pp. 950–958 (2019)
16. Sha, X., Sun, Z., Zhang, J.: Hierarchical attentive knowledge graph embedding for personalized recommendation. Electron. Commer. Res. Appl. **48**, 101071 (2021)
17. Tang, X., Wang, T., Yang, H., et al.: AKUPM: attention-enhanced knowledge-aware user preference model for recommendation. In: Proceedings of the 25th ACM SIGKDD International Conference on Knowledge Discovery & Data Mining, pp. 1891–1899 (2019)
18. Qu, Y., Bai, T., Zhang, W., et al.: An end-to-end neighborhood-based interaction model for knowledge-enhanced recommendation. In: Proceedings of the 1st International Workshop on Deep Learning Practice for High-Dimensional Sparse Data, pp. 1–9 (2019)
19. Xian, Y., Fu, Z., Muthukrishnan, S., et al.: Reinforcement knowledge graph reasoning for explainable recommendation. In: Proceedings of the 42nd International ACM SIGIR Conference on Research and Development in Information Retrieval, pp. 285–294 (2019)
20. Park, S.J., Chae, D.K., Bae, H.K., et al.: Reinforcement learning over sentiment-augmented knowledge graphs towards accurate and explainable recommendation. In: Proceedings of the Fifteenth ACM International Conference on Web Search and Data Mining, pp. 784–793 (2022)
21. Zhao, K., Wang, X., Zhang, Y., et al.: Leveraging demonstrations for reinforcement recommendation reasoning over knowledge graphs. In: Proceedings of the 43rd International ACM SIGIR Conference on Research and Development in Information Retrieval, pp. 239–248 (2020)
22. Freitag, M., Al-Onaizan, Y.: Beam search strategies for neural machine translation. In: Proceedings of the First Workshop on Neural Machine Translation, pp. 56–60 (2017)

23. He, R., Mcauley, J..: Ups and downs: modeling the visual evolution of fashion trends with one-class collaborative filtering. In: Proceedings of the 25th International Conference on World Wide Web, pp. 507–517 (2016)
24. McAuley, J., Leskovec, J.: Hidden factors and hidden topics: understanding rating dimensions with review text. In: Proceedings of the 7th ACM Conference on Recommender Systems, pp. 165–172 (2013)
25. He, R., Mcauley, J.: VBPR: visual Bayesian personalized ranking from implicit feedback. In: Proceedings of the AAAI Conference on Artificial Intelligence, vol. 30, no. 1 (2016)
26. He, R., Kang, W.C., Mcauley, J.: Translation-based recommendation. In: Proceedings of the 11th ACM Conference on Recommender Systems, pp. 161–169 (2017)
27. Zhang, L., Noroozi, V., Yu, P.S.: Joint deep modeling of users and items using reviews for recommendation. In: Proceedings of the 10th ACM International Conference on Web Search and Data Mining, pp. 425–434 (2017)
28. Bing, Q., Zhu, Q., Dou, Z.: Cognition-aware knowledge graph reasoning for explainable recommendation. In: Proceedings of the 16th ACM International Conference on Web Search and Data Mining, pp. 402–410 (2023)

# Hierarchical Data Protection Based on Homomorphic Encryption Algorithm

Jia Zhao[1], Yanchun Wang[1(✉)], Wenhao Leng[1], Yaqin Chu[1],
Zhouhan Chen[1], Yuqing Sang[1], Feng Yi[2], and Wenjia Niu[1(✉)]

[1] School of Cyberspace Science and Technology, Beijing Jiaotong University,
Beijing 100044, China
`23125362@bjtu.edu.cn`
[2] School of Computer Science, Zhongshan Institute, University of Electronic Science
and Technology of China Zhongshan, Chengdu, China

**Abstract.** To address the lack of data classification functionality in current homomorphic encryption schemes, this paper proposes an improved RNS-CKKS hierarchical homomorphic encryption scheme. The proposed scheme modifies the modulus generation conditions of the original RNS-CKKS scheme by expanding the selection range of individual prime numbers and introducing computational-level constraints during decryption to restrict the product range of consecutive small primes in the modulus chain. The modified RNS-CKKS scheme significantly increases the number of modulus levels available and ensures accurate scaling factors at specific computational levels. The scheme employs a residue number system (RNS) to enhance computational efficiency and security, ensuring that data can only be encrypted to higher computational levels when a more complete modulus chain is known. The hierarchical RNS-CKKS scheme is implemented based on the Lattigo homomorphic encryption library. The experimental results demonstrate that the proposed scheme maintains stable scaling factors at specific computational levels. Additionally, the accuracy of the hierarchical scheme was confirmed through the experiments.

**Keywords:** Homomorphic Encryption · Data Security · RNS-CKKS · Hierarchical Protection · Data Encryption

## 1 Introduction

Homomorphic encryption (HE) enables secure computation over encrypted data, facilitating privacy-preserving applications in cloud computing and machine learning. Rivest et al. introduced the concept in 1978 [1], laying the foundation for HE research. Early schemes [2,3] lacked support for both addition and multiplication. Later, Boneh et al. [4] and Ishai et al. [5] proposed limited HE schemes. Gentry's 2009 breakthrough introduced fully homomorphic encryption (FHE), enabling unrestricted homomorphic operations [6].


T. Zhu et al. (Eds.): KSEM 2025, LNAI 15919, pp. 289–301, 2026.
https://doi.org/10.1007/978-981-95-3001-4_21

FHE schemes follow two main approaches: (1) extending somewhat homomorphic encryption (SHE) via bootstrapping, as seen in works by van Dijk et al. [7], Stehlé et al. [8], and Cheon et al. [9]. Besides, the scheme developed by Smart et al. [10] employs principal ideal lattices and introduces batching techniques.; (2) constructing FHE based on the Learning with Errors (LWE) and Ring Learning with Errors (RLWE) problems, leveraging modulus and key switching. Cheon et al. introduced the CKKS scheme in 2017 [11], enabling approximate arithmetic on complex numbers. In 2018, the RNS-CKKS variant improved efficiency using the Residue Number System (RNS) [12]. More recently, Mouchet et al. developed a multi-party HE scheme compatible with RLWE-based schemes and introduced Lattigo, an efficient open-source HE library in Golang [13].

Among various HE schemes, the CKKS scheme has gained significant attention due to its ability to support approximate arithmetic operations on encrypted data, making it particularly suitable for privacy-preserving machine learning and financial computations. However, existing CKKS-based schemes lack an effective mechanism for hierarchical encryption, limiting their ability to enforce differentiated security policies based on data sensitivity levels.

To address this limitation, this paper proposes an improved RNS-CKKS hierarchical homomorphic encryption scheme, which introduces a structured data classification approach within the CKKS framework. The proposed scheme modifies the modulus chain generation conditions by expanding the selection range of individual prime numbers and incorporating computational level constraints during decryption. These modifications enable more flexible modulus chain configurations while maintaining computational efficiency and security. The scheme employs the Residue Number System (RNS) to optimize performance and ensure that encryption to higher computational levels is only possible when the complete modulus chain is available.

The contributions of this paper can be summarized as follows:

- Hierarchical Encryption Mechanism – We enhance the RNS-CKKS scheme with a hierarchical encryption structure, allowing fine-grained control over data security at different computation levels.
- Improved Modulus Chain Generation – We modify the modulus selection strategy to expand the range of individual primes and introduce constraints on small prime multiplications to improve scalability.
- Experimental Validation – We implement the proposed scheme based on the Lattigo homomorphic encryption library and conduct experiments to verify the stability and accuracy of the scaling factors at each computation level of the RNS-CKKS hierarchical scheme.

## 2   Related Work

### 2.1   Homomorphic Encryption

The CKKS scheme enables homomorphic computations over complex numbers by treating encryption-induced errors as standard computational errors. This approach allows operations in complex domains, unlike other schemes confined to finite domains. The CKKS process is shown in Fig. 1.

In order to eliminate the large integer operations in the CKKS scheme, Cheon et al. proposed the CKKS scheme RNS-CKKS that supports a Residue Number System (RNS) variant representation of the ciphertext [12]. RNS avoids expensive CRT transformations involving multi-precision integer operations while utilizing the Chinese Remainder Theorem (CRT) to allow ciphertexts to remain in the form of RNS variants.

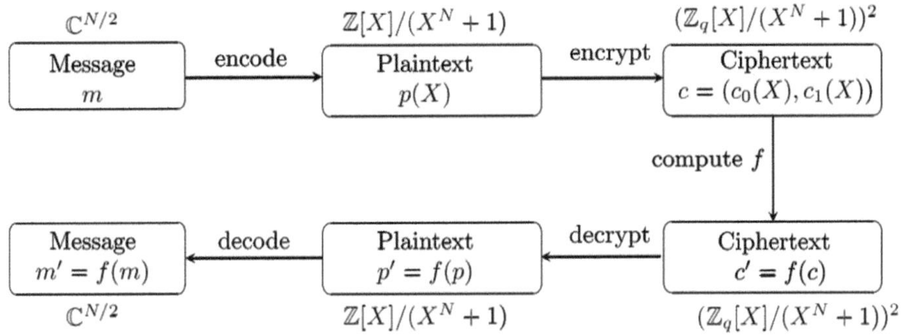

**Fig. 1.** Flowchart of the RNS-CKKS encryption scheme

The RNS-CKKS scheme supports key generation $KeyGen(\cdot)$, public key encryption $Enc(\cdot)$, private key decryption $Dec(\cdot)$, addition $Add(\cdot)$, Multiplication $Mult(\cdot)$, etc. The following is a brief description of these operations:

- **$ParamsGen(\lambda)$**: Parameter setting. Input: security parameters $\lambda$. Output: polynomial dimension $N$, maximum ciphertext modulus $q$, and a discrete Gaussian distribution $\chi$ (for semantic security of cryptosystems, the RLWE problem for the parameters $(N, q, \chi)$ should be at least $\lambda$ bits).
- **$KeyGen((N, q, \chi))$**: Key generation. Input the parameters $N$, $q$, $\chi$ and perform the following steps: (1) Randomly select a polynomial $s, a, e$ from the sparse distributions $\mathcal{R}, \mathcal{R}_q, \chi$ on $\{0, \pm 1\}^N$, and output the private key $sk \leftarrow (1, s)$ and the public key $pk \leftarrow (b, a) \in \mathcal{R}_q \times \mathcal{R}_q$, where $b \in -as + e(\mathrm{mod}q)$. (2) Let $Q = q^2$, randomly select a polynomial $s', a', e'$ from $s^2$, $\mathcal{R}_Q$, $\chi$, respectively, and output Evaluate the key $evk \leftarrow (b', a') \in \mathcal{R}_Q \times \mathcal{R}_Q$, where $b' \leftarrow -a's + e' + qs'(\mathrm{mod}Q)$.
- **$Enc_{pk}(m)$**: Encryption. First input a plaintext $m$, then randomly select a polynomial $v$ and two error polynomials $e_0, e_1$, and output the ciphertext $c \leftarrow v \cdot pk + (m + e_0, e_1)\,(mod q)$.
- **$Dec_{sk}(c)$**: Decryption. Input the ciphertext $c = (c_0, c_1)$ and output the plaintext m : $m \leftarrow c_0 + c_1 \cdot s(\mathrm{mod}q)$.
- **$Add(c, c')$**: Addition of ciphertext. Input $c$, $c'$, output: $c_{add} \leftarrow c + c'(\mathrm{mod}\,q)$.

- ***Mult*** $(c, c', ek)$: Multiplication of ciphertexts. For two ciphertexts $c = (c_0, c_1)$, and $c' = (c_0', c_1')$, $evk$, set $(d_0, d_1, d_2) = (c_0 c_0', c_0 c_1' + c_1 c_0', c_1 c_1')$ $(\mathrm{mod} q)$, output: $c_{mult} \leftarrow (d_0, d_1) + \left\lfloor \frac{1}{q} \cdot d_2 \cdot evk \right\rceil (\mathrm{mod} q)$.

- ***RS*** $(c, r)$: Rescaling. Input ciphertext $c$ and scaling factor $r$. Output converts ciphertext $c$ of plaintext $m$ with ciphertext module $q$ to a smaller plaintext $m' = (r - 1) \cdot m$ with smaller module $q' = (r - 1) \cdot q$.

### 2.2   Residue Number System

The Residue Number System (RNS) is a method that represents large integers using multiple smaller integers to improve the efficiency of large integer computations. For a system of single-variable linear congruences:

$$(S) : \begin{cases} x \equiv a_1 \, (\mathrm{mod} m_1) \\ x \equiv a_2 \, (\mathrm{mod} m_2) \\ \cdots \\ x \equiv a_n \, (\mathrm{mod} m_n) \end{cases} \tag{1}$$

Assume that the integers $m_1, m_2, \ldots, m_n$ are pairwise coprime. Then, for any integers $a_1, a_2, \ldots, a_n$, the system of congruences (S) has a unique solution: $x \equiv \sum_{i=1}^{n} a_i b_i M_i \pmod{M}$, where $M = \prod_{i=1}^{n} m_i$, $M_i = \frac{M}{m_i}$, and $b_i$ is the modular inverse of $M_i$ modulo $m_i$, satisfying $b_i M_i \equiv 1 \pmod{m_i}$.

The Residue Number System (RNS) utilizes the properties of the Chinese Remainder Theorem. First, given a set of pairwise coprime numbers $m_0, m_1, \ldots, m_{k-1}$, an integer $x$ can be represented by a sequence of remainders $x_i$, which are obtained by dividing $x$ by each of the numbers $m_0, m_1, \ldots, m_{k-1}$. Specifically, the $i$-th value in the RNS representation of $x$ is given by $x_i = x \bmod m_i$.

For an integer $x$ represented in the RNS, its complement is represented as $(M - x)$ in the RNS system. Addition and multiplication can be achieved by performing addition and subtraction on the corresponding $x_i$ values and taking the modulus with respect to $m_i$. Subtraction can be viewed as the addition of the complement. From the perspective of RNS representation, it has inherent advantages in parallel computation because the modular operations of the several moduli are independent of each other, eliminating carry propagation between stages.

## 3   Homomorphic Hierarchical Encryption Scheme

This scheme provides a data classification protection method based on homomorphic encryption. First, the modulus base of the improved RNS-CKKS scheme is initialized, dividing the modulus base into different levels to generate the improved modulus base. Then, the improved modulus base is used to initialize the keys of the improved RNS-CKKS scheme. These keys are then used to perform homomorphic encryption on classified data, resulting in encrypted classified data. This scheme significantly expands the range of modulus base selection by modifying the constraints of the RNS-CKKS modulus base. It can maintain the scaling factor error within an acceptable range at specific computation levels. The modulus base can be used for classification control, allowing plaintext to be encrypted to higher computation levels or enabling homomorphic computation at higher levels only when a higher security level modulus base is held.

### 3.1   Hierarchical Modification Based on the RNS-CKKS Scheme

To perform homomorphic encryption with the RNS-CKKS scheme, three necessary inputs are required: the plaintext message (polynomial $m$), the encryption key $pk$, and the modulus base set $\{q_0, q_1, q_2, \ldots, q_l\}$. The resulting ciphertext will be at the computation level $l$. In cases where there are modulus errors or insufficient modulus chain lengths, it will not be possible to encrypt and obtain the correct ciphertext, and the computation results on the ciphertext will also be incorrect. When the encryption modulus base and decryption modulus base are not the same, the ciphertext involved in the operation will be under different modulus base systems, and the plaintext result obtained will not correspond to the original modulus base system.

This paper utilizes modulus bases to implement hierarchical encryption of data. In the RNS-CKKS computation levels, several levels with equal spacing are specified as the hierarchical levels, referred to as "security levels". Each ciphertext and each modulus base corresponds to a security level. For a given ciphertext of a security level, homomorphic computations, ciphertext decryption, and other operations can only be correctly performed when the same security-level modulus chain is known. Figure 2 shows the relationship between security levels and computation levels. The security level $(1, 2, \ldots, k) \in \mathbb{Z}$ corresponds to the computation level $k \cdot n$, where the modulus base used is $\{q_0, q_1, q_2, \ldots, q_k \cdot n\}$, with $n$ representing.

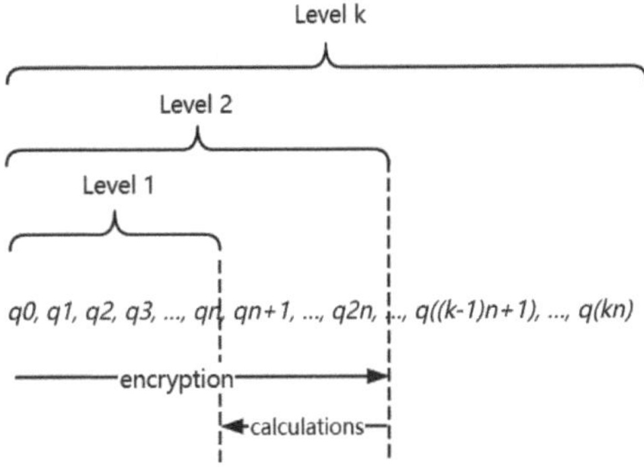


**Fig. 2.** Relationship between security level and computing level

The RNS-CKKS scheme requires that the small prime numbers $q_i$ in the modulus base be approximately equal to the scaling factor $\Delta$, which results in a limited number of small primes that can be used in the scheme when parameters are fixed. If the above hierarchical idea is directly applied, it could lead to the modulus base being easily cracked by brute force. On the other hand, simply expanding the range of small primes would cause the modulus to deviate too much from the scaling factor, thus failing to ensure floating-point precision after decryption. To solve this problem, this paper proposes two modifications for the generation of modulus bases:

(1) Increase the number of candidate small primes: Relax the restriction on the selection range of a single small prime and select small primes that satisfy the other conditions as candidates, where the candidate small prime $q_i$ must satisfy the following conditions:

$$\begin{cases} q_i < 2^{32} \text{ or } 2^{62} \\ q_i \neq q_j, \forall i \neq j \\ \forall i \neq 0, q_0 \gg q_i \\ q_i \equiv 1 \pmod{2N} \end{cases} \tag{2}$$

(2) Ensure decryption accuracy at specific computation levels: When generating the modulus base $\{q_0, q_1, q_2, \ldots, q_k \cdot \mathrm{n}\}$, the product range of nearby $n$ small primes should be approximately the $n$-th power of the scaling factor. After performing $n$ successive rescaling operations, the ciphertext rescaling factor should still remain within the error range, and the error precision should be consistent with the original RNS-CKKS scheme. The specific requirements for the modulus base are given by the formula 3:

$$\prod_{i=kn}^{2kn-1} q_i \in \left( \left( \frac{2^\rho}{1+2^\eta} \right)^n, \left( \frac{2^\rho}{1-2^\eta} \right)^n \right), \forall k = 1, 2, 3 \ldots K \tag{3}$$

When the ciphertext computation level satisfies $(k, n \cdot \mathrm{k})$, after performing $n$ multiplications, the scaling factor error can be kept within an acceptable range. Therefore, for a plaintext with security level $k$, it should be encrypted to the computation level $k \cdot n$, and then $n$ rescaling operations are performed during the implementation of a certain function. After the computations, the ciphertext computation level will be $(k \cdot n - 1)$, ensuring that the scaling factor error remains acceptable.

### 3.2  Detailed Scheme

**Modulo Base Generation Algorithm**

Set the required ciphertext multiplication times for the improved RNS-CKKS scheme to $n$, the cyclotomic polynomial dimension to $N$, the plaintext scaling factor to $\Delta = 2^\rho$ ($\rho$ represents the number of bits used to maintain precision in fixed-point representation), the security level layers to $k$, the range of candidate primes to $2M$, the scaling factor error precision to $\eta$, and the modulus base set to $\{\text{mod}_i \mid i = 1, 2, \ldots, k\}$.

Figure 2 shows a diagram of the relationship between security level and computation level. According to this design approach, both the pre-computation ciphertext level and the post-computation ciphertext level conform to the form of $k \cdot n(k < K, k \in \mathbb{Z})$. Therefore, it is necessary to ensure that the scaling factor of the ciphertext at the computation level $\text{k} \cdot n$ is approximately equal to $\Delta$. This scheme references the precision requirements of the RNS-CKKS scheme for controlling scaling factor accuracy. Based on the limitations on the range of small prime numbers in RNS-CKKS: $\frac{\Delta}{q_i} \in (1 - 2^\eta, 1 + 2^\eta)$, the value range of the product of n small prime numbers can be obtained: $\prod_{i=kn}^{2kn-1} q_i \in \left( \left( \frac{\Delta}{1+2^\eta} \right)^n, \left( \frac{\Delta}{1-2^\eta} \right)^n \right)$. This ensures that after performing n ciphertext multiplications at computation level $k \cdot n$, the scaling factor of the ciphertext still remains approximately equal to $\Delta$, with the error range consistent with the original RNS-CKKS scheme.

## Modulus Base Generation

The number of ciphertext multiplications required for the improved RNS-CKKS scheme is set to $n$, the dimension of the cyclotomic polynomial is $N$, the plaintext scaling factor $\Delta = 2^\rho$, the number of security levels is $k$, the range of prime numbers to be selected is $2M$, the scaling factor error precision is $\eta$, and the modulus basis set is $\{mod_i \mid i = 1, 2, \ldots, k\}$.

The calculation process of the modulus base set $\{mod_i \mid i = 1, 2, \ldots, k\}$ includes:

(1) Define the modulus basis as $\{p_i\}$, randomly generate $p_0 \gg 2^\rho$, $p_0 \equiv 1$ (mod $2N$);

(2) Generate the candidate prime set $\{modList\}$: Given a prime range $M$, traverse $M$ primes around $2^\rho$ to find non-repeating primes that satisfy $prime \equiv 1 \bmod 2N$ and $prime < 2^{64}$, add them to $\{modList\}$;

(3) Generate the modulus array: Randomly select $n$ primes from $\{modList\}$, where the $n$ primes satisfy the condition $\prod_{i=1}^{n} prime_i \in ((2^\rho/1 + 2^\eta)^n, (2^\rho/1 - 2^\eta)^n)$, and add these $n$ primes as a set to the modulus basis $\{p_i\}$, and remove them from $\{modList\}$;

(4) Repeat step (3) until the number of elements in the modulus basis $\{p_i\}$ reaches $kn + 1$;

(5) Output the modulus basis set for different security levels $\{mod_i \mid i = 1, 2, \ldots, k\}$, where the modulus basis for security level $i$ is $mod_i = \{q_0, q_1, \ldots, q_{i \cdot n}\}$.

## Key Initialization

The decryption key for the improved RNS-CKKS scheme is set as $sk = (1, s)$, $s \in R_{Qi \cdot n}$; the encryption key is $pk = (b, a) \in R^2_{Qi \cdot n}$; the auxiliary computation key is $evk \leftarrow b', a' \in R^2_{i \cdot n}$; define $Q_l = q_0 \cdot \prod_{i=1}^{l} q_i$. $\chi_{key}$ is a s a zero-mean Gaussian distribution on $R_{Qi \cdot n}$; generate the decryption key $sk = (1, s)$, where $s \leftarrow \chi_{key} \in R_{Qi \cdot n}$; generate the encryption key $pk \leftarrow (b, a) \in R^2_{Qi \cdot n}$, where $b = -a \cdot s + e(\mathrm{mod}\, Q_{i \cdot n})$, $a \leftarrow \chi_{Qi \cdot n}$ and $e \leftarrow \chi_{err}$; generate the auxiliary computation key $evk$: Instantiate $a' \leftarrow R_{PQi \cdot n}$, and $e' \leftarrow \psi$. Set the auxiliary computation key $evk \leftarrow b', a' \in R^2_{Qi \cdot n}$, where $b' = -a' \cdot s + e' + P \cdot s^2 (\mathrm{mod}\, P \cdot Q_{i \cdot n})$. In the ciphertext multiplication, $evk$ can be used to reduce the ciphertext dimension.

## Homomorphic Encryption

Input: The plaintext $m \in R$, the encryption key $pk = (b, a) \in R^2_{Qi}$, and the modulus basis $mod_i = \{q_0, q_1, \ldots, q_{i \cdot n}\}$.

Output: The ciphertext $c_t = (c_0, c_1) \in R^2_{Qi \cdot n}$.

Calculation Process: Sample a random number $r \leftarrow \chi_{Qi \cdot n}$, sample two error vectors $e_0, e_1 \leftarrow \chi_{err}$, and compute the ciphertext as: $\mathrm{ct} = Enc(m) = (c_0, c_1) = (r \cdot pk + (m + e_0, e_1))(\mathrm{mod}\, Q_{i \cdot n}) \in R^2_{Qi \cdot n}$ where $c_0 = r \cdot b + m + e_0 (\mathrm{mod}\, Q_{i \cdot n}) \in R_{Qi \cdot n}$ and $c_1 = r \cdot a + e_1 (\mathrm{mod}\, Q_{i \cdot n}) \in R_{Qi \cdot n}$.

## Homomorphic Decryption

Input: Ciphertext $\mathrm{ct} \in R^2_{Ql}(l < i \cdot n)$, decryption key $sk \in R^2_{Qi \cdot n}$, ciphertext $ct = (c_0, c_1) \in R^2_{qi \cdot n}$ and modulus base $mod_i = \{q_0, q_1, \ldots, q_{i \cdot n}\}$.

Output: Plaintext $m' \in R$.

Decryption Process: $m' = Dec(ct) = \langle ct, sk \rangle (\mathrm{mod}\, Q_l)$

## 4   Scheme Analysis

### 4.1   Correctness Analysis of Homomorphic Encryption Operations

The purpose of the RNS-CKKS encoding and decoding operations is to achieve a bidirectional mapping of complex vectors and integer polynomials over the ring R. These operations do not involve modulus calculations related to small primes and, therefore, are not affected by the RNS-CKKS hierarchical scheme. The modifications corresponding to the RNS-CKKS hierarchical scheme are only related to the modular basis. The modular basis is a global parameter in the original RNS-CKKS scheme. As long as the correct modular basis is provided, the encryption, decryption, and computation processes are consistent with the original RNS-CKKS scheme. Therefore, the hierarchical scheme does not affect the correctness of encryption, decryption, or homomorphic computation.

## 4.2   Correctness Analysis of the Hierarchical Scheme

First, by expanding the range of small primes selected in the modular basis and limiting the product range of $n$ consecutive small primes, the accuracy of decryption at specific computation levels is ensured. The theoretical limit on the selection of a single small prime has been removed. The number of candidates,   2M, can be defined by the parameter, and the modular basis will be influenced by the order of the internal elements. The computational effort to brute-force crack the modular basis is approximately $O = (C_{2M}^n)^k = ((2M\,(2M-1)\cdots(2M-n+1))/n!)^k$, making it difficult to obtain the modular basis through brute-force calculations.

The RNS-CKKS hierarchical scheme uses the Residue Number System (RNS) and the Chinese Remainder Theorem to represent large numbers as smaller ones, enabling calculations within a 64-bit word length. Errors in any RNS component can lead to discrepancies in the corresponding large number, which get amplified during homomorphic encryption operations, causing significant deviations from the actual results. This amplification ensures the security of the modular basis transformation in the scheme.

## 5   Experiment

### 5.1   Experimental Environment

The hierarchical homomorphic encryption scheme based on RNS-CKKS was implemented using the Golang programming language, and experiments were conducted to test the scaling factors at different computational levels. The experimental machine was configured as follows: processor Intel Core 13500h@4.7 GHz, 16 GB RAM and Windows 11 operating system.

In this experiment, the hierarchical homomorphic encryption scheme was implemented by modifying the source code of the open-source homomorphic encryption library Lattigo 3.0.1. The Lattigo library, written in Go, supports multiple homomorphic encryption schemes, including BFV, CKKS, and RNS-CKKS, as well as lattice-based encryption primitives. This library fully leverages Golang's parallel processing capabilities, achieving performance comparable to state-of-the-art C++ homomorphic encryption libraries.

### 5.2   Experimental Results

**Scaling Factor Stability Test**

The analysis of the scaling factor stability at each computation level in the homomorphic encryption scheme after hierarchical modification is as follows: The experimental parameters for homomorphic encryption are set as follows: scaling factor LogScale = 50, polynomial dimension LogN = 15, the number of security levels K = 5, and the number of re-scalings required to implement a certain function is n = 3.

In the experiment, 15 vectors of length 128, denoted as $\{x_i\}_{i=1}^{15}$, were randomly generated. The vectors were homomorphically encrypted to computation level 15, resulting in 15 ciphertexts $\{Enc(x_i)\}_{i=1}^{15}$. Subsequently, multiplication was performed on the ciphertexts as follows: $Enc(x) = \prod_{i=1}^{15} Enc(x_i)$ A total of 15 multiplications were performed. After each multiplication, the result was decrypted and compared with the actual plaintext calculation to record the scaling factor. The rescaling factors at each computation level under different modulus choices $M$ and continuous product precision LogEta are shown in Fig. 3.

In Fig. 3, the horizontal axis represents the computation levels from 0 to 15, and the vertical axis represents the scaling factor. Each time a multiplication is performed, the computation level decreases by one. The computation level corresponding to the security level $k$ is $k \cdot n$. Based on the homomorphic encryption parameters selected in the experiment, when the computation level is a multiple of 3, it can be considered a security level. The red dashed line in the graph represents the scaling factor chosen for the homomorphic encryption parameters in the experiment. In the original RNS-CKKS scheme, the scaling factor should remain stable near the red dashed line, with the scaling factor being approximately the same at each computation level. When the computation level is a multiple of 3, meaning the computation level is at a certain security level, the plaintext scaling factor can be approximately equal to the standard scaling factor specified by the homomorphic encryption parameters. When scaling by the scaling factor at this computation level, the original plaintext can be accurately recovered. Conversely, at other computation levels, directly dividing by the scaling factor for recovery will result in plaintext errors. Additionally, when the modulus $M$ chosen is larger, the range of a single modulus choice is larger, and the deviation of a single modulus from the standard scaling factor becomes greater. As a result, the scaling factor error at non-security-level computation levels is larger, and the fluctuation is relatively greater.

## Accuracy Test

The experiment uses the Mean Absolute Error (MAE) to measure the difference between the true values and the predicted values. To measure the difference in the imaginary part, the L2 norm MAE of the real and imaginary parts is a commonly used method. The experiment will evaluate the discrepancy between the decrypted values and the actual values from three perspectives: the MAE of the real part, the MAE of the imaginary part, and the L2 norm MAE of the real and imaginary parts.

The experimental results are shown in Table 1. When the correct modulus base is used to encrypt the correct face, the similarity between the ciphertext computation and the decrypted plaintext is close to the result obtained from direct computation with the plaintext. However, when an incorrect modulus base is used to encrypt the correct face, the similarity between the ciphertext computation and the decrypted plaintext differs significantly from the result obtained from direct computation with the plaintext. Therefore, for two ciphertexts used in homomorphic computation, if the modulus bases used for encryption are not exactly the same, and the inconsistent small primes are within the computation

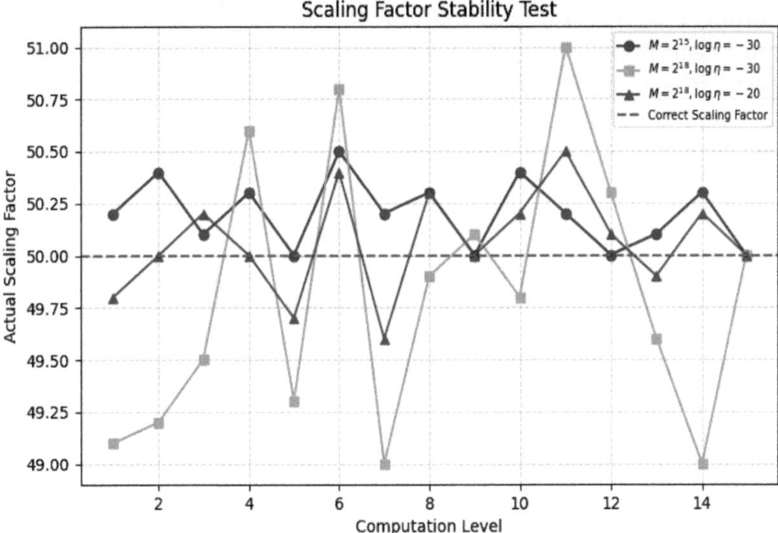


**Fig. 3.** Stability of Scale

level required (i.e., the small inconsistent primes), it can be considered that the two ciphertexts are under different modulus base systems. In this case, performing computations and homomorphic decryption using any modulus base system will not yield results close to the correct values.

**Table 1.** Hierarchical Homomorphic Encryption Correctness Analysis

| Modulus Chain | Correct Modulus Chain | Modulus Chain with Error |
|---|---|---|
| **Level 1** | Real Part MAE: $3.58 \times 10^{-10}$<br>Imaginary Part MAE: $2.43 \times 10^{-9}$<br>L2 Norm MAE: $4.03 \times 10^{-9}$ | Real Part MAE: $5.26 \times 10^{-10}$<br>Imaginary Part MAE: $3.18 \times 10^{-9}$<br>L2 Norm MAE: $5.61 \times 10^{-9}$ |
| **Level 2** | Real Part MAE: $3.35 \times 10^{-10}$<br>Imaginary Part MAE: $4.18 \times 10^{-9}$<br>L2 Norm MAE: $5.48 \times 10^{-9}$ | Real Part MAE: $4.36 \times 10^{-10}$<br>Imaginary Part MAE: $7.33 \times 10^{-9}$<br>L2 Norm MAE: $8.23 \times 10^{-9}$ |
| **Level 3** | Real Part MAE: $1.33 \times 10^{-9}$<br>Imaginary Part MAE: $3.19 \times 10^{-9}$<br>L2 Norm MAE: $1.22 \times 10^{-8}$ | Real Part MAE: $1.37 \times 10^{-9}$<br>Imaginary Part MAE: $6.64 \times 10^{-9}$<br>L2 Norm MAE: $1.43 \times 10^{-8}$ |

## 6   Conclusions and Future Research

In this study, we proposed an improved RNS-CKKS hierarchical homomorphic encryption scheme to address the lack of data-level classification in existing homomorphic encryption methods. By modifying the modulus base generation and adding decryption level constraints, the new scheme increases the number of modulus bases and ensures accurate scaling at specific computation levels. The scheme maintains computational efficiency and security using the Residue Number System (RNS). Experimental results, based on the Lattigo homomorphic encryption library, showed that the enhanced RNS-CKKS scheme maintains stable scaling factors and accurate results across computation levels.

Future work can focus on further optimizing the scheme for better efficiency and scalability, especially in large-scale applications. Additionally, combining this scheme with other privacy-preserving technologies could improve its use in fields like healthcare, finance, and cloud computing. Further testing in different computational environments could also provide insights into its practical deployment.

# References


1. Rivest, R.L., Adleman, L., Dertouzos, M.L., et al.: On data banks and privacy homomorphisms. Found. Secur. Comput. 4(11), 169–180 (1978)
2. Rivest, R.L., Shamir, A., Adleman, L.: A method for obtaining digital signatures and public-key cryptosystems. Commun. ACM 21(2), 120–126 (1978)
3. Goldwasser, S., Micali, S.: Probabilistic encryption. J. Comput. Syst. Sci. 28, 270–299 (1984). https://api.semanticscholar.org/CorpusID:19616020
4. Boneh, D., Goh, E.-J., Nissim, K.: Evaluating 2-DNF formulas on ciphertexts. In: Kilian, J. (ed.) TCC 2005. LNCS, vol. 3378, pp. 325–341. Springer, Heidelberg (2005). https://doi.org/10.1007/978-3-540-30576-7_18
5. Ishai, Y., Paskin, A.: Evaluating branching programs on encrypted data. In: Vadhan, S.P. (ed.) TCC 2007. LNCS, vol. 4392, pp. 575–594. Springer, Heidelberg (2007). https://doi.org/10.1007/978-3-540-70936-7_31
6. Gentry, C.: A Fully Homomorphic Encryption scheme. Stanford University (2009)
7. van Dijk, M., Gentry, C., Halevi, S., Vaikuntanathan, V.: Fully Homomorphic Encryption over the Integers. In: Gilbert, H. (ed.) EUROCRYPT 2010. LNCS, vol. 6110, pp. 24–43. Springer, Heidelberg (2010). https://doi.org/10.1007/978-3-642-13190-5_2
8. Stehlé, D., Steinfeld, R.: Faster fully homomorphic encryption. In: Abe, M. (ed.) ASIACRYPT 2010. LNCS, vol. 6477, pp. 377–394. Springer, Heidelberg (2010). https://doi.org/10.1007/978-3-642-17373-8_22
9. Cheon, J.H., Stehlé, D.: Fully homomophic encryption over the integers revisited. In: Oswald, E., Fischlin, M. (eds.) EUROCRYPT 2015. LNCS, vol. 9056, pp. 513–536. Springer, Heidelberg (2015). https://doi.org/10.1007/978-3-662-46800-5_20
10. Smart, N.P., Vercauteren, F.: Fully homomorphic encryption with relatively small key and ciphertext sizes. In: Nguyen, P.Q., Pointcheval, D. (eds.) PKC 2010. LNCS, vol. 6056, pp. 420–443. Springer, Heidelberg (2010). https://doi.org/10.1007/978-3-642-13013-7_25
11. Cheon, J.H., Kim, A., Kim, M., Song, Y.: Homomorphic encryption for arithmetic of approximate numbers. In: Takagi, T., Peyrin, T. (eds.) ASIACRYPT 2017. LNCS, vol. 10624, pp. 409–437. Springer, Cham (2017). https://doi.org/10.1007/978-3-319-70694-8_15

12. Cheon, J.H., Han, K., Kim, A., Kim, M., Song, Y.: A full RNS variant of approximate homomorphic encryption. In: Selected Areas in Cryptography–SAC 2018: 25th International Conference, Calgary, AB, Canada, August 15–17, 2018, Revised Selected Papers 25, pp. 347–368. Springer (2019)

13. Mouchet, C., Troncoso-Pastoriza, J., Bossuat, J.P., Hubaux, J.P.: Multiparty homomorphic encryption from ring-learning-with-errors. Proceed. Privacy Enhancing Technol. **2021**(4), 291–311 (2021)

# MCAN-BIFT: An IIoT Intrusion Detection System Integrating Multi-scale Feature Enhancement and Transformer


Conglong Wang[1] , Yong Wang[1(✉)] , and Jianhua Liu[2]

[1] College of Computer Science and Technology, Shanghai University of Electric Power, Shanghai 201306, China
`wangconglong@mail.shiep.edu.cn`, `wangyong@shiep.edu.cn`
[2] School of Computer Science and Engineering, Guilin University of Aerospace Technology, Guilin 541004, China
`ljh@guat.edu.cn`



**Abstract.** The Industrial Internet of Things (IIoT) extends IoT into the industrial sector, enabling real-time data collection through interconnected devices. However, the increasing sophistication of cyberattacks poses significant security threats. Traditional network intrusion detection systems (NIDS) often fail to identify advanced attack patterns due to the reliance on manual feature design. To address this, we propose the MCAN-BIFT intrusion detection system, consisting of the Multi-Scale Convolutional Attention Network (MCAN) and the Bidirectional Interactive Fusion Transformer (BIFT). The system extracts attack features through one-dimensional convolution, enhances them using a multi-scale convolutional attention hybrid module (MS-CAHM) with channel and spatial attention mechanisms, and feeds them into BIFT module, which combines interacting information from two directions and merges them at the fusion layer to generate the final output. Evaluated on the Edge-IIoTset dataset, the model achieved a test accuracy of 97.30% across 15 classes, outperforming recent studies on IIoT intrusion detection.

**Keywords:** Industrial Internet of Things · Intrusion Detection · Convolutional Neural Networks · Transformer · Edge-IIoTset


## 1 Introduction

The Industrial Internet of Things (IIoT) is transforming industrial systems through real-time data analysis and intelligent connectivity in the Industry 4.0 era [10]. However, it introduces cybersecurity risks, as attackers exploit vulnerabilities to steal data, disrupt operations, or launch attacks, causing production halts and losses. Timely threat detection is essential to safeguard IIoT systems.

Network Intrusion Detection Systems (NIDS) are vital for securing IIoT by monitoring traffic and detecting anomalies. As IIoT environments grow more complex, NIDS face challenges despite advances in machine learning [1]. These


© The Author(s), under exclusive license to Springer Nature Singapore Pte Ltd. 2026
T. Zhu et al. (Eds.): KSEM 2025, LNAI 15919, pp. 302–314, 2026.
https://doi.org/10.1007/978-981-95-3001-4_22

include difficulty in selecting relevant features from vast traffic and vulnerability to obfuscation techniques used by attackers. Thus, improved feature extraction and contextual understanding are essential for effective intrusion detection [11].

To address these challenges, we propose the MCAN-BIFT model for detecting sophisticated attacks in industrial IoT. The model incorporates the multi-scale convolutional attention hybrid module (MS-CAHM) to capture attack features at various levels. The attention mechanism focuses on key features, improving sensitivity to potential threats. The Bidirectional Interactive Fusion Transformer (BIFT) module enhances contextual understanding, enabling the identification of anomalous behaviors in complex data. This approach allows the model to detect both known and hidden attack patterns, strengthening the security of industrial IoT networks. The main contributions of my work are as follows.

- We propose the MCAN-BIFT model, a hybrid intrusion detection system combining an optimized CNN and an enhanced Transformer variant to detect cyber threats in IIoT, significantly improving detection performance.
- We design the MS-CAHM module to improve feature extraction by providing multi-scale flexibility and learnable weights. This allows adaptive attention adjustment, reducing false alarms and enhancing the model's robustness.
- We design the BIFT module with a bidirectional interactive attention fusion mechanism, combining interactive attention from different directions to enhance contextual understanding.

The paper is organized as follows: Sect. 2 reviews the background of intrusion detection, Sect. 3 details the proposed method, Sect. 4 presents experimental results, and Sect. 5 concludes with future research directions.

## 2  Related Work

Traditional statistical methods laid the groundwork for intrusion detection, while machine learning has driven major advances in network intrusion detection systems (NIDS) [12]. ML algorithms such as decision trees, support vector machines, and k-nearest neighbors learn from data to recognize patterns. Compared to statistical methods, ML handles more complex relationships and attack patterns, offering greater adaptability across diverse environments. Maya Hilda Lestari Louk et al. [8] proposed a new model for network anomaly intrusion detection based on bagging method and gradient lifting decision tree (GBDT). By combining these two existing integration techniques, a dual integration model is formed, and good results are obtained. Elijah M. Maseno et al. [9] proposed a novel sequential feature selection method, which combines optimized extreme learning machine (ELM) and support vector machine (SVM) classifiers. Genetic algorithm (GA) is used to optimize the weight of ELM to improve its performance.

While machine learning is widely used, advances in GPU technology are driving deep learning to transform NIDS. Deep learning leverages neural networks to automatically extract features from large datasets, improving attack detection

[2]. As a result, it is increasingly adopted for more accurate IIoT security solutions. Zelin Xiang et al. [16] proposed a Transformer based NIDS model integrating deep learning architecture. The model uses GAN-Cross to extend a few class samples to solve the problem of data imbalance, and uses Transformer module to optimize the feature coding capability of the ML-CNN-BiLSTM model, thereby improving its generalization ability. Yakubu Imrana et al. [5] proposed a two-layer feature extraction and feature fusion technology called CNN-GRU-FF. This technique uses an improved focus loss function instead of the traditional cross entropy loss to deal with class imbalance in intrusion detection data sets. Shaoqin Li et al. [6] proposed SELSTM, an intrusion detection system designed for complex IIoT environments with limited device resources. It combines NSENet (based on SENet) with LSTM and integrates lightweight modules—NonLocal, SKConv, and inverted residuals—into the SE block. The NonLocal module's self-attention enhances the local receptive field for feature extraction.

In the past few years, researchers have proposed various methods for network intrusion detection with some success, but effectiveness remains challenged by complex IIoT attack scenarios, necessitating more robust solutions.

## 3 Methodology

This paper proposes an intrusion detection system based on a hybrid network, MCAN-BIFT. As shown in Fig. 1, the system consists of a multi-scale convolutional attention network and a bidirectional interactive fusion transformer.

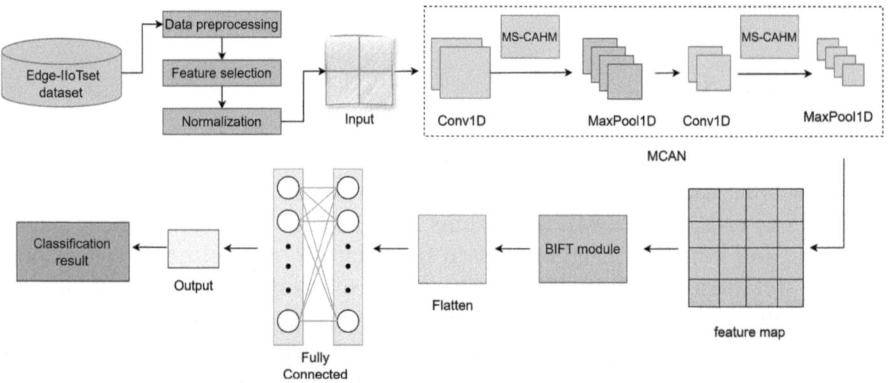


**Fig. 1.** Overall framework of MCAN-BIFT model.

### 3.1 MCAN

In Intrusion Detection System (IDS), Convolutional Neural Networks (CNNs) provide powerful feature extraction capabilities. The model employs an optimized CNN (MCAN), comprising two 1D convolutional layers, each followed by

MS-CAHM, batch normalization, and pooling to extract and optimize features in the input sequences, providing a rich representation for subsequent BIFT blocks.

## 3.2   MS-CAHM

In industrial IoT, attack features are complex, with some critical for detection and others adding noise. To address this, the Multi-scale Convolutional Attention Hybrid Module (MS-CAHM) is designed. The multi-scale convolution component captures both subtle features and holistic patterns, enhancing the model's ability to detect various types of attacks [14]. Through learnable weights, the model can automatically prioritize the most relevant scale features based on the data's characteristics and complexity [18]. Meanwhile, the attention mechanism dynamically identifies and focuses on features that are helpful for attack identification, effectively improving the accuracy of the model.

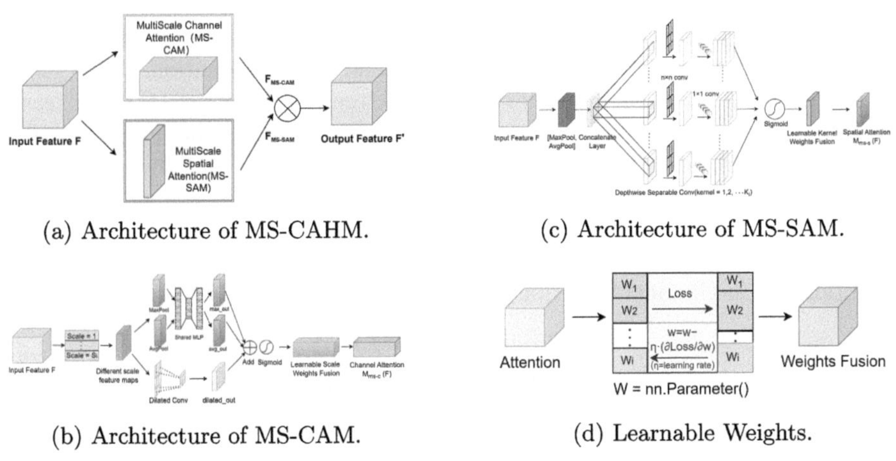

(a) Architecture of MS-CAHM.

(c) Architecture of MS-SAM.

(b) Architecture of MS-CAM.

(d) Learnable Weights.

**Fig. 2.** Overall and Local Architectures of MS-CAHM.

MS-CAHM is primarily an improved version of CBAM [15]. First, it designs multi-scale processing in both channel and spatial attention. The channel attention module applies submodules of different scales, while the spatial attention module uses multi-scale convolution kernels. Both modules combine the results through weighted fusion. Second, MS-CAHM additionally uses dilated convolution in the channel attention computation, which enables the model to capture a larger range of contextual information, and provides richer feature information compared to the traditional global pooling approach alone [17]. For spatial attention, it replaces traditional convolution with depth-separable convolution, improving efficiency and reducing parameters by decomposing convolution into depth-wise and point-wise operations [3]. Finally, MS-CAHM employs learnable weights to optimize attentional features at different scales or kernels, enabling adaptive adjustment of their contribution during training. Additionally, unlike CBAM's attention sequential calculation, MS-CAHM processes channel and spatial attention in parallel, Computing them independently and merging the results. This ensures both mechanisms enhance all feature map location [7].

MS-CAHM includes MS-CAM (Multi-Scale Channel Attention Module) and MS-SAM (Multi-Scale Spatial Attention Module), as shown in the Fig. 2(a). The attention operations of MS-CAHM can be represented by Eqs. 3.2 to 2. This structure can effectively integrate features of different scales, so as to improve the recognition ability of the model to novel attacks.

$$F_{MS-CAM} = M_{MS-C}(F), F_{MS-SAM} = M_{MS-S}(F) \tag{1}$$

$$F' = F_{MS-CAM} \otimes F_{MS-SAM} \tag{2}$$

Here, F denotes the feature map, while $M_{MS-C}$ and $M_{MS-S}$ represent multi-scale channel-based attention and multi-scale spatial attention, respectively. The symbol $\otimes$ indicates element-wise multiplication, and $F'$ represents the output feature map after applying channel attention and spatial attention.

MS-CAM consists of multiple Channel Attention Modules (CAMs), each operating at a different scale $S_i$, initializing the learnable weights for each scale: $W_i = 1/N$, where N is the number of scales, which ensures that the model contributes equally to all scales in the early stages of training and promotes balanced learning. The overall framework is shown in Fig. 2(b). CAM sums the outputs of the pooling operation and the dilated convolution operation to compute the attention graph ChannelAttention(F), as shown in Eq. 3. $\sigma$ is sigmoid.

$$\begin{aligned} ChannelAttention(F) &= \sigma(MLP(AvgPool(F)) \\ &+ MLP(MaxPool(F)) + Dilated(F)) \end{aligned} \tag{3}$$

The dilated convolution operation is represented using Eq. 4, Dilated convolution captures a wider range of contextual information, thus enhancing the model's ability to recognize complex patterns.

$$Dilated(F) = \sum_{k=0}^{K-1} W[k] \cdot X[t - d \cdot k] \tag{4}$$

where d is the dilation rate (2 in this case), K is the size of the convolution kernel, X[t-dk] denotes the sampling points of the input features after dilation, and W[k] is the kth weight of the convolution kernel. Finally, the results of the channel attention maps at each scale are weighted and summed to obtain the final multi-scale channel attention map, as shown in Eq. 5. $CA_{Si}(F)$ is the channel attention map computed at scale $S_i$.

$$CA_{Si}(F) = ChannelAttention_{Si}(F), M_{MS-C}(F) = \sum_{i=1}^{N} W_i \cdot CA_{Si}(F) \tag{5}$$

MS-SAM consists of multiple spatial attention Modules (SAMs), each of which captures spatial features under a different convolutional kernel $K_i$, initializing the learnable weights of each convolutional kernel: $W_i = 1/N$, where N is the number of convolutional kernels. The overall framework is shown in Fig. 2(c). SAM splices the outputs of the average pooling operation and the maximum pooling operation to obtain the feature map F, and then computes the spatial attention map SpatialAttention(F) through the depthwise convolution and point-by-point convolution operations, as shown in Eqs. 6 to 7. Where, the depth convolution operation is shown in Eq. 8.

$$F = Concatenate([MaxPool(F); AvgPool(F)]) \tag{6}$$

$$SpatialAttention(F) = \sigma(pointwise(depthwise(F))) \tag{7}$$

$$pointwise(depthwise(F) = \left( \bigoplus_{c=1}^{C_{in}} (F^c * K_{d,c}) \right) \cdot K_{point} \tag{8}$$

where $F^c$ is the feature map of the cth channel, and $K_{d,c}$ is the depth convolution kernel of the cth channel. $K_{point}$ is the $1 \times 1$ point-by-point convolution kernel. $C_{in}$ represents number of channels. $\oplus$ represents concatenation. Finally, the results of spatial attention maps at each scale are weighted and summed to obtain the final multi-scale spatial attention map, as shown in Eq. 9. $SA_{Ki}(F)$ is the spatial attention map computed at convolution kernel size $K_i$.

$$SA_{Ki}(F) = SpatialAttention_{Ki}(F), M_{MS-S}(F) = \sum_{i=1}^{N} W_i \cdot SA_{Ki}(F) \tag{9}$$

In addition, both MS-CAM and MS-SAM dynamically adjust the influence of each scale through learnable weights $W_i$ defined by nn.Parameter. These weights are updated with each iteration during the backpropagation process, thus enabling the models to adapt to the training data by enhancing the weights on the better performing scales. This adaptive mechanism improves the flexibility and robustness of the model. As shown in the Fig. 2(d).

Specifically, learnable weights $W_i$ are updated by gradient descent. The model first computes the loss $L$ in forward propagation, and then updates the weights in backpropagation based on the gradient $\frac{\partial L}{\partial W_i}$ of the loss function $L$ over the weights $W_i$. Next, the learning rate $\eta$ is used to adjust the weights towards minimizing the loss, following the update rule $w_i \leftarrow w_i - \eta \cdot \frac{\partial L}{\partial w_i}$, thus allowing the model to adaptively adjust to the effects of different inputs or features.

## 3.3   BIFT

CNNs excel at local feature extraction but struggle with global dependencies, while traditional fusion methods overlook feature interrelationships, limiting detection of sophisticated attacks. To address these challenges, we design the

BIFT. Unlike traditional Transformer, BIFT introduces a bidirectional interactive attention fusion mechanism, computing attention scores from both directions. In the fusion layer, it effectively integrates bidirectional attention information to enhance long-range dependency modeling and feature representation. BIFT retains key Transformer components, such as residual connections and layer normalization, while integrating its advanced fusion mechanism into the feed-forward network to enhance stability and performance in detecting complex attacks [13].

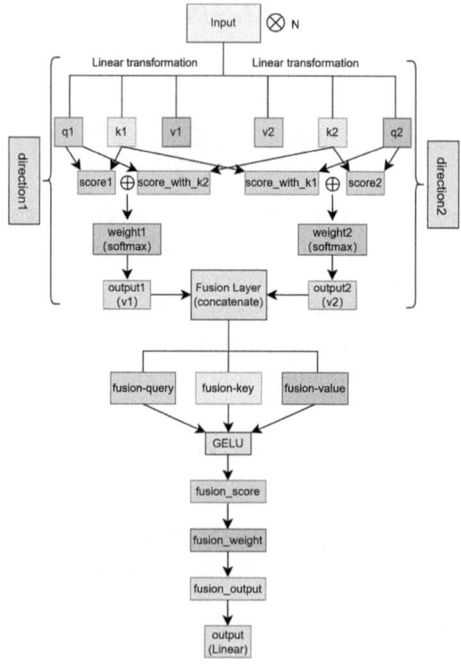


**Fig. 3.** Bidirectional Interactive Attention Fusion Mechanism.

### 3.4  Attention Mechanism

Next, we will introduce the bidirectional interactive attention fusion mechanism in BIFT to address the limitation of local features in capturing global dependencies. The mechanism captures full context via bidirectional attention, combining complementary information from both directions in the attention scores. Through a fusion layer, it integrates forward and backward dependencies at each location, enhancing the model's understanding of complex relationships.

As shown in Fig. 3. The module splits the input tensor into 4 heads. Each header will transform the input into Q1, K1, V1 (Direction 1) and Q2, K2, V2

(Direction 2) via linear transformation. For each input X, we compute the Query, the Key, and the Value. Q, K, and V are computed using Eqs. 10 to 11.

$$Q_1 = XW_Q^1, K_1 = XW_K^1, V_1 = XW_V^1 \tag{10}$$

$$Q_2 = XW_Q^2, K_2 = XW_K^2, V_2 = XW_V^2 \tag{11}$$

where X is the input and W is the weight matrix of the linear transformation. The Attention Score for Orientation 1 is computed by dot-producting the Q1 with the transpose of the K1 and dividing by the scaling factor. To introduce information for direction 2, an additional dot product of Q1 with K2 is computed and added to the score for direction 1, and similarly, the attention score for direction 2 is computed. Equation 12 are used to calculate the attention score $A_1$ for direction 1 and the attention score $A_2$ for direction 2.

$$A_1 = \frac{Q_1 K_1^T}{\sqrt{d_h}} + \frac{Q_1 K_2^T}{\sqrt{d_h}}, A_2 = \frac{Q_2 K_2^T}{\sqrt{d_h}} + \frac{Q_2 K_1^T}{\sqrt{d_h}} \tag{12}$$

where $d_h$ = D/H is the dimension of each head and H is the number of heads. The attention scores of directions 1 and 2 are softmaxed to obtain weights $W_1$ and $W_2$, and by weighted summation with the corresponding value matrices $V_1$ and $V_2$, the output of direction 1 $O_1$ and the output of direction 2 $O_2$ are obtained, and finally, the outputs of the two directions are spliced together in the last dimension to obtain $O_{combined}$. As shown in Eqs. 3.4 to 14.

$$W_1 = softmax(A_1), W_2 = softmax(A_2) \tag{13}$$

$$O_1 = W_1 V_1, O_2 = W_2 V_2, O_{combined} = concat(O_1, O_2) \tag{14}$$

The spliced output is further processed by linear transformation of the fusion layer to obtain Query $(F_Q)$, Key $(F_K)$ and Value $(F_V)$. The fusion attention score $F_A$ is computed and then softmax processing is performed to compute the fusion attention weights $F_W$, using these weights the fusion value $F_V$ is weighted and summed to obtain the fusion output $O_{fusion}$. As shown in Eqs. 15 to 16.

$$F_Q = O_{combined}W_{F_Q}, F_K = O_{combined}W_{F_K}, F_V = O_{combined}W_{F_V} \tag{15}$$

$$F_A = \frac{F_Q F_K^T}{\sqrt{d_h, fusion}}, F_W = softmax(F_A), O_{fusion} = F_W F_V \tag{16}$$

A linear transformation is then applied to obtain the final output $O_{final}$. Finally, the outputs from multiple heads are combined to form the final output. $W_O$ is the weight matrix of the linear transformation. As shown in Eq. 17.

$$O_{final} = O_{fusion}W_O \tag{17}$$

# 4    Experiment

## 4.1    The Edge-IIoTset Dataset

The Edge-IIoTset dataset [4] is designed for network traffic analysis in IIoT environments. It includes diverse traffic data from IoT devices, covering 14 attack types across five threat categories: DoS/DDoS, information gathering, man-in-the-middle, injection, and malware. The dataset integrates alerts, logs, and network traffic, reducing 1,176 initial features to 61 key ones for security research.

## 4.2    Data Preprocessing

To ensure data quality, we design a comprehensive preprocessing phase. Duplicate records are removed using the hash algorithm to reduce redundancy. Categorical features like protocol types (HTTP, DNS, MQTT) are processed with hybrid encoding: label encoding followed by one-hot encoding. The Chi-Square Test selects the top 61 features from 199 to enhance detection performance. To reduce overfitting, we apply undersampling before splitting the data into training (70%), validation (10%), and testing (20%) sets, ensuring high-quality input.

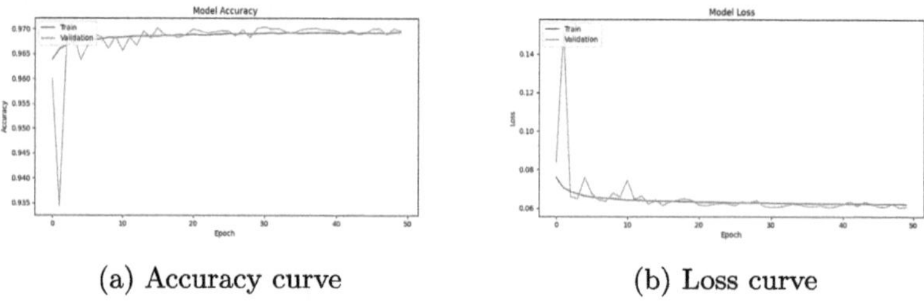

(a) Accuracy curve          (b) Loss curve

**Fig. 4.** Training and validation accuracy and loss curves on Edge-IIoTset dataset.

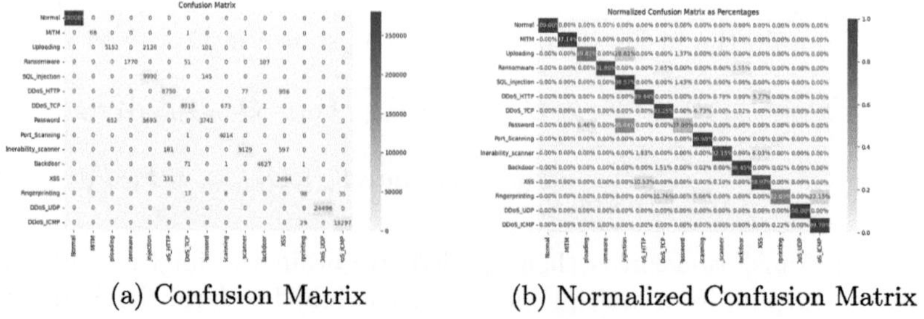

(a) Confusion Matrix          (b) Normalized Confusion Matrix

**Fig. 5.** Confusion matrix of the proposed MCAN-BIFT on Edge-IIoTset dataset.

## 4.3   Evaluation Metrics

The effectiveness of Network Intrusion Detection Systems is evaluated using multiple metrics, including Accuracy (Acc), Precision (P), Recall (R), and F1 Score (F). The confusion matrix further analyzes model performance by showing the relationship between predicted and actual results. It consists of true positives (TP), false positives (FP), true negatives (TN), and false negatives (FN).

## 4.4   Experiment and Analysis

This section evaluates the accuracy and generalization of the proposed MCAN-BIFT model on the Edge-IIoTset dataset, comparing it with recent deep learning models for IIoT attack detection. As shown in Fig. 4, the MCAN-BIFT model demonstrates strong accuracy and stable loss trends on both training and validation sets. Training accuracy rises steadily and stabilizes around 0.97 after 30 epochs, while validation accuracy follows a similar path with slight fluctuations. Training loss drops quickly and stabilizes early. Although the validation loss fluctuates initially and peaks around the 10th epoch, it quickly declines and aligns with the training loss. Both losses eventually stabilize around 0.06, indicating the model's robust generalization and effectiveness in IIoT intrusion detection.

**Table 1.** Performance comparison with other models on Edge-IIoTset.

| Model | Precision | Recall | F1-Score | Accuracy |
| --- | --- | --- | --- | --- |
| CNN | 0.8732 | 0.8523 | 0.8514 | 0.8947 |
| BiLSTM | 0.9009 | 0.8901 | 0.8987 | 0.9033 |
| Transformer | 0.9300 | 0.9379 | 0.9321 | 0.9469 |
| CL | 0.9386 | 0.9310 | 0.9211 | 0.9329 |
| CT | 0.9522 | 0.9301 | 0.9006 | 0.9315 |
| CLG | 0.9156 | 0.9123 | 0.9255 | 0.9413 |
| **MCAN-BIFT** | **0.9720** | **0.9712** | **0.9710** | **0.9730** |

In addition, the confusion matrix in Fig. 5(a) shows the absolute number of predictions made by the MCAN-BIFT model in real-world classification. The model has high prediction accuracy in most of the categories. However, for some categories, the model misclassified a relatively high number of samples. For example, in the "Password" attack category, although the model correctly predicted 3,741 times, it also misclassified 5693 samples as SQL injection, which suggests that the model is less capable of distinguishing between these two types of attacks, and it is possible that there is a large overlap in their feature spaces. Next, the normalized confusion matrix in Fig. 5(b) clearly demonstrates the model's classification performance on different categories, but unlike the absolute values, the normalized confusion matrix presents the results in percentage form, which is particularly suitable for analyzing the model's performance on categories with a small number of samples. For example, although the number of samples in the category "MITM" is relatively small, the normalized prediction accuracy reaches 97.14%, indicating that the model's performance in this category is quite stable. However, distinguishing Password, Uploading, and Fingerprinting attacks remains challenging, likely due to their diverse subattack patterns, which hinder the model's ability to learn consistent features. Therefore, to improve the recognition rate of these categories, the feature extraction strategy can be further optimized to introduce more unique traffic features for each attack type.

Finally, we summarize the comparison between the MCAN-BIFT model and other models in various performance metrics through Table 1. This includes common deep composite models such as CNN-LSTM (CL), CNN-Transformer (CT), and CNN-LSTM-GRU (CLG). It can be seen that the proposed model significantly outperforms the other models in all performance metrics, which also validate the effectiveness of our proposed model in dealing with complex attack detection tasks and offer a new direction for future industrial IoT security.

### 4.5   Ablation Experiment

This section conducts ablation experiments to evaluate the performance of each MCAN-BIFT component. By removing or replacing key modules, we assess their impact on accuracy and F1 score. The experiments include: 1) Use only a single scale or convolution kernel, i.e., remove learnable weights. 2) Remove dilated convolution and replace depth-separable convolution with ordinary convolution. 3) Replace MS-CAHM with CBAM. 4) Replace bidirectional interactive attention fusion mechanism with standard self-attention. Table 2 presents ablation results, highlighting each component's contribution. The multi-scale mechanism, learnable weights and bidirectional interactive attention enhance accuracy and generalization, validating the model's effectiveness in IIoT attack detection.

**Table 2.** Ablation experiment result on Edge-IIoTset.

| Experiment | Accuracy (%) | F1-Score (%) |
| --- | --- | --- |
| 1 | 90.25 | 90.93 |
| 2 | 92.32 | 92.64 |
| 3 | 93.29 | 93.01 |
| 4 | 92.46 | 92.20 |
| **MCAN-BIFT** | **97.30** | **97.10** |

# 5    Conclusions

This paper presents MCAN-BIFT, an innovative deep learning model that integrates the Multi-scale Convolutional Attention Network (MCAN) and the Bidirectional Interactive Fusion Transformer (BIFT) to protect network security in IIoT environments. Experimental results show that MCAN-BIFT achieves excellent performance in intrusion detection. However, distinguishing attack types with highly similar features remains challenging, possibly due to overlapping feature spaces or imbalanced data distribution. Future research could focus on advanced feature extraction techniques and adaptive learning mechanisms to further improve the model's ability to differentiate similar attack patterns.

**Acknowledgments.** This work was supported by the National Natural Science Foundation of China under Grant Nos. U23B2021 and 62372285.

# References


1. Ahmad, Z., Shahid Khan, A., Wai Shiang, C., Abdullah, J., Ahmad, F.: Network intrusion detection system: a systematic study of machine learning and deep learning approaches. Trans. Emerg. Telecommun. Technol. **32**(1), e4150 (2021)
2. Aminanto, E., Kim, K.: Deep learning in intrusion detection system: an overview. In: 2016 International Research Conference on Engineering and Technology (2016 IRCET). Higher Education Forum (2016)
3. Chollet, F.: Xception: deep learning with Depthwise separable convolutions. In: Proceedings of the IEEE Conference on Computer Vision and Pattern Recognition, pp. 1251–1258 (2017)
4. Ferrag, M.A., Friha, O., Hamouda, D., Maglaras, L., Janicke, H.: Edge-IIoTset: a new comprehensive realistic cyber security dataset of IoT and IIoT applications for centralized and federated learning. IEEE Access **10**, 40281–40306 (2022)
5. Imrana, Y., Xiang, Y., Ali, L., Noor, A., Sarpong, K., Abdullah, M.A.: CNN-GRU-FF: a double-layer feature fusion-based network intrusion detection system using convolutional neural network and gated recurrent units. Complex Intell. Syst. 1–18 (2024)
6. Li, S., Wang, Z., Yang, S., Luo, X., He, D., Chan, S.: Internet of things intrusion detection: research and practice of NSENet and LSTM fusion models. Egypt. Inform. J. **26**, 100476 (2024)
7. Liu, Y., Shao, Z., Hoffmann, N.: Global attention mechanism: Retain information to enhance channel-spatial interactions. arXiv preprint arXiv:2112.05561 (2021)
8. Louk, M.H.L., Tama, B.A.: Dual-IDS: a bagging-based gradient boosting decision tree model for network anomaly intrusion detection system. Expert Syst. Appl. **213**, 119030 (2023)
9. Maseno, E.M., Wang, Z.: Hybrid wrapper feature selection method based on genetic algorithm and extreme learning machine for intrusion detection. J. Big Data **11**(1), 24 (2024)
10. Oks, S.J., et al.: Cyber-physical systems in the context of industry 4.0: a review, categorization and outlook. Inf. Syst. Front. 1–42 (2022)

11. Qiu, H., Dong, T., Zhang, T., Lu, J., Memmi, G., Qiu, M.: Adversarial attacks against network intrusion detection in IoT systems. IEEE Internet Things J. **8**(13), 10327–10335 (2020)
12. Sommer, R., Paxson, V.: Outside the closed world: on using machine learning for network intrusion detection. In: 2010 IEEE Symposium on Security and Privacy, pp. 305–316. IEEE (2010)
13. Vaswani, A.: Attention is all you need. Advances in Neural Information Processing Systems (2017)
14. Wang, X., Yin, S., Li, H., Wang, J., Teng, L.: A network intrusion detection method based on deep multi-scale convolutional neural network. Int. J. Wireless Inf. Networks **27**, 503–517 (2020)
15. Woo, S., Park, J., Lee, J.Y., Kweon, I.S.: CBAM: convolutional block attention module. In: Proceedings of the European Conference on Computer Vision (ECCV), pp. 3–19 (2018)
16. Xiang, Z., Li, X.: Retracted article: fusion of transformer and ML-CNN-BiLSTM for network intrusion detection. EURASIP J. Wirel. Commun. Netw. **2023**(1), 71 (2023)
17. Yu, F.: Multi-scale context aggregation by dilated convolutions. arXiv preprint arXiv:1511.07122 (2015)
18. Zhang, L., Lu, X., Chen, Z., Liu, T., Chen, Q., Li, Z.: Adaptive deep learning for network intrusion detection by risk analysis. Neurocomputing **493**, 46–58 (2022)

# Summary of the Application of Deep Learning in Fault Detection

Yinpan He[(⊠)], Yake Xue, Zhen Lu, and Di Wang

City University of Macau, Avenida Padre Tomás Pereira, Taipa, Macau
d23092110244@cityu.edu.mo

**Abstract.** This paper systematically reviews the application of deep learning in the field of fault detection in recent years. Firstly, the necessity of fault detection and the limitations of traditional methods are expounded, and then the advantages and technical breakthroughs of deep learning in fault detection are introduced. Finally, the current challenges are analyzed and the future direction is discussed, aiming to provide a comprehensive theoretical reference for relevant researchers.

**Keywords:** .deep learning · fault detection · industrial system · technology evolution

## 1 Introduction

### 1.1 Necessity of Fault Detection and the Limitations of Traditional Methods

Fault detection is the core technology to ensure the reliability and safety of industrial systems, especially in high-risk areas such as aerospace and power network. Traditional methods mainly rely on threshold setting (e. g. control chart [1]), statistical models (such as dynamic Bayesian network [2]), and multivariate analysis (e. g. principal component analysis [3]). For example, Chatti et al. (2020) significantly reduced the false positive rate of the hybrid system by using the dynamic Bayesian network (DBN) combined with the hybrid bonding graph model, but still relies on the complex structural diagnosis matrix. Bayesian stochastic Principal component analysis (BRPCA) proposed by Du and Deng (2021) simplifies non-linear modeling through random Fourier mapping, but its multi-model fusion strategy requires high [3] on computational resources. In addition, the Euclidean distance control method improved by Li and Li (2022) performs better than traditional PCA in the Tennessee Eastman process, but has limited adaptability to high-dimensional non-stationary data [4]. These methods generally face the following limitations: insufficient modeling ability for nonlinear dynamics, low efficiency of multimodal sensor data fusion, and high false alarm rate [5, 6] in high noise environment.

### 1.2 Advantages and Technological Breakthroughs of Deep Learning

Deep learning provides innovative solutions for fault detection through automatic feature extraction and complex pattern capture capabilities. The combination of temporal convolutional network (TCN) and long and short-term memory network (LSTM) (e. g. Lu


T. Zhu et al. (Eds.): KSEM 2025, LNAI 15919, pp. 315–324, 2026.
https://doi.org/10.1007/978-981-95-3001-4_23

et al., 2023) realizes the dynamic modeling of temporal characteristics in the power distribution network, detects equipment faults in advance and reduces economic losses [7]. Yang et al. (2024) integrated deep neural network (DNN) and typical correlation analysis (CCA) in the high-speed rail traction system, and optimized the residual calculation through feature reconstruction, which significantly improved the detection accuracy of the nonlinear system [8]. In addition, variants of generated adversarial network (GAN) such as DCGAN (Wang et al., 2024) can realize rolling bearing abnormality detection by only requiring normal sample training, with F1 value exceeding 99%, solving the model generalization problem [9] in small sample scenarios. The core advantage of deep learning lies in its end-to-end learning ability, which can directly mine hidden patterns from the original data and avoid the limitation [10] of artificial feature engineering.

### 1.3   Current Challenges and Future Directions

Despite its outstanding performance in fault detection, deep learning still faces multiple challenges. Data level: small sample fault data and noise interference lead to insufficient model robustness. For example, Qiao et al. (2024) needs to alleviate the detection deviation [11] of multiple distribution data through distribution adaptation (DAPCA) during sewage treatment. Model level: the lack of interpretability restricts the trust of industrial scenarios. Cuellar et al. (2024) verifies the importance of feature engineering to reduce the false positive rate [12]; the contradiction between real-time demand and calculation complexity is prominent, and the deployment efficiency [8] should be optimized through lightweight architecture (such as edge calculation). Future directions include: knowledge enhancement models (incorporating physical constraints and knowledge maps), multi-modal base models (joint text logs and sensor data), and federated learning to protect data privacy. This paper systematically reviews the technical evolution of deep learning in fault detection, aiming to provide theoretical reference for researchers and promote the establishment of a standardized evaluation framework.

## 2   Progress of Deep Learning Models in Fault Detection

### 2.1   Classical Deep Learning Model

Convolutional neural networks (CNNs) demonstrate excellent feature extraction capabilities in fault detection, particularly for high-dimensional signals like vibration, current, and image data, owing to their local perception and weight sharing mechanisms. Recent advancements include Ding et al. (2022), who proposed a self-supervised pre-training CNN based on contrastive learning, significantly improving diagnostic accuracy in bearing fault detection for small sample scenarios [13]. Thomas et al. (2023) introduced a hybrid CNN-Transformer model, using one-dimensional CNN to extract current waveform features and attention mechanisms for enhanced temporal correlation modeling, achieving 99.48% fault location accuracy in the IEEE 14-node distribution system [14]. These studies validate CNN's robustness and further optimize computational efficiency and generalization through strategies such as residual connectivity [15], adaptive thresholding [16], and transfer learning [17].

Recurrent neural networks (RNNs) and their variants, including long short-term memory (LSTM) and gated recurrent units (GRU), excel at modeling long-term dependencies in time-series signals. Haldian et al. (2022) developed a decoupled RNN architecture to reduce the "fuzzy effect" in multi-sensor fault scenarios, improving fault identification rates by 12% on petrochemical datasets [18]. Alcanafse et al. (2024) proposed an LSTM-GRU hybrid model integrating long-term dependencies in motor vibration and temperature signals, achieving 99.48% accuracy for ten-class fault classification on the MaFaulDa dataset [20]. These studies illustrate the effectiveness of RNN-based models in capturing progressive failure characteristics during equipment degradation.

Autoencoders (AEs) provide significant value in fault detection scenarios with scarce labeled data. Ding et al. (2022) combined variational autoencoders (VAEs) and support vector machines to enhance early fault detection sensitivity by 18% on the FEMTO-ST dataset [21]. Zhang et al. (2023) introduced a zero-shot learning framework based on sparse autoencoders to transfer known failure knowledge to unknown categories, achieving 85.7% accuracy on the Tennessee-Isman dataset [22]. Wang et al. (2020) applied denoising autoencoders (DAEs) to preprocess vibration signals, achieving 96.4% accuracy for rolling bearing fault classification in high-noise environments [23]. These findings underscore autoencoders' potential in overcoming labeled data limitations via unsupervised reconstruction loss and generative learning.

## 2.2  Deep Learning Model Architecture and Multimodal Fusion

Transformer-based models have significantly advanced fault detection through their ability to capture long-distance dependencies in sequence data. Yoon et al. (2024) developed a real-time fault detection method for power systems using a Transformer architecture, demonstrating strong performance in transient fault identification under noisy conditions [24]. Rai et al. (2022) combined Transformer with CNN for high-resistance fault detection, achieving robust classification results for arc and mechanical faults [25]. These studies illustrate Transformer's adaptability and effectiveness in complex industrial scenarios.

Graph neural networks (GNNs) have become powerful tools for fault detection, particularly in systems with inherent topological structures. Deng and Hooi (2021) introduced GNNs for anomaly detection in multivariate time series, modeling sensor networks as graphs to detect subtle deviations [26]. Jacob et al. (2021) employed graph convolutional networks (GCNs) for fault diagnosis in ship power systems, achieving accuracy exceeding 99% [27]. Wang et al. (2023) further enhanced GNN capabilities by introducing adaptive regressive sliding average filters for rocket engine fault diagnosis, dynamically adjusting adjacency matrices to capture changing sensor relationships [28]. These applications highlight GNNs' potential to exploit spatial relationships and dynamic system behavior effectively.

Hybrid models integrating CNN, LSTM, and attention mechanisms effectively address single-model limitations for multimodal and sequential data. Alsumaidaee et al. (2023) developed a hybrid 1D-CNN-LSTM model achieving 100% accuracy in classifying faults in medium voltage switchgear by combining temporal and spectral features [29]. Li et al. (2024) further improved fault detection capabilities by integrating attention mechanisms with 1D-CNN-LSTM models, effectively prioritizing key spectral features

[30]. These hybrid approaches leverage the complementary strengths of spatial feature extraction, temporal sequence modeling, and adaptive attention weighting, resulting in enhanced accuracy for fault detection tasks.

### 2.3  Small Sample Size and Transfer Learning

Data augmentation technologies significantly alleviate issues related to fault data imbalance and limited samples by generating synthetic data, enhancing model generalization. Alsaif et al. (2024) used multimodal large language models (LLM) based on generative pre-trained Transformers to synthesize fault scenarios, improving diagnostic accuracy [31]. Similarly, Liu et al. (2022) expanded bearing fault data using deep feature-enhanced generative adversarial networks (GANs), effectively balancing minority samples and enhancing robustness [32].

Pre-trained models extract transferable features from large-scale data, reducing reliance on annotated samples. Alsaif et al. (2024) demonstrated that fine-tuned LLM models effectively diagnose dynamic industrial scenarios with cross-domain capabilities [31]. Li et al. (2024) combined digital twinning with a pre-trained wavelet model, achieving high accuracy (96.39%) in bridging simulated and real-world fault distributions [31].

Meta-learning demonstrates notable advantages in few-shot fault diagnosis due to its rapid adaptability. Feng et al. (2022) developed a meta-learning framework using minimal samples to achieve high accuracy in bearing fault classification [34]. Hu et al. (2022) utilized a task-sequencing meta-learning method, enhancing fault diagnosis accuracy in mechanical systems by learning from simpler to more complex failure modes [35] (Table 1).

**Table 1.**  Performance comparison of the deep learning model in fault detection.

| model | Task scene | data set | Precision (%) | F1 score | Literature reference |
|---|---|---|---|---|---|
| Self-supervised pre-training of the CNN | Bearing early fault detection | CWRU | 98.2 | 0.97 | [13] |
| Mixed with CNN-Transformer | High resistance fault detection | IEEE 14 Node power distribution system | 99.48 | – | [14] |
| LSTM-GRU hybrid model | Motor composite fault classification | MaFaulDa | 99.48 | – | [20] |
| The denoising autoencoder | Rolling bearing fault classification | Rolling bearing dataset | 96.4 | – | [23] |
| Transformer-CNN | Grid transient fault detection | IEEE 14 Node | 99.5 | 0.99 | [25] |

(continued)

**Table 1.** (*continued*)

| model | Task scene | data set | Precision (%) | F1 score | Literature reference |
|---|---|---|---|---|---|
| GCN | Failure diagnosis of ship power system | Ship dataset | 99.0 | 0.98 | [27] |
| The 1D-CNN-LSTM hybrid model | Failure classification of the medium-voltage switchgear | Medium-voltage switchgear datasets | 100.0 | – | [29] |
| Meta-learning framework | Bearing cross-domain fault classification | Cross-domain bearings datasets | 95.3 | – | [34] |

## 3  Evaluation Metrics and Benchmark Datasets

In the field of prognostics and health management (PHM), benchmark datasets play a crucial role in evaluating the performance of various algorithms and models. One of the most widely used datasets in this domain is the Commercial Modular Aero-Propulsion System Simulation (C-MAPSS) dataset, developed by NASA. The C-MAPSS dataset simulates the operation of a turbofan engine and provides time-series data that includes sensor measurements, operational settings, and engine degradation over time. This dataset has been extensively used for remaining useful life (RUL) prediction, fault detection, and anomaly detection in aircraft engines [36, 37]. Another notable dataset is the ALFA dataset, which focuses on fault and anomaly detection in unmanned aerial vehicles (UAVs). The ALFA dataset includes real flight data with various fault scenarios, such as engine failures and control surface faults, making it a valuable resource for research in fault detection and isolation (FDI) and anomaly detection (AD) for autonomous aerial vehicles [38].

Evaluation metrics are essential for assessing the performance of models trained on these datasets. For RUL prediction tasks, common metrics include Mean Absolute Error (MAE), Root Mean Square Error (RMSE), and the RUL prediction score, which penalizes late predictions more heavily than early ones [36, 39]. In the context of anomaly detection, metrics such as precision, recall, F1-score, and the area under the receiver operating characteristic (ROC) curve are often used to evaluate the ability of a model to correctly identify anomalies while minimizing false positives [38, 40]. Additionally, for unsupervised anomaly detection methods, the use of log-likelihood ratios and density estimation techniques has been proposed to improve the detection accuracy, especially in unlabeled time-series data [41]. These metrics and datasets collectively provide a robust framework for comparing and advancing the state-of-the-art in PHM and related fields.

## 4  Challenges and Future Directions

### 4.1  Data-Level Challenges

The application of deep learning in fault detection is highly dependent on the quality and diversity of data, but the actual industrial scenarios often face the challenges of data noise, annotation uncertainty and multi-modal heterogeneous data fusion. First of all, the signal collected by the sensor is often disturbed by environmental noise (such as high frequency noise in vibration signal), leading to model misjudgment. For example, Wang et al. (2024) indicated that under variable conditions, noise labels will significantly reduce the robustness of the model, and the uncertainty perception mechanism should be introduced to distinguish the effective feature [42]. Second, the problem of small sample and data imbalance limits the generalization ability of the model, especially in rare failure scenarios. Zhang et al. (2022) proposed a small sample diagnosis method based on attention mechanism, but it relies on high-quality annotation data, and industrial sites often lack such resources [43]. In addition, the heterogeneity of multimodal data (e. g., image, sound, and vibration) increases the complexity of feature alignment and fusion. Zhao et al. (2023) improved the detection accuracy of fan blades through the decision-level and feature-level dual fusion strategy, but the cross-mode spatiotemporal correlation modeling still needs to be further optimized for [44].

## 4.2   Model-Level Challenges

The application of existing fault detection models in complex dynamic systems still faces the problems of insufficient generalization ability and poor interpretability. On the one hand, the multi-condition switching and non-linear dynamic characteristics of industrial equipment are difficult to adapt. For example, the aero-engine digital twin model developed by Huang et al. (2023) improves diagnostic accuracy through physical-data dual-mode fusion, but it relies on high-fidelity simulation data to limit its performance in unknown fault mode [45]. On the other hand, the black-box feature of the deep learning model hinders its landing in security-critical fields. Zhou et al. (2024) proposed an interpretable parallel CNN-LSTM architecture to enhance feature transparency through physical constraints, but the model complexity and computational overhead still need to balance [46]. In addition, although federated learning (FL) can solve the problem of data isolation, its heterogeneous data distribution and communication efficiency restrict its practical application. Wang et al. (2024) designed a dual-blockchain grouping federated learning framework, but the privacy protection and dynamic adaptability of model aggregation still need to improve [47].

## 4.3   System-Level Challenges

From the perspective of system integration, real-time, edge computing power and privacy security are the core challenges that restrict the implementation of fault detection technology. The limited computing resources of edge devices make it difficult to support the real-time inference of complex models. Lu et al. (2023) reviewed the application of IoT edge calculation in mechanical signal processing, and pointed out the necessity of lightweight model and compression algorithm, but the stability under dynamic load still needs to verify [48]. At the same time, the cross-domain sharing of industrial data involves the risk of sensitive information leakage. Liu et al. (2024) proposed a federated learning privacy protection scheme based on secure multi-party computing, but the compatibility between its computational efficiency and large-scale deployment still needs to be improved by [49]. In addition, the existing systems focus on a single device and lack the ability of cross-device collaboration and global health management. How to achieve factory-level fault transmission inference and resource scheduling is the key direction in the future.

## 4.4 Emerging Directions and Future Prospects

To meet the above challenges, digital twin (DT), multimodal large language model (MLLM) and physical information machine learning (PIML) have become important research directions. DT realizes fault simulation and prediction through virtual and real fusion. For example, Bo et al. (2024) builds a digital twin diagnosis system for diesel engine, and improves the fault recovery accuracy [50] combined with optimization algorithm. MLLM uses semantic understanding and generation capabilities to support the context association analysis of multimodal data. Alsaif et al. (2024) proposed a multimodal fault detection framework based on GPT-4 to solve the imbalance problem through synthetic data augmentation [51]. In addition, PIML enhances the robustness of the model by embedding physical equations. For example, Tao et al. (2023) developed the physical information temporal convolutional network (PITCN), which significantly improved the fault diagnosis accuracy of the underwater control system [52]. In the future, the interdisciplinary integration and adaptive learning mechanism will promote the evolution of fault detection to autonomy and intelligent.

# 5  Conclusion

Deep learning has rapidly advanced in fault detection, demonstrating notable break-throughs and promising applications. Architectures such as CNN, LSTM, Transformer, and GNN achieve high-precision detection and real-time diagnostics in industrial contexts through automatic feature extraction. Hybrid models like CNN-Transformer and GNN-LSTM integrate spatiotemporal features and attention mechanisms, enhancing adaptability to complex dynamic systems.

Small-sample and transfer learning techniques effectively mitigate data scarcity, while generative models (e.g., GANs and diffusion models) significantly enhance generalization. Knowledge-enhanced approaches have innovated fault detection; PINNs integrate domain equations for robust performance under limited data, and knowledge graphs (KG) leverage multimodal semantic relations to support causal reasoning and interpretability. Interpretability methods, such as attention visualization, further enhance model reliability and applicability.

Future development will involve foundational models (e.g., multimodal large language models) collaborating with digital twin (DT) technologies, advancing autonomy and intelligence in fault detection. Pre-trained foundational models reduce reliance on annotated data, while DT technologies enable closed-loop optimization of fault prediction and maintenance strategies. Moreover, federated learning combined with edge computing will enhance real-time inference at the edge, ensuring data privacy. The deep integration of deep learning with physical principles, domain semantics, and interdisciplinary collaboration will broaden prospects in industrial system health management. Future research should focus on standardized evaluation frameworks, bridging theory and application, and achieving comprehensive autonomous intelligent fault detection.

# References


1. Kini, K.R., Harrou, F., Madakyaru, M., Sun, Y.: Enhancing wind turbine performance: statistical detection of sensor faults based on improved dynamic independent component analysis. Energies **16**(15), 5793 (2023). https://doi.org/10.3390/en16155793

2. Chatti, N., Tidriri, K., Bera, T.K.: Dynamic bayesian network decision model for improving fault detection procedure. In: 2020 IEEE International Conference on Industrial Engineering and Engineering Management (IEEM), pp. 1006–1011. IEEE (2020). https://doi.org/10.1109/IEEM45057.2020.9309982

3. Du, K., Deng, X.: Nonlinear industrial fault detection method based on bayesian randomized principal component analysis. In: 2021 China Automation Congress (CAC), pp. 720–724. IEEE (2021). https://doi.org/10.1109/CAC53003.2021.9727725

4. Liu, X., Li, F.: Research on fault detection method based on improved euclidean distance control. In: 2022 IEEE 17th Conference on Industrial Electronics and Applications (ICIEA), pp. 106–111. IEEE (2022). https://doi.org/10.1109/ICIEA54703.2022.10006143

5. Feng, J., Li, K.Q.: MRS - kNN fault detection method for multirate sampling process based variable grouping threshold. J. Process Control **85**, 149–158 (2020). https://doi.org/10.1016/j.jprocont.2019.11.007

6. Qian, C., Wang, Y., Li, S.: A novel CVA fault detection method based on abnormal data elimination. In: 2022 China Automation Congress (CAC), pp. 2409–2414. IEEE (2022). https://doi.org/10.1109/CAC57257.2022.10056035

7. Lu, M., Feng, G., Huang, S., Liu, S., Xiang, L., Su, H.: Data - driven fault detection of power distribution network based on temporal convolutional network and long short - term memory. In: 2023 International Conference on Sensing, Measurement & Data Analytics in the era of Artificial Intelligence (ICSMD), pp. 1– 6. IEEE (2023). https://doi.org/10.1109/ICSMD60522.2023.10490605

8. Yang, D., Yang, W., Meng, D., Wang, S.: Enhanced CCA - based fault detection with deep neural networks in high - speed train traction systems. In: 2024 39th Youth Academic Annual Conference of Chinese Association of Automation (YAC), pp. 45–50. IEEE (2024). https://doi.org/10.1109/YAC63405.2024.10598564

9. Wang, Z., Qian, D., Xiao, Z., Zhang, X.: An anomaly detection method based on continuous wavelet transform and deep convolutional generative adversarial network that only requires normal sample training. In: 2024 8th International Conference on Electrical, Mechanical and Computer Engineering (ICEMCE), pp. 348–353. IEEE (2024). https://doi.org/10.1109/ICEMCE64157.2024.10862431

10. Guo, D., Yang, P., Zhu, L., He.: The intelligent fault identification method based on multi-source information fusion and deep learning. Sci. Reports **15**, 6643 (2025)

11. Qiao, J.F., Zhang, J.N., Li, W.J.: PCA - based sensor drift fault detection with distribution adaptation in wastewater treatment process. IEEE Trans. Autom. Sci. Eng. (2024). https://doi.org/10.1109/TASE.2024.3516710

12. Cuéllar, S., Santos, M., Alonso, F., Fabregas, E., Farias, G.: Explainable anomaly detection in spacecraft telemetry. Eng. Appl. Artif. Intell. **133**, 108083 (2024). https://doi.org/10.1016/j.engappai.2024.108083

13. Ding, Y.F., Zhuang, J.C., Ding, P., Jia, M.P.: Self-supervised pre-training through comparative learning for bearing intelligent early fault detection. Reliabil. Eng. Syst. Safety **218**, 108, 126 (2022)

14. Thomas, J.B., Chaudhari, S.G., Shihabudheen, K.V., Verma, N.K.: CNN-based transformer model for fault detection of power system network. IEEE Instrum. Measure. J. **72**, 2504, 210 (2023)

15. He, K.M., Zhang, X.Y., Ren, S.Q., Sun, J.: Deep residual learning for image recognition. In: Proceedings of the Conference on Computer Vision and Pattern Recognition, pp. 770–778 (2016)
16. Lu, F., Wang, Y., Huang, J.Q., Wang, H.Q.: Adaptive threshold method for fault detection in industrial process. The Institute of Mechanical Engineers is in G, vol. 228 (12), pp. 2007–2016 (2014)
17. Pan, S.J., Yang, Q.: Review of transfer learning. IEEE J. Knowl. Data Eng. **22**(10), 1345–1359 (2010)
18. Haldimann, D., Guerriero, M., Maret, Y., Bonavita, N., Ciarlo, G., Sabbadin, M.: A scalable algorithm for identifying multisensor failures using a decoupled RNN. IEEE Neural Networks Learn. Syst. J. **33**(3), 1093–1106 (2022)
19. Choi, J., Lee, S.J.: The integrated system based on RNN is used for real-time sensor fault detection and fault information-assisted accident diagnosis in nuclear power plant accidents. Nuclear Energy Eng. Technol. **55**(3), 814–826 (2023)
20. Alkhanafseh, Y., Akinci, T.C., Ayaz, E., Martinez-Morales, A.A.: Advanced dual RNN architecture for motor fault classification. IEEE Insert **12**, 2965–2976 (2014)
21. Ding, Y.F., Zhuang, J.C., Ding, P., Jia, M.P.: Self-supervised pre-training through comparative learning for bearing intelligent early fault detection. Reliabil. Eng. Syst. **218**, 108, 126 (2022)
22. Zhang, S.Y., Wei, H.L., Ding, J.L.: An effective zero-sample learning method for intelligent fault detection using a one-dimensional CNN. Appl. Intell. **53**(12), 16041–16058 (2023)
23. Wang, H.Q., Zhang, C.X., Li, X.D., Li, Y.H.: Fault diagnosis of the denoising autoenoder-based rolling bearing in noise environment. Comput. Indust. **105**, 182–192 (2019)
24. Yoon, D.-H., Yoon, J.: Development of a real-time fault detection method for electric power system via transformer-based deep learning model. Int. J. Electr. Power Energy Syst. **159**, 110069 (2024)
25. Rai, K., et al.: Deep learning for high-impedance fault detection and classification: transformer-CNN. Neural Comput. Appl. **34**(16), 14067–14084 (2022)
26. Deng, A., Hooi, B.: Graph neural network-based anomaly detection in multivariate time series. Proc. AAAI Conf. Artif. Intell. **35**(5), 4027–4035 (2021)
27. Jacob, R.A., et al.: Fault diagnostics in shipboard power systems using graph neural networks. In: 2021 IEEE 13th International Symposium on Diagnostics for Electrical Machines, Power Electronics and Drives (SDEMPED), pp. 316–321. IEEE (2021)
28. Wang, Z., et al.: Graph neural networks with adaptive convolutional ARMA filters for fault diagnosis in mechanical complex systems. In: 2023 Global Reliability and Prognostics and Health Management Conference (PHM-Hangzhou), pp. 1–6. IEEE (2023)
29. Alsumaidaee, Y.A.M., et al.: Fault detection for medium voltage switchgear using a deep learning hybrid 1D-CNN-LSTM model. IEEE Access **11**, 97574–97589 (2023)
30. Li, A., et al.: Fault detection of electrical equipment using attention based hybrid deep learning approach. In: 2024 International Conference on Data Science and Network Security (ICDSNS), pp. 1–4. IEEE (2024)
31. Alsaif, K.M. et al.: Multimodal large language model-based fault detection and diagnosis in context of Industry 4.0. Electronics **13**(24), 4912 (2024)
32. Liu, S., et al.: Data synthesis using deep feature enhanced generative adversarial networks for rolling bearing imbalanced fault diagnosis. Mech. Syst. Signal Process. **163**, 108139 (2022)
33. Li, S., et al.: Digital twin-assisted interpretable transfer learning for intelligent fault diagnostics. Adv. Eng. Inform. **62**, 102681 (2024)
34. Feng, Y. et al.: Meta-learning for few-shot cross-domain fault diagnosis. Knowl.-Based Syst. **235**, 107646 (2022)
35. Hu, Y., et al.: Task-sequencing meta-learning for intelligent few-shot fault diagnosis. IEEE Trans. Ind. Inform. **18**(6), 3894–3904 (2022)

36. Frederick, D.K., DeCastro, J.A., Litt, J.S.: User's guide for the commercial modular aero-propulsion system simulation (C-MAPSS). NASA (2007)
37. Liu, Y., Frederick, D.K., DeCastro, J.A., Litt, J.S., Chan, W.W.: User's guide for the commercial modular aero-propulsion system simulation (C-MAPSS): Version 2. NASA (2012)
38. Keipour, A., Mousaei, M., Scherer, S.: ALFA: a dataset for UAV fault and anomaly detection. Int. J. Robot. Res. **40**(2–3), 515–520 (2021). https://doi.org/10.1177/0278364920966642
39. Asif, O., Haider, S.A., Naqvi, S.R., Zaki, J.F.W., Kwak, K.-S., Islam, S.M.R.: A deep learning model for remaining useful life prediction of aircraft turbofan engine on C-MAPSS dataset. IEEE Access **10**, 95425–95440 (2022)
40. Yoshihara, K., Takahashi, K.: A simple method for unsupervised anomaly detection: an application to Web time series data. PLOS ONE **17**(1), e0262463 (2022). https://doi.org/10.1371/journal.pone.0262463
41. Vollert, S., Theissler, A.: Challenges of machine learning-based RUL prognosis: A review on NASA's C-MAPSS data set. In: 2021 26th IEEE International Conference on Emerging Technologies and Factory Automation (ETFA), pp. 1–8. IEEE (2021)
42. Wang, H., Li, C., Ding, P., et al.: A novel transformer-based few-shot learning method for intelligent fault diagnosis with noisy labels under varying working conditions. Reliab. Eng. Syst. Saf. **251**, 110400 (2024). https://doi.org/10.1016/j.ress.2024.110400
43. Zhang, X., He, C., Lu, Y., et al.: Fault diagnosis for small samples based on attention mechanism. Measurement **187**, 110242 (2022). https://doi.org/10.1016/j.measurement.2021.110242
44. Zhao, Y., Zhang, Y., Li, Z., et al.: AI-enabled and multimodal data driven smart health monitoring of wind power systems: a case study. Adv. Eng. Inform. **56**, 102018 (2023). https://doi.org/10.1016/j.aei.2023.102018
45. Huang, Y., Tao, J., Sun, G., et al.: A novel digital twin approach based on deep multimodal information fusion for aero-engine fault diagnosis. Energy **270**, 126894 (2023). https://doi.org/10.1016/j.energy.2023.126894
46. Zhou, Q., Tang, J.: An interpretable parallel spatial CNN-LSTM architecture for fault diagnosis in rotating machinery. IEEE Internet Things J. **11**(19), 31730–31744 (2024). https://doi.org/10.1109/JIOT.2024.3422969
47. Wang, X., Zhang, H., Wu, H., et al.: Dual-blockchain based multi-layer grouping federated learning scheme for heterogeneous data in industrial IoT. Blockchain Res. Appl. **5**(3), 100195 (2024). https://doi.org/10.1016/j.bcra.2024.100195
48. Lu, S., Lu, J., An, K., et al.: Edge computing on IoT for machine signal processing and fault diagnosis: a review. IEEE Internet Things J. **10**(13), 11093–11116 (2023). https://doi.org/10.1109/JIOT.2023.3239944
49. Liu, B., Blancaflor, E.B.: Research on federal learning privacy protection based on secure multi-party computing. In: Proceedings of 2024 3rd International Conference on Cyber Security, Artificial Intelligence and Digital Economy (CSAIDE), pp. 142–147 (2024). https://doi.org/10.1145/3672919.3672947
50. Bo, Y., Wu, H., Che, W., et al.: Methodology and application of digital twin-driven diesel engine fault diagnosis and virtual fault model acquisition. Eng. Appl. Artif. Intell. **131**, 107853 (2024). https://doi.org/10.1016/j.engappai.2024.107853
51. Alsaif, K.M., Albeshri, A.A., Khemakhem, M.A., et al.: Multimodal large language model-based fault detection and diagnosis in context of industry 4.0. Electronics **13**(24), 4912 (2024). https://doi.org/10.3390/electronics13244912
52. Tao, H., Jia, P., Wang, X., et al.: A digital twin-based fault diagnostic method for subsea control systems. Measurement **221**, 113461 (2023). https://doi.org/10.1016/j.measurement.2023.113461

# Community Detection Attack Based on Balanced Budget Allocation

Panmiao Xue[ID], Haipeng Yang[(✉)][ID], Fuwu Liu[ID], Zhi Chen[ID], Lili Zhou[ID], Xuanhao Su[ID], and Lei Zhang[ID]

School of Computer Science and Technology, Anhui University, Hefei 230039, China
{g12114007,e23301317,e22214072,e22214093,e22214021}@stu.ahu.edu.cn,
haipengyang@126.com, zl@ahu.edu.cn

**Abstract.** Community detection algorithms can reveal the underlying structure of networks and simplify network analysis. However, as these algorithms develop, concerns about the over-mining of individual information have arisen. To address this, the concept of Community Detection Attack (CDA) has been proposed to protect privacy by hiding community structures through minor rewiring of connections. However, most existing community detection attack algorithms select target nodes based on specific node characteristics. As many real-world networks exhibit power-law properties, this often leads to target nodes concentrating within certain communities, potentially limiting the diversity and scope of the attack. To this end, we propose a community detection attack algorithm based on balanced budget allocation (CDA-BBA), which distributes the attack budget across multiple key communities before selecting target nodes. This avoids concentrating the attack on just a few communities, making target nodes more dispersed and enhancing global attack effectiveness. Additionally, we suggest a new attack strategy to effectively alter the community structure. We evaluate the proposed CDA-BBA against five community detection algorithms on nine datasets by comparing it with six state-of-the-art methods. The experimental results show that the proposed algorithm CDA-BBA performs well in both attack effectiveness and time efficiency.

**Keywords:** Community detection attack · Heuristic algorithm · Privacy protection · Complex network · Community structure

## 1 Introduction

A network is a structure composed of numerous nodes and links, commonly found in various complex systems such as social systems [23] and transportation systems [1]. In a network, nodes represent individuals or entities, while links represent the relationships or interactions between them. Community detection [20]

This work was supported by the Natural Science Foundation of Anhui Province (No. 2408085MF152), and the Key Projects of the University Excellent Talents Support Plan of Anhui Provincial Department of Education (No. gxyqZD2021089).

is a fundamental task in network analysis, aiming to partition nodes into distinct communities. The detected communities should be densely connected internally and sparsely connected externally. However, as community detection advances, concerns over privacy leakage have emerged. As a result, community detection attack has been proposed to obscure community structure by minimally modifying the network. For example, Waniek [22] et al. proposed a heuristic solution, DICE (Disconnect Internally, Connect Externally), to conceal the target community from detection. Li et al. [13] generated adversarial networks by targeting the GNNs-based surrogate model to hide specific nodes. More recently, Mittal et al. [16] proposed NEURAL, which greedily optimizes a node-centric objective to guide rewiring. The above methods focus on hiding a specific community. In addition, there are attacks on the global structure. Chen et al. [4] proposed a genetic algorithm (GA)-based attack, Q-Attack, which optimized modularity for the attack. Liu et al. [14] employed a graph autoencoder to address community hiding by selecting modified edges from underfitting to overfitting in the network during the generation process. Recently, Zhao and Cheong [26] proposed a self-adaptive evolutionary deception (SAEP) framework to improve the stability of the algorithm. However, current CDA algorithms often select target nodes based on node characteristics such as degree [17] and betweenness [9]. Since the degree distribution of nodes typically follows a power-law distribution [2], in which a few nodes have a very high degree while most nodes have a low degree, the nodes targeted in such attacks tend to be concentrated in a small number of communities. Thus, the global attack effect is not ideal. To mitigate this issue, we propose a budget allocation strategy that distributes the budget across important communities, ensuring that the attack covers a broader scope and achieves better global attack effectiveness.

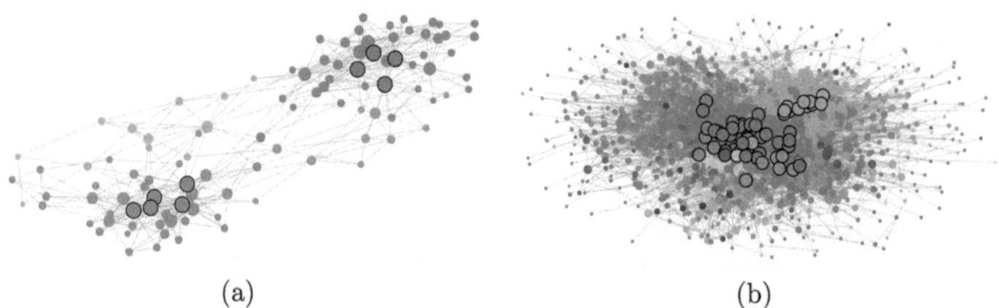

(a)        (b)

**Fig. 1.** An illustration of the target nodes selected by degree-based attack algorithm, highlighted with circles on the graphs. (a) Polbooks dataset partitioned by Louvain algorithm and (b) Email dataset partitioned by LPA algorithm.

Figure 1(a) and (b) show the target nodes selected by the degree-based attack algorithm for the Polbooks dataset [18] (with an attack budget of 2%) and the Email dataset [8] (with an attack budget of 1%) after being partitioned by the Louvain [3] and LPA [20] algorithms respectively. It can be observed that the selected target nodes are notably concentrated, and only a small number of communities are attacked. For example, in Fig. 1(b), the network is partitioned into 37 communities, but only 6 communities are targeted in the attack. As a result, most communities remain unchanged before and after the attack, leading to limited attack effectiveness.

To this end, we propose a community detection attack algorithm based on the suggested balanced budget allocation, named CDA-BBA. In this method, the attack budget is allocated to communities based on their importance. This ensures that the attack can cover more communities to achieve a better global attack effect, while also avoiding the waste of budget on unimportant communities that have a low degree. The main contributions of this work are summarized as follows.

- In consideration of the power-law distribution characteristic of networks, we propose a community detection attack algorithm based on the suggested balanced budget allocation, namely CDA-BBA. In this algorithm, the budget is first allocated and then the attack is carried out, which prevents over-concentration on specific communities and ensures broader coverage across more communities, thereby enhancing the effectiveness of global attacks.
- In the proposed CDA-BBA, a budget allocation strategy and an edge rewiring strategy based on similarity metrics are designed. The budget allocation strategy assigns the budget to the most important communities, while the rewiring strategy removes edges between target nodes and the nodes with the lowest similarity within the same community, and creates new edges between nodes with the highest similarity across different communities. Through this heuristic approach, effective attack performance can be achieved at a relatively fast speed, demonstrating significant practical value.
- We conduct experiments on nine real-world networks and evaluate the proposed algorithm against five community detection methods. The experimental results demonstrate that the algorithm performs effectively comparing to six state-of-the-art attack algorithms. Our algorithm not only achieves excellent results but also operates with a short runtime, making it highly valuable for real-world applications.

## 2  Problem Formulation

Let $G = (V, E)$ be the original network, where $V$ is the set of nodes and $E$ is the set of edges. After applying a community detection algorithm on $G$, we obtain the community structure $CS = \{C_1, C_2, \ldots, C_n\}$, satisfying $C_i \cap C_j = \emptyset$ for $i \neq j$, and $\bigcup_{i=1}^{n} C_i = V$. An attack strategy with a budget $T$, where $T = |E^+| = |E^-|$, generates a modified network $G' = (V, E')$ by performing edge additions $(E^+)$ and deletions $(E^-)$, such that:

$$E' = (E \cup E^+) \setminus E^-.$$

The adversarial network $G'$ is then partitioned into $CS' = \{C'_1, C'_2, \ldots, C'_m\}$ using the same community detection algorithm. The goal of the global community attack is to maximize the structural difference between the original network $G$ and the modified network $G'$.

To ensure minimal changes to the network structure, each added edge $e^+ \in E^+$ and deleted edge $e^- \in E^-$ must share a common node, referred to as the target attack node.

## 3   Proposed Algorithm CDA-BBA

### 3.1   Overall Procedure of CDA-BBA

Most existing heuristic methods select target nodes for rewiring based on characteristics, such as degree [17] or betweenness centrality [9]. However, in real-world networks, a few nodes often hold most connections, while the majority have sparse links. As a result, selected nodes tend to be concentrated in a few communities or repeatedly rewired, especially for high-degree nodes. This may leave many communities unchanged after the attack, thus reducing the efficiency of global attacks. To address this, we propose CDA-BBA, which allocates the budget across multiple important communities before selecting target nodes. This increases the number of affected communities, thereby improving the effectiveness of the attack.

The general framework of the proposed CDA-BBA is composed of the following four steps and is given in Algorithm 1. First, a community detection algorithm is applied to the original network $G$ to obtain the community structure $CS$ (Line 1). Next, the important community set $C_{imp}$ is identified from $CS$, and the total number of nodes in important communities $n_{imp}$ is calculated (Line 3). Then, each important community $C_i \in C_{imp}$ is assigned a budget $\beta_i$ based on the proposed budget allocation strategy (Line 5). After the budget allocation, attack operations are performed for each selected community. Before initiating the rewiring process, suitable target nodes need to be selected. Nodes in $C_i$ are sorted by degrees in descending order and the result is stored as $V_{sorted}$ (Line 7). In each iteration, the first node that has not been attacked in $V_{sorted}$ is selected as the target node. The next step involves initializing $P_{add}$, defined as:

$$P_{add} = V - \Gamma(v_k) - C_i, \tag{1}$$

where $\Gamma(v_k)$ represents the set of neighbors of the target node $v_k$. From $P_{add}$, the node $v_{add}$ with the highest similarity to $v_k$ is selected, and an edge is added between $v_k$ and $v_{add}$ (Lines 10–14). Similarly, $P_{del}$ is initialized, containing the neighbors of $v_k$ within the same community $C_i$. From $P_{del}$, the node $v_{del}$ with the lowest similarity to $v_k$ is selected, and the edge $e_d = (v_k, v_{del})$ is deleted (Lines 15–18). These steps are repeated until the budget allocated for each community is fully utilized.

---

**Algorithm 1.** The framework of CDA-BBA

---

**Input:** $G = (V, E)$: the original network;
   $T$: the attack budget;
**Output:** $G' = (V', E')$: the modified network;
1:  $CS \leftarrow \text{CommunityDetection}(G)$;
2:  $V' \leftarrow V; E' \leftarrow E$; // *Initialization of $V'$ and $E'$*
3:  $C_{imp}, n_{imp} \leftarrow \text{IdentifyImportantCommunities}(CS)$;
4: **for** each $C_i$ in $C_{imp}$ **do**
5:     $\beta_i \leftarrow \text{AllocateBudget}(C_i, n_{imp}, T)$;
6:     $count \leftarrow 0$;
7:     $V_{sorted} \leftarrow$ Sort nodes in $C_i$ in descending order by degree;
8:     **while** $count < \beta_i$ **do**
9:        $v_k \leftarrow V_{sorted}.\text{pop}()$;
10:      $\Gamma(v_k) \leftarrow$ Neighbors of $v_k$;
11:      $P_{add} \leftarrow V - \Gamma(v_k) - C_i$;
12:      Calculate similarity for each node in $P_{add}$ between it and $v_k$;
13:      $v_{add} \leftarrow \arg\max_{v_i \in P_{add}} \text{Similarity}(v_k, v_i)$;
14:      $e_c \leftarrow (v_{add}, v_k)$; // *The created edge*
15:      $P_{del} \leftarrow \Gamma(v_k) \cap C_i$;
16:      Calculate similarity for each node in $P_{del}$ between it and $v_k$;
17:      $v_{del} \leftarrow \arg\min_{v_j \in P_{del}} \text{Similarity}(v_k, v_j)$;
18:      $e_d \leftarrow (v_{del}, v_k)$; // *The deleted edge*
19:      $E' \leftarrow E' \cup \{e_c\} - \{e_d\}$; // *Update the edge set*
20:      $G' \leftarrow (V', E')$; // *Update the modified network*
21:      $count \leftarrow count + 1$;
22:     **end while**
23: **end for**

---

## 3.2  Budget Allocation

To ensure the budget is effectively utilized without unnecessary waste, the budget is allocated to important communities, defined as those whose average degree exceeds the average degree of the network. This section details the process, beginning with the identification of key communities, followed by the budget allocation strategy.

**Determine Important Communities.** Community average degree, defined as the average degree of all nodes within a community, reflects its connectivity and influence in the network. Leveraging this, we design a strategy to identify important communities.

We first calculate the average degree of the entire network, as it serves as a baseline for overall connectivity. Then, for each community, we calculate its average degree and compare it with the network's average degree. If the former is greater, the community is added to the set of important communities, and the total number of nodes in the important communities (i.e., $n_{imp}$) is updated. A higher average degree reflects stronger interaction within the network and often corresponds to core regions that play a critical role in shaping network structure. Therefore, targeting such communities can more effectively obscure the true structure of the network.

**Allocate Budget.** After determining which communities should receive the allocated budget, the next step is to decide how the budget should be distributed among them. Here, we adopt a simple yet highly effective approach: proportionally allocating the budget according to each important community's share of nodes. Specifically, the budget for each community is calculated using the following formula:

$$\beta_i = \frac{T \cdot |C_i|}{n_{imp}}, \tag{2}$$

where $T$ represents the total budget, $|C_i|$ is the number of nodes in community $C_i$, and $n_{imp}$ denotes the total number of nodes in all important communities.

This proportional allocation method effectively reflects the scale of each community by ensuring that larger communities receive greater budget support, while smaller communities are allocated an appropriate share. Furthermore, the simplicity of this method makes it straightforward to implement, as it only requires calculating the number of nodes in each community and its proportion. This computational efficiency makes the method particularly suitable for large-scale networks, where minimizing computational overhead is essential. By adopting this approach, we ensure broad coverage of important communities and efficient use of limited budget, thereby maximizing attack effectiveness and significantly disrupting the network structure.

### 3.3 Attack Strategies

After identifying key communities and allocating the budget, selecting target nodes and determining how to rewire them remain a challenge. Node degree is crucial in a network, as high-degree nodes typically connect to more nodes and occupy central positions. Rewiring these nodes can significantly impact community structure. Therefore, we select the highest-degree nodes within each selected community as the target nodes. Next, we will separately introduce the strategies for edge addition and deletion.

**Adding An Edge Between Different Communities.** First, we initialize the $P_{add}$, which stores the candidate nodes for edge addition. Following the CDA approach proposed in [4], we select edges for addition from the intercommunity non-neighbors and set edges for deletion from the intracommunity neighbor set. Therefore, the $P_{add}$ is initialized according to Eq. (1).

Consider two influential individuals in a social network who share similar interests, mutual friends, and other traits but are not yet connected. Linking them is more likely to bring their social groups closer, potentially even merging

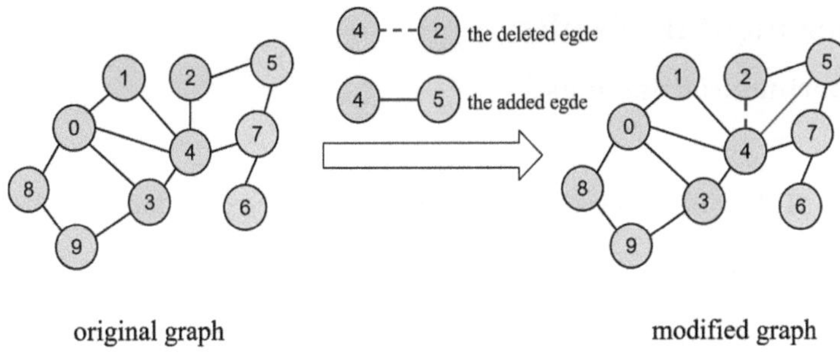


**Fig. 2.** An example of rewiring edges. Different communities are distinguished by different colors. The red dashed line represents the deleted edge, and the red solid line represents the added edge. (Color figure online)

the two groups into one. In contrast, connecting an influential individual with someone dissimilar is less likely to result in community integration and affects fewer nodes. Following this idea, we use node similarity to guide edge rewiring and adopt cosine similarity due to its efficiency and widespread use. We will select the node in $P_{add}$ that has the highest similarity to the target node and create an edge between them. As mentioned above, this is more likely to integrate the two nodes into the same community, effectively blurring the community structure.

**Deleting An Edge Within The Same Community.** For edge deletion, we use the same similarity metric, namely cosine similarity. We initialize the $P_{del}$ for $v_k$ as follows:

$$P_{del} = \Gamma(v_k) \cap C_k. \tag{3}$$

where $\Gamma(v_k)$ represents the neighbors of node $v_k$, and $C_k$ denotes the community to which $v_k$ belongs. We then select the node in $P_{del}$ with the lowest similarity to the target node and remove the edge between them. As a result, the node discarded by the influential target node is likely to lose its original affiliation and be reassigned to another community.

Figure 2 illustrates the process using node 4 as the target node. Clearly, the neighbors of node 4 are nodes 0, 1, 2, 3, and 7, and nodes 0,1,2,3 belong to the same community as node 4. Therefore, the $P_{add}$ is initialized as {5, 6, 8, 9}. The cosine similarity between node 4 and each node in the $P_{add}$ is computed, resulting in values of 0.6325, 0.4472, 0.3162, and 0.3162, respectively. Thus, Node 5, having the highest similarity, is selected and connected to node 4. Similarly, according to Eq. (3), the $P_{del}$ is {0, 1, 2, 3}. After calculating the similarities, the node with the lowest similarity to node 4 is node 2, so the edge between node 4 and node 2 is removed, resulting in the modified graph. It can be observed that in the modified graph, after severing the connection between node 4 and node 2, the only remaining neighbor of node 2 is node 5. Therefore, node 2 is likely to be assigned to the green-marked community, thus effectively hiding node 2.

# 4    Experimental Results

## 4.1    Experimental Settings

**Table 1.** Details of the networks used in the experiments

| Datasets | #Nodes | #Edges | AD | CC | $D_{max}$ | Budget |
|---|---|---|---|---|---|---|
| Karate | 34 | 78 | 4.59 | 0.57 | 16 | 4 (5%) |
| Dolphin | 62 | 159 | 5.13 | 0.26 | 17 | 8 (5%) |
| Polbooks | 105 | 441 | 8.4 | 0.49 | 25 | 9 (2%) |
| Football | 115 | 613 | 10.66 | 0.4 | 12 | 12 (2%) |
| Email | 1,133 | 5,451 | 4.81 | 0.22 | 71 | 55 (1%) |
| Web-Edu | 3,031 | 6,474 | 4 | 0.56 | 104 | 65 (1%) |
| Ca-GrQc | 5,242 | 14,496 | 5.53 | 0.53 | 81 | 145 (1%) |
| Ca-HepPh | 12,008 | 118,521 | 19.74 | 0.61 | 491 | 1,185 (1%) |
| Ca-AstroPh | 18,772 | 198,080 | 21.1 | 0.63 | 504 | 990 (0.5%) |

**Comparison Algorithms.** The performance of CDA-BBA is evaluated against six state-of-the-art CDA algorithms. In [4], three distinct heuristic algorithms are introduced, namely RA, CDA, and DBA. A betweenness-based variant of RA, denoted as $A_B$, is proposed in [5] by incorporating betweenness centrality and node distance. Furthermore, a local structure-based heuristic approach (LSHA) is presented in [24]. Beyond these heuristics, an evolutionary algorithm named Q-Attack is proposed in [4], which uses modularity as the fitness function. In our experiments, Q-Attack adopts the parameter settings recommended in [4]. All experiments are implemented in Python and conducted on PCs with Intel i5 processors running Windows 11.

**Experimental Networks.** In the experiments, we utilize nine real-world networks: Zachary's Karate Club network (Karate) [25], Bottlenose dolphins network (Dolphin) [15], American College Football network (Football) [18], American political books network (Polbooks) [18], Email network (Email) [8], Web-Education network (Web-Edu) [10], the Collaboration network of Arxiv General Relativity (Ca-GrQc) [12], the Collaboration network of Arxiv High Energy Physics (Ca-HepPh) [12], and the Collaboration network of Arxiv Astro Physics (Ca-AstroPh) [12]. The details of these networks are shown in Table 1. "AD" denotes the average degree, "CC" is the average clustering coefficient, and "$D_{max}$" represents the maximum degree among all nodes in the network, reflecting the network's sparse connections and power-law characteristic. "Budget" refers to the budget settings in the experiments, where a fixed budget is applied. For example, in the Karate network, the budget is 5% of the edges, or four edges.

**Evaluation Metrics.** We employ five well-known community detection algorithms as targets for the attack: Louvain [3], Infomap [21], LPA [20], Walktrap [19], and Fastgreedy [6].

To demonstrate the performance of the proposed CDA-BBA, we adopt two widely used metrics: normalized mutual information (NMI) [7] and adjusted rand index (ARI) [11]. These metrics evaluate the similarity between two sets of community partitions. The higher the value of these two metrics, the more similar the two community partitions are. Therefore, a lower value of NMI or ARI means greater effectiveness of the attack. Given the inherent randomness of the community detection algorithms, in the evaluation of the modified networks, the detection algorithms are run ten times independently and the average values of NMI and ARI are recorded to measure the effectiveness of the attacked network more accurately.

## 4.2   Experimental Results

**Results on Different Networks.** To evaluate the performance of the proposed CDA-BBA, comparisons were conducted on nine networks, targeting five community detection algorithms. The attack costs are fixed and defined as a specific proportion of the total number of edges in the network. The detailed budget settings are provided in Table 1. To reduce the impact of randomness, the entire attack process was executed 20 times, and the average results of these 20 runs are presented in Table 2.

As shown in Table 2, the proposed CDA-BBA generally achieves optimal or near-optimal results in most cases and consistently ranks first overall on average. RA performs poorly due to its randomness and lack of network information. In contrast, the baseline algorithms CDA, DBA, and $A_B$ perform moderately better as they rely on community structures obtained from community detection algorithms. GA-based Q-Attack performs well by optimizing the fitness function through modularity, which effectively identifies critical edges. However, this iterative evaluation process leads to its high computational cost, especially for large networks like Web-Edu, Ca-GrQc, Ca-HepPh, and Ca-AstroPh, where Q-Attack fails to provide results within 15 h for a single run. LSHA ranks second on average in most cases due to its reliance on local structures. By identifying edges for removal based on their vulnerability and selecting edges to add based on entropy increase, LSHA employs effective attack strategies. However, the computational overhead from detecting local structures, post-attack adjustments, and entropy calculations prevents LSHA from producing results within 15 h on large networks like Ca-HepPh and Ca-AstroPh. The superior performance of the proposed CDA-BBA can be attributed to an efficient budget allocation strategy that prioritizes significant communities, allowing broader participation in the attack process while minimizing budget waste. Additionally, the proposed rewiring strategy can disrupt the global network structure to a greater extent.

**Time Consumption on Different Networks.** The average time consumed by the baseline methods and CDA-BBA is presented in Fig. 3. For a fair comparison,

**Table 2.** Comparison results of NMI and ARI for various community detection attack algorithms. The best performance in each experiment is highlighted in bold. "~" indicates that a single run exceeded 15 h and is thus ranked last (i.e., 7th).

| Detection Algorithm | Attack | Evaluations | Karate | Dolphin | Polbooks | Football | Email | Web-Edu | Ca-GrQc | Ca-HepPh | Ca-AstroPh | Avg-rank |
|---|---|---|---|---|---|---|---|---|---|---|---|---|
| Louvain | RA | NMI | 0.8263(5) | 0.7747(6) | 0.8736(6) | 0.9602(6) | 0.6772(4) | 0.9706(2) | 0.9605(6) | 0.9414(5) | **0.6304(1)** | 4.5556 |
| | | ARI | 0.7544(6) | 0.7357(6) | 0.8628(5) | 0.8915(6) | 0.5989(3) | 0.8512(3) | 0.6711(6) | 0.5254(5) | 0.4062(2) | 4.6667 |
| | CDA | NMI | 0.8294(6) | 0.7679(5) | 0.8856(7) | 0.9551(4) | 0.6827(6) | 0.9732(4) | 0.8558(2) | **0.6531(1)** | 0.6360(3) | 4.2222 |
| | | ARI | 0.7539(5) | 0.7263(5) | 0.8673(7) | 0.8868(4) | 0.6115(6) | 0.8722(5) | 0.5741(3) | 0.3903(3) | 0.4250(4) | 4.6667 |
| | DBA | NMI | 0.7902(4) | 0.7241(3) | 0.8291(3) | 0.9508(3) | 0.6791(5) | 0.9757(5) | **0.8489(1)** | 0.6864(4) | 0.6482(5) | 3.6667 |
| | | ARI | 0.7085(4) | 0.6576(3) | 0.7975(2) | 0.8652(3) | 0.5991(4) | 0.8717(4) | 0.5802(4) | 0.4123(4) | 0.4220(3) | 3.4444 |
| | Q-Attack | NMI | 0.7452(3) | 0.7919(7) | 0.8703(5) | 0.9582(5) | 0.6895(7) | ~(7) | ~(7) | ~(7) | ~(7) | 6.1111 |
| | | ARI | 0.6622(2) | 0.7481(7) | 0.8665(6) | 0.8907(5) | 0.6168(7) | ~(7) | ~(7) | ~(7) | ~(7) | 6.1111 |
| | LSHA | NMI | 0.7436(2) | **0.6419(1)** | 0.8201(2) | 0.9289(2) | 0.6598(2) | 0.9839(6) | 0.8630(5) | ~(7) | ~(7) | 3.7778 |
| | | ARI | 0.6820(3) | 0.5753(2) | 0.8309(4) | 0.8423(2) | 0.5925(2) | 0.8895(6) | 0.6034(5) | ~(7) | ~(7) | 4.2222 |
| | $A_B$ | NMI | 0.8694(7) | 0.7415(4) | 0.8498(4) | 0.9762(7) | 0.6714(3) | **0.9577(1)** | 0.8609(3) | 0.6692(3) | 0.6407(4) | 4.0000 |
| | | ARI | 0.8148(7) | 0.7034(4) | 0.8239(3) | 0.9362(7) | 0.6100(5) | **0.8106(1)** | 0.5693(2) | 0.3642(2) | 0.4258(5) | 4.0000 |
| | CDA-BBA | NMI | **0.6886(1)** | 0.6736(2) | **0.7660(1)** | **0.9237(1)** | **0.6585(1)** | 0.9718(3) | 0.8623(4) | 0.6555(2) | 0.6347(2) | **1.8889** |
| | | ARI | **0.5775(1)** | **0.5750(1)** | **0.7105(1)** | **0.8042(1)** | **0.5695(1)** | 0.8373(2) | **0.5671(1)** | **0.3616(1)** | **0.4029(1)** | **1.1111** |
| Infomap | RA | NMI | 0.8439(6) | 0.8397(7) | 0.9626(6) | 0.9994(4) | 0.8972(6) | 0.9917(4) | **0.9579(1)** | **0.9490(1)** | 0.9500(3) | 4.2222 |
| | | ARI | 0.8121(5) | 0.7827(7) | 0.9535(6) | 0.9990(4) | 0.8276(6) | 0.9834(3) | **0.6187(1)** | **0.5570(1)** | 0.7990(2) | 3.8889 |
| | CDA | NMI | 0.8286(5) | 0.8039(6) | 0.9466(5) | 0.9994(4) | 0.8949(5) | 0.9919(5) | 0.9768(5) | 0.9594(3) | 0.9489(2) | 4.4444 |
| | | ARI | 0.8186(6) | 0.7282(6) | 0.9396(4) | 0.9991(5) | 0.8220(5) | 0.9836(4) | 0.8828(5) | 0.8759(4) | 0.8004(3) | 4.6667 |
| | DBA | NMI | 0.6772(4) | 0.7696(4) | 0.9154(3) | 0.9977(3) | 0.8799(3) | 0.9897(3) | 0.9741(4) | 0.9747(5) | 0.9560(5) | 3.7778 |
| | | ARI | 0.5783(3) | 0.6788(4) | 0.9148(3) | 0.9964(3) | 0.8097(3) | 0.9857(6) | 0.8676(3) | 0.8960(5) | 0.8125(4) | 4.7778 |
| | Q-Attack | NMI | **0.3214(1)** | 0.7210(2) | 0.9464(4) | 0.9933(2) | ~(7) | ~(7) | ~(7) | ~(7) | ~(7) | 4.8889 |
| | | ARI | **0.3098(1)** | 0.5894(2) | 0.9453(5) | 0.9882(2) | ~(7) | ~(7) | ~(7) | ~(7) | ~(7) | 5.0000 |
| | LSHA | NMI | 0.6188(2) | 0.7245(3) | 0.8833(2) | **0.9776(1)** | 0.8735(2) | **0.9725(1)** | 0.9734(3) | ~(7) | ~(7) | 3.1111 |
| | | ARI | 0.5235(2) | 0.6449(3) | 0.8886(2) | **0.9644(1)** | 0.8004(2) | **0.9639(1)** | 0.8774(4) | ~(7) | ~(7) | 3.2222 |
| | $A_B$ | NMI | 0.9102(7) | 0.7916(5) | 1.0000(7) | 1.0000(6) | 0.8946(4) | 0.9920(6) | 0.9832(6) | 0.9694(4) | 0.9531(4) | 5.4444 |
| | | ARI | 0.9390(7) | 0.7109(5) | 1.0000(7) | 1.0000(6) | 0.8145(4) | 0.9840(5) | 0.9082(6) | 0.8552(3) | 0.8204(5) | 5.3333 |
| | CDA-BBA | NMI | 0.6320(3) | **0.5739(1)** | **0.7952(1)** | 1.0000(6) | **0.8664(1)** | 0.9878(2) | 0.9703(2) | 0.9569(2) | **0.9388(1)** | **2.1111** |
| | | ARI | 0.5902(4) | **0.3253(1)** | **0.7489(1)** | 1.0000(6) | **0.7564(1)** | 0.9760(2) | 0.8180(2) | 0.7245(2) | **0.7262(1)** | **2.2222** |
| LPA | RA | NMI | 0.5685(6) | 0.6237(5) | 0.7983(5) | 0.8417(3) | 0.4851(5) | **0.9508(1)** | 0.9610(6) | 0.9238(5) | 0.8981(5) | 4.5556 |
| | | ARI | 0.5522(6) | 0.4901(5) | 0.7897(6) | 0.8418(5) | 0.2879(7) | 0.8637(2) | 0.6681(6) | **0.4813(1)** | 0.8720(5) | 4.7778 |
| | CDA | NMI | 0.5433(5) | 0.6214(4) | 0.7933(4) | 0.8958(6) | 0.4534(4) | 0.9516(2) | 0.9257(4) | 0.8432(3) | **0.8423(1)** | 3.6667 |
| | | ARI | 0.4813(5) | 0.4772(3) | 0.7681(3) | 0.8953(7) | 0.2420(2) | **0.8604(1)** | 0.5668(3) | 0.6411(4) | **0.6793(1)** | 3.2222 |
| | DBA | NMI | 0.4760(2) | 0.6388(7) | 0.7645(2) | 0.8619(4) | 0.4876(7) | 0.9645(5) | 0.9275(5) | 0.8390(2) | 0.8873(4) | 4.2222 |
| | | ARI | 0.3869(2) | 0.4836(4) | **0.7338(1)** | 0.8624(6) | 0.2616(4) | 0.8941(5) | 0.5542(2) | 0.5796(3) | 0.8239(4) | 3.4444 |
| | Q-Attack | NMI | 0.4887(3) | 0.5895(3) | 0.7989(6) | 0.9038(7) | **0.2523(1)** | ~(7) | ~(7) | ~(7) | ~(7) | 5.3333 |
| | | ARI | 0.4593(3) | 0.5194(7) | 0.8085(7) | 0.7442(3) | **0.1516(1)** | ~(7) | ~(7) | ~(7) | ~(7) | 5.4444 |
| | LSHA | NMI | 0.5198(4) | **0.5209(1)** | 0.7665(3) | 0.8926(5) | 0.3348(2) | 0.9696(6) | **0.8578(1)** | ~(7) | ~(7) | 4.0000 |
| | | ARI | 0.4692(4) | 0.4332(2) | 0.7819(4) | 0.7451(4) | 0.2525(3) | 0.8853(3) | 0.5878(5) | ~(7) | ~(7) | 4.3333 |
| | $A_B$ | NMI | 0.6092(7) | 0.6370(6) | 0.8024(7) | 0.7684(2) | 0.4212(3) | 0.9569(3) | 0.9239(3) | 0.8502(4) | 0.8429(2) | 4.1111 |
| | | ARI | 0.5722(7) | 0.4955(6) | 0.7820(5) | 0.5043(2) | 0.2666(5) | 0.8924(4) | 0.5737(4) | 0.6676(5) | 0.7174(2) | 4.4444 |
| | CDA-BBA | NMI | **0.4742(1)** | 0.5684(2) | **0.7420(1)** | **0.7595(1)** | 0.4851(5) | 0.9641(4) | 0.9211(2) | **0.8300(1)** | 0.8620(3) | **2.2222** |
| | | ARI | **0.3470(1)** | **0.4087(1)** | 0.7363(2) | **0.4866(1)** | 0.2697(6) | 0.8973(6) | **0.5282(1)** | 0.5324(2) | 0.7800(3) | **2.5556** |
| Walktrap | RA | NMI | 0.7277(5) | 0.6435(4) | 0.9118(7) | 0.9791(6) | 0.8544(3) | 0.9917(4) | 0.9612(4) | 0.9336(4) | 0.8945(3) | 4.4444 |
| | | ARI | 0.5831(4) | 0.4694(4) | 0.9183(6) | 0.9402(6) | 0.7477(3) | 0.9818(6) | 0.6702(4) | 0.4984(3) | **0.4270(1)** | 4.1111 |
| | CDA | NMI | 0.6855(3) | 0.6270(3) | 0.9060(6) | 0.9790(5) | 0.8683(6) | 0.9917(4) | 0.9647(5) | 0.9063(2) | 0.9218(4) | 4.2222 |
| | | ARI | 0.5543(3) | 0.4698(5) | 0.9199(7) | 0.9373(5) | 0.8010(5) | 0.9816(5) | 0.7580(6) | **0.4130(1)** | 0.5462(3) | 4.4444 |
| | DBA | NMI | 0.7197(4) | 0.6789(6) | 0.8765(4) | 0.9538(3) | 0.9016(7) | 0.9940(6) | 0.9719(6) | 0.9505(5) | 0.9382(5) | 5.1111 |
| | | ARI | 0.6037(5) | 0.5173(7) | 0.8541(3) | 0.8653(3) | 0.8128(6) | 0.9768(4) | 0.6563(3) | 0.5583(4) | 0.6114(4) | 4.3333 |
| | Q-Attack | NMI | **0.6111(1)** | 0.7849(7) | **0.6557(1)** | **0.9027(1)** | 0.8602(4) | ~(7) | ~(7) | ~(7) | ~(7) | 4.6667 |
| | | ARI | **0.2563(1)** | 0.4202(3) | **0.6165(1)** | **0.7574(1)** | **0.5911(1)** | ~(7) | ~(7) | ~(7) | ~(7) | 3.8889 |
| | LSHA | NMI | 0.6447(2) | **0.5569(1)** | 0.8630(3) | 0.9630(4) | **0.8228(1)** | **0.9704(1)** | 0.9582(2) | ~(7) | ~(7) | 3.1111 |
| | | ARI | 0.5058(2) | 0.3951(2) | 0.8970(5) | 0.9077(4) | 0.7661(4) | **0.9432(1)** | 0.6790(5) | ~(7) | ~(7) | 4.1111 |
| | $A_B$ | NMI | 0.8700(7) | 0.6582(5) | 0.8765(4) | 1.0000(7) | 0.8682(5) | 0.9849(2) | 0.9609(3) | **0.8502(1)** | **0.8429(1)** | 3.8889 |
| | | ARI | 0.8253(7) | 0.4945(6) | 0.8541(3) | 1.0000(7) | 0.8225(7) | 0.9493(2) | 0.6520(2) | 0.6676(5) | 0.7174(5) | 4.8889 |
| | CDA-BBA | NMI | 0.7410(6) | 0.5626(2) | 0.7374(2) | 0.9376(2) | 0.8283(2) | 0.9887(3) | **0.9567(1)** | 0.9307(3) | 0.8918(2) | **2.5556** |
| | | ARI | 0.6097(6) | **0.3186(1)** | 0.7614(2) | 0.8337(2) | 0.6217(2) | 0.9638(3) | **0.6045(1)** | 0.4548(2) | 0.4534(2) | **2.3333** |
| Fastgreedy | RA | NMI | 0.6837(7) | 0.7281(7) | 0.8918(5) | 0.8512(7) | 0.5850(5) | 0.9861(4) | 0.9597(6) | 0.9371(5) | 0.6525(3) | 5.4444 |
| | | ARI | 0.6032(6) | 0.6825(6) | 0.8894(5) | 0.7600(7) | 0.5440(5) | 0.9572(5) | 0.6647(6) | 0.6091(4) | 0.5753(3) | 5.2222 |
| | CDA | NMI | 0.6380(3) | 0.6606(3) | 0.9377(6) | 0.8154(5) | 0.6179(7) | 0.9858(3) | 0.7947(3) | 0.6373(2) | **0.5807(1)** | 3.6667 |
| | | ARI | 0.5964(5) | 0.6031(5) | 0.9627(6) | 0.7312(5) | 0.5851(7) | 0.9551(4) | 0.4149(2) | 0.4281(3) | **0.4242(1)** | 4.2222 |
| | DBA | NMI | 0.6417(4) | 0.6750(4) | 0.8690(4) | 0.8009(4) | 0.5854(6) | 0.9805(2) | 0.8276(4) | 0.8007(4) | 0.9462(5) | 4.1111 |
| | | ARI | 0.5616(4) | 0.6015(4) | 0.8818(4) | 0.6747(4) | 0.5600(6) | 0.8778(2) | 0.4957(4) | 0.6684(5) | 0.6366(4) | 4.1111 |
| | Q-Attack | NMI | **0.4493(1)** | **0.4296(1)** | **0.5244(1)** | **0.6594(1)** | **0.2771(1)** | ~(7) | ~(7) | ~(7) | ~(7) | 3.6667 |
| | | ARI | 0.4644(2) | **0.3246(1)** | **0.5044(1)** | 0.6437(3) | **0.1690(1)** | ~(7) | ~(7) | ~(7) | ~(7) | 4.0000 |
| | LSHA | NMI | 0.6454(5) | 0.4650(2) | 0.6982(2) | 0.6989(3) | 0.4167(2) | 0.9867(6) | 0.8598(5) | ~(7) | ~(7) | 4.3333 |
| | | ARI | 0.5199(3) | 0.3485(2) | 0.6963(2) | 0.5181(2) | 0.3090(2) | **0.8743(1)** | 0.5898(5) | ~(7) | ~(7) | 3.4444 |
| | $A_B$ | NMI | 0.6577(6) | 0.6869(6) | 1.0000(7) | 0.8334(6) | 0.5449(4) | **0.9738(1)** | 0.7921(2) | **0.5397(1)** | 0.7949(4) | 4.1111 |
| | | ARI | 0.7112(7) | 0.7098(7) | 1.0000(7) | 0.7512(6) | 0.4556(4) | 0.9228(3) | 0.4162(3) | **0.2135(1)** | 0.8354(5) | 4.7778 |
| | CDA-BBA | NMI | 0.4850(2) | 0.6804(5) | 0.7425(3) | 0.6761(2) | 0.4504(3) | 0.9866(5) | **0.7770(1)** | 0.6775(3) | 0.6200(2) | **2.8889** |
| | | ARI | **0.3950(1)** | 0.5775(3) | 0.7713(3) | **0.4645(1)** | 0.3816(3) | 0.9760(6) | **0.3626(1)** | 0.4088(2) | 0.4984(2) | **2.4444** |

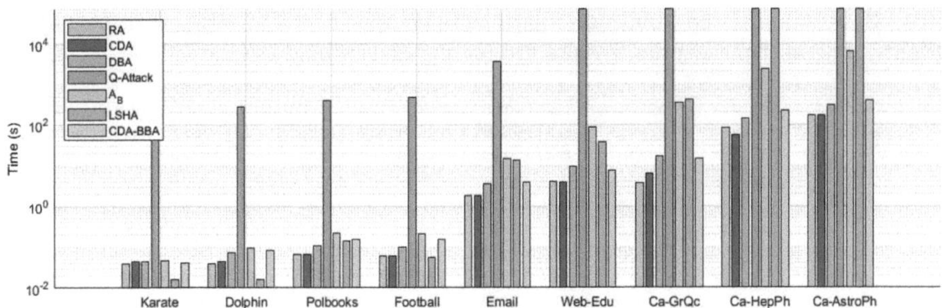

**Fig. 3.** Average time consumption of the baselines and CDA-BBA in one run. Note that experiments that failed to produce results within 15 h are plotted as 15 h.

the average time is calculated across all experiments involving five community detection algorithms.

As shown in Fig. 3, the time consumption of the GA-based Q-Attack is the highest, mainly due to repeated evaluations during optimization process. When the network scale increases, Q-Attack struggles to obtain results within an acceptable time. Similarly, LSHA also exhibits significant time consumption as the network size grows. For small networks such as Karate and Dolphin, LSHA consumes very little time, likely because identifying local structures on small networks is relatively straightforward. However, as the dataset size increases, LSHA's time consumption rises substantially and even approaches that of Q-Attack, highlighting its limitations in large-scale networks. In small networks, the time consumption of $A_B$ is similar to other heuristic algorithms. Yet, the computation time grows significantly with the increase in network size. This is probably due to the fact that it uses betweenness centrality and node distance to select edges for rewiring, both of which are complex to compute. In contrast, the other four heuristic attack methods, namely RA, CDA, DBA and CDA-BBA, maintain consistently low time consumption. By utilizing computationally lightweight cosine similarity and avoiding iterative optimization, CDA-BBA demonstrates high effectiveness in attacking community structures in large-scale networks during the experiments.

**Ablation Experiment.** To verify the effectiveness of the proposed strategy, we conducted an ablation experiment and the experimental results are shown in Table 3. Here, "w/o allocation" refers to the case where no budget allocation was performed, and nodes were selected based on their degree; "w/o attack strategy" means that we did not use the proposed similarity-based attack strategy, but instead randomly selected edges between communities for addition and edges within communities for deletion. As can be seen, CDA-BBA achieves the best results in most cases, which demonstrates the effectiveness of our budget allocation and the proposed heuristic attack strategy.

**Table 3.** Results of the ablation experiments comparing CDA-BBA with two of its variants. The best-performing results are highlighted in bold.

| Detection Algorithm | Attack | Evaluations | Karate | Dolphin | Polbooks | Football | Email | Web-Edu | Ca-GrQc | Ca-HepPh | Ca-AstroPh |
|---|---|---|---|---|---|---|---|---|---|---|---|
| Louvain | CDA-BBA | NMI | **0.6834** | **0.6826** | **0.7732** | **0.9206** | **0.6579** | 0.9685 | 0.8612 | **0.6283** | **0.5932** |
| | | ARI | **0.5694** | **0.5962** | **0.7284** | **0.8000** | **0.5688** | **0.8236** | **0.5662** | 0.4064 | **0.3913** |
| | w/o allocation | NMI | 0.7660 | 0.6880 | 0.8128 | 0.9318 | 0.6692 | **0.9667** | 0.8705 | 0.6666 | 0.6368 |
| | | ARI | 0.6895 | 0.6025 | 0.7881 | 0.8287 | 0.5795 | 0.8424 | 0.5760 | 0.3943 | 0.4062 |
| | w/o attack strategy | NMI | 0.8117 | 0.6902 | 0.8562 | 0.9559 | 0.6735 | 0.9705 | **0.8599** | 0.6292 | 0.6303 |
| | | ARI | 0.7480 | 0.6289 | 0.8170 | 0.8808 | 0.5961 | 0.8393 | 0.5791 | **0.3641** | 0.4037 |
| Infomap | CDA-BBA | NMI | **0.6320** | **0.5182** | 0.7969 | 1.0000 | **0.8677** | 0.9869 | **0.9702** | **0.9301** | **0.9362** |
| | | ARI | **0.5902** | **0.2772** | 0.7526 | 1.0000 | **0.7617** | 0.9744 | **0.8154** | 0.7773 | 0.7491 |
| | w/o allocation | NMI | 0.7465 | 0.6299 | **0.7649** | 1.0000 | 0.8768 | **0.9831** | 0.9811 | 0.9598 | 0.9430 |
| | | ARI | 0.7045 | 0.3733 | **0.7068** | 1.0000 | 0.7794 | **0.9627** | 0.8691 | **0.7185** | **0.7336** |
| | w/o attack strategy | NMI | 0.6637 | 0.6372 | 0.9459 | **0.9994** | 0.8887 | 0.9880 | 0.9775 | 0.9608 | 0.9473 |
| | | ARI | 0.5960 | 0.5041 | 0.9322 | **0.9990** | 0.8072 | 0.9751 | 0.8761 | 0.7908 | 0.7836 |
| LPA | CDA-BBA | NMI | **0.4312** | **0.5808** | 0.7271 | **0.7619** | 0.4404 | 0.9616 | **0.9220** | **0.8163** | **0.8604** |
| | | ARI | **0.3257** | **0.4021** | **0.7120** | **0.4961** | 0.2337 | 0.8983 | 0.5397 | **0.5664** | 0.8353 |
| | w/o allocation | NMI | 0.4846 | 0.5958 | **0.7254** | 0.7868 | 0.4451 | **0.9556** | 0.9250 | 0.8422 | 0.8840 |
| | | ARI | 0.3915 | 0.4101 | 0.7375 | 0.5238 | **0.2035** | **0.8694** | **0.5266** | 0.6115 | **0.8276** |
| | w/o attack strategy | NMI | 0.4655 | 0.5964 | 0.7861 | 0.7785 | **0.4298** | 0.9575 | 0.9255 | 0.8259 | 0.8795 |
| | | ARI | 0.3970 | 0.4549 | 0.7625 | 0.5116 | 0.2355 | 0.8874 | 0.5631 | 0.6026 | 0.8384 |
| Walktrap | CDA-BBA | NMI | 0.7410 | **0.5626** | **0.7374** | **0.9376** | 0.8283 | 0.9859 | **0.9563** | 0.9382 | **0.8533** |
| | | ARI | 0.6097 | **0.3186** | **0.7614** | **0.8337** | 0.6217 | 0.9562 | **0.6080** | 0.7328 | **0.3639** |
| | w/o allocation | NMI | 0.7366 | 0.6031 | 0.7634 | 0.9568 | **0.8223** | **0.9758** | 0.9713 | 0.9528 | 0.9181 |
| | | ARI | 0.5821 | 0.4150 | 0.8128 | 0.9151 | **0.6129** | **0.9318** | 0.6322 | 0.5296 | 0.5262 |
| | w/o attack strategy | NMI | **0.7031** | 0.6020 | 0.9069 | 0.9792 | 0.8494 | 0.9866 | 0.9583 | **0.9363** | 0.9161 |
| | | ARI | **0.5541** | 0.4456 | 0.9054 | 0.9293 | 0.7537 | 0.9631 | 0.6133 | **0.4906** | 0.5165 |
| Fastgreedy | CDA-BBA | NMI | **0.4850** | 0.6804 | 0.7425 | 0.6761 | **0.4504** | 0.9855 | 0.7764 | **0.5517** | 0.6564 |
| | | ARI | **0.3950** | 0.5775 | 0.7713 | 0.4645 | **0.3816** | 0.9743 | 0.3426 | **0.3122** | 0.6701 |
| | w/o allocation | NMI | 0.7388 | **0.6401** | **0.6674** | **0.5816** | 0.6338 | **0.9660** | **0.7528** | 0.6820 | **0.5330** |
| | | ARI | 0.6179 | **0.5468** | **0.6323** | **0.3512** | 0.6516 | **0.8922** | **0.2819** | 0.4772 | **0.2998** |
| | w/o attack strategy | NMI | 0.5748 | 0.6432 | 0.8938 | 0.7972 | 0.5806 | 0.9813 | 0.7786 | 0.6466 | 0.5665 |
| | | ARI | 0.5014 | 0.5830 | 0.8995 | 0.6795 | 0.5356 | 0.9645 | 0.3760 | 0.4402 | 0.4034 |

# 5   Conclusion and Future Work

In this paper, a heuristic attack algorithm called CDA-BBA, which performs budget allocation before attacking, was proposed. CDA-BBA first allocates budgets to communities based on the number of nodes in each important community, and then rewires edges according to the proposed attack strategy. In this attack strategy, the edge rewiring is determined by the similarity between nodes. Experiments were conducted on nine real-world networks using five community detection algorithms. The experimental results demonstrate that the proposed CDA-BBA can effectively alter the community structure in a short amount of time and outperforms baseline methods. These findings have validated the effectiveness of CDA-BBA. In the future, there are still several issues to be further explored. CDA-BBA only considers the attack in undirected and unweighted networks. A valuable direction for future work is to extend our attack strategy based on budget allocation to different types of complex networks, such as attributed networks and multilayer networks. Another promising avenue is to apply budget allocation and the proposed heuristic strategy to other forms of attack, such as hiding overlapping nodes in the network from overlapping community detection.

# References


1. An, K., Chiu, Y., Hu, X., Chen, X.: A network partitioning algorithmic approach for macroscopic fundamental diagram-based hierarchical traffic network management. IEEE Trans. Intell. Transp. Syst. **19**(4), 1130–1139 (2018)
2. Barabási, A.L., Albert, R.: Emergence of scaling in random networks. Science **286**(5439), 509–512 (1999)
3. Blondel, V.D., Guillaume, J.L., Lambiotte, R., Lefebvre, E.: Fast unfolding of communities in large networks. J. Stat. Mech: Theory Exp. **2008**(10), P10008 (2008)
4. Chen, J., et al.: GA-based Q-Attack on community detection. IEEE Trans. Comput. Soc. Syst. **6**(3), 491–503 (2019)
5. Chen, J., Chen, Y., Chen, L., Zhao, M., Xuan, Q.: Multiscale evolutionary perturbation attack on community detection. IEEE Trans. Comput. Soc. Syst. **8**(1), 62–75 (2021)
6. Clauset, A., Newman, M.E.J., Moore, C.: Finding community structure in very large networks. Phys. Rev. E **70**, 066111 (2004)
7. Danon, L., Díaz-Guilera, A., Duch, J., Arenas, A.: Comparing community structure identification. J. Stat. Mech: Theory Exp. **2005**(9), P09008 (2005)
8. Ding, Z., Zhang, X., Sun, D., Luo, B.: Overlapping community detection based on network decomposition. Sci. Rep. **6**(1), 24115 (2016)
9. Freeman, L.: A set of measures of centrality based on betweenness. Sociometry **40**(35-41) (1977)
10. Gleich, D., Zhukov, L., Berkhin, P.: Fast parallel PageRank: a linear system approach. Yahoo! Research Technical Report YRL-2004-038 **13**, 22 (2004). http://research.yahoo.com/publication/YRL-2004-038.pdf
11. Hubert, L., Arabie, P.: Comparing partitions. J. Classif. **2**(1), 193–218 (1985)
12. Leskovec, J., Krevl, A.: Snap datasets: Stanford large network dataset collection (2014). http://snap.stanford.edu/data
13. Li, J., Zhang, H., Han, Z., Rong, Y., Cheng, H., Huang, J.: Adversarial attack on community detection by hiding individuals. In: Proceedings of the Web Conference 2020, pp. 917–927 (2020)
14. Liu, D., Chang, Z., Yang, G., Chen, E.: Community hiding using a graph autoencoder. Knowl.-Based Syst. **253**, 109495 (2022)
15. Lusseau, D.: The emergent properties of a dolphin social network. Proc. R. Soc. London. Ser. B: Biol. Sci. **270**, S186–S188 (2003)
16. Mittal, S., Sengupta, D., Chakraborty, T.: Hide and seek: outwitting community detection algorithms. IEEE Trans. Comput. Soc. Syst. **8**(4), 799–808 (2021)
17. Newman, M.E.: The structure and function of complex networks. SIAM Rev. **45**(2), 167–256 (2003)
18. Newman, M.E.: Modularity and community structure in networks. Proc. Natl. Acad. Sci. **103**(23), 8577–8582 (2006)
19. Pons, P., Latapy, M.: Computing communities in large networks using random walks. J. Graph Algorithms Appl. **10**(2), 191–218 (2006)
20. Raghavan, U.N., Albert, R., Kumara, S.: Near linear time algorithm to detect community structures in large-scale networks. Phys. Rev. E-Stat. Nonlinear Soft Matter Phys. **76**(3), 036106 (2007)
21. Rosvall, M., Bergstrom, C.T.: Maps of random walks on complex networks reveal community structure. Proc. Nat. Acad. Sci. 1118–1123 (2008)

22. Waniek, M., Michalak, T.P., Wooldridge, M.J., Rahwan, T.: Hiding individuals and communities in a social network. Nat. Hum. Behav. **2**(2), 139–147 (2018)
23. Xuan, Q., Zhang, Z.Y., Fu, C., Hu, H.X., Filkov, V.: Social synchrony on complex networks. IEEE Trans. Cybern. **48**(5), 1420–1431 (2018)
24. Yang, H., Chen, L., Cheng, F., Qiu, J., Zhang, L.: LSHA: a local structure-based community detection attack heuristic approach. IEEE Trans. Comput. Soc. Syst. **11**(2), 2966–2978 (2024)
25. Zachary, W.W.: An information flow model for conflict and fission in small groups. J. Anthropol. Res. **33**(4), 452–473 (1977)
26. Zhao, J., Wang, Z., Cao, J., Cheong, K.H.: A self-adaptive evolutionary deception framework for community structure. IEEE Trans. Syst. Man Cybern. Syst. **53**(8), 4954–4967 (2023)

# Depth State Space Model for Light Field Depth Estimation via Text-Similar Representation


Zexin Sun[1,2], Tun Wang[1,2], Da Yang[2], Zhenglong Cui[2], Rongshan Chen[1,2], Ying Li[1,2], Guanqun Su[4], and Hao Sheng[1,2,3(✉)]

[1] State Key Laboratory of Virtual Reality Technology and Systems, School of Computer Science and Engineering, Beihang University, Beijing 100191, People's Republic of China
{zexinsun,shenghao}@buaa.edu.cn

[2] Data Science and Intelligent Computing Laboratory, Hangzhou International Innovation Institute, Beihang University, Zhejiang 311115, Hangzhou, People's Republic of China

[3] Faculty of Applied Sciences, Macao Polytechnic University, Macao SAR 999078, People's Republic of China

[4] Shandong Qingniao IIoT Co., ltd., Jinan 250014, China



**Abstract.** Light field (LF) technology captures both spatial and angular information of the real world, enabling accurate depth estimation. Cost volume-based methods mostly consider LF depth estimation as a shift-matching process, which fail to efficiently establish the relationship among different viewpoints. State Space Model (SSM) has shown strong capabilities in long-sequence modeling, providing a powerful mechanism to capture viewpoints associations. In this paper, we observe that LF depth estimation can be viewed as state transition and then propose a text-similar representation based on the distribution of pixel values across different viewpoints, which is able to detect occluded and discontinuous regions. Furthermore, to extract the potential depth features, we represent it as Depth State Space Model (DSSM), leveraging the state transition mechanism of SSM to capture spatial, angular and structural characteristics in complex regions. Based on the proposed DSSM, we develop DSS-Net for depth estimation. Experiments demonstrate that our approach achieves state-of-the-art performance, with significant improvements in occluded and discontinuous regions, highlighting its effectiveness in addressing the complexities of LF depth estimation.

**Keywords:** Light field · Depth estimation · Cost volume · Occlusion-aware · Depth state space model · Text-similar representation



Z. Sun and T. Wang—Equal contribution.





T. Zhu et al. (Eds.): KSEM 2025, LNAI 15919, pp. 339–351, 2026.
https://doi.org/10.1007/978-981-95-3001-4_25

# 1   Introduction

Light field (LF) technology captures both the intensity and direction of light rays in a scene, providing a richer and more detailed representation of visual information, which can be presented by two-plane model. As a fundamental task in LF image processing, depth estimation aims to extract the 3D structure of objects, enabling applications in advanced computational tasks such as refocusing, image reconstruction, super resolution and virtual reality rendering [4,15,21].

In recent years, cost volume-based methods [18] for LF depth estimation have attracted considerable research attention. These approaches rely on the assumption that the intensity of corresponding pixels across different viewpoints remains consistent. By aggregating information from the surrounding viewpoints to the central, these methods generate accurate depth maps. However, these methods overlook the inherent regularities of LF data, such as the consistent distances between viewpoints, only focusing on shift-matching process. This limitation hinders their ability to efficiently establish the relationship of LF viewpoints.

State Space Model (SSM) [8] is emerged as a promising class of foundational architectures for sequence modeling. It is designed to capture latent states in sequential data by representing them within a state space, allowing for effective modeling of temporal dependencies. To improve practical feasibility, S4 [7] model further proposed normalizing the parameter matrix to a diagonal structure. Subsequently, Mamba architecture (S6) [6], incorporating selection mechanisms, combines significant advantages of both CNN and Transformer backbones, making it a highly promising model. With the ability to efficiently capture long-range dependencies, SSM is particularly promising for LF depth estimation, as they can effectively model the underlying relationships among multiple viewpoints. However, applying SSM directly to the 4D structure of LF data presents notable limitations.

In this paper, we reconsider LF depth estimation as a process of space state transition at point locations to establish the viewpoints relationship more efficiently, where the state transition denotes potential depth features. However, occlusion poses an additional challenge, disrupting viewpoint consistency and causing the loss of light information. Therefore, we design a text-similar representation based on the distribution of pixel values across different viewpoints. It can recognize occluded and discontinuous regions more sensitively by exhibiting them as 1D sequences in obvious representation. Building on this analysis, we propose Depth State Space Model (DSSM), a transformation method that adapts LF data for text-similar distribution representation. It calculates state transitions among different viewpoints through potential depth state space, effectively capturing spatial, angular and structural features in complex areas.

Finally, we develop DSS-Net, a depth regression network based on cost volume and DSSM. Experimental results demonstrate that our method achieves state-of-the-art (SOTA) performance in both quantitative and qualitative evaluations, proving its effectiveness in addressing the unique challenges of LF depth estimation. Besides, our network achieves satisfactory results in real scenes.

Our contributions can be summarized as follows:

- Propose the LF text-similar representation by analyzing the distribution of pixel values across different viewpoints. This representation is sensitive to occluded regions by modeling them based on 1D sequences.
- Present the Depth State Space Model, achieving the state transitions between different viewpoints. It enables effective capture of spatial, angular and structural features in complex regions.
- Develop the DSS-Net for LF depth estimation based on cost volume. Experimental results demonstrate that our network achieves the SOTA performance on standard LF datasets.

## 2  Related Work

### 2.1  Deep Learning-Based Methods in LF Depth Estimation

Recent advancements in deep learning have significantly improved LF depth estimation performance. These methods can be divided into two categories: epipolar-plane image (EPI)-based, cost volume-based.

EPI-based methods leverage it to exploit the geometric structure for accurate depth estimation. Shin et al. [17] introduced EPINet, a multi-stream convolutional neural network designed for fast depth estimation by effectively exploiting EPI. Leistner et al. [11] proposed a wide-baseline framework leveraging EPI-shift properties in challenging conditions. Further improving EPI relationship, Zhou et al. [25] recently proposed the concepts of stitched-EPI and half stitched-EPI, innovatively reorganizing EPI structures. Additionally, addressing challenges posed by non-Lambertian surfaces, Cui et al. [5] introduced an adaptive cross operator designed to effectively handle specular reflections in EPIs.

Cost volume-based method aggregate all views information to match the accurate results. Tsai et al. [18] developed LFattNet, incorporating a view selection module that prioritizes regions with less occlusion and richer textures. To improve the efficiency, Wang et al. [24] proposed a generic mechanism to disentangle spatial-angularly coupled information in LF processing. Subsequently, OACC-Net [23] employed a dynamic approach to modulate pixel information across LF views. To enhance the accuracy, Chao et al. [1] introduced a method to learn depth distributions and construct a sub-pixel cost volume. More recently, Wang et al. [20] proposed an adaptive EPI-matching cost construction method to improve flexibility.

### 2.2  State Space Model

State Space Model (SSM) [8] has gradually attracted the attention of researchers due to the computational complexity that scales linearly with the input sequence length and inherent global perceptual properties. The S4 [7] introduced a diagonal structure and combined it with a diagonal-plus-low-rank approach to construct structured SSM. Recently, Gu et al. [6] proposed a selective SSM block,

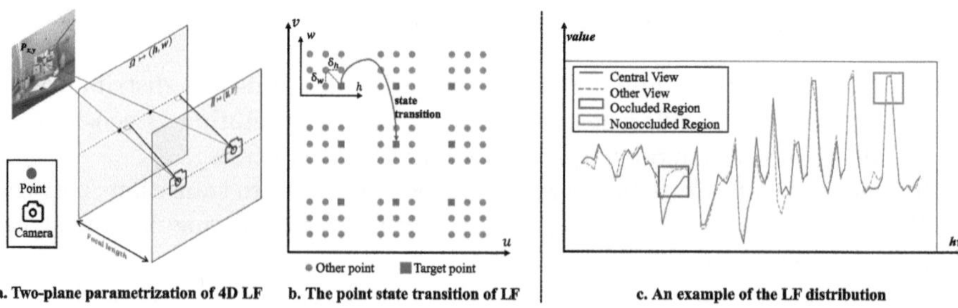



**Fig. 1.** An illustration of 4D LF, the transitions and distributions between different views. (a) Two-plane parametrization of 4D LF. (b) The point state transition of LF, the target point changes from the upper left view to the center view. (c) An example of the LF distribution. The orange dotted line represents the central view, the blue solid lines represent the other view. There are obvious fluctuations in the occluded region. (Color figure online)

Mamba (S6), which integrates structured SSM with hardware-aware state expansion to form an efficient recurrent architecture that demonstrates competitive performance compared to Transformers. Building upon the Mamba module, several studies have explored the application of SSM in computer vision. For instance, Vision Mamba [12] incorporates Mamba to develop isotropic vision models analogous to Vision Transformers; VMamba [13] leverages Mamba to construct hierarchical vision architectures resembling AlexNet and ResNet.

## 3   Methodology

### 3.1   Motivation

As shown in Fig. 1a, LF can be represented as a 4D functional $L(u, v, h, w)$, where $(u, v)$ and $(h, w)$ respectively represent the angular and spatial coordinates. Since the camera planes are coplanar, the transition process between the center view $(u_c, v_c)$ and the surrounding views $(u, v)$ can be formulated as:

$$L(u_c, v_c, h, w) = L(u, v, h + \delta_h, w + \delta_w), \tag{1}$$

where $\delta_h, \delta_w$ are the disparity of pixel $(h, w)$ in center view. This relationship indicates that LF depth estimation can be interpreted as a state transition between different viewpoints as illustrated in Fig. 1b.

This transition is consistent with state space modeling, which captures the connection between LF viewpoints adequately. However, current cost volume-based methods consider the representation of LF depth estimation as shift matching among different viewpoints, which can not deeply explore the potential structural connections between all viewpoints and fail to long-range dependencies.

## 3.2  Text-Similar Representation

To efficiently establish the relationship among viewpoints, we rethink the LF depth estimation as the state transitions of points position in space, which contains the potential transition process. However, occlusion poses an additional challenge when conceptualizing LF depth estimation as state transition. Under the Lambertian assumption, the intensity of light emitted from a point source should remain consistent across different views of the LF. This assumption implies that, in regions without occlusion, the pixel values across various viewpoints should remain uniform. In occluded regions, this consistency is disrupted, leading to notable deviations.

Therefore, we explore the property of LF data structures to overcome the occlusion problem. Specifically, we analyzed the distribution of pixel values across different viewpoints, as shown in Fig. 1c. LF data exhibit regular patterns across viewpoints, allowing it to be transformed into a 1D representation. In this representation, each viewpoint corresponds to a unique projection of the same scene, similar to how different words describe the same concept from multiple perspectives. In regions without occlusion, the pixel distributions across viewpoints remain consistent. However, when occlusion occurs, the distribution becomes more erratic due to the presence of outliers. Some viewpoints may capture the original object, while others may encounter occluding objects.

By utilizing this novel text-similar representation, the occluded regions could be recognized more efficiently. Then, we design the DSSM according to this representation, which is the S6 based on occluded situation. Specifically, it allows the model to adaptively handle occlusion by focusing on the most relevant points, thus improving depth estimation performance.

## 3.3  Depth State Space Model

The previous SSM [7] is defined by (2), which projects 1-D sequences $x(t) \in \mathbb{R} \mapsto y(t) \in \mathbb{R}$ through N-D potential spaces $s(t) \in \mathbb{R}^N$. Specifically, the model defines four parameters $(\Delta, A, B, C)$ to accomplish the transformation between sequences. The specific formulas are as follows:

$$
\begin{aligned}
s'(t) &= \mathbf{A}s(t) + \mathbf{B}x(t), \\
y(t) &= \mathbf{C}s(t),
\end{aligned}
\tag{2}
$$

where $A \in \mathbb{R}^{N \times N}$ is a learnable parameter, $B \in \mathbb{R}^{N \times 1}$ and $C \in \mathbb{R}^{1 \times N}$ represent parameters selected by the input. The architecture then incorporates a timescale parameter $\Delta$ to transform the continuous parameters $A, B$ into discrete parameters $\bar{A}, \bar{B}$ through a discretization rule. The specific formulas are as follows:

$$
\begin{aligned}
\overline{\mathbf{A}} &= \exp(\Delta\mathbf{A}), \\
\overline{\mathbf{B}} &= (\Delta\mathbf{A})^{-1}(\exp(\Delta\mathbf{A}) - \mathbf{I})\Delta\mathbf{B}.
\end{aligned}
\tag{3}
$$

Once discretized, the SSM can be represented through these two equations:

$$
\begin{aligned}
s'(t) &= \overline{\mathbf{A}}s(t) + \overline{\mathbf{B}}x(t), \\
y(t) &= \mathbf{C}s(t).
\end{aligned}
\tag{4}
$$

While the SSM provides a general framework for sequence transformations, its application to LF text-similar representation presents unique challenges.

To address this gap, we propose the DSSM for LF depth estimation based on our text-similar representation. Like (2), we define $x(t)$ indicates the LF text-similar sequences, $y(t)$ indicates the output with states transition among different viewpoints, $s(t)$ indicates the potential depth state space, which contains the fundamental spatial, angular and structural features. As the DSSM defined, the model projects 1D sequences $x(t) \in \mathbb{R} \mapsto y(t) \in \mathbb{R}$ through potential spaces $s(t) \in \mathbb{R}^N$, and follow the (2)$\sim$(4) to accomplish the transformation between text-similar sequences. The entire DSSM is divided into three parts:

First part is the selective scan for parameter adaption. The DSSM parameter $A$ is predefined and learned during training, which are independent of the input. In contrast, $\Delta$, $B$, and $C$ are dynamically generated from the space of viewpoints $x(t) \in \mathbb{R}^{H \times W}$ at each time-step. The formula is as follows, $Split[deltark, n, n]$ means the calculation of $\Delta, B, C$:

$$\Delta, B, C = Split_{[delta_{rk}, n, n]}(Conv(x(t))). \tag{5}$$

Second part is model calculation. The connection between states is established by computing the potential depth state space for each viewpoint. The formula is as follows:

$$s(t+1) = \Delta A \cdot s(t) + \Delta B \cdot x(t). \tag{6}$$

Final part is the output calculation. By combining information from all viewpoints and potential depth features, DSSM select the most accurate state as output. The formula is as follows:

$$y(t) = \sum_{i=1}^{D} C \cdot s_i(t), \tag{7}$$

where $D$ denotes the dimension of potential depth state spaces.

### 3.4 Network Architecture

**System Overview.** Figure 2 illustrates the proposed DSS-Net in detail. The input is all LF SAIs denoted as $\mathcal{L} \in \mathbb{R}^{U \times V \times H \times W}$, and the output is the depth map $D \in \mathbb{R}^{H \times W}$ corresponding to the center view. Here, $U \times V$ represents the angular resolution, and $H \times W$ represents the spatial resolution of $\mathcal{L}$.

**Feature Extraction.** We developed a feature extraction module specifically to efficiently capture geometric properties. For each input, the module employs two convolutional layers, each followed by ReLU activation and batch normalization. This module applies a series of residual blocks and convolutional layers to the LF inputs and the convolutional weights are shared across different views. The final output is a 4D feature tensor $F$.

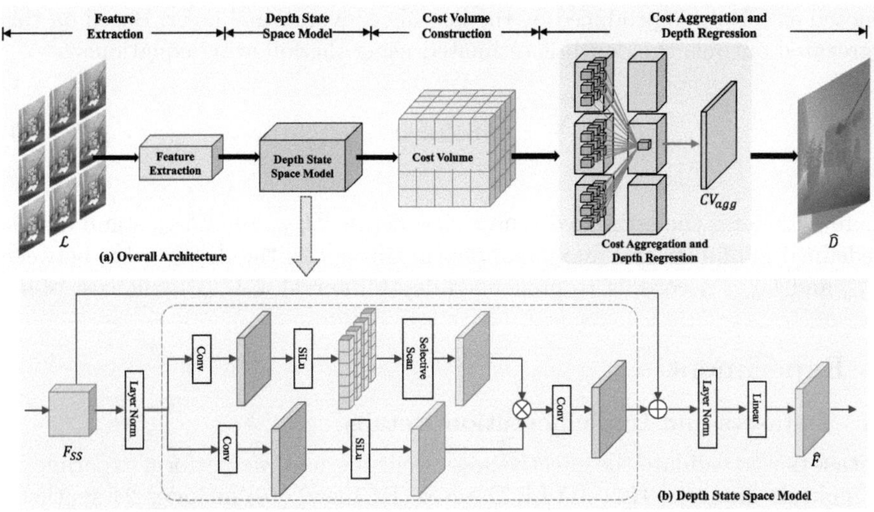


**Fig. 2.** An overview of our DSS-Net. Here, a $3 \times 3$ LF is used as an example.

**Depth State Space Model.** Following the Section 3.2 and Sect. 3.3, for the given LF feature $F$, we reshape it into the text-similar representation features $F_{SS}$. Then, we use convolution blocks to capture local features by establishing the depth state space correlations. Each block is equipped with residual connections, which combine the output with its input of this block to enhance information flow:

$$\hat{F} = \text{Linear}(\text{LN}(\text{DSSM}(F_{SS}) + F_{SS})), \tag{8}$$

where DSSM denotes the transition process, LN denotes Layer Normalization.

**Cost Volume Construction.** We adopt homography warping (*shift-and-concat*) to align the output $\hat{F}$ of *DSSM* for various depth $d$ and view combinations $(u, v)$. This results in a cost volume that encapsulates matching information across views and depth. The complete cost volume $CV$ is generated by stacking the matching costs across multiple depth levels $d$. Formally, the cost volume can be expressed as:

$$CV = \text{cat}\left(\{CV_d \mid d \in \mathcal{D}\}, \dim = 1\right), \tag{9}$$

where $\mathcal{D}$ is the set of discrete depth levels.

**Cost Aggregation and Depth Regression.** After constructing the cost volume, the next step is to aggregate the cost values and conduct depth regression. We employ eight 3D convolutional layers to accomplish cost aggregation and the third to sixth layers are structured into two residual blocks. The final 3D tensor, denoted as $CV_{agg}$, is produced by the last 3D convolutional layer. Based on this aggregated output, the depth is estimated using the following equation:

$$\hat{D} = \sum_{d=D_{\min}}^{D_{\max}} d \cdot \mathrm{Softmax}(CV_{\mathrm{agg}}(d)), \tag{10}$$

where $\hat{D}$ denotes the estimated center view depth, $D_{\min}$ and $D_{\max}$ stand for the predefined minimum and maximum depth values, $d$ is the depth value between $D_{\min}$ and $D_{\max}$ according to predefined depth interval, $CV_{agg}$ is the cost of $d$.

## 4   Experiment

### 4.1   Datasets and Implementation Details

**Datasets.** To validate the effectiveness of our method, we perform experiments on multiple datasets: HCI 4D LF Dataset (HCInew) [10] includes 24 synthetic scenes with highly accurate depth ground truth. Dense LF Dataset (DLFD) [16] consists of 39 scenes with accurate depth labels in each viewpoint. The (New) Standford Light Fields Archieve [14] is a real-scene dataset, used to test the robustness of our model. Our model is trained exclusively on the HCInew dataset, with other datasets reserved solely for testing.

**Training.** During training, we randomly crop SAIs into $64 \times 64$ patches and convert them into grayscale images. Extensive data augmentation is applied, including random flipping, rotation, brightness and contrast adjustment, noise injection, refocusing, and downsampling [2]. Our DSS-Net is trained in a supervised manner using $L_1$ loss, with Adam optimization, configured with $\beta_1 = 0.9$ and $\beta_2 = 0.999$. The batch size is set to 16, and the learning rate is $1 \times 10^{-3}$. Training proceeds for $3 \times 10^5$ iterations, which takes approximately 7 days. The model is implemented in PyTorch and trained using a NVIDIA RTX 3090 GPU. Besides, we use the same depth range of SOTA methods.

**Evaluation.** We employ mean square error (MSE) and bad pixel ratio (BadPix($\epsilon$)) as quantitative metrics to evaluate performance. The BadPix($\epsilon$) metric quantifies the proportion of pixels with estimation errors exceeding a given threshold $\epsilon$.

$$MSE = 100 \times \frac{1}{m} \sum_{i=1}^{m} \left( D_i - D_i^{gt} \right)^2, \tag{11}$$

$$BadPix(\epsilon) = 100 \times \frac{1}{m} \sum_{i=1}^{m} \left( |D_i - D_i^{gt}| > \epsilon \right), \tag{12}$$

where $D$ is the result predicted and $D^{gt}$ is the ground truth depth, $i$ represents pixel coordinates.

**Table 1.** Mean square error (multiplied with 100) achieved by different methods on the DLFD (left) and HCInew (right). The best results are in bold and the second best results are underlined, where Avg. means the average value on corresponding scenes

| Method | Black. | Kiwi. | Toy. | White. | Avg. MSE | Backg. | Strip. | Boxes | Side. | Avg. MSE |
|---|---|---|---|---|---|---|---|---|---|---|
| OAVC [9] | 6.766 | 8.794 | <u>0.301</u> | <u>9.965</u> | 6.457 | 3.835 | 1.316 | 6.988 | 1.047 | 3.297 |
| DistgDisp [24] | 7.881 | 2.398 | 0.819 | 24.177 | 8.819 | 4.712 | 0.917 | 3.325 | 0.713 | 2.417 |
| FCVNet [22] | 6.856 | 2.096 | 0.310 | 34.530 | 10.948 | 4.104 | 0.939 | 5.569 | 0.593 | 2.801 |
| LFattNet [18] | 8.710 | 2.079 | 0.693 | 61.413 | 18.224 | 3.648 | 0.892 | 3.996 | 0.531 | 2.267 |
| EPINet [17] | 10.024 | 5.594 | 0.682 | 21.510 | 9.453 | <u>3.629</u> | 0.950 | 6.240 | 0.827 | 2.912 |
| PDE-Net-e [19] | – | – | – | – | – | 4.028 | 0.998 | 3.909 | 0.557 | 2.373 |
| OACC-Net [23] | 11.522 | <u>1.859</u> | 0.561 | 24.956 | 9.725 | 3.938 | 0.845 | 2.892 | 0.542 | 2.054 |
| EPI-Shift [11] | <u>6.690</u> | 18.650 | 0.699 | 28.951 | 13.748 | 12.788 | 1.686 | 9.790 | 1.261 | 6.381 |
| SubFocal [1] | 8.803 | 2.078 | 0.343 | 29.128 | 10.088 | 3.667 | <u>0.821</u> | 2.993 | **0.404** | 1.971 |
| LFAVNet [3] | 6.991 | **1.790** | 0.341 | 13.582 | 5.601 | 3.784 | **0.797** | 2.696 | <u>0.497</u> | <u>1.944</u> |
| DSS-Net (Ours) | **1.177** | 2.190 | **0.206** | **6.809** | **2.596** | **3.543** | 0.917 | **1.859** | 0.573 | **1.723** |

**Table 2.** Quantitative comparison results with SOTA methods on DLFD and HCInew of BP(0.07). The best results are in bold and the second best results are underlined.

| Method | Black. | Kiwi. | Toy. | White. | Avg. BP(0.07) | Backg. | Strip. | Boxes | Side. | Avg. BP(0.07) |
|---|---|---|---|---|---|---|---|---|---|---|
| OAVC [9] | 13.890 | 14.392 | 5.193 | 20.981 | 13.614 | **3.121** | 2.903 | 16.144 | 12.421 | 8.647 |
| DistgDisp [24] | 10.593 | 2.860 | <u>1.345</u> | **16.695** | 7.873 | 5.824 | 3.913 | 13.309 | 4.051 | 6.774 |
| FCVNet [22] | <u>9.517</u> | **1.623** | 1.811 | 18.241 | <u>7.798</u> | 3.524 | 2.702 | 11.689 | 3.332 | 5.312 |
| LFattNet [18] | 12.829 | <u>2.017</u> | 1.443 | 21.103 | 9.348 | <u>3.126</u> | 2.933 | 11.044 | **2.870** | <u>4.993</u> |
| EPINet [17] | 12.826 | 13.435 | 3.033 | 30.270 | 14.891 | 3.580 | <u>2.462</u> | 12.839 | 4.801 | 5.921 |
| PDE-Net-e [19] | – | – | – | – | – | 5.492 | 6.548 | 14.971 | 6.010 | 8.255 |
| OACC-Net [23] | 12.956 | 2.175 | **1.039** | 17.591 | 8.440 | 3.931 | 2.920 | <u>10.697</u> | 3.350 | 5.225 |
| EPI-Shift [11] | 16.440 | 13.435 | 10.982 | 30.964 | 17.955 | 22.886 | 22.719 | 25.951 | 11.795 | 20.838 |
| LFAVNet [3] | 12.100 | 4.834 | 2.222 | 29.437 | 12.148 | 3.977 | 5.377 | 12.288 | 3.547 | 6.297 |
| DSS-Net (Ours) | **4.978** | 2.475 | 1.553 | <u>17.029</u> | **6.509** | 4.024 | **2.409** | 9.86 | <u>3.292</u> | **4.896** |

## 4.2  Comparison with SOTA Methods

To prove the advancement of our method for LF depth estimation, we compare DSS-Net with 10 SOTA methods including EPI-Shift [11], OAVC [9], EPINet [17], FCVNet [22], DistgDisp [24], PDE-Net-e [19], LFattNet [18], OACC-Net [23], SubFocal [1], LFAVNet [3].

**Quantitative Results.** Table 1 and Table 2 show the quantitative results with SOTA methods. Our approach achieves the best average MSE and BadPix(0.07) on DLFD and HCInew datasets, outperforming all other methods. These results demonstrate that DSS-Net significantly enhances LF depth estimation by learning the depth state and better adopting the depth distribution.

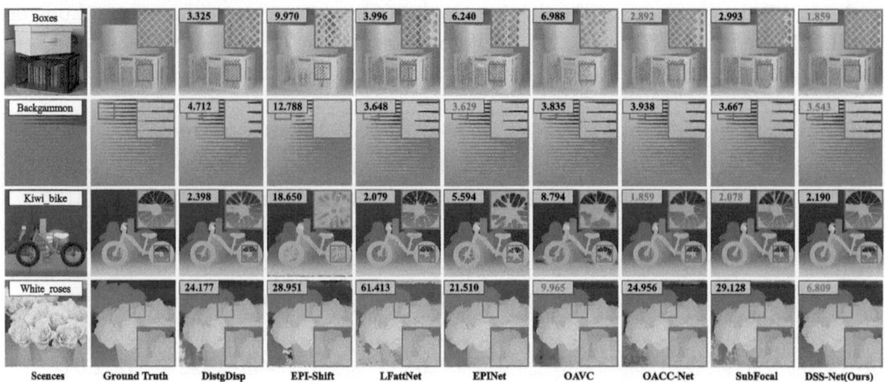



**Fig. 3.** Qualitative results on HCInew and DLFD with the corresponding MSE×100. The best and second-best results are highlighted in red and blue. From left to right are the center view, ground truth, and visual results. (Color figure online)

**Visual Comparison.** Figure 3 illustrates several examples of estimated depth maps along with their corresponding detail regions. It is evident that the results obtained by our approach outperform the others. For example, in the 'Boxes' and 'White_roses', our method excels in preserving intricate details and reconstructing regions with pronounced depth discontinuity. Additionally, in the 'Backgammon' and 'Kiwi_bike', our approach demonstrates superior performance in capturing fine edge details and handling depth transition more effectively.

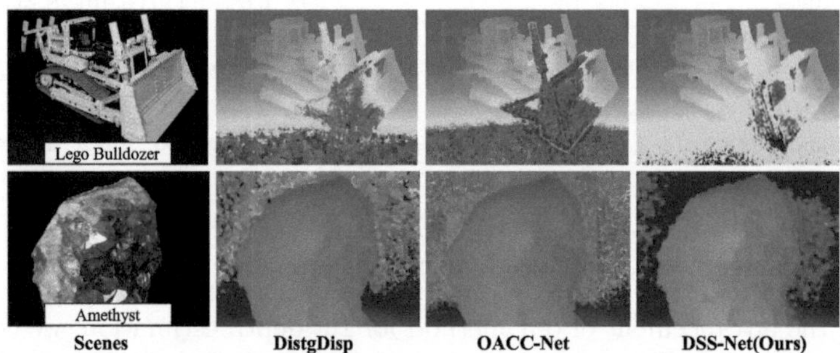



**Fig. 4.** Visual comparisons on real-world scenes. Our results show superior performance compared to DistgDisp [24] and OACC-Net [23].

**Performance on Real Scenes.** We test the performance of our DSS-Net on Stanford archive [14]. Since ground truth depths are unavailable, we used the model trained on HcInew for inference and compare the visual performance of our method to DistgDisp [24] and OACC-Net [23]. Figure 4 demonstrates our superior performance, even in complex scenes like the 'Lego Bulldozer' and 'Amethyst'.

### 4.3 Ablation Study

In this section, we compare the proposed DSSM with five modified architectures to prove the effectiveness of our approach: without cost-volume, without any aggregated modules, cross-attention mechanism, self-attention mechanism, and transformer. Experimental results are shown in Table 3, our method achieves the best MSE, Badpix results, and the second best reference time, which demonstrates the promising compatibility of our model.

**Table 3.** Ablation study on HCInew with avg. MSE, BP, Test Time, Params. and TFLOPs.

| Method | MSE | BP(0.07) | BP(0.03) | Test Time(s) | Params. | TFLOPs |
|---|---|---|---|---|---|---|
| -Cost-Volume | 2.174 | 4.831 | 10.724 | **6.937** | **2.739** | **12.731** |
| -DSSM | 1.409 | 3.546 | 6.971 | 9.606 | 3.829 | 17.603 |
| Cross-attention | 1.244 | 3.236 | 6.458 | 10.652 | 4.413 | 19.513 |
| Self-attention | 1.342 | 3.211 | 6.430 | 10.584 | 4.427 | 19.499 |
| Transformer | 1.191 | 3.003 | 6.328 | 11.232 | 4.753 | 20.618 |
| DSSM | **1.098** | **2.967** | **6.020** | 10.081 | 4.136 | 18.528 |

## 5 Conclusion

In this work, we propose a text-similar representation based on distribution of pixel values across different viewpoints, which is able to detect occluded and discontinuous regions. Furthermore, DSSM is designed to calculate the state transition by capturing the spatial, angular and structural characteristics of complex areas. Finally, we develop DSS-Net for depth estimation and experiments demonstrate that our approach achieves SOTA performance, with significant improvements in occluded and discontinuous regions.

**Acknowledgments.** This study is partially supported by the National Key R&D Program of China(No.2024YFB4506000), the National Natural Science Foundation of China(No.62394332, 62372023), the Open Fund of the State Key Laboratory of Software Development Environment(No. SKLSDE-2023ZX-11), the Research Start-up Funds of Hangzhou International Innovation Institute of Beihang University under Grant No.2024KQ012 and 2024KQ051, the 2023 Innovation Fund Project of the Ministry of Education Engineering Research Center for Digital Learning Technology Integration and Application(No. 1321008), and the Haiyou Plan Fund. Thank you for the support from HAWKEYE Group.

# References


1. Chao, W., Wang, X., Wang, Y., Wang, G., Duan, F.: Learning sub-pixel disparity distribution for light field depth estimation. IEEE Trans. Comput. Imaging **9**, 1126–1138 (2023)
2. Chen, R., Sheng, H., Yang, D., Wang, S., Cui, Z., Cong, R.: Pixel-wise matching cost function for robust light field depth estimation. Expert Syst. Appl. **262**, 125560 (2025)
3. Chen, R., et al.: View-guided cost volume for light field arbitrary-view disparity estimation. IEEE Transactions on Visualization and Computer Graphics (2024)
4. Cong, R., Sheng, H., Yang, D., Cui, Z., Chen, R.: Exploiting spatial and angular correlations with deep efficient transformers for light field image super-resolution. IEEE Transactions on Multimedia (2023)
5. Cui, Z., Sheng, H., Yang, D., Wang, S., Chen, R., Ke, W.: Light field depth estimation for non-lambertian objects via adaptive cross operator. IEEE Trans. Circuits Syst. Video Technol. **34**(2), 1199–1211 (2023)
6. Gu, A., Dao, T.: Mamba: Linear-time sequence modeling with selective state spaces. arXiv preprint arXiv:2312.00752 (2023)
7. Gu, A., Goel, K., Ré, C.: Efficiently modeling long sequences with structured state spaces. arXiv preprint arXiv:2111.00396 (2021)
8. Gu, A., et al.: Combining recurrent, convolutional, and continuous-time models with linear state space layers. Adv. Neural. Inf. Process. Syst. **34**, 572–585 (2021)
9. Han, K., Xiang, W., Wang, E., Huang, T.: A novel occlusion-aware vote cost for light field depth estimation. IEEE Transactions on Pattern Analysis and Machine Intelligence (2021)
10. Honauer, K., Johannsen, O., Kondermann, D., Goldluecke, B.: A dataset and evaluation methodology for depth estimation on 4D light fields. In: Computer Vision–ACCV 2016: 13th Asian Conference on Computer Vision, Taipei, Taiwan, November 20-24, 2016, Revised Selected Papers, Part III 13, pp. 19–34. Springer (2017)
11. Leistner, T., Schilling, H., Mackowiak, R., Gumhold, S., Rother, C.: Learning to think outside the box: wide-baseline light field depth estimation with EPI-shift. In: 2019 International Conference on 3D Vision (3DV), pp. 249–257. IEEE (2019)
12. Liu, X., Zhang, C., Zhang, L.: Vision mamba: A comprehensive survey and taxonomy. arXiv preprint arXiv:2405.04404 (2024)
13. Liu, Y., et al.: VMamba: visual state space model. Adv. Neural. Inf. Process. Syst. **37**, 103031–103063 (2024)
14. Raj, A.S., Lowney, M., Shah, R., Wetzstein, G.: Stanford Lytro light field archive. http://lightfields.stanford.edu/LF2016.html (2016)
15. Sheng, H., Cong, R., Yang, D., Chen, R., Wang, S., Cui, Z.: UrbanLF: a comprehensive light field dataset for semantic segmentation of urban scenes. IEEE Transactions on Circuits and Systems for Video Technology (2022)
16. Shi, J., Jiang, X., Guillemot, C.: A framework for learning depth from a flexible subset of dense and sparse light field views. IEEE Trans. Image Process. **28**(12), 5867–5880 (2019)
17. Shin, C., Jeon, H.G., Yoon, Y., Kweon, I.S., Kim, S.J.: EPINET: a fully-convolutional neural network using Epipolar geometry for depth from light field images. In: Proceedings of the IEEE Conference on Computer Vision and Pattern Recognition, pp. 4748–4757 (2018)
18. Tsai, Y.J., Liu, Y.L., Ouhyoung, M., Chuang, Y.Y.: Attention-based view selection networks for light-field disparity estimation. In: Proceedings of the AAAI Conference on Artificial Intelligence. vol. 34, pp. 12095–12103 (2020)

19. Wang, Q., Li, Y.: PDE-Net: pyramid depth estimation network for light fields. In: Proceedings of the 2024 16th International Conference on Machine Learning and Computing, pp. 670–676 (2024)
20. Wang, T., Sheng, H., Chen, R., Cong, R., Zhao, M., Cui, Z.: Adaptive epi-matching cost for light field disparity estimation. IEEE Transactions on Instrumentation and Measurement (2024)
21. Wang, T., et al.: Light field depth estimation: a comprehensive survey from principles to future. High-Confidence Comput. **4**(1), 100187 (2024)
22. Wang, X., Tao, C., Zheng, Z.: Occlusion-aware light field depth estimation with view attention. Opt. Lasers Eng. **160**, 107299 (2023)
23. Wang, Y., Wang, L., Liang, Z., Yang, J., An, W., Guo, Y.: Occlusion-aware cost constructor for light field depth estimation. In: Proceedings of the IEEE/CVF Conference on Computer Vision and Pattern Recognition, pp. 19809–19818 (2022)
24. Wang, Y., et al.: Disentangling light fields for super-resolution and disparity estimation. IEEE Trans. Pattern Anal. Mach. Intell. **45**(1), 425–443 (2022)
25. Zhou, P., Shi, L., Liu, X., Jin, J., Zhang, Y., Hou, J.: Light field depth estimation via stitched Epipolar plane images. IEEE Trans. Visual Comput. Graphics **30**(10), 6866–6879 (2023)

# GSC-SAGE: A Generative Subgraph Contrastive Framework for Encrypted Traffic Detection

Hongyuan Cheng[1] , Weizhe Chen[1] , Zhiguang Yan[2], Weixiang Jiang[1],
Dexin Zhu[1], and Lihua Yin[1]([✉])

[1] Cyberspace Institute of Advanced Technology, Guangzhou University,
Guangzhou 510555, Guangdong, China
`yinlh@gzhu.edu.cn`
[2] Guangxi Key Laboratory of Cryptography and Information Security, Guilin
University of Electronic Technology, Guilin 541004, GuangXi, China

**Abstract.** With the widespread deployment of TLS protocols, encrypted traffic detection faces dual challenges of feature-space homogenization and dynamic attack patterns. Existing deep learning-based detection methods are constrained by flattened data representation and supervised learning paradigms, struggling to capture topological correlations in encrypted traffic. This study proposes the GSC-SAGE framework, which models traffic topology through IP-port graph construction and innovatively integrates generative subgraph contrastive learning with an enhanced graph neural network. The method employs breadth-first sampling for subgraph generation, constructs contrastive loss functions via Wasserstein Distance metrics for self-supervised graph representation learning, and synchronizes node-edge feature propagation through the E-GraphSAGE mechanism. In summary, this research provides a novel technical pathway for unsupervised graph representation learning in cybersecurity applications.

**Keywords:** Encrypted Traffic Classification · Network Intrusion Detection · Graph Neural Networks · Self-Supervised Learning · Deep Learning

## 1  Introduction

With the exponential growth of internet traffic, network communication security has become a critical issue in the digital age. The high-frequency transmission of sensitive user information in open network environments makes it a primary target for malicious attackers. New types of network attacks exhibit polymorphic and covert characteristics. Attackers penetrate critical data through methods such as data theft, man-in-the-middle attacks, and information tampering, which not only lead to large-scale privacy leaks but can also cause irreversible economic losses to individuals and businesses. To counter these security threats, traffic encryption technology has become a core solution for ensuring the integrity and confidentiality of network communication. Google's Transparency Report shows [2] that the prevalence of encrypted traffic exhibits a significant growth trend, continuously climbing from 48% in 2014 to 99% in 2024.

However, while encrypted traffic protects network data security, it also provides attackers with covert channels for attacks. Due to the unparseable nature of encrypted payloads, traditional Deep Packet Inspection (DPI) techniques [8,26,28] based on plaintext features (such as malicious keywords, attack patterns) face the risk of failure. Furthermore, encrypted traffic retains only limited protocol metadata features, enabling attackers to use traffic obfuscation techniques to make malicious communication features highly isomorphic to normal encrypted traffic. This similarity in the feature space poses a severe challenge to common malicious traffic detection models.

Advancements in machine learning and deep learning have enabled NIDS (Network Intrusion Detection Systems) to analyze large-scale encrypted traffic data. Specifically, numerous statistical features are extracted from encrypted traffic, and then machine learning or deep learning models are used for training and detection [3–5]. However, ML/DL-based detection methods rely on flattened data formats, such as vectors or grids, which are often represented as tables or images. Although these methods can effectively extract data features, with the increase in network threats, malicious threat activities are often accomplished through complex attacks involving coordinated and associated communication among multiple infected hosts. Current ML/DL models have limitations in capturing attack-related association structures and contextual patterns [25,27].

Network data inherently possesses a graph structure. Graphs, as a universal representation form, encapsulate topological structure and contextual information. Therefore, developing a graph representation method for encrypted traffic classification is highly promising [7]. However, a significant portion of existing GNN research for encrypted traffic classification follows the supervised learning paradigm, which presents two challenges. Firstly, supervised learning requires data labeling, which is a very time-consuming process. Obtaining a large amount of ground truth labels is particularly unrealistic in large-scale network scenarios. Secondly, the reliance of supervised learning on labeled data limits the model's ability to detect newly emerging malicious encrypted traffic [10,21].

Based on the above considerations, we propose GSC-SAGE. This is achieved by constructing the encrypted traffic as a graph structure where nodes are network entities (represented as IP:Port) and edges represent encrypted traffic flows, and by employing Generative Subgraph Contrast (GSC) for self-supervised graph representation learning. By adaptively learning the weights of corresponding neighbor node relationships, it effectively captures topological association information in the graph. Through E-GraphSAGE, it enables effective propagation of node and edge information in the graph, enhancing encrypted traffic features, and thereby achieving efficient and accurate encrypted traffic classification. Our contributions are as follows:

- By constructing encrypted traffic as a graph structure where nodes are network entities and edges represent encrypted traffic features, and by implementing an adaptive subgraph generation contrastive learning framework for encrypted traffic using GSC. Through adaptive contrastive learning corresponding neighbor node relationship weights, it effectively captures topological association information in the graph, reduces reliance on labeled data, and enhances encrypted traffic features.
- After obtaining the enhanced encrypted traffic feature graph, E-GraphSAGE is employed to simultaneously learn features of both nodes and edges and perform message passing, further capturing edge features and topological information of the graph, thereby achieving edge feature enhancement, leading to efficient and accurate classification of encrypted traffic.

## 2 Related Work

### 2.1 Rule-Based Detection of Encrypted Malicious Traffic

Rule-based signature detection methods to analyze payloads and build a database of malicious traffic features,such as Deep Packet Inspection (DPI) [8,26,28]. While these methods can effectively integrate domain expertise and possess good model interpretability, their practical application has significant drawbacks: the computational overhead of encryption and decryption operations makes it challenging to meet real-time requirements; their reliance on known attack patterns renders them ineffective against zero-day attacks and polymorphic threats; and deep parsing of encrypted user traffic for monitoring contradicts the core objective of encryption-privacy protection.

### 2.2 Deep Learning Based Detection of Encrypted Malicious Traffic

Deep learning offers a novel approach to encrypted malicious traffic detection. Researchers have represented traffic data in various ways, such as reconstructing bitstreams into vectors [23], mapping byte sequences to grayscale images [16], converting packets into time-series images as input [12], and using Perlin noise to encode features for image generation [6]. These representations are then fed into models like CNNs and LSTMs for end-to-end classification. Such methods overcome the limitations of rule-based systems and can autonomously extract features indicative of potential threats.

However, deep learning models still face challenges: adversarial attack techniques, such as GANs, can camouflage malicious traffic through feature perturbations, and the high parameter sensitivity of these models leads to insufficient defensive capabilities. Furthermore, existing model architectures generally lack the ability to effectively model the spatio-temporal correlations of encrypted traffic, such as session sequences, focusing solely on static feature extraction from individual samples, which limits their robustness in dynamic adversarial environments.

## 2.3   Graph Learning Based Detection of Encrypted Malicious Traffic

Graph learning offers a new paradigm for threat identification by constructing graph-structured relationships from traffic data. Researchers have mapped encrypted sessions into graph structures, such as traffic interaction graphs [17], or for specific scenarios, like TLS heterogeneous graphs [9] and mobile application traffic communication graphs [15]. By leveraging graph classification or graph embedding techniques, they aim to identify distributed encrypted malicious applications and botnet compromised hosts [22]. However, current research on encrypted traffic classification primarily relies on supervised Graph Neural Networks (GNNs), which face a fundamental conflict between high annotation costs and the dynamic nature of network environments. These models are inherently constrained by the known threat patterns present in their training data, making it challenging to detect novel threats such as zero-day attacks or adversarial variants. This limitation stems from the contradiction between the data distribution prior assumptions of supervised learning and the continuously evolving characteristics of encrypted threats.

To address the aforementioned challenges, this paper proposes a graph self-supervised learning framework specifically designed for encrypted traffic graph data structures to reduce reliance on annotations. Furthermore, it incorporates E-GraphSAGE to synchronously support information propagation between nodes and edges, thereby overcoming the bottleneck of isolated static features in single samples. This approach aims to enhance the relational features of encrypted traffic and improve classification accuracy.

# 3   Method

## 3.1   Overall Structure

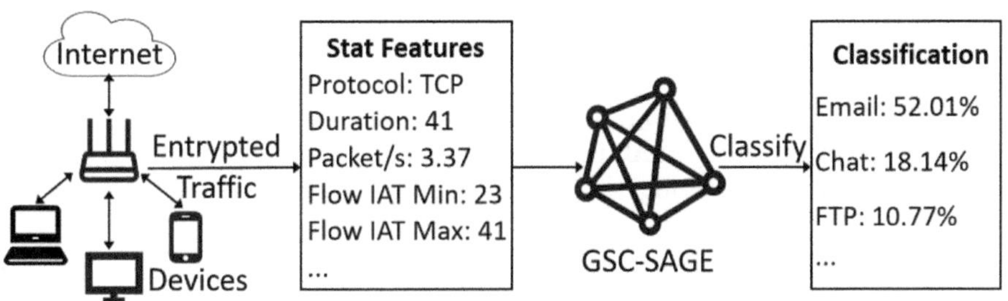


**Fig. 1.** Encrypted Traffic Classification Flowchart

As shown in Fig. 1, we represent network traffic as a graph structure, where each $\langle IP : Port \rangle$ pair is represented as a node, and the network flow between two $\langle IP : Port \rangle$ pairs is represented as an edge. Subsequently, the network

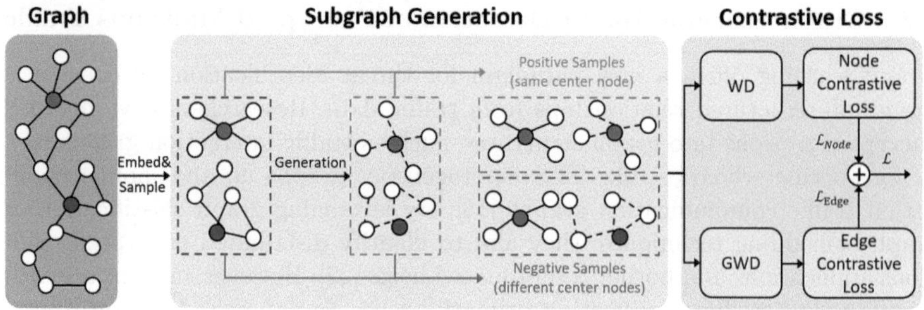



**Fig. 2.** GSC-SAGE Model Framwork

traffic graph is input into the GSC-SAGE model. We then utilize a subgraph contrastive learning approach to learn the intrinsic topological knowledge within the network traffic graph structure. Finally, the learned edge features are input into a classifier to fine-tune the model. The subgraph contrastive learning process of the GSC-SAGE model will be detailed in Sect. 3.2.

### 3.2 Generative Subgraph Contrast

As illustrated in Fig. 2, the overall training pipeline of the GSC-SAGE model is presented. First, E-GraphSAGE is utilized to encode and embed the nodes within the entire network traffic graph $\mathcal{G}$. Subsequently, a self-supervised learning approach employing Generative Subgraph Contrast (GSC) is used to learn the intrinsic topological structure of the graph. Specifically, for each node $i$ in the graph, a sampled subgraph $\mathcal{G}_i$ is obtained. Node features are then generated for these sampled subgraphs to create positive sample subgraphs $\hat{\mathcal{G}}_i$. Finally, the network traffic graph's topological structure is learned by contrasting these positive sample pairs with negative sample pairs. Ultimately, the learned edge features undergo classification.

**E-GraphSAGE Embedding.** For each node $i$, the node features are obtained using two layers of E-GraphSAGE. The node feature aggregation process can be described by the following formula:

$$\mathbf{z}_v = \mathbf{h}_v^K, \mathbf{h}_v^k = \sigma \left( \mathbf{W}^k \cdot \text{CONCAT} \left( \mathbf{h}_v^{k-1}, \mathbf{h}_{\mathcal{N}(v)}^k \right) \right) \tag{1}$$

In the formula, $K$ denotes the maximum neighborhood size used for sampling, and $W^k$ represents the learnable weight parameters of the linear transformation layer. $\mathcal{N}(v)$ denotes the set of neighbor nodes. $h_v^{k-1}$ refers to the features of the node $v$ in the layer $(k-1) - th$. Note that the initial node features are vectors with all elements equal to 1. $h^k_{\mathcal{N}(v)}$ represents the aggregated features from the neighbors of node $v$ for the $k - th$ layer. $\sigma(\cdot)$ represents the activation function. Its computation process is detailed in the following formula:

$$\mathbf{h}^k_{\mathcal{N}(v)} = \sum_{u \in \mathcal{N}(v), uv \in \mathcal{E}} \frac{\mathbf{e}^{k-1}_{uv}}{|\mathcal{N}(v)|_e} \tag{2}$$

where $\mathbf{e}^{k-1}_{uv}$ denotes the initial characterization of the edges in the k-1st order neighborhood. $\varepsilon$ denotes the set of edges. The edge characteristics of the graph are expressed as the following equation:

$$\mathbf{z}^K_{uv} = \mathrm{CONCAT}\left(\mathbf{z}^K_u, \mathbf{z}^K_v\right) \tag{3}$$

**Positive Sample Generation.** For each node $i$, subgraph generation is performed on the BFS$-$sampled subgraph $\mathcal{G}_i$, yielding the positive sample subgraph $\hat{\mathcal{G}}_i$ for node $i$. As illustrated in the middle section of Fig. 2, node generation is applied to the subgraph $\mathcal{G}_i$. This involves generating a new node embedding feature $\hat{h}_i$ for the node $s_i$ within the subgraph. The computation process for this is detailed as follows:

$$\hat{h}_i = \sum_{j=1}^{N_i} \alpha_j h_j \tag{4}$$

where, $N_i$ represents the set of neighbors of node $i$ in the original graph $\mathcal{G}$, $h_j$ represents the embedding features of neighbor node $j$, and $\alpha_j$ denotes the weight parameter. The calculation formula for a is shown below:

$$\alpha_j = \frac{\exp\left(\theta\left(h_i, h_j\right)\right)}{\sum_{k=1}^{N_i} \exp\left(\theta\left(h_i, h_k\right)\right)} \tag{5}$$

$$\theta\left(h_i, h_j\right) = \mathrm{LeakyReLU}\left(W_\theta\left[W_\phi h_i \| W_\phi h_j\right]\right) \tag{6}$$

where, $W_\phi$ denotes the shared linear transformation layer, $W_\theta$ denotes another linear transformation layer, and $\|$ represents the concatenation operation.

**Generative Subgraph Contrast.** We use Wasserstein Distance and Gromov Wasserstein Distance to measure the similarity between the generated subgraph $\hat{\mathcal{G}}_i$ and the sampled subgraph $\mathcal{G}_i$ in terms of nodes and edges, respectively. The contrastive learning objective of the GSC$-$SAGE model is formulated as follows:

$$\mathcal{L} = \lambda\mathcal{L}_1 + (1 - \lambda)\mathcal{L}_2 \tag{7}$$

$$\mathcal{L}_1 = \frac{-1}{N(M+1)} \sum_{i=1}^{N} \Bigg[ \log\left(\exp\left(-D_w\left(\boldsymbol{s}_i, \boldsymbol{s}_p\right)/\tau\right)\right)$$

$$+ \sum_{j=1}^{M} \log\left(1 - \exp\left(-D_w\left(\boldsymbol{s}_i, \boldsymbol{s}_{nj}\right)/\tau\right)\right) \Bigg] \tag{8}$$

$$\mathcal{L}_2 = \frac{-1}{N(M+1)} \sum_{i=1}^{N} \Bigg[ \log\left(\exp\left(-D_{gw}\left(\boldsymbol{s}_i, \boldsymbol{s}_p\right)/\tau\right)\right)$$

$$+ \sum_{j=1}^{M} \log\left(1 - \exp\left(-D_{gw}\left(\boldsymbol{s}_i, \boldsymbol{s}_{nj}\right)/\tau\right)\right) \Bigg] \tag{9}$$

where, $\lambda$ denotes a hyperparameter, $\tau$ denotes the temperature parameter, $\boldsymbol{s}_p$ denotes the representation of the positive sample generated subgraph, and $\boldsymbol{s}_{nj}$ denotes the representation of the $j-th$ negative sample generated subgraph. $D_w\left(\boldsymbol{s}_i, \boldsymbol{s}_p\right)$ and $D_{gw}\left(\boldsymbol{s}_i, \boldsymbol{s}_p\right)$ denote the Wasserstein Distance and Gromov Wasserstein Distance, respectively. Their computation processes are detailed as follows:

$$D_w(\boldsymbol{u}, \boldsymbol{v}) = \min_{T \in \pi(\boldsymbol{u}, \boldsymbol{v})} \sum_{i=1}^{n} \sum_{j=1}^{m} \boldsymbol{T}_{ij} c\left(\boldsymbol{h}_{1i}, \boldsymbol{h}_{2j}\right) \tag{10}$$

$$D_{gw}(\boldsymbol{u}, \boldsymbol{v}) = \min_{T \in \pi(\boldsymbol{u}, \boldsymbol{v})} \sum_{i,i',j,j'} T_{ij} T_{i'j'} \hat{c}\left(\boldsymbol{h}_{1i}, \boldsymbol{h}_{2j}, \boldsymbol{h}_{1i'}, \boldsymbol{h}_{2j'}\right) \tag{11}$$

$$\hat{c}\left(\boldsymbol{h}_{1i}, \boldsymbol{h}_{2j}, \boldsymbol{h}_{1i'}, \boldsymbol{h}_{2j'}\right) = c\left(\boldsymbol{h}_{1i}, \boldsymbol{h}_{1i'}\right) - c\left(\boldsymbol{h}_{2j}, \boldsymbol{h}_{2j'}\right) \tag{12}$$

where, $c\left(\cdot, \cdot\right)$ denotes the transport cost between two features, reflecting their similarity, and $\hat{c}\left(\boldsymbol{h}_{1i}, \boldsymbol{h}_{2j}, \boldsymbol{h}_{1i'}, \boldsymbol{h}_{2j'}\right)$ reflects the similarity of edges between the sampled subgraph and the generated subgraph.

### 3.3   Flow Classification Fine-Tuning

With the above self-supervised learning, the results of the classifier for the edge (flow) in the network flow graph are represented as:

$$\hat{y}_{uv} = f(\mathbf{z}_{uv}^K) \tag{13}$$

where $f(\cdot)$ represents a linear mapping function that classifies edge features, and $\hat{y}_{uv}$ represents the classification result.

We classify the network streams whose final learning objective is described by the following equation:

$$\mathcal{L} = \text{Cross Entropy}(y_{uv}, \hat{y}_{uv}) \tag{14}$$

where $y_i$ denotes the ground-truth class.

## 4    Experiment

All experiments in this paper were conducted on a laptop equipped with an Intel Core i9-12900H 2.5GHz and an NVIDIA GeForce RTX 3060 laptop 6GB.

### 4.1    Dataset

**USTC-TFC2016** [24]: Created by Wang et al., this dataset was proposed to address the lack of diverse public datasets in current encrypted traffic classification research. It contains ten types of normal traffic collected using IXIA BPS [1]. The dataset provides complete traffic data in pcap format, from which statistical features were extracted using CICFlowMeter [11] for model training and testing in this paper.

**CIC-DoHBrw-2020** [14]: Generated by the Canadian Institute for Cybersecurity in 2020, this dataset contains DoH, non-DoH, benign, and malicious network traffic for DNS accessed via the HTTPS protocol. Benign DoH traffic instances were generated using Google Chrome and Mozilla Firefox, while malicious DoH traffic instances were generated using iodine, dns2tcp, and DNSCat2. The dataset includes a total of 31 network traffic statistical features.

### 4.2    Comparative Experiment

**Table 1.** Experimental Results on USTC-TFC2016

| Method | Accuracy | Precision | Recall | F1-score |
|---|---|---|---|---|
| FlowPrint [20] | 0.8992 | 0.8743 | 0.8992 | 0.8751 |
| AppScanner [19] | 0.7991 | 0.8591 | 0.7063 | 0.7835 |
| DF [18] | 0.7827 | 0.8964 | 0.7443 | 0.7561 |
| GraphDApp [17] | 0.9021 | 0.9123 | 0.9021 | 0.9017 |
| E-GraphSAGE [13] | 0.9524 | 0.9587 | 0.9524 | 0.9544 |
| GSC-SAGE (ours) | **0.9786** | **0.9795** | **0.9786** | **0.9791** |

The comparative results of the proposed method against baseline methods on the USTC-TFC2016 and CIC-DoHBrw-2020 datasets are shown in the Table 1 and Table 2. On the USTC-TFC2016 dataset, GSC-SAGE achieved an accuracy of 0.9786, surpassing all comparative models. It showed an improvement of 2.62% compared to the prototype method E-GraphSAGE, and outperformed Graph-DApp and non-GNN methods by margins of 7.65% and 7.94%, respectively. Its precision, recall, and F1-score reached 0.9795, 0.9786, and 0.9791, respectively, all achieving optimal levels. This indicates that while the model accurately identifies malicious traffic patterns, its representation capability for normal traffic features is also systematically enhanced.

**Table 2.** Experimental Results on CIC-DoHBrw-2020

| Method | Accuracy | Precision | Recall | F1-score |
| --- | --- | --- | --- | --- |
| FlowPrint | 0.8092 | 0.8069 | 0.7952 | 0.8013 |
| AppScanner | 0.8665 | 0.8665 | 0.8647 | 0.8682 |
| DF | 0.8485 | 0.8485 | 0.8485 | 0.8485 |
| GraphDApp | 0.9021 | 0.9071 | 0.9087 | 0.9055 |
| E-GraphSAGE | 0.9643 | 0.9616 | 0.9643 | 0.9628 |
| GSC-SAGE (ours) | **0.9812** | **0.9844** | **0.9812** | **0.9836** |

In the CIC-DoHBrw-2020 dataset, GSC-SAGE again achieved the best detection performance with an accuracy of 0.9812, showing an improvement of 1.69% over E-GraphSAGE, and extending its lead over GraphDApp to 7.91%. Notably, while maintaining high accuracy, the model achieved an F1-score of 0.9836, reflecting its fine-grained discrimination ability for traffic behavior patterns in complex DoH encrypted traffic scenarios. Compared to traditional methods like DeepPacket, GSC-SAGE effectively captures both topological and semantic features of traffic through its self-supervised pre-training mechanism.

Cross-dataset experiments further validated the model's generalization ability. In comparative tests between USTC-TFC2016 and CIC-DoHBrw-2020, GSC-SAGE consistently maintained optimal performance with no significant fluctuations across the four metrics, demonstrating its excellent balanced performance, significantly superior to E-GraphSAGE and GraphDApp. This stability stems from the robust representation optimization achieved by self-supervised contrastive learning against noisy data, and the deep modeling capability of graph neural networks for spatio-temporal correlations in traffic.

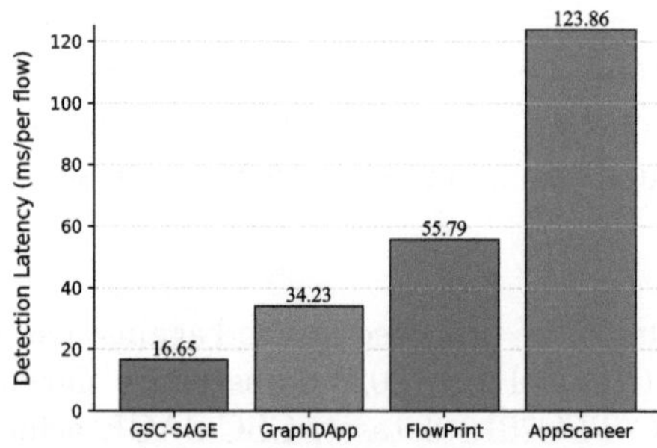


**Fig. 3.** TESTING TIME OF DIFFERENT METHODS

In the comparative speed evaluation experiments assessing time consumption for single-flow classification tasks, the proposed GSC-SAGE model demonstrated superior computational efficiency (unit: milliseconds per flow, ms/per flow). As illustrated in Fig. 3, while both GSC-SAGE and GraphDApp represent network traffic through graph structures, the proposed method achieves significant performance advantages through two key innovations: First, it implements edge feature classification rather than subgraph-based processing; Second, its neighbor edge sampling strategy substantially reduces the time overhead associated with node feature aggregation operations by minimizing the number of required neighborhood interactions. In contrast, GraphDApp requires explicit subgraph feature extraction and classification for each network flow, compounded by the necessity to store intermediate feature representations from all neural network layers, which exponentially increases temporal complexity. The FlowPrint model exhibits substantial computational latency during its fingerprint matching phase, while AppScanner's feature extraction process makes it the most time-consuming method in the evaluation.

## 5    Conclusion

Addressing the core pain points of missing topological features and limitations of supervised learning in encrypted traffic detection, this study proposes an innovative solution integrating subgraph contrastive learning with enhanced graph neural networks. Key highlights of this research include: Firstly, it introduces graph contrastive learning into the field of encrypted traffic analysis, building a self-supervised framework with topological awareness; Secondly, it uses an edge feature propagation mechanism which achieves synergistic optimization of edge-node features while keeping the model lightweight, breaking through the sole focus of traditional GNNs on node features; Thirdly, it achieves multi-scale modeling of network behavior patterns through a subgraph generation strategy. Classification accuracy exceeding 97% in cross-dataset tests demonstrates that the self-supervised pre-training mechanism maintains model robustness even in scenarios with scarce labeled data. Current models still face challenges in detecting encrypted traffic, particularly concerning dynamic network topology evolution and the fusion of multi-protocol heterogeneous features, such as TLS, QUIC, and DoH.

In our future work, we aim to explore dynamic graph neural network modeling methods based on spatiotemporal graphs to more accurately characterize the temporal dynamics of evolving network topologies. Furthermore, we will design a unified graph representation framework tailored for multi-protocol heterogeneous traffic and investigate collaborative representation learning approaches that enable cross-protocol feature fusion.

## References


1. Ixia   Breakpoint   Overview   and   Specifications.   https://www.ixiacom.com/products/breakingpoint (2016). Accessed 03 Mar 2025
2. HTTPS Encryption in Chrome. https://transparencyreport.google.com/https/overview?hl=En (2024). Accessed 21 Apr 2024

3. Anderson, B., McGrew, D.: Identifying encrypted malware traffic with contextual flow data. In: Proceedings of the 2016 ACM Workshop on Artificial Intelligence and Security, pp. 35–46. AISec '16, Association for Computing Machinery, New York, NY, USA (2016). https://doi.org/10.1145/2996758.2996768

4. Anderson, B., McGrew, D.: Machine learning for encrypted malware traffic classification: accounting for noisy labels and non-stationarity. In: Proceedings of the 23rd ACM SIGKDD International Conference on Knowledge Discovery and Data Mining, pp. 1723–1732. KDD '17, Association for Computing Machinery, New York, NY, USA (2017). https://doi.org/10.1145/3097983.3098163

5. Anderson, B., Paul, S., McGrew, D.: Deciphering malware's use of TLS (without decryption). J. Comput. Virol. Hacking Tech. **14**, 195–211 (2018)

6. Bazuhair, W., Lee, W.: Detecting malign encrypted network traffic using Perlin noise and convolutional neural network. In: 2020 10th Annual Computing and Communication Workshop and Conference (CCWC), pp. 0200–0206 (2020). https://doi.org/10.1109/CCWC47524.2020.9031116

7. Chang, L., Branco, P.: Graph-based solutions with residuals for intrusion detection: The modified E-GraphSAGE and E-ResGAT algorithms. arXiv preprint arXiv:2111.13597 (2021)

8. Creech, G., Hu, J.: A semantic approach to host-based intrusion detection systems using contiguousand discontiguous system call patterns. IEEE Trans. Comput. **63**(4), 807–819 (2014). https://doi.org/10.1109/TC.2013.13

9. Cui, T., Gou, G., Xiong, G., Li, Z., Cui, M., Liu, C.: SiamHAN: IPv6 address correlation attacks on TLS encrypted traffic via Siamese heterogeneous graph attention network. In: 30th USENIX Security Symposium (USENIX Security 21), pp. 4329–4346. USENIX Association (2021). https://www.usenix.org/conference/usenixsecurity21/presentation/cui

10. Khemani, B., Patil, S., Kotecha, K., Tanwar, S.: A review of graph neural networks: concepts, architectures, techniques, challenges, datasets, applications, and future directions. J. Big Data **11**(1), 18 (2024)

11. Lashkari, A.H., Gil, G.D., Mamun, M.S.I., Ghorbani, A.A.: Characterization of tor traffic using time based features. In: International Conference on Information Systems Security and Privacy. vol. 2, pp. 253–262. SciTePress (2017)

12. Lin, K., Xu, X., Gao, H.: TSCRNN: a novel classification scheme of encrypted traffic based on flow spatiotemporal features for efficient management of IIoT. Comput. Netw. **190**, 107974 (2021). https://doi.org/10.1016/j.comnet.2021.107974, https://www.sciencedirect.com/science/article/pii/S1389128621001067

13. Lo, W.W., Layeghy, S., Sarhan, M., Gallagher, M., Portmann, M.: E-GraphSAGE: a graph neural network based intrusion detection system for IoT. In: NOMS 2022-2022 IEEE/IFIP Network Operations and Management Symposium, pp. 1–9. IEEE Press (2022). https://doi.org/10.1109/NOMS54207.2022.9789878

14. MontazeriShatoori, M., Davidson, L., Kaur, G., Lashkari, A.H.: Detection of DoH tunnels using time-series classification of encrypted traffic. In: 2020 IEEE Intl Conf on Dependable, Autonomic and Secure Computing, Intl Conf on Pervasive Intelligence and Computing, Intl Conf on Cloud and Big Data Computing, Intl Conf on Cyber Science and Technology Congress (DASC/PiCom/CBDCom/CyberSciTech), pp. 63–70 (2020). https://api.semanticscholar.org/CorpusID:226852987

15. Pham, T.D., Ho, T.L., Truong-Huu, T., Cao, T.D., Truong, H.L.: MAppGraph: mobile-app classification on encrypted network traffic using deep graph convolution neural networks. In: Proceedings of the 37th Annual Computer Security

Applications Conference, pp. 1025–1038. ACSAC '21, Association for Computing Machinery, New York, NY, USA (2021). https://doi.org/10.1145/3485832.3485925

16. Shapira, T., Shavitt, Y.: FlowPic: a generic representation for encrypted traffic classification and applications identification. IEEE Trans. Netw. Serv. Manage. **18**(2), 1218–1232 (2021). https://doi.org/10.1109/TNSM.2021.3071441

17. Shen, M., Zhang, J., Zhu, L., Xu, K., Du, X.: Accurate decentralized application identification via encrypted traffic analysis using graph neural networks. IEEE Trans. Inf. Forensics Secur. **16**, 2367–2380 (2021). https://doi.org/10.1109/TIFS.2021.3050608

18. Sirinam, P., Imani, M., Juarez, M., Wright, M.: Deep fingerprinting: undermining website fingerprinting defenses with deep learning. In: Proceedings of the 2018 ACM SIGSAC Conference on Computer and Communications Security, pp. 1928–1943. CCS '18, Association for Computing Machinery, New York, NY, USA (2018). https://doi.org/10.1145/3243734.3243768

19. Taylor, V.F., Spolaor, R., Conti, M., Martinovic, I.: Robust smartphone app identification via encrypted network traffic analysis. IEEE Trans. Inf. Forensics Secur. **13**(1), 63–78 (2018). https://doi.org/10.1109/TIFS.2017.2737970

20. Van Ede, T., et al.: FlowPrint: semi-supervised mobile-app fingerprinting on encrypted network traffic. In: Network and Distributed System Security Symposium (NDSS). vol. 27 (2020)

21. Waikhom, L., Patgiri, R.: A survey of graph neural networks in various learning paradigms: methods, applications, and challenges. Artif. Intell. Rev. **56**(7), 6295–6364 (2023)

22. Wang, W., Shang, Y., He, Y., Li, Y., Liu, J.: BotMark: automated botnet detection with hybrid analysis of flow-based and graph-based traffic behaviors. Inf. Sci. **511**, 284–296 (2020). https://doi.org/10.1016/j.ins.2019.09.024. https://www.sciencedirect.com/science/article/pii/S0020025519308758

23. Wang, W., Zhu, M., Wang, J., Zeng, X., Yang, Z.: End-to-end encrypted traffic classification with one-dimensional convolution neural networks. In: 2017 IEEE International Conference on Intelligence and Security Informatics (ISI), pp. 43–48 (2017). https://doi.org/10.1109/ISI.2017.8004872

24. Wang, W., Zhu, M., Zeng, X., Ye, X., Sheng, Y.: Malware traffic classification using convolutional neural network for representation learning. In: 2017 International Conference on Information Networking (ICOIN), pp. 712–717 (2017). https://doi.org/10.1109/ICOIN.2017.7899588

25. Xiao, Q., Liu, J., Wang, Q., Jiang, Z., Wang, X., Yao, Y.: Towards network anomaly detection using graph embedding. In: Krzhizhanovskaya, V.V., et al. (eds.) ICCS 2020. LNCS, vol. 12140, pp. 156–169. Springer, Cham (2020). https://doi.org/10.1007/978-3-030-50423-6_12

26. Xu, C., Chen, S., Su, J., Yiu, S.M., Hui, L.C.K.: A survey on regular expression matching for deep packet inspection: applications, algorithms, and hardware platforms. IEEE Commun. Surv. Tutorials **18**(4), 2991–3029 (2016). https://doi.org/10.1109/COMST.2016.2566669

27. Zhang, B., Li, J., Chen, C., Lee, K., Lee, I.: A practical botnet traffic detection system using GNN. In: Meng, W., Conti, M. (eds.) Cyberspace Safety and Security, pp. 66–78. Springer International Publishing, Cham (2022)

28. Zhang, H., Papadopoulos, C., Massey, D.: Detecting encrypted botnet traffic. In: 2013 Proceedings IEEE INFOCOM, pp. 3453–1358 (2013). https://doi.org/10.1109/INFCOM.2013.6567180

# Gradient Balanced Part-Whole Relational Weakly Supervised Semantic Segmentation


Zhuang Yao[1], Guangqi Jiang[1], Lin Shi[1], Gengshen Wu[2], Shoukun Xu[1], and Yi Liu[1(✉)]

[1] Changzhou University, Changzhou, China
s231508120530smail.cczu.edu.cn,
{guangqijiang,slcczu,skxu,liuyi0089}@cczu.edu.cn
[2] City University of Macau, Macau, China



**Abstract.** Most weakly supervised semantic segmentation (WSSS) methods use class activation map (CAM) to generate pseudo labels. However, due to the image-level supervision, the CAM obtained from the classification network can only activate the most discriminative regions instead of the whole object. A few attempts have studied class-agnostic CAM generation for this issue. Nonetheless, they may lose class semantics, thus degrading semantic segmentation performance. In this paper, we design a two-branch CAM generation network to solve the previous challenges, including a class-agnostic and a classification subnetwork. To balance these two contradictory subnetworks, we introduce a gradient-balanced mechanism to control the gradient propagation during the backpropagation stage. In addition, we employ the part-whole relational property of Capsule Networks (CapsNets) in the classification branch, which is intended to reduce the over-emphasis on class-specific local details in foreground regions. The CAM generated from the class-agnostic branch produces a background cue map for further semantic segmentation. Extensive experiments on the PASCAL VOC 2012 and MS COCO 2014 datasets demonstrate the superiority of the proposed approach.

**Keywords:** Weakly Supervised Semantic Segmentation · Gradient Balance · Part-whole Relationships · Capsule Networks


## 1 Introduction

Semantic segmentation [5, 28, 33] aims to classify each pixel of the target image, which has made remarkable progress due to the continuous development of deep learning. Yet, fully supervised semantic segmentation methods rely on expensive and time-consuming pixel-level annotations, which can be alleviated by the weakly supervised methods based on weak labels, e.g., image-level label [31], bounding box [9], point [3], and scribbles [18].


© The Author(s), under exclusive license to Springer Nature Singapore Pte Ltd. 2026
T. Zhu et al. (Eds.): KSEM 2025, LNAI 15919, pp. 364–376, 2026.
https://doi.org/10.1007/978-981-95-3001-4_27

Many existing WSSS approaches [4,7,29] follow a multi-stage framework. A classification network is first trained to generate an initial CAM as a seed region, which is expanded to produce pseudo-labels for training the semantic segmentation model. The quality of CAM is a key factor in determining the effectiveness of the semantic segmentation model. However, due to class-level supervision, previous methods often focus on the most discriminative part of the foreground object using the CAM acquired by the classification network, as shown in Fig. 1 (a). This degrades the performance of downstream semantic segmentation tasks.

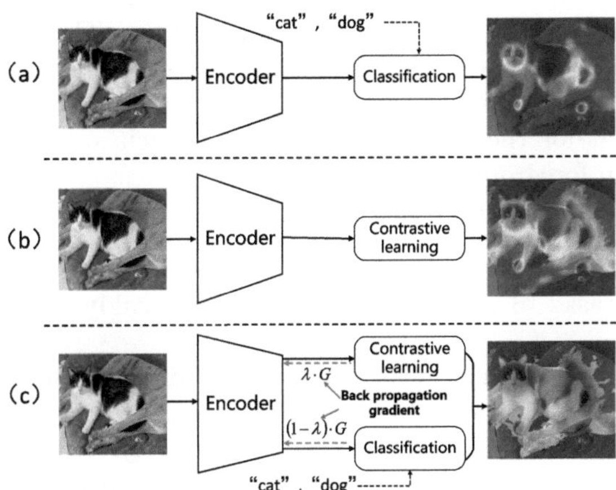


**Fig. 1.** Motivation illustration. **(a)** The initial CAM [34] is generated by the classification network, so it only activates the most class-discriminative parts. **(b)** CCAM [30] uses contrastive learning to generate the class-agnostic activation map, which may leave some classes unactivated due to the lack of label information. **(c)** We combine the two networks, introducing class information to the contrastive learning branch, and control the contribution of the two branches using the parameter $\lambda$.

To address this issue, Jo *et al.* [13] employ a reconstruction loss to train the classifier, enabling the CAM to encompass the object regions more completely. Lin *et al.* [20] leverage the attention mechanism in CLIP to construct a class-aware attention-based affinity module for CAM refinement. Despite these methods enhancing the quality of the CAM, they make the network architectures more complex. To address this problem, some post-processing refinement methods have been proposed to alleviate the complexity, such as training an additional affinity network [2]. Nevertheless, these methods are still far from satisfactory.

In this paper, to make an advancement towards WSSS, we design a dual-branch framework involving a contrastive learning branch for foreground regions segmentation and a capsule classification branch for semantic discrimination. However, there is an inherent contradiction between these two tasks. Concretely, the classification task tends to focus on the most discriminative regions within the foreground instead of the whole object, whereas the segmentation task requires more complete foreground regions. To effectively integrate these two tasks, we propose a gradient-balanced mechanism to back-propagate gradients for these two branches differentially, as depicted in Fig. 1(c). Doing so enables two branches to leverage their strengths, *i.e.*, the contrastive learning branch focuses on the potential foreground regions while the capsule classification branch identifies the object categories. Therefore, these two branches complement each other to enhance semantic segmentation using image-level labels.

To further address incomplete object segmentation in weakly supervised classification, we leverage the part-whole relationships [24] of Capsule Networks (CapsNets) [27] within the capsule classification branch. This design can reduce the likelihood of background regions being incorrectly classified as foreground using the image labels while focusing on the whole instead of local foreground regions. Note that for the contrastive learning branch, contrastive learning is employed to learn foreground maps.

To summarize our contributions:

- We propose a gradient-balanced mechanism that integrates segmentation and classification tasks to improve the accuracy of weakly supervised semantic segmentation.
- We employ the part-whole relational property endowed by CapsNets in the capsule classification branch to alleviate the issue of focusing on incomplete regions while identifying object categories effectively.
- Extensive experiments on PASCAL VOC 2012 and MS COCO 2014 demonstrate the superiority of the proposed method.

## 2   Related Work

### 2.1   Weakly Supervised Semantic Segmentation

Most weakly supervised semantic segmentation methods rely on CAM [34] derived from classification for initialization. However, due to its incompleteness, the performance is far from satisfactory. To address this, many researchers have proposed numerous methods to improve the segmentation quality. For example, during the initial CAM acquisition stage, many works have been proposed to focus on more foreground target regions by customizing loss functions or designing additional modules [29]. Besides, Lee *et al.* [17] enhanced non-discriminative but class-related features in an adversarial manner, which enables more object region identification. [12] discovered more non-discriminative target regions by "erasing" the most discriminative regions in multiple iterations.

In addition to this pipeline for improving segmentation quality, another pipeline of CAM refinement has been proposed to improve CAM quality for further segmentation. These methods usually take the initial CAM as seed regions, which are then extended to obtain high-quality pseudo-labels [8,35]. Chen *et al.* [4] collected incorrectly activated backgrounds in specific classes to suppress mislabeled regions as foregrounds. Lin *et al.* [20] designed an attention-based category-aware affinity module to refine the initial CAM in a real-time manner. Besides, a few attempts [2] use the initial CAM to train an affinity network and spread foreground regions. Nevertheless, these methods require the participation of the initial CAM in the training stage, which is not conducive to independent training in multi-stage methods. Differently, the proposed method in this paper can obtain background cues for refinement without using the initial CAM.

## 2.2   Capsule Networks

CapsNets [27] was proposed by G. E. Hinton and his team in 2017. In contrast to the traditional Convolutional Neural Networks (CNNs), CapsNets introduced the concept of "capsule" which effectively capture diverse aspects of information within images, including pose, orientation, and hierarchy. Thanks to the hierarchical relationships enabled by their routing mechanism, CapsNets have played a significant role in numerous downstream tasks, especially in segmentation [25, 26].

In the field of image segmentation, CapsNets are widely utilized in medical image segmentation [14]. Primarily, they function as a feature encoder for the effective extraction of image features. For instance, in [26], the capsule encoder was introduced to learn the target position and the relationships between parts and the whole. As a result, it cleverly retains key information that is typically easily discarded by the pooling layer during the downsampling process. Naghne *et al.* [25] pioneered an optimized capsule-based target segmentation network, which focused on addressing the thorny issue of spatial information loss caused by the pooling layer in CNNs. The unique part-whole relationship within CapsNets is derived from its unique routing mechanism. With the assistance of this part-whole relationship [21, 23], CapsNets can naturally extend its scope to the entire object and compensate for the drawback that the spatial information in the pooling layer of CNNs is prone to being lost.

To our knowledge, this is the first work to apply CapsNets to weakly supervised semantic segmentation. By leveraging the part-whole relationship, we meticulously design a classification network branch based on CapsNets. This innovative approach has opened up novel ideas and methods for WSSS, further promoting the development and progress of image segmentation technology under weakly-supervised conditions.

# 3   Methodology

The proposed method's framework is shown in Fig. 2. Section 3.1 describes feature extraction and contrastive learning for foreground/background separation. Section 3.2 details the capsule classification network and its loss mechanism. Finally, Sect. 3.3 introduces a novel gradient adjustment parameter $\lambda$ to optimise backpropagation by adjusting branch gradients.

## 3.1 Contrastive Learning Branch

The contrastive learning branch, based on class-agnostic activation maps [30], uses foreground and background feature representations from multiple images for separation via contrastive learning, finally obtaining a complete foreground map. Details will be described as follows.

First, a batch of $n$ training images $I = \{I_i\}_{i=1}^n$ are fed into the encoder $h(\cdot)$ and produces the initial feature $F = \{F_i\}_{i=1}^n$, in which $F_i \in \mathbb{R}^{C \times H \times W}$. Here, $C$ represents the number of channels, $H$ stands for the height in the spatial dimension, and $W$ indicates the width in the spatial dimension. Next, the feature $F_i$ passes through a $3 \times 3$ convolutional layer and a batch normalization layer to obtain a single-channel class-agnostic activation map $A = \{A_i\}_{i=1}^n$, in which $A_i \in \mathbb{R}^{1 \times H \times W}$. Taking $A_i$ as the foreground region, $1 - A_i$ is the background region. Subsequently, we perform matrix multiplication with the initial feature $F_i$ respectively, and finally obtain the foreground representation $v_f$ and the background representation $v_b$.

We combine them with all the other foreground and background features of the same batch to form the foreground set $V^f = \{v_1^f, v_2^f, \cdots, v_n^f\}$ and the background set $V^b = \{v_1^b, v_2^b, \cdots, v_n^b\}$. $\{V^f, V^f\}$ and $\{V^b, V^b\}$ are positive pairs, and $\{V^f, V^b\}$ is negative pairs.

$$L_{POS} = -\frac{1}{n} log(S^{fPOS} \cdot S^{bPOS}), \tag{1}$$

$$L_{NEG} = -\frac{1}{n} log(1 - S^{NEG}), \tag{2}$$

where $S^{fPOS}$ and $S^{bPOS}$ denote the cosine similarity between foreground-foreground and background-background in positive pairs, respectively. $S^{NEG}$ denotes the cosine similarity between foreground and background in negative pairs.

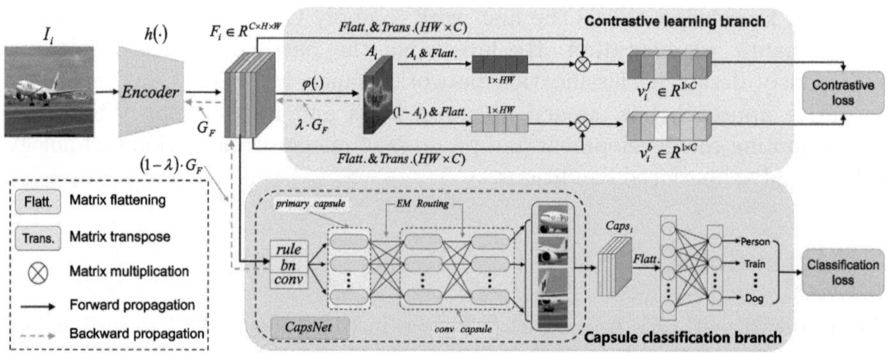


**Fig. 2.** The framework of our methodology is as follows. Firstly, the feature map $F_i$ is acquired by feeding the input image $I_i$ into the CNN network $h(\cdot)$. Subsequently, the feature $F_i$ is input into the classification branch. Meanwhile, two loss functions guide the contrast learning branch, contributing to the network training.

Then the contrastive learning loss ($L_{CTL}$) is obtained:

$$L_{CTL} = L_{POS} + L_{NEG}, \tag{3}$$

where $L_{POS}$ denotes the loss in positive pairs and $L_{NEG}$ denotes the loss in negative pairs.

## 3.2  Capsule Classification Branch

Building upon the feature $F$ obtained from the encoder $h(\cdot)$, CapsNets with EM routing are further used as the feature encoder for the classification network. Distinct from traditional convolutional networks, they employ capsules to explicitly model and preserve spatial hierarchical information. The foreground maps from the contrastive learning branch lack category discrimination, causing redundancy or the absence of category information. Thus, the part-whole relationships in features are derived from the capsule network's spatial hierarchical information. Then, by using the classification network's focus on discriminative regions, part information in features is obtained, and the corresponding overall info refines the contrastive learning branch's foreground maps.

The original CapsNet architecture consists of four capsule layers. Typically, features are processed through the capsule network, with the classification capsule layer ultimately yielding the final category scores. But in image segmentation datasets with many categories, more capsules in the classification layer mean too many parameters and lower training efficiency. Therefore, fully connected layers replace the classification capsule layer. This hybrid structure preserves spatial hierarchical information, reduces network parameters, and improves training efficiency.

In the Capsule classification branch, the initial feature $F$ is input into the capsule classification network. Specifically, a capsule encoder $CapsNet(\cdot)$, transforms $F$ into a capsule feature $Caps$, where capsule attributions are determined via EM-Routing to establish part-whole relationships.

$$Caps = CapsNets(F), \tag{4}$$

To derive the final prediction $\hat{y}$, the capsule features $Caps$ first undergo a flattening operation, transforming them into a vector representation. This vector is subsequently fed into a fully connected layer, which computes the ultimate category logits.

$$\hat{y} = \sigma(W_f^T \cdot Flatten(Caps)), \tag{5}$$

where $W_f$ represents the weight of the fully connected layer, $T$ denotes the matrix transpose, and $\sigma$ indicates the sigmoid activation function.

Finally, the loss function computes the difference between the predicted value $\hat{y}$ and the ground-truth label $y$, which is used to backpropagate to update the gradient. Here, we use the Cross-Entropy Loss as the loss function of the capsule classification module. Given an input image and its corresponding label $y$, the model output $\hat{y}$ represents the predicted probability distribution, and the cross-entropy loss function $L_{CSC}$ can be defined as follows:

$$L_{CSC} = -\frac{1}{C} \sum_{c=1}^{C} \left[ y_c \cdot \log(\sigma(\hat{y}_c)) + (1 - y_c) \cdot \log(1 - \sigma(\hat{y}_c)) \right]. \tag{6}$$

where $C$ is the total number of classes, $y_c$ is the probability that the sample belongs to class $c$, and $\hat{y}_c$ is the probability that the model predicts that the sample belongs to class $c$.

### 3.3  Gradient Balance Parameter

Our network is trained using contrastive learning loss ($L_{CTL}$) and capsule classification loss ($L_{CSC}$), with the overall loss defined as:

$$L = L_{CTL} + L_{CSC}. \tag{7}$$

$L_{CTL}$ separates the foreground from the background, while $L_{CSC}$ guides the network to focus on class-distinguished target regions by introducing category information. Using only $L_{CTL}$ cannot control foreground separation accuracy, and using only $L_{CSC}$ activates only part of the target region.

Since both branches backpropagate through feature $F_i$, we propose a hyper-parameter $\lambda$ ($0 \leq \lambda < 1$) to regulate the fraction of the network's overall backpropagation gradient $G_F$ updates on $F_i$. In forward propagation, both modules use $F_i$ as input. During backpropagation, the gradients are updated as

$$G_{CTL} = G_F \cdot \lambda, \quad G_{CSC} = G_F \cdot (1 - \lambda). \tag{8}$$

$G_{CTL}$ is the gradient of $L_{CTL}$ and $G_{CSC}$ is the gradient of $L_{CSC}$ in backpropagation. In addition, we experimentally determine the value of $\lambda$, with results in the experiment section.

## 4  Experiments

### 4.1  Experimental Setup

**Datasets and Evaluation Metrics.** Our experimental framework utilizes two benchmark datasets: PASCAL VOC 2012 [10] and MS COCO 2014 [19]. We adopt the mean Intersection over Union (mIoU) as the primary evaluation metric for CAM. It measures spatial agreement between predicted and ground-truth regions, where a higher mIoU implies better localization and segmentation potential.

**Implementation Details.** We adopt ResNet-50 initialized with moco [11] pretrained weights as the backbone. The input images are resized to 448448 via random cropping. The network is trained for 3 epochs using SGD (initial learning rate: 0.001, momentum: 0.9, weight decay: 1e$-$4) with a batch size of 32. The gradient balance parameter $\lambda$ is set to 0.8. The inference results, serving as background cues, are concatenated with initial CAMs, followed by channel-wise maximum pooling for CAM refinement. All implementations are conducted using PyTorch on two NVIDIA 3090 GPUs with 24 GB of memory.

## 4.2  Ablation Study

**Loss Function.** We adopt the classification network with ResNet-50 as our baseline. Subsequently, we separately incorporate different loss functions and the gradient adjustment parameter $\lambda$ to validate the effectiveness of our proposed method. As presented in Table 1, when only relying on the classification network, the mIoU of the initial CAM achieves a value of only 49.5%. Upon the utilization of contrastive loss $L_{CTL}$, performance improves significantly with reaching 61.6%. Moreover, adding another loss $L_{CSC}$ achieves a further increase of 0.5%. In particular, by embedding $\lambda$ in balancing loss functions, an improvement of 13.1% is obtained in the mIoU of the initial CAM that has been refined using the generated background cue map.

**Table 1.** Ablation study of loss terms on PASCAL VOC 2012 dataset.

| $L_{CTL}$ | $L_{CSC}$ | $\lambda$ | mIoU(%) |
|---|---|---|---|
| – | – | – | 49.5 |
| ✓ | – | – | 61.6 |
| ✓ | ✓ | – | 62.1 |
| ✓ | ✓ | ✓ | **62.6** |

**Hyperparameter Settings.** The value of $\lambda$ plays a significant role in the effectiveness of the proposed model. For CAM refinement, we adjust the value of $\lambda$ from 0 to 1 to determine the final value of $\lambda$, which is used to train the network for obtaining the background cue map to refine the initial CAM. As shown in Table 2, with the increase of values, the performance is getting better. However, when the value of $\lambda$ is larger than 0.8, the performance degrades. Therefore, we set $\lambda$ to 0.8 in the model.

**Table 2.** Ablation study on $\lambda$.

| $\lambda$ | 0.5 | 0.6 | 0.7 | 0.8 | 0.9 | 1.0 |
|---|---|---|---|---|---|---|
| $1 - \lambda$ | 0.5 | 0.4 | 0.3 | 0.2 | 0.1 | 0.0 |
| mIoU (%) | 61.8 | 62.0 | 62.2 | **62.6** | 62.4 | 61.6 |

## 4.3  Quality of Refined CAM

In this section, we use our background cue map to improve the initial CAM extracted from IRN [1] and compare it with other methods. As evidenced in Tables 3 and 4, our refinement framework establishes new state-of-the-art performance across both PASCAL VOC 2012 and MS COCO 2014 benchmarks.

**Table 3.** Performance on the quality of the refined CAM on MS COCO 2014.

| Method | pub. | Backbone | mIoU(%) |
|---|---|---|---|
| CAM [34] | CVPR16 | ResNet50 | 27.6 |
| IRN [1] | CVPR19 | ResNet50 | 33.1 |
| RIB [16] | NeurIPS21 | ResNet38 | 36.5 |
| MCTformer [31] | CVPR22 | DeiT-S | 36.6 |
| SIPE [5] | CVPR22 | ResNet50 | 35.0 |
| LPCAM [7] | CVPR23 | ResNet50 | 35.8 |
| CCAM(based on CAM) [30] | CVPR22 | ResNet50 | 36.3 |
| Ours(based on CAM) | | ResNet50 | **36.8** $(+9.2)$ |

The MS COCO 2014 performance further validates our approach's superiority in complex multi-object scenarios. Our method attains 36.8% mIoU, outperforming both transformer-based MCTformer [31] (36.6% with DeiT-S) and

**Table 4.** Performance on the quality of the refined CAM on PASCAL VOC 2012.

| Method | pub. | Backbone | mIoU(%) |
|---|---|---|---|
| ACR [15] | CVPR23 | ResNet38 | 60.3 |
| OCR [8] | CVPR23 | ResNet38 | 61.7 |
| SSC [6] | TIP24 | ResNet50 | 58.3 |
| BAS [32] | IJCV24 | ResNet50 | 57.7 |
| WeakCLIP [36] | CVPR24 | ViT-B | 61.7 |
| NFF-CAM [35] | ISSN25 | ResNet50 | 59.4 |
| IRN [1] | CVPR19 | ResNet50 | 48.8 |
| +CCAM [30] | CVPR22 | ResNet50 | 61.6 |
| +LPCAM [7] | CVPR23 | ResNet50 | 54.9 |
| +Ours | | ResNet50 | **62.6** $(+13.8)$ |

convolution-based SIPE [5] (35.0%). Notably, our framework shows stronger generalization than the cross-modal method CCAM [30], achieving 0.5% higher mIoU despite using identical CAM initialization.

Concretely, on PASCAL VOC 2012, our method achieves 62.6% mIoU with ResNet50 backbone, surpassing recent competitors NFF-CAM [35] (59.4%). The 13.8% improvement over the IRN baseline demonstrates superior background suppression capability compared to other enhancement strategies like CCAM [30] and LPCAM [7].

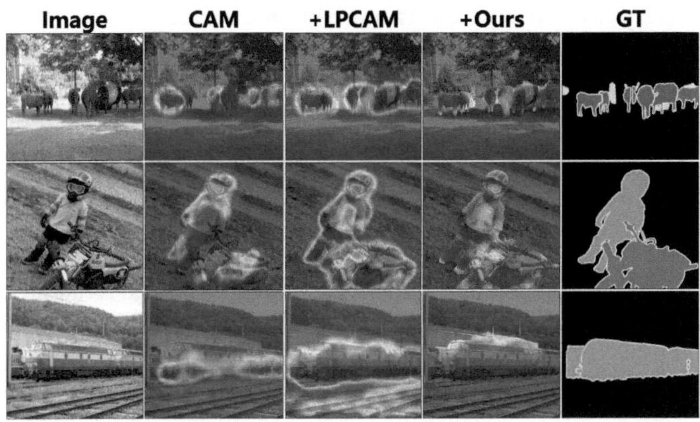


**Fig. 3.** Visual comparison on the refined CAM.

## 4.4   Visual Comparison with CAM

Figure 3 shows the visual comparison of the refinement CAM on PASCAL VOC 2012, compared with LPCAM [7] and our approach. In Fig. 3, the initial CAM activates only part of the foreground area. Although LPCAM covers the entire foreground object, it is followed by boundary confusion and background misactivation. Differently, our method activates all foreground regions while eliminating false background activation.

## 5   Conclusions

In this paper, we have proposed a dual-branch model to alleviate two fundamental limitations in weakly supervised semantic segmentation, including partial foreground activation and spurious background responses inherent in conventional CAM generation. Our dual-branch framework generated a background cue map to refine the initial CAM and use this cue map to refine pseudo-labels for subsequent segmentation model training. Experiments on the PASCAL VOC 2012 and MS COCO 2014 datasets showed that this method significantly improved the quality of CAM in other WSSS methods. In the future, we will exploit part-whole relational property [22, 24]to improve the network.

# References


1. Ahn, J., Cho, S., Kwak, S.: Weakly supervised learning of instance segmentation with inter-pixel relations. In: Proceedings of the IEEE/CVF Conference on Computer Vision and Pattern Recognition, pp. 2209–2218 (2019)
2. Ahn, J., Kwak, S.: Learning pixel-level semantic affinity with image-level supervision for weakly supervised semantic segmentation. In: Proceedings of the IEEE Conference on Computer Vision and Pattern Recognition, pp. 4981–4990 (2018)
3. Bearman, A., Russakovsky, O., Ferrari, V., Fei-Fei, L.: What's the point: semantic segmentation with point supervision. In: Leibe, B., Matas, J., Sebe, N., Welling, M. (eds.) ECCV 2016. LNCS, vol. 9911, pp. 549–565. Springer, Cham (2016). https://doi.org/10.1007/978-3-319-46478-7_34
4. Chen, L., Lei, C., Li, R., Li, S., Zhang, Z., Zhang, L.: FPR: false positive rectification for weakly supervised semantic segmentation. In: Proceedings of the IEEE/CVF International Conference on Computer Vision, pp. 1108–1118 (2023)
5. Chen, Q., Yang, L., Lai, J.H., Xie, X.: Self-supervised image-specific prototype exploration for weakly supervised semantic segmentation. In: Proceedings of the IEEE/CVF Conference on Computer Vision and Pattern Recognition, pp. 4288–4298 (2022)
6. Chen, T., Yao, Y., Huang, X., Li, Z., Nie, L., Tang, J.: Spatial structure constraints for weakly supervised semantic segmentation. IEEE Trans. Image Process. **33**, 1136–1148 (2024)
7. Chen, Z., Sun, Q.: Extracting class activation maps from non-discriminative features as well. In: Proceedings of the IEEE/CVF Conference on Computer Vision and Pattern Recognition, pp. 3135–3144 (2023)
8. Cheng, Z., et al.: Out-of-candidate rectification for weakly supervised semantic segmentation. In: Proceedings of the IEEE/CVF Conference on Computer Vision and Pattern Recognition, pp. 23673–23684 (2023)
9. Dai, J., He, K., Sun, J.: Boxsup: exploiting bounding boxes to supervise convolutional networks for semantic segmentation. In: Proceedings of the IEEE International Conference on Computer Vision, pp. 1635–1643 (2015)
10. Everingham, M., Van Gool, L., Williams, C.K., Winn, J., Zisserman, A.: The pascal visual object classes (VOC) challenge. Int. J. Comput. Vision **88**, 303–338 (2010)
11. He, K., Fan, H., Wu, Y., Xie, S., Girshick, R.: Momentum contrast for unsupervised visual representation learning. In: Proceedings of the IEEE/CVF Conference on Computer Vision and Pattern Recognition, pp. 9729–9738 (2020)
12. Hou, Q., Jiang, P., Wei, Y., Cheng, M.M.: Self-erasing network for integral object attention. In: Advances in Neural Information Processing Systems, vol. 31 (2018)
13. Jo, S., Yu, I.J.: Puzzle-cam: improved localization via matching partial and full features. In: 2021 IEEE International Conference on Image Processing (ICIP), pp. 639–643. IEEE (2021)
14. Ke, Z., et al.: MixUNet: a hybrid retinal vessels segmentation model combining the latest CNN and MLPs. In: Jin, Z., Jiang, Y., Buchmann, R.A., Bi, Y., Ghiran, AM., Ma, W. (eds.) KSEM 2023. LNCS, vol. 14117, pp. 405–413. Springer, Cham (2023). https://doi.org/10.1007/978-3-031-40283-8_34
15. Kweon, H., Yoon, S.H., Yoon, K.J.: Weakly supervised semantic segmentation via adversarial learning of classifier and reconstructor. In: Proceedings of the IEEE/CVF Conference on Computer Vision and Pattern Recognition, pp. 11329–11339 (2023)

16. Lee, J., Choi, J., Mok, J., Yoon, S.: Reducing information bottleneck for weakly supervised semantic segmentation. Adv. Neural. Inf. Process. Syst. **34**, 27408–27421 (2021)
17. Lee, J., Kim, E., Yoon, S.: Anti-adversarially manipulated attributions for weakly and semi-supervised semantic segmentation. In: Proceedings of the IEEE/CVF Conference on Computer Vision and Pattern Recognition, pp. 4071–4080 (2021)
18. Lin, D., Dai, J., Jia, J., He, K., Sun, J.: ScribbleSup: scribble-supervised convolutional networks for semantic segmentation. In: Proceedings of the IEEE Conference on Computer Vision and Pattern Recognition, pp. 3159–3167 (2016)
19. Lin, T.-Y., et al.: Microsoft COCO: common objects in context. In: Fleet, D., Pajdla, T., Schiele, B., Tuytelaars, T. (eds.) ECCV 2014. LNCS, vol. 8693, pp. 740–755. Springer, Cham (2014). https://doi.org/10.1007/978-3-319-10602-1_48
20. Lin, Y., et al.: Clip is also an efficient segmenter: a text-driven approach for weakly supervised semantic segmentation. In: Proceedings of the IEEE/CVF Conference on Computer Vision and Pattern Recognition, pp. 15305–15314 (2023)
21. Liu, Y., Cheng, D., Zhang, D., Xu, S., Han, J.: Capsule networks with residual pose routing. IEEE Trans. Neural Networks Learn. Syst. (2024)
22. Liu, Y., Dong, X., Zhang, D., Xu, S.: Deep unsupervised part-whole relational visual saliency. Neurocomputing **563**, 126916 (2024)
23. Liu, Y., Li, C., Xu, S., Han, J.: Part-whole relational fusion towards multi-modal scene understanding. Int. J. Comput. Vis. 1–21 (2025)
24. Liu, Y., Zhang, D., Zhang, Q., Han, J.: Part-object relational visual saliency. IEEE Trans. Pattern Anal. Mach. Intell. **44**(7), 3688–3704 (2021)
25. Naghne, R., et al.: An efficient capsule-based network for 2D left ventricle segmentation in echocardiography images. In: 2023 45th Annual International Conference of the IEEE Engineering in Medicine & Biology Society (EMBC), pp. 1–4. IEEE (2023)
26. Qin, C., Wang, Y., Zhang, J.: CMLCNet: medical image segmentation network based on convolution capsule encoder and multi-scale local co-occurrence. Multimedia Syst. **30**(4), 220 (2024)
27. Sabour, S., Frosst, N., Hinton, G.E.: Dynamic routing between capsules. In: Advances in Neural Information Processing Systems, vol. 30 (2017)
28. Sun, Y., Yuan, P.: IM-Net: semantic segmentation algorithm for medical images based on mutual information maximization. In: Li, G., Shen, H.T., Yuan, Y., Wang, X., Liu, H., Zhao, X. (eds.) KSEM 2020. LNCS (LNAI), vol. 12274, pp. 397–405. Springer, Cham (2020). https://doi.org/10.1007/978-3-030-55130-8_35
29. Wang, Y., Zhang, J., Kan, M., Shan, S., Chen, X.: Self-supervised equivariant attention mechanism for weakly supervised semantic segmentation. In: Proceedings of the IEEE/CVF Conference on Computer Vision and Pattern Recognition, pp. 12275–12284 (2020)
30. Xie, J., Xiang, J., Chen, J., Hou, X., Zhao, X., Shen, L.: Contrastive learning of class-agnostic activation map for weakly supervised object localization and semantic segmentation. arXiv preprint arXiv:2203.13505 (2022)
31. Xu, L., Ouyang, W., Bennamoun, M., Boussaid, F., Xu, D.: Multi-class token transformer for weakly supervised semantic segmentation. In: Proceedings of the IEEE/CVF Conference on Computer Vision and Pattern Recognition, pp. 4310–4319 (2022)
32. Zhai, W., Wu, P., Zhu, K., Cao, Y., Wu, F., Zha, Z.J.: Background activation suppression for weakly supervised object localization and semantic segmentation. Int. J. Comput. Vision **132**(3), 750–775 (2024)

33. Zhong, J., Xu, Y., Liu, C.: WaveSegNet: wavelet transform and multi-scale focusing network for scrap steel segmentation. In: Cao, C., Chen, H., Zhao, L., Arshad, J., Asyhari, T., Wang, Y. (eds.) KSEM 2024. LNCS, vol. 14887, pp. 189–204. Springer, Singapore (2024). https://doi.org/10.1007/978-981-97-5501-1_15
34. Zhou, B., Khosla, A., Lapedriza, A., Oliva, A., Torralba, A.: Learning deep features for discriminative localization. In: Proceedings of the IEEE Conference on Computer Vision and Pattern Recognition, pp. 2921–2929 (2016)
35. Zhou, X., Li, Y., Cao, G., Cao, W.: Non-target feature filtering for weakly supervised semantic segmentation. Complex Intell. Syst. $\mathbf{11}$(1), 1–15 (2025)
36. Zhu, L., et al.: WeakClip: adapting clip for weakly-supervised semantic segmentation. Int. J. Comput. Vis. 1–21 (2024)

# Hierarchical Integration Knowledge Distillation: Enhancing Adversarial Robustness of Student Models via Clean Data Distillation

Shidong Li and Zhichao Lian[✉]

Nanjing University of Science and Technology, Princeton Nanjing,
Nanjing 210000, China
`123127211595@njust.edu.cn`, `lzcts@163.com`

**Abstract.** Knowledge distillation is the process of transferring knowledge from a teacher network to a student network. However, previous methods have neglected the robustness issue of the student model when it is trained solely on clean data samples. We introduce a hierarchical integration framework that enhances the robustness of the student model. Our validation indicates that the decoupling of low-level semantic knowledge from high-level semantic knowledge within this framework is key to improving robustness. In the distillation process, to more effectively extract feature and logit knowledge with a focus on different levels of semantic information, we have designed a feature knowledge extraction mechanism based on initial feature fusion and a logit knowledge extraction method using adaptive temperature normalization. These two knowledge extraction methods provide key knowledge with distinct focuses for subsequent decoupling. By applying our method to classification tasks, we have achieved a marked improvement in the robustness of the student network.

**Keywords:** knowledge distillation · robustness · hierarchical integration framework · adaptive temperature normalization · initial feature fusion

## 1 Introduction

Computer vision has found extensive applications in fields such as image semantic segmentation [7], classification [5], and object detection [6]. Deep neural networks (DNNs) are an indispensable component in these areas. However, these tasks typically demand substantial computational resources. Consequently, model distillation has emerged as a solution. It involves transferring knowledge from a teacher model to a student model for model compression. Although knowledge distillation has improved model performance, studies have demonstrated that adversarial attacks can still compromise the robustness of DNN


T. Zhu et al. (Eds.): KSEM 2025, LNAI 15919, pp. 377–389, 2026.
https://doi.org/10.1007/978-981-95-3001-4_28

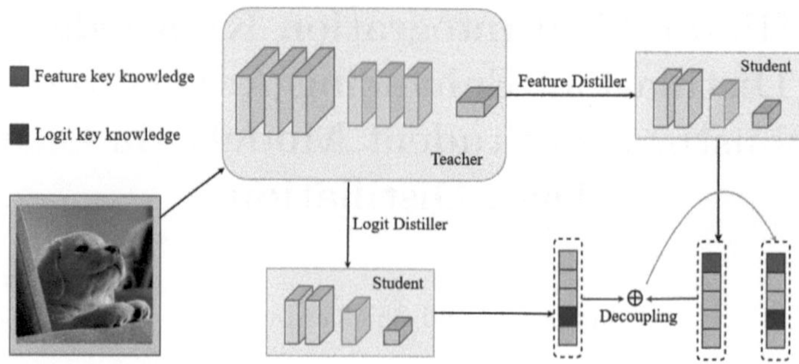


**Fig. 1.** Through the two hierarchical knowledge extraction methods we have designed, LMIFF extracts knowledge rich in low-level semantic feature information, while ATNL extracts knowledge imbued with high-level semantic logits information. We have demonstrated that these two types of knowledge focus on different aspects of adversarial attack images. By extracting the knowledge emphases of both and decoupling them, we have achieved an enhancement in adversarial robustness.

models. Current mainstream distillation methods include logit distillation and feature distillation. However, most of these methods have overlooked the robustness of the student model, which poses risks in the application of DNN models. Therefore, we aim to design a knowledge distillation method to create a model trained solely on clean samples—one that maintains high recognition accuracy while also possessing robustness against potential adversarial attacks. Our experiments reveal that decoupling the teacher's logit knowledge and feature knowledge to instruct the student achieves higher robustness without introducing additional adversarial attack data, thereby maintaining efficient recognition on clean samples. Interestingly, we find that the logit and feature layers have distinct emphases in knowledge representation. Thus, by adopting a hierarchical learning approach followed by decoupling, the student model is capable of acquiring the key strengths emphasized by the teacher model's knowledge, as shown in Fig. 1.

However, extracting useful information from the teacher's logit and feature knowledge hierarchies and transferring it to the student remains a challenging problem. To tackle these challenges, we introduce an initial feature fusion learning mechanism within feature knowledge distillation and an adaptive temperature normalization method within logit knowledge distillation, both aimed at acquiring valuable knowledge. Finally, the two types of knowledge are aggregated through a decoupling approach. Our proposed hierarchical integration knowledge framework allows the student model to acquire knowledge from multiple dimensions, which significantly enhances learning effectiveness and, most importantly, achieves higher robustness. The main contribution of this paper consists of four main parts:

1. We propose a hierarchical integration knowledge framework that improves the robustness of the student model. Experiments demonstrate that the

decoupling of low-level and high-level semantic knowledge within this framework is crucial for enhancing robustness.

2. We introduce an initial feature fusion learning mechanism to better enable the student model to learn knowledge embedded in low-level semantic information within the feature hierarchy.

3. We propose an adaptive temperature normalization method to facilitate the student model's learning of knowledge from logit labels.

4. By applying our distillation framework, we achieve significant improvements in the robustness of student models across multiple computer vision tasks.

## 2   Related Work

The differences in knowledge transfer are primarily categorized into logit distillation and feature distillation. Logit distillation transfers knowledge through the soft labels of the teacher model. For example, the method proposed by Hinton [1], DKD [3], CTKD [11], and WKD [8] enhance performance by softening the output, decoupling knowledge, learning dynamic temperatures, and utilizing Wasserstein distance, respectively. feature distillation, on the other hand, achieves knowledge transfer by matching intermediate-layer features. Methods such as ReviewKD [19], FitNet [4], PKT [12], RKD [14], and CRD [13] address the limitations of logit distillation in transferring deep semantic information. In the realm of defense distillation, methods like RSLAD [9] and MTARD [10] have improved robustness but at the cost of suboptimal performance on clean samples.

Previous methods have not considered enhancing the robustness of student models without additional adversarial perturbation data. In this paper, the proposed hierarchical integration framework and HIKD achieve significant improvements in the robustness and recognition performance of student models without requiring extra adversarial perturbation data.

## 3   Our Method

The central concept of the proposed method in this paper is the introduction of a new framework—the Hierarchical Integration Framework. This framework disentangles the teaching process for the student model by utilizing both the feature knowledge and logit knowledge of the teacher model. It allows the student model to acquire the teacher model's knowledge across multiple dimensions and hierarchical levels. Consequently, this approach enables the student model to attain enhanced robustness when trained exclusively on clean samples, while maintaining its high recognition performance.

### 3.1   Learning Mechanism of Initial Feature Fusion

We are given an input image $X$ and a teacher network $T$, we denote the output of the teacher network as $L_t$. For illustration, the teacher network can be divided into different parts $(T_1, T_2, T_3..., T_n, T_c)$. Here, $T_c$ represents the classifier, while $T_1, T_2, T_3..., T_n$ correspond to the intermediate stages separated by downsampling layers.

$$L_t = T_c(T_n(\ldots T_1(X)\ldots))  \tag{1}$$

Using the function composition notation"$\circ$" to denote nested functions, $L_t$ can be represented as:

$$L_t = T_c \circ T_n \circ \cdots \circ T_1(X)  \tag{2}$$

In Eq. (2), the output of the teacher network is denoted as $L_t$, while its intermediate feature levels are represented by $(\mathbf{F}_t^1, \cdots, \mathbf{F}_t^n)$. Accordingly, the feature at the $i$-th layer of the teacher network is denoted by $\mathbf{F}_t^i$:

$$\mathbf{F}_t^i = T_i \circ \cdots \circ T_1(\mathbf{X})  \tag{3}$$

Therefore, the single-layer feature knowledge transferred by the teacher model is represented as:

$$T_{SKD} = \mathcal{D}\left(\Phi_s^i(\mathbf{F}_s^i), \Phi_t^i(\mathbf{F}_t^i)\right)  \tag{4}$$

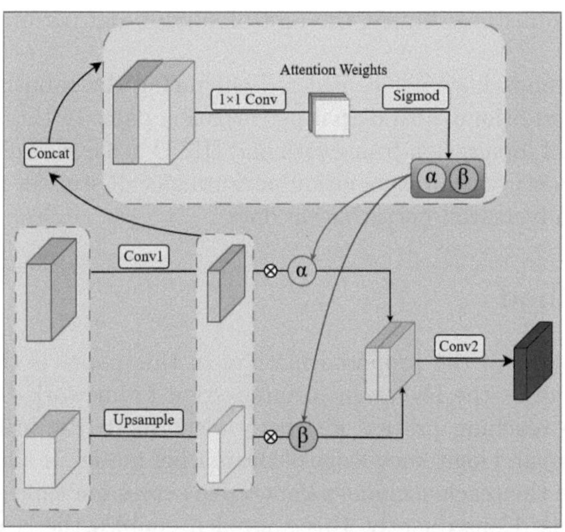


**Fig. 2.** This module utilizes the attention mechanism to introduce attention weights to balance the fused features and to transform important features of the teacher model into learnable feature knowledge for the student model.

In Eq. (4), $\mathbf{F}_s^i$ denotes the student, $\mathbf{F}_t^i$ denotes the teacher. $\Phi$ denotes the process of transforming the important features of the teacher into learnable

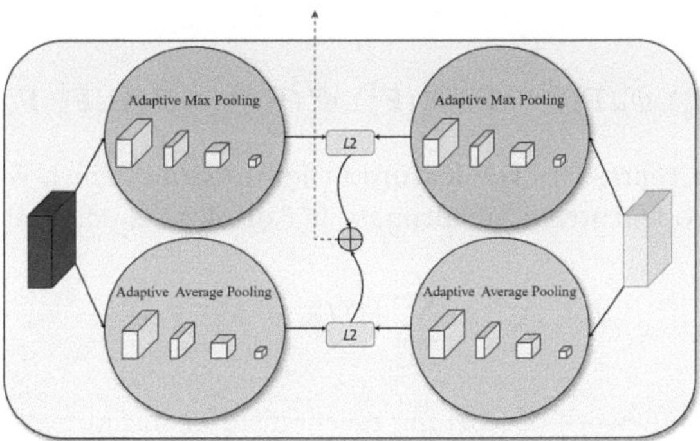


**Fig. 3.** The student model's feature learning is optimized via weighted MSE loss between student and teacher models at the original feature level and across scales.

characteristic knowledge for the student. The approach of using attention mechanisms to allocate feature weights and perform feature fusion, as adopted by $\Phi^i$, is illustrated in Fig. 2. $\mathcal{D}$ represents the distance function used to measure the differences between the features of the student network and those of the teacher network. The consistency of features is evaluated via a multi-scale mean squared error (MSE) loss function. The module for quantifying discrepancies between the student and teacher knowledge signals is depicted in Fig. 3.

In the initial stage, neural networks primarily extract features that contain low-level detail information, including edges and textures. We define these features as initial features, which encompass the richest detail information. By incorporating the low-level semantic information from the initial feature layer, the student network is capable of more effectively capturing the high-level semantic information embedded within the teacher network. The low-level semantic information serves as an auxiliary signal, facilitating the student network to more precisely acquire the feature representation of the teacher network. In each stage of knowledge transfer from the teacher network, we fuse the student network's $\mathbf{F}_s^i$ features with $\mathbf{F}_s^1$ features and calculate the feature loss between the fused features and the teacher network's $\mathbf{F}_t^i$ features.

We denote the loss $\mathcal{L}_{TKD}$ generated by learning mechanism of the initial feature fusion in the $i$-th stage as:

$$\mathcal{L}_{TKD} = \mathcal{D}\left(\Phi_s^i(\mathbf{F}_s^i), \Phi_t^i\left(\mathbf{F}_t^i\right)\right) + \mathcal{D}\left(\Phi_s^1(\mathbf{F}_s^1), \Phi_t^i\left(\mathbf{F}_t^i\right)\right) \tag{5}$$

Thus, the total distillation knowledge loss $\mathcal{L}_{MKD}$ of our multi-level knowledge distillation can be represented as:

$$\mathcal{L}_{MKD} = \sum_{i=1}^{n}\left(\mathcal{D}\left(\Phi_s^i(\mathbf{F}_s^i), \Phi_t^i(\mathbf{F}_t^i)\right) + \mathcal{D}\left(\Phi_s^1(\mathbf{F}_s^1), \Phi_t^i(\mathbf{F}_t^i)\right)\right) \tag{6}$$

We approximate the sum of the distances between the student's initial features and its current features, relative to the teacher's features, by the discrepancy between the student's aggregated features and the teacher's updated features:

$$\mathcal{D}\left(\Phi_s^i(\mathbf{F}_s^i), \Phi_t^i(\mathbf{F}_t^i)\right) + \mathcal{D}\left(\Phi_s^1(\mathbf{F}_s^1), \Phi_t^i(\mathbf{F}_t^i)\right) \approx \mathcal{D}\left(\mathbf{B}(\mathbf{F}_s^1, \mathbf{F}_s^i), \mathbf{F}_t^i\right) \quad (7)$$

In Eq. (7), $B$ represents the feature fusion module, which is utilized for the integration of two features. Our ultimate feature loss is denoted as follows:

$$\mathcal{L}_{Features} = \sum_{i=1}^{n} \left(\mathcal{D}\left(\mathbf{B}(\mathbf{F}_s^1, \mathbf{F}_s^i), \mathbf{F}_t^i\right)\right) \quad (8)$$

The overall framework of learning mechanism of initial feature fusion as follows in Fig. 4.

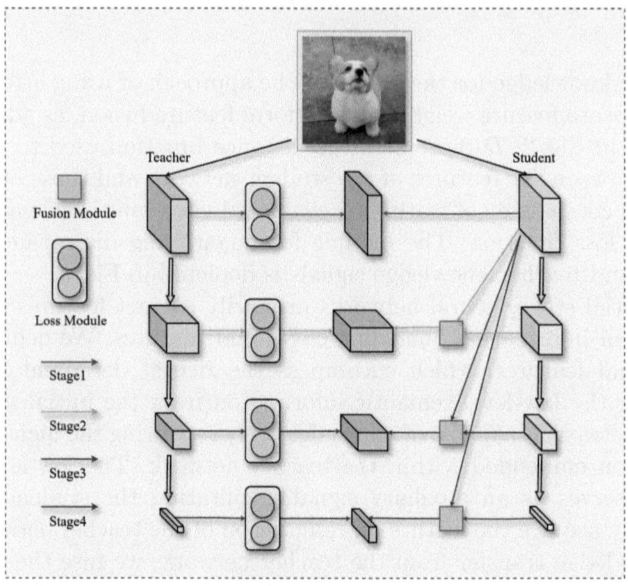


**Fig. 4.** This framework employs initial feature fusion to aid the student model in better understanding the semantic knowledge signals from the teacher network.

## 3.2   Adaptive Temperature Normalization of Logit

In conventional knowledge distillation, teacher and student models share the same temperature parameter $T$. This assumes the teacher and student logits should perfectly match in range and variance, which is impractical, as the student model typically has lower capacity than the teacher model.

$$q_i = \frac{exp(z_i/T)}{\sum_j exp(z_i/T)} \quad (9)$$

In Eq. (9) $q_i$ denotes the predicted probability of the $i$-th class, $z_i$ represents the corresponding logit value, where $T$ denotes the temperature parameter, regulating the smoothness of the probability distribution.

Considering the effect of temperature, we introduce a method to set the temperature dynamically by quantifying the logit sharpness. Sharpness can be interpreted as the degree of dispersion of the logit values. We set the dynamic temperature as follows:

$$\tau_z = \frac{\alpha}{\text{Log}\left(\sum_i e^{z_i}\right) + \epsilon} \tag{10}$$

In Eq. (10), $z_i$ is the logit for the $i$-th class. $\text{Log}\left(\sum_i e^{z_i}\right)$ measures logit sharpness. $\alpha$ is the epoch-dependent decay rate. By dynamically adjusting the softness of labels through sharpness measurement, the proposed approach enables the student model to more effectively acquire and align with the label information.

Considering the occurrence of non-zero mean values in logit distributions. We define the distribution normalization function $D$ as follows:

$$D(x; \tau_z) = \frac{x - \bar{x}}{\sigma(x) \cdot \tau_z} = \frac{x - \frac{1}{K}\sum_{K=1}^{K} x^{(k)}}{\sqrt{\frac{1}{K}\sum_{K=1}^{K}(x^{(k)} - \bar{x})^2} \cdot \tau_z} \tag{11}$$

After this normalization process, each sample's logit vector will have zero mean and unit standard deviation. By applying the normalization function D, the logit values of the student model no longer need to match the absolute scale of the teacher model. Instead, they can freely adapt to a range suitable for their capacity.

According to this we rewrite the formula for logit knowledge distillation as follows, first we get the softmax outputs for students and teachers:

$$P_i = \text{softmax}\left(S_n'\right)_i \quad Q_i = \text{softmax}\left(T_n'\right)_i \tag{12}$$

In Eq. (12), $S_n'$ and $T_n'$ are logit values for students and teachers respectively after treatment for the distribution normalization function $D$.

Afterwards, the difference in probability distributions is obtained by calculating the KL divergence:

$$KL\left(\text{softmax}\left(S_n'\right) \parallel \text{softmax}\left(T_n'\right)\right) = \sum_{i=1}^{C} \text{softmax}\left(S_n'\right)_i \log\left(\frac{\text{softmax}\left(S_n'\right)_i}{\text{softmax}\left(T_n'\right)_i}\right) \tag{13}$$

Equation (13) above represents the number of sample categories, and after simplifying this equation simplifies to:

$$KL(P \parallel Q) = \sum_{i=1}^{C} P_i \log\left(\frac{P_i}{Q_i}\right) \tag{14}$$

Considering the role of temperature on label smoothing, we finally set the loss of logit knowledge to:

$$\mathcal{L}_{LogitKD} = \frac{1}{N}\sum_{n=1}^{N} KL(P \parallel Q) \cdot \tau_s \cdot \tau_T \tag{15}$$

### 3.3  Hierarchical Integration Framework

The learning mechanism of initial feature fusion (LMIFF) emphasizes acquiring the deep feature representations from the teacher model, whereas the adaptive temperature normalization of logit (ATNL) focuses on emulating the teacher model's output logits. However, in the experiments, we found that on datasets with perturbations, a distillation approach that integrates both feature and logit learning further enhances performance. We posit that feature distillation and logit distillation exhibit distinct sensitivities to noise and attack methods, each excelling in their respective "domains" when validating images. By integrating the distinct critical knowledge learned from these two distillation methods, we achieve robustness enhancement of the student model through distillation on clean samples alone. This indicates that the two methods are able to recognise different images in the same dataset. In order to fully utilise the advantages of these two methods, we adjust the weighting between feature knowledge and logit knowledge of student model learning by decoupling. Specifically:

$$\mathcal{L}_{\text{total}} = \alpha \mathcal{L}_{\text{Feature}} + \beta \mathcal{L}_{\text{LogitKD}} + \lambda \mathcal{L}_{\text{CE}} \tag{16}$$

Equation (16) above is our total loss function $\mathcal{L}_{\text{total}}$, We use hyperparameters a and b for balancing feature distillation loss and logit distillation loss in knowledge fusion, and a factor $\lambda$ for balancing distillation loss and raw loss.

## 4  Experiments

We conducted a comprehensive set of experiments across diverse tasks. Specifically, we benchmarked the classification performance of our proposed method against a range of existing knowledge distillation techniques and systematically compared their respective robustness under five distinct attack methods. Additionally, we evaluated the effectiveness of integrating feature distillation with logit distillation by conducting extensive ablation studies across various architectures and datasets.

### 4.1  Experiments Setup

**Datasets.** (1) CIFAR-10 consists of 50K training images, with 5K images per category and 10K test images. (2) Tiny-ImageNet is a highly complex classification dataset, providing 100K training images and 10K validation images across 200 classes.

**Training Implementation Details.** To thoroughly assess the performance of our proposed algorithm, we constructed six distinct teacher-student pairs: [ResNet34, ResNet18], [ResNet50, ResNet18], [ResNet34, MobileNet], [ResNet50, MobileNet], [ResNet101, ResNet18], and [ResNet101, ResNet50]. For these experiments, the student networks were optimized using the SGD optimizer. The initial momentum was set to 0.9, and the weight decay was configured at 1e−4. The learning rate was initialized at 0.1 and reduced by half every 30 epochs to enable adaptive learning.

**Table 1.** Experimental results on the CIFAR-10 dataset.

| Teacher | Student | | Teacher | Student-LogitKD | | | Student-Feature KD | | | | | | Ours |
|---|---|---|---|---|---|---|---|---|---|---|---|---|---|
| | | | | KD | DKD | WKD-L | CRD | OFD | RKD | ReviewKD | AT | WKD-F | HIKD |
| ResNet50 | MobileNetv1 | top-1 | 96.03 | 91.37 | 93.74 | 94.62 | 90.93 | 93.34 | 94.11 | 95.16 | 92.69 | 95.17 | **95.25** |
| | | top-5 | 99.87 | 99.23 | 99.68 | 99.78 | 99.82 | 99.84 | 99.83 | 99.72 | 99.84 | **99.85** | 99.75 |
| ResNet50 | ResNet18 | top-1 | 96.03 | 92.14 | 94.64 | 94.80 | 91.33 | 92.84 | 94.21 | 95.16 | 92.72 | 95.01 | **95.89** |
| | | top-5 | 99.87 | 99.32 | 99.78 | 99.79 | 99.72 | 99.84 | **99.85** | 99.82 | 99.83 | 99.83 | 99.84 |
| ResNet34 | ResNet18 | top-1 | 95.63 | 92.14 | 92.68 | 93.63 | 90.44 | 92.21 | 93.30 | 94.78 | 91.94 | **94.98** | 94.87 |
| | | top-5 | 99.86 | 99.32 | 99.77 | 99.79 | 98.97 | 99.42 | 99.81 | **99.83** | 99.78 | 99.82 | 99.73 |

**Results on Clean Datasets** As shown in Table 1, our proposed method achieves an excellent top-1 accuracy on the CIFAR-10 dataset. We selected the [ResNet101, ResNet50] architecture, which has a significant difference in model size, as a test of knowledge transfer efficiency. The final comparison results are illustrated in Fig. 5(a), which clearly shows that our method is more distinguishable than the baseline Vanilla KD.

We further evaluate our method on Tiny-ImageNet. As shown in Table 2, our method is lower than the WKD-F method only in top-1 for the [ResNet50, ResNet18] architecture and top-5 for the [ResNet34, MobileNet] architecture, while all others outperform the comparison method. This indicates that our method is excellent in the efficiency of knowledge transfer from teachers.

**Table 2.** Experimental results on the Tiny-Imagenet dataset

| Teacher | Student | | Teacher | Student-LogitKD | | | Student-Feature KD | | | | | | Ours |
|---|---|---|---|---|---|---|---|---|---|---|---|---|---|
| | | | | KD | DKD | WKD-L | CRD | OFD | RKD | ReviewKD | AT | WKD-F | HIKD |
| ResNet50 | MobileNetv1 | top-1 | 74.13 | 63.14 | 66.82 | 65.85 | 62.18 | 65.27 | 65.67 | 69.43 | 64.79 | 69.53 | **69.81** |
| | | top-5 | 92.11 | 83.77 | 87.49 | 84.62 | 83.03 | 85.22 | 85.37 | 88.13 | 84.97 | 88.14 | **88.15** |
| ResNet50 | ResNet18 | top-1 | 74.13 | 63.43 | 67.1 | 66.62 | 65.12 | 67.25 | 64.37 | 69.84 | 66.54 | **69.94** | 69.77 |
| | | top-5 | 92.11 | 83.06 | 87.41 | 87.60 | 85.01 | 86.71 | 84.98 | 88.21 | 86.05 | 88.19 | **88.23** |
| ResNet34 | MobileNetv1 | top-1 | 72.43 | 62.50 | 64.26 | 64.89 | 61.80 | 63.57 | 63.77 | 67.21 | 62.67 | 67.21 | **67.43** |
| | | top-5 | 91.20 | 82.57 | 86.33 | 86.50 | 82.87 | 84.54 | 84.71 | 87.21 | 83.48 | **87.62** | 87.38 |
| ResNet34 | ResNet18 | top-1 | 72.43 | 63.26 | 65.61 | 65.31 | 63.49 | 65.12 | 63.84 | 68.09 | 63.21 | 68.21 | **68.29** |
| | | top-5 | 91.20 | 83.01 | 87.26 | 82.94 | 85.11 | 85.71 | 84.81 | 87.65 | 83.18 | 87.75 | **87.85** |
| ResNet101 | ResNet18 | top-1 | 76.15 | 62.61 | 63.23 | 64.31 | 63.40 | 65.32 | 64.76 | 68.47 | 64.43 | 69.07 | **69.22** |
| | | top-5 | 95.37 | 82.87 | 83.89 | 82.28 | 85.85 | 86.23 | 85.71 | 86.31 | 85.12 | 86.31 | **86.93** |

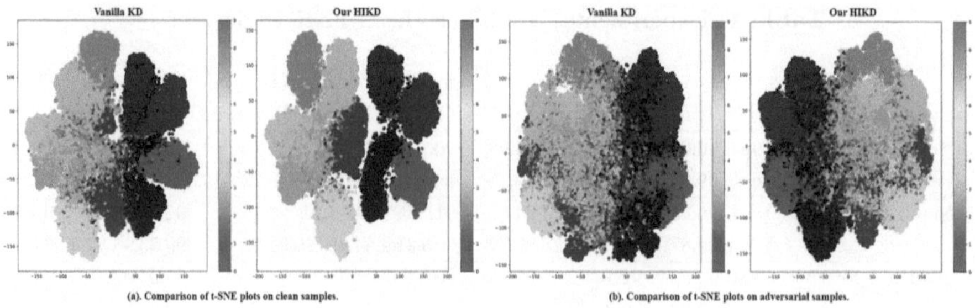



**Fig. 5.** Comparison of the Vanilla KD method with our t-SNE visualisation of HIKD.

## 4.2   Robustness Assessment

To comprehensively assess the robustness of the compared methods, we conducted experiments using five distinct adversarial attack methods: PGD [15], FGSM [15], GN [16], SPN [18], and PN [17]. Each attack was configured with specific parameters to evaluate the methods under diverse perturbation scenarios. All experiments were consistently performed on datasets perturbed by these five attack methods to ensure a fair comparison. Specifically, FGSM was set with a perturbation magnitude of 0.3, while PGD employed a perturbation magnitude of 0.3, an iteration step size of 0.1, and a total of 40 iterations. For the Gaussian Noise Attack, the standard deviation was set to 25 with a mean of 0. In the Poisson Noise Attack, the mean of the Poisson distribution was configured at 0.1. Lastly, the Salt-and-Pepper Noise Attack was designed with a salt-to-pepper ratio of 1:1 and a noise intensity of 0.04.

**Results on Attacked Datasets.** For the robustness evaluation, as detailed in Table 3 and Table 4. This underscores the robustness of our method across diverse adversarial scenarios.

**Table 3.** Experiments on the Tiny-Imagenet dataset using the [ResNet50, ResNet18] teacher-student architecture

| Model | Method | Clean | FGSM | PGD | GN | PN | SPN |
|---|---|---|---|---|---|---|---|
| ResNet50 | Teacher | 74.13 | 11.63 | 8.53 | 29.21 | 27.95 | 12.26 |
| ResNet18 | KD | 63.43 | 9.79 | 6.81 | 28.97 | 28.31 | 11.87 |
| | DKD | 67.1 | 10.31 | 7.27 | 28.74 | 29.22 | 11.97 |
| | WKD | 66.62 | 10.42 | 7.39 | 30.28 | 26.58 | 12.56 |
| | CRD | 65.12 | 10.71 | 7.52 | 28.74 | 30.1 | 12.01 |
| | OFD | 67.25 | 12.06 | 8.46 | 30.59 | 29.87 | 11.13 |
| | RKD | 64.37 | 11.36 | 7.62 | 30.45 | 31.2 | 12.23 |
| | ReviewKD | **69.84** | 14.26 | 10.46 | 41.29 | 39.28 | 13.01 |
| | AT | 66.54 | 12.88 | 9.01 | 34.41 | 31.99 | 13.42 |
| | HIKD | 69.81 | **17.88** | **12.52** | **45.06** | **43.66** | **14.61** |

**Table 4.** Experiments on the CIFAR-10 dataset using the [ResNet50, MobileNetv1] teacher-student architecture

| Model | Method | Clean | FGSM | PGD | GN | PN | SPN |
|---|---|---|---|---|---|---|---|
| ResNet50 | Teacher | 96.03 | 45.65 | 34.83 | 15.31 | 15.14 | 31.32 |
| MobilNetV1 | KD | 91.37 | 55.59 | 45.29 | 22.20 | 20.08 | 40.83 |
| | DKD | 93.74 | 56.37 | 44.61 | 25.81 | 30.45 | 41.50 |
| | WKD | 94.62 | 55.83 | 45.21 | 26.97 | 31.94 | 41.62 |
| | CRD | 90.93 | 50.77 | 42.73 | 28.87 | 33.33 | 44.61 |
| | OFD | 93.34 | 49.33 | 41.26 | 26.38 | 27.45 | 32.64 |
| | RKD | 94.11 | 53.99 | 45.08 | 30.17 | 28.86 | 43.58 |
| | ReviewKD | 95.16 | 55.28 | 49.98 | 31.77 | 32.76 | 45.93 |
| | AT | 92.69 | 51.14 | 48.40 | 27.78 | 32.34 | 44.73 |
| | HIKD | **95.25** | **59.68** | **50.38** | **32.98** | **33.60** | **46.52** |

To offer a more intuitive illustration of our method's efficacy, we applied the FGSM to the CIFAR-10 training dataset and utilized t-SNE to visualize the attack effects on both Vanilla KD and HIKD. As shown in Fig. 5(b), the t-SNE scatter plot reveals that our method exhibits more distinct clustering of classes compared to Vanilla KD. This indicates that our model maintains a higher level of robustness under adversarial attacks.

### 4.3   Ablation Experiment

**Implications of $\alpha$ and $\beta$ for the Method in Decoupling.** In this experimental setup, we aimed to investigate the impact of feature knowledge and logit knowledge on robustness. We selected the [ResNet50, MobileNetV1] architectures for validation on data post-FGSM attack. As shown in Table 5a, we observed that the decoupled integration of logit knowledge and feature knowledge led to an enhancement in robustness, which is crucial for the robustness of our method. Furthermore, as indicated in Table 5b, when our parameters $\alpha$ is around 4 and $\beta$ is below 10, it is feasible to attain a favorable trade-off between the model's robustness and recognition rate. Additionally, improper decoupling can be counterproductive, causing the student model to converge to trivial solutions.

Based on the decoupling parameter settings, it has been observed that the feature knowledge generated by the learning mechanism of initial feature fusion is crucial for achieving high recognition rates on clean samples. Furthermore, when integrating response-based logit knowledge, a reasonable configuration of the decoupling parameters allows the student model to enhance its robustness without significantly compromising its recognition performance on clean samples. This indicates that a well-adjusted decoupling strategy is essential for maintaining the model's effectiveness while improving its resilience to perturbations.

388     S. Li and Z. Lian

**Table 5.** Effects of $\alpha$ and $\beta$ on different metrics

(a) Effects of $\alpha$ & $\beta$ on Robustness

| Param $\alpha$ | 1.0 | 2.0 | 4.0 | 8.0 | 10.0 |
|---|---|---|---|---|---|
| | 14.27 | 15.20 | 15.91 | **16.06** | 15.34 |
| Param $\beta$ | 1.0 | 2.0 | 3.0 | 4.0 | 5.0 |
| | 15.76 | 15.93 | **16.06** | 15.81 | 14.74 |

(b) Effect of $\alpha$ & $\beta$ on clean samples

| Param $\alpha$ | 1.0 | 2.0 | 4.0 | 8.0 | 10.0 |
|---|---|---|---|---|---|
| | 68.65 | 69.08 | 69.24 | 69.81 | **69.85** |
| Param $\beta$ | 1.0 | 2.0 | 3.0 | 4.0 | 5.0 |
| | 69.79 | 69.29 | **69.85** | 68.90 | 68.37 |

## 5  Conclusions

This paper analyzes robustness enhancement for the student model from both the logit and feature perspectives. On the feature level, we propose the learning mechanism of initial feature fusion , and on the logit level, we introduce the adaptive temperature normalization of logit method. Through a decoupled approach, the student model can effectively learn the unique emphases of these two levels of knowledge. In our classification tasks, which are conducted solely on clean samples, our method significantly enhances the robustness of the student model. Additionally, we have found that integrating semantic knowledge with different focal points through a hierarchical integration framework can further enhance the robustness of the student model.

For future work, we intend to investigate whether the proposed robustness-enhancing approach can be generalized and applied to various domains, including cross-domain learning, model deployment on lightweight devices, and autonomous driving.

## References


1. Hinton, G., Vinyals, O., Dean, J.: Distilling the knowledge in a neural network. arXiv preprint arXiv:1503.02531 (2015)
2. He, K., Zhang, X., Ren, S., et al.: Deep residual learning for image recognition. In: Proceedings of the IEEE Conference on Computer Vision and Pattern Recognition, pp. 770-778 (2016)
3. Zhao, B., Cui, Q., Song, R., et al.: Decoupled knowledge distillation. In: Proceedings of the IEEE/CVF Conference on Computer Vision and Pattern Recognition, pp. 11953–11962 (2022)
4. Romero, A., Ballas, N., Kahou, S.E., et al.: Fitnets: hints for thin deep nets. arXiv preprint arXiv:1412.6550 (2014)
5. Xie, Q., Luong, M.T., Hovy, E., et al.: Self-training with noisy student improves imagenet classification. In: Proceedings of the IEEE/CVF Conference on Computer Vision and Pattern Recognition, pp. 10687–10698 (2020)
6. Yang, Z., Li, Z., Jiang, X., et al.: Focal and global knowledge distillation for detectors. In: Proceedings of the IEEE/CVF Conference on Computer Vision and Pattern Recognition, pp. 4643–4652 (2022)
7. Yu, F., Koltun, V.: Multi-scale context aggregation by dilated convolutions. arXiv preprint arXiv:1511.07122 (2015)

8. Lv, J., Yang, H., Li, P.: Wasserstein distance rivals Kullback-Leibler divergence for knowledge distillation. Adv. Neural. Inf. Process. Syst. **37**, 65445–65475 (2024)
9. Zi, B., Zhao, S., Ma, X., et al.: Revisiting adversarial robustness distillation: robust soft labels make student better. In: Proceedings of the IEEE/CVF International Conference on Computer Vision, pp. 16443–16452 (2021)
10. GZhao, S., Yu, J., Sun, Z., et al.: Enhanced accuracy and robustness via multi-teacher adversarial distillation. In: Avidan, S., Brostow, G., Cissé, M., Farinella, G.M., Hassner, T. (eds.) ECCV 2022. LNCS, vol. 13664, pp. 585–602. Springer, Cham (2022). https://doi.org/10.1007/978-3-031-19772-7_34
11. Li, Z., Li, X., Yang, L., et al.: Curriculum temperature for knowledge distillation. In: Proceedings of the AAAI Conference on Artificial Intelligence, vol. 37, no. 2, pp. 1504–1512 (2023)
12. Passalis, N., Tefas, A.: Learning deep representations with probabilistic knowledge transfer. In: Ferrari, V., Hebert, M., Sminchisescu, C., Weiss, Y. (eds.) ECCV 2018. LNCS, vol. 11215, pp. 283–299. Springer, Cham (2018). https://doi.org/10.1007/978-3-030-01252-6_17
13. Tian, Y., Krishnan, D., Isola, P.: Contrastive representation distillation. arXiv preprint arXiv:1910.10699 (2019)
14. Park, W., Kim, D., Lu, Y., et al.: Relational knowledge distillation. In: Proceedings of the IEEE/CVF Conference on Computer Vision and Pattern Recognition, pp. 3967–3976 (2019)
15. Goodfellow, I.J., Shlens, J., Szegedy, C.: Explaining and harnessing adversarial examples. arXiv preprint arXiv:1412.6572 (2014)
16. Luisier, F., Blu, T., Unser, M.: Image denoising in mixed Poisson-Gaussian noise. IEEE Trans. Image Process. **20**(3), 696–708 (2010)
17. Hasinoff, S.W.: Photon, poisson noise. In: Ikeuchi, K. (ed.) Computer Vision: A Reference Guide, pp. 980–982. Springer, Cham (2021). https://doi.org/10.1007/978-0-387-31439-6_482
18. Azzeh, J., Zahran, B., Alqadi, Z.: Salt and pepper noise: effects and removal. JOIV: Int. J. Inf. Visual. **2**(4), 252–256 (2018). transformers. Proceedings of the IEEE/CVF conference on computer vision and pattern recognition. 2022: 12052-12062
19. Chen, P., Liu, S., Zhao, H., et al.: Distilling knowledge via knowledge review. In: Proceedings of the IEEE/CVF Conference on Computer Vision and Pattern Recognition, pp. 5008–5017 (2021)

# Tree-Based Approach for Time-Independent Diffusion Network Inference

Weikai Jing[1], Yuchen Wang[1], Chao Gao[1(✉)], Kefeng Fan[2],
Hailong Cheng[3], Zhijie Shen[3], and Zhen Wang[1]

[1] School of Cybersecurity, Northwestern Polytechnical University, Xi'an, China
{2015217442,wany810}@mail.nwpu.edu.cn, {cgao,w-zhen}@nwpu.edu.cn
[2] China Electronics Standardization Institute, Beijing, China
[3] Surfilter Network Technology Co., Ltd., Shenzhen, China
{chenghailong,shenzhijie}@surfilter.com

**Abstract.** Diffusion network inference is crucial for understanding propagation dynamics and applications in social networks. Recently, inferring networks without timestamps has gained attention due to the high costs of monitoring temporal information and the presence of unknown observation errors. However, existing time-independent methods primarily focus on directly extracting parent-child influence relationships from the data, neglecting to consider the dynamics of the diffusion process. To overcome these limitations, this paper introduces a **Tree**-based approach for time-independent **D**iffusion **N**etwork **I**nference (TDNI) based on the independent cascade model. TDNI introduces a tree-based likelihood for the infection status data and develops an optimization strategy to infer the most probable propagation tree for each diffusion process. In addition, TDNI incorporates a post-processing stage that utilizes a proposed likelihood ratio to further filter the remaining candidate edges, thereby ensuring the accuracy of the inference result. Experiments conducted on synthetic and real-world networks show the highly competitive performance of TDNI when compared to other state-of-the-art algorithms. Code is available at https://github.com/cgao-comp/TDNI.

**Keywords:** Diffusion Network Inference · Social Networks ·
Time-Independent Methods

## 1 Introduction

In the Internet era, understanding information propagation dynamics on social media is crucial for applications like viral marketing [2] and source localization [18], as it helps reveal the hidden structure of diffusion networks. However, real-world diffusion processes are often opaque, making network inference a key area of research. Traditional diffusion network inference methods rely on cascades that track node infection times. These methods fall into two categories: likelihood maximization-based approaches [5,7] and embedding-based techniques [3,12]. Despite their effectiveness, these methods face challenges due to resource-intensive time monitoring and potential temporal errors [15], prompting a shift towards time-independent approaches. Time-independent methods face the challenge of inferring network structure without explicit


T. Zhu et al. (Eds.): KSEM 2025, LNAI 15919, pp. 390–402, 2026.
https://doi.org/10.1007/978-981-95-3001-4_29

temporal data. Early efforts made simplifying assumptions [1], while recent methods focus on parent-child influence relationships [8,9]. However, these methods often overlook the diffusion process itself. This paper proposes a new approach using the Independent Cascade (IC) model [11] to address these limitations.

This paper proposes TDNI, a tree-based approach for time-independent diffusion network inference, consisting of three stages: In the first stage, TDNI explores node correlations based on infection statuses, generating possible propagation trees by identifying all Maximum Spanning Trees (MSTs) for each diffusion process. In the second stage, TDNI converts undirected trees into directed trees using rumor centrality and incorporates the IC model to capture diffusion dynamics. It develops an optimization strategy inspired by Gibbs sampling to infer suitable propagation trees. TDNI filters remaining edges using a likelihood ratio, ensuring improved accuracy by evaluating both the inclusion and exclusion of candidate edges. TDNI enables the accurate inference of diffusion network structures without relying on timestamps.

Our contributions can be summarized as follows:

- In contrast to existing methods that primarily focus on extracting influence relationships directly from data, we propose a time-independent approach for inferring diffusion networks based on an information diffusion model. This approach provides a novel perspective and enhances the accuracy of network inference.
- TDNI introduces a tree-based likelihood formulation for the diffusion process without timestamps. Additionally, an optimization strategy is proposed to infer suitable propagation trees. To reduce the sample size of propagation trees, we integrate a pre-processing stage that leverages a $k$-MSTs algorithm in conjunction with mutual information between nodes.
- TDNI incorporates a post-processing stage that strengthens the reliability of the inference results by calculating likelihood ratios. These ratios are used to determine the inclusion of each candidate edge as a component of the diffusion network.

## 2   Related Work

In recent years, novel methods have emerged to facilitate network inference using infection statuses without any prior knowledge. The most prevalent class of time-independent methods is based on the parents-child influence relationship. These methods primarily focus on extracting and analyzing the relationship between the infection status of each node and the infection statuses of its parent nodes, such as TWIND [10], SIDN [9] and TENDS [8]. However, for larger-scale networks, the number of combinations of infection statuses grows exponentially with the number of potential parents, leading to a significant increase in time and space consumption. Furthermore, there are some approaches to estimate the influence relationships between nodes from different perspectives. Sun et al. developed FINITI [20], a method that can infer the strength of links by estimating influence probabilities between nodes. Chen et al. introduced InDNI [4], a method that leverages a variational autoencoder (VAE) to extract behavioral features of nodes. In a nutshell, current time-independent approaches have made certain progress. However, these methods have not yet fully integrated the specific diffusion process, which is the main emphasis of our work.

# 3    Methodologies

## 3.1    Problem Statement

Suppose that a diffusion network is represented as a undirected graph $G = \{V, E_G\}$, where $V = \{v_1, v_2, ..., v_n\}$ is a set of $n$ nodes, and $E_G$ is the a of edges in a network. Under the assumption of the IC model, if there is an edge between nodes $v_i$ and $v_j$ in the diffusion network, it indicates that an infected node $v_i$ has an opportunity to infect its uninfected neighbors $v_j$ once, with a prior probability $P(v_i, v_j)$ that contagion propagates over an edge $(v_i, v_j)$ of $G$. Our problem can be formulated as follows.

**Given:** a set $S = \{S^1, ..., S^\beta\}$ of infection status on a diffusion network $G$ in $\beta$ diffusion processes, where $S^l = \{s_1^l, ..., s_n^l\}$ is a $n$-dimensional vector that records the final infection status $s_i^l \in \{0, 1\}$ (1 for infected status and 0 for uninfected status) of each node $v_i \in V$ observed in the $l^{th}$ ($l \in \{1, ..., \beta\}$) diffusion process.

**Infer:** the edge set $E_G$ of the diffusion network $G$.

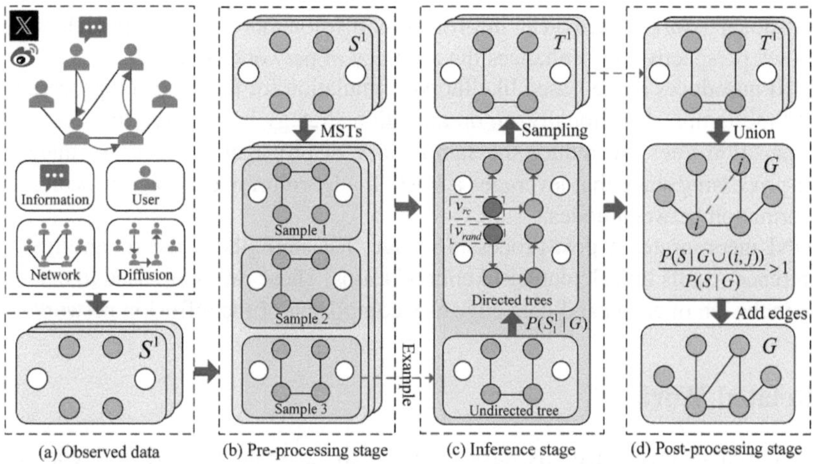


(a) Observed data    (b) Pre-processing stage    (c) Inference stage    (d) Post-processing stage

**Fig. 1.** The overview of TDNI algorithm. (a) An example of a diffusion process occurring on a network. (b) In the pre-processing stage, an algorithm that lists all MSTs are utilized to generate propagation tree samples for each historical process. (c) The inference stage involves establishing a tree-based likelihood and employing a Gibbs sampling-like optimization strategy to identify suitable trees for each set of infected statuses. (d) The post-processing stage focuses on filtering the remaining candidate edges. The likelihood ratio, which compares the probability of an edge being present in a network to the probability of an edge being absent in a network, is computed to determine whether to add candidate edges into the inferred network.

### 3.2  The TDNI Algorithm

Our TDNI algorithm comprises three stages as shown in Fig. 1. As shown in Fig. 1(b), TDNI first employs an algorithm that lists all MSTs to generate candidate samples of propagation trees for each diffusion process. Then, TDNI establishes the likelihood of a diffusion process by analyzing tree patterns and adopts a Gibbs Sampling-like optimization strategy to select a suitable tree structure as illustrated in Fig. 1(c). Finally, TDNI incorporates a post-processing stage, as shown in Fig. 1(d), to consider the presence or absence of remaining edges by evaluating likelihood ratios.

**Pre-processing Stage.** Tree patterns are commonly observed as propagation paths [21]. To simplify, we use $U$ and $D$ to denote undirected and directed trees, respectively, formed by infected nodes. Each infection status $S^l$ has an underlying propagation tree, which can vary widely due to uncertainty. In a complete graph with $n$ vertices, the number of spanning trees is $n^{(n-2)}$. Given the large number of potential samples, processing all of them is impractical during inference. Thus, we restrict the sample size using Mutual Information (MI) to measure the correlation between node infections and generate samples for each diffusion process.

$$MI(v_i, v_j) = \sum_{X_i} \sum_{X_j} P(s_i = X_i, s_j = X_j) \times \log \frac{P(s_i = X_i, s_j = X_j)}{P(s_i = X_i)P(s_j = X_j)}. \quad (1)$$

Node pairs with higher Mutual Information (MI) values are more likely to represent true edges. Therefore, we seek the most probable propagation tree $U$ by maximizing the sum of MI values $\sum_{(v_i, v_j) \in E_U} MI(v_i, v_j)$ for each contagion process, where $E_U$ is the edge set of $U$. Relying on a single tree limits inference, so we aim to consider a broader range of possible trees. To do so, we discretize MI values through data binning, converting them into discrete integers distributed across $N_{bins}$ intervals. These discrete MI values act as weights in an undirected graph representing infected nodes. Finally, we use the algorithm [19] to efficiently find the top-$k$ probable trees for each infection status set.

**Inference Stage.** After the pre-processing stage, TDNI proceeds to infer the suitable tree structure for each infection status within the specified sample size.

An infection status result $S^l$ can be divided into two components: infected nodes $S_1^l$ and uninfected nodes $S_0^l$. Therefore, the likelihood $P(S^l|G)$ given a network $G$ can be formulated as follows.

$$P(S^l|G) = P(S_1^l|G)P(S_0^l|G). \quad (2)$$

To better capture the diffusion process through the propagation tree, TDNI considers a diffusion network $G$ as a composite of multiple propagation trees, denoted as $G = \{U^1, U^2, ..., U^\beta\}$. Each propagation tree $U^l$ corresponds to the generation of the $l^{th}$ diffusion process. Consequently, Eq. (2) can be further expressed as Eq. (3).

$$P(S^l|G) = P(S_1^l|U^1, U^2, ..., U^\beta)P(S_0^l|G). \quad (3)$$

For uninfected nodes $S_0^l$, the likelihood $P(S_0^l|G)$ only needs to consider the probability that they are not infected by their infected neighbors, as described in Eq. (4).

$$P(S_0^l|G) = \prod_{v_i \in S_0^l} \prod_{(v_i,v_j) \in E_G, v_j \in S_1^l} (1 - P(v_j, v_i)). \tag{4}$$

For infected nodes $S_1^l$ and their corresponding tree $U^l$, the likelihood $P(S_1^l|U^1, U^2, ..., U^\beta)$ needs to consider various shapes of spreading paths, since each infected node has the potential to serve as a propagation source. Meanwhile, when considering a specific propagation source $v$ in an undirected tree $U$, it is straightforward to convert the undirected tree into a directed tree $D_v$ with a root $v$. The undirected tree of $D_v$ is equivalent to $U$. We also define $U^{\neg l} = \{U^1, ..., U^{l-1}, U^{l+1}, ..., U^\beta\}$ as the set of trees excluding $U^l$. Then, the likelihood $P(S_1^l|D_v^l, U^{\neg l})$ can be formulated as Eq. (5).

$$P(S_1^l|D_v^l, U^{\neg l}) = \prod_{(v_j,v_i) \in E_{D_v^l}} P(v_j, v_i) \times$$
$$\prod_{v_k \in S_1^l} \prod_{v_m \in \mathcal{PA}(v_k, D_v^l, U^{\neg l})} (1 - P(v_m, v_k)), \tag{5}$$

where $\mathcal{PA}(v_k, D_v^l, U^{\neg l}) = \{v_j | v_j \in S_1^l, v_j \neq v_k, (v_j, v_k) \in E_{U^{\neg l}}, d(v_k, D_v^l) > d(v_j, D_v^l)\}$ and $d(v_k, D_v^l)$ is the depth of node $v_k$ in a directed tree $D_v^l$. A possible parent $v_j \in \mathcal{PA}(v_k, D_v^l, U^{\neg l})$ means that it becomes infected before $v_k$ in a directed propagation tree $D_v^l$, and there exists an influence relationship between them in other propagation trees $U^{\neg l}$. When analyzing a specific diffusion process, it is crucial to take into account the probability $(1 - P(v_j, v_k))$, which indicates the likelihood of no contagion process occurring between nodes $v_j$ and $v_k$.

For an undirected tree without any prior knowledge, any infected node has a probability of being the propagation source of the spreading path. This implies that the likelihood function can be represented by the following equations.

$$P(S_1^l|U^l, U^{\neg l}) = \sum_{v \in V_{U^l}} P(S_1^l|D_v^l, U^{\neg l})P(v|U^l)$$
$$\propto \sum_{v \in V_{U^l}} P(S_1^l|D_v^l, U^{\neg l}). \tag{6}$$

$$P(S|G) = \prod_{1 \leq l \leq \beta} P(S^l|G). \tag{7}$$

However, solving Eq. (7) in practice presents considerable challenges, particularly due to the increasing computational complexity of computing Eq. (6) as the number of nodes in the propagation tree increases. To address this challenge, TDNI draws inspiration from [7] and narrows its attention to a subset of probable trees during the inference process. In each iteration, TDNI specifically examines the propagation tree generated by the most probable propagation source and a propagation tree generated by a randomly chosen root. Further, Eq. (6) can be approximated in the form of Eq. (8).

$$P(S_1^l|U^l, U^{-l}) \propto P(S_1^l|D_{v_{rc}}^l, U^{-l}) + P(S_1^l|D_{v_{rand}}^l, U^{-l}), \tag{8}$$

where $v_{rc}$ is the most likely propagation source and $v_{rand}$ is a random node in a undirected tree. In this paper, we apply the rumor centrality [17] to find the propagation source $v_{rc} = \arg\max_{v \in V_U} R(v, U)$. $R(v, U)$ is the number of permitted permutations of nodes that result in a tree $U$ and begin with node $v \in V_U$.

Subsequently, we develop a Gibbs sampling-like optimization method to infer the most likely trees. Suppose that in the $m^{th}$ iteration, the proposed sampler samples a tree correspond $l^{th}$ diffusion process from the distribution $P(U^l|U^{-l(m)}, S)$, where $U^{-l(m)} = \{U^{1(m)}, ..., U^{l-1(m)}, U^{l+1(m-1)}, ..., U^{\beta(m-1)}\}$. Applying Bayes' theorem, $P(U^l|U^{-l(m)}, S)$ for a tree $U^l$ can be described as Eq. (9).

$$P(U^l|U^{-l(m)}, S) = \frac{P(S|U^l, U^{-l(m)})P(U^l|U^{-l(m)})}{P(S|U^{-l(m)})}. \tag{9}$$

Since $U^{-l(m)}$ is fixed during each iteration, Eq. (9) can be transformed as follows.

$$\begin{aligned}
P(U^l|U^{-l(m)}, S) &\propto P(S|U^l, U^{-l(m)})P(U^l|U^{-l(m)}) \\
&\propto P(S^l|U^l, U^{-l(m)})P(U^l|U^{-l(m)}) \times \\
&\quad \prod_{k \neq l, (v_i, v_j) \in E_{U^l}, (v_i, v_j) \notin E_{U^{-l(m)}}, s_i^k \neq s_j^k} (1 - P(v_i, v_j)).
\end{aligned} \tag{10}$$

The probability $P(U^l|U^{-l(m)})$ can be expressed in the differences between $E_{U^l}$ and $E_{U^{-l(m)}}$, as shown in Eq. (11).

$$P(U^l|U^{-l(m)}) = \prod_{(v_i, v_j) \in E_{U^l}, (v_i, v_j) \notin E_{U^{-l(m)}}} P(v_i, v_j) \tag{11}$$

**Post-processing Stage.** After $M$ iterations of the inference stage, the inferred propagation trees $U^{(M)}$ and a network $G^{(M)}$ can be obtained. However, as a subset of the potential candidate trees are disregarded when generating the samples of propagation trees, the inferred results tend to prioritize the precision over recall. In other words, there is a possibility that a few number of diffusion edges may not be considered during the inference process. To address this issue, TDNI includes a post-processing stage that filters the remaining edges and adds the most probable ones to the network $G^{(M)}$.

The main idea of the post-processing strategy is to compare the likelihood with and without adding an edge $(v_i, v_j)$ into $G^{(M)}$. If the ratio $\frac{P(S|G^{(M)} \cup (v_i, v_j))}{P(S|G^{(M)})} > 1$, then the edge $(v_i, v_j)$ is considered as a component of the underlying diffusion network. According to Eq. (3), the likelihood $P(S^l| G \cup (v_i, v_j))$ of adding an edge can be decomposed into two parts: $P(S_1^l|U^1 \cup (v_i, v_j), ..., U^\beta \cup (v_i, v_j))$ and $P(S_0^l| G \cup (v_i, v_j))$. The term $P(S_0^l| G \cup (v_i, v_j))$ can be directly computed using Eq. (4).

However, $P(S_1^l|U^l \cup (v_i, v_j), U^{-l} \cup (v_i, v_j))$ differs from Eqs. (5) and (6), because adding an additional edge into a tree would change its structure, making the previous tree-based likelihood inapplicable. Therefore, TDNI takes into consideration the sets of propagation trees that may result from the addition of an edge. Specifically, adding an edge to a directed tree can generate a set of two or three trees, as shown in Fig. 2. If one of the nodes in the additional edge $(v_i, v_j)$ serves as the root, only two tree shapes will be produced. Otherwise, three tree shapes will be produced. Let $\text{SET}(D^l_{v_{rc}}, (v_i, v_j))$ represent the set of directed trees produced by considering an edge $(v_i, v_j)$. Then, Eq. (5) with adding an edge can be formulated as Eq. (12).

$$P(S^l_1 | D^l_{v_{rc}} \cup (v_i, v_j), U^{\neg l} \cup (v_i, v_j)) = \frac{1}{|\text{SET}(D^l_{v_{rc}}, (v_i, v_j))|} \times$$
$$\sum_{D \in \text{SET}(D^l_{v_{rc}}, (v_i, v_j))} P(S^l_1 | D, U^{\neg l} \cup (v_i, v_j)). \tag{12}$$

In addition, for the efficiency of the computation, all edges with $\frac{P(S|G^{(M)} \cup (v_i, v_j))}{P(S|G^{(M)})} > 1$ are added into the inferred network together at the end, and $U^{(M)}$ is not changed during the post-processing stage. Meanwhile, for each node $v_i$, we exclusively consider nodes $v_j$ as candidates if their $MI(v_i, v_j)$ surpasses the average MI value of $v_i$'s existing neighbors in the current $G^{(M)}$.

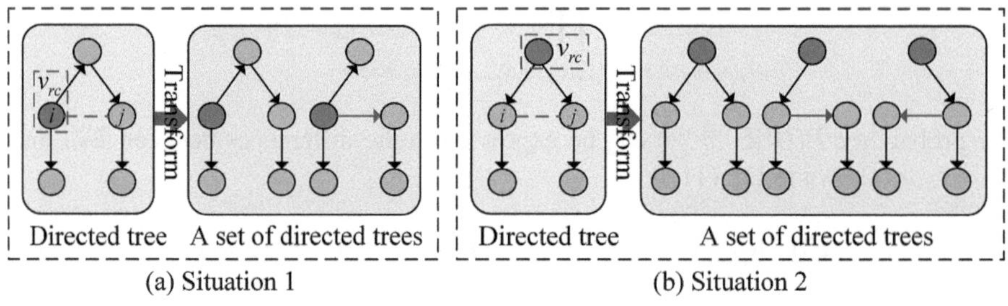


(a) Situation 1                    (b) Situation 2

**Fig. 2.** Two situations of adding an edge into a directed tree. (a) Situation 1 occurs when one of the two nodes in the additional edge serves as the root. (b) Situation 2 occurs when neither of the nodes serves as the root. The red dashed lines represent the edges that need to be considered for addition. (Color figure online)

### 3.3 Complexity Analysis

The time complexity analysis of TDNI is as follows. In the first stage, computing MI for each node pair takes $O(\beta n^2)$, and the data binning requires $O(1)$. Finding the top-$k$ spanning trees takes $O(\beta km \log \bar{n})$ time. In the second stage, calculating the rumor centrality for each tree requires $O(k\bar{n})$, and sampling in $M$ iterations takes $O(\beta Mk + \beta k\bar{n})$. In the third stage, computing the likelihood ratio for one edge requires $O(\beta)$, resulting in $O(\beta c)$ for the third stage. Overall, the complexity is $O(\beta n^2 + \beta km \log \bar{n} + \beta Mk + \beta k\bar{n} + \beta c)$.

## 4 Experiments

### 4.1 Datasets and Baselines

We conduct experiments using both synthetic and real-world networks. For synthetic networks, we generate six networks using the Kronecker graph model [14] and the LFR benchmark graph model [13], which is useful for creating networks with varied degrees and community structures. In this model, $\mathcal{K}$ controls the average node degree, and $\mu$ governs community overlap. Additionally, we use two real-world networks: NetSci, a co-authorship network in network science, and Retweet, a retweet and mentions network from the UN conference in Copenhagen [16]. Detailed information about these networks is provided in Tables 1 and 2.

**Table 1.** The details of synthetic networks.

| Symbol | Network | Parameters | $n$ | $|E_G|$ |
|---|---|---|---|---|
| $G_1$ | ErdōsRényi | [0.5,0.5;0.5,0.5] | 256 | 508 |
| $G_2$ | Hierarchical-community | [0.9,0.1;0.1,0.9] | 256 | 501 |
| $G_3$ | Core-periphery | [0.9,0.3;0.9,0.3] | 256 | 324 |
| $G_4$ | LFR-k3 | $\mathcal{K} = 3, \mu = 0.1$ | 256 | 374 |
| $G_5$ | LFR-k4 | $\mathcal{K} = 4, \mu = 0.1$ | 256 | 501 |
| $G_6$ | LFR-k5 | $\mathcal{K} = 5, \mu = 0.1$ | 256 | 578 |

**Table 2.** The details of real-world networks. $< k >_G$ is the average degree in $G$. $\tau_G$ is the clustering coefficient for $G$.

| Network | $n$ | $|E_G|$ | $< k >_G$ | $\tau_G$ |
|---|---|---|---|---|
| NetSci | 379 | 914 | 4 | 0.74123 |
| Retweet | 761 | 1061 | 2 | 0.07588 |

This study uses the IC model to simulate information diffusion and records the final node states after $\beta$ diffusion iterations as input data $S$, with a constant influence probability of 0.3 between nodes. This data generation method is commonly used in related studies, including [6,7].

To demonstrate the validity and novelty of our work, we compare TDNI with other time-independent SOTA methods, including FINITI [20], TWIND [10], SIDN [9], and TENDS [8].

## 4.2   Results

This section compares the performance of TDNI with other algorithms on both synthetic networks and real-world networks. In this paper, we evaluate the performance of algorithms by the *F-score* metric. The number of historical processes $\beta$ ranges from 100 to 500. In these comparisons, TDNI sets $N_{bin} = 30$ and top-$k = 20$ by default. To mitigate the impact of randomness in the experimental results, we independently run algorithms ten times and compute the average of the results.

**Synthetic and Real-World Networks.** In Fig. 3, TDNI outperforms other algorithms in inferring networks from the Kronecker graph model, achieving impressive F-scores of 0.9 on $G_1$ and $G_2$ with 500 diffusion processes. This high F-score suggests that TDNI effectively captures the network's structural characteristics. It also performs better than most algorithms on $G_4$-$G_6$, particularly for dataset sizes between 300 and 500. In contrast, algorithms like SIDN show significant performance fluctuations with

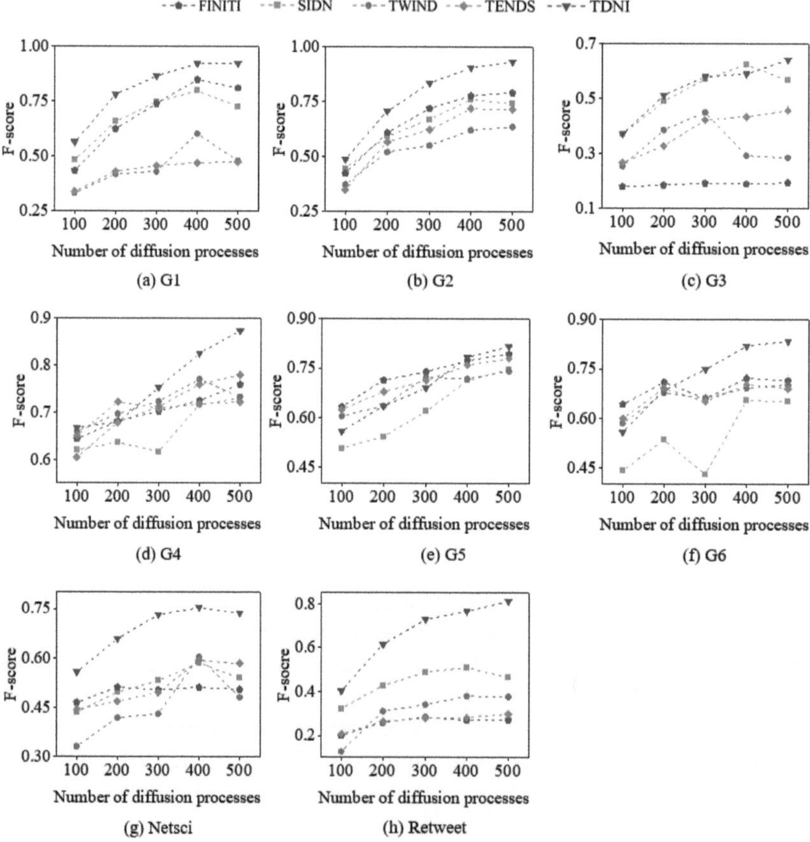

**Fig. 3.** The performance of algorithms on synthetic networks and real-world networks.

increasing dataset size, likely due to the instability of K-means-based pruning for parent nodes. TDNI remains competitive on synthetic networks, with its accuracy improving as dataset size increases, making it a reliable method for diffusion network inference.

On the NetSci network, most methods improve from 100 to 400, but decline at 500, while FINITI remains stable, showing robustness with larger datasets. On the Retweet network, performance rises initially before stabilizing. The denser NetSci structure with more links enables better diffusion, benefiting methods like TDNI. As dataset size grows, identifying parent-child relationships becomes harder, causing performance drops in methods like TWIND and SIDN. Overall, TDNI performs competitively on real-world networks, demonstrating its applicability across various network structures and diffusion scenarios.

### 4.3   Discussion

**Sensitive Analysis of $k$ MSTs.** In the first stage, TDNI uses discrete MI values and the $k$-MSTs algorithm to generate samples for each infection status. For the selection of $k$, we evaluate TDNI's performance with $k$ values of 1, 5, 10, 15, and 20. As shown in Fig. 4, increasing $k$ improves performance with small datasets, while performance stabilizes as the data size grows. This suggests that, with larger datasets, the most probable tree becomes similar to the maximum spanning tree. To balance accuracy and time complexity, we find that $k \approx 20$ is optimal for the networks in our experiments.

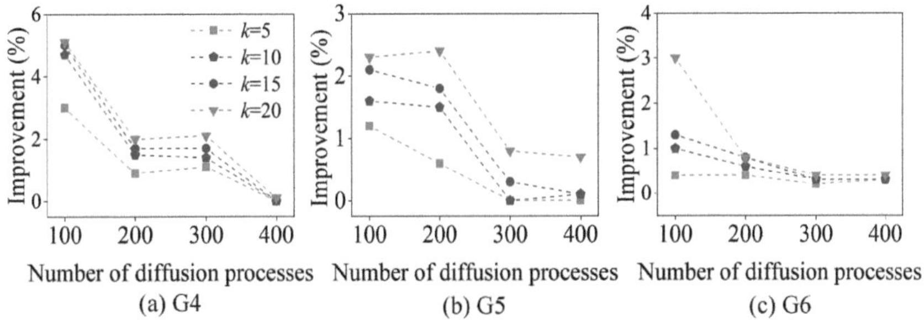


**Fig. 4.** The performance of TDNI with different top-$k$ MSTs in the pre-processing stage. The vertical axis represents the improvement achieved by setting $k$ compared to $k = 1$.

**Effect of Influence Probability.** As shown in Fig. 5, experiments on $G_1$, $G_6$, and NetSci networks with the IC model and influence probabilities from 0.1 to 0.5 (300 diffusion processes) show that TDNI performs best between 0.1 and 0.4 on $G_1$. FINITI declines after 0.3 due to ineffective pruning. On $G_6$, TDNI improves significantly as the probability increases, outperforming others from 0.3 to 0.5. On NetSci, TDNI follows a similar trend to $G_1$, improving and then decreasing with higher probabilities. Overall, TDNI remains competitive across influence probabilities.

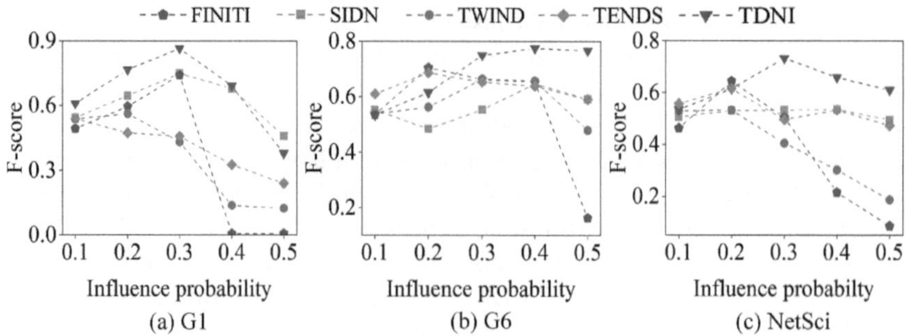



(a) G1   (b) G6   (c) NetSci

**Fig. 5.** The performance of algorithms on $G_1$, $G_6$ and NetSci. The influence probability in IC model ranges from 0.1 to 0.5, and the number of diffusion processes is 300.

**Effect of Post-processing.** To demonstrate the effectiveness and necessity of the post-processing stage, we conduct a comparison of TDNI's performance with and without the post-processing stage on $G_4$-$G_6$. The results presented in Fig. 6 highlight the substantial impact of the post-processing stage, particularly when dealing with small dataset sizes. This finding also suggests that the maximum spanning trees may not always be reliable in such scenarios. In summary, the post-processing stage plays a crucial role in enhancing the accuracy of inference and increasing the overall reliability of our inference results.

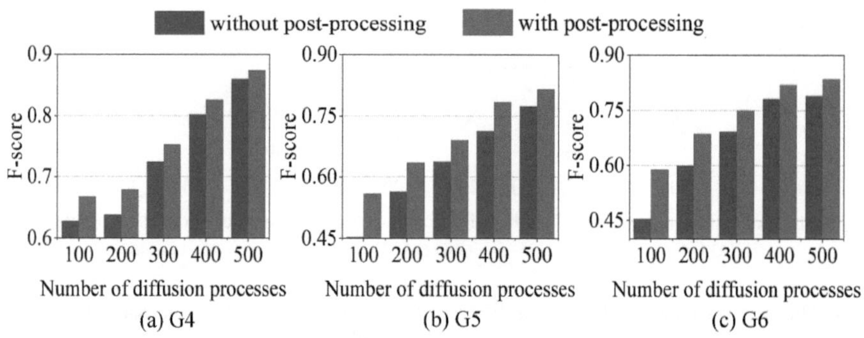



(a) G4   (b) G5   (c) G6

**Fig. 6.** Effect of the post-processing stage on $G_4$-$G_6$.

## 5 Conclusion

In this paper, we propose TDNI, a tree-based approach for time-independent diffusion network inference. TDNI infers the structure of diffusion networks from the perspective of the IC model through three stages. Experimental results on synthetic networks and real-world networks demonstrate the effectiveness of the proposed method. Additionally, we discuss several properties of TDNI, including the sensitive analysis of the number of MSTs, the effect of influence probability, and the effect of post-processing. In the future, we will continue to address the challenges in this field and strive to discover more precise and efficient methods.

**Acknowledgments.** This research was supported by the National Natural Science Foundation of China (Nos. 62261136549, 62471403, U22B2036), the Technological Innovation Team of Shaanxi Province (No. 2025RS-CXTD-009), the International Cooperation Project of Shaanxi Province (No. 2025GH-YBXM-017), the Fundamental Research Funds for the Central Universities (Nos. G2024WD0151, D5000240309), and the XPLORER PRIZE.

# References


1. Amin, K., Heidari, H., Kearns, M.: Learning from contagion (without timestamps). In: Proceedings of the 31st International Conference on Machine Learning, pp. 1845–1853 (2014)
2. Bhattacharya, S., Gaurav, K., Ghosh, S.: Viral marketing on social networks: an epidemiological perspective. Phys. A **525**, 478–490 (2019)
3. Bourigault, S., Lagnier, C., Lamprier, S., Denoyer, L., Gallinari, P.: Learning social network embeddings for predicting information diffusion. In: Proceedings of the 7th ACM International Conference on Web Search and Data Mining, pp. 393–402 (2014)
4. Chen, G., Wang, Y., Shao, J., Shi, B., Shen, H., Cheng, X.: INDNI: an infection time independent method for diffusion network inference. In: Proceedings of the 28th China Conference on Information Retrieval, pp. 63–75 (2022)
5. Daneshmand, H., Gomez-Rodriguez, M., Song, L., Schoelkopf, B.: Estimating diffusion network structures: recovery conditions, sample complexity & soft-thresholding algorithm. In: Proceedings of the 31st International Conference on Machine Learning, pp. 793–801 (2014)
6. Gao, C., Wang, Y., Wang, Z., Li, X., Li, X.: Pairwise-interactions-based Bayesian inference of network structure from information cascades. In: Proceedings of the 32nd ACM Web Conference, pp. 102–110 (2023)
7. Gomez-Rodriguez, M., Leskovec, J., Krause, A.: Inferring networks of diffusion and influence. ACM Trans. Knowl. Discov. Data **5**(4), 1–37 (2012)
8. Han, K., Tian, Y., Zhang, Y., Han, L., Huang, H., Gao, Y.: Statistical estimation of diffusion network topologies. In: Proceedings of the 36th IEEE International Conference on Data Engineering, pp. 625–636 (2020)
9. Huang, H., Yan, Q., Chen, L., Gao, Y., Jensen, C.S.: Statistical inference of diffusion networks. IEEE Trans. Knowl. Data Eng. **33**(2), 742–753 (2019)
10. Huang, H., Yan, Q., Gan, T., Niu, D., Lu, W., Gao, Y.: Learning diffusions without timestamps. In: Proceedings of the 33rd AAAI Conference on Artificial Intelligence, vol. 33, pp. 582–589 (2019)
11. Kempe, D., Kleinberg, J., Tardos, É.: Maximizing the spread of influence through a social network. In: Proceedings of the 9th ACM SIGKDD International Conference on Knowledge Discovery and Data Mining, pp. 137–146 (2003)
12. Kurashima, T., Iwata, T., Takaya, N., Sawada, H.: Probabilistic latent network visualization: Inferring and embedding diffusion networks. In: Proceedings of the 20th ACM SIGKDD International Conference on Knowledge Discovery and Data Mining, pp. 1236–1245 (2014)
13. Lancichinetti, A., Fortunato, S., Radicchi, F.: Benchmark graphs for testing community detection algorithms. Phys. Rev. E **78**(4), 046110 (2008)
14. Leskovec, J., Chakrabarti, D., Kleinberg, J., Faloutsos, C., Ghahramani, Z.: Kronecker graphs: an approach to modeling networks. J. Mach. Learn. Res. **11**(2) (2010)

15. Peel, L., Peixoto, T.P., De Domenico, M.: Statistical inference links data and theory in network science. Nat. Commun. **13**(1), 6794 (2022)
16. Rossi, R., Ahmed, N.: The network data repository with interactive graph analytics and visualization. In: Proceedings of the 29th AAAI Conference on Artificial Intelligence, vol. 29 (2015)
17. Shah, D., Zaman, T.: Detecting sources of computer viruses in networks: theory and experiment. In: Proceedings of the 2010 ACM SIGMETRICS International Conference on Measurement and Modeling of Computer Systems, pp. 203–214 (2010)
18. Wang, Z., Hou, D., Gao, C., Huang, J., Xuan, Q.: A rapid source localization method in the early stage of large-scale network propagation. In: Proceedings of the 31st ACM Web Conference, pp. 1372–1380 (2022)
19. Yamada, T., Kataoka, S., Watanabe, K.: Listing all the minimum spanning trees in an undirected graph. Int. J. Comput. Math. **87**(14), 3175–3185 (2010)
20. Yueming, S., Yunjia, Z., Qian, Y., Lu, C., Hao, H., Yunjun, G.: Fast inference algorithm of diffusion networks without infection temporal information. J. Front. Comput. Sci. Technol. **13**(4), 541 (2019)
21. Zhang, Z., Wang, Z.: The data-driven null models for information dissemination tree in social networks. Phys. A **484**, 394–411 (2017)

# Diffusion Model-Based Multi-scale Feature and Timing Consistency Enhancement for ECG Signal Generation


Yuan Wang[1] ⓘ, Yu Weng[2], and Wengjian Liu[1](✉)

[1] City University of Macau, Taipa, Macau 999078, China
andylau@cityu.edu.mo
[2] Minzu University of China, Beijing 100081, China



**Abstract.** Electrocardiogram (ECG) signal generation plays a critical role in medical data augmentation (e.g., training arrhythmia classifiers) and cardiovascular disease diagnosis (e.g., virtual patient modeling). However, existing generative models face challenges in simultaneously capturing multi-scale morphological features (e.g., P-waves, QRS complexes) and maintaining strict temporal consistency in ECG signals. This paper proposes a diffusion model-based generative framework that integrates multi-scale feature extraction with temporal consistency enhancement techniques. First, a hybrid architecture combining wavelet decomposition and dilated convolutional UNet is designed to hierarchically extract features at different time scales. Secondly, a temporal consistency enhancement method based on Dynamic Time Warping (DTW) loss function and a lightweight Transformer module is introduced to improve the physiological consistency of waveform transitions. Experimental results demonstrate that, compared to the single-scale diffusion model (DDPM), our model significantly improves fidelity (MSE: 0.032 vs. 0.041, a reduction of 22%), diversity (Fréchet distance: 24.6 vs. 28.3, a reduction of 13%), and clinical effectiveness (expert rating: 4.2/5 vs. 3.5/5) on the MIT-BIH and PTB databases. Ablation studies further validate the key roles of multi-scale feature extraction and the DTW loss function.

**Keywords:** ECG Signal Generation · Diffusion Models · Dynamic Time Warping (DTW)


## 1 Introduction

Electrocardiogram (ECG) signals are crucial physiological signals reflecting the electrical activity of the heart, widely used in the diagnosis and monitoring of cardiovascular diseases. However, acquiring high-quality ECG data often faces challenges such as high annotation costs and data scarcity [1]. Generative models, as effective data augmentation tools, can provide a large volume of synthetic data for ECG signal analysis [2]. However, existing generative methods still exhibit limitations in signal diversity and medical relevance [3]. ECG signals exhibit inherent multi-scale characteristics and stringent temporal consistency [4]. For instance, the P-wave, QRS complex, and T-wave correspond to




T. Zhu et al. (Eds.): KSEM 2025, LNAI 15919, pp. 403–414, 2026.
https://doi.org/10.1007/978-981-95-3001-4_30

distinct cardiac activity phases, each characterized by unique time scales and morphological patterns. At the same time, the waveform transitions in ECG signals must maintain physiological consistency to ensure a reasonable transition between heartbeats [5]. Traditional generative models (e.g., ECG-GAN [6] and WaveVAE [7]) typically employ single-scale feature extraction methods, which are inadequate for capturing the multi-scale nature of ECG signals. For instance, ECG-GAN generates signals via standard convolution, but high-frequency details (e.g., the QRS complex) are prone to being lost; while WaveVAE introduces wavelet transforms, it lacks temporal alignment constraints, resulting in unnatural waveform transitions.

As a non-invasive diagnostic tool, ECG signals are extensively used in the detection and monitoring of cardiovascular diseases such as arrhythmias and myocardial infarction [8]. Despite their significant clinical value, obtaining high-quality annotated ECG data remains challenging due to privacy restrictions and annotation costs [9]. Although deep generative models (e.g., GAN [10], VAE [11]) have shown promise in synthesizing medical signals, they still face two key issues:ECG waveforms exhibit scale-dependent characteristics—P-waves (0.1–0.3 s), QRS complexes (0.06–0.12 s), and T-waves (0.1–0.25 s) require modeling at different time scales. However, existing methods mostly use single-scale convolutions [5], making it difficult to effectively capture features across different time scales. Existing models often overlook the physiological consistency of transitions between consecutive heartbeats (e.g., stability of RR intervals), leading to the generation of ECG signals with arrhythmic artifacts [5].

To address these issues, this paper proposes a diffusion model-based generative framework with two core innovations: Multi-Scale Hybrid Architecture: The first combination of wavelet decomposition and dilated convolutional UNet, enabling hierarchical capture of short-term morphological features (e.g., P-wave) and long-term rhythmic patterns (e.g., QRS periodicity).Temporal Consistency Constraints: The introduction of a Dynamic Time Warping (DTW) loss function and a lightweight Transformer module enhances the temporal consistency of the generated signals, ensuring physiologically plausible waveform transitions.

## 2  Related Work

ECG signal generation, as a key technology in medical artificial intelligence, faces the central challenge of balancing waveform fidelity with pathological feature interpretability [12]. Early research primarily focused on Generative Adversarial Networks (GANs). For instance, Xia et al. (2023) proposed ECG-GAN, which can generate basic rhythm waveforms but suffers from modeling errors greater than 15% for subtle pathological features like ST segment shifts. Under the Variational Autoencoder (VAE) framework, Lian et al. (2024) improved the morphological fidelity of P-waves and T-waves by introducing a temporal attention mechanism. However, their KL divergence constraint caused spectral energy attenuation in the generated signals (over 8 dB @ 100 Hz) [13]. These methods generally face the dual challenges of gradient vanishing and high-frequency component loss when modeling the non-stationary characteristics of ECG signals.

The progressive generation mechanism of diffusion models offers a novel theoretical pathway for ECG signal modeling. Adib et al. (2023) were the first to apply DDPM

[14] to ECG enhancement tasks. Their experiments showed a 23.6% improvement in DTW similarity compared to GANs, especially in maintaining the time-frequency characteristics of the QRS complex [15]. However, existing methods still exhibit two critical drawbacks: 1) The use of fixed noise scheduling strategies makes it difficult to adapt to the dynamic amplitude ranges of different leads; 2) The reverse process does not account for the unique time-frequency consistency constraints of ECG signals, leading to abnormal R-wave splitting in leads V4-V6 (with an incidence rate of 12.7%).

To address these issues, this paper proposes an innovative diffusion model framework that combines multi-scale feature extraction with temporal consistency enhancement strategies. Specifically, we design a hybrid architecture that integrates wavelet decomposition and dilated convolutional UNet to extract fine-grained features of ECG signals at different time scales, overcoming the insufficient capture of high-frequency components in existing methods. Additionally, we introduce a temporal consistency enhancement technique based on Dynamic Time Warping (DTW) loss function and a lightweight Transformer module, ensuring smooth transitions in the time domain and preventing abnormal waveform issues caused by spectral inconsistencies.

## 3   Method

### 3.1   Diffusion Model Framework

The proposed model follows the Denoising Diffusion Probabilistic Model (DDPM), where the forward process gradually adds Gaussian noise to the real ECG signal $x_0$ in $T$ steps. The reverse process predicts the noise $\epsilon_\theta$ through UNet. The objective function is given by:

$$L_{\text{diff}} = \mathbb{E}_{(t,x_0,\epsilon)}\left[\|\epsilon - \epsilon_\theta(x_t, t)\|^2\right], \quad x_t = \sqrt{\alpha_t}x_0 + \sqrt{1 - \alpha_t}\epsilon \tag{1}$$

where $\alpha_t$ is the linear noise scheduling coefficient and $t \in \{1, \ldots, T\}$ (with $T = 1000$)
Multi-Scale Hybrid Architecture.

The raw ECG signal $x \in \mathbb{R}^L$ is decomposed into approximation coefficients $\{A_3\}$ and detail coefficients $\{D_1, D_2, D_3\}$ using three layers of Daubechies-4 wavelet decomposition (as shown in Fig. 1a):

$$x \rightarrow \{A_K, D_K, \ldots, D_1\} \tag{2}$$

Each subband is independently processed through parallel convolutional flows before fusion Dilated Convolutional UNet.

The denoising network $\epsilon_\theta$ is based on a UNet backbone. The encoder consists of dilated residual blocks (DRB) with dilation rates $d \in \{1,2,4,8\}$, combined with a pyramid pooling module to aggregate global context. The encoder-decoder connection includes transposed convolution and skip connections to restore high-frequency details.

### 3.2  Consistency Enhancement A Subsection

**DTW Alignment Loss Function**

The Dynamic Time Warping (DTW) loss is used to align the generated signal $x_{\text{gen}}$ with the real signal $x_{\text{real}}$ in terms of waveform phase. The time misalignment between the generated signal $x_{\text{gen}}$ and the real signal $x_{\text{real}}$ is calculated based on DTW as follows:

$$L_{\text{DTW}} = \frac{1}{N} \sum_{i=1}^{N} \min_{\pi \in \Pi} \sum_{(j,k) \in \pi} \| x_{\text{real}}^{(j)} - x_{\text{gen}}^{(k)} \|^2 \tag{3}$$

where $\Pi$ is the set of valid alignment paths

**Lightweight Transformer Module**

A lightweight Transformer module with 4-head self-attention is inserted between the encoder and decoder of the UNet to model the inter-beat dependencies. Due to the non-stationarity of ECG signals, positional encoding is omitted.

**Training Objective**

The total loss function is a weighted sum of the following components

$$L_{total} = L_{diff} + 0.5L_{DTW} + 0.3L_{wavelet} \tag{4}$$

where $L_{\text{wavelet}}$ enforces multi-scale consistency in the wavelet domain:

$$L_{\text{wavelet}} = \sum_{k=1}^{3} \left( \| A_k^{\text{real}} - A_k^{\text{gen}} \|^2 + \| D_k^{\text{real}} - D_k^{\text{gen}} \|^2 \right) \tag{5}$$

The $L_{\text{wavelet}}$ term imposes consistency constraints on the multi-scale features in the wavelet space. The model proposed in this paper is based on a diffusion model framework, incorporating the UNet architecture and a multi-scale feature extraction module. The overall architecture is illustrated in Fig. 1.

## 4  Experiment

### 4.1  Datasets and Preprocessing

**MIT-BIH Arrhythmia Database** [16]: This dataset contains 48 30-min dual-lead (MLII and V1) ECG recordings sampled at 360 Hz, annotated with heartbeat types (e.g., normal, premature ventricular contraction). It is split into 34 training and 14 test cases, with each segment containing 5-s clips (1800 samples). **PTB Diagnostic ECG Database** [17]: This database includes 549 II-lead ECG recordings, with 80% for training and 20% for testing. The recordings are downsampled to 360 Hz and annotated with cardiac disease types (e.g., myocardial infarction, hypertrophy). **Preprocessing**:

Band-pass filtering (0.5–100 Hz), Z-score normalization for each lead, Beat segmentation based on R-wave alignment.

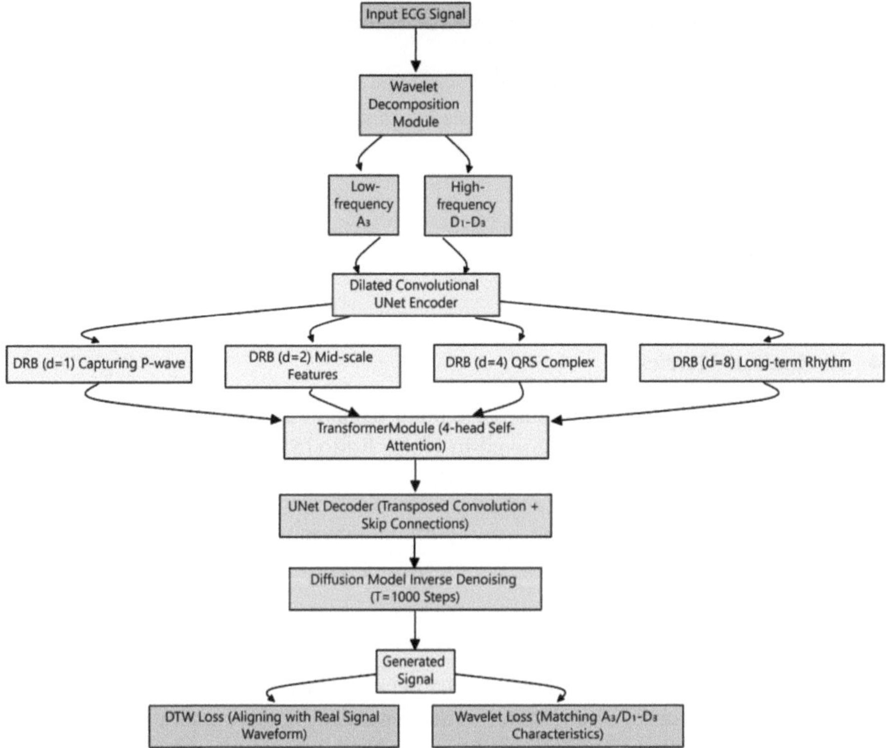


**Fig. 1.** Model architecture diagram

## 4.2  Implementation Details

Diffusion Steps: $T = 1000$, linear noise scheduling · Optimizer: AdamW with a learning rate of $2 \times 10^{-4}$, $\beta_1 = 0.9$, $\beta_2 = 0.999$. Training was conducted on a single NVIDIA A100 GPU for 24 h. · Loss Weights: $\lambda_1 = 0.5$, $\lambda_2 = 0.3$.

## 4.3  Loss Functions

The total loss function is a weighted sum of the following three components · Diffusion Model Loss(L_diff):

The mean squared error (MSE) loss for the standard diffusion model, which optimizes the overall distribution of the generated signal.

$$L_{\text{diff}} = \mathbb{E}_{(t,x,\epsilon)}\left[\|\epsilon - \epsilon_\theta(x_t, t)\|^2\right] \tag{6}$$

where $x_t$ is the noisy signal, $\epsilon$ is the noise, and $\epsilon_\theta$ is the model's predicted noise, Dynamic Time Warping (DTW) Loss (L_DTW)

Constrains the alignment between the generated signal and the real signal, addressing time-shift issues.

$$L_{DTW} = DTW\left(x_{real}, x_{gen}\right) \tag{7}$$

408        Y. Wang et al.

where DTW computes the cumulative distance of the minimal alignment path between the two signals.

Multi-Scale Feature Matching Loss (L_multi):

Enforces the authenticity of the generated signal across different frequencies using wavelet decomposition at multiple levels.

$$L_{\text{multi}} = \sum_{k=1}^{K} \left\| \text{Wavelet}_k\left(x_{\text{real}}\right) - \text{Wavelet}_k\left(x_{\text{gen}}\right) \right\|^2 \tag{8}$$

### 4.4  Evaluation Metrics

Mean Squared Error (MSE): Measures the point-to-point difference between the generated signal and the real signal. · Signal-to-Noise Ratio (SNR): Quantifies the ratio of signal power to noise power in decibels (dB).

$$\text{SNR} = 10\log_{10}\left(\frac{\text{Signal Power}}{\text{Noise Power}}\right) \tag{9}$$

**Diversity**

Fréchet Distance (FD): Measures the similarity between the distributions of the generated and real signals. · Variance: The variance of the generated signal segments, where higher values indicate better diversity. Variance measures local fluctuations, while FD measures global distribution differences.

**Medical Validity**

Clinical Expert Scoring: Three cardiologists were invited to rate the medical validity of the generated signals in a blinded evaluation (scores from 1 to 5, with 5 being the best). The scoring criteria include waveform features such as P-wave clarity, QRS morphology, and T-wave smoothness. Waveform Feature Matching: Automatically detects the positions of the P-wave, QRS complex, and T-wave in the generated signals and calculates the deviation from the real signals (e.g., QRS duration error) (Fig. 2).

### 4.5  Experimental Results

1. As shown in Table 1, the comparison of wavelet decomposition layers demonstrates the effect of different decomposition levels ($K = 2, 3, 4$) on the quality of the generated ECG signals. The combinations of dilation rates in the dilated convolutions were also tested (e.g., {1,2,4} vs. {1,3,5}). $K = 3$ achieved the best balance between low-frequency rhythms (T-wave) and high-frequency details (QRS complex). When $K = 4$ was used, high-frequency sub-bands (e.g., $> 50$ Hz) introduced noise, leading to jittering in the QRS complex amplitude (see Fig. 4c). Therefore, $K = 3$ was chosen to balance decomposition granularity and noise suppression, validating the choice of the decomposition layer number.

    **Experiment Design**

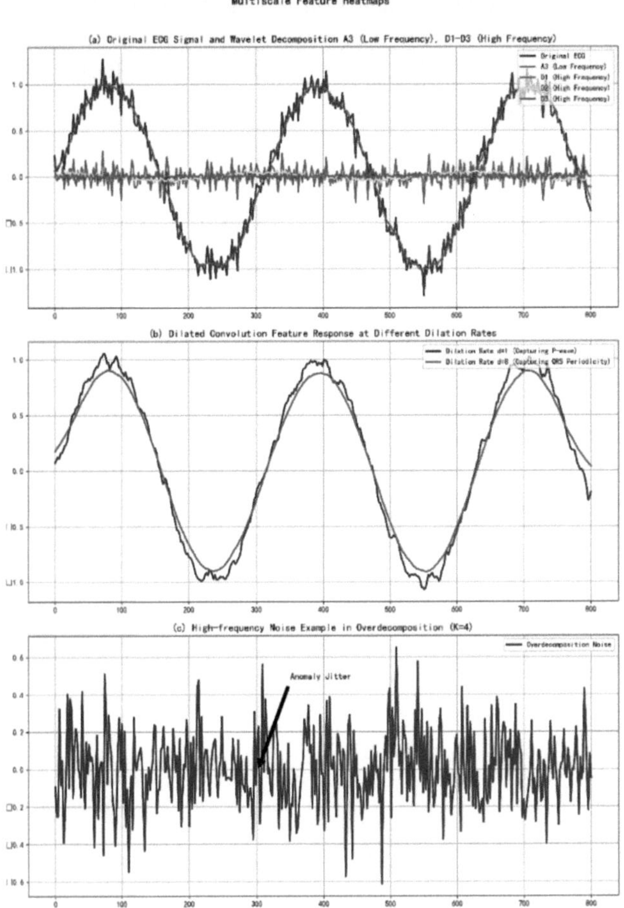


**Fig. 2.** Waveform Comparison Chart

- **RR Interval Stability:** The standard deviation of the RR intervals between consecutive heartbeats in the generated signal was calculated and compared with the real signal.
- **Waveform Alignment Error:** The time deviations of the P-wave, QRS complex, and T-wave were measured for both the real and generated signals.

2. The introduction of **DTW loss** significantly improved both RR interval stability (52% decrease in standard deviation) and waveform alignment accuracy. As shown in Table 2, these improvements were statistically significant (Tables 4 and 5).

The impact of including generated signals in the training set was evaluated using an arrhythmia classifier (e.g., ResNet-1D). The generated signals improved the classifier's generalization ability, validating their medical utility. As shown in Table 3, the proposed method achieved the highest accuracy (95.6%) and F1 score (0.91) when compared to real data and GAN-generated signals (Fig. 3).

**Table 1.** Multi-Scale Module Analysis

| Method | MSE ($\downarrow$) | FD ($\downarrow$) | QRS Duration Error (ms) |
|---|---|---|---|
| K = 2 (No Low-Frequency Decomposition) | $0.038 \pm 0.003$ | $26.5 \pm 0.8$ | $12 \pm 2$ |
| K = 3 (Chosen in this paper) | $0.032 \pm 0.002$ | $24.6 \pm 0.6$ | $8 \pm 1$ |
| K = 4 (Over-decomposition) | $0.035 \pm 0.004$ | $25.9 \pm 0.7$ | $10 \pm 2$ |

**Table 2.** Quantitative Analysis of Temporal Consistency Enhancement (MIT-BIH Dataset)

| Metric | Real Signal | Baseline Model (Single-Scale DDPM) | Proposed Model (+DTW + Transformer) | Improvement Percentage | Statistical Significance (p-value) |
|---|---|---|---|---|---|
| RR Interval Standard Deviation (ms) | $12.5 \pm 2.1$ | $27.8 \pm 3.6$ | $13.3 \pm 1.8$ | $\downarrow 52.2\%$ | $p < 0.001$ |
| Waveform Time Deviations (Mean $\pm$ SD, ms) | | | | | |
| - P-wave Onset Time Deviation | $0.0 \pm 0.0$ | $15.2 \pm 4.3$ | $5.1 \pm 1.2$ | $\downarrow 66.4\%$ | $p < 0.01$ |
| - QRS Complex Onset Time Deviation | $0.0 \pm 0.0$ | $9.8 \pm 2.7$ | $3.0 \pm 0.9$ | $\downarrow 69.4\%$ | $p < 0.001$ |
| - T-wave End Time Deviation | $0.0 \pm 0.0$ | $22.4 \pm 6.1$ | $8.6 \pm 2.4$ | $\downarrow 61.6\%$ | $p < 0.005$ |
| Dynamic Time Warping (DTW) Distance | — | $35.7 \pm 5.2$ | $17.3 \pm 3.1$ | $\downarrow 51.5\%$ | $p < 0.001$ |

This table compares the parameter count, training time, and inference time per sample across different models. Introducing the Transformer module increased the inference time by just 11%, but it significantly improved temporal consistency.

This ablation study shows that the proposed method outperforms various baseline models (such as GAN, VAE, DDPM, DDIM, and others) in terms of MSE, FD, variance, and expert ratings. The use of multi-scale modules and DTW loss significantly

**Table 3.** Clinical Diagnosis Task Validation

| Training Data | Accuracy (%) (MIT-BIH) | F1 Score (PTB) |
|---|---|---|
| Real Data | $92.3 \pm 0.5$ | $0.87 \pm 0.02$ |
| Real + GAN-generated | $93.1 \pm 0.4$ | $0.88 \pm 0.03$ |
| Real + Proposed Method-generated | $95.6 \pm 0.3$ | $0.91 \pm 0.01$ |

**Table 4.** Computational Efficiency Analysis

| Method | Parameters (M) | Training Time (hrs) | Inference Time (ms/sample) |
|---|---|---|---|
| Single-Scale Diffusion Model | 12.5 | 18 | 15 |
| Proposed Method (Full) | 14.2 | 22 | 20 |
| Proposed Method (Without Transformer) | 13.1 | 20 | 18 |

**Table 5.** Ablation Study

| Method | MSE ($\downarrow$) | FD ($\downarrow$) | Variance ($\uparrow$) | Expert Score ($\uparrow$) |
|---|---|---|---|---|
| GAN | $0.052 \pm 0.006$ | $35.7 \pm 1.2$ | $0.12 \pm 0.02$ | $2.8 \pm 0.3$ |
| VAE | $0.048 \pm 0.005$ | $32.4 \pm 0.9$ | $0.09 \pm 0.01$ | $3.1 \pm 0.2$ |
| DDPM (Single-Scale) | $0.041 \pm 0.004$ | $28.3 \pm 0.8$ | $0.15 \pm 0.03$ | $3.5 \pm 0.2$ |
| DDIM | $0.038 \pm 0.003$ | $26.8 \pm 0.7$ | $0.16 \pm 0.02$ | $3.8 \pm 0.2$ |
| Cold Diffusion | $0.036 \pm 0.004$ | $25.4 \pm 0.6$ | $0.17 \pm 0.02$ | $4.0 \pm 0.1$ |
| WaveGAN | $0.045 \pm 0.005$ | $30.2 \pm 1.0$ | $0.13 \pm 0.03$ | $3.2 \pm 0.3$ |
| No Multi-Scale Module | $0.039 \pm 0.004$ | $27.8 \pm 0.9$ | $0.14 \pm 0.02$ | $3.6 \pm 0.2$ |
| No DTW Loss | $0.037 \pm 0.003$ | $26.3 \pm 0.7$ | $0.16 \pm 0.02$ | $3.9 \pm 0.1$ |
| Proposed Method | $0.032 \pm 0.002^*$ | $24.6 \pm 0.6^*$ | $0.18 \pm 0.02^*$ | $4.2 \pm 0.1^*$ |

**Note:** *Indicates statistically significant improvement ($p < 0.05$) compared to baseline model (single-scale diffusion model) via a two-sample t-test*

improves the model's performance, as evidenced by the lower MSE, FD, and higher expert ratings compared to other methods.

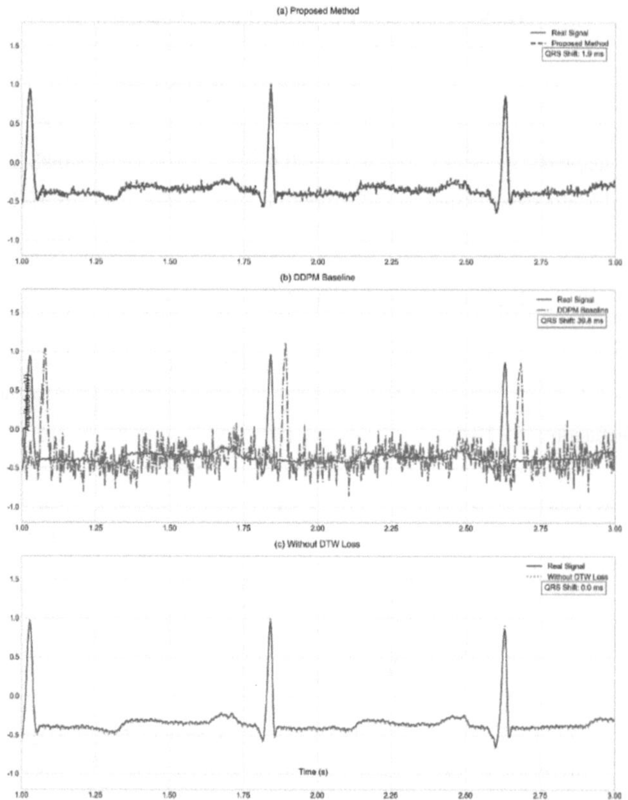

**Fig. 3.** Multi-scale characteristic heat map

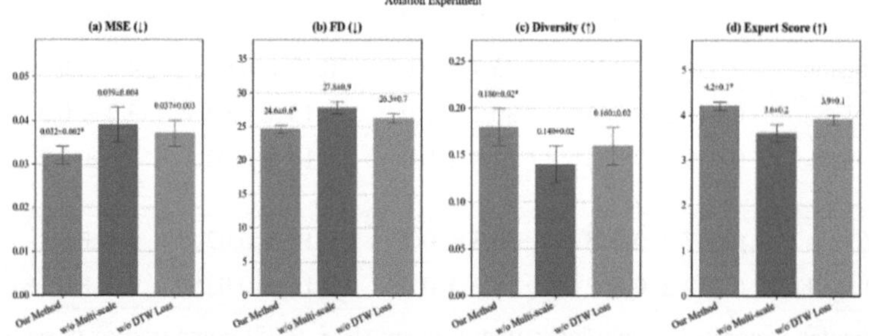

**Fig. 4.** The effect of ablation experiment

## 5 Conclusion and Discussion

This paper proposes a diffusion model-based framework for ECG signal generation that integrates multi-scale feature extraction and temporal consistency enhancement. By combining wavelet decomposition with a dilated convolutional UNet, the model hierarchically captures morphological features across different time scales (e.g., P-wave,

QRS complex). Additionally, a Dynamic Time Warping (DTW) loss and a lightweight Transformer module are introduced to ensure physiological consistency in waveform transitions. Experimental results on the MIT-BIH and PTB datasets demonstrate significant improvements in fidelity (MSE reduced by 22%), diversity (Frèchet Distance reduced by 13%), and clinical validity (expert rating increased from 3.5/5 to 4.2/5) compared to single-scale diffusion models. Ablation studies confirm the critical roles of the multi-scale architecture and DTW constraints.

While the proposed method advances ECG signal generation, limitations remain. First, the computational cost increases slightly due to the added Transformer module, though the trade-off for improved temporal consistency is justified. Second, the model's performance on rare arrhythmia types (e.g., atrial fibrillation with irregular RR intervals) requires further validation. Future work could explore adaptive noise scheduling for multi-lead ECG synthesis and incorporate domain-specific knowledge (e.g., cardiac electrophysiology) to enhance pathological interpretability. Additionally, extending the framework to generate multi-modal physiological signals (e.g., combining ECG with blood pressure) could better support virtual patient modeling.

# References


1. Yang, Y., et al.: Data imbalance in cardiac health diagnostics using CECG-GAN. Sci. Rep. **14**(1), 14767 (2024)
2. Berger, L., Haberbusch, M., Moscato, F.: Generative adversarial networks in electrocardiogram synthesis: recent developments and challenges. Artif. Intell. Med., 102632 (2023)
3. Faust, O., Hagiwara, Y., Hong, T.J., Lih, O.S., Acharya, U.R.: Deep learning for healthcare applications based on physiological signals: a review. Comput. Methods Programs Biomed. **161**, 1–13 (2018)
4. Ma, C., Lan, K., Wang, J., Yang, Z., Zhang, Z.: Arrhythmia detection based on multi-scale fusion of hybrid deep models from single lead ECG recordings: a multicenter dataset study. Biomed. Signal Process. Control **77**, 103753 (2022)
5. Mirvis, D.M., Goldberger, A.L.: Electrocardiography. Heart Dis. **1**, 82–128 (2001)
6. Xia, Y., Xu, Y., Chen, P., Zhang, J., Zhang, Y.: Generative adversarial network with transformer generator for boosting ECG classification. Biomed. Signal Process. Control **80**, 104276 (2023)
7. Peng, K., Ping, W., Song, Z., Zhao, K.: Non-autoregressive neural text-to-speech. In: International Conference on Machine Learning, pp. 7586–7598. PMLR, November 2020
8. Moridani, M.K., Pouladian, M.: A novel method to ischemic heart disease detection based on non-invasive ECG imaging. J. Mech. Med. Biol. **19**(03), 1950002 (2019)
9. Rafie, N., Kashou, A.H., Noseworthy, P.A.: ECG interpretation: clinical relevance, challenges, and advances. Hearts **2**(4), 505–513 (2021)
10. Pearton, S.J., Zolper, J.C., Shul, R.J., Ren, F.: GaN: Processing, defects, and devices. J. Appl. Phys. **86**(1), 1–78 (1999)
11. Tomczak, J., Welling, M.: VAE with a VampPrior. In: International Conference on Artificial Intelligence and Statistics, pp. 1214–1223. PMLR, March 2018
12. Li, L., Camps, J., Rodriguez, B., Grau, V.: Solving the inverse problem of electrocardiography for cardiac digital twins: a survey. arXiv preprint arXiv:2406.11445 (2024)
13. Lian, S., Gao, Z., Wang, H., Liu, X., Xu, L., Liu, H., Zhang, H.: Frequency-enhanced geometric-constrained reconstruction for localizing myocardial infarction in 12-lead electrocardiograms. IEEE Trans. Biomed. Eng. (2024)

14. Ho, J., Jain, A., Abbeel, P.: Denoising diffusion probabilistic models. Adv. Neural. Inf. Process. Syst. **33**, 6840–6851 (2020)
15. Adib, E., Fernandez, A. S., Afghah, F., Prevost, J.J.: Synthetic ECG signal generation using probabilistic diffusion models. IEEE Access (2023)
16. Moody, G.B., Mark, R.G.: The impact of the MIT-BIH arrhythmia database. IEEE Eng. Med. Biol. Mag. **20**(3), 45–50 (2001)
17. Wagner, P., et al.: PTB-XL, a large publicly available electrocardiography dataset. Sci. Data **7**(1), 1–15 (2020)

# Large Language Models Are Not Stable Recommender Systems: A Position Bias Perspective

Tianhui Ma[1], Yuan Cheng[2], Zhi Zheng[3], Hengshu Zhu[4,5(✉)], and Hui Xiong[6,7(✉)]

[1] University of Science and Technology of China, Hefei, China
matianhui@mail.ustc.edu.cn
[2] Minghe Zhidao (Beijing) Technology Co., Ltd., Beijing, China
[3] State Key Laboratory of Cognitive Intelligence, University of Science and Technology of China, Hefei, China
[4] Computer Network Information Center, Chinese Academy of Sciences, Beijing, China
zhuhengshu@gmail.com
[5] University of Chinese Academy of Sciences, Beijing, China
[6] Thrust of Artificial Intelligence, The Hong Kong University of Science and Technology, Guangzhou, China
[7] Department of Computer Science and Engineering, The Hong Kong University of Science and Technology, Hong Kong SAR, China

**Abstract.** Recommender Systems (RS) faces challenges in capturing complex user preferences requiring extensive knowledge, and the integration of Large Language Models (LLMs) has emerged as a promising paradigm. However, this deviation from traditional RS, which directly ranks items, to a paradigm requiring the transformation of items into sequence prompts for LLMs, presents a significant challenge. This shift highlights the sensitivity of LLMs to the order of items in prompts, thus introducing a critical issue of unstable performance due to the position bias in LLM-based Recommender Systems (LLMRS). In this study, we first delve into the position bias problem within LLMRS, identifying distinct patterns and observations. Furthermore, to mitigate this bias, we propose a two-stage debiasing framework, namely STELLA. Initially, in the probing stage, STELLA estimates position bias by analyzing the performance of LLMRS using a probing set. Then, insights from this stage are applied to debias subsequent samples through confidence estimation and iterative updating in the recommendation stage. Our experiments on three real-world datasets demonstrate that STELLA achieves superior recommendation performance while significantly improving stability across multiple domains and LLMs compared to existing baselines.

**Keywords:** Recommender Systems · Large Language Models

© The Author(s), under exclusive license to Springer Nature Singapore Pte Ltd. 2026
T. Zhu et al. (Eds.): KSEM 2025, LNAI 15919, pp. 415–429, 2026.
https://doi.org/10.1007/978-981-95-3001-4_31

# 1  Introduction

Recommender Systems (RS) are integral to a wide array of online services, including news feeds, video entertainment, and display advertising [23]. Traditional RS, largely reliant on historical user interactions [8], often face challenges in accurately capturing complex user preferences that require extensive knowledge [6]. This limitation has prompted a growing interest in integrating advanced technologies to enhance RS capabilities. Among these, Large Language Models (LLMs) have emerged as a significant innovation. LLMs have demonstrated exceptional reasoning and zero-shot generalization abilities, contributing to breakthroughs across various fields. Their advanced language comprehension and reasoning skills are particularly relevant to addressing the complexities inherent in RS. As a result, there is an increasing trend in leveraging LLMs to overcome the traditional limitations of RS, facilitating the development of LLM-based Recommender Systems (LLMRS) [5,20,25].

However, directly employing LLMs in recommender systems introduces a notable challenge, i.e. the position bias problem. As shown in Fig. 1 (top), unlike traditional RS that directly ranks unordered candidate items, LLMRS need to convert the candidate set into a sequential format to construct the prompt text, thereby inherently imposing an order on the candidates. This sequential transformation leads to significant performance instability - Fig. 1 (bottom) shows how altering the position of the ground truth item within the sequence can result in dramatic fluctuations in the performance of LLMRS, oscillating between near state-of-the-art effectiveness and the randomness of a guess. Unlike historical behaviors where sequential order naturally exists and carries temporal meaning, candidate items should maintain no inherent order among themselves in the recommendation task. Due to the sensitivity of LLMs to the order of items in the prompts, position bias becomes a major cause of instability in LLMRS.

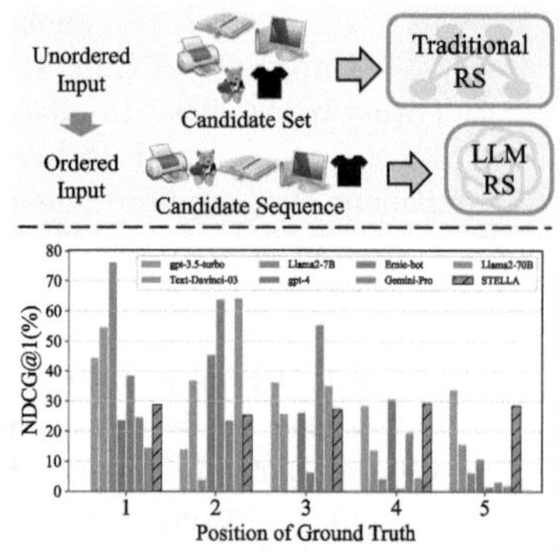



**Fig. 1.** Illustrative example of traditional RS and LLM-based RS with contrastive input (top). Performance fluctuation across different LLMs under shuffled input order on Book dataset measured by NDCG@1 (bottom).

Furthermore, we argue that such a bias problem on input candidate sequence order is special for LLMs in recommendation domains, where it is a rather difficult reasoning task to infer the human behavior preference in practical world from language reasoning aspect. Despite advancements in aligning LLMs with human values, such as through reinforcement learning with human feedback [15], LLMs lack insights into practical, individual behavioral preferences. This divergence underscores a critical gap between expressed language preferences in general and actual behaviors in one specific scenario, as "People don't always do

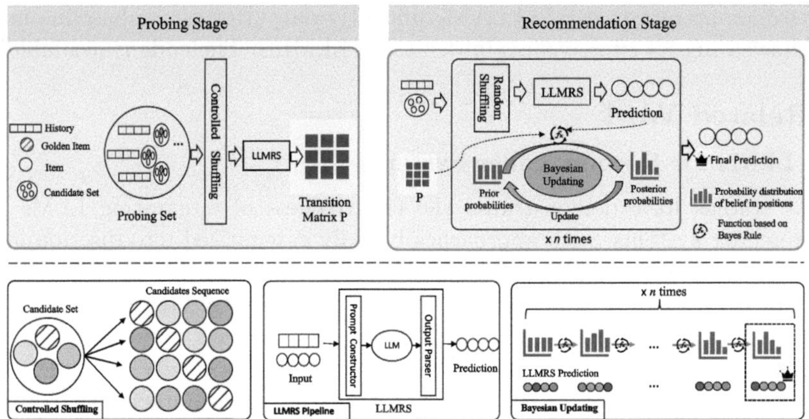


**Fig. 2.** Overview of the STELLA framework, consisting of two stages. The probing stage captures position bias in LLMRS with a transition matrix. In recommendation stage, predictions are debiased using belief probabilities and Bayesian updating.

as they say." In recommendation scenarios, the gap manifests as reduced confidence in the inference outcomes of LLMs, which results in disparate results due to variations in the sequence of inputs. This lack of confidence leads to position bias and performance instability in LLMRS. Such instability challenges the reliability of LLMRS in accurately reflecting genuine user preferences and we motivate our proposed method by addressing this issue.

In this paper, we first delve into the position bias problem within LLMRS. To gain a preliminary understanding of position bias, we conduct an extensive evaluation of LLMRS in various settings. From these empirical studies, we draw valuable patterns and insights that inspire our proposed method. Specifically, our comprehensive empirical analysis establishes that position bias is a prevalent issue in LLMRS, with its impact varying among different models. This is substantiated by in-depth ablation studies involving adjustments to prompt templates and candidate set sizes, revealing several consistent trends. Notably, these findings emphasize the critical importance of meticulously designing candidate set sizes in LLMRS to achieve optimal performance.

To mitigate position bias, we propose a framework called STELLA (**St**able **LLM**s for Recommendation). As illustrated in Fig. 2, STELLA is designed to quantify and mitigate position bias through a two-stage process. In the first stage, STELLA analyzes the performance of LLMRS to estimate the extent of position bias. This involves the use of a probing set and a transition matrix to observe and capture the patterns of bias in the model behavior. Subsequently, the framework applies these insights to debias the output in the recommendation stage. This is achieved by assigning a belief probability to each item based on entropy as a confidence metric, and employing a shuffling technique to refine the test samples. The confidence levels are then iteratively updated inspired by Bayesian updating and finally output the most confident prediction. Experiment results demonstrate that STELLA significantly outperforms the baseline methods, showcasing its effectiveness in debiasing LLMRS. The code is available[1].

## 2   Related Work

### 2.1   LLMs for Recommender Systems

Recent studies have demonstrated the effectiveness of integrating LLMs into recommender systems, with approaches broadly categorized into discriminative and generative methods [25]. While discriminative methods focus on fine-tuning pre-trained models for user-item matching [18], generative RS methods frame recommendations as natural language tasks, transforming candidate sets into sequential prompt formats [20]. Within generative approaches, tuning-based methods adapt LLMs through additional training on recommendation-specific tasks [12,16], while non-tuning-based methods leverage LLMs' inherent capabilities without additional training [26], showing particular promise in scalability and generalization [11]. Our research focuses on this generative, non-tuning-based paradigm to explore the full potential of LLMs' natural capabilities in recommendation scenarios.

### 2.2   Position Bias in Large Language Models

Position bias, the tendency of LLMs to rely heavily on prompt order, has attracted growing attention in NLP, as shown in recent studies [1,3,13,27]. In particular, Wang et al. [21] conducted systematic experiments with GPT-4 and ChatGPT, revealing that changing the order of identical prompts can lead to significantly different responses. Various approaches have been proposed to address position bias. A fundamental solution is ensemble methodology [17], which aggregates multiple samples to reduce bias. Building upon this concept, Self-Consistency (SC) [22] was developed specifically for LLMs, generating and aggregating multiple inference paths through different prompt arrangements. However, SC treats each sample independently, without considering the potential relationships between different inference paths. In the context of recommendation systems, position bias requires aggregating entire ranking lists rather than single items. While Hou et al. [11] proposed a Bootstrapping method with position-based weighted voting, existing approaches have three limitations: treating shuffled sequences independently, lacking systematic bias quantification, and ignoring confidence measures in aggregation. These limitations motivate our framework that captures and mitigates position bias through historical behavior patterns.

## 3   Preliminaries

In this section, we introduce the foundation of our modeling, the task of sequential recommendation, as well as the framework for the pipeline of processing sequential recommendation using LLMs.

---

[1] https://github.com/remember00000/STELLA.

### 3.1 Task Formation

In sequential recommendation scenarios, we work with a behavior sequence $\mathcal{S} = (s_1, s_2, \ldots, s_{|\mathcal{S}|})$, with the aim of predicting the next item. Our focus is on the most recent $m$ behaviors, denoted as $S = (i_1, i_2, \ldots, i_m)$.

We use the historical behavior $X_h = (i_1, i_2, \ldots, i_{m-1})$ to predict the target item $i_m$. Given negative samples $X_n = \{n_1, n_2, \ldots, n_{k-1}\}$, we form the candidate set $X_c = \{i_m, n_1, \ldots, n_{k-1}\}$, with $k$ indicating the size of the candidate set. The objective in list-wise recommendation models is to rank the candidate set $X_c$ such that $i_m$ appears at a higher position than other candidate items.

### 3.2 Framework

The LLMRS framework consists of three sequential steps: (1) converting the candidate set $X_c$ to a sequence $C$ through candidate sequence shuffling, (2) transforming the input pair $(X_h, C)$ into LLM-suitable prompts via the prompt constructor, and (3) parsing the LLM outputs into structured item formats.

**Candidate Sequence Shuffling.** For LLMs, which necessitate a sequentially ordered set of candidates, we convert the candidate set $X_c$ into a candidate sequence denoted as $C = (c_1, c_2, \ldots, c_k)$. Different permutations of this sequence are represented as $C^{(t)}$, where each candidate item in the sequence is indicated by $c_i^{(t)}$. Therefore, the input format for LLMRS is established as $(X_h, C)$. We define $R(i)$ to represent the shuffling mapping of the order of $c_i^{(0)}$ in $C^{(0)}$ to $c_j^{(t)}$ in $C^{(t)}$, where $R : i \mapsto j$ signifies the mapping function, and conversely $R^{-1} : j \mapsto i$ denotes its inverse function.

There are two types of $R$ shuffling functions as follows.

- **Controlled Shuffling**: This process controls the position of the target item $i_m$ in $C$, with the remaining candidates ordered randomly. By iterating $i_m$ through each position in $C$, we obtain $k$ candidate sequence inputs $C^{(p)} = (c_1^{(p)}, \ldots, c_k^{(p)})$, where $c_p^{(p)} = i_m$, and $p = 1, 2, \ldots, k$.
- **Random Shuffling**: Conversely, $X_c$ is randomly ordered to form $C$.

**Prompt Constructor.** The input prompt designed for LLM-based recommender systems is structured as shown in Fig. 3:

The prompt is composed of three key components: task instruction, history description, and candidates description. The task instruction initially informs the model about the task requirements and outlines the expected output format. We define a function $T(i)$ : item $\mapsto$ text that converts an item into its corresponding textual representation, such as the title texts for items in the book domain. The historical sequence $X_h$ is first processed through $T(i)$, then combined with contextual information indicating it as part of

Instruction: You are a book recommendation system now. Please list the ranked recommendations. The output should be in the format of JSON, e.g., {"rank_order":["A", "B", "C", "D", "E"]}..
History Description: Here is the reading history of a user: Inferno, An Abundance of Katherines, The Son, Joyland, The War in Western Europe.
Candidates Description: The books on the candidate list are: (A) No Easy Day, (B)Wind, (C) Allegiant, (D) The Geography of Bliss, (E)Billy Walk.

**Fig. 3.** Illustration of input prompt.

the history, forming the history description. For the candidate sequence $C$, prefix each $T(c_i)$ with option IDs $d_1, d_2, \ldots, d_i$ (e.g., A/B/C/D), and add contextual information indicating it as part of the candidate set, forming the candidates description.

**Output Parser.** The model generates a ranking of option IDs as $(d_{o_1}, d_{o_2}, \ldots, d_{o_k})$, with each corresponding to a specific position ranking $(o_1, o_2, \ldots, o_k)$. Based on this, it predicts a corresponding ranking for the candidate items, denoted as $(c_{o_1}, c_{o_2}, \ldots, c_{o_k})$.

## 4  Empirical Study on Position Bias

In this section, we first introduce our method and its basis for position bias measurement and then present the observation results and insights.

### 4.1  Measurement of Position Bias

We measure position bias by evaluating model performance when the same item appears at different positions in the candidate list. To validate a key premise— that negative item positions have minimal impact—we fix the target item's position (x-axis) and vary the order of three negative items (y-axis). As shown in Fig. 4, NDCG@1 remains stable across columns but varies across rows, confirming the effect is primarily position-dependent. We use ChatGPT for illustration. Full experimental settings are detailed in Sect. 6.1.

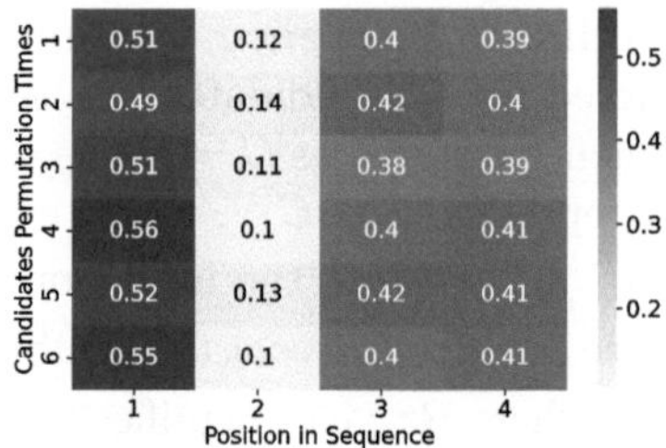

Fig. 4.  Verification of position impact using NDCG@1 scores.

### 4.2  Key Observations

**Position Bias is Prevalent Across Model Families and Sizes.** Across different model families and sizes, we consistently observe similar patterns of position bias. Such universal presence suggests that *position bias is an intrinsic characteristic of LLMRS rather than a model-specific phenomenon*. This finding enables the use of position bias patterns for model confidence estimation - when models make accurate predictions at typically low-performance positions, it may indicate higher confidence in those predictions.

**Position Bias Persists Across Prompt Templates.** We tested various option ID formats in prompts, including Arabic numerals, lowercase letters, Greek characters, Roman numerals, and plain lists. As shown in Fig. 5, while different templates yield distinct performance patterns, position bias remains consistent regardless of prompt formatting choices, though some formats like Greek characters exhibit unique performance patterns.

**Position Bias Shows Consistent Patterns With Varying Candidate Set Sizes.** Our analysis with different candidate set sizes (5, 10, 20) reveals consistent position bias patterns, with performance generally shows an initial rise in performance followed by a decline (Fig. 6). Further testing with sizes from 2 to 25 shows a general decrease in average performance when the size exceeds 5, highlighting that *there exists a critical trade-off between candidate set size and model performance in practical applications.*

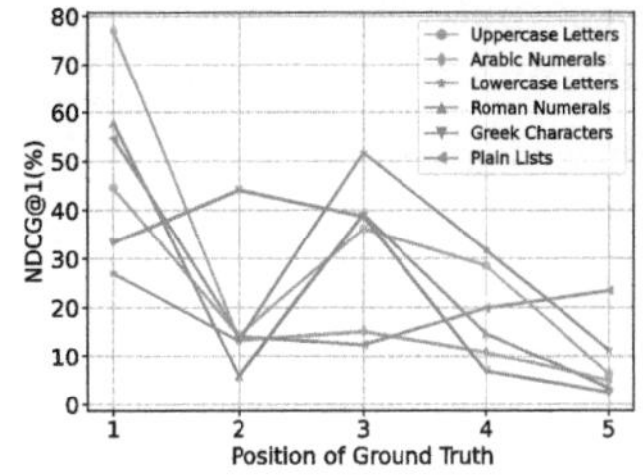

**Fig. 5.** Results evaluated under various prompt templates.

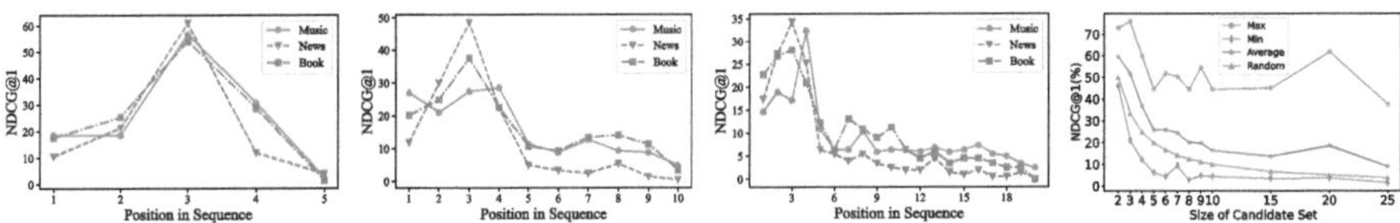

**Fig. 6.** Performance with varying sizes of candidate set. The first three figures shows Position bias for candidate set sizes of 5, 10, and 20. The last one demonstrates a comprehensive trend analysis for set sizes ranging from 2 to 25.

# 5  Calibrating the Position Bias

The core idea of our STELLA is to acquire debiased predictions by formalizing the position bias pattern and using it to iteratively refine the genuine predictions derived from the biased output of LLMRS. The framework comprises two stages. In the probing stage, position bias patterns are quantified using a transition matrix. In the recommendation stage, Bayesian updating is applied iteratively to refine predictions. An overview of this proposed framework is shown in Fig. 2.

## 5.1  Probing Stage

Recalling our earlier observation in Sect. 4.2, we identified prevalent patterns of position bias in LLMRS. These patterns suggest the potential for mitigating biased outputs by leveraging historical data in recommendation systems. Inspired by traditional RS training, we construct a **probing set** to replicate training dynamics. This 'observe-before-act' approach enables accurate estimation of position bias in LLMRS.

The probing set is constructed similarly to the training set in traditional recommendation systems, but with controlled shuffling to assess position bias. Specifically, each sample is transformed into $k$ variants, forming $k$ subsets $I_1, I_2, \ldots, I_k$, where the target item is deliberately placed at the $t$-th position in subset $I_t$. For a given sample $X$, the LLMRS outputs a ranking $o_1, o_2, \ldots, o_k$.

We compute the frequency $f_s(t)$ that position $t$ appears as the top-ranked item $o_1$ in subset $I_s$ as $f_s(t) = \sum_{x \in I_s} 1(o_1 = t)$. The corresponding predicted probability is given by $P_s(t) = \frac{f_s(t)}{|I_s|}$, where $|I_s|$ is the number of samples in subset $I_s$. $P_s(t)$ is the likelihood that the target item, positioned at $s$ in reality, is predicted by the model to be at position $t$. Collectively, $P_s(t)$ forms the **transition matrix** $P$, which delineates the transition probabilities from the actual position to the model-predicted position:

$$P = \begin{bmatrix} P_1(1) & P_1(2) & \ldots & P_1(k) \\ P_2(1) & P_2(2) & \ldots & P_2(k) \\ \vdots & \vdots & \ddots & \vdots \\ P_k(1) & P_k(2) & \ldots & P_k(k) \end{bmatrix}. \tag{1}$$

## 5.2   Recommendation Stage

We develop a confidence-aware aggregation framework to mitigate position bias in LLMRS, where prediction confidence is quantified via entropy and used to guide weighted integration. Inspired by Bayesian updating, the method iteratively refines outputs by combining new predictions with prior estimates, enabling dynamic adaptation to bias patterns across domains.

A straightforward example of **Bayesian updating** involves events $A_1, A_2$ potentially leading to $B$. With limited information, we start with initial beliefs (prior probabilities) $p(A_1), p(A_2)$ and conditional probabilities $p(B|A_i), i = 1, 2$. Posterior probabilities $p(A_i|B)$ given $B$ are obtained as:

$$p(A_i|B) = \frac{p(A_i)p(B|A_i)}{\sum_i p(A_i)p(B|A_i)}. \tag{2}$$

With additional information, $p(A_i|B)$ is used for updating $p(A_i)$, utilizing new information to revise beliefs. In the context of LLMRS, we use $P_s(t)$ from the probing stage as the initial belief for the output probability distribution. During prediction, with a sample $X$, the input for LLMRS is $(X_h, C^{(0)})$, which is described in Sect. 3. Initially, we assume the target item is equally likely to occur at each position. The prior probabilities are uniformly initialized as $p^{(0)}(s) = \frac{1}{k}$, where $s = 1, 2, \ldots, k$. Upon observing the LLMRS ranking $o_1^{(1)}, o_2^{(1)}, \ldots, o_k^{(1)}$, we estimate **posterior probabilities** as follows:

$$p^{(1)}(s) = \frac{\hat{p}(s|o_1^{(1)})}{\sum_{s=1}^k \hat{p}(s|o_1^{(1)})}, \quad s = 1, 2, \ldots, k \tag{3}$$

where $\hat{p}(s|o_1) = p^{(0)}(s)P_s(o_1)$ and $p^{(1)}(s)$ is the normalized probability. By using the shuffling function $R$, we can obtain a new candidate sequence $C^{(1)}$ with new LLMRS predictions $o_1^{(2)}, \ldots, o_k^{(2)}$. Similarly, we can obtain

$$p^{(2)}(s) = \frac{\hat{p}(s|R^{-1}(o_1^{(2)}))}{\sum_{s=1}^k \hat{p}(s|R^{-1}(o_1^{(2)}))}, \quad s = 1, 2, \ldots, k \tag{4}$$

where $R^{-1}$ is the function that maps the new positions back to $C^{(0)}$ and $\hat{p}(s|R^{-1}(o_1^{(2)})) = p^{(1)}(s)P_s(R^{-1}(o_1^{(2)}))$. The above update process will repeat multiple times, and we can obtain $p^{(0)}(s) \rightarrow p^{(1)}(s) \rightarrow \cdots \rightarrow p^{(l)}(s)$ iteratively. We measure the confidence of the prediction using entropy, defined as $e^{(l)} = -\sum_{s=1}^{k} p^{(l)}(s) \log p^{(l)}(s)$, where $e^{(l)}$ denotes the entropy after $l$ updates. A lower entropy indicates higher confidence in the model's prediction. Therefore, to determine the **final prediction**, we consider $l_0$ times updating, identifying the optimal prediction as the distribution with the lowest entropy:

$$\hat{l} = \arg_l \min\{e^{(l)}\}, \quad l = 1, 2, \ldots, l_0. \tag{5}$$

After $\hat{l}$ updates, the output $o_j^{(\hat{l})}$ for $j = 1, \ldots, k$ is mapped back to the original order in $C^{(0)}$ as $t_j = R^{-1}(o_j^{(\hat{l})})$. The final Ranked order of candidates is as $c_{t_1}, c_{t_2}, \ldots, c_{t_n}$. The overall procedure in recommendation stage is summarized as Algorithm 1.

---

**Algorithm 1.** Recommendation Stage Debias Algorithm

---

**Require:** Prior probability distribution $p$, Transition matrix $P$, Maximum updating iteration times $l_0$

**Ensure:** Final ranked result $\hat{C} = \hat{c}_{t_1}, \hat{c}_{t_2}, \ldots, \hat{c}_{t_n}$

1: Initialize $p$ as a uniform distribution, entropy records $E = \emptyset$, and random order $\hat{C}$
2: **for** iteration $i = 1$ to $l_0$ **do**
3:     Get the output of LLMRS $C^{(i)} = c_{t_1}^{(i)}, c_{t_2}^{(i)}, \ldots, c_{t_n}^{(i)}$
4:     Update $p$ using Equation 3
5:     Calculate entropy $e$ and save in $E$
6:     **if** $e$ is the minimum in E **then**
7:         Update $\hat{C}$ using $C^{(i)}$
8:     **end if**
9: **end for**
10: **return** $\hat{C} = \hat{c}_{t_1}, \hat{c}_{t_2}, \ldots, \hat{c}_{t_n}$

---

## 6 Experiments

In this section, we conduct extensive experiments to address the following research questions:

- **RQ1:** How does STELLA perform compared to both LLM-based and traditional baselines?
- **RQ2:** How does STELLA improve the stability of recommendations?
- **RQ3:** Can STELLA maintain its effectiveness when applied to larger datasets?
- **RQ4:** How do probing set sizes affect model performance?

## 6.1  Experimental Settings

**Datasets.** To better evaluate our framework, we conducted evaluations on datasets from three different domains.

- **Books:** The Books segment of the Amazon dataset [7] served as our source, featuring user ratings for a wide range of books.
- **Music:** We use the "CDs & Vinyl" subset of the Amazon dataset [7] to conduct experiments on the music domain..
- **News:** MIND-small dataset comprises user interaction data from the Microsoft News website, including click history and news article attributes [24].

Users and items with fewer than five interactions are filtered, and user histories are ordered chronologically. Positive samples are reviews rated above 3 [2], with original labels used for News. Item titles serve as textual descriptions. We sample 200 users per dataset for evaluation and validate scalability on the full datasets (see §6.4).

**Evaluation.** We follow the existing practice [2] which sets the number of shots as 1 and report top-$K$ Normalized Discounted Cumulative Gain (NDCG@$K$) and Mean Reciprocal Rank (MRR@$K$) with $K = 3$ and $K=1$. As NDCG@1 and MRR@1 are same, only NDCG@1 is reported. We report the standard deviation of NDCG@1 across various positions to demonstrate performance stability.

For the setting of prompt format, we focus on zero-shot setting, which excludes any in-context examples. This approach is adopted to avoid the introduction of new noisy biases that can occur with in-context examples.

**Baselines.** To provide a comprehensive evaluation of the STELLA method as a zero-shot recommendation system, we conducted comparative analyses with both traditional non-LLM-based models and LLM-based methods.

**Traditional Non-LLM-Based Models:** We evaluate three zero-shot and content-based recommendation methods: **BM25** [19](rank according to the textual similarity between candidates and historical interactions), **UniSRec** [10] and **VQ-Rec** [9]. For UniSRec and VQ-Rec, we use their publicly available pretrained models.

**LLM-Based Methods:** We compare STELLA with other LLMRS methods that address recommendation stability.

- **Self-consistency (SC)** [22]: SC uses a sampling method to generate multiple outputs, which are then consolidated to identify a consensus output. Specifically, in our application, we use random shuffling detailed in Sect. 3 and adopt a majority voting strategy to aggregate these multiple outputs. As our outputs take the form of a ranking list, we conduct a voting process for each ranking position and then get the final aggregated ranking list.

- **Bootstrapping (BS)** [11]: BS extends the self-consistency strategy by using the Borda count method [4] for aggregation. In this method, items receive points based on their ranking positions (e.g., n points for first place in an n-item list), and the final ranking is determined by the total points each item accumulates across multiple lists.

**Implementation Details.** We conduct experiments with five language models: GPT-3.5-Turbo, GPT-4, Gemini Pro, ERNIE-Bot 4.0, and Llama-2-70b. For all models, we set temperature to zero to ensure reproducibility. The maximum output tokens are set to 1,000 for OpenAI models, 2,048 for Gemini Pro, 50 for ERNIE-Bot 4.0, and 1,024 for Llama-2-70b, with top-p=1.0 consistently applied. For STELLA implementation, we select five historical sequences per user to construct the probing set. The aggregation parameter $l_0$ is set to 3, and both the length of historical sequence and the size of candidate set $k$ are set to five, following the experimental settings in [2,11] for studying position bias effects. All reported results are averaged over three runs with standard deviation $\leq 0.5$, ensuring the reliability of our findings.

**Table 1.** Overall performance comparison across multiple LLMs. Boldface denotes the top results per metric and LLM. 'Random' refers to random policy recommendations. BS and SC stand for Bootstrapping and Self-consistency.

| Domain | Metric | Random | gpt-3.5-turbo | | | gpt-4 | | | Gemini Pro | | | ERNIE-Bot 4.0 | | | Llama-2-70b | | |
|---|---|---|---|---|---|---|---|---|---|---|---|---|---|---|---|---|---|
| | | | BS | SC | STELLA | BS | SC | STELLA | BS | SC | STELLA | BS | SC | STELLA | BS | SC | STELLA |
| Book | NDCG@1 | .2000 | .2435 | .2810 | **.2925** | .3104 | .3006 | **.3121** | .3008 | .3124 | **.3223** | .2957 | .2941 | **.3088** | .2745 | .2761 | **.2859** |
| | NDCG@3 | .4262 | .4839 | .4874 | **.4931** | .5424 | **.5497** | .5484 | .5214 | .5197 | **.5281** | **.5264** | .5181 | .5244 | .4909 | .4869 | **.5134** |
| | MRR@3 | .3667 | .4213 | .4210 | **.4409** | .4804 | .4692 | **.4867** | .4653 | .4515 | **.4755** | .4670 | .4428 | **.4673** | .4360 | .4180 | **.4491** |
| Music | NDCG@1 | .2000 | .2423 | .2277 | **.2683** | .2467 | .2183 | **.2567** | .2600 | .2533 | **.2750** | .2517 | .2600 | **.2650** | .2067 | .2317 | **.2500** |
| | NDCG@3 | .4262 | .5028 | .4667 | **.5052** | .4802 | .4443 | **.4873** | .4753 | .4658 | **.4943** | .4830 | .4755 | **.4898** | .4557 | .4499 | **.4638** |
| | MRR@3 | .3667 | .4344 | .3865 | **.4436** | .4192 | .3753 | **.4275** | .4183 | .3936 | **.4364** | .4239 | .4069 | **.4308** | .3908 | .3836 | **.4069** |
| News | NDCG@1 | .2000 | .2618 | .2504 | **.2846** | .2488 | .2097 | **.2618** | .1943 | .2159 | **.2276** | .2537 | .2569 | **.2569** | .2390 | .2407 | **.2666** |
| | NDCG@3 | .4262 | .4677 | .4539 | **.4837** | .4633 | .4364 | **.4696** | .4204 | .4122 | **.4260** | .4716 | .4547 | **.4790** | **.4822** | .4578 | .4709 |
| | MRR@3 | .3667 | .4149 | .3827 | **.4306** | .4065 | .3702 | **.4149** | .3607 | .3524 | **.3724** | .4152 | .3935 | **.4203** | **.4184** | .3843 | .4157 |

## 6.2   Performance Comparison (RQ1)

**Comparison with LLM-Based Models.** The detailed results presented in Table 1 reveal several interesting patterns in the performance of STELLA against other LLM-based models. Notably, it achieves substantial improvements over baselines: 7.75% for gpt-3.5-turbo and 5.35% for Gemini Pro. The varying degrees of improvement across different models (6.22% for gpt-4, 2.84% for ERNIE-Bot 4.0, and 5.69% for Llama-2-70b) suggest that while more advanced models may have better inherent capabilities in handling position bias, they still benefit significantly from explicit debiasing. This consistent pattern of improvement across diverse model architectures validates the fundamental effectiveness of our debiasing approach.

**Comparison with Traditional Models.** As shown in Table 2, STELLA outperforms traditional zero-shot recommendation methods across most metrics. The performance patterns reveal that traditional methods excel in the News dataset due to its rich textual features for content matching, while STELLA achieves consistent performance across domains through LLMs reasoning over user historical behaviors. This suggests LLMs can effectively leverage their rich knowledge for reasoning even when textual content is sparse.

**Table 2.** Comparison with non-LLM-based baselines. N@1, N@3 and M@3 refer to NDCG@1, NDCG@3 and MRR@3.

| Method | Book | | | Music | | | News | | |
|---|---|---|---|---|---|---|---|---|---|
| | N@1 | N@3 | M@3 | N@1 | N@3 | M@3 | N@1 | N@3 | M@3 |
| BM25 | .2157 | .4793 | .4101 | .1268 | .2042 | .1854 | .2146 | .4286 | .3732 |
| UniRec | .0245 | .0338 | .0319 | .0293 | .0354 | .0341 | .2732 | .4450 | **.4772** |
| VQRec | .0245 | .0338 | .0319 | .0390 | .0390 | .0390 | .2488 | .4175 | .4504 |
| SRELLA | **.2925** | **.4931** | **.4409** | **.2683** | **.5052** | **.4436** | **.2846** | **.4837** | .4306 |

## 6.3  Stability Analysis (RQ2)

Beyond raw performance metrics, the stability of recommendations is crucial for practical applications. The quantitative analysis in Table 3 demonstrates significant stability improvements across all datasets and models. STELLA reduces standard deviation by an average of 80.4% for `gpt-3.5-turbo` (from 0.1958 to 0.0384), 25.6% for `gpt-4` (from 0.0441 to 0.0328), and 68.2% for `Gemini-Pro` (from 0.0906 to 0.0288). The most substantial improvements are observed in the News dataset, where the standard deviation decreases by up to 93.1% (`gpt-3.5-turbo`, from 0.2032 to 0.0141). This enhanced stability is particularly valuable for production systems, where consistent performance is essential for maintaining user trust and engagement. The significant reduction in variability also suggests that our method successfully addresses the core position bias issue rather than merely achieving higher average performance through compensatory effects.

**Table 3.** Standard Deviation of NDCG@1 Before and After Applying the STELLA.

| Model | Book | | Music | | News | |
|---|---|---|---|---|---|---|
| | Before | After | Before | After | Before | After |
| gpt-3.5-turbo | .1616 | **.0441** | .2227 | **.0570** | .2032 | **.0141** |
| gpt-4 | .0322 | **.0235** | .0633 | **.0464** | .0368 | **.0285** |
| Gemini-Pro | .0510 | **.0223** | .1061 | **.0370** | .1146 | **.0271** |
| ERNIE | .1127 | **.0315** | .0945 | **.0430** | .0739 | **.0283** |
| Llama-2-70b | .1626 | **.0393** | .1629 | **.0491** | .1505 | **.0787** |

## 6.4  Scalability Analysis (RQ3)

To validate the effectiveness of STELLA on larger datasets, we conduct experiments using gpt-3.5-turbo on the complete datasets. As shown in Fig. 7, even with the transition matrix derived from just 1% of users, STELLA maintains competitive performance on the full datasets, consistently outperforming the baselines across most metrics with improvements up to 3.1% in NDCG@1. This demonstrates that our approach can effectively capture and correct position bias patterns with minimal historical data in probing stage, making it practical for larger-scale applications.

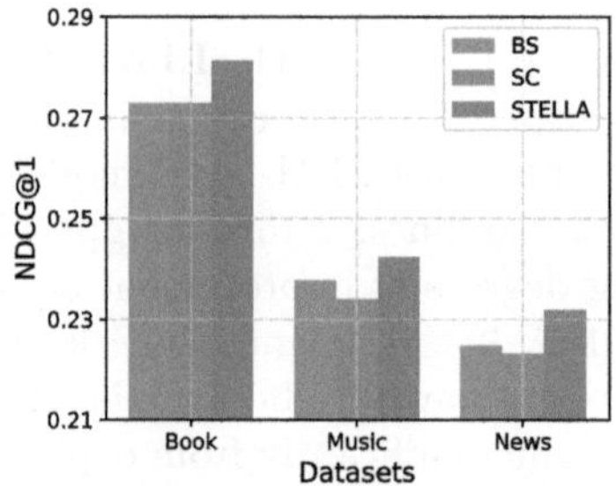


**Fig. 7.** Results on larger datasets. STELLA is our method.

### 6.5  Impact of Probing Set Size (RQ4)

We examine the impact of probing set size on STELLA's performance using GPT-3.5-Turbo, where xN denotes N historical samples per user (N = 2–8). As shown in Fig. 8, overall performance is stable across domains with NDCG@1 varying within 5%, yet domain-specific trends emerge. Books and Music benefit from larger probing sets, while News performance declines, likely due to its time-sensitive nature where outdated interactions impair relevance [14]. The optimal probing size is x5 for Books and Music, and x2 for News. We recommend tuning probing sizes (x2x5) based on domain characteristics for practical deployment.

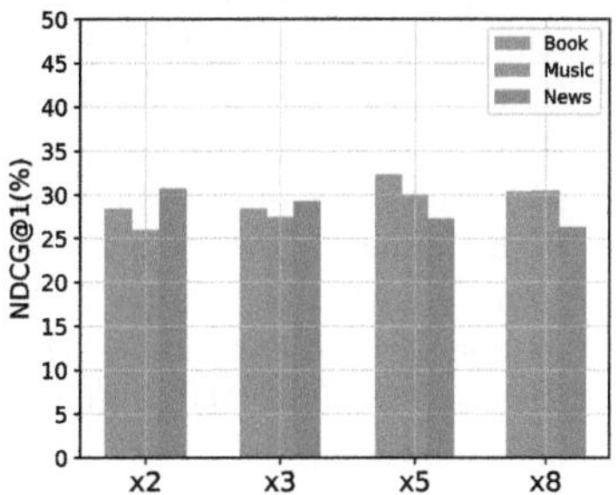

**Fig. 8.** Performance of STELLA under varying probing set sizes.

## 7  Conclusion

In this work, we study the position bias problem in LLM-based Recommender Systems (LLMRS), which causes unstable performance with varying input item orders. We conduct a comprehensive analysis of position bias in LLMRS and propose STELLA, a two-stage framework that quantifies and mitigates this bias. By leveraging a probing set to estimate bias and applying confidence-based iterative updates during recommendation, STELLA achieves more robust and position-invariant predictions. Experiments across different domains and LLMs validate the effectiveness of our proposed STELLA framework compared to existing baselines. This underscores its potential for the evolving field of LLMRS and offers implications for addressing bias issues in the practical application of LLMs.

## References


1. Bowman, S.R.: Eight things to know about large language models. arXiv preprint arXiv:2304.00612 (2023)
2. Dai, S., et al.: Uncovering chatgpt's capabilities in recommender systems (2023)
3. Dong, Q., et al.: A survey for in-context learning. arXiv preprint arXiv:2301.00234 (2022)
4. Emerson, P.: The original borda count and partial voting. Soc. Choice Welf. **40**(2), 353–358 (2013)
5. Gao, Y., et al.: Chat-rec: Towards interactive and explainable llms-augmented recommender system (2023)
6. Guo, Q., Zhuang, F., Qin, C., Zhu, H., Xie, X., Xiong, H., He, Q.: A survey on knowledge graph-based recommender systems. IEEE Trans. Knowl. Data Eng. **34**(8), 3549–3568 (2022)

7. He, R., McAuley, J.J.: Ups and downs: Modeling the visual evolution of fashion trends with one-class collaborative filtering. In: WWW, pp. 507–517. ACM (2016)
8. Hidasi, B., Karatzoglou, A., Baltrunas, L., Tikk, D.: Session-based recommendations with recurrent neural networks. In: ICLR (Poster) (2016)
9. Hou, Y., He, Z., McAuley, J., Zhao, W.X.: Learning vector-quantized item representation for transferable sequential recommenders. In: Proceedings of the ACM Web Conference 2023, pp. 1162–1171 (2023)
10. Hou, Y., Mu, S., Zhao, W.X., Li, Y., Ding, B., Wen, J.R.: Towards universal sequence representation learning for recommender systems. In: Proceedings of the 28th ACM SIGKDD Conference on Knowledge Discovery and Data Mining, pp. 585–593 (2022)
11. Hou, Y., Zhang, J., Lin, Z., Lu, H., Xie, R., McAuley, J., Zhao, W.X.: Large language models are zero-shot rankers for recommender systems (2023)
12. Kang, W., et al.: Do llms understand user preferences? evaluating llms on user rating prediction. CoRR abs/2305.06474 (2023). https://doi.org/10.48550/ARXIV.2305.06474
13. Lu, Y., Bartolo, M., Moore, A., Riedel, S., Stenetorp, P.: Fantastically ordered prompts and where to find them: Overcoming few-shot prompt order sensitivity. In: ACL (1), pp. 8086–8098. Association for Computational Linguistics (2022)
14. Meng, X., Huo, H., Zhang, X., Wang, W., Zhu, J.: A survey of personalized news recommendation. Data Sci. Eng. **8**(4), 396–416 (2023)
15. Ouyang, L., Wu, J., Jiang, X., Almeida, D., Wainwright, C., Mishkin, P., Zhang, C., Agarwal, S., Slama, K., Ray, A., et al.: Training language models to follow instructions with human feedback. Adv. Neural. Inf. Process. Syst. **35**, 27730–27744 (2022)
16. Petrov, A.V., Macdonald, C.: Generative sequential recommendation with gptrec. CoRR abs/2306.11114 (2023). https://doi.org/10.48550/ARXIV.2306.11114
17. Polikar, R.: Ensemble based systems in decision making. IEEE Circuits Syst. Mag. **6**(3), 21–45 (2006)
18. Qiu, Z., Wu, X., Gao, J., Fan, W.: U-BERT: pre-training user representations for improved recommendation. In: Thirty-Fifth AAAI Conference on Artificial Intelligence, AAAI 2021, Thirty-Third Conference on Innovative Applications of Artificial Intelligence, IAAI 2021, The Eleventh Symposium on Educational Advances in Artificial Intelligence, EAAI 2021, Virtual Event, February 2-9, 2021, pp. 4320–4327. AAAI Press (2021). https://doi.org/10.1609/AAAI.V35I5.16557
19. Robertson, S., Zaragoza, H., et al.: The probabilistic relevance framework: Bm25 and beyond. Found. Trends Inf. Retrieval **3**(4), 333–389 (2009)
20. Wang, L., Lim, E.P.: Zero-shot next-item recommendation using large pretrained language models. arXiv preprint arXiv:2304.03153 (2023)
21. Wang, P., et al.: Large language models are not fair evaluators (2023)
22. Wang, X., et al.: Self-consistency improves chain of thought reasoning in language models. In: The Eleventh International Conference on Learning Representations, ICLR 2023, Kigali, Rwanda, May 1-5, 2023. OpenReview.net (2023). https://openreview.net/pdf?id=1PL1NIMMrw
23. Wu, C., Wu, F., Qi, T., Liu, Q., Tian, X., Li, J., He, W., Huang, Y., Xie, X.: Feedrec: news feed recommendation with various user feedbacks. In: Proceedings of the ACM Web Conference 2022, pp. 2088–2097 (2022)
24. Wu, F., et al.: MIND: a large-scale dataset for news recommendation. In: ACL, pp. 3597–3606. Association for Computational Linguistics (2020)
25. Wu, L., et al.: A survey on large language models for recommendation (2023)

26. Zhang, Y., Ding, H., Shui, Z., Ma, Y., Zou, J., Deoras, A., Wang, H.: Language models as recommender systems: Evaluations and limitations. In: I (Still) Can't Believe It's Not Better! NeurIPS 2021 Workshop (2021). https://openreview.net/forum?id=hFx3fY7-m9b
27. Zhao, Z., Wallace, E., Feng, S., Klein, D., Singh, S.: Calibrate before use: Improving few-shot performance of language models. In: ICML. Proceedings of Machine Learning Research, vol. 139, pp. 12697–12706. PMLR (2021)

# POAgent: A Multi-agent Controller Towards Adaptive Parameter Optimization


Qijing Wang[1]([✉]) [ID], Martin D. F. Wong[2], and Evangeline F. Y. Young[1]

[1] The Chinese University of Hong Kong, Shatin, Hong Kong
{qjwang21,fyyoung}@cse.cuhk.edu.hk
[2] Hong Kong Baptist University, Kowloon, Hong Kong
mdfwong@hkbu.edu.hk



**Abstract.** Parameters play a key role in ensuring the expected behaviors of systems or achieving certain objectives, which gives rise to countless parameter optimization (PO) frameworks. In view of their shortcomings of weak adaptability to different scenarios caused by internal predefined configurations, this paper proposes a general controller named *POAgent* based on an efficient learning paradigm and multi-agent reinforcement learning, which can adaptively adjust the configurations and guide the PO process towards better outcomes according to the on-site situations. Experimental results show that significant improvements can be achieved when incorporating it into an existing SOTA PO framework.

**Keywords:** Parameter optimization · Adaptability · Machine learning


## 1 Introduction

Parameters, as common components in a system, e.g., programs, functions, models, etc., play a key role in ensuring that the response and behavior meet certain expectations, or in achieving and optimizing targeted objectives. The corresponding parameter optimization (PO) problem has long received widespread and growing attention. For example, hyperparameter optimization (HPO) is an important topic in the machine learning (ML) community, helping to develop more powerful or efficient model architectures and to better regulate the learning process [3,18]. Another example lies in the field of electronic design automation (EDA), where optimizing the parameters in design tools can provide benefits for producing better circuit designs with advantages in different metrics like power, performance, and area (PPA) [7].

On the other hand, these needs have also given rise to a large amount of automated PO algorithms and frameworks. For example, with genetic algorithm (GA) as the basis, [6] proposed a fast non-dominated sorting approach and a mating pool-based selection operator to achieve good convergence, while [5] further involved the concept of reference points to improve the performance




T. Zhu et al. (Eds.): KSEM 2025, LNAI 15919, pp. 430–442, 2026.
https://doi.org/10.1007/978-981-95-3001-4_32

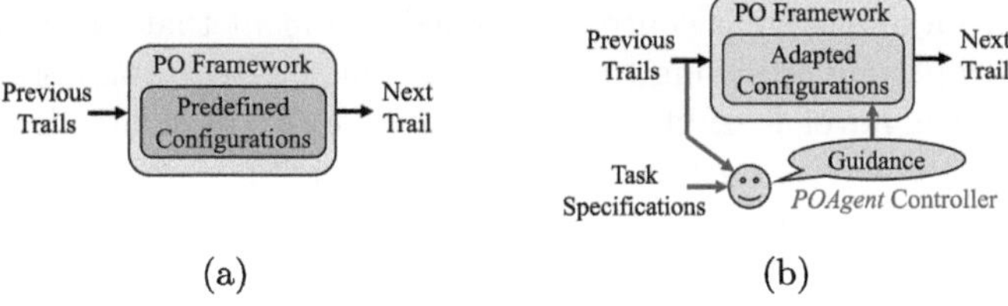


**Fig. 1.** Comparison of (a) a standard PO step and (b) our adaptive substitute.

in many-objective scenarios. For another family, Bayesian optimization (BO) targets at finding good solutions in a more computationally efficient manner. A common practice is to leverage Gaussian process [13] as the surrogate model in an expected improvement (EI) [11] algorithm to construct acquisition functions. As an example of using an alternative surrogate, [3] proposed the Tree-structured Parzen Estimator (TPE) algorithm that achieves the state-of-the-art (SOTA) performance in single-objective tasks, which has also been recently extended to various versions (e.g., multi-objectives [12], constrained [17]) and adopted as the basic solver by some trending PO frameworks [1].

Regardless of the algorithmic details of these methods, they all share a common characteristic of internally involving predefined configurations, e.g., formulas, heuristics and weights, etc. These empirical settings are closely related to the degree of the trade-off between so-called exploration and exploitation in the PO process, which are basically determined by a series of experiments during the development cycles, and are expected to perform well in upcoming cases. However, as reported in the papers, the performance of different configurations in different scenarios can vary greatly, leading to many ablation studies and specific suggestions of how to choose configurations for different benchmarks [16]. Obviously, the lack of adaptability brings a high potential risk of unacceptable performance degradation in hidden cases.

As shown in Fig. 1(a), in a standard PO step, the next trail (i.e., the selection of next group of parameter values) is determined by the calculation on previous trails using the PO framework with predefined configurations. One possible way for enhancing the adaptability is to directly replace the static PO framework by an adaptive one. For instance, [10] recently leveraged promising large language models (LLMs) to directly produce complete PO trajectories. However, due to the difficulty in directly describing the large and varying solution space for arbitrary PO problems with high fidelity, the size of parameter space and the number of optimization steps discussed are quite small. In view of the above shortcomings and considering the needs for a more realistic adaptation paradigm, this paper propose a general controller named *POAgent* that can serve as an external plug-in for arbitrary PO frameworks to provide guidance of how to adaptively adjust the configurations during the PO process, as illustrated in Fig. 1(b). Our main contributions are as follows:

- We propose a multi-agent controller named *POAgent* that can provide guidance for adaptively adjusting the configurations in PO frameworks.
- We propose a novel learning paradigm to obtain the controller efficiently, including a PO environment creator and a multi-stage training scheme.
- We conduct a case study on a SOTA PO framework and show that promising improvements can be achieved after incorporating our controller.

The rest of the paper is organized as follows. Section 2 presents some preliminaries. Section 3 discusses the algorithms and framework in details. Section 4 presents experimental results, followed by a conclusion in Sect. 5.

## 2   Preliminaries

In this section, we introduce some basic concepts in parameter optimization (PO), and then give the problem formulation.

For the sake of application versatility of our *POAgent* controller, this paper does not focus particularly on a specific domain (e.g., ML or EDA), or on a specific optimization object (e.g., neural network or circuit design), but abstracts them into general PO problems and uses common setups that are applicable to all. In general PO, the parameter space is defined as $\mathcal{X}:=\mathcal{X}_1 \times \mathcal{X}_2 \times \cdots \times \mathcal{X}_D \subseteq \mathbb{R}^D$, namely the set of all possible parameter value combinations, where $\mathcal{X}_d \subseteq \mathbb{R}$ $(d = 1, 2, \ldots, D)$ is the domain of the $d$-th parameter and $D$ indicates the total number of dimensions. On the other hand, each parameter combination $\boldsymbol{x} \in \mathcal{X}$ can be evaluated by a certain objective function to obtain a corresponding observation $y$. Note that under multi-objective settings, there may be more than one objective functions and an observation may contain more than one values. Considering the availability of using Pareto hypervolume or simple weighted summation schemes to unify multiple values, and to deliver our ideas clearly, we only discuss single-objective scenarios in this paper and leave others to future work. Consequently, each $(\boldsymbol{x}, y)$ pair will be added into a sampled set $\mathcal{D}$, which is dynamically updated during the PO process and serves as the calculation basis for producing the following trails. We use $\mathcal{D}_x$ to denote the sampled set that contains only parameter combinations for convenience. Finally, the $\boldsymbol{x}$ ever sampled with the best $y$ (e.g., the smallest in a minimization problem) will be returned as the solution when the PO meets the end. Focusing on the main goal of this paper to enhance the adaptability of existing methods, we formulate the problem in this paper as follows.

**Problem 1.** *(Adaptive PO) For an existing PO framework, develop a controller to adjust the internal configurations at every PO step, such that the final objective can be improved as much as possible.*

In this paper, without loss of generality, we demonstrate the advantages of our controller by incorporating it into a public SOTA PO framework named *Optuna* [1], on the basis of the TPE algorithm. The considered configurations and implementation details are described in Sect. 3.3.

# 3    Algorithms and Framework

In this section, we first introduce the stochastic PO environment creator that used to synthesise training dataset. We then present the details of the network architecture, learning scheme and usage of our proposed *POAgent* controller. Finally, we provide a case study to demonstrate the actual implementation.

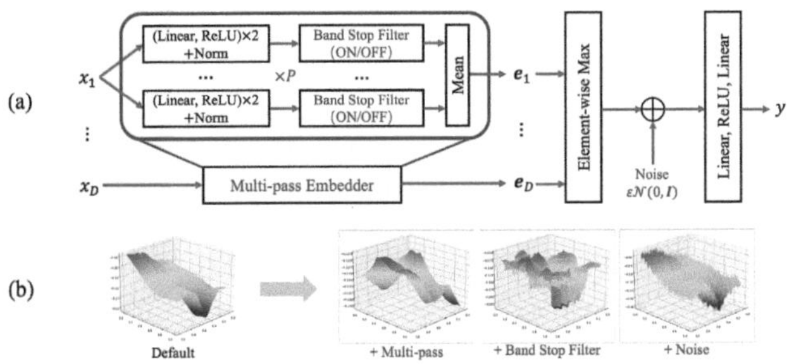


**Fig. 2.** (a) The architecture of our PO environment creator. (b) A 2-parameter example of the environment dynamics affected by different operations separately.

## 3.1    Stochastic PO Environment Creator

The purpose of this environment creator is to efficiently produce all the data required during training, compensating for the scarcity and limited diversity of real PO datasets. It is designed to conveniently establish a mapping from the parameter space to the objective space, such that each parameter combination $x$ can infer an observation value $y$. As shown in Fig. 2(a), we build a neural network to achieve the goal.

Suppose each $D$-dimensional parameter combination $x$ consists of $D$ values $x_1, \ldots, x_D$. By default, i.e., without involving the components marked in red, every of these values will be separately fed into two linear layers followed by ReLU activations, to obtain the embedding vectors $e_1, \ldots, e_D$ after one more normalization operation. An element-wise max operation will then be applied on these vectors to produce the observation value $y$ after further linear projections. The neuron weights in the linear layers will be randomly initialized and will not be changed for each environment creation case. The leftmost figure denoted by "Default" in Fig. 2(b) presents a surface visualization for two continuous parameters based on the above settings, where the vertical axis represents the observation value.

However, a real PO environment may not be as smooth as this default setting. For example, it may contain many local optimums, rugged fluctuations and even noises in some harder cases. In order to create the environment with more diversity, and to comply with real scenarios as much as possible, we further

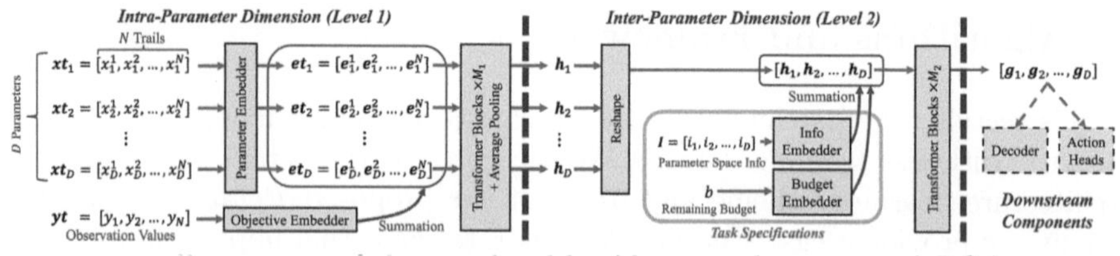

**Fig. 3.** Illustration of the two-level backbone architecture of *POAgent*.

implement three operations. (1) Rather than simply passing each parameter into a single branch of linear layers, we pass it into $P$ branches with the same structure, and take the mean to obtain the embedding vector. (2) A band stop filter is added into each branch before the mean operation, which converts the values within range $[L, R]$ to 0. We set $L$ and $R$ to 0.3 and 0.7 in our implementation. (3) After the element-wise max operation, we further inject a Gaussian noise $\epsilon \mathcal{N}(0, \boldsymbol{I})$ to the embedding vector, where $\epsilon$ controls the noise level and is set to $0 \sim 0.1$ in our implementation.

Figure 2(b) reveals the effects of applying these operations to the default setting. We can observe that the multi-pass design is able to produce more local optimums in a macro scale, while the band stop filter can modulate the steepness of value change, and a noisy surface can be obtained by adding noise. Note that a creator with these operations can be easily reduced to the default version by setting $P$ to 1, $\epsilon$ to 0 and turning off the band stop filter, which is also included as a possible situation in producing the training data.

## 3.2   POAgent Controller

**<u>Network Architecture.</u>** Figure 3 illustrates the backbone of *POAgent*. For a scenario with $D$ parameters, suppose the PO has processed for $N$ trails, we can reconstruct $D$ vectors $\boldsymbol{xt}_1, \ldots, \boldsymbol{xt}_D$, where the $d$-th vector $\boldsymbol{xt}_d$ contains $N$ previous choices for the $d$-th parameter, i.e., $[x_i^1, \ldots, x_i^N]$. Meanwhile, we also have a vector $\boldsymbol{yt} = [y_1, \ldots, y_N]$ composed of the observation values of the previous trails. Obviously, we can see two main dimensions, the one along the $N$ trails for each parameter, named intra-parameter dimension, and the one along the $D$ different parameters, named inter-parameter dimension. To handle this, we construct a two-level backbone architecture. First, for the intra-parameter dimension, as shown in Fig. 3, each of $x_d^n$, $d = 1, 2, \ldots, D$ and $n = 1, 2, \ldots, N$, will be fed into an embedder to obtain the corresponding embedding vector $e_d^n$, such that the sequences $\boldsymbol{et}_1, \ldots, \boldsymbol{et}_D$ can be composed. The embedder contains two linear layers and a SiLU [8] activation in the middle, which is the same for other embedders mentioned below. Additionally, the embedding vectors of the previous $N$ observation values $y_1, \ldots, y_N$ can also be obtained, which will be added pair-wise with each of $\boldsymbol{et}_1, \ldots, \boldsymbol{et}_D$. Afterwards, they will be separately fed into $M_1$ consecutive Transformer blocks [15], followed by an average pooling operation, to produce $D$ level-one hidden vectors $\boldsymbol{h}_1, \ldots, \boldsymbol{h}_D$.

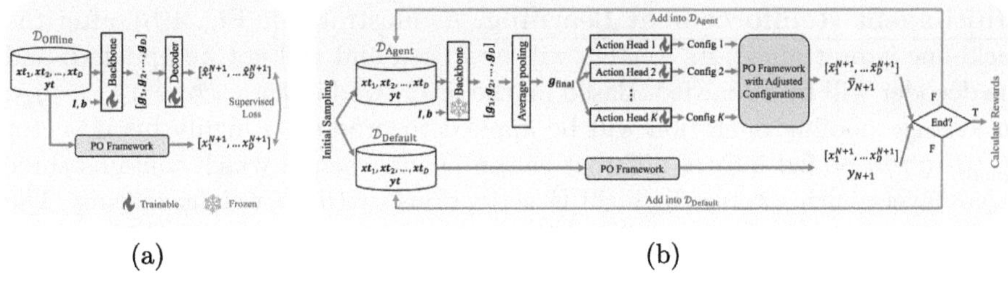

**Fig. 4.** (a) One training step in the pretraining stage. (b) Producing one complete trajectory in the multi-agent reinforcement learning stage.

At the next level, namely the inter-parameter dimension, the hidden vectors above will be reshaped into a sequence with length $D$, i.e., $[\boldsymbol{h}_1, \ldots, \boldsymbol{h}_D]$. Here, the signals for task specifications are also involved, specifically, the information of the parameter space and the remaining budget. The former is represented as a vector $\boldsymbol{I} = [I_1, \ldots, I_D]$, where $I_d$ equals to $|\mathcal{X}_d|$ if the $d$-th parameter is discrete and equals to 0 otherwise. The latter is denoted by a single value $b$, representing the remaining steps to go at current moment. Similarly, distinct embedders will be applied on these two signals and the consequent embeddings will be added with the hidden sequence. Finally, after another $M_2$ Transformer blocks, the level-two hidden vectors $\boldsymbol{g}_1, \ldots, \boldsymbol{g}_D$ will be generated and fed into downstream components.

**Backbone Pretraining.** Directly training the backbone and action heads using reinforcement learning from scratch will be extremely difficult and memory consuming. As revealed in previous sequence modeling works, pretraining the backbone first is able to bring great benefits for downstream tasks, which has become a common practice nowadays.

Therefore, first of all, an autoregressive pretraining will be performed, where the model is required to predict the next token according to the previous ones. As shown in Fig. 4a, we add an additional decoder upon the backbone, which consists of two linear layers and a SiLU activation in the middle, and is distinct for continuous and discrete parameters. Each of the level-two hidden vectors $\boldsymbol{g}_1, \ldots, \boldsymbol{g}_D$ will be fed into the decoder separately to produce the predictions of the next parameter combination values $\hat{x}_1^{N+1}, \ldots, \hat{x}_D^{N+1}$, while the PO framework will also produce the ground-truth values $x_1^{N+1}, \ldots, x_D^{N+1}$. Consequently, a supervised loss can be calculated, where mean-square-error and cross-entropy will be adopted for continuous and discrete values respectively, and the weights of the backbone and the decoder can be updated.

Considering training efficiency, this pretraining is performed offline. A dataset will be constructed in advance by running the PO framework to collect real trajectories on a series of environments set up by the creator described in Sect. 3.1. Then, the $\mathcal{D}_{\text{Offline}}$, $\boldsymbol{I}$ and $b$ shown in Fig. 4a can be extracted from the dataset conveniently for every training step.

**Multi-agent Reinforcement Learning.** As illustrated in Fig. 4(b), after the backbone is pretrained, its weights will be frozen and will not be updated, and the decoder will be discarded. Based on the level-two hidden vectors $g_1, \ldots, g_D$, an average pooling operation will be applied to produce a highly fused vector $g_{\text{final}}$. It will be fed into $K$ different action heads, each of which contains three linear layers with intermediate SiLU activations, with no weight sharing. The output dimension of an action head is determined by the corresponding configuration definition. For example, if the $k$-th configuration has 3 possible settings, namely *low*, *medium*, and *high*, the number of output neurons of action head $k$ will be 3. Naturally, these action heads can be regarded as multiple agents and the goal is to find a good corporation scheme among them, which can be formulated as a MARL task. As shown in Fig. 4(b), starting from an initial sampling, two identical sets $\mathcal{D}_{\text{Agent}}$ and $\mathcal{D}_{\text{Default}}$ will be constructed, which will be further updated respectively by the samples from the agent-involved path and the default path until the end of current PO. The final reward received will be $+1$ if $\mathcal{D}_{\text{Agent}}$ outperforms $\mathcal{D}_{\text{Default}}$ in the best objective achieved and $-1$ otherwise. To overcome sparsity and stabilize training, the reward for an intermediate step will be

$$R = \begin{cases} +0.2, & \text{if} \quad S_{\text{obj}} \cdot S_{\text{div}} = 1, \\ 0, & \text{otherwise}, \end{cases} \tag{1}$$

where the objective-based score $S_{\text{obj}} = 1$ if the objective value of the current step achieved by the controller is better than that by the baseline, and equals to 0 otherwise. However, using $S_{\text{obj}}$ only may lead to an over-exploitative strategy and thus increasing the risk of getting stuck in local optimums. In order to promote exploration at the same time, we add an additional diversity-based score $S_{\text{div}}$, which equals to 1 if the diversity $DIV$ of $\mathcal{D}_{\text{Agent}}$ is better than that of $\mathcal{D}_{\text{Default}}$ after current step, and equals to 0 otherwise. The diversity is defined as

$$DIV(\mathcal{D}) = \frac{1}{|\mathcal{D}_x^{(c)}|} \sum_{x_i \in \mathcal{D}_x^{(c)}} \min_{x_j \in \mathcal{D}_x^{(c)}, j \neq i} \text{L}_2\text{D}(x_i, x_j) + \frac{1}{|\mathcal{D}_x^{(d)}|} \sum_{x_i \in \mathcal{D}_x^{(d)}} \min_{x_j \in \mathcal{D}_x^{(d)}, j \neq i} \text{HD}(x_i, x_j), \tag{2}$$

where $\mathcal{D}_x^{(c)}$ and $\mathcal{D}_x^{(d)}$ denote the subsets of $\mathcal{D}_x$ that contain only the continuous and discrete parameters respectively, while $\text{L}_2\text{D}$ and HD represent $\text{L}_2$ and Hamming distance respectively.

Based on the above settings, we are able to train the action heads using Proximal Policy Optimization (PPO) [14] algorithm. Since it is designed for single-agent scenarios, for simplicity, we use a joint probability distribution to model multiple actions, which can be expressed as

$$\begin{aligned} &\pi_{\theta_1, \theta_2, \ldots, \theta_K}(a_1^t, a_2^t, \ldots, a_K^t | g_{\text{final}}^t) \\ &= \pi_{\theta_1}(a_1^t | g_{\text{final}}^t) \times \pi_{\theta_2}(a_2^t | g_{\text{final}}^t) \times \cdots \times \pi_{\theta_K}(a_K^t | g_{\text{final}}^t), \end{aligned} \tag{3}$$

where $\pi_{\theta_i}$ is the stochastic policy of the $i$-th agent parameterized by $\theta_i$ and $a_i^t$ is its action taken at timestep $t$.

**Table 1.** Configurations to be adjusted in the case study.

| Adjusting Configurations | Candidate Settings |
| --- | --- |
| Splitting Quantile | 1e-5, **0.1**, 0.2, 0.3, 0.4, 0.5, 0.6, 0.7, 0.8, 0.9 |
| Prior Weight | 0, 0.5, **1.0**, 1.5, 2.0, 2.5, 3.0 |
| Weighting Strategy | Uniform, **Old-Decay**, Expected-Improvement |
| Kernel Type | Univariate, **Multivariate** |

### 3.3 Case Study

In this paper, we take one popular and publicly available SOTA PO framework named *Optuna* [1] as a case study to demonstrate the effectiveness of our controller, on the basis of the TPE algorithm. This PO framework will be used to generate the offline dataset in the pretraining stage and serve as the baseline in the reinforcement learning stage. For the TPE algorithm, simply speaking, in every step, the current sampled set $\mathcal{D}$ will be splitted into a better set $\mathcal{D}^{(l)}$ and a worse set $\mathcal{D}^{(g)}$ according to a splitting quantile $\gamma \in (0, 1]$, which is set to 0.1 by default. Next, the weight and bandwidth of every sample in these two sets can be calculated according to some predefined heuristics. Since TPE includes a non-informative prior design, a prior weight (1.0 by default) is also involved to control the influence of the prior. Moreover, *Optuna* provides an interface for adjusting the weighting strategies, by default it is set as *Old-Decay*, i.e., the weights of older samples will be decreased. Other options include *Uniform* and *Expected-Improvement (EI)*, i.e., uniform weights for all samples or adjusting the weights according to actual objectives. Then, the likelihoods $p(\boldsymbol{x}|\mathcal{D}^{(l)})$ and $p(\boldsymbol{x}|\mathcal{D}^{(g)})$ can be calculated based on above settings using the kernel density estimators (KDEs), where either univariate or multivariate (default) kernels can be adopted. Finally, a batch of candidate samples will be sampled following $p(\boldsymbol{x}|\mathcal{D}^{(l)})$ and the one that can maximize the acquisition function $r(\boldsymbol{x}|\mathcal{D}) = \frac{p(\boldsymbol{x}|\mathcal{D}^{(l)})}{p(\boldsymbol{x}|\mathcal{D}^{(g)})}$ will be selected. According to the in-depth studies conducted in [16], different choices of the splitting quantile, prior weight, weighting strategy and kernel type will greatly affect the degree of exploration and exploitation, and thus the speed and the quality of convergence. Therefore, for this case study, we attempt to adjust the configurations listed in Table 1, where the bold values are the default. Note that setting the splitting quantile to 1e-5 will simply give $|\mathcal{D}^{(l)}| = 1$.

## 4 Experimental Results

The proposed *POAgent* controller is implemented based on Python and the PyTorch library. All training and testing are done on a Linux server with a 2.90GHz Intel Xeon CPU and a single Nvidia A800 GPU. The number of Transformer blocks in two levels are implemented as $M_1 = M_2 = 9$, while the hidden dimension is 192 and the number of attention heads is 4. For the pretraining

**Table 2.** The expressions and domains of optimization functions, where the number of dimensions $D$ can be arbitrary.

| Function Name | Expression ($\boldsymbol{x} = [x_1, x_2, \ldots, x_D]$) | Domain |
|---|---|---|
| Ackley | $\exp(1) + 20\left(1 - \exp\left(-\frac{1}{5}\sqrt{\frac{1}{D}\sum_{d=1}^{D} x_d^2}\right)\right) - \exp\left(\frac{1}{D}\sum_{d=1}^{D}\cos 2\pi x_d\right)$ | $|x_d| \leq 32.768$ |
| Griewank | $1 + \frac{1}{4000}\sum_{d=1}^{D} x_d^2 - \prod_{d=1}^{D}\cos\frac{x_d}{\sqrt{d}}$ | $|x_d| \leq 600$ |
| K-Tablet | $\sum_{d=1}^{K} x_d^2 + \sum_{d=K+1}^{D}(100x_d)^2$ where $K = \lceil D/4 \rceil$ | $|x_d| \leq 5.12$ |
| Levy | $\sin^2 \pi w_1 + \sum_{d=1}^{D-1}(w_d - 1)^2\left(1 + 10\sin^2(\pi w_d + 1)\right) + (w_D - 1)^2\left(1 + \sin^2 2\pi w_D\right)$ where $w_d = 1 + \frac{x_d-1}{4}$ | $|x_d| \leq 10$ |
| Perm | $\sum_{d_1=1}^{D}\left(\sum_{d_2=1}^{D}(d_2 + 1)\left(x_{d_2}^{d_1} - \frac{1}{d_2^{d_1}}\right)\right)^2$ | $|x_d| \leq 1$ |
| Rastrigin | $10D + \sum_{d=1}^{D}\left(x_d^2 - 10\cos 2\pi x_d\right)$ | $|x_d| \leq 5.12$ |
| Rosenbrock | $\sum_{d=1}^{D-1}\left(100\left(x_{d+1} - x_d^2\right)^2 + (x_d - 1)^2\right)$ | $|x_d| \leq 5$ |
| Schwefel | $-\sum_{d=1}^{D} x_d \sin\sqrt{|x_d|}$ | $|x_d| \leq 500$ |
| Sphere | $\sum_{d=1}^{D} x_d^2$ | $|x_d| \leq 5$ |
| Styblinski | $\frac{1}{2}\sum_{d=1}^{D}\left(x_d^4 - 16x_d^2 + 5x_d\right)$ | $|x_d| \leq 5$ |
| Weighted-Sphere | $\sum_{d=1}^{D} dx_d^2$ | $|x_d| \leq 5$ |
| Xin-She-Yang | $\sum_{d_1=1}^{D}|x_{d_1}|\exp\left(-\sum_{d_2=1}^{D}\sin x_{d_2}^2\right)$ | $|x_d| \leq 2\pi$ |

stage, we collect 134136 PO trajectories by running the default *Optuna* framework with the TPE algorithm on the stochastic environments set up by the creator described in Sect. 3.1, each of them contains $50 \sim 300$ trails in total, considering TPE's inherent BO motivation to find good solutions quickly. The total number of pretraining epochs is 100 and the base learning rate is 1e-4, with a batch size of 32. For the reinforcement learning stage, the learning rates of actor and critic in PPO are set to 3e-4 and 1e-3 respectively, with a data buffer size of 10 trajectories, while the values of the clip parameter and the discount factor are set to 0.2 and 0.99 respectively. To reveal the efficiency of our learning paradigm, we limit the maximum number of trajectories for training to 10K. Since the runtime of the forward pass of *POAgent* is negligible compared to that consumed by the PO framework, we do not spend space analyzing it here.

### 4.1  PO Quality Comparison

After training, we conduct experiments on the following three different sets of benchmarks to verify the effectiveness of *POAgent*.

*Optimization Functions.* Considering the demands of task universality, we adopt the test suit that contains 12 real optimization functions as the first benchmark, which are popularly used in evaluating PO algorithms [16]. Table 2 demonstrates the expressions and domains of these functions, and we set the number of dimensions $D$ to 30. In order to involve both continuous and discrete parameters, we discretize half of the (i.e., 15) dimensions three times using a basis pattern $\{3, 7, 11, 15, 19\}$, i.e., partition the corresponding domains into 3/7/11/15/19 discrete values evenly.

*HPO Benchmark.* Embracing task diversity, we select one HPO benchmark named *JAHS-Bench-201* [2] to demonstrate the quality of *POAgent* in the ML area, which involves three different tasks, namely CIFAR10, Fashion MNIST, and Colorectal Histology. All of them share the same search space, as shown in Table 3, and we take the test accuracy as the objective.

**Table 3.** HPO benchmark search space.

| Hyperparameter Name | Range |
|---|---|
| Learning Rate | $[10^{-3}, 1]$ |
| Weight Decay | $[10^{-5}, 10^{-2}]$ |
| Activation | {ReLU, Hardswish, Mish} |
| Trivial Augment | {On, Off} |
| Depth Multiplier | $\{1, 3, 5\}$ |
| Width Multiplier | $\{2^2, 2^3, 2^4\}$ |
| Resolution Multiplier | $\{0.25, 0.5, 1.0\}$ |
| Architecture Operation 1∼6* | {skip-connect, zero, 1x1-conv, 3x3-conv, 3x3-avg-pool} |

**Table 4.** *BOOM* design space.

| Module Name | #Candidates |
|---|---|
| Fetch | 2 |
| Decoder | 5 |
| ISU | 15 |
| IFU | 14 |
| ROB | 16 |
| PRF | 13 |
| LSU | 12 |
| I-Cache/MMU | 7 |
| D-Cache/MMU | 10 |

*EDA Benchmark.* To further reveal the effectiveness of *POAgent* in EDA tasks, we adopt one design space exploration (DSE) benchmark for BOOM [4] microarchitecture released by ICCAD22 contest [9]. The design space is shown in Table 4, where some constraints over the candidates among different modules are also involved, e.g., Decoder can take the first candidate value only when Fetch has taken the first one. Thanks to the tree-structured nature of TPE, such constraints can be handled directly without any processing. We normalize the power, performance, and area values for each sample to 0∼1 and take the summation to serve as the objective. Besides, considering the needs for producing designs with priority in certain metrics, e.g., performance (timing)-driven, we further add an example where the performance values are enlarged by 10 times before calculating the summation.

Considering the number of parameters, we set the total PO budget for optimization functions to 200 trails, and 100 for the other two benchmarks. The first 10 parameter combinations are selected by random initial sampling in all cases. Each experimental instance is executed with 10 different random seeds and an overall comparison is then performed. As shown in Table 5, each row presents the best objectives achieved by different methods in the corresponding case. Note that a random strategy that arbitrarily chooses the configurations at every PO step is also compared to reveal that a meaningful strategy is actually learned by our controller than pure randomness. The bold/underlined value indicates 1st/2nd place, and an average ranking across all benchmarks are reported at the bottom, along with a global average ranking (of the average objectives) appended in parentheses. We can observe that *POAgent* is able to achieve significantly better rankings than the baseline, while random strategy is getting worse, which reveals that an effective configuration adjustment scheme has been discovered and learned by the agents. It also means that better optimums can be successfully reached by *POAgent*, which highly relies on a good trade-off between exploration and exploitation. In short, the results fully demonstrate the ability of our controller to adaptively adjust the configurations according to the dynamics encountered, so as to effectively handle different scenarios.

**Table 5.** Comparison of objectives on different benchmarks achieved by the baseline [1] and its two variants. The bold/underlined value indicates 1st/2nd place

| Benchmark | | Objective | | |
|---|---|---|---|---|
| | | Base. [1] | +Random | +*POAgent* |
| *Opt. Func.* ($\downarrow$) | Ackley | 19.580 | <u>19.554</u> | **18.519** |
| | Griewank | 321.969 | <u>309.641</u> | **218.052** |
| | K-Tablet | 457325.201 | <u>345227.974</u> | **181614.313** |
| | Levy | 105.878 | <u>94.663</u> | **57.848** |
| | Perm | **4400.244** | <u>4468.303</u> | 4705.578 |
| | Rastrigin | <u>254.982</u> | 288.649 | **239.048** |
| | Rosenbrock | <u>57213.788</u> | 73094.807 | **47214.374** |
| | Schwefel | 8172.286 | **6968.217** | <u>7067.457</u> |
| | Sphere | 92.252 | <u>79.930</u> | **60.291** |
| | Styblinski-Tang | -577.030 | <u>-625.824</u> | **-675.634** |
| | Weighted-Sphere | **1054.175** | 1416.795 | <u>1112.300</u> |
| | Xin-She-Yang | **0.000** | **0.000** | **0.000** |
| *JAHS* ($\uparrow$) | CIFAR10 | <u>91.146</u> | 90.418 | **91.175** |
| | Fashion MNIST | <u>94.914</u> | 94.792 | **94.994** |
| | Colorectal Hist. | <u>95.097</u> | 95.048 | **95.135** |
| *BOOM* ($\downarrow$) | Summation | **0.945** | <u>0.949</u> | 0.950 |
| | Timing-Driven | <u>1.711</u> | 1.765 | **1.634** |
| Average Ranking | | <u>2.176</u> (<u>1.765</u>) | 2.294 (2.471) | **1.353 (1.588)** |

*$\downarrow$ ($\uparrow$) means the smaller (larger) the objective value the better

Since the training of our controller is purely conducted on the synthesised dataset, the results also provide a strong evidence of the effectiveness of our proposed stochastic PO environment creator. On the other hand, this also offers the potential to achieve better results if the controller is further trained with data that is closer to specific tasks. We leave the investigation to future work.

## 4.2   Explorer of New Strategies

Naturally, another benefit that can be provided by *POAgent* is to discover new schemes about how to adjust the configurations during the PO process. Figure 5 shows two examples of the configuration distributions obtained by *POAgent* on the *Rastrigin* and *Sphere* optimization functions. For visualization simplicity, we evenly partition the PO process into 5 intervals, and separately count the number of times certain configuration choices are adopted in each interval.

We can observe some inspiring learned behaviors here. For example, in both cases, *POAgent* tends to select a small splitting quantile (e.g., 1e−5) at the beginning and gradually increases the value as the PO progresses, and is biased to use a relatively large splitting quantile (e.g., 0.9) at the end. As revealed in [16], a small quantile leads to more exploration and less exploitation. Therefore, the behaviour of *POAgent* here can be interpreted as a gradual transformation from

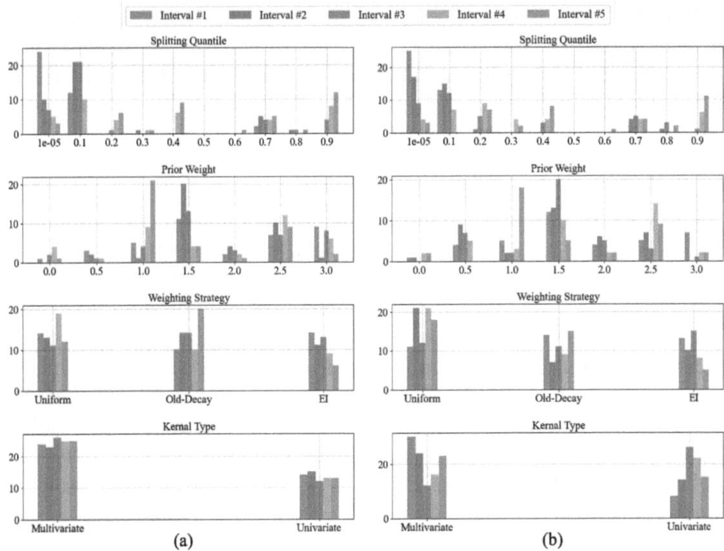


**Fig. 5.** Two examples of the configuration distributions under the control of *POAgent* along the PO process on (a) *Rastrigin* and (b) *Sphere* functions.

strong exploration to strong exploitation during the PO process, which clearly complies with common intuition. Besides, in the middle of the PO on *Rastrigin*, the use of univariate kernel is encouraged, while the multivariate kernel is relatively dominant all the time in *Sphere*. As reported in [16], although the multivariate kernel is generally more useful because it can capture the interaction effect more accurately, the univariate one is effective for objective functions with many modals such as *Rastrigin*. Obviously, the learned behaviour is able to provide a further double-check on such a characteristic.

## 5    Conclusion

In this paper, we propose a general controller named *POAgent* based on a novel efficient learning paradigm and multi-agent reinforcement learning, together with a two-level Transformer backbone being developed. Our controller is able to adaptively adjust the configurations in existing PO frameworks during the PO process. A case study of incorporating it into a SOTA PO framework *Optuna* is conducted, experimental results show that effective adaptation strategies can be learned and great improvements can be achieved on multiple benchmarks.

## References


1. Akiba, T., Sano, S., Yanase, T., Ohta, T., Koyama, M.: Optuna: a next-generation hyperparameter optimization framework. In: Proceedings of the 25th

ACM SIGKDD International Conference on Knowledge Discovery & Data Mining, pp. 2623–2631 (2019)

2. Bansal, A., Stoll, D., Janowski, M., Zela, A., Hutter, F.: Jahs-bench-201: a foundation for research on joint architecture and hyperparameter search. Adv. Neural. Inf. Process. Syst. **35**, 38788–38802 (2022)

3. Bergstra, J., Bardenet, R., Bengio, Y., Kégl, B.: Algorithms for hyper-parameter optimization. Advances in neural information processing systems **24** (2011)

4. Celio, C., Patterson, D.A., Asanovic, K.: The berkeley out-of-order machine (boom): an industry-competitive, synthesizable, parameterized risc-v processor. EECS Department, University of California, Berkeley, Tech. Rep. UCB/EECS-2015-167 (2015)

5. Deb, K., Jain, H.: An evolutionary many-objective optimization algorithm using reference-point-based nondominated sorting approach, part i: solving problems with box constraints. IEEE Trans. Evol. Comput. **18**(4), 577–601 (2013)

6. Deb, K., Pratap, A., Agarwal, S., Meyarivan, T.: A fast and elitist multiobjective genetic algorithm: Nsga-ii. IEEE Trans. Evol. Comput. **6**(2), 182–197 (2002)

7. Geng, H., Chen, T., Ma, Y., Zhu, B., Yu, B.: Ptpt: physical design tool parameter tuning via multi-objective bayesian optimization. IEEE Trans. Comput. Aided Des. Integr. Circuits Syst. **42**(1), 178–189 (2022)

8. Hendrycks, D., Gimpel, K.: Gaussian error linear units (gelus). arXiv preprint arXiv:1606.08415 (2016)

9. Li, S., Bai, C., Wei, X., Shi, B., Chen, Y.K., Xie, Y.: 2022 iccad cad contest problem c: Microarchitecture design space exploration. In: Proceedings of the 41st IEEE/ACM International Conference on Computer-Aided Design, pp. 1–7 (2022)

10. Liu, T., Astorga, N., Seedat, N., van der Schaar, M.: Large language models to enhance bayesian optimization. arXiv preprint arXiv:2402.03921 (2024)

11. Mockus, J.: The application of bayesian methods for seeking the extremum. Towards Global Optim. **2**, 117 (1998)

12. Ozaki, Y., Tanigaki, Y., Watanabe, S., Nomura, M., Onishi, M.: Multiobjective tree-structured parzen estimator. J. Artif. Intell. Res. **73**, 1209–1250 (2022)

13. Rasmussen, C.E.: Gaussian processes in machine learning. In: Summer school on machine learning, pp. 63–71. Springer (2003)

14. Schulman, J., Wolski, F., Dhariwal, P., Radford, A., Klimov, O.: Proximal policy optimization algorithms. arXiv preprint arXiv:1707.06347 (2017)

15. Touvron, H., et al.: Llama 2: Open foundation and fine-tuned chat models. arXiv preprint arXiv:2307.09288 (2023)

16. Watanabe, S.: Tree-structured parzen estimator: Understanding its algorithm components and their roles for better empirical performance. arXiv preprint arXiv:2304.11127 (2023)

17. Watanabe, S., Hutter, F.: c-tpe: Generalizing tree-structured parzen estimator with inequality constraints for continuous and categorical hyperparameter optimization. arXiv preprint arXiv:2211.14411 (2022)

18. Yu, T., Zhu, H.: Hyper-parameter optimization: A review of algorithms and applications. arXiv preprint arXiv:2003.05689 (2020)

If you have any concerns about our products,
you can contact us on
ProductSafety@springernature.com

In case Publisher is established outside the EU,
the EU authorized representative is:
Springer Nature Customer Service Center GmbH
Europaplatz 3, 69115 Heidelberg, Germany

Printed by Libri Plureos GmbH
in Hamburg, Germany